D0099992

THE NEW JOURNALISM
A Historical Anthology

Also by NICOLAUS MILLS:

Comparisons: A Short Story Anthology
American and English Fiction in the Nineteenth Century
The Great School Bus Controversy

THE NEW JOURNALISM

A Historical Anthology

NICOLAUS MILLS

McGRAW-HILL BOOK COMPANY

New York   St. Louis   San Francisco   Düsseldorf   Johannesburg
Kuala Lumpur   London   Mexico   Montreal   New Delhi   Panama
Paris   São Paulo   Singapore   Sydney   Tokyo   Toronto

1234567890 MUMU 7987654

This book was set in Times Roman by University
Graphics, Inc. The editors were David Edwards
and Susan Gamer; the designer was Nicholas
Krenitsky; and the production supervisor was Bill
Greenwood.
The Murray Printing Company was the printer and
binder.

Library of Congress Cataloging in Publication Data

Mills, Nicolaus, comp.
    The new journalism.

    1. Journalism—United States. I. Title.
PN4726.M5   081   73-16122
ISBN 0-07-042349-0
ISBN 0-07-042350-4 (pbk.)

ACKNOWLEDGMENTS

Neil Armstrong, Michael Collins, and Edwin E. Aldrin, Jr., from *First On the Moon*
written with Gene Farmer and Dora Jane Hamblin. Copyright © 1970 by Little,
Brown and Company. Reprinted by permission of Little, Brown and Co.

Alfred G. Aronowitz, "The Great Rock Pileup," "Rock Festival Health Crisis,"
"Benign Monster Devoured Music," and "Aftermath at Bethel: Garbage and
Creditors," © 1969 by the New York Post Corporation. Reprinted by permission
of the *New York Post*.

Ingrid Bengis, *Heavy Combat in the Erogenous Zone,* copyright 1970 by The Village Voice, Inc. Reprinted by permission of *The Village Voice*.

Jimmy Breslin "How He Saw the War in Vietnam," from *The World of Jimmy Breslin* by Jimmy Breslin. Copyright © 1965 by Jimmy Breslin. All rights reserved. Reprinted by permission of The Viking Press.

Paul Bullock, "The Riot," from *Watts: The Aftermath.* Copyright © 1969 by Paul Bullock. Reprinted by permission of Grove Press, Inc.

Peter Collier, "Apollo 11: The Time Machine," © 1969 by *Ramparts* magazine, Inc. Reprinted by permission of the author.

Robert Conot, from *Rivers of Blood, Years of Darkness.* Copyright © 1967 by Bantam Books, Inc. Published by William Morrow & Company, Inc., and Bantam Books, Inc. All rights reserved. Reprinted by permission of the publisher.

Donald Duncan, "The Whole Thing Was a Lie!" © 1966 by *Ramparts* magazine, Inc. Reprinted by permission of the editors.

John Gregory Dunne, from *Delano.* Copyright © 1967, 1971 by John Gregory Dunne. Reprinted with the permission of Farrar, Straus & Giroux, Inc.

F. W. Dupee, "The Uprising at Columbia," copyright © 1968 by New York Review, Inc. Reprinted with permission from *The New York Review of Books.*

Edgar Z. Friedenberg, "Another America," from *The New York Review of Books.* Copyright © 1966 by New York Review, Inc. Reprinted with permission from *The New York Review of Books.*

Richard Goldstein, "The Groovy Revolution: Fold, Spindle, Mutilate," copyright 1968 by The Village Voice, Inc. Reprinted by permission of *The Village Voice.*

Vivian Gornick, "Consciousness ♀" in *New York Times Magazine,* Jan. 10, 1971. Copyright © 1971 by Vivian Gornick. Reprinted by permission of The Sterling Lord Agency, Inc.

Germaine Greer, "McGovern, the Big Tease," copyright © 1972, by Minneapolis Star and Tribune Co., Inc. Reprinted from the October 1972 issue of *Harper's magazine* by permission of the author's agent.

David Halberstam, from *The Making of a Quagmire,* copyright © 1964, 1965 by David Halberstam. Reprinted by permission of Random House, Inc.

Pete Hamill, "Two Minutes to Midnight: The Very Last Hurrah," copyright 1968 by The Village Voice, Inc. Reprinted by permission of *The Village Voice.*

William H. Honan, "*Le Mot Juste* for the Moon," © 1969 by Esquire, Inc. Reprinted by permission of *Esquire* magazine.

Jill Johnston, "The March of the Real Women," copyright 1972 by The Village Voice, Inc. Reprinted by permission of *The Village Voice.*

Elizabeth Kaye, "The Man Who Held RFK in His Arms," copyright 1972 by The Village Voice, Inc. Reprinted by permission of *The Village Voice.*

Sally Kempton, "Cutting Loose: A Private View of the Women's Uprising," © 1970 by Esquire, Inc. Reprinted by permission of *Esquire* magazine.

Andrew Kopkind, "The Woodstock Music and Art Fair," from *Rolling Stone,* © 1969 by Straight Arrow Publishers, Inc. All rights reserved. Reprinted by permission.

James Simon Kunen, "The Shit Hits the Fan," from *The Strawberry Statement* by James Simon Kunen. Copyright © 1968, 1969 by James S. Kunen. Reprinted by permission of Random House, Inc.

Michael P. Lerner, "Mayday: Anatomy of the Movement," © *Ramparts* magazine, Inc., 1971. Reprinted by permission of the editors.

David McReynolds, "Notes on Another Death—And Our Shadowed Future," copyright 1968 by The Village Voice, Inc. Reprinted by permission of *The Village Voice.*

Norman Mailer, "A Sleep on the Moon," from *Of a Fire on the Moon* by Norman Mailer. Copyright © 1969, 1970 by Norman Mailer. Includes 1,200 words from *First on the Moon* by Neil Armstrong, Michael Collins, and Edwin E. Aldrin, Jr., copyright © 1970 by Little, Brown and Company. Reprinted by permission of Little, Brown and Company, and by permission of the author and the author's agents, the Scott Meredith Literary Agency, Inc., 580 Fifth Avenue, New York.

Greil Marcus, "The Woodstock Festival," from *Rolling Stone,* © 1969 by Straight Arrow Publishers, Inc. All Rights Reserved. Reprinted by permission.

Peter Matthiessen, from *Sal Si Puedes,* copyright © 1969 by Peter Matthiessen. A substantial portion of this material originally appeared in *The New Yorker* in different form. Reprinted by permission of Random House, Inc.

Arthur Miller, "Making Crowds," first published in *Esquire* magazine. Copyright © 1972 by Arthur Miller. Reprinted by permission of International Famous Agency.

Nicolaus Mills, "The Whip and the Bee: Diary from the Grape Strike," copyright 1973 by Nicolaus Mills. Originally published in *Dissent.* Reprinted by permission of the publisher.

Malcolm Muggeridge, "The Elevation of Senator Robert F. Kennedy," copyright © 1968 by Esquire, Inc. First published in *Esquire* magazine. Reprinted by permission of Harold Ober Associates, Inc.

Jack Newfield, "Columbia Coverage: Pre-Fitting the News at the Paper of Record," copyright 1968 by The Village Voice, Inc. Reprinted by permission of *The Village Voice.*

Thomas Pynchon, "A Journey into the Mind of Watts," © 1966 by The New York Times Company. Reprinted by permission of *The New York Times* and Robert Lantz-Candida Donadio Literary Agency, Inc.

Dotson Rader, "One Weekend in May," copyright © 1971 by Dotson Rader. Reprinted by permission of Dotson Rader c/o International Famous Agency, Inc.

Richard Reeves, "Mike Lang (Groovy Kid from Brooklyn) Plus John Roberts (Unlimited Capital) Equals Woodstock," © 1969 by The New York Times Company. Reprinted by permission.

Errata
The following credits should appear on page vii:

CREDITS FOR PHOTOGRAPHS

Page 54: Donald McCullin/Magnum

Page 118: Bonnie Freer

Page 160: Bonnie Freer

Page 206: Wide World

Page 226: Wide World

Page 290: Burk Uzzle/Magnum

Page 320: R. Freeman/Magnum

Page 354: Bonnie Freer

Page 392: Leonard Freed/Magnum

The following credit should appear on page 393:

Tom Hayden, as quoted in an interview by Tim Findley, *Rolling Stone,* November 9, 1972, p. 55. © 1972 by Straight Arrow Publishers, Inc. All Rights Reserved. Reprinted by permission.

Mills: THE NEW JOURNALISM 1/1

0-07-042350-4 SC
0-07-042349-0 HC

Robin Reisig, "The Vets and Mayday," copyright 1971 by The Village Voice, Inc. Reprinted by permission of *The Village Voice.*

Jonathan Schell, from *The Village of Ben Suc.* Copyright © 1967 by Jonathan Schell. Reprinted by permission of Alfred A. Knopf, Inc. Originally appeared in *The New Yorker* in slightly different form.

Wilfrid Sheed, "Donkey Serenade," copyright © 1972 by *Saturday Review of the Arts,* Volume LV, Number 33. Reprinted by permission of Robert Lantz-Candida Donadio Literary Agency, Inc.

Hunter S. Thompson, "Fear and Loathing in Miami Beach," from *Rolling Stone,* © 1972 by Straight Arrow Publishers, Inc. All Rights Reserved. Reprinted by permission.

Nicholas von Hoffman, "Washington: On the Ropes," "Peace Freaks," and "Nyaa, Nyaa, We Won," from the Washington Post, May 5, 7, and 10, 1971. Copyright 1971 by the Washington Post. Reprinted by permission.

Tom Wolfe, from *The Pump House Gang,* copyright © 1966 by the World Journal Tribune Corporation, copyright © 1968 by Tom Wolfe. Reprinted with the permission of Farrar, Straus & Giroux, Inc.

FOR

Kermit
Fran
Ross
Julia
Alexandra

Acknowledgment

For the putting-together of this book, I owe a special debt to Dave
Edwards, Alice Felbinger, Susan Gamer, and Robert Randall.
Were it not for Bob Rodgers, it all would have been stillborn.

Contents

Introduction

When we think of the forces that since the mid-1960s have been changing American life, our first instinct is still to hold our breath, to want more time to sort out what seems permanent from what seems faddish. We have surprisingly little trouble accepting the picture of America that Norman Mailer draws at the end of *Armies of the Night* when he describes the country in the turmoil of childbirth:

> Brood on that country who expresses our will. She is·America, once a beauty of magnificence unparalled, now a beauty with leprous skin. She is heavy with child—no one knows if legitimate—and languishes in a dungeon whose walls are never seen. Now the first contractions of her fearsome labor begin—it will go on: no doctor exists to tell the hour. It is only known that false labor is not likely on her now, no, she will probably give birth, and to what?—the most fearsome totalitarianism the world has ever known? or can she, poor giant, tormented lovely girl, deliver a babe of a new world, tender, artful and wild?*

---

* Norman Mailer, *Armies of the Night,* New American Library, New York, 1968, p. 320, Signet edition.

When we recall all that has happened in America since 1965, we know, for example, the "system" has proved more resilient than its radical critics supposed. It has not collapsed nor even changed in ways they predicted. Yet we also know that during these years there has been a black movement, a student movement, a women's movement of unparalleled dimension and promise, and that even among professional workers, dissatisfaction runs deeper than they or anyone else thought possible.

What follows in this anthology is an attempt to explore the changes that have been taking place in America since the mid-1960s through the body of writing that came into existence with them and, perhaps more than any other, goes to their center—the new journalism. The term itself is not without limitations. Even someone as closely identified with the new journalism as Tom Wolfe has complained that he has never liked the term, doesn't know when it was coined or exactly who coined it, and thinks anyone using it is "begging for trouble." Wolfe's remarks are to be taken as a warning, not a prohibition, however. For we can, without fear of creating an artificial literary category, begin to speak of the new journalism as opposed to the old, trace its origins as well as general acceptance, and by example argue for the importance of the picture it gives of contemporary America.

II

There is no better starting point for an understanding of the new journalism than this description by one of its early practicioners, Gay Talese:

> The new journalism, though often reading like fiction, is not fiction. It is, or should be, as reliable as the most reliable reportage although it seeks a larger truth than is possible through the mere compilation of verifiable facts, the use of direct quotations, and adherence to the rigid organizational style of the older form. The new journalism allows, demands in fact, a more imaginative approach to reporting, and it permits the writer to inject himself into the narrative if he wishes. . . .*

The practical significance of Talese's description comes into focus the minute we compare a traditional and new journalistic account of the same event. The following excerpts from stories about Robert Kennedy's assassination offer a case in point. The first passage is from a story by Warren Weaver, Jr., in the *New York Times:*

> Senator Robert F. Kennedy was shot and critically wounded by an unidentified gunman this morning just after he made his victory speech in the California primary election.

*From FAME AND OBSCURITY: PORTRAITS BY GAY TALESE, Copyright © 1970 by Gay Talese. With permission of Thomas Y. Corwell Co., Inc.

> Moments after the shots were fired, the New York Senator lay on the cement floor of a kitchen corridor outside the ballroom of the Ambassador Hotel while crowds of screaming and wailing supporters crowded around him.*

The second passage is from Pete Hamill's account in *The Village Voice:*

> The scene assumed a kind of insane fury, all jump cuts, screams, noise, hurtling bodies, blood. The shots went pap-pap, pap-pap-pap, small sharp noises like a distant firefight or the sound of firecrackers in a backyard. . . .
> I saw Kennedy lurch against the ice machine, and then sag, and then fall forward slowly, to be grabbed by someone, and I knew then that he was dead. . . . his face remainded me somehow of Benny Paret the night Emile Griffith hammered him into unconsciousness.†

As the *Times* story illustrates, it is most important for the traditional journalist to describe what happened in terms of the facts themselves and to let the facts determine the structure and tone of his report. In this, Weaver succeeds perfectly. From his account we know exactly when and where Robert Kennedy was shot and that an unidentified gunman did it. From the new journalist Pete Hamill's account, on the other hand, we eventually get the same information, but not at all on the basis of an order dictated by the facts. Above all else, Hamill wants us to feel what it was like to be near Robert Kennedy when he died, and so he describes the sound of the shots, not just the shooting, the way Kennedy fell, not just Kennedy's death, and his own reaction, not merely the crowd's screams.

When we go beyond such specific examples and try to distinguish the new journalism from the old in more systematic ways, it means confronting two basic issues: the shape of the new journalism and the writer's relationship to it. Certainly nothing is more obvious about the new journalism than the ways in which it reads differently from the old. As a practical matter, the new journalism may take a hybrid form or utilize neglected possibilities of traditional journalism, but the thrust of the new journalism is in a very different direction from that of the old—toward fiction. The structure, the language, the point of view of the new journalism all go against the grain of the ordered, objective, detached approach of established reporting. The fear of getting too close to a subject or developing a prose style that contradicts the image of the reporter as "clerk of fact" is not the worry of the new journalist. As Tom Wolfe observed of his own first attempt at new journalism, the great "plus" it offered was freedom to use any literary device—from stream-of-consciousness to traditional dialogue—that might involve a reader more deeply in events.

---

* Warren Weaver, *The New York Times,* June 5, 1968, p. 1. © 1968 by the New York Times Company. Reprinted by permission.

† Pete Hamill, "Two Minutes to Midnight," *The Village Voice,* June 13, 1968, p. 1. © 1968 by The Village Voice, Inc. Reprinted by permission of The Village Voice.

What these changes mean as far as a definition of new journalism goes is that it must be seen as a freer and more ambitious type of reporting that makes special use of the techniques of fiction. The structure of a new journalistic story will, for example, tend to be based on a dramatic rather than a chronological narrative of events. For the new journalist it is "the scene" that is crucial, and he will make every effort to construct his story in terms of scenes, even if it means sacrificing other kinds of order. The same distinction applies to dialogue. For the new journalist the value of dialogue, in contrast to an isolated quotation or a "statement to the press," is that it grows out of a context in which people reveal themselves spontaneously, and how they speak becomes as important as what they say. The extended dialogue in so many new journalistic accounts frequently establishes character more swiftly than any description can. There are similar reasons for the new journalist's tendency to write from his own point of view or that of a character he is describing. For in both cases he has moved his reader closer to events by getting him to see them from the perspective of someone caught up by them.

The form of the new journalism tells only part of the story when it comes to distinguishing it, however. There is also the new journalist's relationship to his writing. Here it is important to bear in mind Dan Wakefield's observation that "in a supernation the gathering of information is usually carried on by vast networks and organizations, equipped with computers, recording machines, scientific questionnaires, and various other highly technical apparatus." The new journalist has put himself in direct opposition to this kind of corporate journalism. Not only does he do his own legwork and research, he makes sure each of his stories bears his imprint. "I do not write differently for any particular magazine—nor for any editor," Gay Talese declares. "I write for myself, usually selecting subjects that interest me and are part of something larger than the magazine subject."

In terms of political stands, this personal quality of the new journalism is especially apparent. To be sure, few new journalists have gone as far as Andrew Kopkind in declaring "objectivity is the rationalization for moral disengagement, the classic cop-out from choice making." But not at all uncommon are the views of a politically committed reporter like Jack Newfield:

> Participation and advocacy remain the touchstones of the new insurgent journalism. The evidence now seems overwhelming that the closer a serious writer gets to his material, the more understanding he gets, the more he is there to record the decisive moments of spontaneity and authenticity. . . . He does not have to write about impersonal public rituals like ghost-written speeches, well-rehearsed concerts, and stated and managed press conferences. He is there to see and react to the human reflexes exposed late at night that illuminate a man's character.
>
> The advocacy journalist breaks down the artificial barrier between work and leisure; between private and public knowledge. He can do this because he is

writing, by choice, about subjects that excite his imagination, rather than ful-filling an assignment made by the city desk, and that needs to be approved and edited by the copy desk. He is a free man, relying on his instincts, intelligence, and discipline, liberated from all the middlemen who try to mediate between the writer and reality.*

The difference between the old and new journalists' relationships to their writing is perhaps most strikingly illustrated by the fact that when we think of the old journalism at its best, we generally think of newspapers, e.g., the *New York Times,* the *St. Louis Post-Dispatch,* the *Christian Science Monitor;* but when we think of the new journalism, it is generally the writers who come to mind first: Jimmy Breslin and Pete Hamill more than the *New York Post,* Tom Wolfe and Gay Talese more than *Esquire* magazine. Equally revealing, when we think of the new journalists, it is not only their writing that comes to mind but who they are. For example, we have a good idea of Pete Hamill's closeness to his father or how Tom Wolfe dresses or whom Jimmy Breslin trusts, and this knowledge influences the way we judge their reporting.

III

It is more difficult to be precise about when the new journalism began. Tom Wolfe contends that around 1965 newspaper and magazine writers began experimenting with what became known as the new journalism and that by late 1966 people started talking about the new journalism. Certainly the 1965–1966 period offers the first solid evidence that the new journalism was being practiced by a number of writers and developing an audience of its own. In addition to Wolfe, one could by this time identify Gay Talese, Jimmy Breslin, Dick Schaap, and Terry Southern as new journalists and point to *Esquire* and *The New York Herald Tribune* as places where the new journalism had found a home. By 1966 there were even whole books of new journalism, ranging from Hunter Thompson's *Hell's Angels* to George Plimpton's *Paper Lion,* as well as a sudden flour-ishing of "offbeat" newspapers practicing new journalism. The circulation of the *Village Voice* skyrocketed during these years, while papers like the *Berkeley Barb* got their start and the Underground Press Syndicate was formed.

The 1965–1966 period also saw a body of criticism begin to develop around the new journalism. Some of the criticism was, of course, hostile. In mid-1965 Dwight Macdonald charged, "A new kind of journalism is being born or spawned. It might be called 'parajournalism,' from the Greek *para, 'beside'* or *'against'*: something similar in form but different in func-tion. . . . It is a bastard form, having it both ways, exploiting the factual authority of journalism and the atmospheric license of fiction." But much

---

* Jack Newfield, "Journalism: Old, New, and Corporate," *Dutton Review,* number 1, pp. 164–165. Copyright © 1970 by E. P. Dutton & Company, Inc., Publishers, and used with their permission.

of the criticism surrounding the new journalism was favorable and helped to develop it. In the year following Macdonald's attack, Dan Wakefield, who would later make a one-man tour of the United States and write *Super-nation at War and Peace,* observed in an article called "The Personal Voice and the Impersonal Eye" that nonfiction was now being treated as a serious art form, and Truman Capote changed the whole critical climate in which new journalism was received with his publication of *In Cold Blood* and his insistence on a new literary genre, "the nonfiction novel."

The new journalism has never been so new that it was without precedent, however. There is much truth in Jack Newfield's observation, "Defoe, Addison and Steele, Stephen Crane, and Mark Twain were all new journalists according to most definitions." For what the work of these men points up is that, long before the new journalism developed into a distinguishable body of writing, there was literature that combined the techniques of fiction and journalism and emphasized the importance of authorial involvement in describing events. Defoe in his *Journal of the Plague Year* was, for example, able to make such effective use of old records and a seemingly true personal narrative that his book was often taken as a historical account rather than fiction, and Mark Twain in his *Life on the Mississippi* was able to weave his own adventures and observations into a narrative far more penetrating than any standard journalistic account of America in those years.

Since the 1930s the precedents for the new journalism have come even closer to the mark. George Orwell's account of the Spanish Civil War in *Homage to Catalonia,* James Agee's description of the life of Southern tenant farmers in *Let Us Now Praise Famous Men,* John Hersey's story of the effect of the atomic bomb on the Japanese in *Hiroshima* all employed new journalistic techniques in innovative ways. The following description by James Agee of picking cotton provides a perfect illustration of a pre-new journalist using new journalistic techniques to make his reader *feel* what it was like to work as a tenant farmer:

> Over the right shoulder you have slung a long white sack whose half length trails the ground behind. You work with both hands as fast and steadily as you can. The trick is to get the cotton between your fingertips at its very roots in the burr in all three or four gores at once so that it is brought out clean in one pluck. It is easy enough with one burr in perhaps ten, where the cotton is ready to fall; with the rest the fibers are more tight and tricky. So another trick is, to learn these several different shapes of burr and resistance as nearly as possible by instinct, so there will be no second trying and delay. . . .*

By the 1950s the circle of writers doing new journalism, or work very close to it, had grown even wider. It included, among others, a veteran newsman

---

*James Agee and Walker Evans, *Let Us Now Praise Famous Men,* Houghton Mifflin Company, Boston, 1939, p. 306, Ballentine-Walden edition.

like A. J. Liebling reporting on the press, James Baldwin writing on race, and Jimmy Cannon on sports.

What sets off modern new journalism from these earlier efforts is the way in which it has developed into a more clearly definable literary form and grown into a sizable body of writing. But *why* the new journalism should have come into its own in the mid-1960s is a different question. And in this regard it is helpful to examine its relation to other forces in American life. Certainly nothing contributed more to the success of the new journalism than the failures of the old. Bill Moyers' observation, "I learned at the White House that of all the great myths of American journalism, objectivity is the greatest," tells a good part of the story. But it was not just the failure of the traditional journalists to practice the objectivity they preached that helped the new journalism along. Equally important was the caution of the old journalists and their papers. In an era of great turmoil, when what was being challenged were the aims and not merely the details of American society, there was nothing the old journalism missed so completely as the spirit of the challengers. A who, what, where, when, why style of reporting could not begin to capture the anger of a black power movement or the euphoria of a Woodstock. At best it could give the external shape of such events, and even in this effort it did not possess the immediacy of television. For an audience either deeply concerned or directly involved in the changes going on in America, it was necessary to report events from the inside out, and this is what the new journalism attempted to do. When it failed, it was not out of coldness or want of sympathy but for a quality its audience was prepared to understand: the blindness that comes from getting too close to an event. As a result, when the new journalism came into prominence in the mid-1960s, it was supported on one side by tremendous changes in social consciousness and on the other by changes produced through the media. The combination was more than enough to make new journalism profitable. The best reporters were drawn to it, and novelists like Norman Mailer, Truman Capote, and Kurt Vonnegut, Jr., did some of their finest work in it.

IV

The forty pieces of new journalism that make up this anthology are indicative of its scope as well as the commitment the new journalists have made to covering public events in terms of their effect on individual lives. The articles in this collection are not, however, limited to "pure" new journalism. They reflect the way the new journalism often takes a hybrid form that amalgamates old and new journalistic techniques, and is especially appropriate to a magazine like *Rolling Stone,* for example, which, in the words of its editor, Jann Wenner, is "on the line between under-ground versus above-ground press, between newspaper and magazine, between being a trade paper and a consumer paper, between dope and music." For new journalistic purists, such an approach is bound to be irritating because it makes the category of new journalism too broad. And for traditional journalists opposed to the new journalism, such an approach is only likely to stir the observation that the new journalism isn't so new after all. The answer to both these criticisms is that for all practical purposes the new journalism is recognizable by the *varying degrees* in which its innovations carry it beyond the bounds of established journalism. In speaking of the new journalism as a distinguishable form of writing, it need not appear as a consistently pure form.

In this regard it is also important to emphasize the diversity within the category of new journalism. (Indeed, some of the writers included in this anthology would probably argue that they were not new journalists.) There are a number of new journalists who have written for the same magazine or same editors and who have been influenced by one another. But categorizing these writers as new journalists, like categorizing a series of 1960s painters as pop artists, only touches on the general direction of their work, not its individuality. It is still necessary to acknowledge that Tom Wolfe, for example, does not generally use point of view the way Norman Mailer does. Jimmy Breslin's style is not like David Halberstam's, and the tone of Jack Newfield's writing in no way resembles that of Truman Capote's.

In this anthology we have chosen to deal with these and other differences by exploring the new journalism as it reflects upon ten events that have taken place since the mid-1960s. The advantage of such an approach is that it offers a way of judging the new journalism in comparison with itself and in terms of contemporary America. But it also means that we have abandoned certain alternatives. Collecting the most outstanding pieces of new journalism in a book that might have been called *The Best of the New Journalism* has not been done on the grounds that the qualitative merit of such an anthology would not offset its lack of any greater order. Similarly, a collection that would be only chronological or would progress from a study of established journalism, to combinations of old and new journalism, to pure new journalism has not been tried on the grounds that it sacrifices too much of the historical depth of the new journalism.

More difficult to justify are the choices that have been made in regard to the events and movements on which this anthology is based:

1. The American Racial Divide: Black Power in Watts
2. Crusade in Asia: Vietnam before Tet
3. Organizing the Unorganized: The California Grape Boycott
4. Students in Revolt: Crisis at Columbia
5. The Politics of Assassination: The Death of Robert Kennedy
6. Conquest of Space: The Apollo 11 Moon Landing
7. The Counter Culture in Action: Woodstock
8. The Protest to End Protests: Mayday in Washington

It is easy to point to all that such a list leaves out, and the only general defense we can offer is that, in any anthology of less than encyclopedic size, quantity is always an issue. We think it is essential, however, to answer in detail two other questions: What overall logic is behind these sections? Within this framework what priorities were established?

The answer to the first question is that since 1965 the most important developments in America are those that have challenged the basis of national life. In contrast to the 1950s, when so much stress was placed on maintaining traditional values, or the early years of President Kennedy's administration, when new energy went into old battles (America would meet the Russian challenge by closing the missile gap), from the middle 1960s on, the most crucial events are those that have put in doubt the established order. The black power movement, for example, does not ask white Americans to admit black Americans to white institutions. It challenges white Americans to let black Americans form their own institutions. The Vietnam protest goes far beyond America's role in Asia. It questions our national morality and role as world policeman. Even Woodstock, in contrast to a 1950s Newport Jazz Festival, raises fundamental doubts about a national life style: about sex, about traditional families, about drugs.

The merit of these challenges to a traditional America is a different question. Indeed, it is the question with which the new journalism of this book struggles. To present the overriding issues in America from 1965 on as ones involving challenge and doubt is not to preclude the judgment Daniel Bell gives when he describes the predominant sensibility of this period as "a longing for the lost gratifications of an idealized childhood." What the individual sections of this anthology attempt to do is focus on and clarify the most significant points of challenge and conflict. Thus, there is a section on Watts rather than Selma, because we judged that after 1965 the black power movement was more important than the civil rights movement. Similarly, in dealing with the politics of assassination, it is Robert Kennedy's death, rather than any other that is analyzed, because we thought his murder brought into perspective the deaths of President Kennedy, Malcolm X, and Martin Luther King. By contrast, Vietnam before Tet is the subject of a section, because after the Tet offensive opposition to the war became easier and less politically revealing. Perhaps most surprising of all is a section devoted to the 1972 Democratic Convention in Miami instead of the 1968 Democratic Convention in Chicago. The choice in this case was made on the grounds that, although the first convention was more shocking to the country, the second convention offered a chance to see if the lessons of the first had been absorbed.

The result is admittedly a collection that raises questions in its own right.

But any other approach risks too little. It minimizes the way the literary innovations of the new journalism are a response to the pressures of American life, and above all, it diverts us from seeing how coming to terms with a history of the new journalism means coming to terms with the new journalism as history.

The American Racial Divide: Black Power in Watts

By almost any historical standard 1965 looked as if it were going to be *the year* for the civil rights movement. In the spring the Selma march—despite numerous arrests and the murders of Jimmy Lee Jackson, the Reverend James Reeb, and Viola Liuzzo—ended on a note of triumph with 25,000 people gathering at a rally in front of the old state capitol in Montgomery, Alabama. Five months later, on August 6, President Johnson signed into the law the long-awaited Voting Rights Act. Yet in terms of America's racial climate, the most significant chain of events in 1965 began on August 11 with the start of the Watts riot in Los Angeles.

In six days of rioting 34 persons were killed, 1,032 injured, 3,952 arrested. Property damage totaled an estimated $140 million, and 14,000 National Guardsmen were called into action. The result was not only a change in the racial climate of America, but the start of a new era in black thinking and black–white political relations. After Watts, a black power movement would begin to replace an essentially integrationist, nonviolent civil rights effort. Eldridge Cleaver, although he was in Folsom Prison at the time of Watts, would sense these changes immediately. "Watts was a place of shame," he wrote. "We used to use Watts as an epithet in much the same way as city boys used 'country' as a term of derision. . . . But now blacks are seen in Folsom saying, 'I'm from Watts, Baby!'—whether true or no, but I think their meaning is clear. Confession: I, too, have participated in this game, saying, I'm from Watts. In fact, I did live there for a time, and I'm proud of it, the tired lamentations of Whitney Young, Roy Wilkins, and The Preacher notwithstanding."

The spark that set off the Watts riot was the arrest of Marquette Frye, a Watts resident, one block from his home on a charge of drunk driving. In short order, however, the immediate cause of the riot was obscured by deeper grievances. The best and the worst neighborhoods in Watts were not far apart in their response. As compared to 25.6 percent of those in the worst neighborhoods, 18 percent of those in the best neighborhoods in Watts joined the riot. What they shared, beyond all else, was the Watts experience: few good jobs and an adult unemployment rate of 30 percent; a public transportation system often requiring a domestic worker to spend $1.50 in fare and two hours on the bus traveling to a job paying $7 a day; no nearby hospital; and a police department unsympathetic to the Watts community, with only 200 of its 25,000 officers black. The five accounts that follow all concern themselves directly or indirectly with these facts of life in Watts. Where they differ and invite special comparison is in the perspective from which they are written.

Robert Conot's "Stranger in the City," the first chapter of his Watts study, *Rivers of Blood, Years of Darkness,* focuses on the incident from which the Watts riot stemmed—the arrest of Marquette Frye on a charge of drunk driving. In typical new journalist fashion Conot has gone to great lengths to recapture not only the scene, but the point of view of the Frye family and their friends. His story begins with a history of the Frye family and how Marquette Frye, who was born in the coal mining town of Hanna, Wyoming (population 625), still felt like a stranger in Los Angeles after living there for eight years. To reconstruct the arrest scene on Avalon Boulevard, Conot has gone to the Los Angeles County District Attorney's records, court transcripts, interviews with police officers and witnesses to the arrest, and then has woven his information into a drama that moves between what people were thinking and what was actually happening. It is these shifts in consciousness that give his report its force. For as the drama builds from a driver's being stopped for speeding, to a charge of drunk driving, to a fight involving the Frye family, to a battle between the police and the crowd, Conot's narrative makes clear how this escalation stems from the racial tensions of Los Angeles in particular and the country in general. It is the logic of all that took place after Frye's arrest, not the unexpectedness of it, by which we are struck.

Paul Bullock's "Riot" begins two days after Frye's arrest. Bullock is most concerned with capturing the viewpoint of the Watts rioters, and by way of introduction, he tells of the time in World War II he and his army buddies looted a German factory. For Bullock and his friends there was little guilt attached to their actions. The Germans, they felt, were responsible for enormous crimes, and their own looting was a personal gesture of revenge. Bullock finds a similar pattern in the Watts riot, noting that certain "fair" stores were left untouched. Bullock does not, like Conot, attempt to reconstruct scenes, however. Instead, he lets the Watts residents tell their own stories. It is these accounts, with their concern for the anguish the rioting reflected and caused, that gives "The Riot" its true center.

By contrast, Tom Wolfe's "Pump House Gang" offers a total shift in perspective on the Watts riot—to that of a La Jolla teen-age surfing gang. In his typical chameleon fashion Wolfe manages to write not merely from the point of view of the Pump House gang but often in a style that duplicates their language and their values. The gang went to Watts during the riot, Wolfe observes, because Watts "just happened to be what was going on at the time as far as the netherworld of La Jolla surfing was concerned." But how could the gang come to think this way? What combination of indifference and preoccupation with sensation lay behind their action? These are questions Wolfe attempts to answer not by analyzing the gang but, as the following scene shows, by entering their minds and trying to express the world as they see it:

> The party got *very Dionysian* that night and somebody put a hole through one wall, and everybody else decided to see if they could make it bigger. Everybody was stoned out of their hulking gourds, and it got to be about 3:30 a.m. and everybody decided to go see the riots. There were the riots in Watts. The Los Angeles *Times* and the San Diego *Union* were all saying, WATTS NO-MAN'S LAND and STAY AWAY FROM WATTS YOU GET YO'SE'F KILLED, but naturally nobody believed that. Watts was a blast, and the Pump House gang was immune to the trembling gourd panic rattles of the L. A. *Times* black pan-thuhs. Immune!

In the end it is clear that nothing that happened in Watts, as long as it remained confined to Watts, could ever reach the La Jolla world of the Pump House gang.

The final report in this section, novelist Thomas Pynchon's "Journey into the Mind of Watts," was written in the year following the riot, when another police incident, the shooting of Leonard Deadwyler, as he was driving his pregnant wife to the hospital, threatened a second round of bloodshed. As far as Pynchon can see, very little is different from the summer of 1965. "The neighborhood may be seething with social workers, data collectors, VISTA volunteers and other assorted members of the humanitarian establishment, all of whose intentions are the purest in the world. But somehow nothing much has changed." The more Pynchon examines Watts after the riot, the more it seems like Watts before the riot. In the end, we cannot help wondering if the clearest perspective on Watts was not expressed by the crowd on Avalon Boulevard that saw the Frye family arrested and refused to swallow their anger.

A Stranger in the City

Robert Conot

Robert Conot has been a newspaper reporter, a television writer, and an editor. A graduate of Standford University, Mr. Conot is the author of *Ministers of Vengeance* and *Rivers of Blood, Years of Darkness*.

Marquette Frye had lived in Los Angeles for eight years, but he was still a stranger in the city. He had grown up in the coal-mining town of Hanna, Wyoming, where every one of the 625 residents was a neighbor to everyone else, and he had had a sense of belonging. Not here. Here he didn't know what he was. He didn't know what he was, because he didn't know what he could be, or what he was supposed to be. He had no plans, because it seemed to him as if he had been dumped into a dead end— a dead end with but one exit: an exit that both frightened and repelled him.

And so he was lost. Lost within his cul-de-sac, that in itself was lost amidst the labyrinths of the city.

Hanna sits astride the Continental Divide just south of what had been the great Overland Trail up the Platte and down the Sweetwater River; and the high, rolling land retains much of the flavor that had greeted the settlers. The population of Carbon County, an area about the size of Vermont, still is less than 15,000, 9,000 of whom are crowded into the city of Rawlins. For the first 13 years of his life Marquette had the great all-American boyhood of romantic legend. The fact that he was a Negro had made no impact upon him. There was a large Greek community, and they had a Mediterranean tolerance for dark-skinned people. Most of the neighbors were white. His friends were white. He would go over to their houses for dinner, and they would come and spend the night with him. They were different from him and his brothers and sisters, but it

was a difference like that of brown and blond hair or gray and blue eyes.

Then, in the mid-1950's, the operation of the coal mine in Hanna, like that of many small mines from Kentucky to Washington, had begun to peter out. Wallace Frye, an Oklahoma cotton farmer who had been recruited by the United Mine Workers in 1944 when there had been a shortage of miners, had to start thinking about moving. Nor was it only· a question of moving. Wallace Frye had two skills: cotton farming and coal mining. Technological changes had made a manpower surplus in both. Now, in middle age, he was cast out to become part of that vast minority army, jobless and with no real prospect of ever again being able to gain anything but marginal employment. Having relatives in Los Angeles, he decided to transport his second wife Rena, his stepson Marquette, and the other children to Southern California.

The Fryes arrived in Los Angeles in 1957. From a truly integrated community they were plunged into the heart of a ghetto, where a white face was seen more rarely than in Negro sections of the Black Belt. Wallace Frye went from job to job—service-station attendant, paper-factory worker, parking-lot attendant. Rena supplemented his income by working as a domestic. The children, who hardly knew what a policeman was, were picked up on their very first day in the city.

They had gone out to get some ice cream, when they were spotted by a truant officer. He took them home, and, when it was explained to him that they were not in school because they had just arrived, he tried to give the family an insight into the area. He warned the children that they would have to work at staying out of trouble—there was an element in the community that would do its best to draw them into it.

For no one was the transition so difficult as it was for Marquette. A thin, intelligent 13-year-old who had all of his life lived as part of a white community, he was suddenly dropped, like a character from a Jules Verne balloon, into a new environment where almost all the faces he saw were colored. In them he could see himself—yet he felt no identity with them. He felt different. He was different. And his problems began.

"Hey! How come you talks funny like that? 'You from Mars or somethin'?" The other kids in the junior high school, the substantial majority of whom had migrated from the South or had parents who came from the South, challenged his English. It was not difficult for them to sense that he did not feel himself part of them. They retaliated by ostracizing him.

"White boy, what happened to you? You fall in a puddle of ink and come up black?"

He was an outsider. He was lost in the impersonality of the 35-pupils-per-class school. Not knowing who he was, or where he belonged—and, even more important where he was heading—his motivation dropped off, he became like a badly tuned engine chugging desperately up a hill. He didn't make it. In his senior year at Fremont High School he became a dropout.

The first time he was picked up by the police was a month before his sixteenth birthday. He was only doing what a lot of the other kids—the ones who always seemed to have change in their pockets—bragged about doing: rifling a coin machine. Telephone booths, coin-operated laundries, soft drink machines—all are easy pickings.

At 77th St. station, the police gave him a talking to. They tried to impress upon him, as they try every year to impress upon a hundred other kids picked up for the first time, what lay ahead of him if he didn't straighten out. It is a brimstone-and-hell admonition, and sometimes it works.

Sometimes.

More often, though, it becomes a joke.

"See, they can't do nothing to you!" the other kids told him after he'd been released. "The law don't allow 'em to!"

This is patently untrue, but it is believed by many, because few juveniles are ever filed on for first offenses; or even for second or third.

The fact that he'd gotten into trouble with the law brought Marquette a measure of acceptance from many of his schoolmates. The law is white. The law was against him. So Marquette had to be true black after all.

In March of the next year, 1961, he was caught taking wine, cigars, and chewing gum from a grocery store. This time a juvenile court hearing was set, and he went before the judge on May 18. The case was continued, pending the filing of a probation report.

Few days later he and some other kids, including several girls, were hanging around outside a laundromat when an older man began egging them on. Very soon Marquette found himself dared into snatching a purse, containing $18, from a woman doing her laundry. The man took the purse, and Marquette was in the process of making his escape, when the police came and collared the girls he had been with. Gallantly he returned, and gave himself up. On June 15 he was placed in the custody of the L.A. County Probation Department and sent to a forestry camp.

He stayed there two years, until he was 19 years old. Then he was released on parole. For five months thereafter he worked as a pickup and delivery man for an auto dealer. But he wasn't satisfied. He wanted something better.

"A man may be willing to swallow his pride and eat humble pie if he thinks it's going to get him somewhere," he says. "But what's the use of going hat in hand if it doesn't get you nowhere no way?"

For the next 18 months he worked only desultorily. When he is in his element he has a jaunty, Sammy Davis-like way about him that often charms people and makes them laugh. Emphasizing a point, he will take quick, small dancing steps back and forth, using his hands as if he were sparring, putting his whole body into the conversation. He has a collegiate sophistication, smoking a pipe and wearing fashionable clothes. When he puts on his wrap-around sunglasses, he looks like a swinger. Within his own age group he is popular. Yet with the anomalies and inconsistencies of a socio-economic structure dominated by whites —a white world which resembled not at all that in which he had grown up—he did not know how to cope. It was always a white man to whom he had to go looking for a job; a white man who would inspect and interrogate him as if he were a piece of material for sale. Under those conditions, he always went on the defensive. He was made to feel, as he said, "like nothing but a piece of shit."

On Wednesday, August 11, 1965, he had slept late. He had slept late because he often stayed out late at night, and there wasn't any point in getting up early. When he did get up the room was already stuffy from the sun's rays ricocheting off the windows. Until a few days before it had been one of the city's really cool summers, with the temperature scarcely rising above 80. But on Monday the heat wave had descended, smothering, like a brooding hen onto an egg; and from mid-morning until late afternoon south-central Los Angeles sim-

mered in 95-degree temperatures beneath a yellow-gray coverlet of smog. As Marquette splashed water onto his face and pulled on his slim, Italian-style pants, he decided he would accompany two of his friends, Pete and Milton, to court in Inglewood where, that afternoon, Milton was scheduled to appear for preliminary hearing on a burglary charge.

All in all, Marquette thought, things weren't too bad. Since getting out of the camp he had kept his nose clean. On July 3 he had successfully completed his two years of probation. Now, for the first time in five years, he was out from under the gun. Then, too, his stepbrother, Ronald, a year older than he, had arrived from Wyoming on Monday, and yesterday evening he had taken him around the neighborhood to introduce him to a few girls. They had had a good time partying.

Yet, one way or another, there were always problems. He hadn't had a job for months; and his girl friend, Gloria, had just told him she was pregnant.

He had his mother's gray-white 1955 Buick; and, after the hearing, he decided to go home and pick up Ronald before going over to Milton's house. It was 5 o'clock, and the breeze sucked seaward from the mountains was beginning to wipe away the pollution like grime from a dirty window. Still, the heat hadn't abated much, and it was a real pleasure when he and Ronald got over to Milton's place and were able to relax with cooling screwdrivers—vodka and orange juice.

The girls they were expecting didn't show up, so they just sat and talked. They had three or four drinks. A few minutes before 7 o'clock, when Marquette decided they'd better head home for dinner, he'd had just enough vodka to make him feel as if the world was a good place to live in after all.

He drove with verve. Slightly too fast, and not altogether in conformity with traffic regulations. As he turned north from El Segundo onto Avalon Blvd., a Negro, driving a pickup truck and waiting for the light to change, thought his behavior erratic. Coincidentally, just before the light turned green, a California Highway Patrol motorcycle officer pulled up. The truck driver, leaning from the cab, shouted to him that there seemed to be something the matter with the driver of a Buick heading north on Avalon. In response to the officer's query, he said that he "looked like he might be drunk or something."

Officer Lee Minikus gave him an informal salute in acknowledgement, gunned the cycle, and swung up Avalon Blvd. after the Buick, which was already a couple of blocks ahead.

At 65 miles an hour Minikus sped up the broad, heavily traveled street. To his right was an undeveloped area of open fields and small manufacturing plants, to his left junkyards and small businesses. Crossing 120th St. the roadway narrowed; there were stores, a café, a laundry, a beauty parlor, a neighborhood grocery featuring accounting and income-tax services. A couple of blocks farther north the neighborhood became mainly residential, consisting of recently built two-story apartment houses, interspersed here and there with old dwellings dating back to a time when the area had been used for truck farms. Lining the side streets were neat, single-family residences with well-kept lawns and plots of flowers—differing little, if at all, from other middle-class suburban neighborhoods.

As Marquette drove past 117th St., Ronald became aware of the sharp red light reflected in the rear-view mirror. He called his brother's attention to it. Marquette slowed down, then brought the car to a halt against the curb a half block north of 116th Place, stopping a few feet behind a car already parked. It just so happened that he was only a block from home— he had been planning to make a left turn onto

116th St., then left again onto Towne, which parallels Avalon.

It was just a minute or two after 7 o'clock.

At that moment, highway patrol Officer Bob Lewis, Lee Minikus's partner, was cruising on his cycle near the Harbor Freeway, six blocks to the west. Officier Wayne Wilson sat astride his cycle, watching for speeders, at an El Segundo intersection. And Officer Larry Bennett, in a CHP car, was patrolling in unincorporated county territory in the vicinity of Athens Park.

At Avalon Blvd. and 118th St., a location that Officer Minikus had just passed, Walter Gaines was working late in his barbershop. Mr. Gaines had worked long hours all of his life in order to support his closely knit family— a wife and seven children. Although he had spent most of his 40-odd years in Stockton, in the north-central part of the state, he had decided to move to Los Angeles seven years before, because Los Angeles had a barbering college, and the Stockton area, at that time, had not. Knowing that he could not afford to send his children through college, he had been determined that each of them would have a trade before he left home. So, in their early teens, while still attending high school, boys and girls alike, off he sent them to barbering school. Each of them, by the time he received his high-school diploma, also had his barbering license.

Two of his daughters were working in the shop. The younger, Joyce Ann, who would be 21 in December, had been in the shop with him until after 6 o'clock, when she had decided to go to Vergie Nash's beauty parlor, a block down on Avalon, to have her hair set.

When Marquette opened the door of the car and stepped out, he wasn't really concerned. He knew the psychology of police officers, and he was confident he would be able to handle the situation. "Mostly when an officer stops you, he'll come up to you harshly, you know. This isn't because the officer is trying to be mean to you, but because he's trying to find out what type of person you are. I mean, if you're going to be an asshole, you know he's going to treat you as such."

These were his thoughts; and he was determined that he would disarm the officer by his friendly manner.

Lee Minikus, putting down the kickstand on the cycle and taking off his gloves, saw a smiling, jaunty Marquette Frye approaching him. Marquette had on a stingy brimmed hat; pointed, Italian-style shoes; narrow, cuffless trousers; and a tailored sport shirt: they accentuated his slenderness, and made him look as if he might have stepped out of a production of *Ana Lucasta*. Minikus, on the other hand, with his boots and baggy-hipped riding trousers, his waist encircled by his gun belt, his head and face virtually hidden by the white and black crash helmet and the dark goggles covering his eyes, had the impersonality of a comic strip Batman.

Beneath this exterior he was, in actuality, a rather good-natured man with sandy red hair, a windburned face, and a prominent nose. Like so many other officers, after a hitch in the service and a brief stint at a sedentary job, he had chosen the highway patrol as a means of escaping the eight-to-five office routine. In his middle thirties, married and with three children, he had been with the CHP almost 10 years.

"Can I see your driver's license, please?" he asked Marquette.

"Well, as it happens, you see, I was down at the New Pike in Long Beach a few days ago, and it fell out of my pocket, or some follow could have taken it. You know how it is. I lost it, and I just haven't had time to get me a new one."

It was the truth. He had lost his driver's license. But it didn't improve the situation.

"You know you were going 50 miles an hour in a 35-mile zone?" Minikus continued.

"Aw, officer. That old car wouldn't do more than 35 if you shoved it off a cliff!" Marquette laughed.

Marquette had come right up to him. Minikus, smelling his breath, asked, "Have you been drinking?"

"Well, you see," Marquette replied, "my brother, he's been in the service, and he just came in from Wyoming. So we went over to these girls and we were sort of having a party —and I had two or three screwdrivers. But I'm not drunk, officer, if that's what you mean."

In recent years, different jurisdictions have adopted a number of different tests in order to determine whether a person is intoxicated. The California Highway Patrol has chosen to retain the field sobriety test, a method of making the determination based on the person's physical behavior. This places a considerable burden on the officer's judgment. After checking the vehicle registration—which noted that the car belonged to Rena Frye, of 11620 Towne Ave.—and asking Marquette his name, Minikus ordered him to walk a straight line along the sidewalk, where a dirt strip divides the pavement from the curbing.

Marquette did as he was ordered. And did it rather successfully, *he* thought. "Now, would you like me to walk it backward?" he asked.

"No. Just stand there. Close your eyes. Put your finger to your nose." Minikus went on to the next test.

After Marquette's performance on that and one further test, Minikus decided that he had a 502—a drunk driver—on his hands. He went to the motorcycle, unhooked the radio mike, and called for his partner, Bob Lewis. He also asked for a transportation car to take Marquette to jail.

Returning to Marquette, Minikus began filling out a ticket. Since Marquette had no driver's license, it was necessary to ask him for all of the information—his birth date, address, the color of his eyes, the color of his hair.

"It's black, man!" Marquette replied. "I'm black all over, can't you see!" He was still jovial, doing a little jig.

"You're a real comedian, aren't you?" Minikus said good-humoredly.

While Marquette was taking his tests, people had begun to be attracted by his antics. A good many of them had been sitting on their steps or out on the lawns, and some had been congregating at the Oasis Shoeshine Stand, a hangout for Muslims, down toward Imperial Highway. A couple of dozen of them now stood around, watching the proceedings, laughing, talking among themselves, now and then making some jocose remark to Marquette or Minikus. It was a pleasant evening, a half hour before sunset.

Walking home from the store, Rosalie Sanders and her daughter Pearlie noticed the gathering. Marquette Frye had dated Pearlie, who was now married, some years before, and Rosie, as Rosalie was known, considered herself a friend of the Frye family.

"Isn't that Marquette standing there with that officer?" she asked Pearlie.

Pearlie, looking over in the indicated direction, replied that she believed it was.

Threading her way among the people, Rosie asked one of the bystanders what was going on. He answered that it looked like the boy had had a little too much to drink, and that they were going to take him to jail.

Alarmed, Rosie set out to tell Rena Frye. On the east side of Avalon Blvd., where the action was taking place, one apartment house runs lengthwise along the street, presenting its facade to the sidewalk. To the west, however, the apartment houses are aligned perpendicular to the boulevard, so that it is possible to walk between them and reach the next row of apartments facing on Towne Ave. It would

take Rosie a minute, at the most, to get to the Frye apartment.

Marquette, in the meantime, although still in good humor, was becoming concerned. Minikus continued writing the ticket. Another motorcycle officer pulled up.

"Officer, you don't have to give me a ticket or take me to jail," Marquette said, talking with his hands, and using his whole body for emphasis, the way he always did when he became excited. "I live here, half a block, right around the corner. You can let my brother Ronny drive the car home, and let me walk home. I'd appreciate it, because I done came from El Segundo and Wilmington, you know, and being a half block away from home, you could, you know, let me get by with that." Having said his piece, he started to wander off.

Officer Bob Lewis had parked his cycle. "What have you got?" he inquired of Minikus. "A deuce!" he replied, using police slang for 502.

"Who's the one under arrest?" Lewis asked, as there were now several persons within a few feet radius of the motorbike.

Minikus pointed to Marquette, who, seeing he was the subject of discussion, returned.

"Man, I'm not drunk," Marquette said. "Can't you see I'm a good fellow who wouldn't diddledybop nobody?" Still trying to make light of it, he put one hand on Minikus's cycle.

"Get your hands off that bike!" Lewis ordered.

"Now, you don't have to do me like that," Marquette replied, feeling unjustly chastened.

Although beneath their regalia it would have been difficult to tell them apart, and both had had much the same experience on the highway patrol, in personality and looks Lewis was quite different from Minikus. An extrovert, with shortcropped light hair and a full-fleshed face, Lewis laughs easily, likes his good time, and, since divorcing his wife, has had a sharp eye for the girls. After spending seven years in the southeast Los Angeles sector, he had, in 1964, been transferred to Lake Tahoe. A few months at the California-Nevada resort had convinced him that, with nightclubs and casinos all around, the cost of living was too high. So he had asked for, and received, a transfer back to Los Angeles.

Ronald, during this time, had not stirred from the front seat of the car. He was 22 years old, the youngest of four children of Wallace Frye's previous marriage to Mary Etta Riggs. Born in Arkansas, he had been raised in Superior, Wyo., where his mother had remarried after the divorce. In 1961, following graduation from high school, he had joined the air force, becoming a mechanic and reaching the rank of airman second class. Discharged in June, he had come to Los Angeles, hoping to enroll in IBM School. Slow-spoken and quite handsome, his temperament was the opposite of Marquette's mercurial one. He figured that, whatever trouble Marquette was in, it would be better to let him work out of it by himself.

"Do you want to store the vehicle?" Lewis asked Minikus. It is standard procedure to have a car put in storage when the driver is unable to operate it, since, if it is left on the street, there is danger of its being stripped.

Minikus replied in the affirmative. Lewis started walking back toward his cycle to get a storage report form. As he did, the transportation car, driven by Officer Bennett, arrived. Almost simultaneously, a truck from the South East Tow Co. in Compton, three miles away, appeared.

The driver, Joseph Lee Gabel, inquired as to which vehicle was involved. Lewis indicated to him that he was to take the Buick.

As Ronald saw the tow truck stop, then back around the parked car with apparent intent to hook onto the Buick, he decided that he'd better intervene. He went back to the motor-cycle, identified himself to Minikus, told him he was Marquette's brother, and asked him if he could take the car. Minikus wanted to know if he had identification, and Ronald pulled out his wallet to show him his driver's license.

That was when Rena, wearing a loose shift, her hair in disarray, came hurrying across the street. The past spring she had had a major operation, from which she was only now fully recovering.

Seeing the tow truck operator unwinding the hook, she went up to him, and, out of breath, asked him what was going on. When he replied that he was going to tow the car away, she remonstrated with him, telling him it was hers.

"Lady, I got nothing to do with it," he answered. "You'd better talk to them officers."

Catching sight of Ronald conversing with Minikus, she went back to where they were standing. Having had the foresight to bring her driver's license along, she showed it to Minikus. Since it checked with the registration of the car, he agreed, after momentary consultation with Lewis, that she could take the Buick. Walking forward, he informed Gabel that they were making out a "no hold" on the vehicle, and that he wouldn't be needed.

Observing his mother arrive on the scene, Marquette had moved around one of the trees and toward the wall of the apartment house, some 15 feet from the curb. A couple of the men were kidding him about going to jail. From his euphoric mood he was plunging into despair. After two years of watching his step and not getting into any trouble, here he was in a mess again. Nothing ever seemed to go right for him. Nothing.

The crowd continued to swell. One lane of the street was blocked. Cars were slowing down, their occupants craning their necks. Some of the drivers parked and joined the onlookers, more than 30 of whom were now gathered on the east side in the vicinity of the vehicles, with another 15 or 20 watching from across the boulevard.

One of the spectators had engaged Minikus in conversation. Lewis was replacing the storage forms in the cycle box. Bennett had alighted from the patrol car to join them. Rena was walking over toward Marquette.

"Let me have the keys to the car," she said to him. "You know better than to drive after you've been drinking."

"Momma, I'm not going to jail. I'm *not* drunk and I am *not* going to jail." He pulled away from her.

The noise the people were making was increasing. As Lewis straightened up from the cycle he thought, for a moment, that Marquette had disappeared. Then he spotted him by the building, and called to Minikus, "We're going to have to get Frye out of that crowd!"

They started toward Marquette, whose unhappiness was increasing. As he spoke to his mother, his voice broke. He was almost crying. Spotting the officers, he started backing away, his feet shuffling, his arms waving.

"Come on, Marquette, you're coming with us." Minikus reached toward him.

Marquette slapped his hand away. "I'm not going to no sonofabitching jail!" he cried out. "I haven't did anything to be taken to jail."

"Go with them and make it easy on yourself," Rena said, caught between him and the officers.

All the old anger, the old frustration, welled up within Marquette. What right had they to treat him like this?

"You motherfucking white cops, you're not taking me anywhere!" he screamed, whipping his body about as if he were half boxer, half dancer.

There was a growl from the crowd, now about 100 in number. Many had just arrived, and, not having witnessed the beginning of the incident, had little knowledge of what the dispute was about. Marquette's defiance struck a responsive chord. The officers were white; they were outsiders; and, most of all, they were police. Years of reciprocal distrust, reciprocal contempt, and reciprocal insults had created a situation in which the residents assumed every officer to be in the wrong until he had proven himself right, just as the officers assumed every Negro guilty until he had proven his innocence. The people began to close in on the three highway patrolmen. What, a few minutes before, had seemed to be an entirely innocuous situation, was taking on an ugly tenor.

Lewis returned quickly to the motorcycle to broadcast a Code 1199—Officer Needs Help!—over the radio. Minikus retrieved the riot baton from Lewis's motorcycle, and Bennett got his shotgun from the patrol car. Together Minikus and Bennett advanced on the crowd, pushing the people back.

In the vicinity, when the Code 1199 call went out, were motorcycle Officers Wayne Wilson and Veale J. Fondville of the highway patrol. Turning on their red lights, and with their sirens screaming, they headed for Avalon and 116th Place.

Minikus and Bennett were once more within striking distance of Marquette. While Bennett used the shotgun to keep spectators at bay, Minikus tried to duck beneath Marquette's flailing arms in order to grab him from behind.

"Hit those blue-eyed bastards!" a voice yelled.

Marquette and Minikus came into contact. Marquette, grabbing for the riot baton, got one hand on it—there was a brief scuffle before Minikus was able to regain control of it.

"Go ahead, you motherfuckers! Why don't you kill me? You'll have to kill me before you take me to jail!" Marquette shouted, dancing away from Minikus. At that moment, it would have been easy enough for Marquette to escape into the crowd, but he made no effort to do so.

Nearby, Ronald, involved despite himself,

concerned about Marquette being hurt, was remonstrating with Lewis.

"You'll have to stay out of the way!" Lewis tried to brush past him.

"But he's my brother!" Ronald pleaded.

Officer Wilson, as he arrived on the scene, riot baton in hand even before he had the kickstand of the motorcycle down, was confronted by an image of blurred chaos. A chunky man, about 40, with a reddish face and short-cropped hair, he went into action with no more opportunity to assess the situation than those Negro spectators who had arrived late and assumed from what they saw that there was violent conflict between Marquette and the officers.

Wilson glimpsed the crowd—grown to perhaps 150, but seeming larger and more menacing because of the noise and the narrow confines of the action. He heard them shouting. He was well aware of their hostility. Close by he saw one officer in what appeared to be a dispute with a Negro youth. A few feet farther off, there was a fight between another Negro and an officer.

Rushing toward Ronald and Lewis, and without speaking to either, Wilson jabbed the riot baton into the pit of Ronald's stomach. As Ronald doubled over, he jabbed again. Ronald rolled to the ground.

With one adversary dispatched, it was but a half dozen steps to where Marquette was fending off Minikus. Wilson swung the baton. He caught Marquette with a glancing blow to the forehead, above the left eye. As Marquette turned instinctively to meet him, Wilson jabbed him hard in the stomach. Marquette doubled over. Instantly Minikus caught his head in a vise, and, with the fight gone out of him, had no trouble leading him to the patrol car. Throwing him across the front seat, Minikus pulled Marquette's arms behind him, and, bending over him, started to handcuff his wrists.

Rena Frye, distraught at having seen both Ronald and Marquette struck down, believed the latter to be under further attack in the police car. Rushing to his aid and trying to pull Minikus away, she, a foot shorter than the officer, sprawled awkwardly across his back. As she pulled at him she suddenly felt herself lifted up. Struggling, the back of Minikus's shirt bunched in her fist, she was torn away by Officer Fondville. Off balance, a strip of the ripped shirt in her hand, she stumbled onto the the back of Officer Wilson. Both momentarily went to the ground.

Straightening up, Rena was grabbed by Fondville. Bending her over the trunk of the car, he forced her arms behind her, handcuffed her, and placed her in the rear seat.

"Put your legs inside," he ordered her.

"I wouldn't do anything for you, you white Southern bastard!" she spat at him, tears streaming down her face.

Ronald objected: "What are you arresting her for?"

Getting no answer, he became more insistent. A moment later he received his reply. Handcuffed, he too was placed inside the car.

The Negro crowd, continuing to swell, incensed by the altercation, pressed in. There were isolated shouts of: "Come on, let's get them!" "Leave the old lady alone!" "We've got no rights at all—it's just like Selma!" "Those white motherfuckers got no cause to do that!"

More highway patrol officers were arriving. With riot batons and shotguns, they kept the people back from the car.

In the front seat, Minikus had finished handcuffing Marquette. Pulling him upright on the seat, he was closing the door when Marquette, cursing, lashed out with his foot. He caught the door sharply, swinging it open, and partially springing it. As he did, one of the newly arrived officers, Taylor, kicked his feet back inside of the car, then helped Minikus cuff Marquette's legs together.

The sound of sirens was exploding from all

directions as Los Angeles police sped to the scene to assist. As Sgt. V. Nicholson of the highway patrol arrived, it became evident to him that the cars converging at high speed were in danger of crashing into each other. Since the situation appeared now to be under control, he went on the radio to order the units to veer off.

Responding to the lure of the sirens, hundreds of people flocked to the area. Four blocks south of 116th Place, at Virgie Nash's beauty parlor, Joyce Ann Gaines and Joan Nash, Virgie's daughter, were unable to suppress their curiosity. Despite the fact that Joyce Ann had a headful of pink curlers and was wearing a green barber's smock to protect her white capris, they ventured into the street. As they kept asking people what was happening, and received vague, or unknowing answers in reply, they drifted farther and farther to the north, until, finally they came upon the scene shortly before 7:30 p.m.—just as all of the Fryes had been hustled into the police car.

Joyce Ann Gaines, a sociology student at Compton Junior College, is a slender, eye-catchingly attractive girl with light brown hair and a matching complexion; even the fact that she was walking around with her hair up in curlers could not hide this attractiveness. As she made her way toward the front of the crowd and asked what had happened, people were quick to tell her, "The boy in the front seat, he was already bleeding and handcuffed, and one of the cops kicked him!"

"That lady in back—they jerked her around till she was screaming with the pain!"

"With all those cops, you'd think they were fighting in Vietnam!"

"We can't even go peaceful in our own way. It's just like the South!"

Joe Gabel, under the direction of Minikus, was once more hitching the Buick onto his tow truck when Jimmy Ticey walked up to him. The Ticey brothers operate the T and T

Wrecking Yard twenty blocks to the south on Avalon Blvd., and Jimmy, drawn like the others by the sirens, had arrived two or three minutes before.

"Why," he asked Gabel, "are you impounding this boy's car? I mean, being legally parked, why are you all impounding?"

"What's it to you?" An officer snapped back at him. "You want to get yourself in trouble?"

"No. No." Ticey shrugged. "It's nothing to me."

He walked off, and, caught up in the agitation of the crowd, was pushed toward the spot where Joyce Ann Gaines was standing. Among the police he noticed an officer he knew, Bill Davis. Davis, because of his size—six feet five inches, and 235 pounds—stood out clearly from the rest. The residents of the area called him "Wild Bill."

Traffic on Avalon Blvd. had come to a halt. A half block to the south, one of the well-worn red buses of the South Los Angeles Transportation Co.—a subsidiary concern servicing the area, since the city does not feel it worthwhile to send its buses that far out—had had to stop. Behind it a number of cars and trucks were stacking up. The sun had disappeared into the haze of the Pacific Ocean, leaving only a few red reflections in a sky that was rapidly darkening. Driven by Bennett, the CHP car with the Fryes pulled away from the curb. Behind it, the tow truck, with the Buick hanging from its winch like a slaughtered animal, was escorted from the scene.

The police prepared to withdraw. There was the throaty sound of motorcycle engines being kicked into life as the officers separated themselves from the crowd and waited for the signal to be given to leave.

"Come on," Joan Nash said to Joyce Gaines. "Let's get back. I've got customers waiting for me."

Officers Vaughan and Taylor of the highway patrol were on their cycles, their backs half turned to the people. There were taunts from the crowd:

"Look at the yellow-bellies run!"

"Stay a while. We'll make it interesting for you mothers!"

The officers ignored the taunts. Then, suddenly, Vaughan felt something sting the back of his neck. Instinctively slapping his hand to the area, his fingers came off wet. Whirling around he saw, disappearing among the people, the back of a girl with pink curlers in her hair.

"Goddam! She spit on me!" he exclaimed to Sgt. Nicholson, who was sitting on a cycle a few feet away. Nicholson, and his partner, Gilbert, jumped off their bikes and plunged into the crowd after the girl.

"Let it go! It's not worth it!" another officer called out. But it was too late. The two highway patrolmen had been swallowed up by the people.

Within seconds the other officers dismounted to go to their assistance. At the point where they disappeared into the crowd seething agitation began. Officer Pattee, fearful, broadcast a new Code 1199—Officer Needs Help!—call. The first cars that had left the scene, already a block or two away, swung back. Several new units, including some from the Sheriff's Department, raced to respond.

"Hey, pink lady!" someone called to Joyce Ann Gaines as she made her way through the crowd. They kidded her about the curlers in her hair, and she laughed. Then with startling suddenness, an arm snaked itself about the lower part of her face; she felt herself pulled backward.

"Who's that? What are you doing?" she giggled, thinking it was someone playing a joke. Dragged backward, trying to turn her head, she started to lose her balance and instinctively put out her arms to support herself.

Officer Gilbert, certain in his own mind after Vaughan's indication that the girl had spit on a fellow officer, was determined to bring her out of the crowd. Joan Nash grabbed Joyce Ann's extended arm and hung on. Pulled in opposite directions, Joyce Ann, struggling, called for help.

"She hasn't did a thing, and look at what they're doing to her!" Joan cried.

Jimmy Ticey, going to Joan Nash's aid, attempted to wrest Joyce Gaines away from Gilbert.

Other officers became involved in the melee.

"Wild Bill! Help us! Look at what they're doing to her. Don't let 'em do that to her, Wild Bill!" Jimmy Ticey shouted to Off. Davis.

Several patrolmen, not knowing to whom Ticey was calling, presumed he was exhorting others in the crowd to help Joyce Ann Gaines resist arrest. They jumped on him, pinioning his arms.

An officer, shorter than the others, broke Joan Nash's hold on her friend. He drew back his baton, threatening her.

"Go ahead, I dare you to hit me!" she screamed. "I dare you to hit me, 'cause I haven't did a thing!"

"You leave my sister alone!" Janet Nash hurled at him.

Gilbert, not for one moment releasing his hold on Joyce Ann, the elbow of his arm clamped tightly across her chin, half walked, half dragged her backward out into the street. As she struggled and kicked, the pink curlers in her hair loosened and were scattered about the pavement. Bent backward, wearing the barber's smock, she took on a pregnant appearance. Away from the crowd, out as she was in the arena of the street, hundreds of people could see her.

"Look at what they're doing to that pregnant girl!" a woman shouted.

"Oh those motherfuckers!" an anguished voice cried out.

One Negro officer, Ronald Farwell, of the Los Angeles police was among those attempting to contain the crowd. "What kind of a brother are you, when you let them do that to a girl?" he was castigated and cursed.

As Sgt. Nicholson was handcuffing Jimmy Ticey, the latter was still called out to "Wild Bill" for help. Davis came over and told him to calm down.

"Just go quietly, and you'll be all right," he promised him.

Lee Castruita, of the LAPD, had been one of those leaving the scene when another officer had called out: "There they go again!" Returning, he found himself rushing to the assistance of Officer Gilbert. As Gilbert held Joyce Gaines, Castruita handcuffed her, then started walking her toward his patrol car. Despite the handcuffs, she was more than he could handle.

"Someone give me a hand!" Castruita called out, and Los Angleles police officer Harvey Eubank ran to help him.

Together they walked the girl to Castruita's patrol car, only to discover it immovably jammed between several others. Continuing along the line of police cars, they found one at the end that had the key in the ignition. Placing Joyce Ann in the car, the officers jumped in. Unable to turn the auto around, Castruita backed it rapidly two blocks north on Avalon Blvd., to the intersection of Imperial. Here he swung into a service station and made his turn.

"Help me! Help me! Don't let the bastards take me to jail!" Joyce Gaines called out. Her resentment flaring, she bombarded the officers with invectives.

Returning to his patrol car, LAPD Officer C. A. Willig of the 77th St. division discovered that it had been stolen.

Heading north on Avalon toward the 77th St. station, Castruita and Eubank heard on the radio that they were driving a stolen car.

"Be quiet!" Castruita snapped at Joyce Gaines. He had unhooked the radio mike, and was attempting to report that he was transporting a prisoner to the station in Willig's car. "Can't you see I'm trying to broadcast?"

"I don't have to be quiet—I don't give a good goddam if you ever broadcast!" she cried, starting a shouting match between her and the officers.

Several blocks farther on, Castruita hailed a police car heading in the opposite direction. He asked them to call the station and report he was bringing in a prisoner.

Eubank got out and exchanged places with the passenger officer in the other car. The exchange between Joyce Ann and the new officer became even more acerbic.

"Why? Why? Why," she shouted, "are you doing this to me? What have I done?" She leaned forward awkwardly in the seat, trying to get an answer out of Castruita.

The new officer pulled her back. She lashed out at him with her foot.

"If you try that once more, I'll give you a kick that'll push your teeth down your throat!" he snapped.

"I'd look right stupid trying to kick you with these handcuffs on me!" she retorted, falling silent for the remainder of the five-minute ride to the station.

Along the two-block stretch of Avalon Blvd., decades of distrust, of resentment, of antipathy, of pride ground into the dust had found a focal point in the arrest of Joyce Ann Gaines. In the manner with which the police had handled the girl the people saw, or thought they saw, the contempt of the white man for the Negro. They felt, collectively, his heel grinding in their faces. They were stricken once more by the sting of his power.

"Goddam!" a woman called out. "Goddam! They'd never treat a white woman like that!"

"What kind of men are you, anyways?" another challenged. "What kind of men are you, anyways, to let them do that to our people?"

"It's a shame! It's a pitiful, crying shame!"

"Blue-eyed white devils! We is going to get you! Oh shit! We is going to get you!"

"Motherfuckers!" It came from all sides of the crowd. "Motherfuckers!"

The police officers, although they had long worked in a culture of antagonism, had never seen hatred of such intensity. Sgt. Richard Rankin—a sergeant of two weeks' standing—of the 77th St. police station was the senior city police officer on the scene. To him it seemed, and rightly so, that the continued presence of the officers could only incite the crowd furthur; that it would only lead to one incident after another, each bigger than the one before. Over the loudspeaker mounted on his patrol car he ordered his men to re-form and withdraw. Once more they began disengaging themselves from the crowd.

Gabriel Pope had made his way to the scene from the corner of Imperial and Avalon Blvd. at about 7:15. For the past 30 minutes, a two-thirds empty pop bottle in his hand, he had been wandering back and forth between 116th Place and the rose-lavender painted church at the corner of 116th St. and Avalon. Strongly built, just slightly over six feet tall, he had been born in Los Angeles in 1946, the fourth child of Sam and Tessie Pope. Sam and Tessie had both been raised in Woodville, Miss. In 1942, shortly after the beginning of the war, Sam Pope had gone to work in the Armstrong Rubber Co. plant in Natchez. Two years later he had moved his parents and his family to the West Coast, where, in the same job, the money was better. By the time Gabriel was born, however, returning veterans had begun to press Sam Pope for his job, and, under the pressure, his marriage had started showing cracks.

When Sam picked up Tessie at the hospital after she had given birth to Gabriel, they had stopped off at his parents' place to show them the child.

"What a beautiful baby!" his mother had exclaimed. "I'd like to have another beautiful baby like that myself!"

Two weeks later Tessie had returned with the baby and its accoutrements. She hadn't seen Sam for 10 days, and three children were enough for her to take care of, she said. So, since Sam's mother liked the baby so much, she might as well have it for a while.

Gabriel stayed with his paternal grandparents for the next eight years. For him, they became his parents. He saw his father every two or three months, and his mother even less frequently. Then, in 1954, his grandmother died. His grandfather, past 75, was not able to take care of himself, much less an 8-year-old boy.

Gabe, as everyone called him, returned to live with his mother.

In the intervening years she had had three more children, the last two by Thomas Wicket, the man who was living with her, and whom Gabe was instructed was his stepfather. He wasn't really, his brothers and sisters told him. Their mother made a big to-do about how they were married, but that was just for show.

For Gabe, his life collapsed. He was a stranger in his own family. Though his older sister tried to be kind to him, the others ignored him. The apartment had only two bedrooms. His mother and stepfather slept in one; four of the children in the second; Gabe and the youngest of his stepbrothers shared the couch in the living room. At his grandparents he had not only had his own bed, but his own room. He felt as if he were an orphan.

He moped. He didn't eat. He picked fights with the other children. He generated conflict between Thomas Wicket and his mother.

After two months, Tessie took Gabe aside. She suggested that he wasn't happy living with them. Gabe agreed. Wouldn't he, Tessie asked,

like it better going to live with his grandparents? Gabe thought she was asking if he
would like to return to his grandfathers house,
and his heart leaped with joy. Yes, he said, he
would like that.

Two days later, to his bewilderment, he was
placed on a bus headed for Woodville, Miss.
He was going to be making his home with Oss
and Millie Davis, Tessie's parents.

Oss Davis was in his middle fifties. He had
worked hard all of his life. He had kept his
place. He owned his own farm of 30 acres between Woodville and Centreville. Maybe the
house he lived in wasn't much, but it had
electricity, and he'd never in all his life lived in
a place that had indoor plumbing, so, as he
said, he didn't think he would care for it anyhow. He grew cotton and corn, he raised pigs
and chickens, and he had his own cow for milk.
His proudest possession was a 1937 Ford from
which parts kept dropping off like dry scales
from a fish. The fewer parts it had, the better
it seemed to run.

When he received the telegram that his
grandson was coming to visit, he was per-
plexed, but he didn't let it worry him. He and
Millie had brought eight children into the
world. Three of them had died before they
were a year old, and four had survived to adult-
hood. He believed he had raised them right—
they had gone to church every Wednesday
evening and twice on Sundays. He knew,
though, that in a lot of ways they thought different from him, and, as he said, he was suspi-
cioning that all wasn't right with Tessie.

Bewildered as he was, Gabe didn't put up
much of a fight against Oss at first. What he
missed most of all was television, and what he
hated most were the seemingly endless sessions
in church. When he saw Oss go out and chop
off the head of a chicken, or, at pig-killing time,
string the pig up upside down and then slit its
throat, he was, initially, shocked and nause-

ated. But soon he got used to it, and would be
no more squeamish about wielding an ax than
Oss. What he couldn't get used to were Oss's
constant warnings about being careful, his
admonitions that a boy must know his place.
When Oss really got going on the subject he
would tell of the time that "one of them un-
godly niggers" had stirred up the white community, and they had hung him up by his heels
from a tree and taken turns shooting at him.
Every time a shot had hit him he'd twitched
and hollered for mercy, but it hadn't done him
any good, because he didn't know his God.

Gabe had asked Oss what God had had to
do with it. Oss, drawing back his hand as if to
slap him, had warned him not to sass him.
Gabe knew then that, despite all of his preten-
sions, Oss lived in fear. And he saw him as less
than a man.

By the time he was 13 years old, there was
rebellion in Gabe's heart. There was no longer
much that Oss could do to handle him. White
people whom Oss had known all of his life
shook their heads and counseled him to do
something about that boy. Oss tried. But the
more he tried, the more recalcitrant Gabe
seemed to become.

The final straw had come the next year,
when Gabe was 14. He was standing in line in
the post office in Woodville when a white man
had come up and said, "Let me get by, boy,
I'm in a hurry!"

"Man, I'm just as much in a hurry as you is,"
Gabe had replied, and stood his ground.

In the ensuing altercation, the white man
had shoved Gabe. Gabe had shoved him back!
It had been a scandal.

"We kaint keap him no more," Oss had
written to Tessie. "We is feared for his sake,
and our too."

Six years after he had left, Gabriel Pope
returned to Los Angeles. He was big for his
age. He had been toughened on the farm. And

he had a cockiness that made others wary of him.

His mother was now living in the Jordan Downs Housing Project in Watts. Thomas Wicket, although he still came around periodically, was no longer living with her, and she hadn't had any real contact for years with Sam Pope. All of her children by Pope were being supported by the Bureau of Public Assistance, and Gabe was simply added to the list.

He enrolled in Edwin Markham Junior High School, and the next year he was passed, not graduated, on to Jordan High. He wasn't graduated, since he obviously lacked qualifications. But, since he was 15, he was out of place and a disturbing influence in the junior high school. They had to do something with him. So they gave him to Jordan.

When he went to Jordan, Gabe decided that he would do well. This determination quickly went to pieces when he discovered the books he was given might just as well have been printed in Chinese. He couldn't read them. Most of what his teachers said in class, about mathematics and English, seemed gibberish. He sat there bored. He gave his teachers a hard time. He flirted outrageously with the girls. He got into trashcan fights and threw food across the tables in the cafeteria. He became quickly identified as a hardhead. His counselor tried at first to work with him, but there was no communication between them. To the counselor, who had four times the load he should have, Gabe fell into a pattern. He was one of those tough cases that, lacking the wherewithal, just had to be shrugged off.

Gabe failed 10B twice, and then was passed on to 10A. It was the only practical thing to do with him. If all those failing were forced to repeat the same grades endlessly, the schools would soon be so clogged as to collapse the entire educational structure. Anyone who keeps his nose clean has a reasonable opportunity of, sooner or later, being pushed out at the top by the mass of new students coming in at the bottom. Whether he knows anything or not is irrelevant.

Gabe didn't keep his nose clean. He ditched classes whenever he felt like it, and he was suspended several times. He decided that, if he were going to continue going to school, he had to have better clothes. Clothes are the symbol of status. And status is the most important thing in the school.

He began working at a car wash on weekends. It was mean and dirty work, and it paid only $1 an hour. More often than not he had to fight to keep the man from cheating him even out of some of that.

Still, he now had $15 to $20 a week he could call his own. He bought himself some jazzy slacks and sport shirts, and a coat. He could take out a girl, and not feel like dirt. It really perked him up.

That lasted for five months. Then his mother inadvertently let it slip to the social worker that Gabriel had a job, and the next month he was deducted from the check. His mother told him he would have to give her money with which to buy him food—so there he was, working for nothing. He really hated his mother for being so stupid.

He quit his job. That created more problems with the BPA. The next fall his counselor at Jordan suggested that perhaps he might be happier with a work-study program, in which he would have a job and go to school only part time. He agreed, and found a job in an auto wrecking yard. He went to classes in the evening a couple of times, and then didn't bother to return. Once there was a question as to why he wasn't attending, but it was a perfunctory one. There were too many other problems for school officials to be worrying about Gabriel Pope.

He worked desultorily. He would hold a job

for a few months, then something would happen and he would be out of work for an equal period of time. He'd hustle at pool halls; he'd do odd jobs for one of the numerous bookies in the area; if things got really bad, he'd go out with the gang and clout some cars.

Before he was 18 he'd been stopped and questioned by the police twice, both times for curfew violation. Los Angeles had an ordinance prohibiting any person below the age of 18 from being on the street after 10 p.m. unless accompanied by a near relative. From a practical standpoint the ordinance is difficult to enforce, and on Friday and Saturday nights Hollywood Blvd. is jammed with teenagers that the police ignore as long as they behave themselves. In the high crime area of southeast Los Angeles, however, anything that moves at night is liable to be stopped, and the ordinance provides a handy catch-all.

In the summer of 1964 Gabe was working 103rd St. in Watts, peddling bennies, red devils, and some of the numerous other pick-me-up, lay-you-down drugs for which the middle-class American has little trouble getting his doctor to write a prescription, but for which the less affluent society is willing to pay a premium. Every so often he would run into the well-dressed, quiet-spoken representative of the Muslims who stood in front of the Food Giant Market, selling *Muhammad Speaks.* Gabriel would sometimes stop to needle him: "They turned you paper boys into real dudes, ain't they? I bet you wears a coat and tie when you takes your bath!"

The Muslim, in turn, would say to him, "You are letting *the man*[1] twist you around his little finger. Here you is, penny picking, and putting yourself right where he wants you, like a mouse tickling a cat's whiskers. Pretty soon that cat's gonna jump, and you're gonna be in jail, which is where he wants to see you. Listen

to us, brother. Live up to your heritage. Don't let *the man* degrade you!"

Gabe did not believe in the Muslims. His thinking was that all the preachers were out only to feather their own nests, and he couldn't see that the Muslims were much different.

But he did think about what the Muslim had said. Right about the same time he began going steady with Lada Young, whom he'd met that spring. Lada had finished high school. She was working as a waitress and was going to secretarial school during the daytime. He liked her and kept asking her, "What for are you doing all this? You know nothing's never going to happen." But she refused to believe that. She said she would make it happen.

He would say, "Shit, you don't know what you talking about!" But he had doubts about his own convictions.

Then a couple of the other peddlers in the neighborhood got arrested. And that thing about penny picking really started nagging him.

He found work in the tire department of an automotive center, and it turned out to be a job more to his liking than any he'd had before. In November he bought a 1956 Chevy. Spending all of his spare time working on it, scrounging parts here and there, within a couple of months he had it looking like a pretty sharp model. He felt good when he took Lada out in it; he felt good when he would see his friends on the street, and could wave to them, knowing that in their eyes he was making it.

Every so often Michael Lasky, white, a former UCLA student, and a Marxist-Leninist Communist (as he calls himself), would come by the Pastrami-dip place where the automotive center's Negro employees went to lunch and try to organize them. He usually had a white girl carrying a few copies of the *Peking Review,* containing such statements by Mao Tse-tung as:

"On behalf of the Chinese people, I wish to

[1] The white man.

take this opportunity to express our resolute support for the American Negroes in their struggle against racial discrimination and for freedom and equal rights. . . . The evil system of colonialism and imperialism grew up along with the enslavement of Negroes and the trade in Negroes, and it will surely come to its end with the thorough emancipation of the black people."

"The Martin Luther Kings, Farmers, Randolphs, Formans and all the other sell-outs such as Ferrell and Hawkins,[2] by casting their vote for the 'democracy' of the white ruling class, keep the Negroes in bondage," Lasky averred, passing out handbills urging, "Support the people's revolutionary union!"

They were polite to him, but they laughed, asking, "Is them white Chinese, or black Chinese?"

"Mr. Charley is the snarling, ugly face with the bloody fangs," Lasky declared. But Lasky himself was a Mr. Charley, and there had been too many white men before him who, protesting that they were there to help the Negro, had only made use of him. They couldn't see where Lasky was much different. They didn't believe him. They didn't trust him.

It was around Easter time that, as Gabe was driving down Central Ave. with Lada in the car, the police stopped him. They made him get out of the car and stand spreadeagled against its side as they searched him. When he protested and wanted to know what it was all about, they told him to shut up:

"We can do it here, or down at the station, buddy. Take your choice!"

After patting him down, they made Lada get out of the car also. Then they took out the seats, and threw them onto the sidewalk. After that, they did the same with the paraphernalia in the trunk. When they couldn't find any

[2] Douglas Ferrel is a state assemblyman; Gus Hawkins a congressman. Both are Negroes, representing the southeast Los Angeles area.

contraband, they called in on the police radio to run a make on him, and, while waiting for a reply, filed out an FI (field interrogation) slip on him. When he continued to press them as to what it was about they said that there had been a burglary in the area, and that his vehicle fitted the description of the one used by the suspects. He knew that wasn't true. He knew—in his own mind—they'd stopped him only because he had a sharp-looking car, and they wanted to harass him.

When they got the word back on the radio, they said, "It looks like you check out okay, Gabriel."

They handed him back his driver's license and drove off, leaving him standing there with the car gutted and its contents piled in a heap. "Motherfuckers!" he cried in rage after them, shaking with the fury and the helplessness of his humiliation.

Here, in August, four months later, all that old feeling welled up in him as he watched the police pull out. All the old feeling of being stomped into the ground, of having no right to his own manhood, of having to crawl before the white man. Of the white man abusing Negro women, and the Negro man standing by in cowardly indifference—the girl with the pink curlers could just as well have been Lada.

"It burn your soul, but what can you do?" said a woman next to him, and her words were like a solo to the orchestra of imprecations rising about him. Without conscious thought of his action he darted into the street and hurled the empty pop bottle in his hand toward the last of the departing black-and-white cars. Striking the rear fender of Sgt. Rankin's car, it scattered. And it was as if in that shattering the thousand people lining the street found their own release. It was as if in one violent contortion the bonds of restraint were snapped. Rocks, bottles, pieces of wood and iron— whatever missiles came to hand—were projected against the sides and windows of the bus and automobiles that, halted for the past 20 minutes by the jammed street, unwittingly started through the gauntlet. The people had not been able to overcome the power of the police. But they could, and would, vent their fury on other white people. The white people who used the police to keep them from asserting their rights.

It was 7:45 p.m. Amidst the rending sounds of tearing metal, splintering glass, cries of bewilderment and shouts of triumph, the Los Angeles uprising had begun.

The Riot

Paul Bullock

Paul Bullock worked in Watts long before the riots in 1965. An Associate Research Economist for the Institute of Industrial Relations at UCLA, Mr. Bullock has authored articles for the New Republic, *Journal of Negro Education, Industrial Relations,* and *Dissent.* He specializes in employment and educational problems of minority groups in the Los Angeles area, and his findings on minority unemployment and underemployment between 1963 and 1965 were published by the Government Printing Office in *Hard-Core Unemployment and Poverty in Los Angeles.*

It goes without saying that the massive riot of August, 1965, remains the most significant event in the lives of the people of Watts. Although the actual curfew zone covered more than forty-six square miles in the heart of Los Angeles County, headlines and history have already identified it for all time as the area of the "Watts riot." Some of the most spectacular damage, it is true, did occur along 103rd Street, the main commercial center of Watts, since dubbed "Charcoal Alley." Yet it is equally true that much of the burning and looting took place elsewhere in the south central ghetto, on Central Avenue, Broadway, Florence, Vermont, and even Western Avenues—many miles to the west of Watts itself. Significantly, all of the damage was done *within* the ghetto; lily-white communities like South Gate and Huntington Park, Inglewood and Gardena, were untouched, though some of them are literally within a stone's throw of Watts.

The police action that triggered the four days of destruction seemed almost routine at the time. The arrest of the two Frye brothers on a drunk-driving charge, about a half-mile west of Watts on a hot Wednesday evening, had elements of ineptitude and misunderstanding, but it rated only a brief item on the third page of the *Los Angeles Times* the next morning. Though there was some violence following that incident, the next day appeared calm and tranquil, until darkness fell. I journeyed to Watts in the afternoon to keep an appointment, driving down 103rd Street to Wilmington Avenue, where the office of the Watts Labor Community Action Committee was then located. No expectation of imminent violence was in my mind, though rumors were spreading that the police had assaulted a pregnant woman the night before. A few hours later, after my return to the west side, the first reports of renewed and intensified activity in the area were broadcast. The volcano had erupted.

Friday was "Watts day." For the first time,

103rd Street was struck en masse, and the buildings housing stores became infernos. The small department stores, clothing stores, pawn shops, liquor stores, and many grocery stores were special targets, but there was never a completely consistent pattern. The relatively new Safeway store on Imperial and the Shop Rite store on Central went up in flames, but the infamous Giant Food Market on 103rd, whose white owner had an unenviable reputation in the community, was amazingly unscathed. (Apparently he had mobilized his own private army of employees.) On the other hand, the three ABC markets in the south central area were undamaged, though they were, and are, white-owned; their reputation for fairness, service, and cleanliness is good. It is probably accurate to say that with a very few fortuitous exceptions like the one noted above, the stores with especially unfavorable reputations in the area were uniformly hit, but beyond this it is difficult to generalize.

One may, of course, argue a different case, depending on one's ideological viewpoint. The conservatives suggest, on the basis of almost no evidence, that the "rioting" is either the work of criminals or malcontents or the result of a "conspiracy" by radical and militant groups. The militants sometimes respond that the "riot" is really a justified protest against police brutality, commercial exploitation, and general subjugation of the ghetto by white outsiders. My own reflections lead me to the conclusion that the conservative position is totally wrong and that the militant view is vastly oversimplified.

Perhaps a simple but critical point should be made first. The basic middle-class rules of morality become meaningless whenever "law and order" in the accepted sense have become inoperative. In no way is this a racial or cultural phenomenon as my own experience in the American army during World War II will attest. In those days of rigid segregation, my battalion in the 102nd Infantry Division was lily white and, essentially, a pretty representative cross-section of the dominant racial and cultural groups in America. Yet, as we proceeded through Germany in the wartime years of 1944 and 1945, we looted and stole and, sometimes, raped. Even the most moral and moralistic among us felt no guilt about taking "souvenirs" from the closets and drawers of houses in which we were bivouacked, including items of some value. The High Command issued directives that the looting must stop, particularly in the light of criticisms directed against the Russians for the same practice, but they had little effect in my outfit.

A particularly apt example comes to mind. Two of my closest buddies were devoutly religious, extremely moral young men, who were among the very few soldiers to respect the established rule against fraternization with *fräuleins* while it was in effect. One day, in the near-destroyed town of Krefeld, the three of us stumbled upon a large safe in the ruins of a bombed-out factory building. Without hesitation, my buddies proceeded to round up all usable tools and force open the door to the safe. To our amazement, they discovered the equivalent of several hundred dollars in negotiable Dutch currency, which was promptly removed and later sent home over a period of time. (I had wandered away before the safe was opened and the loot liberated, thereby invalidating my claim to a full share.) The prize was so embarassingly ample that it became necessary to fabricate a plausible and acceptable explanation. The explanation decided upon, if any question should arise, was that the money had been won through gambling. I do not know whether an explanation was ever demanded, but, if so, it would have had a most suspicious ring. My buddies were perhaps the only two persons in the platoon (possibly in the battalion) who *never* gambled, as a matter of principle.

I could multiply this example many times over. These same buddies, for instance, regularly collected items of German photographic equipment which we often encountered in houses, buildings, and stores, and put together a most impressive picture-taking and picture-developing operation. All of us, at one time or another, "liberated" liquor, articles of clothing, guns, watches, silverware, radios, and anything else that we valued and could carry. We felt especially justified in these practices because we were taking from the Germans, who had systematically looted and pillaged throughout Europe and murdered millions of innocent people. We reasoned that the Germans were the last people on earth who had any right to complain if we recaptured, individually or collectively, some of the material possessions which they had reaped directly or indirectly through the brutal, if efficient, workings of the Nazi system. Furthermore, some of us thought that the Germans (even the Nazis) would be on top again in a few years, suffering none of the burdens which they had imposed on others. Our "looting" was actually a small and inadequate punishment.

I hope that the analogy between our "white" behavior during World War II and the "black" reasoning during the riot is now somewhat clear to the reader. A riot certainly has many of the aspects of a war, and in the case of a black-white confrontation, the "enemy" is relatively easy to define. The whites, especially the white merchants, are seen as exploiters and parasites, and the decades of brutality, discrimination, and repression directed by whites against blacks become highly relevant. If stores are burned and goods are looted, this must be measured against the *systematic* exploitation of blacks by whites throughout a long and painful history. I do not claim an ability to penetrate the mind of a black "rioter" while in the act of "rioting," but surely some of my own reasoning in our confrontation with the Germans must be identical to his. The conditions and circumstances are remarkably parallel.

This attempted explanation undoubtedly overstates the degree of conscious reasoning exercised by a potential rioter. Once the spark has been ignited, even from accidental or spontaneous combustion, the conflagration gathers a force and momentum of its own. At a certain point, it is no longer necessary or even possible to reason in specific terms: it simply becomes clear that the goods will be taken by someone, and "it might as well be me." This, after all, is an old American principle, fully consistent with the moral bases of the capitalistic system. Is not the entire system based upon the relentless and single-minded pursuit of one's own self-interest?

An incident during the riot will illustrate the point clearly. A young friend of mine had ventured into a Watts store to secure a new broom for his mother. Having made his selection, he left the premises and headed back toward his pad. A couple of blocks away he encountered a policeman, who eyed him incredulously. "For Christ's sake," the cop said, "why don't you pick up something worthwhile?" My friend turned around, returned to 103rd Street, and did precisely that.

In retrospect, perhaps the most astonishing thing about the 1965 violence is that so little of it, relatively, was directed against white civilians. Indeed, the official records tell us that not a single white person was killed by a black, but that thirty-one blacks lost their lives. In view of the reports of widespread sniping and attacks on whites in certain stages of the riot, the statistics seem almost incredible. We are forced to one or more of three conclusions: (1) The published figures do not tell the whole story; (2) the accounts of sniping and black violence directed against persons were exaggerated for one reason or another; (3) the snipers and attackers were woefully inaccurate in aim or inefficient in execution, or perhaps did not intend murder. The reminiscences of the three teen-agers in this chapter, plus the news reports, confirm that some whites were assaulted and injured, but we are told that no fatalities resulted.

This is all the more remarkable in the light of the location of Watts in relation to the white communities to the east and to the west of it. Imperial Highway, which forms the southern boundary of Watts where "Mudtown" once stood, is one of those unique east–west roads which almost spans the entire width of Los Angeles County. Across Alameda and along Imperial lie lily-white cities like South Gate, Lynwood, Bell, and another vast Anglo region, and a few miles to the west are Inglewood, Gardena, Westchester, and more Anglo territory. Each day, especially at peak traffic hours, thousands of whites traverse Imperial Highway on their way to work, home, the beach, or Disneyland. If the riot reflected a militant or antiwhite conspiracy, it was poorly executed indeed.

There is, in fact, no evidence that the riot was organized or planned in any way. It is probable that in certain cases, small bands of teen-agers or young adults moved from one store to another, or from one area to another, after the rioting had started, but their organization was spontaneous and informal and had no ideological meaning. The resentments expressed against white-controlled stores and police practices have provided the basis for the suggestion that the riot was actually an uprising which reflected frustration and social protest. Without doubt, this was a powerful motivation behind much of the riot activity, but to many of the teen-age participants, the riot was primarily an exciting incident which destroyed the boredom of hot summer days and offered an unexpected opportunity to obtain a few of those possessions which TV commercials identify to them as essential parts of the "American way of life."

In the following section some of the residents, mainly teen-agers, reminisce about their actions and experiences during the riot, and provide a bit of insight into attitudes toward the police, the merchants, and whites in general. Mike is the youngest; born in the East but a long-time resident of Watts, he is quick-witted and articulate. Despite a sharp mind, he had not gotten along well in school, had been in frequent difficulty with school officials and the law, and had dropped out (or been kicked out). Henry is Mike's buddy, though somewhat older. Born in Louisiana, he has been in Watts since 1956, living first in a private home near Mike's place and later moving into a housing project with his mother and four brothers. He graduated from high school in the mid-sixties, and is intelligent and alert. At the time of the riot his record was clean, but he subsequently got into trouble, along with his buddy, in an incident involving a car. Mel is somewhat younger than Henry, a product of Mississippi, but again a long-time Watts resident. He disliked school and dropped out in the eleventh grade. Highly verbal, he has a flair for drama and music, but is handicapped by a weakness in reading and by a "record" which resulted from hustling.

For obvious reasons, the names of persons referred to in the following section, in most instances, have been changed.

Mike: Let me see, first night when it got started. Henry and I were on our way home from a party they were having in my older sister's house; they was having an anniversary party that night. Me and Henry got off the bus down on 108th and Avalon, and we just saw a whole lot of people starting to run; I thought maybe somebody was fighting or something like that, or there had been an accident, so Henry and I went down to investigate. I saw a lot of police. I saw cars turned over on the street, and bricks, bottles, and a whole lot of glass lying around. I looked at Henry . . . and started laughing. So we decided to go on down further. I looked around, a whole big crew of policemen just ran by us. They were running opposite directions; I didn't know what was happening. I just turned back to Henry, and we thought we'd come home before we got killed. You know, "Wow," and I'd got down on 109th and Avalon, about 112th and Avalon, and so we decided we'd then just go along home, and we passed by another group of policemen, and they stopped us. They asked us where we was going. Henry told him we were on our way home, and he asked us where we live, and we responded and told him, and he told us where were we going and where were we coming from. Of course, Henry and I were scared, so I said, "We just got off work. . . ." We took a couple more steps, and he grabbed me by my shoulders, and I turned around and asked him what was wrong with him, and he swung at me with his night stick, but he missed. And I grabbed his arm and knocked his arm down, and I was going to hit him. Then a whole police gang got around him, and they had us circled. We just stood there, and he says, "Where did you say you was going?" I say, "I'm going along," and he says, "Let me see you get along." . . . He swung at me again, and he hit me on the leg. Then immediately I knew what was he talking about, you know.

We started running, and we got down by the corner. We were going to be smart, so I called him a name, and we took off again. We were in an open field, and we looked around, and a whole bunch of lights were flashing over that way, and we paused for a moment, then we looked back over there again, and there were nine or ten police cars behind us. So me and Henry started running again, and all of a sudden we thought, "here is the law." We thought somebody was shooting at us, and they got to ricocheting kind of close. I finally realized that we was being shot at, so me and Henry, we hit the dirt and we were crawling across this big open field. They was shining a big old spotlight, trying to find us, so we made it over near the railroad tracks, and about that time, a train was coming, and I say, "Henry, man, let's hop on this train and get away from here," so I hopped on the train. We were leaving, you know. I looked around and said, "Come on, Henry, man, get on, man, get on." The train was increasing its speed quite a bit. I just got on, and I didn't see Henry. I looked around and Henry was laying there against the fence. So I got off the train; I say, "Come on, Henry." Henry was limping a little, and we got down on Central and Lanzit Avenue. . . . Right there you can just look up the creek . . . over near 103rd Street . . . and I looked up and I just saw a fire; the air was just full of smoke, and I glanced over and I saw a large fire over toward where I live at; I just saw things burning, burning, burning. Everywhere I looked, I saw a fire.

And I got all scared, and Henry was living around the corner from me at the time. So we took all the back streets and all the dark streets to the pad, and when I got home, I just sat down and looked at TV, and still I didn't feel, I didn't know, it was a riot. This was the first night [probably Thursday], and I finally . . . figured in the pad that there was a riot outside. At the last minute I suddenly realized that that was where I just came from. So my mother, she tried to encourage me to stay in the pad where I wouldn't get into no trouble, and all that, but you know me. She got to telling me about the looting; there wasn't nobody saying nothing about it. . . . So I got back out in the street again and participated and threw a few rocks, and looted a little case and stuff like that, and . . . I was on the street till they called out the National Guard, and that's when I decided to go back to the pad, 'cause the National Guard they weren't jiving.

Mel: I was, so happened to be, on 114th the night that this happened, all this occurred. I was over at my girl friend's house. At the time, we were all in the house watching television, and after we were watching television, we heard over the news that there was a riot in Watts, that peoples were burning up and looting. We had overheard the sirens outside, all the calling, hollering, and screaming, and peoples hollering "Whitey, kill Whitey," and all this different stuff, so my girl friend's mother wouldn't let me out of the house. My girl friend's sister's boy friend was over, so myself and him and his brother, we tried to get out the house; we tried to sneak out the house. We finally sneaked out after everyone had went to bed that night.

So, across over on Imperial and Central, over a gas station called United gas station, there was a liquor store called Rocket. Peoples started running from the project, from across Imperial over, getting, just taking what they want, anything, all kinds of liquor, just from the store. This upset my mind, you know; I never seen anything like this. But at first I was really frightened, because I had heard about riots in other countries, but never a riot in America. Never had I realized what a riot really was. So I went in the store, and I was panicky. Everybody was knocking down, peoples grabbing stuff, grabbing wine, bottles, beer; stuff was all over the floor; people were just taking what they want.

Little kids was all out on the streets. Peoples were shooting guns, and the sky was just black, like the world was going to come to an end. People was running out, and there was this one lady, she was hollering, "Stop, you peoples don't know what you're doin'," and all this different stuff. It was in the afternoon, and people were coming from work, I guess. They was white people, Caucasian people coming from work, and they would have to take this route to get to Bellflower or South Gate, down Central and Avalon. And this was just horrible because colored peoples over there they just

took advantage of them. They even detoured the buses through the projects, and why they do this, I do not know, because I was giving it up. They was just telling them, "Come on, you can do anything you want" . . . and it was horrible; I just didn't think stuff like that would exist, and I heard of wars and all this. . . .

People was turnin' over people's cars. . . . They ran over to the gas station, on Imperial; they took over the man's gas station, United. They started takin' gas out of the pump, putting 'em in Coca-Cola bottles, and beer bottles, and anything they could, big jugs, and scratchin' a match, and puttin' it to it, and throwin' it to a car, and blowin' it up, taking alcohol and making cocktail bombs out of 'em, whatever you want to call 'em, and just catch a car on fire in a matter of seconds, and peoples just lost their whole car, and some people even lost their lives in the car because they couldn't get out. . . .[1]

I saw cars with kids, this is what made me want to stop, because I saw little kids, seven or eight years old, Caucasian kids, in the cars flying down the street. Their fathers, their mothers, were driving; they had big holes in their heads, and all the windows were broken out of their cars. Peoples were hollering; every time a car would come by, everybody would jump over the fence and run at it, and it would look like a torch or something, like someone putting you in a room and just throwin' down on you with bottles, and bricks, and cans, anything they had, sticks. I saw one boy run after a car and had a big two by four in his hand, and the man came out, he was shooting a gun. He was just starting to shoot; the boy, he hit him across the head with the two by four and five or six other ones just beat him to death, beat

[1] The official records of the riot do not list any deaths of Caucasians, other than two policemen accidentally killed by fellow officers and a fireman killed by a falling wall. However, it is certain that many whites were assaulted and some seriously hurt.

him so bad, they beat all the clothes off of him. He was beaten badly. They tore all his clothes off him, the skin all off his back, all off the side of his face. It was just horrible.

I will be truthful with you. About two or three days after the thing happened, everybody was getting what they could get; I figure, well, I might as well get all what I could get. So people started talking about they coming down 103rd; they was burning up 103rd. They said the whole 103rd was on fire. This I could not believe. They said they was running into the pawn shop, getting guns, rifles, and machetes, all this other thing; so myself and a friend of mine and my brother-in-law we went to walking down 103rd; we saw these peoples running with suits in their hands; I never owned a suit in my life, and this just excited me. And when I got there, everybody was running with stuff, tape recorders, and record players; people were— even little kids—pushing washing machines down the street. And the first thing I saw was a stamp machine, a government stamp machine, and I thought about all the dimes that was in that stamp machine, and I pulled the stamp machine off the wall in the liquor store. And by the time I tore it off, all the dimes fell on the floor, there wasn't any dimes left because everybody else beat me to these dimes. Everybody pushed me out of the way, so I didn't get but maybe thirty, forty cents worth of dimes. So I saw a chance to get me a couple record players; I took those and then went over to Shop Rite market and got a little stuff.

We went over there, and the supply houses, they had boxes and boxes of beans in the back. They had beans, all kinds of canned goods, anything you wanted, just like a free for all; everybody could get what they wanted. . . . It wasn't on fire at the time, but . . . what made it so bad, the people who were throwing [Molotov cocktail] bombs, they would give you a limited time to be in there and tell you to get

out. If you don't get out, they would throw them in there, and you would be caught. So I was in there, had a basket, just shopping for what I wanted. I was taking bread, sardines, crackers, everything my hand got on. I put it in the basket and rolled it down the street. I had bunches of greens, all in the basket; I had everything, and I got to my mother's car, put it all in the car, driving home; the police, they couldn't do nothing. The police couldn't . . . it seemed like the world was just out of hand.

The police were standing around looking, but they couldn't do nothing about it, and it was just like a Vietnam hand-to-hand combat war with rifles. On one side of the street were officers, on the other side was the citizens, and they were shooting at one another just like Dodge City, Tombstone Territory, anything you want to call it. They were shooting back at one another. . . .

Then this incident happened where this lady was coming through the project. She was a Caucasian lady and must have been about, I would say, about twelve or one o'clock at night, and this was on a Friday, I think it was. And she had a purse sitting beside her as she was coming through, and she had to stop for a red light. I opened the door, and I said, "Give me that purse," you know, like that, and it frightened her. She panicked, and I grabbed the purse, and I slammed the door, and I started running. By the time I started running, there were about ten other dudes behind me, and her money was in the purse. When I opened the purse up, I found a little chump change, which was about thirty or forty cents, and three packages of Pall Mall cigarettes, which I do not smoke. That is all.

This boy was a Western Union; he was on one of those little Honda 55's. He was coming by, I guess he didn't see that trash can, because a friend of mine took this trash can and knocked him off his bicycle, and I jumped on his Honda and started riding it around the project, started hollering, "Ride!" People start taking hose pipe, sticking them through the windows of their houses, running hot, scalding water out through the hose pipe. They put . . . hot water on Caucasian people there as they come by. . . . Peoples is all up on top of the project, sniping at the policemen, and they couldn't do nothing. A helicopter was coming down, and they was shooting at the helicopter.

It was just horrible. If I could do it all over again, I don't think I would do anything, because after I looked at the television and looked at everything, looked at how the smoke was smoking, it looked like the world was coming to an end; I was sitting out in my front yard wondering what tomorrow was going to hold. And that Saturday, that whole weekend, people just took what they want; they just ran all the white peoples away from Watts as far as they could; just tore it up, just drank it; wine, the winos had so much wine till they couldn't drink; the dope addicts had so much dope, they couldn't smoke it all, they couldn't take it all. The hypes had all they could have, and it was just a free for all, for everybody. And at the time, myself, I didn't have enough because I was scared. I was really scared.

Chuck: This is the way it happened to me. I got home around midnight, and at the time . . . Snick [SNCC—Student Nonviolent Coordinating Committee] had this house about three doors down from our house, and it was ran mostly by a Caucasian. Negroes were involved in the program, but the Caucasians would travel in during the day and leave during the night, but yet and still the Negroes that was working with this group would sort of hang around, would stay at the house, taking care of the house. This girl and I and three more of her friends were riding down Imperial Highway. They [the SNCC group] had this little teen-ager, named Eddie, he was in a car. They

was coming across this canal. There around a corner was a taxi, and the driver that was killed, hit all in the head with bricks and stuff thrown. People got to calling Eddie "Whitey-lover." So finally . . . they rushed back to the house. People on my street were getting panicky, running all out of the house, hollering at "Whitey". . . . People started hollering, "Get out, Whitey, get out, Whitey." So all of a sudden, they [SNCC members] jumped in their car and split; we never hear anything else from them. . . . We never saw them again.

So, the next morning, Eddie and his sister, my next-door neighbor, we was going down 103rd; she was going down there to shop; people just standing around, standing around the street . . . like it was to watch a parade or something, walking back and forth, police down at the other end. All of a sudden, this big noise, people get this hollering and screaming going on. But it was a funny thing, on one side of the tracks they would do something over here, and the police from this end come over here, and this police go down there, and in the meantime while the police is transferring, they'd start hitting the buildings in between. Finally, the whole of 103rd was just up in flames. I stayed a while on 103rd, just to look; in other words, just to see could I see anything I wanted, like everybody, free.

I got off in this pawn shop, when the window was broken. . . . I got scared, broke another window . . . and finally . . . came to the door . . . . The police car was screaming and going on, and meanwhile . . . this man, he grabbed a box in the pawn shop. . . . He got to cut on it, he cuts it up, and I'm standing around, waiting, and hoping he gets money out, so I'd get a little bit. He cuts, he cuts, and cuts, and came to a little box in it, up in the center of it. He opened the box, and there aren't nothing but watches in the box; I am disappointed.

I went out to the back, you know, the room

with the radios . . . tried to find something that I liked. Finally, I got AM-FM; it was black, short wave, AM-FM, and a guy sees me as I walked to the door; he snatched it out of my hand, so I turned around and go back and get another one. I went back home, put that down, because if they catch you with it, they are going to take it back, but I figure I will get that off my hands. During that time, the whole street was empty, just like it's dead down 103rd Street. This lady next door to me, her grandfather's friend had a big truck. So I jumped on the truck, went down to 103rd; she started loading up TV, washing machines. National Guard's coming back across the tracks on Santa Ana, on Graham. The National Guard stopped the truck, told everybody to get out back and front . . . so the man still sitting behind the wheel, and everybody else is out. . . .

So going home, my mother tells me to stay in the house, but I just find excuses to get out. Let's see, yeah, it was Eddie . . . at the time, he needed a battery for his car. Safeway had these Delco batteries, exactly the kind he wanted, so we get in the truck, and we split down to Safeway. When the riot broke out, we just broke and . . . put it all on the truck. We get back to the pad. We split that up. It was night. In the meanwhile, we went down to 103rd Street. Martin Luther King[2] is coming down on a truck with PA system: "My black brothers, why don't you go home?" People just ignore him, start throwing stuff at him. Along 103rd, everything was just burned, ashes . . . . National Guards were there, so they had those signs, TURN OR GET SHOT, and the brother of a friend of mine was killed just by disobeying one of those signs.

Mel: That Sunday . . . when everything had cooled off, and the National Guards had arrived. And I had this radio, this FM, I had

looted out of the store, my personal self, and we was sitting off in the project . . . over by Bob's liquor store on 103rd, they said everybody . . . had to make a curfew at eight o'clock. We didn't believe this curfew. So we's sitting down drinking up wine. Everybody got something else; they got wine, whisky, beer, and everything; everybody sitting out at the project socializing, talking about what they looted, what they stole, and all this. So this man comes over, this colored dude comes over with a tape recorder; he gets to talking about what's our names, you know, and all this stuff. We had a fifth of corn whisky. He asked us all our names. We gave him all phony names. He said, "I know this is phony." I said, "If you know it, why do you want to ask?" He was supposed to have been a newspaper reporter, or something . . . tennis shoes, levis; he had a tape recorder. I thought he was losing his mind, you know.

All of a sudden, we heard shots, five minutes to eight, just boom, boom, boom, boom. I just grabbed my radio. I had to go over to my friend's house to stay all night, because I couldn't get out, and I saw everybody at Bob's liquor store. National Guard had one of those big, old 21 BM's,[3] whatever you want to call it, just sitting it up on the air, just blow out a whole light pole . . . with one shot, blowed the whole light out and people standing like fools, standing over there on the property shooting at him with little, old .45's and the Guards had great big machine guns, and tearing the brick walls up, tearing the whole wall up with three or four shots. . . .

Let me tell you, and this is the truth. I saw a 1964 or '65 Dodge with a Caucasian, it got stopped on Wilmington right at 105th. . . . They stopped him early in the morning, Monday, must be about 6:30 or 7:30 in the morning,

---

[2] It was undoubtedly another "civil rights" leader.

[3] The speaker probably is referring to a 20 mm. gun.

and they opened the trunk of that man's car. He had rifles for an army; he had rifles; he had machine guns; they opened up the back of his seat, he had so many bullets that he could start anything he wanted. He was over there selling that stuff to them colored peoples. That is the truth, and the National Guard catch him, held him there until the police came. . . . White people, they did a hell of a lot in the riot.

Mike: I saw one incident where two Caucasians were driving an old model car, and they stopped at a red light, and they spotted these police, and they took off, but the police caught them; I would say [they were] about our age. They found guns in the car that had been fired recently. . . . They came over from South Gate, Lynwood, Bellflower, Huntington Park.

I saw another incident that I thought was pretty cold. I had figured the world was coming to an end, so I decided to go to church that night, and we was going down Alameda, the only way we can come down and go where the church was is to come down Alameda to Imperial from where we live and . . . we were coming down Imperial, and right there by the corner of Mona and Imperial, there is a liquor store. We was riding alongside of a sheriff's car at the time. And after that, we were coming to a light, and for some reason, I don't know why, I just decided I would pull behind the sheriff's car instead of pulling up next to it, for the lane was free; we stopped at a light, and something just told me to pull up behind them, and as soon as I pulled up behind, three or four shotguns came out the window, boom, boom, boom, out at the store, where people were off in there looting. Before I knew how to start beating it, I just saw the shotgun for a minute and closed my eyes, and I looked back up, I saw the sheriff's car taking off right quick. As it pulled off, I saw this man coming; I saw

him come staggering out the liquor store, and he fell dead, dead.

We was walking down from 107th and Graham, from the Teen Post, on Friday night, and this time, the police was riding four deep with shotguns hanging out the window. They stopped us; they stopped us all at once and told us to put our hands against the wall, and we had this truant officer with us named Jim. He was supposed to have been a probation officer. They made *him* get up beside the wall, and we was all up beside the wall till Ricky said—this one boy name Ricky—he said, "What did we do? We didn't do nothing." So the police kicked him, then took his jacket, took this big stick he had out and poked Ricky with it. He told Ricky, "You are getting smart." Ricky didn't say nothing; Ricky just couldn't say nothing; he had all the wind out of him. Then he [the cop] came over to me, and he started talking to me; he said, "You want to get smart?" I said, "No, sir. I ain't said nothing, sir," just like that. So he went where Henry was; he put his knee up on Henry's butt and told Henry to straighten up and kick, open his legs up, you know, and I thought he was beating on his behind, myself, so I started laughing. So he came back to me and asked me what was funny. I told him, "Nothing." He grabbed me in the back of my neck, and he slugged me down; he told me, and he told all of us, to go. He told all of us to get on home were we was going. He said, "You are going to walk down the street; you are not going to look back, and you aren't going to think no nasty names in your mind to call us, are you?" And I said, "No, sir, we are going on home." So we were going home.

So this SA [Spanish-American, or Mexican-American] Johnny Garcia, he was walking down the street, and he was walking minding his own business; the police flashed a light in his face and told him to stop, and he was walking and looking at him. He told him to come here, and the Mexican fellow was walking over, blocking the light out of his eyes. By the time he got up on him, the police hit him, wham, wham, slapped him upside and pushed him, told him to get on, just like that. We felt like running; we all started running and started laughing about it, and later we got together, we called ourselves camouflaged police that night. We started throwing bricks and bottles; that was what started us; that's what really started us. Like we get dog dukey, put it in a bottle, throw it on them, messing them up, that was what we did after they did that. We weren't thinking about it at first, you know.

A Teen-Ager: Another night . . . the police and some National Guard had camped in the Teen Post when the Teen Post was at the Art Center, so all that night we was gonna go and get them, and we ran around, trying to find some gasoline. There was a big old truck and we wanted to set the truck on fire, and the National Guard overheard us, but anyway we got ourselves together to set the Teen Post on fire to burn them up in there with it. . . . The truck caught on fire; this dude burned the truck, but the Teen Post wouldn't burn. . . .

Some residents react to the question of whether there was some sort of pattern to the rioting, and why the stores in nearby Caucasian areas were not hit.

Sam: I never did myself go out for that "brothers" talk, that "black power" talk, until after the riot; that is when I really got involved in it; that's when everyone really got involved in it. They started reading this literature and started getting interested.

Sam, Chuck, and *Bill:* No, there was no pattern, just as it went. . . . The bus drivers let you ride free on the buses. . . . They stole most of the buses from the bus company and took them way out in the country in Compton and hid 'em. It was something else. . . . They

sound like they are unbelievable, but everything is true. I never in my life experienced things like this till I came to California.

I hope there will never be another riot. A lot of people think there is going to be another riot, but I don't think there will ever be another riot in Watts, because if there will be another riot, I feel there will be a nuclear war between Caucasians and Colored people.

[White areas weren't hit] because for the simple reason . . . the merchants that owns the stores in Watts, they would take money out of [the community] this is where they get . . . their hustle. This is how they work. They would come in and open up a business here, and they would charge you $20 for a pair of shoes. You can go to Huntington Park or anywhere else and get it for $8.01 or so. Go to Kinney's and get it even for $7.98. They felt that they would just go in and take these suckers. . . . They call them [the merchants] the blue-eyed devils. We gonna take these devils' business so he can't make it no more. That is why everybody did that: that's why. A lot of people owed them for the rest of their lives, see what I mean, and they said we are going to destroy these records; they won't find no records so I won't owe a damn thing, and get away with it.

Sam: I was in Mississippi until I was ten years old. I could see how the black man could live in the state of Mississippi, Georgia, Arkansas, anywhere else you want, for $2.50 a week. They can go over to the store and buy a can of beer, salt meat, a loaf of bread or more for a dollar. When you come here, there's bread here, 41¢ a loaf. How's a man going to live in Los Angeles, 41¢ a loaf? When you are . . . living in the [housing] project, you go to stores, these prices are jacked up so high till if a lady got eight or nine kids and living in a project, she might as well give it up. . . .

Al and *Sam:* I noticed that when I was

around a Negro neighborhood . . . the food is jacked up sky high, but you go the white man's neighborhood, like you go to Baldwin Hills, somewhere like that, you can get it real cheap. . . .

I think . . . taxes are higher in Watts. We went over to Compton and bought cigarettes for 25¢ a pack; we get back over here, cigarettes cost 40¢ a pack. You know why? Because there is a difference in the community. It is where you live, is what you pay. A business . . . in a Negro area . . . is taxed to death.

Sam, Chuck and *Bill:* See, in this community the Jews and the Mexicans usually own the liquor stores, and Chinese own some of the food stores. They will go back home, and think, "Well, we got the Negroes over there." They know you got to buy the stores' stuff to survive off of. . . . You can go to Hollywood and buy soda water from any store. You can buy some cheaper than you can in Watts. What they got here in Watts is jacked up so high that people in Hollywood wouldn't dare drive those prices up so high.

I think Watts is definitely better off without Martin's. [One of the stores that was burned in the riot.] For furniture, jewelry, clothes, you always pay more in Watts. Like, you go up there and get a watch, they say they have diamonds in it. You take the watch, it cost you two or three hundred in Watts; it's not even worth $75. Then they had this layaway plan: they'd charge you for layaway.

Mrs. Williams: You know, I once got some clothes for my children at _____. [A store which was burned.] The clothes fell to pieces, but they are still trying to collect $25 from me. The records were burned in the fire, but they still harass me with bills. I went to the man [at Neighborhood Legal Service, an OEO-funded agency to help poor people with legal problems] and told him I only owed about $15, which I would pay. He phoned them and they

said they would accept the $15. I sent a money order for the exact amount to the man at Legal Service, so he could send it in and know I was paying the bill. The store got my money, but they are still sending me bills for more money.[4]

You can go down there [to 103rd Street], you are going there to buy a belt, you pay three or four dollars for that belt, but you can go downtown and get a belt for $1.79. . . . I'll tell you why people shop in Watts; they don't have no way of getting rides to the stores [in other areas].

Chuck: You could go down to _____ loan company, and say, "I am going to pawn this $200 watch," and throw it up there on the table; the man grabbed it and looked at it. "This ain't no $200 watch, what's wrong with you? Who sold you this watch for $200?" And looked at him like he is a fool, and . . . he looked all over to see [if] diamond is in it; if the diamond is in it, he don't know if there is any diamond in it. He is looking all in the back of it, checking in it, and tearing it all up. "I will give you $15 cash money, that's all I can lend, that's it." And the man has been trading there ever since 1900. That don't mean a thing. "Mr. _____," he said, "I can't give you no more than that." They'll rob you for this money. It's just like a pack of wolves. . . . They will con you out of every dime you got, every dime.

Sam and *Chuck:* Most people don't know what it's like in Watts. They [Caucasians outside Watts] never experienced poverty in their lives; they never seen ignorance; they never seen disease like there is in Watts; they never seen crime like there is in Watts; they never really known what poorness is; they never really experienced anything bad in their lives . . . . And they figure, especially in Washington or downtown at the City Hall . . . the south Los Angeles is a bad place. . . . "There is a bunch

---

[4] The editor can verify the truth of these statements.

of colored peoples out there; they are no good," this and that. They put all this in the people's head in Beverly Hills, and Malibu, and we go out there looking for jobs, and we couldn't get hired.

One day . . . someone brought up the subject about looking at the paper for jobs. So we all got together, six or seven of us, looking through the paper for jobs. So three of us hit on the same job, on Washington. . . . We were supposed to be selling these magazines. The first question the man asked, after he looked over our application and everything, he said, "Oh, I see. You young men are from the south central area." I said, "Yes, we are from Watts," like this. He looked as though he was objecting to us, like we was no good. He just told us, "Well, I will see what I can do, I will call you if I need you." That was the only reply we got from this man. . . . That's the only reply we got from any Caucasian person that we went to get hired from. . . . I know one person that had gotten a job, but he's Mexican-American.

The Pump House Gang

Tom Wolfe

Tom Wolfe has been credited with creating the nonfiction short story. He, more modestly, describes himself as a proponent of new journalism. Wolfe worked as a staff writer with the *Washington Post* from 1959 to 1962. He joined the *New York Herald Tribune* in 1962 but took advantage of the 1963 *Tribune* strike to do an article for *Esquire* magazine on customized cars in California. He returned with plenty of notes but no story. The notes were run as is, liberated from traditional journalistic form, and were followed by some forty more impressionistic articles over the next two years. His books include *The Pump House Gang* and *The Electric Kool-Aid Acid Test*.

Our boys never hair out. The black panther has black feet. Black feet on the crumbling black panther. Pan-thuh. Mee-dah. Pam Stacy, 16 years old, a cute girl here in La Jolla, California, with a pair of orange bell-bottom hip-huggers on, sits on a step about four steps down the stairway to the beach and she can see a pair of revolting black feet without lifting her head. So she says it out loud, "The black panther."

Somebody farther down the stairs, one of the boys with the *major* hair and khaki shorts, says, "The black feet of the black panther."

"Mee-dah," says another kid. This happens to be the cry of a, well, *underground* society known as the Mac Meda Destruction Company.

"The pan-thuh."

"The poon-thuh."

All these kids, seventeen of them, members of the Pump House crowd, are lollygagging around the stairs down to Windansea Beach, La Jolla, California, about 11 a.m., and they all look at the black feet, which are a woman's pair of black street shoes, out of which stick a pair of old veiny white ankles, which lead up like a senile cone to a fudge of tallowy, edematous flesh, her thighs, squeezing out of her bathing suit, with old faded yellow bruises on them, which she probably got from running eight feet to catch a bus or something. She is standing with her old work-a-hubby, who has on *san*dals: you know, a pair of navy-blue anklet socks and these sandals with big, wide, new-smelling tan straps going this way and that, *for keeps.* Man, they look like orthopedic sandals, if one can imagine that. Obviously, these people come from Tucson or Albuquerque or one of those hincty adobe towns. All these hincty, crumbling black feet come to La Jolla-by-the-sea from the adobe towns for the weekend. They even drive in cars all full of thermos bottles and mayonnaisey sandwiches and some kind of latticework wooden-back support for the old crock who drives and Venetian blinds on the back window.

"The black panther."

"Pan-thuh."

"Poon-thuh."

"Mee-dah."

Nobody says it to the two old crocks directly. God, they must be practically 50 years old. Naturally, they're carrying every piece of garbage imaginable: the folding aluminum chairs, the newspapers, the lending-library book with the clear plastic wrapper on it, the sunglasses, the sun ointment, about a vat of goo—

It is a Mexican standoff. In a Mexican standoff, both parties narrow their eyes and glare but nobody throws a punch. Of course, nobody in the Pump House crowd would ever even jostle these people or say anything right to them; they are too cool for that.

Everybody in the Pump House crowd looks over, even Tom Coman, who is a cool person. Tom Coman, 16 years old, got thrown out of his garage last night. He is sitting up on top of the railing, near the stairs, up over the beach, with his legs apart. Some nice long willowy girl in yellow slacks is standing on the sidewalk but leaning into him with her arms around his body, just resting. Neale Jones, 16, a boy with great lank perfect surfer's hair, is standing nearby with a Band-Aid on his upper lip, where

the sun has burnt it raw. Little Vicki Ballard is up on the sidewalk. Her older sister, Liz, is down the stairs by the Pump House itself, a concrete block, 15 feet high, full of machinery for the La Jolla water system. Liz is wearing her great "Liz" styles, a hulking rabbit-fur vest and black-leather boots over her Levis, even though it is about 85 out here and the sun is plugged in up there like God's own dentist lamp and the Pacific is heaving in with some fair-to-middling surf. Kit Tilden is lollygagging around, and Tom Jones, Connie Carter, Roger Johnson, Sharon Sandquist, Mary Beth White, Rupert Fellows, Glenn Jackson, Dan Watson from San Diego, they are all out here, and everybody takes a look at the panthers.

The old guy, one means, you know, he must be practically 50 years old, he says to his wife, "Come on, let's go farther up," and he takes her by her fat upper arm as if to wheel her around and aim her away from here.

But she says, "No! We have just as much right to be here as they do."

"That's *not the point*—"

"Are you going to—"

"Mrs. Roberts," the work-a-hubby says, calling his own wife by her official married name, as if to say she took a vow once and his word is law, even if he is not testing it with the blond kids here—"farther up, *Mrs. Roberts.*"

They start to walk up the sidewalk, but one kid won't move his feet, and, oh, god, her work-a-hubby breaks into a terrible shaking Jello smile as she steps over them, as if to say, Excuse me, sir, I don't mean to make trouble, please, and don't you and your colleagues rise up and jump me, screaming *Gotcha*—

Mee-dah!

But exactly! This beach *is* verboten for people practically 50 years old. This is a segregated beach. They can look down on Windansea Beach and see nothing but lean tan kids. It is posted "no swimming" (for safety reasons), meaning surfing only. In effect, it is segregated by age. From Los Angeles on down the California coast, this is an era of age segregation. People have always tended to segregate themselves by age, teenagers hanging around with teenagers, old people with old people, like the old men who sit on the benches up near the Bronx Zoo and smoke black cigars. But before, age segregation has gone on within a larger community. Sooner or later during the day everybody has melted back into the old community network that embraces practically everyone, all ages.

But in California today surfers, not to mention rock 'n' roll kids and the hot-rodders or Hair Boys, named for their fanciful pompadours—all sorts of sets of kids—they don't merely hang around together. They establish whole little societies for themselves. In some cases they live with one another for months at a time. The "Sunset Strip" on Sunset Boulevard used to be a kind of Times Square for Hollywood hot dogs of all ages, anyone who wanted to promenade in his version of the high life. Today "The Strip" is almost completely the preserve of kids from about 16 to 25. It is lined with go-go clubs. One of them, a place called It's Boss, is set up for people 16 to 25 and won't let in anybody over 25, and there are some terrible I'm-dying-a-thousand-deaths scenes when a girl comes up with her boyfriend and the guy at the door at It's Boss doesn't think she looks under 25 and tells her she will have to produce some identification proving she is young enough to come in here and live The Strip kind of life and—she's *had* it, because she can't get up the I.D. and nothing in the world is going to make a woman look stupider than to stand around trying to argue *I'm younger than I look, I'm younger than I look.* So she practically shrivels up like a Peruvian shrunken head in front of her boyfriend and he trundles her off, looking for some place you can get an old doll like this into. One of the few remaining clubs for "older people," curiously, is the Play-

boy Club. There are apartment houses for people 20 to 30 only, such as the Sheri Plaza in Hollywood and the E'Questre Inn in Burbank. There are whole suburban housing developments, mostly private developments, where only people over 45 or 50 can buy a house. Whole towns, meantime, have become identified as "young": Venice, Newport Beach, Balboa—or "old": Pasadena, Riverside, Coronado Island.

Behind much of it—especially something like a whole nightclub district of a major city, "The Strip," going teenage—is, simply, money. World War II and the prosperity that followed pumped incredible amounts of money into the population, the white population at least, at every class level. All of a sudden here is an area with thousands of people from 16 to 25 who can get their hands on enough money to support a whole nightclub belt and to have the cars to get there and to set up autonomous worlds of their own in a fairly posh resort community like La Jolla—

—Tom Coman's garage. Some old bastard took Tom Coman's garage away from him, and that means eight or nine surfers are out of a place to stay.

"I went by there this morning, you ought to see the guy," Tom Coman says. Yellow Stretch Pants doesn't move. She has him around the waist. "He was out there painting and he had this brush and about a thousand gallons of ammonia. He was really going to scrub me out of there."

"What did he do with the furniture?"

"I don't know. He threw it out."

"What are you going to do?"

"I don't know."

"Where are you going to stay?"

"I don't know. I'll stay on the beach. It wouldn't be the first time. I haven't had a place to stay for three years, so I'm not going to start worrying now."

Everybody thinks that over awhile. Yellow

Stretch just hangs on and smiles. Tom Coman, 16 years old, piping fate again. One of the girls says, "You can stay at my place, Tom."

"Um. Who's got a cigarette?"

Pam Stacy says, "You can have these."

Tom Coman lights a cigarette and says, "Let's have a destructo." A destructo is what can happen in a garage after eight or 10 surfers are kicked out of it.

"Mee-dah!"

"Wouldn't that be bitchen?" says Tom Coman. Bitchen is a surfer's term that means "great," usually.

"Bitchen!"

"Mee-dah!"

It's incredible—that old guy out there trying to scour the whole surfing life out of that garage. He's a pathetic figure. His shoulders are hunched over and he's dousing and scrubbing away and the sun doesn't give him a tan, it gives him these . . . *mottles* on the back of his neck. But never mind! The hell with destructo. One only has a destructo spontaneously, a Dionysian . . . *bursting out,* like those holes through the wall during the Mac Meda Destruction Company Convention at Manhattan Beach—Mee-dah!

Something will pan out. It's a magic economy—yes!—all up and down the coast from Los Angeles to Baja California kids can go to one of these beach towns and live the complete surfing life. They take off from home and get to the beach, and if they need a place to stay, well, somebody rents a garage for twenty bucks a month and everybody moves in, girls and boys. Furniture—it's like, one means, you know, one *appropriates* furniture from here and there. It's like the Volkswagen buses a lot of kids now use as beach wagons instead of woodies. Woodies are old station wagons, usually Fords, with wooden bodies, from back before 1953. One of the great things about a Volkswagen bus is that one can . . . *exchange* motors in about three minutes. A good VW motor exchanger can go up to a parked Volkswagen, and a few ratchets of the old wrench here and it's up and out and he has a new motor. There must be a few nice old black panthers around wondering why their nice hubby-mommy VW's don't run so good anymore—but—then—they—are—probably—puzzled—about—a—lot of things. Yes.

Cash—it's practically in the air. Around the beach in La Jolla a guy can walk right out in the street and stand there, stop cars and make the candid move. Mister, I've got a quarter, how about 50 cents so I can get a *large* draft. Or, I need some after-ski boots. And the panthers give one a Jello smile and hand it over. Or a guy who knows how to do it can get $40 from a single night digging clams, and it's nice out there. Or he can go around and take up a collection for a keg party, a keg of beer. Man, anybody who won't kick in a quarter for a keg of beer is a jerk. A couple of good keg collections—that's a trip to Hawaii, which is the surfer's version of a trip to Europe: there is a great surf and great everything there. Neale spent three weeks in Hawaii last year. He got $30 from a girl friend, he scrounged a little here and there and got $70 more and he headed off for Hawaii with $100.02, that being the exact plane fare, and borrowed 25 cents when he got there to . . . blast the place up. He spent the 25 cents in a photo booth, showed the photos to the people on the set of *Hawaii* and got a job in the movie. What's the big orgy about money? It's warm, nobody even wears shoes, nobody is starving.

All right, Mother gets worried about all this, but it is limited worry, as John Shine says. Mainly, Mother says, *Sayonara,* you all, and you head off for the beach.

The thing is, everybody, practically everybody, comes from a good family. Everyone has been . . . *reared well,* as they say. Everybody is very upper-middle, if you want to bring it down to that. It's just that this is a new order. Why hang around in the hubby-mommy household with everybody getting neurotic hang-ups with each other and slamming doors and saying, Why can't they have some privacy? Or, it doesn't mean anything that I have to work for a living, does it? It doesn't mean a thing to you. All of you just lie around here sitting in the big orange easy chair smoking cigarettes. I'd hate for you to have to smoke standing up, you'd probably get phlebitis from it— Listen to me, Sarah—

—why go through all that? It's a good life out here. Nobody is mugging everybody for money and affection. There are a lot of bright people out here, and there are a lot of interesting things. One night there was a toga party in a garage, and everybody dressed in sheets, like togas, boys and girls and they put on the appropriated television set to an old Deanna Durbin movie and turned off the sound and put on Rolling Stones records, and you should have seen Deanna Durbin opening her puckered kumquat mouth with Mick Jagger's voice bawling out, *I ain't got no satisfaction.* Of course, finally everybody started pulling the togas off each other, but that is another thing. And one time they had a keg party down on the beach in Mission Bay and the lights from the amusement park were reflected all over the water and that, the whole design of the thing, those nutty lights, that was part of the party. Liz put out the fire throwing a "sand potion" or something on it. One can laugh at Liz and her potions, her necromancy and everything, but there is a lot of thought going into it, a lot of, well, mysticism.

You can even laugh at mysticism if you want to, but there is a kid like Larry Alderson, who spent two years with a monk, and he learned a lot of stuff, and Artie Nelander is going to spend next summer with some Outer Mongolian tribe; he really means to do that. Maybe the "mysterioso" stuff is a lot of garbage, but still, it is interesting. The surfers around the Pump House use that word, mysterioso, quite

a lot. It refers to the mystery of the Oh Mighty Hulking Pacific Ocean and everything. Sometimes a guy will stare at the surf and say, "Mysterioso." They keep telling the story of Bob Simmons' wipeout, and somebody will say "mysterioso."

Simmons was a fantastic surfer. He was fantastic even though he had a bad leg. He rode the really big waves. One day he got wiped out at Windansea. When a big wave overtakes a surfer, it drives him right to the bottom. The board came in but he never came up and they never found his body. Very mysterioso. The black panthers all talked about what happened to "the Simmons boy." But the mysterioso thing was how he could have died at all. If he had been one of the old pan-thuhs, hell, sure he could have got killed. But Simmons was, well, one's own age, he was the kind of guy who could have been in the Pump House gang, he was . . . *immune*, he was plugged into the whole pattern, he could feel the whole Oh Mighty Hulking Sea, he didn't have to think it out step by step. But he got wiped out and killed. Very mysterioso.

Immune! If one is in the Pump House gang and really keyed in to this whole thing, it's—well, one is . . . *immune,* one is not full of black panthuh panic. Two kids, a 14-year-old girl and a 16-year-old boy, go out to Windansea at dawn, in the middle of winter, cold as hell, and take on 12-foot waves all by themselves. The girl, Jackie Haddad, daughter of a certified public accountant, wrote a composition about it, just for herself, called "My Ultimate Journey":

"It was six o'clock in the morning, damp, foggy and cold. We could feel the bitter air biting at our cheeks. The night before, my friend Tommy and I had seen one of the greatest surf films, *Surf Classics.* The film had excited us so much we made up our minds to go surfing the following morning. That is what brought us down on the cold, wet, soggy sand of Windansea early on a December morning.

"We were the first surfers on the beach. The sets were rolling in at eight to 10, filled with occasional 12-footers. We waxed up and waited for a break in the waves. The break came, neither of us said a word, but instantly grabbed our boards and ran into the water. The paddle out was difficult, not being used to the freezing water.

"We barely made it over the first wave of the set, a large set. Suddenly Tommy put on a burst of speed and shot past me. He cleared the biggest wave of the set. It didn't hit me hard as I rolled under it. It dragged me almost 20 yards before exhausting its strength. I climbed on my board gasping for air. I paddled out to where Tommy was resting. He laughed at me for being wet already. I almost hit him but I began laughing, too. We rested a few minutes and then lined up our position with a well known spot on the shore.

"I took off first. I bottom-turned hard and started climbing up the wave. A radical cutback caught me off balance and I fell, barely hanging onto my board. I recovered in time to see Tommy go straight over the falls on a 10-footer. His board shot nearly 30 feet in the air. Luckily, I could get it before the next set came in, so Tommy didn't have to make the long swim in. I pushed it to him and then laughed. All of a sudden Tommy yelled, 'Outside!'

"Both of us paddled furiously. We barely made it up to the last wave, it was a monster. In precision timing we wheeled around and I took off. I cut left in reverse stance, then cut back, driving hard toward the famous Windansea bowl. As I crouched, a huge wall of energy came down over me, covering me up. I moved toward the nose to gain more speed and shot out of the fast-flowing suction just in time to kick out as the wave closed out.

"As I turned around I saw Tommy make a beautiful drop-in, then the wave peaked and fell all at once. Miraculously he beat the suction. He cut back and did a spinner, which followed with a reverse kick-up.

"Our last wave was the biggest. When we got to shore, we rested, neither of us saying a word, but each lost in his own private world of thoughts. After we had rested, we began to walk home. We were about half way and the rain came pouring down. That night we both had bad colds, but we agreed it was worth having them after the thrill and satisfaction of an extra good day of surfing."

John Shine and Artie Nelander are out there right now. They are just "outside," about one fifth of a mile out from the shore, beyond where the waves start breaking. They are straddling their surfboards with their backs to the shore, looking out toward the horizon, waiting for a good set. Their backs look like some kind of salmon-colored porcelain shells, a couple of tiny shells bobbing up and down as the swells roll under them, staring out to sea like Phrygian sacristans looking for a sign.

John and Artie! They are—they are what one means when one talks about the surfing life. It's like, you know, one means, they have this life all of their own; it's like a glass-bottom boat, and it floats over the "real" world, or the square world or whatever one wants to call it. They are not exactly off in a world of their own, they are and they aren't. What it is, they float right through the real world, but it can't touch them. They do these things, like the time they went to Malibu, and there was this party in some guy's apartment, and there wasn't enough *legal* parking space for everybody, and so somebody went out and painted the red curbs white and everybody parked. Then the cops came. Everybody ran out. Artie and John took an airport bus to the Los Angeles Airport, just like they were going to take a plane, in khaki shorts and T-shirts with Mac Meda

Destruction Company stenciled on them. Then they took a helicopter to Disneyland. At Disneyland crazy Ditch had his big raincoat on and a lot of flasks strapped onto his body underneath, Scotch, bourbon, all kinds of stuff. He had plastic tubes from the flasks sticking out of the flyfront of his raincoat and everybody was sipping whiskey through the tubes—

—Ooooo-eeee-Mee-dah! They chant this chant, Mee-dah, in a real fakey deep voice, and it *really bugs people.* They don't know what the hell it is. It is the cry of the Mac Meda Destruction Company. The Mac Meda Destruction Company is ... an *underground* society that started in La Jolla about three years ago. Nobody can remember exactly how; they have arguments about it. Anyhow, it is mainly something to *bug* people with and organize huge beer orgies with. They have their own complete, bogus phone number in La Jolla. They have Mac Meda Destruction Company decals. They stick them on phone booths, on cars, any place. Some mommy-hubby will come out of the shopping plaza and walk up to his Mustang, which is supposed to make him a hell of a tiger now, and he'll see a sticker on the side of it saying, "Mac Meda Destruction Company," and for about two days or something he'll think the sky is going to fall in.

But the big thing is the parties, the "conventions." Anybody can join, any kid, anybody can come, as long as they've heard about it, and they can only hear about it by word of mouth. One was in the Sorrento Valley, in the gulches and arroyos, and the fuzz came, and so the older guys put the young ones and the basket cases, the ones just too stoned out of their gourds, into the tule grass, and the cops shined their searchlights and all they saw was tule grass while the basket cases moaned scarlet and oozed on their bellies like reptiles

and everybody else ran down the arroyos, yelling Mee-dah.

The last one was at Manhattan Beach, inside somebody's poor hulking house. The party got *very Dionysian* that night and somebody put a hole through one wall, and everybody else decided to see if they could make it bigger. Everybody was stoned out of their hulking gourds, and it got to be about 3:30 a.m. and everybody decided to go see the riots. These were the riots in Watts. The Los Angeles *Times* and the San Diego *Union* were all saying, WATTS NO-MAN'S LAND and STAY WAY FROM WATTS YOU GET YO' SE'F KILLED, but naturally nobody believed that. Watts was a blast, and the Pump House gang was immune to the trembling gourd panic rattles of the L.A. *Times* black pan-thuhs. Immune!

So John Shine, Artie Nelander and Jerry Sterncorb got in John's VW bus, known as the Hog of Steel, and they went to Watts. Gary Wickham and some other guys ran into an old man at a bar who said he owned a house in Watts and had been driven out by the drunk niggers. So they drove in a car to save the old guy's house from the drunk niggers. Artie and John had a tape recorder and decided they were going to make a record called "Random Sounds from the Watts Riots." They drove right into Watts in the Hog of Steel and there was blood on the streets and roofs blowing off the stores and all these apricot flames and drunk Negroes falling through the busted plate glass of the liquor stores. Artie got a nice recording of a lot of Negroes chanting, "Burn, baby, burn." They all got out and talked to some Negro kids in a gang going into a furniture store, and the Negro kids didn't say Kill Whitey or Geed'um or any of that. They just said, Come on, man, it's a party and it's free. After they had been in there for about three hours talking to Negroes and watching drunks collapse in the liquor stores, some cop with a helmet on came roaring up and said, "Get the hell out of here, you kids, we cannot and will not provide protection."

Meantime, Gary Wickham and his friends drove in in a car with the old guy, and a car full of Negroes *did* stop them and say, Whitey, Geed'um, and all that stuff, but one of the guys in Gary's car just draped a pistol he had out the window and the colored guys drove off. Gary and everybody drove the old guy to his house and they all walked in and had a great raunchy time drinking beer and raising hell. A couple of Negroes, the old guy's neighbors, came over and told the old guy to cut out the racket. There were flames in the sky and ashes coming down with little rims of fire on them, like apricot crescents. The old guy got very cocky about all his "protection" and went out on the front porch about dawn and started yelling at some Negroes across the street, telling them "No more drunk niggers in Watts" and a lot of other unwise slogans. So Gary Wickham got up and everybody left. They were there about four hours altogether and when they drove out, they had to go through a National Guard checkpoint, and a lieutenant from the San Fernando Valley told them he could not and would not provide protection.

But exactly! Watts just happened to be what was going on at the time, as far as the netherworld of La Jolla surfing was concerned, and so one goes there and sees what is happening and comes back and tells everybody about it and laughs at the L.A. *Times.* That is what makes it so weird when all these black panthuhs come around to pick up "surfing styles," like the clothing manufacturers. They don't know what any of it means. It's like archaeologists discovering hieroglyphics or something, and they say, god, that's neat—Egypt!—but they don't know what the hell it is. They don't

know anything about it . . . *The Life.* It's great to think of a lot of old emphysematous panthuhs in the Garment District in New York City struggling in off the street against a gummy 15-mile-an-hour wind full of soot and coffee-brown snow and gasping in the elevator to clear their old nicotine-phlegm tubes on the way upstairs to make out the invoices on a lot of surfer stuff for 1966, the big nylon windbreakers with the wide, white horizontal competition stripes, nylon swimming trunks with competition stripes, bell-bottom slacks for girls, the big hairy sleeveless jackets, vests, the blue "tennies," meaning tennis shoes, and the . . . *look,* the Major Hair, all this long lank blond hair, the plain face kind of tanned and bleached out at the same time, but with big eyes. It all starts in a few places, a few strategic groups, the Pump House gang being one of them, and then it moves up the beach, to places like Newport Beach and as far up as Malibu.

Well, actually there is a kind of back-and-forth thing with some of the older guys, the old heroes of surfing, like Bruce Brown, John Severson, Hobie Alter and Phil Edwards. Bruce Brown will do one of those incredible surfing movies and he is out in the surf himself filming Phil Edwards coming down a 20-footer in Hawaii, and Phil has on a pair of nylon swimming trunks, which he has had made in Hawaii, because they dry out fast—and it is like a grapevine. Everybody's got to have a pair of nylon swimming trunks, and then the manufacturers move in, and everybody's making nylon swimming trunks, boxer trunk style, and pretty soon every kid in Utica, N.Y., is buying a pair of them, with the competition stripe and the whole thing, and they never heard of Phil Edwards. So it works back and forth—but so what? Phil Edwards is part of it. He may be an old guy, he is 28 years old, but he and Bruce Brown, who is even older, 30, and John Severson, 32, and Hobie Alter, 29, never haired out to the square world even though they make thousands. Hair refers to courage. A guy who "has a lot of hair" is courageous; a guy who "hairs out" is yellow.

Bruce Brown and Severson and Alter are known as the "surfing millionaires." They are not millionaires, actually, but they must be among the top businessmen south of Los Angeles. Brown grossed something around $500,000 in 1965 even before his movie *Endless Summer* became a hit nationally; and he has only about three people working for him. He goes out on a surfboard with a camera encased in a plastic shell and takes his own movies and edits them himself and goes around showing them himself and narrating them at places like the Santa Monica Civic Auditorium, where 24,000 came in eight days once, at $1.50 a person, and all he has to pay is for developing the film and hiring the hall. John Severson has the big surfing magazine, *Surfer*. Hobie Alter is the biggest surfboard manufacturer, all hand-made boards. He made 5,000 boards in 1965 at $140 a board. He also designed the "Hobie" skate boards and gets 25 cents for every one sold. He grossed between $900,000 and $1 million in 1964.

God, if only everybody could grow up like these guys and know that crossing the horror dividing line, 25 years old, won't be the end of everything. One means, keep on living *The Life* and not get sucked into the ticky-tacky life with some insurance salesman sitting forward in your stuffed chair on your wall-to-wall telling you that life is like a football game and you sit there and take that stuff. The hell with that! Bruce Brown has the money and *The Life*. He has a great house on a cliff about 60 feet above the beach at Dana Point. He is married and has two children, but it is not that hubby-mommy you're-breaking-my-gourd scene. His office is only two blocks from his

house and he doesn't even have to go on the streets to get there. He gets on his Triumph scrambling motorcycle and cuts straight across a couple of vacant lots and one can see him . . . *bounding* to work over the vacant lots. The Triumph hits ruts and hummocks and things and Bruce Brown bounces into the air with the motor—*thragggggh*—moaning away, and when he gets to the curbing in front of his office, he just leans back and pulls up the front wheel and hops it and gets off and walks into the office barefooted. *Barefooted;* why not? He wears the same things now that he did when he was doing nothing but surfing. He has on a faded gray sweatshirt with the sleeves cut off just above the elbows and a pair of faded corduroys. His hair is the lightest corn yellow imaginable, towheaded, practically white, from the sun. Even his eyes seem to be bleached. He has a rain-barrel old-apple-tree Tom-Sawyer little-boy roughneck look about him, like Bobby Kennedy.

Sometimes he carries on his business right there at the house. He has a dugout room built into the side of the cliff, about 15 feet down from the level of the house. It is like a big pale green box set into the side of the cliff, and inside is a kind of upholstered bench or settee you can lie down on if you want to and look out at the Pacific. The surf is crashing like a maniac on the rocks down below. He has a telephone in there. Sometimes it will ring, and Bruce Brown says hello, and the surf is crashing away down below, roaring like mad, and the guy on the other end, maybe one of the TV networks calling from New York or some movie hair-out from Los Angeles, says:

"What is all that noise? It sound like you're sitting out in the surf."

"That's right," says Bruce Brown, "I have my desk out on the beach now. It's nice out here."

The guy on the other end doesn't know what to think. He is another Mr. Efficiency who just got back from bloating his colon up at a three-hour executive lunch somewhere and now he is Mr.-Big-Time-Let's-Get-This-Show-on-the-Road.

"On the beach?"

"Yeah. It's cooler down here. And it's good for you, but it's not so great for the desk. You know what I have now? A warped leg."

"A warped leg?"

"Yeah, and this is an $800 desk."

Those nutball California kids—and he will still be muttering that five days after Bruce Brown delivers his film, on time, and Mr. Efficiency is still going through memo thickets or heaving his way into the bar car to Darien—in the very moment that Bruce Brown and Hobie Alter are both on their motorcycles out on the vacant lot in Dana Point. Hobie Alter left his surfboard plant about two in the afternoon because the wind was up and it would be good catamaranning and he wanted to go out and see how far he could tip his new catamaran without going over, and he did tip it over, about half a mile out in high swells and it was hell getting the thing right side up again. But he did, and he got back in time to go scrambling on the lot with Bruce Brown. They are out there, roaring over the ruts, bouncing up in the air, and every now and then they roar up the embankment so they can . . . fly, going up in the air about six feet off the ground as they come up off the embankment—*thraaagggggh*—all these people in the houses around there come to the door and look out. These two . . . nuts are at it again. Well, they can only fool around there for 20 minutes, because that is about how long it takes the cops to get there if anybody gets burned up enough and calls, and what efficient business magnate wants to get hauled off by the Dana Point cops for scrambling on his motorcycle in a vacant lot.

Bruce Brown has it figured out so no one in the whole rubber-bloated black pan-thuh world can trap him, though. He bought a forest in the Sierras. There is nothing on it but trees. His own wilds: no house, no nothing, just Bruce Brown's forest. Beautiful things happen up there. One day, right after he bought it, he was on the edge of his forest, where the road comes into it, and one of these big rancher king moteroos with the broad belly and the $70 lisle Safari shirt comes tooling up in a Pontiac convertible with a funnel of dust pouring out behind. He gravels it to a great flashy stop and yells:

"Hey! You!"

Of course, what he sees is some towheaded barefooted kid in a torn-off sweatshirt fooling around the edge of the road.

"Hey! You!"

"Yeah?" says Bruce Brown.

"Don't you know this is private property?"

"Yeah," says Bruce Brown.

"Well, then, why don't you get your ass off it?"

"Because it's mine, it's my private property," says Bruce Brown. "Now you get *yours* off it."

And Safari gets a few rays from that old apple-tree rain-barrel don't-cross-that-line look and doesn't say anything and roars off, slipping gravel, the dumb crumbling pan-thuh.

But . . . perfect! It is like, one means, you know, poetic justice for all the nights Bruce Brown slept out on the beach at San Onofre and such places in the old surfing days and would wake up with some old crock's black feet standing beside his head and some phlegmy black rubber voice saying:

"All right, kid, don't you know this is private property?"

And he would prop his head up and out there would be the Pacific Ocean, a kind of shadowy magenta-mauve, and one thing, *that* was nobody's private property—

But how many Bruce Browns can there be? There is a built-in trouble with age segregation.

Eventually one *does* reach the horror age of 25, the horror dividing line. Surfing and the surfing life have been going big since 1958, and already there are kids who—well, who aren't kids anymore, they are pushing 30, and they are stagnating on the beach. Pretty soon the California littoral will be littered with these guys, stroked out on the beach like beached white whales, and girls, too, who can't give up the mystique, the mysterioso mystique, Oh Mighty Hulking Sea, who can't *conceive* of living any other life. It is pathetic when they are edged out of groups like the Pump House gang. Already there are some guys who hang around with the older crowd around the Shack who are stagnating on the beach. Some of the older guys, like Gary Wickham, who is 24, are still in *The Life,* they still have it, but even Gary Wickham will be 25 one day and then 26 and then . . . and then even pan-thuh age. Is one really going to be pan-thuh age one day? Watch those black feet go. And Tom Coman still snuggles with Yellow Slacks, and Liz still roosts moodily in her rabbit fur at the bottom of the Pump House and Pam still sits on the steps contemplating the mysterioso mysteries of Pump House ascension and John and Artie still bob, tiny pink porcelain shells, way out there waiting for godsown bitchen *set,* and godsown sun is still turned on like a dentist's lamp and so far—

—the panthers scrape on up the sidewalk. They are at just about the point Leonard Anderson and Donna Blanchard got that day, December 6, 1964, when Leonard said, Pipe it, and fired two shots, one at her and one at himself. Leonard was 18 and Donna was 21—21!—god, for a girl in the Pump House gang that is almost the horror line right there. But it was all so mysterioso. Leonard was just lying down on the beach at the foot of the Pump House, near the stairs, just talking to John K. Weldon down there, and then Donna appeared at the top of the stairs and Leonard got up and went up the stairs to meet her, and they didn't say anything, they weren't *angry* over anything, they never had been, although the police said they had, they just turned and went a few feet down the sidewalk, away from the Pump House and—blam blam!—these two shots. Leonard fell dead on the sidewalk and Donna died that afternoon in Scripps Memorial Hospital. Nobody knew what to think. But one thing it seemed like—well, it seemed like Donna and Leonard thought they had lived *The Life* as far as it would go and now it was running out. All that was left to do was—but that is an *insane* idea. It can't be like that, *The Life* can't run out, people can't change all that much just because godsown chronometer runs on and the body packing starts deteriorating and the fudgy tallow shows up at the thighs where they squeeze out of the bathing suit—

Tom, boy! John, boy! Gary, boy! Neale, boy! Artie, boy! Pam, Liz, Vicki, Jackie Haddad! After all this—just a pair of bitchen black panther bunions inching down the sidewalk away from the old Pump House stairs?

A Journey into the Mind of Watts

Thomas Pynchon

Thomas Pynchon, a graduate of Cornell University, has written articles for *Epoch, Kenyon Review,* the *Saturday Evening Post,* and the *New York Times Magazine.* Acclaimed as a novelist in 1963 for his book *V,* he won the William Faulkner Foundation First Novel Award. His second novel, *The Crying of Lot 49,* was published in 1966. His latest novel is *Gravity's Rainbow.*

The night of May 7, after a chase that began in Watts and ended some 50 blocks north, two Los Angeles policemen, Caucasians, succeeded in halting a car driven by Leonard Deadwyler, a Negro. With him were his pregnant wife and a friend. The younger cop (who'd once had a complaint brought against him for rousting some Negro kids around in a more than usually abusive way) went over and stuck his head and gun in the car window to talk to Deadwyler. A moment later there was a shot; the young Negro fell sideways in the seat, and died. The last thing he said, according to the other cop, was, "She's going to have a baby."

The coroner's inquest went on for the better part of two weeks, the cop claiming the car had lurched suddenly, causing his service revolver to go off by accident; Deadwyler's widow claiming it was cold-blooded murder and that the car had never moved. The verdict, to no one's surprise, cleared the cop of all criminal responsibility. It had been an accident. The D.A. announced immediately that he thought so too, and that as far as he was concerned the case was closed.

But as far as Watts is concerned, it's still very much open. Preachers in the community are urging calm—or, as others are putting it: "Make any big trouble, baby, The Man just going to come back in and shoot you, like last time." Snipers are sniping but so far not hitting much of anything. Occasional fire bombs are being lobbed at cars with white faces inside, or into empty sports models that look as if they might be white property. There have been a few fires of mysterious origin. A Negro Teen Post—part of the L.A. poverty war's keep-them-out-of-the-streets-effort—has had all its windows busted, the young lady in charge expressing the wish next morning that she could talk with the malefactors, involve them, see if they couldn't work out the problem together. In the back of everybody's head, of course, is the same question: Will there be a repeat of last August's riot?

An even more interesting question is: Why is everybody worrying about another riot—haven't things in Watts improved any since the last one? A lot of white folks are wondering. Unhappily, the answer is no. The neighborhood may be seething with social workers, data collectors, VISTA volunteers and other assorted members of the humanitarian establishment, all of whose intentions are the purest in the world. But somehow nothing much has changed. There are still the poor, the defeated, the criminal, the desperate, all hanging in there with what must seem a terrible vitality.

The killing of Leonard Deadwyler has once again brought it all into sharp focus; brought back longstanding pain, reminded everybody of how very often the cop does approach you with his revolver ready, so that nothing he does with it can then really be accidental; of how, especially at night, everything can suddenly reduce to a matter of reflexes: your life trembling in the crook of a cop's finger because it is dark, and Watts, and the history of this place and these times make it impossible for the cop to come on any different, or for you to hate him any less. Both of you are caught in something neither of you wants, and yet night after night, with casualties or without, these traditional scenes continue to be played out all over the south-central part of this city.

Whatever else may be wrong in a political way—like the inadequacy of Great Depression techniques applied to a scene that has long outgrown them; like an old-fashioned grafter's glee among the city fathers over the vast amounts of poverty-war bread that Uncle is now making available to them—lying much closer to the heart of L.A.'s racial sickness is the co-existence of two very different cultures: one white and one black.

While the white culture is concerned with various forms of systematized folly—the economy of the area in fact depending on it—the black culture is stuck pretty much with basic realities like disease, like failure, violence and death, which the whites have mostly chosen—and can afford—to ignore. The two cultures do not understand each other, though white values are displayed without let-up on black people's TV screens, and though the panoramic sense of black impoverishment is hard to miss from atop the Harbor Freeway, which so many whites must drive at least twice every working day. Somehow it occurs to very few of them to leave at the Imperial Highway exit for a change, go east instead of west only a few blocks, and take a look at Watts. A quick look. The simplest country which lies, psychologically uncounted miles further than most whites seem at present willing to travel.

On the surface anyway, the Deadwyler affair hasn't made it look any different, though underneath the mood in Watts is about what you might expect. Feelings range from a reflexive, angry, driving need to hit back somehow, to an anxious worry that the slaying is

just one more bad grievance, one more bill that will fall due some warm evening this summer. Yet in the daytime's brilliance and heat, it is hard to believe there is any mystery to Watts. Everything seems so out in the open, all of it real, no plastic faces, no transistors, no hidden Muzak, or Disneyfied landscaping, or smiling little chicks to show you around. Not in Raceriotland. Only a few historic landmarks, like the police substation, one command post for the white forces last August, pigeons now thick and cooing up on its red-tiled roof. Or, on down the street, vacant lots, still looking charred around the edges, winking with emptied Tokay port and sherry pints, some of the bottles peeking out of paper bags, others busted.

A kid could come along in his bare feet and step on this glass—not that you'd ever know. These kids are so tough you can pull slivers of it out of them and never get a whimper. It's part of their landscape, both the real and the emotional one: busted glass, busted crockery, nails, tin cans, all kinds of scrap and waste. Traditionally Watts. An Italian immigrant named Simon Rodia spent 30 years gathering some of it up and converting a little piece of the neighborhood along 107th Street into the famous Watts Towers, perhaps his own dream of how things should have been: a fantasy of fountains, boats, tall openwork spires, encrusted with a dazzling mosaic of Watts debris. Next to the Towers, along the old Pacific Electric tracks, kids are busy every day busting more bottles on the steel rails. But Simon Rodia is dead, and now the junk just accumulates.

A few blocks away, other kids are out playing on the hot blacktop of the school playground. Brothers and sisters too young yet for school have it better—wherever they are they have yards, trees, hoses, hiding places. Not the crowded, shadeless tenement living of any Harlem; just the same one- or two-story urban sprawl as all over the rest of L.A., giving you some piece of grass at least to expand into when you don't especially feel like being inside.

In the business part of town there is a different idea of refuge. Pool halls and bars, warm and dark inside, are crowded; many domino, dice and whist games in progress. Outside, men stand around a beer cooler listening to a ball game on the radio; others lean or hunker against the sides of buildings—low, faded stucco boxes that remind you, oddly, of certain streets in Mexico. Women go by, to and from what shopping there is. It is easy to see how crowds, after all, can form quickly in these streets, around the least seed of a disturbance or accident. For the moment, it all only waits in the sun.

Overhead, big jets now and then come vacuum-cleaning in to land; the wind is westerly, and Watts lies under the approaches to L.A. International. The jets hang what seems only a couple of hundred feet up in the air; through the smog they show up more white than silver, highlighted by the sun, hardly solid, only the ghost, or possibilities, of airplanes.

From here, much of the white culture that surrounds Watts—and, in a curious way, besieges it—looks like those jets: a little unreal, a little less than substantial. For Los Angeles, more than any other city, belongs to the mass media. What is known around the nation as the L.A. scene exists chiefly as images on a screen or TV tube, as four-color magazine photos, as old radio mikes, as new songs that survive only a matter of weeks. It is basically a white Scene, and illusion is everywhere in it, from the giant aerospace firms that flourish or retrench at the whims of Robert McNamara, to the "action" everybody mills along the Strip on weekends looking for, unaware that they, and their search which will end, usually, unfulfilled, are the only action in town.

Watts lies impacted in the heart of this white fantasy. It is, by contrast, a pocket of bitter reality. The only illusion Watts ever allowed itself was to believe for a long time in the white version of what a Negro was supposed to be. But with the Muslim and civil-rights movements that went, too.

Since the August rioting, there has been little building here, little buying. Lots whose buildings were burned off them are still waiting vacant and littered with garbage, occupied only by a parked car or two, or kids fooling around after school, or winos sharing a pint in the early morning. The other day, on one of them, there were ground-breaking festivities, attended by a county supervisor, pretty high-school girls decked in ribbons, a white store owner and his wife, who in the true Watts spirit busted a bottle of champagne over a rock—all because the man had decided to stay and rebuild his $200,000 market, the first such major rebuilding since the riot.

Watts people themselves talk about another kind of aura, vaguely evil; complain that Negroes living in better neighborhoods like to come in under the freeway as to a red-light district, looking for some girl, some game, maybe some connection. Narcotics is said to be a rare bust in Watts these days, although the narco people cruise the area earnestly, on the lookout for dope fiends, dope rings, dope peddlers. But the poverty of Watts makes it more likely that if you have pot or a little something else to spare you will want to turn a friend on not sell it. Tomorrow, or when he can, your friend will return the favor.

At the Deadwyler inquest, much was made of the dead man's high blood alcohol content, as if his being drunk made it somehow all right for the police to shoot him. But alcohol is a natural part of the Watts style; as natural as LSD is around Hollywood. The white kid digs hallucination simply because he is conditioned to believe so much in escape, escape as an integral part of life, because the white L.A. Scene makes accessible to him so many different forms of it. But a Watts kid, brought up in a pocket of reality, looks perhaps not so much for escape as just for some calm, some relaxation. And beer or wine is good enough for that. Especially good at the end of a bad day.

Like after you have driven, say, down to Torrance or Long Beach or wherever it is they're hiring because they don't seem to be in Watts, not even in the miles of heavy industry that sprawl along Alameda Street, that gray and murderous arterial which lies at the eastern boundary of Watts looking like the edge of the world.

So you groove instead down the freeway, maybe wondering when some cop is going to stop you because the old piece of a car you're driving, which you bought for $20 or $30 you picked up somehow, makes a lot of noise or burns some oil. Catching you mobile widens The Man's horizons; gives him more things he can get you on. Like "excessive smoking" is a great favorite with him.

If you do get to where you were going without encountering a cop, you may spend your day looking at the white faces of personnel men, their uniform glaze of suspicion, their automatic smiles, and listening to polite putdowns. "I decided once to ask" a kid says, "one time they told me I didn't meet their requirements. So I said: 'Well, what are you looking for? I mean, how can I train, what things do I have to learn so I can meet your requirements?' Know what he said? 'We are not obligated to tell you what our requirements are.'"

He isn't. That right there is the hell and headache: he doesn't have to do anything he doesn't want to do because he is The Man. Or he was. A lot of kids these days are more apt to be calling him the *little* man—meaning not so much any member of the power structure as just your average white L.A. taxpayer, registered voter, property owner; employed, stable, mortgaged and the rest.

The little man bugs these kids more than The Man ever bugged their parents. It is the little man who is standing on their feet and in their way; he's all over the place, and there is not much they can do to change him or the way he feels about them. A Watts kid knows more of what goes on inside white heads than possibly whites do themselves; knows how often the little man has looked at him and thought "Bad credit risk"—or "Poor learner," or "Sexual threat," or "Welfare chiseler"—without knowing a thing about him personally.

The natural, normal thing to want to do is hit the little man. But what, after all, has he done? Mild, respectable, possibly smiling, he has called you no names, shown no weapons. Only told you perhaps that the job was filled, the house rented.

With a cop it may get more dangerous, but at least it's honest. You understand each other. Both of you silently admitting that all the cop really has going for him is his gun. "There was a time," they'll tell you, "you'd say, 'Take off the badge, baby, and let's settle it.' I mean he wouldn't, but you'd say it. But since August, man, the way I feel, hell with the badge—just take off that gun."

The cop does not take off that gun; the hassle stays verbal. But this means that, besides protecting and serving the little man, the cop also functions as his effigy.

If he does get emotional and say something like "boy" or "nigger," you then have the option of cooling it or else—again this is more frequent since last August—calling him the name he expects to be called, though it is understood you are not commenting in any literal way on what goes on between him and his mother. It is a ritual exchange, like the dirty dozens.

Usually—as in the Deadwyler incident—it's the younger cop of the pair who's more troublesome. Most Watts kids are hip to what's going on in this rookie's head—the things he feels he has to prove—as much as to the elements of the ritual. Before the cop can say, "Let's see your I.D.," you learn to take it out politely and say, "You want to see my I.D.?" Naturally it will bug the cop more the further ahead of him you can stay. It is flirting with disaster, but it's the cop who has the gun, so you do what you can.

You must anticipate always how the talk is going to go. It's something you pick up quite young, same as you learn the different species of cop: the Black and White (named for the color scheme of their automobiles), who are L.A. city police and in general the least flexible; the L.A. county sheriff's department, who style themselves more of an elite, try to maintain a certain distance from the public, and are less apt to harass you unless you seem worthy; the Compton city cops, who travel only one to a car and come on very tough, like leaning four of you at a time up against the wall and shaking you all down; the juvies, who ride in unmarked Plymouths and are cruising all over the place soon as the sun goes down, pulling up alonside you with pleasantries like, "Which one's buying the wine tonight?" or, "Who are you guys planning to rob this time?" They are kidding, of course, trying to be pals. But Watts kids, like most, do not like being put in with winos, or dangerous drivers or thieves, or in any bag considered criminal or evil. Whatever the cop's motives, it *looks* like mean and deliberate ignorance.

In the daytime, and especially with any kind of crowd, the cop's surface style has changed some since last August. "Time was," you'll hear, "man used to go right in, very mean, pick maybe one kid out of the crowd he figured was the troublemaker, try to bust him down in front of everybody. But now the people start yelling back, how they don't want no more of that, all of a sudden The Man gets very meek."

Still, however much a cop may seem to be following the order of the day read to him every morning about being courteous to everybody, his behavior with a crowd will really depend as it always has on how many of his own he can muster, and how fast. For his Mayor, Sam Yorty, is a great believer in the virtues of Overwhelming Force as a solution to racial difficulties. This approach has not gained much favor in Watts. In fact, the Mayor of Los Angeles appears to many Negroes to be the very incarnation of the little man: looking out for no one but himself, speaking always out of expediency, and never, never to be trusted.

The Economic and Youth Opportunities Agency (E.Y.O.A.) is a joint city-county "umbrella agency" (the state used to be represented, but has dropped out) for many projects scattered around the poorer parts of L.A., and seems to be Sam Yorty's native element, if not indeed the flower of his consciousness. Bizarre, confused, ever in flux, strangely ineffective, E.Y.O.A. hardly sees a day go by without somebody resigning or being fired, or making an accusation, or answering one—all of it confirming the Watts Negroes' already sad estimate of the little man. The Negro attitude toward E.Y.O.A. is one of clear mistrust, though degrees of suspicion vary, from the housewife wanting only to be left in peace and quiet, who hopes that maybe The Man is lying less than usual this time, to the young, active disciple of Malcolm X who dismisses it all with a contemptuous shrug.

"But why?" asked one white lady volunteer. "There are so many agencies now that you can go to, that can help you, if you'll only file your complaint."

"They don't help you." This particular kid had been put down trying to get a job with one of the larger defense contractors.

"Maybe not before. But it's different now."

"Now," the kid sighed, "*now*. See, people been hearing that '*now*' for a long time, and I'm just tired of The Man telling you, '*Now* it's OK, *now* we mean what we say.'"

In Watts, apparently, where no one can afford the luxury of illusion, there is little reason to believe that now will be any different, any better than last time.

It is perhaps a measure of the people's indifference that only 2 per-cent of the poor in Los Angeles turned out to elect representatives to the E.Y.O.A. "poverty board." For a hopeless minority on the board (7 out of 23), nobody sees much point in voting.

Meantime, the outposts of the establishment drowse in the bright summery smog; secretaries chat the afternoons plaintively away about machines that will not accept the cards they have punched for them; white volunteers sit filing, doodling, talking on the phones, doing any kind of busy-work, wondering where the "clients" are; inspirational mottoes like SMILE decorate the beaverboard office walls along with flow charts to illustrate the proper disposition of "cases," and with clippings from the slick magazines about "What Is Emotional Maturity?"

Items like smiling and Emotional Maturity are in fact very big with the well-adjusted, middle-class professionals, Negro and white, who man the mimeographs and computers of the poverty war here. Sadly, they seem to be smiling themselves out of any meaningful communication with their poor. Besides a 19th-century faith that tried and true approaches—sound counseling, good intentions, perhaps even compassion—will set Watts straight, they are also burdened with the personal attitudes they bring to work with them. Their reflexes—especially about conformity, about failure, about violence—are predictable.

"We had a hell of a time with this one girl," a Youth Training and Employment Project counselor recalls. "You should have seen those hairdos of hers—piled all the way up to here. And the screwy outfits she'd come in with, you just wouldn't believe. We had to take her aside and explain to her that employers just don't go for that sort of thing. That she'd be up against a lot of very smooth-looking chicks, heels and stockings, conservative hair and clothes. We finally got her to come around."

The same goes for boys who like to wear Malcolm hats, or Afro haircuts. The idea the counselors push evidently is to look as much as possible like a white applicant. Which is to say, like a Negro job counselor or social worker. This has not been received with much enthusiasm among the kids it is designed to help out, and is one reason business is so slow around the various projects.

There is a similar difficulty among the warriors about failure. They are in a socio-economic bag, along with the vast majority of white Angelenos, who seem more terrified of failure than of death. It is difficult to see where any of them have experienced significant defeat, or loss. If they have, it seems to have been long rationalized away as something else.

You are likely to hear from them wisdom on the order of: "Life has a way of surprising us, simply as a function of time. Even if all you do is stand on the street corner and wait." Watts is full of street corners where people stand, as they have been, some of them, for 20 or 30 years, without Surprise One ever having come along. Yet the poverty warriors must believe in this form of semimiracle, because their world and their scene cannot accept the possibility that there may be, after all, no surprise. But it is something Watts has always known.

As for violence, in a pocket of reality such as Watts, violence is never far from you: because you are a man, because you have been put down, because for every action there is an equal and opposite reaction. Somehow, sometime. Yet to these innocent, optimistic child-bureaucrats, violence is an evil and an illness, possibly because it threatens property and status they cannot help cherishing.

They remember last August's riot as an outburst, a seizure. Yet what, from the realistic viewpoint of Watts, was so abnormal? "Man's got his foot on your neck," said one guy who was there, "sooner or later you going to stop *asking* him to take it off."[1] The violence it took to get that foot to ease up even the little it did was no surprise. Many had predicted it. Once it got going, its basic objective—to beat the Black and White police—seemed a reasonable one, and was gained the minute The Man had to send troops in. Everybody seems to have known it. There is hardly a person in Watts now who finds it painful to talk about, or who regrets that it happened—unless he lost somebody.

But in the white culture outside, in that creepy world full of pre-cardiac Mustang drivers who scream insults at one another only when the windows are up; of large corporations where Niceguymanship is the standing order regardless of whose executive back one may be endeavoring to stab; of an enormous priest caste of shrinks who counsel moderation and compromise as the answer to all forms of hassle; among so much well-behaved unreality, it is next to impossible to understand how Watts may truly feel about violence. In terms of strict reality, violence may be a means to getting money, for example, no more dishonest than collecting exorbitant carrying charges from a customer on relief, as white merchants here still do. Far from a sickness, violence may be an attempt to communicate, or to be who you really are.

"Sure I did two stretches," a kid says, "both times for fighting, but I didn't deserve either one. First time, the cat was bigger than I was; next time, it was two against one, and I was the one." But he was busted all the same, perhaps because Whitey, who knows how to get everything he wants, no longer has fisticuffs available as a technique, and sees no reason why everybody shouldn't go the Niceguy route. If you are thinking maybe there is a virility hang-up in here, too, that putting a Negro into a cor-

rectional institution for fighting is also some kind of neutering operation, well, you might have something there, who knows?

It is, after all, in white L.A.'s interest to cool Watts any way it can—to put the area under a siege of persuasion; to coax the Negro poor into taking on certain white values. Give them a little property, and they will be less tolerant of arson; get them to go in hock for a car or color TV, and they'll be more likely to hold down a steady job. Some see it for what it is—this come-on, this false welcome, this attempt to transmogrify the reality of Watts into the unreality of Los Angeles. Some don't.

Watts is tough; has been able to resist the unreal. If there is any drift away from reality, it is by way of mythmaking. As this summer warms up, last August's riot is being remembered less as chaos and more as art. Some talk now of a balletic quality to it, a coordinated and graceful drawing of cops away from the center of the action, a scattering of The Man's power, either with real incidents or false alarms.

Others remember it in terms of music; through much of the rioting seemed to run, they say, a remarkable empathy, or whatever it is that jazz musicians feel on certain nights; everybody knowing what to do and when to do it without needing a word or a signal: "You could go up to anybody, the cats could be in the middle of burning down a store or something, but they'd tell you, explain very calm, just what they were doing, what they were going to do next. And that's what they'd do; man, nobody had to give orders."

Restructuring of the riot goes on in other ways. All Easter week this year, in the spirit of the season, there was a "Renaissance of the Arts," a kind of festival in memory of Simon Rodia, held at Markham Junior High, in the heart of Watts.

Along with theatrical and symphonic events, the festival also featured a roomful of sculptures fashioned entirely from found objects—found, symbolically enough, and in the Simon Rodia tradition, among the wreckage the rioting had left. Exploiting textures of charred wood, twisted metal, fused glass, many of the works were fine, honest rebirths.

In one corner was this old, busted, hollow TV set with a rabbit-ears antenna on top; inside, where its picture tube should have been, gazing out with scorched wiring threaded like electronic ivy among its crevices and sockets, was a human skull. The name of the piece was "The Late, Late, Late Show."

Section Two

Crusade in Asia: Vietnam Before Tet

Unlike the battle of Dien Bien Phu, which led to French withdrawal from Indochina, the 1968 Tet offensive did not force the United States out of Vietnam. In contrast to the French, who had no more than 80 combat planes at their disposal during Dien Bien Phu, the American army did have the fire power to save itself. Yet from a political point of view, the Tet offensive was the American equivalent of Dien Bien Phu. When on January 31, 1968, the second day of Tet, the lunar new year, 84,000 Viet Cong attacked five of South Vietnam's six major cities, 36 of 40 provincial capitals, and 64 district capitals, they shattered once and for all the official American version of the war. As Frances Fitzgerald wrote in her *Fire in the Lake,* public support for the war was never the same after Tet:

> The Tet offensive had an electric effect on popular opinion in the United States. The banner headlines and the television reports of fighting in the cities brought the shock of reality to what was still for many Americans a distant and incomprehensible war. The picture of corpses in the garden of the American embassy cut through the haze of argument and counterargument, giving flat contradiction to the official optimism about the slow but steady progress of the war. Those who

55

had long felt doubts and reservations now felt their doubts confirmed. For the first time the major news magazines, *Time, Life,* and *Newsweek* began to criticize the war policy. . . .*

The reporting in this section all centers on the period before Tet, when criticism of the war was neither easy nor fashionable. As might be expected, the indictment it presents of the United States in Vietnam is far-ranging. It includes military bungling, government deception, the calculated destruction of village life, and racial hostility toward *all* Vietnamese. Indeed, it is the very inclusiveness of the indictment that raises the question that must be continually asked as we examine the new journalist attack against the war: *What were its motives?* Did it have a center? Was it concerned with unveiling the moral and political judgments that led to Vietnam? Or was it merely concerned with showing the ineptitude of American conduct toward the war? Did it take so long to change public opinion because the public was "dead" or because even among the best reporters there was confusion as to what was wrong in Vietnam?

Our judgment is bound to be influenced by our knowledge of the price of Vietnam: 897,000 soldiers from the North and the South killed, 400,000 civilians from the South alone killed, 45,928 Americans dead and over 300,000 wounded, 7.1 million tons of bombs dropped (almost three times that of World War II and Korea), six million acres of land defoliated, additional acreage, equivalent in size to Rhode Island, leveled by bulldozer, $137 billion budgeted for the war between 1965 and its end in 1973. Yet this kind of hindsight *is* necessary for an accurate appraisal of the new journalist attack against the war. Without it we are back to the time when critical reports on Vietnam were never as widely believed as the government's interpretation of events: when the Kennedy administration could send 10,000 "advisors" without opposition, when the Johnson administration, as a result of the 1964 Gulf of Tonkin resolution, could gain nearly unlimited war powers.

The chapter included here from David Halberstam's *Making of a Quagmire* shows that by 1963 reporters in Vietnam had their own war to fight with government officials and censors. Halberstam's report centers on the period during the summer of 1963 when the United States government was urging President Diem to widen his base of support, and Diem's brother, Ngo Dinh Nhu, and sister-in-law, Madame Nhu, were urging him to crush all opposition, particularly that of the Buddhists. The events Halberstam describes are those that led up to the government's attack on the Buddhists on August 21, the day before Henry Cabot Lodge was due to arrive in Saigon to replace the outgoing American ambassador. The drive against the Buddhists, plus the declaration of martial law, were designed to present

*Frances Fitzgerald, *A Fire in the Lake,* Little, Brown and Company in association with Atlantic Monthly Press, Boston, 1972, pp. 393–394.

Ambassador Lodge with a *fait accompli;* and the major part of Halberstam's narrative is devoted to the machinations of the Nhus and their military ally, Colonel Tung. But the most far-reaching part of Halberstam's story is his account of the difficulty he and other reporters had getting their copy out of the country. (President Kennedy would later personally complain to the *New York Times* of Halberstam's coverage of events.) It makes clear why, ten years before the war ended, many of the best reporters in Vietnam had come to see their role as an adversary one.

Just what the Americans and South Vietnamese had to fear from accurate reporting is made amply clear by Jonathan Schell's story of the village of Ben Suc. Schell tells what happened in Ben Suc during operation Cedar Falls, the largest search and destroy mission carried on in 1967. His account is, however, really a description of the American army making enemies and refugees of people it was officially defending. Like so many stories of Vietnam, Schell's deals with deliberate cruelty—the torture of a prisoner, the machine gunning of a man and a woman having a picnic. But what gives his story its true force is his account of the ease with which a village possessing a written history dating back to the Nguyen Dynasty in the eighteenth century was dismantled. At the end of the Cedar Falls operation, Ben Suc no longer exists. All the men in Ben Suc between the ages of 15 and 45 are taken to provincial police headquarters, while their families are shipped by Chinook helicopter to Phu Loi, a village overcrowded with other Vietnamese taken from their homes.

The final two reports in this section provide no less grim an account of Vietnam. But they are most concerned with giving a picture of Vietnam that reflects the thinking of the Americans fighting the war. Jimmy Breslin's "How He Saw the War in Vietnam" shows an American army unable to fight a guerrilla war. But for Breslin, the military failures of America in Vietnam are more than strategic failures. They reflect the degree to which America is only prepared to commit itself to wars like World War I and II, wars involving overriding life and death questions. As Breslin notes in his concluding description of the aircraft carrier *Independence,* "Its planes can knock out a city. But there are no cities to knock out in Viet Nam. . . . It is not the kind of war they were thinking of in Brooklyn when they came to work every morning to build the *Independence.*" In Breslin's eyes America in Vietnam has ignored its own heritage. It has "reached back in ancient history" and chosen to rely on "men who fight a war because they get paid for it." The wounded and the dead are present in nearly every scene Breslin describes, but their suffering is never meaningful, never provides anything except negative insight.

The concluding report, "The Whole Thing Was a Lie," by Donald Duncan, contains the harshest indictment of all on the war in Vietnam. Significantly, it is the analysis of a man who once supported the war, a former career soldier with ten years in the army, six of them in Special Forces.

Duncan desperately wanted to believe in the Vietnam War and only quit the army after he continually found himself lied to. The turning point for him was not a single incident but an accumulation of incidents: the racism of the Special Forces (from which a special effort was made to exclude blacks), the racism in Vietnam, where even South Vietnam troops were known as "slopes" and "gooks," and the disregard of American officers for Vietnamese life (Duncan was instructed to murder Viet Cong prisoners, and South Vietnamese troops he helped train were casually sent off on a suicidal mission). "I had to accept the fact that, Communist or not, the vast majority of the people were pro-Viet Cong and anti-Saigon," he writes. "I had to accept also that the position, 'We are in Vietnam because we are in sympathy with the aspirations and desires of the Vietnamese people,' was a lie." In the end Duncan's chief regret is, "I had to wait until I was 35 years old, after spending 10 years in the army and 18 months personally witnessing the stupidity of the war, before I could figure it out."

The Making of a Quagmire
David Halberstam

David Halberstam worked for newspapers in Mississippi and Tennessee before joining the *New York Times* in 1960. A correspondent in Vietnam from 1962 to 1963, he was awarded the Pulitzer Prize for international reporting for his coverage of the war. His first major book, *The Making of a Quagmire*, deals with Vietnam. Mr. Halberstam is also the author of *The Noblest Roman, One Very Hot Day, The Unfinished Odyssey of Robert Kennedy,* and the recent bestseller *The Best and the Brightest,* which was nominated for the 1973 National Book Award.

By August [1963] it was clear that it was only a matter of time before one of two things happened: either there would be a coup d'état, or Nhu would strike against the pagodas. There was also the possibility of a Nhu coup, which would include an attempt to crush the Buddhist movement.

It was in this tense atmosphere that the Central Intelligence Agency began to take on considerable importance. Just as the other divisions of the American mission had failed—the embassy in converting Diem, the military in having its advice accepted and in assessing the war correctly—the CIA was doomed to fail in its intelligence role.

Although essentially the CIA's lack of success was due to the broad failure of our whole Vietnamese policy, that old problem of the CIA's—whether it was simply an intelligence-gathering agency or whether it was to implement policy as well—was also partially to blame. By and large the CIA's inadequacies in Vietnam were minor compared to the failings of the military mission and the embassy; yet since returning to this country I have been surprised by the public suspicion of its role in general, and of its performance in Vietnam in particular. There still remains a feeling that the CIA was somehow responsible for the continuation of Diem's rule long after it was obvious that he was not the right man for the job. This is not true; admittedly the CIA had something to do with early American support of Diem, but at the time this seemed to be a wise appraisal. Nor is it true, at least during the time I was in Saigon, that the CIA was in conflict with other parts of the mission, that it was foiling the plans of more honorable and better-behaved agencies. Indeed, just the opposite is true, and that was precisely the trouble: there was no conflict between the various elements of the mission at all. The CIA was not a dispassionate analyst of the situation; it was actively on the team.

I suspect that part of the inherent suspicion of the CIA is the outgrowth of its bogeyman image among liberals; the other side of the coin is the conservatives' suspicion of foreign aid programs. Both of these concerns are products of the frustration of trying to promote America's interests in a complex world where the best intentioned and most enlightened of policies, often carried out by the ablest of public servants, do not necessarily work. When these policies fall short of success, as they frequently do, U.S. citizens tend to look for scapegoats and conspiracies; naturally they seek these largely according to their own political predilections, and inevitably they are apt to find the philosophy they are against in domestic affairs conspiring against our policy overseas.

But the world and our foreign policy are not that simple. By and large, domestic ideologies are not effective in foreign countries, and the leaders we support abroad have the unpleasant habit of not conforming as Republicans or Democrats would wish. Diem, for instance, was not the conservative Vietnamese that many Americans think he was. He was suspicious of businessmen and capitalism, and his influential brother Nhu was probably inclined toward socialism, but the Government was mandarin rather than right or left wing.

What happened to the CIA in Vietnam sheds some light on the immensely difficult task it has, and on the conflict between this country's traditional view of itself, its policies and the necessities forced on it by the Cold War. I am not familiar with the intricacies of CIA operations or techniques, and I am not an intelligence expert. But many CIA agents in Saigon were my friends, and I considered them among the ablest Americans I had seen overseas or at home. They were placed in the most difficult jobs, often victims of the enormous disparity between their own high ideals and the vastly different motivations of their Asian ally. Writing only as a layman who was on the scene, I will try to give the best account I can of the role of the agency, culminating in its failure to predict and analyze correctly the crackdown on the pagodas.

Within weeks of my arrival in Saigon in 1962 I had lunch with John Richardson, the chief of the CIA in Vietnam. He was a good man, honest and dedicated, and in his personal philosophy he leaned toward the viewpoint of the American right—though this was not by any means reflected in his operatives. Our talk was pleasant that day, but peculiarly involved in a long, abstract discussion on the nature of coun-

terinsurgency. I was never quite sure that I understood Richardson correctly, for our terms and points of reference were so different.

One part of that first conversation I remember distinctly: our discussion of the Nhus. Nhu, Richardson said, was a great nationalist. When I mentioned some of Nhu's anti-American remarks and the resentment many anti-Communists felt toward him, Richardson said that the anti-Americanism was simply a product of Nhu's nationalism. He was a proud Asian, but he was also for us; more important, he was the one man who understood the strategic hamlet program. As for Mrs. Nhu, she too was a nationalist, according to Richardson—perhaps a bit extreme occasionally, and sometimes a little emotional, but that was typical of women who entered politics—look at Mrs. Roosevelt.

I was new in Saigon at the time, but I was not that new. On the way back to town our host, one of the embassy officials, suggested that I write a story about what he termed the change in Nhu: "The new Nhu." I said that I would wait.

What happened in the following months convinced me that Nhu was anything but a nationalist: he seemed to me to be a born intriguer, suspicious of his ally, taking great delight in dividing his people and in controlling the population—altogether a brilliant but warped man.

The disparity between Richardson's and my views evolved in part from the different nature of our jobs. The CIA was not simply a group of sophisticated young Americans who were predicting events in a somewhat predictable nation. Had this been its role it would have accomplished it handily—but it would also have exposed the weakness of our policy. The fact was, the CIA was not in Saigon just to analyze and evaluate, it was a participant in some of our programs, trying to make them work in order to turn our overall policy into a success. I am not familiar with the full extent of the

CIA's responsibilities in Vietnam, but I do know that it was directly involved in the montagnard arming and training program, as well as in the operation of the strategic hamlet program in some areas. Also, part of Richardson's assignment was "to get close to Nhu." Since Nhu was the key man in the Ngo family, and therefore of the Government, it followed that in Vietnam part of the CIA's role was to influence the Government in the direction we wanted it to take.

In Vietnam there were two major problems facing the CIA in the execution of its basic function—that of gathering intelligence. The first was that no man, once his career and prestige are committed to working for the success of a policy—and once he has told his superiors that such a policy will work—retains his objectivity. From then on, to justify his participation, he is apt to do his utmost to *make* the policy work, regardless of the consequences—witness Nolting's remarkable statements at the end of his tour. Events and indices tending to show that the policy is not working are shrugged off in favor of those which show that it is; agents or individuals who consistently report to the contrary are disregarded in favor of those who are committed to the same vision. Consciously or subconsciously, intelligence becomes tailored to fit the policy.

Richardson, who enthusiastically believed in the policy, had the assignment to gain Nhu's trust, and this constituted the second problem. In Richardson's eyes Nhu was the most influential man in the country (which perhaps he was), not the most hated man (which he certainly was). In staying close to Nhu, Richardson had to pay the price of taking Nhu's words for an event, even of seeing the situation through his eyes. Consequently, it would have placed his position with Nhu in jeopardy if his agents were working the other side of the street and gleaning intelligence—as they should have been—from anti-Nhu sources.

Furthermore, since Nhu and his wife were hated and feared in Vietnam, the fact that our intelligence chief was close to Nhu placed a considerable damper on the gathering of intelligence. One of the most frequent criticisms about the CIA by responsible Vietnamese—indeed about the entire American mission—was that information given Americans about the Ngos went right back to the Palace, apparently in an attempt to buy confidence from the suspicious family. (An American professor in this country told me recently that in September of 1963 he had a student who was the son of a high Vietnamese official. After the pagoda crackdown the official had written his son a letter giving details about Nhu's plans, and the student had shown it to the professor. Sensing that the information was important and significant, the professor passed it on to the State Department. Evidently the information was then turned over to the CIA, because the professor—who had thought he was acting in confidence—was accosted by a very angry Vietnamese student several days later. The boy had a letter from his father saying that a high CIA official had visited him in Saigon with an official cable referring to the professor's call to Washington and asking him to confirm or deny the information.)

Thus, with the onset of the American buildup the CIA was operating under considerable pressure in Saigon. As the situation there became more tense, many wary Vietnamese would tell reporters or young political officers what they were hesitant to take to higher embassy officials or the CIA. This was the penalty suffered by an agency whose top members were part of the team.

As the Buddhist crisis developed, the tension and uncertainty in Saigon continued to build. Amid all the rumors it became obvious that two main coups were in the works. It pointed up the degree of the Government's alienation that both revolts were headed by men who until recently had been among the last of Diem's loyal followers. One coup was the senior officers' plot, headed by Duong Van Minh, Le Van Kim and Tran Van Don; the other was the junior officers' coup, and during early August this seemed the more likely one to materialize. Eventually, under somewhat different circumstances, the latter did take place as the Nguyen Khanh coup replacing the older officers' junta, but at the time many of us thought it would take place immediately because its planning was extremely advanced and its leaders impressed us as being bolder than the generals. However, the generals had a habit of ordering key battalions out of town every time the young Turks were ready to strike.

One day in August an important Vietnamese whom I trusted said he wanted me to have lunch with him and one of his friends. After lunch we repaired to the friend's house in Cholon, the Chinese section of Saigon, where I was told that my two companions were part of the young officers' group which was planning a coup. I was surprised to be given this information, but even more surprised when they told me that they wanted me to cover the story from the inside. They could guarantee nothing if things went sour. Certainly, if the coup failed I would have to leave the country, and there might be even more unpleasant results.

I left them to consider the proposal for a while, talked with Sheehan, decided that journalistically it was worth the risk for such a story, and agreed. Burt Glinn, a photographer then in Saigon for the *Saturday Evening Post,* was also told of the plan, and he too was ready to try his luck. The leaders of the coup gave us a military radio and we were assigned a band and call numbers. We were to be "kidnaped" by the coup plotters and taken to their headquarters; they thought that this would give us

a measure of protection if the coup backfired. After that, there was nothing to do but sit back and wait nervously. On several occasions during the next few weeks we were alerted, but each time the generals, now preparing their own coup, switched battalions on the plotters.

But during this same period CIA agents were telling me that their superiors in Vietnam were still so optimistic that they were not taking the turmoil and unrest very seriously. Yet it was well known that the Nhus were angry over what they felt was Diem's weak handling of the Buddhists, and there were reliable reports that Nhu was planning a coup of his own, which would begin with an attack on the Buddhists and would end by making him the strongest man in the country. Finally this became more than a rumor; details of the plan began to filter down. Hearing these, Nick Turner of Reuters went to see Nhu. "I hear you are planning a coup and that you will raze Xa Loi," Nick said. (Only a Reuters man can make a statement like that and get away with it.)

Nhu smiled. At first he denied it; then he began to talk. He said that if the Buddhist question were not solved, it would soon lead to a coup which would be anti-American, anti-Buddhist and anti-weak Government. If such a coup took place, say, at midnight, Xa Loi would be razed by 2 A.M. (Actually Nhu's timing was slightly off; the raid on Xa Loi began at 12:30 A.M. and ended at 2:30 A.M.) There was only one man capable of leading such a coup: Nhu himself. After Turner filed his remarkable story, he was called to the American embassy and asked if he believed Nhu was serious; he answered that he was 99 percent certain.

By this time Nhu had brought his personal military arm, the special forces under Colonel Le Quang Tung, into the city. Tung's troops were an American brain child. Selected for their physique, specially trained, specially well paid, they were conceived by the American military as an elite force to be employed in counterguerrilla warfare. But the Ngo family had seen fit to make them the political and protective private army of the family, and they had done very little guerrilla fighting. Two battalions of these troops had quietly been brought into Saigon in July, making a total of four in the city.

On August 17 I cabled my office and suggested to my editors that they use every single word coming out of Saigon. Something was on the way, I said, and it was not just Henry Cabot Lodge.

The Buddhists themselves appeared to be at least as much aware of all developments, and their protest seemed to have a mounting intensity. On Sunday, August 18, they put on one of their most impressive demonstrations. Fifteen thousand enthusiastic people, many of them young, flocked to the Xa Loi pagoda. Nguyen Ngoc Rao, the UPI reporter, said that it was the only emotional crowd he could recall since the early days of Diem. The streets were jammed, and when it began to rain the people refused to go home.

It was also a joyous, boisterous crowd. Filming the proceedings on top of the pagoda were two ABC-TV reporters, one of whom was Charles P. Arnot. Suddenly a priest gestured toward the two reporters and spoke a few words; a tremendous roar of laughter went up from the mob. "Thich Quang Do has just told the Buddhists that the foreign correspondents have pledged to go on a \day-long hunger strike," Rao whispered to me. Then Quang Do asked the correspondents to address the crowd. Arnot replied that he would be delighted to, but that he would have to cable New York for permission.

The mood of the demonstration was buoyant, but if the priests had said the word, fifteen thousand Buddhists would have marched on Gia Long Palace immediately. However, Lodge was due in a week, and the Buddhists were clearly holding their fire for his arrival. As I wrote two days later—on the eve of what was to be the pagoda crackdown—the Buddhists were playing "a fast and dangerous game."

On Monday, August 19, a Vietnamese friend called; he was much more cautious than usual, and we made an appointment to walk together along the river front. There he told me that Nhu planned to raid the pagodas and that Colonel Tung's troops would be used. That same day we learned that Nhu had held a meeting of the generals and had chastised them for not taking sufficient precautions against a coup. He told them that one was likely to take place, and that if it did, the family planned to evacuate to a hiding place outside the city while the generals surrounded the capital and razed it with artillery instead of fighting at close quarters. If there was a coup, Nhu said, it would be inspired by the intellectuals and would have Western support. (Incidentally, this was the second time that Nhu had talked to the generals about the possibility of a coup; on the first occasion he said that he had heard rumors of one, and that perhaps some of them knew about it. If so, he suggested that they stay and talk with him after the meeting. None stayed.)

That night I filed complete details, including verbatim dialogue, about Nhu's second meeting with the generals, which had taken place only thirty-six hours earlier. I asked a Vietnamese friend what Nhu's reaction would be to the story.

"It will make him glad," the Vietnamese said.

"Why?"

"Because it will make him think that he can't trust the generals," the Vietnamese said. I still did not understand.

"He already distrusts the generals, and this will convince him that he is right and that he is brilliant," the Vietnamese answered.

On the surface, Saigon went its charming, attractive, corrupt way; the security precautions remained tight, the girls remained pretty, and a reporter could write whatever kind of mood piece he wanted ("In this tense city . . ." "In this happy city where tension lurks beneath the tranquil surface . . ." "The tense surface of Saigon today belies . . .") By this time Sheehan, Perry, Turner, Rao, An and myself had created a small but first-rate intelligence network. Each of us had a different specialty and area: An, for instance, had the best military contacts in the country, since he had served in the Army with many of the majors and lieutenant colonels as a young officer; Rao, by courage and endless hard work, had built a network within Diem's secret police force—such a good network, in fact, that after the coup he was ineffective as a reporter for several weeks because all of his sources were in hiding. We had long suspected that a showdown was coming, and each of us had carefully been cultivating sources so that we would be ready for it. Now, that Monday, a long afternoon of checking on the part of all of us indicated that something was imminent—Rao, for instance, had found that the secret and combat police were on some sort of alert—but we failed to find out exactly what it was. We were all exhausted; for the past five days Sheehan, Turner and I had taken turns staying up all night in order to warn the others in case something broke. Tired and irritable, that evening we decided that the strike would have to come to us.

But on Tuesday afternoon, August 20, I had a drink with Dang Duc Khoi, Diem's information officer who had long since become disenchanted with the President and tired of all the intrigue. "On that matter you inquired about yesterday [the raid on the pagodas]," he said, "I think it will come tonight or tomorrow." I checked another source and received confirmation, then returned to the office and filed a story which said that despite all of the American and Vietnamese officials' talk about the dispute having ended, nothing had been settled, that the Government and the Buddhists were further apart than ever, that the Buddhists were not eager for a settlement, that the Government's initiative had been reduced to deciding whether or not it should keep the bodies of burned monks, that Nhu was restless—and that a showdown was near.

We prepared for a long wait; not sure whether the climax would come that night, the next day or at all, we decided to carry on as if the situation were normal. Several of us were eating at the Faas-Halberstam villa when Mert Perry arrived in a cab. An anonymous Buddhist had just called our office and warned that the crackdown was coming that night. The Buddhists, it turned out later, were tipped off by two sources. First, the Buddhist wives of some of the combat police had called and said that their husbands were going to arrest the Buddhist leaders that night; second, people living in areas around the pagodas had warned that secret policemen had been moving into the neighborhood all day. This was an excellent example of the advantage of having the population on your side in a political war.

The group split up and we each started checking different areas. Mert and I toured the pagodas. They were all tightly locked; they were expecting the raid, and the streets around them were deserted and quiet. At the An Quang pagoda the young priests were overjoyed to see us; they must have thought that our presence meant protection. At Xa Loi everything was calm, and some of the leaders were asleep. When we woke them they told us that they knew about the raid, and then went back to bed. Mert and I hurried out, we suspected that the attack was near, and we didn't want to be caught in it.

Mert returned to the office and I to the house, but I had no sooner settled down than Sheehan raced up the driveway in a cab, shouting that he had just seen three trucks filled with troops roar past the house headed in the direction of the An Quang pagoda. I leaped into his cab and we headed for Xa Loi, which was four blocks in the other direction. On the way we passed the Third District police station; in the lot by the headquarters were hundreds of troops in full battle gear and about twenty trucks, some of which were already setting out in the direction of Xa Loi.

It was a warm and pleasant night. I had that rubbery feeling that comes to an athlete before a game, or that one feels in the last few minutes before a helicopter assault—a period when one's senses are frighteningly acute. I can remember Sheehan cursing and shouting at the driver in Vietnamese, *"Di di. Di di!"* like a man in a harness race. We sped toward Xa Loi, our driver terrified of being involved in whatever was going to happen, but almost equally terrified of his passengers.

We arrived at the pagoda as convoys converged from every direction; it was like being caught in the middle of a vast military operation. Though two hundred troops could have accomplished the mission, several thousand seemed to have been assigned. We were caught in a sea of soldiers; a block and a half from the pagoda there was a traffic jam of troop trucks, and we jumped out of the cab. I later learned that Sheehan, racing to find a phone to try to start emergency filing (we assumed, correctly, that the regular cable facilities would be closed), managed to worm his way into the United States Operations Mission next to the pagoda, and from this vantage point saw and heard much of the action. I could only get to within a block of the pagoda; I could see most of what went on, but every time I tried to edge up closer I was pushed back by a tide of police.

What followed was a horror spectacle. Had Nhu wanted to arrest the Buddhist leaders it could have been accomplished efficiently in a few moments, but these troops were enacting a passion play of revenge and terror. Hundreds of them charged inside, and the night was filled with a discordant jumble of the screams of the Buddhists, the shouts and cries of the attackers, the shattering of glass, the cracking of pistols and occasional explosions—all this punctuated by the sound of the gong on top of the pagoda being struck wildly back and forth, clanging desperately in the dark. Around me Vietnamese officers barked orders; unit after unit moved up and charged into the pagoda as if they were sure that the Buddhists had a battalion inside and reinforcements were needed.

There was one particularly chilling sight. A squad of Colonel Tung's special forces, identifiable by their berets and their size, trotted forward in a V-form riot formation, each carrying submachine guns at high port. As they pranced into the pagoda, looking something like a smart football team coming up to the line of scrimmage, the mark of American instruction was all over them, and the endless clanging of that gong seemed to me to signal the end of a foreign policy.

At that moment, similar units were breaking into pagodas in Hué, smashing the giant statue of Buddha and killing, according to the American consul, thirty priests and students. But as I stood listening to the screams in Saigon and watching Buddhists being carried out, it was impossible for me to tell how many were killed and injured; later I learned that several monks were listed as missing and that about thirty were injured or wounded, but the true toll was never known.

At one point three troopers came up and started shoving me back. As they became more insistent I feared that they would arrest me, so I used a trick I had learned from Jean Louis Arnaud, an Agence France Presse reporter in the Congo. Once during the fighting in Katanga, Arnaud was being pushed around by road guards demanding cigarettes; Arnaud suddenly turned on his tormentors and asked *them* for a cigarette. The Congolese, first stunned and then delighted, produced a whole pack and insisted that Arnaud take it, and immediately the manhandling ceased. Now I borrowed a cigarette from the Vietnamese troopers, smiled, talked fast and convinced them that I was not supposed to move.

The orgy lasted for about two hours because many Buddhists had barricaded themselves inside various rooms of the pagoda and the troops had to take doors off hinges to reach their victims. Though the Buddhists were certainly not cooperating in their arrest, I was puzzled that some of the leaders had not fled to a hiding place, once they knew that the strike was coming. After the coup I asked Thich Quang Do about this, and he answered, "We had done nothing wrong; therefore we could not flee. If we had, it would have been an admission that we were guilty." But my own impression was that the Buddhists were ready to have some martyrs and also that they might have miscalculated the extent of the crackdown; that night raids were conducted not only in Hué and Saigon, but in every major city in the central coastal region; thousands of priests were picked up. There was another possibility: an expectation on the part of the leadership that at the last minute there would be a countercoup by the generals or the junior officers.

At this point my problems changed: I had the story, but wasn't sure how to get it out. I slipped away and returned to Sheehan's office. It was two-thirty in the morning, which meant that it was two-thirty in the afternoon in New York. Neil and I compared notes; his vantage point had been better and he had more details than I did. Then we began to try to file. Neil managed to reach the U.S. Army's communications system and was able to talk a specialist there into sending out about a hundred and fifty words—complete with pistol shots and screams—that gave him a world beat. Then

we went to the embassy to see what we could find out from them, and whether they would file our stories for us.

There was nothing to learn there, for to our astonishment the embassy had been caught completely unaware by the raids. Another good story, I thought. One of the top officials asked, "Why didn't you tell us?" It seemed incredible that all those people who had been tipping us off for the last thirty-six hours had either not called the embassy—or that if they had, the report had not reached the top oficials who were still being assured by the Ngos that there would be no raids. But what happened in the next few days was even more astounding: the raids having taken place, the embassy was unable to learn what had happened or who had been responsible.

Through one more private channel Sheehan and I sent out brief additional reports of three hundred words on what was at least a fifteen-hundred-word story. While this was enough to satisfy my editors in New York, I felt terribly frustrated; there was so much more to report. Even in that first story, however, I had noted that the raids bore the stamp of Ngo Dinh Nhu; I felt that I had never made a safer assumption.

At about four-thirty we returned to Sheehan's office. There we found an exhausted Rao lying on the bed, listening to troop movements which were being broadcast on the military radio that had been given to me earlier. On a map of Saigon he had marked tank companies and battalion after battalion as they took up positions ringing the city. Was this a coup? Rao stayed behind, tracing the moves, while Sheehan and I toured the city. We saw the tanks and troops, but of course we could not tell who was ordering their movements. When we returned to the office a couple of hours later, there were new developments: martial law had been proclaimed, as well as curfew, the Army had allegedly taken over all civilian functions, and strict censorship was enforced. We found out later that way back in July the generals had decided that one way to get troops into the city for their own coup was to impose a state of martial law; they figured that after Diem had declared it, the troops which would be moved into the city to enforce it could stage their revolt. But when this idea was suggested to the brothers, Nhu, who had been planning the pagoda crackdown, saw it as a perfect cover for his own plot. Adopting the generals' plan in part, he raided the pagodas, using only his own special troops; the Army had taken the initial blame, and the generals had been beaten to the punch.

Early in the morning Major General Tran Van Don broadcast several new orders as part of the martial-law regulations. He claimed that the Army was assuming command of the country because enemies of the people were working hand in hand with the Communists and imperialists. Supposedly General Don was in charge, but later we were told that he had said to General Dinh, the one general with any power, "Tomorrow you may be giving the order to have me arrested. Be good to me, eh? Get me a nice cell and put a pretty girl in it."

Plastered to store fronts in Saigon was a long and involved handbill, supposedly written by the Army, which announced that its day of nationalism had finally come. Though the tone of this broadside sounded like something that Nhu, not the Army, had written, everyone's confusion at this point was understandable. The city was filled with troops, and the declaration of martial law and the alleged role of the Army were matters we hadn't counted on and which had to be explained. In our stories written on August 21 we reported the martial law, but added that the exact role of the Army was unclear and that Nhu had obviously played a strong part in what had taken place.

At noon on August 21, under the most dif-

ficult conditions—after almost no sleep, with tension everywhere, great fear on the part of our best Vietnamese sources, the curfew which made travel at night impossible, and no communications lines—we went to work to track down the real story.

It was a time of rumors, and thus a time not to be too hasty at the typewriter. In such circumstances a prominent person who has not been seen is often alleged to be either in power or dead, and a reporter can dig up anything he wants to hear. Information is everywhere; it is the evaluation both of the intelligence and of the people who give it which becomes all-important. In trying to determine what had happened and who was in power, our appraisal of the facts as we knew them went something like this:

1 The strike had all the characteristics of the one proposed by Nhu and repeated to us by knowledgeable friends. In addition, the Buddhist sources had confirmed that virtually the same plan was to be executed at that particular moment. Moreover, on the night of the raids I had identified Tung's special forces and two of Nhu's top aides directing actions at Xa Loi. Lastly, one of our Vietnamese friends had talked to an air-borne soldier who was very angry because many of Tung's troops were wearing air-borne uniforms that night. The implications of this disguise were obvious.

2 It seemed very unlikely to us that the Army would have staged a coup with a blood bath. Though there might be some officers who were annoyed with the Buddhists, one of the first things the Army would seek if it came to power was a rapprochement with the Buddhists.

3 The Ngo family distrusted, feared and felt contempt for the Army, and the purpose of much of its intrigue was to divide it. Yet according to the announcement, the Army and the Ngo family were now sharing power. It was not like the Ngo family to share power with anyone, or any institution—least of all the Army.

4 One correspondent had an interview with Madame Nhu on the day after the pagoda raids. She was in a state of euphoria, chattering like a schoolgirl after a prom. She told the reporter that the Government had crushed the Communist-Buddhists, and referred to this as "the happiest day in my life since we crushed the Binh Xuyen in 1955." In many ways Madame Nhu was the most forthright member of the family, and she could not possibly have been overjoyed at the idea of the family turning over part of its power to the military. Since for a long time she had been the most active proponent of a strong policy against the Buddhists, it seemed probable that she was celebrating the Ngo family's victory.

5 I knew General Tran Van Don fairly well, and had spent some time with him in Da Nang. He had impressed me as a thoughtful, candid man with a considerable amount of integrity; he had even permitted me to use his name in an interview I had with him—a highly unusual circumstance. He was very much the Vietnamese aristocrat, urbane, born and educated in France, and it was hard to believe that he had authorized the pagoda strike.

6 There were constant humiliations of American officials on the day after the raids. Telephone lines to the houses of the top officials were cut, and the car of the head of the USOM, Joe Brant, was stopped and searched at the entrance on his way to and from work. Other Americans were kept waiting interminably for appointments with Government officials and in securing permits to drive after curfew hours. If the Army had really been in charge, it would immediately have moved to reassure the Americans that it wanted them there and that it needed their support. (Indeed, the Army did exactly this after the November 1 coup; it was so public-relations

conscious that it withheld from distribution the photographs of the bodies of Diem and Nhu because it feared they might offend American and world opinion, even though there was tremendous pressure to release the pictures to prove to the population, who doubted that the two brothers would ever die, that their rule was over at last.)

All of these factors were in my mind when I started my leg work; it would take very hard evidence indeed to convince me that the pagoda raids had been the Army's show. On the morning of August 22 everything pointed in the other direction.

One of the first conversations I had that morning was with John Richardson, who had asked to see me. In the first hours after the pagoda raids there was already a rumor spreading around among responsible Vietnamese that the CIA had known of the crackdown, indeed had given its approval, and that the event had been specifically timed to occur between American ambassadors so that the United States would not be embarrassed by the affair. In Vietnamese minds this was a logical extension of Richardson's close relationship with Nhu and the CIA's with Colonel Tung. It was inconceivable to the Vietnamese that the CIA had not known of the raid, and they were therefore sure that the CIA had sponsored it indirectly or at the very least permitted it. The Vietnamese were ready and anxious to believe the very worst about the Americans at that time.

That morning Richardson was a tired and shaken man. He refuted the rumor immediately. "It's not true," he said. "We just didn't know. We just didn't *know,* I can assure you."

After I left Richardson's office, I continued to check details. Soon a pattern began to develop. Shortly I met an American intelligence friend and asked him who was responsible.

"Nhu and Colonel Tung," he said, and then

listed the units which had been involved. "It didn't have a damn thing to do with the Army," he said.

"Why didn't you know?" I asked.

"We should have known," he said. "We had every damn warning you can get. We kept telling *them*—meaning his CIA superiors— "that Tung had his special forces in town and that something like this might happen. We could have been spared this. We could have headed it off."

Like every other American at this moment he was bitter and angry. The violence of the pagoda raids had come as a shock to almost all the Westerners in Vietnam, and now, as people had time to think, the implications of the event were becoming clear. It meant the death of a policy; it was the end of trying to fool ourselves about our conciliatory effect on Diem, for now the Government would be even more under the influence of the Nhus. Further, since American equipment and American-trained troops had been used, the population would have even less confidence in the United States.

Finally, the violation of sacred promises was a direct slap at the Americans, and since this humiliation had come just as a new American ambassador was on his way, it limited his actions by presenting him with a *fait accompli.* (On the night of August 22, General Ton That Dinh, the one general who had been in on the planning of the strike, told a friend of mine, "I, Dinh, am a great national hero. I have defeated the American Cabot Lodge. He was on his way here to pull a coup d'état, but I, Dinh, the hero, have foiled him.")

However, gathering news and writing it was by then a secondary problem. All normal means of communication were now useless because of the heavy-handed censorship of the regime, and no serious reporter wanted his name to appear over a story which had been strained through censorship. So that day we began to use pigeons: civilians or military personnel flying to other Asian cities who could carry our copy out and then relay it to our home offices. From then on, this meant late-morning deadlines in order to catch the plane, which in turn meant that we had to be at work by 7 A.M., rushing to see sources, often allowing not more than thirty minutes for the actual writing of a story, and then racing to the airport to smuggle out the copy with the passenger. Fortunately most of the airport security men were fed up with the regime; our biggest problem was with our own military mission. Colonel Basil Lee Baker, the chief PIO, who had never been considered the reporters' best friend, was true to form during these frantic days. On one occasion, hearing that we were trying to send stories out with servicemen who were flying to Bangkok on a military plane, he called Major General Richard Weede, Harkins' chief of staff, to find out if regulations permitted this. The answer was no, so Baker sent an officer out to the airport to board the plane and announce that it was a court-martial offense to carry out press packets; the officers had no choice but to return the material to us. The incident did not serve to strengthen the existing bonds between Colonel Baker and the reporters; thereafter we had to resort to commercial transport only.

On August 22 we worked all day to put together a full picture of what had happened. Back at the office Sheehan and I swapped notes and then began writing. It seemed obvious that Nhu had used the Army as a front for his strike, in order to hide his own hand and to give the impression that the raid enjoyed far broader backing than it did—that this was an action of national unity. The story caused the *Times* some confusion because it conflicted directly with what the State Department was telling Washington reporters. The *Times* editors fretted for a while and then ran the two stories side by side on the front page under a headline reading: "Two Versions of the Crisis in Vietnam; One Lays Plot to Nhu, Other to Army." The paper introduced the two pieces with a statement which said:

> The confused situation in South Vietnam was reflected yesterday in conflicting versions of the role played by the Army high command in the Saigon regime's attacks this week against the Buddhists. A dispatch from Saigon quoted reliable sources there as having said that the drive had been planned and executed in its initial stage without the knowledge of the Army. But information received in Washington pictured South Vietnam's Army commanders as having put pressure on President Ngo Dinh Diem to persuade him to act.

My story began: "Highly reliable sources here said today that the decision to attack Buddhist pagodas in South Vietnam was planned and executed by Nhu," that the Army had not seized power and in fact knew nothing about it until the raids were well under way. It said that the troops involved were under the command of Colonel Tung, and that Nhu had acted to teach the Buddhists and the Americans a lesson, and to present Lodge with a *fait accompli.*

Our Washington story showed that Nhu had succeeded in confusing the issue by his use of the Army, for it stated that it was the generals who had pressured Diem into acting.

That night we went to the airport to greet Lodge. The PIO's had spent the whole day getting permission for us to violate the curfew by watching the arrival of the new ambassador. We were herded into a special bus, and on reaching the airport found the heads of the American mission awaiting the new chief. At this point we still had no idea that the mission was accepting Nhu's account. While waiting for Lodge at the airport I was talking to Bob Trumbull, my chief from Hong Kong who had arrived earlier that day to beef up the bureau during the crisis, when I saw a high member of the American mission. I introduced Trumbull to him; in the conversation that

followed I made it clear that I thought the raid had been engineered by Nhu, but the official said that he believed the Army had forced Nhu's hand. My private reaction was one of anger; it had never occurred to me that the American mission still believed this, and I assumed that it was said for the benefit of a newly arrived reporter—that it was more of the same old policy line, which I had felt sure was out of date at last. For once I should have taken the line at face value; the fact was that the embassy had misreported the raid.

When Lodge arrived shortly before midnight he was immediately presented with a curfew pass so that he could travel at night. He shook hands with Harkins and Trueheart and then turned toward us. "Where are the gentlemen of the press?" he asked. Clearly the attitude toward us had begun to change.

When we returned to the censor's office to file, every reference indicating that there was any unrest in the country in my brief story on Lodge's arrival was stricken out. All our attempts to slip out the news that Vu Van Mau, the Foreign Minister, had resigned were caught except Mal Browne's; Mal got it through by typing the news onto the caption of a photo of some soldiers and sending it out by wirephoto.

Sheehan, Rao and I spent the night at Mecklin's immense house. There was a reason for this; we had been warned that we were now high on Nhu's list, and both our Vietnamese and American intelligence sources told us that grenades might be thrown into our living quarters. Sheehan lived in the back room of a small apartment with only one exit, and the villa Faas and I had just moved into was away from the center of town and had no telephone.

The next morning Lee Griggs of *Time* flew to Manila, and since he was a reliable pigeon who would make sure that all the copy got out, I sent four stories with him. One, written just before he left, was the daily story on the latest events and maneuverings, and on Lodge's arrival. A second piece described the situation in which Lodge found himself, how it had gotten that way and how serious it was; it was used in the "News of the Week in Review" section on the following Sunday. The third story was a profile of Colonel Tung and how he had come to power. "He has shown over the years that he can be absolutely trusted, that he carries out all orders faithfully, that he has no power impulses of his own and that he keeps his mouth shut," the story said. This ran as a "Man in the News" profile.

The fourth piece, an analysis of the American mission, which ran beside the one on Tung, connected our policy over the past two years to the failures surrounding the pagoda raids. Though it was written in ignorance of the fact that the embassy had blamed the raids on the Army, it said that our mission's lack of knowledge about what was going on in the country could be traced to the fact that it had cut off normal channels of intelligence, had depended excessively on official accounts and had not listened to its junior officers and young civilians. The story continued:

The entire episode has underlined what some sources here consider to be one of the gravest sicknesses of the huge and talented mission here—a vast divergence between what the people in the field are seeing and reporting and what the highest Americans are reporting, because of the ties of the Ngo family to the chiefs of the mission. The fact that Ngo Dinh Nhu with Colonel Tung as his military arm was planning something was not really a secret. Whether it would materialize was another question, because certain aspects of the planning were hard to believe. What was particularly humiliating was that Colonel Tung and his special forces were an American brain child: they were an American idea, to be the proud Vietnamese counterpart of our own elite Special Forces, better equipped and better paid than regular troops. We financed them, we paid them, and we had advisers with them.

With those four stories out, I relaxed a little; a year's hard work had just paid off, and we had told our readers what they needed to know.

That night I had drinks with two friends in the CIA. They were exceptionally bitter, and though they didn't blame any single individual for the agency's failure, they clearly were not happy with Richardson. We discussed the problem of service in a faraway country about which few United States citizens knew or cared. They were both dedicated men, and the risks that they had to take and the immense personal sacrifices they had to make meant a deep commitment on their part. But in this corner of the world such dedication often was not matched by the Asians, and in an atmosphere of despair there was sometimes a tendency to listen too much to Vietnamese who reflected what you wanted to hear.

My two friends were also angry because they felt that the CIA would be blamed unfairly for our whole policy. They were sure that the fault was more Washington's than Saigon's, and they were quite explicit in explaining why. Periodically, as if he were sure that no one would ever believe it, one or the other would say wearily, "Goddamn it! We told them it would happen." I assumed that "them" meant Saigon; it was clear that they felt that Saigon had been caught in Washington's trap. He added, "You give every goddamn thing you have, and you end up with this. I came halfway around the world to get my face rubbed in _____." Altogether, it was a sad conversation; it revealed to me how difficult such a job was, and it made me glad that I was a reporter.

Later Sheehan and I tried as best we could to reconstruct what had happened in the embassy after the raid.

In general the inclination—indeed, the policy—had been to believe what the Ngo family said. With Nolting gone, Richardson was probably the most influential American in the mission; Diem would not see Trueheart, but Nhu would talk to Richardson. Undoubtedly Nhu fed Richardson his version of the pagoda raids—that the generals had forced the hand of the brothers. The Vietnamese generals had almost no confidence in General Harkins; evidently they were not able to state their case strongly enough to the American military mission and had to turn to lower-ranking CIA agents.

Richardson had always seen events as Nhu wanted him to; like Harkins, the CIA chief felt that our policy was working and the war being won. While high American officials were very unhappy about the pagoda raids, they realized—consciously or subconsciously—that a rejection of Nhu's version meant a complete reevaluation of our stand. Since these American officials were very much a part of that policy and had publicly committed their careers to it, they were in no hurry to write it off. Moreover, Richardson did not have the private sources which would refute Nhu's story, for to have listened to such voices earlier would have been to doubt the effectiveness of the policy. And so Saigon misinformed Washington. It was the last stammer of the old guard.

Meanwhile we reporters continued to file stories in a vacuum; we didn't know what was getting out, what was being printed or what play it was getting if a story was used. Then, four days later, Lee Griggs returned from Manila with a folder filled with messages. My pieces were getting into the paper, it turned out, and there were some complimentary notes, including a particularly nice cable from James Reston: KEEP GOING BECAUSE WE'RE ONLY GETTING PROPAGANDA THIS END. I also received my first inkling that Washington had been wrong on what had happened: YOUR STORY ON NHU TWINED WITH SZULCS WASHINGTON SAYS GENERALS FORCED NHU TO SILENCE BUDDHISTS. Finally, there was a cable from our foreign desk: STATE DEPARTMENT NOW COMING AROUND TO YOUR VIEW WHAT HAPPENED AND WHO DID IT AT PAGODAS STOP CHEERS AND MORE CHEERS.

Sitting in the office, I clutched the cables and yelled for Sheehan. Hearing the commotion, Mert Perry came downstairs and read the message; together the three of us laughed and laughed. Mert said that it appeared that Washington had finally got the little picture, and went upstairs to get beer for us. Charley Mohr said, "You guys are the first reporters I've ever known who scooped the State Department by four days."

Holding up the cables proudly, I said to Charley, "Well, that's the end of the press controversy out here. We've finally broken through. Now they'll understand."

I was wrong; the stakes were simply bigger from then on, and the press controversy had just begun.

The Village of Ben Suc

Jonathan Schell

Jonathan Schell accompanied the Cedar Falls operation of January 1967, in which American forces launched a surprise assault on the village of Ben Suc. The mission was to envelop this formidable Viet Cong stronghold, seal it off, remove its inhabitants, and destroy all physical trace of its existence. Schell's book *The Village of Ben Suc* was followed in 1968 by *The Military Half,* which deals with the destruction of rural South Vietnam by bomb attacks. Originally appearing in the *New Yorker,* the book recounts Mr. Schell's experience in Vietnam with fliers of the Forward Air Control planes.

With the attack over, the tricky task of distinguishing V.C.s from the civilians moved from the battlefield into the interrogation room. First, under the direction of the Americans, ARVN soldiers segregated the villagers by age level, sex, and degree of suspiciousness. All males between the ages of fifteen and forty-five were slated to be evacuated to the Provincial Police Headquarters in the afternoon. From among them, all who were suspected of being Vietcong and a smaller group of "confirmed V.C.s" were singled out. Some of these men were bound and blindfolded, and sat cross-legged on the ground just a few yards from the large assemblage of women, children, and aged. They were men who had been caught hiding in their bomb shelters or had otherwise come under suspicion. One group, for example, was unusually well dressed and well groomed. Instead of bare feet and pajamalike garb, these men wore Japanese foam-rubber slippers and short-sleeved cotton shirts. Standing over them, his arms akimbo, an American officer remarked, "No question about these fellas. Anyone in this village with clothes like that is a V.C. They're V.C.s, all right." A group of about a dozen men categorized as defectors were singled out to be taken to the special Open Arms center near Phu Cuong.

The Americans interrogated only the prisoners they themselves had taken, leaving the prisoners taken by the Vietnamese to the Vietnamese interrogators. The American interrogations were held in a large, debris-strewn room of the roofless schoolhouse. Four interrogating teams worked at the same time, each consisting of one American and an interpreter from the Vietnamese Army. The teams sat on low piles of bricks, and the suspects sat on the floor, or on one brick. These sessions did not uncover very much about the enemy or about the village of Ben Suc, but I felt that, as the only extensive spoken contact between Americans and the Ben Suc villagers throughout the Cedar Falls operation, they had a certain significance. Approximately forty people were questioned the first day.

In one session, a stout American named Martinez questioned, in a straightforward, businesslike manner, a small, barefoot, gray-haired man with a neat little gray mustache, who wore a spotlessly clean, pure-white loose-fitting, collarless shirt and baggy black trousers. First, Martinez asked to see the old man's identification card. By law, all South Vietnamese citizens are required to carry an identification card issued by the government and listing their name, date and place of birth, and occupation. (The Americans considered anyone who lacked this card suspicious, and a man who last registered in another village would have to supply a reason.) This suspect produced an I.D. card that showed him to be sixty years old and born in a village across the river. A search of his pockets also revealed an empty tobacco pouch and a small amount of money.

"Why did he come to Ben Suc?" Throughout the session, Martinez, who held a clipboard in one hand, spoke to the interpreter, who then spoke to the suspect, listened to his reply, and answered Martinez.

"He says he came to join relatives."

"Has he ever seen any V.C.?"

"Yes, sometimes he sees V.C."

"Where?"

"Out walking in the fields two weeks ago, he says."

"Where were they going?"

"He says he doesn't know, because he lives far from the center of the village. He doesn't know what they were doing."

"Does he pay any taxes?"

"Yes. The V.C. collect two piastres a month."

"What's his occupation?"

"He says he is a farmer."

"Let's see his hands."

Martinez had the man stand up and hold out his hands, palms up. By feeling the calluses on the palms, Martinez explained, he could tell whether the man had been working the fields recently. Aside from asking questions, Martinez employed only this one test, but he employed it on the majority of his suspects. He squeezed the old man's palms, rubbed the calves of his legs, then pulled up his shirt and felt his stomach. The old man looked down uneasily at Martinez's big hands on his stomach. "He's not a farmer," Martinez announced, and then, with a touch of impatience and severity, he said, "Ask him what he does."

The interpreter talked with the suspect for

about half a minute, then reported, "He says that recently he works repairing bicycles."

"Why did he say he was a farmer?"

"He says he has repaired bicycles only since he finished harvesting."

Deliberately accelerating the intensity of the interrogation, Martinez narrowed his eyes, looked straight at the suspect crouching below him, and, in a suddenly loud voice, snapped, "Is he a V.C.?"

"No, he says he's not," the interpreter announced, with an apologetic shrug.

Martinez relaxed and put his clipboard down on a table. A weary smile took the place of his aggressive posture. "O.K. He can go now," he told the interpreter.

The interpreter, a thin young man with sunglasses, who had spoken to the suspect in a courteous, cajoling manner throughout the questioning, seemed pleased that the interrogation was to involve nothing more unpleasant than this. He gave the old man a smile that said, "You see how nice the Americans are!" and then patted him on the shoulder and delivered him into the hands of a guard.

After the old man had gone, Martinez turned to me with the smile of a man who has some inside information and said confidentially, "He was a V.C. He was probably a tax collector for the V.C." After a moment, he added, "I mean, that's my supposition, anyway."

The other interrogations were very similar. Martinez asked the same questions, with little variation: "Where does he live?" "Is he a farmer?" (Then came the touch test.) "Has he seen any V.C.?" And, finally, "Is *he* a V.C.?" And the suspects, instead of insisting that the National Liberation Front actually governed the village and involved the entire population in its programs, supported him in his apparent impression that the Front was only a roving band of guerrillas. To judge by their testimony to Martinez, the villagers of Ben Suc knew the Front as a ghostly troop of soldiers that appeared once a fortnight in the evening on the edge of the forest and then disappeared for another fortnight. ·When one young suspect was asked if he had "ever seen any V.C.s in the area," he answered that he had seen "fifty armed men disappearing into the forest two weeks ago." Another man, asked if he knew "any V.C.s in the village," answered in a whisper that he knew of *one*—a dark-complexioned man about forty-five years old named Thang. Still another man said that he had been "taken into the jungle to build a tunnel a year ago" but couldn't remember where it was. I had the impression that the suspects were all veterans of the interrogation room. For one thing, they were able to switch immediately from the vocabulary of the Front to the vocabulary of the American and South Vietnamese-government troops. It is a measure of the deep penetration of propaganda into every medium of expression in wartime Vietnam that few proper names serve merely as names. Most have an added propagandistic import. Thus, to the Americans the actual *name* of the National Liberation Front is "Vietcong" (literally, "Vietnamese Communists")—a term that the Front rejects on the ground that it represents many factions besides the Communists. Likewise, to the Front the actual *name* of the Army of the Republic of Vietnam is "Puppet Troops." Even the names of the provinces are different in the two vocabularies. The Front refuses to comply with a presidential decree of 1956 renaming the provinces, and insists on using the old names—calling Binh Duong, for instance, by its old name of Thu Dau Mot. There is no middle ground in the semantic war. You choose sides by the words you use. The suspects made the necessary transitions effortlessly. (Confronted with this problem myself, I have tried in this article to use for each organization the name that its own side has chosen for it.)

Several women were brought into the schoolhouse for interrogation, sometimes carrying a naked child balanced astride one hip. Unlike the men, they occasionally showed extreme annoyance. One young woman only complained loudly, and did not answer any of the questions put to her. Her baby fixed the interrogator with an unwavering, open-mouthed stare, and an old woman, squatting next to the suspect looked at the ground in front of her and nodded in agreement as the young mother complained.

"Do you know any V.C.s in this village?" the interrogator, a young man, asked.

The interpreter, having tried to interrupt the woman's complaining, answered, "She says she can't remember anything. She doesn't know anything, because the bombs were falling everywhere."

"Tell her to just answer the question."

"She says she couldn't bring her belongings and her pig and cow here." The interpreter shook his head and added, "She is very angry."

The interrogator's face grew tense for a moment, and he looked away, uncertain of what to do next. Finally, he dismissed the woman and impatiently turned his pad to a fresh sheet.

The Vietnamese troops had their own style of interrogation. At eleven o'clock that morning, an ARVN officer stood a young prisoner, bound and blindfolded, up against a wall. He asked the prisoner several questions, and, when the prisoner failed to answer, beat him repeatedly. An American observer who saw the beating reported that the officer "really worked him over." After the beating, the prisoner was forced to remain standing against the wall for several hours. Most of the ARVN interrogations took place in a one-room hut behind the school where the Americans were carrying on their interrogations. The suspects, bound and blindfolded, were led one by one into the hut. A group of ten or twelve fatherless families sitting under the shade of a tree nearby heard the sound of bodies being struck, but there were no cries from the prisoners.

As one young man was being led by one arm toward the dark doorway of the interrogation hut, a small boy who was watching intently burst into loud crying. I went inside after the suspect, and found that three tall, slender, boyish Vietnamese lieutenants, wearing crisp, clean American-style uniforms crisscrossed with ammunition belts, and carrying heavy new black pistols at their hips, had sat the young man against the wall, removed his blindfold, and spread a map on the floor in front of him. Pointing to the map, they asked about Vietcong troop movements in the area. When he replied that he didn't have the answers they wanted, one lieutenant beat him in the face with a rolled-up sheet of vinyl that had covered the map, then jabbed him hard in the ribs. The prisoner sat wooden and silent. A very fat American with a red face and an expression of perfect boredom sat in a tiny chair at a tiny table near the door, looking dully at his hands. The three lieutenants laughed and joked · among themselves, clearly enjoying what seemed to them an amusing contest of will and wits between them and the silent, unmoving figure on the floor in front of them. Looking at the prisoner with a challenging smile, the lieutenant with the map cover struck him again, then asked him more questions. The prisoner again said he couldn't answer. Suddenly noticing my presence, all three lieutenants turned to me with the wide, self-deprecating grins that are perhaps the Vietnamese soldiers' most common response to the appearance of an American in any situation. Realizing that I could not speak Vietnamese, they called in an American Intelligence officer—Captain Ted L. Shipman, who was their adviser, and who could speak Vietnamese fluently. They asked him who I was, and, upon learning that I was not a soldier but a reporter, they looked at each other knowingly, saluted me, and con-

tinued their interrogation, this time without beatings. A few minutes later, however, Captain Shipman, who had been standing beside me, said that he was extremely sorry but they wanted me to leave. When we were outside, Captain Shipman, a short man with small worried eyes behind pale-rimmed glasses, drew me aside and, shaking his head, spoke with considerable agitation. "You see, they *do* have some—well, methods and practices that *we* are not accustomed to, that we wouldn't use if we were doing it, but the thing you've got to understand is that this is an Asian country, and their first impulse is force," he said. "Only the fear of force gets results. It's the Asian mind. It's completely different from what we know as the Western mind, and it's hard for us to understand. Look—they're a thousand years behind us in this place, and we're trying to educate them up to our level. We can't just do everything for them ourselves. Now, take the Koreans—they've got the Asian mind, and they really get excellent results here. Of course, we believe that that's not the best way to operate, so we try to introduce some changes, but it's very slow. You see, we know that the kind of information you get with these techniques isn't always accurate. Recently, we've been trying to get them to use some lie detectors we've just got. But we're only advisers. We can tell them how we think they should do it, but they can just tell us to shove off if they want to. I'm only an adviser, and I've made suggestions until I'm *blue in the face!* Actually, though, we've seen some improvement over the last year. This is a lot better than what we used to have."

I asked if the day's interrogations had so far turned up any important information.

"Not much today," he answered. "They're not telling us much. Sometimes they'll just tell you, 'Hey, I'm a V.C., I'm a V.C.' You know—proud. Today, we had one old man who told us his son was in the V.C. *He* was proud of it." Then, shaking his head again, he said with emphasis, as though he were finally putting his finger on the real cause of the difficulty, "You know, they're not *friendly* to us at this place, that's the problem. If you build up some kind of trust, then, once some of them come over to your side, they'll tell you anything. Their brother will be standing near them and they'll tell you, 'Him? He's my brother. He's a V.C.' It's hard for us to understand their mentality. They'll tell you the names of their whole family, and their best friends thrown in." Of the Front soldiers he said, "They don't know what they're doing half the time. Outside of the hard-core leaders, it's just like those juvenile delinquents back home, or those draft-card burners. They're just kids, and they want excitement. You give those kids a gun and they get excited. Half of the V.C.s are just deluded kids. They don't know what they're doing or why. But the V.C. operates through terror. Take this village. Maybe everybody doesn't want to be a V.C., but they get forced into it with terror. The V.C. organizes an association for everyone—the Farmers' Association, the Fishers' Association, the Old *Grandmothers'* Association. They've got one for everybody. It's so mixed up with the population you can't tell who's a V.C. Our job is to separate the V.C. from the people."

At that moment, a helicopter came in sight five hundred yards away, cruising low over the woods and emitting a steady chattering sound that was too loud to be the engine alone. Breaking off his explanation to look up, Captain Shipman said, "Now, there's a new technique they've developed. That sound you hear is the 7.62-calibre automatic weapon on the side. They have a hell of a time finding the V.C. from the air, so now when they hear that there's a V.C. in the area they'll come in and spray a whole field with fire. Then, you see, any V.C.s hiding below will get up and run, and you can go after them."

Captain Shipman went off to attend to other business, and I walked back to the interroga-

tion hut. The fat American in the tiny chair was still looking at his hands, and the prisoner was still sitting stiff-spined on the floor, his lips tightly compressed and his gaze fixed in front of him. The young lieutenant with the map cover held it above the suspect's face and stared intently down at him. All three lieutenants were wholly engrossed in their work, excited by their power over the prisoner and challenged by the task of drawing information out of him. After twenty seconds or so, the American looked up and said to me, "They been usin' a little water torture." In the water torture, a sopping rag is held over the prisoner's nose and mouth to suffocate him, or his head is pushed back and water is poured directly down his nostrils to choke him. Again the lieutenants had not noticed me when I entered, and when the American spoke one of them looked up with a start. The tension and excitement in his expression were immediately replaced by a mischievous, slightly sheepish grin. Then all three lieutenants smiled at me with their self-deprecating grins, inviting me to smile along with them.

Captain Shipman came in, looking even more harried than before. One of the lieutenants spoke to him in a sugary, pleading tone, and Captain Shipman turned to me with a fatalistic shrug and said, "Look, I'm really sorry, but I get it in the neck if I don't take you away." Glancing over my shoulder as I left, I saw that the lieutenants were already crouching around their prisoner again and were all watching my exit closely. Outside again, Captain Shipman explained that this was only a preliminary interrogation—that a more extensive session, by the Province Police, would be held later. He pointed out that American advisers, like him, would be present at the police interrogation.

At the end of an interrogation, the questioner, whether American or Vietnamese, tied an eight-inch cardboard tag around the neck of the bound prisoner. At the top were the words "Captive Card," in both Vietnamese and English, and below were listed the prisoner's name, address, age, occupation, and the kind of weapon, if any, he was carrying when caught. None of the captive cards on the first day listed any weapons.

At one o'clock, the official count of "V.C.s killed" stood at twenty-four, with no friendly casualties reported. Soldiers on the spot told me of six shootings. I learned that three men had crawled out of a tunnel when they were told that the tunnel was about to be blown up. "One of them made a break for it, and they got him on the run," the soldier said. An officer told me that a man and a woman were machine-gunned from a helicopter while they were "having a picnic." I asked him what he meant by a picnic, and he answered, "You know, a *picnic*. They had a cloth on the ground, and food—rice and stuff—set out on it. When they saw the chopper, they ran for it. They were both V.C.s. She was a nurse—she was carrying medical supplies with her, and had on a kind of V.C. uniform—and he was, you know, sitting right there with her, and he ran for it, too, when the chopper came overhead." A soldier told me that down near the river three men with packs had been shot from a distance. Inspection of their packs revealed a large quantity of medical supplies, including a surgical kit, anti-malaria pills, a wide assortment of drugs, and a medical diary, with entries in a small, firm hand, that showed the men to have been doctors. (The *Stars and Stripes* of January 12th gave an account of seven additional shootings: "UPI reported that Brigadier General John R. Hollingsworth's helicopter accounted for seven of the Vietcong dead as the operation began. The door gunner, personally directed by the colorful assistant commander of the 1st. Inf. Div., shot three V.C. on a raft crossing the Saigon River, another as he tried to sneak across camouflaged by lily-pads, and three more hiding in a creek nearby.")

I asked the officer tabulating the day's achievements how the Army disposed of enemy corpses. He said, "We leave the bodies where they are and let the people themselves take care of them." It occurred to me that this was going to be difficult, with only women and children left in the area. Later in the afternoon, I heard the following exchange on the field radio:

"Tell me, how should we dispose of the bodies, sir? Over."

"Why don't you throw them in the river? Over."

"We can't do that, sir. We have to drink out of that river, sir."

The captured-weapons count stood at forty-nine—forty booby traps, six rifle grenades, two Russian-made rifles, and one American submachine gun. All were captured in caches in tunnels.

In the early afternoon, I went over to the field where the Americans were resting to ask them about the attack in the morning and what their feelings were concerning it. When I told one soldier that I was interested in finding out what weapons, if any, the Vietnamese dead had been carrying, he stiffened with pride, stared me straight in the eye, and announced, "What do you mean, 'Were they carrying weapons?' Of course they were carrying weapons! Look. I want to tell you one thing. *Anyone killed by this outfit was carrying a weapon.* In this outfit, no one shoots unless the guy is carrying a weapon. You've got to honor the civilian, that's all." With that, he terminated our conversation. Later, he and I walked over to a small tent where several men sat on the ground eating Spam and turkey from canned rations. They ate in silence, and, in fact, most of the men preferred to be alone rather than talk over the morning's attack. The men who did say anything about it laconically restricted themselves to short statements—such as "C Company had some light contact in the woods over there. Snipers mainly"—usually brought out in an almost weary tone, as though it were over-dramatic or boastful to appear ruffled by the day's events. Nor did they kid around and enjoy themselves, like the ARVN soldiers. One young soldier, who looked to be not out of his teens, did come riding by on a small bicycle he had found near one of the houses in the village and cried out, with a big, goofy smile, "Hey! Look at this!," but the other men ignored him coldly, almost contemptuously.

I entered into conversation with Major Charles A. Malloy. "We're not a bunch of movie heroes out here," he said. "I think you'll find very few guys here who really hate the V.C. There's none of that stuff. I'll tell you what every soldier was thinking about when he stepped out of the helicopter this morning: Survival. Am I going to make it through? Am I going to see my wife and kids again? O.K., so some people without weapons get killed. What're you going to do when you spot a guy with black pajamas? Wait for him to get out his automatic weapon and start shooting? I'll tell you I'm not. Anyway, sometimes they throw away their weapon. They'll throw it into the bushes. You go and look at the body, and fifty yards away there's the weapon in the bushes. You can't always tell if they were carrying a weapon. Now, this man here has just heard that his wife had his first kid, a baby girl." He indicated a short, young-looking soldier with bright-red hair. "Now, if I told any one of these men they could go home tomorrow, they'd be off like a shot." The men listened with quiet faces, looking at the ground. "No, there's very little fanatic stuff here," he went on. At that moment, a middle-aged Vietnamese wearing the customary black floppy clothing was led by, his arms bound behind his back. Major Malloy looked over his shoulder at the prisoner and remarked, "There's a V.C. Look at those black clothes. They're no good for working in the fields. Black absorbs heat. This is a hot country. It doesn't make any sense. And look

at his feet." The prisoner had bare feet, like many of the villagers. "They're all muddy from being down in those holes." In a burst of candor, he added, "What're you going to do? We've got people in the kitchen at the base wearing those black pajamas."

At three-forty-five, the male captives between the ages of fifteen and forty-five were marched to the edge of the helicopter pad, where they squatted in two rows, with a guard at each end. They hid their faces in their arms as a Chinook double-rotor helicopter set down, blasting them with dust. The back end of the helicopter was lowered to form a gangplank, leading to a dark, square opening. Their captive cards flapping around their necks, the prisoners ran, crouching low under the whirling blades, into the dim interior. Immediately, the gangplank drew up and the fat bent-banana shape of the Chinook rose slowly from the field. The women and children braved the gale to watch its rise, but appeared to lose interest in its flight long before it disappeared over the trees. It was as though their fathers, brothers, and sons had ceased to exist when they ran into the roaring helicopter.

Inside the Chinook, the prisoners were sitting on two long benches in a dim tubular compartment, unable to hear anything over the barely tolerable roaring of the engines, which, paradoxically, created a sensation of silence, for people moved and occasionally talked but made no sound. Many of the prisoners held their ears. Up front, on each side, a gunner wearing large earphones under a helmet scanned the countryside. The gunners' weapons pointed out, and there was no guard inside the helicopter. A few of the prisoners—some bold and some just young—stood up and looked out of small portholes in back of their seats. For the first time in their lives, they saw their land spread below them like a map, as the American pilots always see it: the tiny houses in the villages, the green fields along the river pockmarked with blue water-filled bomb craters (some blackened by napalm), and the dark-green jungles splotched with long lines of yellow craters from B-52 raids, the trees around each crater splayed out in a star, like the orb of cracks around a bullet hole in glass.

That night, the women, children, and old people were allowed to return to their houses under a guard of ARVN soldiers. Being of peasant stock themselves for the most part, the ARVN soldiers knew just how to catch, behead, and pluck a chicken. Most of the battalion helped itself to fried chicken—a rare luxury for them. In the hot sun the next day, they went inside the houses to keep cool. Except for the guards on the perimeter of the village, the Americans stayed apart in the field next to the landing pad; even so, a few of them managed to get some chicken to fry.

The next morning, trucks arrived in Ben Suc to begin the evacuation. The Americans on the scene were not sure just how many possessions the villagers were supposed to take with them. The original orders were to "bring everything." In practice, the villagers were allowed to take anything that they themselves could carry to the trucks. Families near the spot where a truck was drawn up took furniture, bedclothes, bags of rice, pigs, cooking utensils, agricultural tools, and just about anything else they wanted to, but, without their men to help them, families living at any distance from a truck could carry only clothing, a few cooking utensils, and one or two bags of rice. By government decree, any rice beyound fifteen bushels per family was to be confiscated as "surplus," potentially intended for the enemy, but although many families had as much as four times this amount at their houses, they could never carry more than fifteen bags with them to the trucks, so no scenes of confiscation took place at the loading. (During the next few days, all the cattle still in or near the village were

rounded up and brought to join the villagers.) Several of the ARVN soldiers helped the women and children load the heavy pigs and bags of rice on the trucks. Later, an American officer who saw this exclaimed in amazement, "You saw it! The Arvins loaded those trucks. We've never seen anything like it." ARVN's willingness to load and unload trucks during this whole operation became quite famous, evoking a few compliments for the ARVN troops amid the usual barrage of American criticism. Hearing about the truck-loading, another officer remarked, "You pat the little Arvin on the ass and he just might do a good job." Because the Americans were very eager to find the Front's storage places for the rice collected as taxes, they had a Vietnamese officer announce to the assembled women that by divulging where this rice was they would gain permission to take it with them to the resettlement area, but no one responded. Several Americans speculated about whether this showed loyalty to the Vietcong.

Jammed with people, animals, and bundles of possessions, the trucks left Ben Suc in convoys of ten. The first few miles of the journey took them along a bumpy dirt road in a choking cloud of dust, which quickly coated everything. After an hour, they turned onto another road, near Phu Cuong, and headed for Phu Loi, their destination. Finally, the trucks swung right into a vast field of at least ten acres, empty except for a row of a dozen or more huts standing in the shade of a line of low palm trees along a narrow dirt road. Since there was nothing resembling a camp for the villagers, the American drivers brought their charges to these huts—the only shelter in sight. They were the houses of families who farmed fields nearby and who were totally surprised to discover themselves playing host to several thousand strangers—strangers not only from Ben Suc but from several other villages. Earlier that day, truckloads of people from other villages in the Iron Triangle had been arriving in a steady stream. ARVN soldiers again won praise by helping to unload the trucks, and American soldiers also gave a hand with the unloading. Dusty, squealing, desperately kicking pigs were slid to the ground down ramps improvised from boards. One American soldier put his hands under the arms of a tiny, very old deaf woman and whisked her to the ground, setting her gently down as though she were as light as a bunch of straw. Several children smiled at seeing the old lady lifted down. As for the lady herself, she simply stood motionless among the pigs and rice bags, staring in front of her with blank unconcern; apparently she was too old to realize that she had just flown through the air from truck to ground. The Americans also lifted down several small, amazed, pantless children. After the unloading was finished, some of the Ben Suc people jammed themselves into the already jammed houses of the Phu Loi peasants, and others simply tried to find some shade. Soon they began to talk with the people from the other villages, who had their own tales of misfortune to tell.

How He Saw the War in Viet Nam

Jimmy Breslin

Jimmy Breslin was a sportswriter for the *Journal American* until hired by the *New York Herald Tribune* in 1963. His distinctive writing style has been vital in the development of new journalism. Author of the novel *The Gang That Couldn't Shoot Straight,* he ran on the same ticket with Norman Mailer and Gloria Steinem in the 1968 mayoral campaign in New York City. A collection of his essays appears in his book *The World of Jimmy Breslin.* His most recent novel is *World Without End, Amen.*

VISIT TO A LITTLE WAR

Travis Air Force Base, California
The ground-crew man kept waving his black-gloved hands for them to keep coming, and they moved slowly over the white concrete runway toward him. The blue truck came first. The big jet transport, which had no windows on its sides, was behind it. Then there were two red firetrucks which always come out when they land a plane that carries people who are wounded. Otherwise, there was no change in the routine of the air base. Transport planes taxied onto runways and took off. Straight across the field, in front of low sand-colored hills, B-52 bombers waited in the dusk with their nuclear bombs inside them. The ground-crew man's black gloves still waved and the truck led the plane right up to a knot of people who stood with their hands over their ears. The jet's engines roared and the kerosene fumes were thick in the air. Then its engines ran out in a whine.

A wide cargo door in the side of the plane came open. A nurse stood in the doorway with a clipboard in her hands. She was dark-haired and tanned, and wearing blue slacks and shirt and a heavy flying jacket with captain's bars on it.

"How many do you have?" one of the officers on the runway said.

She looked down at the mimeographed sheets. "Twenty-six from Viet Nam." She shook her head. "No, I missed one. Twenty-seven from Viet Nam."

"All litters?" the officer said.

"No, we have twelve ambulatory," she said. "And one psychiatric."

The ground crew pushed a covered chute up to the plane. The officers who had been standing on the runway started walking up the chute. A hospital bus backed up to the chute; white-uniformed medics ran out of the bus and up the ramp and into the plane.

The litters were stacked in tiers. The inside of the plane was warm. Only sheets covered their broken bodies. The medics carried them up to the hatch and into the cold Northern California breeze. Each time, the nurse told the medics to put the litter down.

"You have to cover up," she said, and she bent down and pulled olive-drab blankets over them and tucked the blankets in. Then she looked at them. "Now lie on your back, please," she said. The young, smooth faces went back and the white pillows came up around their cheeks. They were silent. Their eyes, opened very wide, looked straight up.

They came, one after another, in casts and with bloodstains on their sheets, and the nurse's tanned hands pulled olive-drab blankets over their broken bodies and she talked quietly and looked into the face of each of them. Then he would be gone and the medics would put another piece of the war in Viet Nam at her feet. And she would bend over and reach for blankets.

She did not bend over when they brought Sergeant Philip Vogel out. He was the last. Both of his legs were in casts that were dark from the blood seeping through them. The

bandages on his body began at his chest. A sheet covered part of him. Plastic bags and tubes from a colostomy showed from under the sheet.

"Don't put anything on my legs, please," Philip Vogel said.

She shook her head. "No, I won't put anything over you," she said. She stood and looked at him. "Get him out of the cold right away," she said. The medics took Philip Vogel down the ramp and into the bus. The doors shut and the bus rolled away and went off the runway and up a hill to the light green hospital building.

They bring them in like this almost every night at Travis Air Force Base. Broken bodies from a small war in a place in Asia. They come in on jet planes that land unnoticed while the nation watches programs on television. They used to come home as heroes. Now they are a way of life.

They put Philip Vogel in a room on the first floor of the hospital. They gave him a cigarette and lit it up for him and then the medic went to get a doctor for him. Vogel's brown eyes looked up at the ceiling. There was no animation in his long, straight face. He took the cigarette out of his mouth and, without being asked a question, he started talking.

"On the second night," he said. "They attacked us on the second night. According to the S-2 there were four hundred guerrillas. It was only my second day there and I got hit. A hand grenade. The VC hit me with a hand grenade. No, what's the use of saying that? I was in a foxhole one night at 10:30 on guard duty and the guy with me was asleep in the higher portion of it. I heard a noise. I didn't want to fire and give away my position. I tried to get out a hand grenade and it didn't clear the bunker and it came back and got me. It bounced right back. Right back at my feet and got me everywhere. I have a colostomy. I'm twenty-five and I have a colostomy. I was going to marry a girl. She's in Pennsylvania. If I ever heal up I can marry her. We got the most modern weapons in the world. I never saw one of them. Never saw one. They move in the grass like snakes. Hey, aren't you gonna do anything about my feet, man?"

The medic heard him and came into the room. He started to take the pillow out from under Vogel's feet. Somebody across the hall began to scream that he couldn't breathe. Then there was a gagging sound. The medic let go of the pillow and ran out of the room.

Vogel looked around the room. "May I have an ashtray, please?" he said.

"Where are you from?" he was asked.

"Baltimore."

"What are you going to do with yourself when you're finished with this?"

"Do? I don't know what I'm going to do. I like the Army. The Army's good. I didn't want to go to Viet Nam. The second lieutenant, he was running to different men's positions. He got shot right in the head. I saw it."

He closed his eyes. "It hurts," he said. His teeth came down and dug into his lip. He started to moan. His teeth came up from his lip and a yell came out of his mouth. A doctor and a nurse came into the room and they bent over Philip Vogel, who had a hand grenade bounce back at him on his second night in Viet Nam.

In an office at the end of the corridor, Ben Griffin, an officer from the base, sat at a desk and went through some forms.

"We got a plane coming in from Viet Nam tomorrow," he said quietly. "This one is carrying coffins."

COLONEL SAM

Saigon

The first time Sam Wilson came to Asia, he walked into the jungles of Burma with a carbine in his hands. He was a captain of the lead detachment of a group which the records say was the 5307th Composite Unit (Provisional). The newspaper and movie people called it Merrill's Marauders. The enemy in Asia then was the Japanese, and Sam Wilson spent three years fighting them behind their lines.

Sam Wilson is back in Asia again, this time as a colonel. He is back in a gabardine suit with a red tie and he stands at the candlelit bar of his huge apartment, a half-gallon of Chivas Regal in front of him, a houseboy padding in with a bucket of ice, and Nat Cole's voice coming over the stereo set. There are no guns lying around the place. There is very little talk of them, either.

At forty-one, and after twenty-four years in the Army, Sam Wilson says that killing people doesn't accomplish a damn thing.

"The Big Red One," he was saying, talking about the United States 1st Infantry Division here in South Viet Nam. "Let's roll them in here, they say. Roll in the Big Red One. We'll flatten these bastards and then go home.

"Oh, Christ, what a waste of time. You roll in the Big Red One here and, do you know what you're doing? Just taking the tarpaulin off the field so you can start to play a ball game. This is a political fight we're in here. It has violent military overtones. But it's going to be won or lost politically. Not with any big firefights."

Wilson tipped the Scotch bottle and poured another round. The room next to the bar had tile walks going around a garden that was lit with Japanese lamps. The center of the ceiling was made of a wire screen. Rain made a waterfall sound as it came through the screen and into a pond in the middle of the garden. Sam Wilson wants to live good. He is going to be here a long time. He is in the Special Forces, but he is attached to the United States Operations Mission. He is in charge of political action in the thatched-roof hamlets and villages which make up this country. Canned milk for babies is Sam Wilson's top weapon.

He is six foot two, 195 pounds, with blue eyes

and light wavy hair and outdoors on his face
and big hands. He is practically inaccessible
around Saigon because he works an eighteen-
hour day between his office and the hamlets
out around the country where he has men
stationed.

He is in the school of Edward Lansdale, the
retired major general who has come here to
direct counterinsurgency operations. And
those who know something of Viet Nam tell
you to see Sam Wilson if you want to find
something hopeful.

"Once the Viet Cong get into a hamlet and
establish this VC infrastructure, as the book
calls it, once they digest the hamlet, you can
roll in the Marines and bring all the firepower
in the world with you," he was saying. "And
for that month that you're in there, you own
the hamlet. But when the tail end of that column leaves the hamlet, the VC owns it again.
And don't you try and go back and spend the
night there. So how can you win here with a
gun?"

"I'm proud I'm a soldier. Hell, I should be
out fighting to be a brigade commander in the
101st Airborne. Only we're doing it differently
now. We're developing a new kind of soldier.
A politico–military breed. Take me. I spent
most of the last five years in Russia and the
satellite countries. I'm 95 per cent fluent in
English and 100 per cent fluent in Russian.
And the job here is to fight them for the people. Get the people. They do it with a tight,
cohesive organization. They make every man
a chairman of something in the hamlet. They
give the man dignity. Even if he's the chairman
of the firewood-organizing committee, he gets
a chance to conduct a meeting once a month
and be on top.

"The other government, the one that runs
Viet Nam, that stops at the district level.
Saigon? That's a word to most of these farmers.
Some place distant. Once in his life the farmer
might meet his district chief. The farmer lives
and works in hamlets and villages. That's

where there is no government influence. Our
job is to bridge the gap and put something in
there. We don't do that, then we win nothing
around here. Shoot 'em up. Christ, shoot hell
out of them. But you win around here by doing
things that aren't exciting."

Wilson's job sounds like another of these ad-
vance-social-worker affairs which, after a
few successes with much fanfare, amount to
a few drops of rain into the sand. But it is the
only way out in this intricate country. Every
aluminum casket shoved onto a freight plane at
Ton San Nhut for delivery to a house in America is a life lost for nothing unless these social
and political things take hold.

"I'd like to go and get a look at those caves
they were hiding in," the Marine colonel at
Chu Lai was told recently.

"Oh, you can't see them now," he said.

"Why?"

"Because our people are out of the area now
and the VC has moved back in. You'll get shot
if you go near them."

These were the caves the Marine operation
swept through in the big American battle they
fought here. The operation was a smashing
success. Except you can't go back, or the VC
will shoot you in the back.

"Rice," Sam Wilson was saying, "they need
rice and old tires to make more sandals out of,
and cloth so they can make some clothes, and
salt. And nuoc mam, the fish sauce they put
over everything. And canned milk for babies.
Past this they don't know about anything, and
they don't need anything. Get in there with
supplies. Then work with them. Make them
understand the only way they can have a free
life is by a decent government. I got men all
over the country living in these hamlets with
them. They're the ones who are going to be
the success around here. If there's ever any
sucess.

"Force? Here, look at this picture. I'll show
you what force does."

He took out a copy of the English-language

newspaper published in Saigon. The front page had a picture of a big Negro Marine holding a rifle on six Viet Cong prisoners. The Viet Cong sat on the ground, with that on-purpose scrawny look they can affect so quickly.

"If those six prisoners had their chance, they would take that Marine and mutilate him while he was still breathing. We know that," Wilson said. "But the people looking at the paper only see this big round-eye standing over the six poor Viet Cong prisoners. Even the Vietnamese people on our side, they don't say anything about it, but they resent that round-eye towering over the poor prisoners."

"The Marine is a Negro. Doesn't that make any difference?"

"As long as he has round eyes, the black guy is a white guy to them. They don't like him. Let me tell you, the more roundeyes we bring over here in our Big Red Ones, the more people we're getting into an area where all the people are going to resent us."

He finished his drink and looked at his watch. "When a kid gets killed over here, he's just as dead as they were in those great big wonderful battles in the forties. You got to work for these kids. Work to try and straighten this out for them. Come on, I have to go out with my troops."

Sam Wilson's troops were in a villa twenty minutes away by car through the rain. The troops were sitting with Vietnamese girls on a tile floor, drinking orange soda. A Vietnamese man with tinted glasses sat on a stool in the middle of the floor, playing a guitar and singing little songs the troops seemed to know. Sam Wilson stood by the door and watched.

"The man playing the guitar is Pham Duy. He's the leading composer in Viet Nam," Wilson said. "The troops are college students who came over here for the summer. I worked their asses off. They got put in hamlets and they stayed here all summer. Some of them

got shot at, some had bombs thrown at them, all of them were threatened. But they worked and got things done. You're looking at one of the only success stories in this war."

Roger Montgomery, a student at Wesleyan in Connecticut, came out on the floor and sat down with the guitar and started to sing, "Michael row the boat ashore." The students and Vietnamese girls sang with him.

"You're a colonel of the coffee house," Wilson was told.

He called one of them over. The student had glasses and a mustache. His name was Allan Samson. He was twenty-six and a graduate student at the University of California at Berkeley.

"This is a much more useful thing to do than student demonstrations," he said. "It's difficult to learn anything in the United States about the problem here. I feel the information put out by the government about Viet Nam is not worthy of an intelligent person. I feel my being here is a channel of protest against the government's information policies. Let them tell the truth. Then one can see more readily that we should be here. McNamara said there is only a nine-thousand difference in the weapons captured by both sides. The figures he used were true. But he slanted them badly. The VC capture mortars and we capture homemade weapons."

"Where did you spend the summer?"

"In Vinh Long, in the delta. A couple of pot-shots at me. But that was nothing. Everybody who comes here gets shot at. It's the initiation."

"Did you get anything done?"

"We accomplished quite a bit," he said. "The picture changed in our area. Not forever. You've got to remain working. But it did change."

Another one came up. He introduced himself as Dan Grady, twenty-five, who attends the Fletcher Law and Diplomacy School at Tufts.

"I worked with VC defectors in Phan Thiet," he said. "Returnees in that area were averaging 2.5 a month until July and August. Then it went up to 19 per cent. I think we had someting to do with it. They are drafting thirteen-year-olds. They're hurting themselves. And we worked on our program. We're beating them in that region now.

"But the American military are hurting us. They should get their ass kicked," Grady said.

"Here you go," Sam Wilson said.

"Well, they should get their ass kicked," Grady said. "The indiscriminate use of air power here is hurting our effort. A lot of civilians have been killed by air strikes that don't accomplish a thing except to make some general feel good."

"Someday I'm going to get used to my men talking like this," Sam Wilson said. "Someday."

"Look what we're working with," Grady said. "They have a sect here, the Cao Dai. They worship Victor Hugo and Winston Churchill as their saints. It takes great patience and understanding to get to them. Then some ass orders an air strike and an American bomb kills one of their sect. How can we talk to them then?"

Sam Wilson was outside the room, standing under a portico and looking at the rain.

"I know there's no sex appeal in it," he said. "We can't give out big stories about operations we went on and how many people we killed. But I'm going to tell you something. I've tried it both ways. I killed more sonsofbitches than you've seen. Killed all the time. Christ, shot them right in the goddamned head. And I'm telling you what we're doing here is the only way."

All around Saigon, planes were dropping immense flares to light up the ground for strikes at the Viet Cong, who creep up from the ground when it becomes dark. American soldiers were on duty everywhere, their weapons aimed through coils of barbed wire. Sam Wilson's troops sat on the floor and drank orange soda. He said they were more important than regular soldiers.

"You can win a war with these kids," he said, "not with any soldiers."

A LITTLE WAR OF RATS

Saigon

George Sunderland rolled over on his cot in the hut and his foot caught the mosquito netting and pulled part of it onto the bed. Mosquito netting should hang straight, from the rod on the ceiling over the cot down to the floor, so that the rat crawling up it follows the netting to the ceiling and does not get a grip on the cot with its feet. Sunderland's foot made a fold in the netting and the rat crawling up it came into the fold and onto the bed. The rat's small mouth moved and its teeth came through the netting and into Sunderland's foot. Sunderland kicked the rat and the rat fell under the cot. The rat crept away with its tail dragging across the dirt floor.

George Sunderland, who is a sergeant in the Special Forces, had to be taken out of his camp at a place called Plateau GI the next morning. The doctors started treating him for rabies by sticking aluminum needles into his stomach.

Viet Nam, which is a little war of rats, is like this always. It is a place of sneaking and gnawing and of people who see nothing and hear nothing and spend days finding nothing, and who are hit in the back by a shot that comes from nowhere. Nothing seems to happen, and then a Marine battalion is sent home after seven months and it has not been in one action and it has 10 per cent casualties.

It is a place where people are hurt and die in little situations, and very little is heard of it because it is all so scattered. But it is here.

The big-bladed fan in the ceiling spun slowly over Richard Nixon's head while he sat on a couch Saturday night and said he thought the military part of the war could go on for two or three more years. He was sitting in the tile-floored living room of a house that is three blocks away from a street called Pasteur. On Pasteur one night this week, the four Air Force men were standing and waiting for a bus to take them to the airport, and one of them saw the hand come over the wall and he let out a yell when he saw the grenade fall onto the pavement. The four started to run but the grenade went off and caught them all in the back.

Everywhere in Viet Nam the days gnaw at people who live them. In a place called Can Tho, which is in the delta area, the Vietnamese have a hospital building, a sickly-yellow place with blue shutters, and behind the building is a sluice and hands and arms and legs are always in the sluice, because Vietnamese army doctors do not repair things the way Americans do. They amputate.

And at a place called Duc Co the two Vietnamese questioned the Viet Cong prisoner who had just been caught out in the thick forests which surround the camp. The Vietnamese were in fatigues. The Viet Cong prisoner wore black. The three squatted down, which is the way Vietnamese talk best. The two soldiers spoke in the bird language of the country and the Viet Cong answered them. The two soldiers showed no anger. One of them reached out with his hands and took the prisoner's right hand and held it. He seemed to be talking to the prisoner with feeling. Then the soldier gripped the prisoner's middle finger and began to bend it back. The soldier's voice did not change. He kept talking in one tone while his hands brought the finger straight up, a brown muddy finger rising from the prisoner's hand. Then the soldier tipped the finger straight back and there was a little sound when the bone of the finger and the knuckle of the hand broke.

The prisoner let out a little cry. Tears came out of his eyes. The soldier let go of the finger. He clasped his hands and put them between his knees. He squatted there and kept talking. The prisoner squatted in front of him, the brown muddly finger back on the top of his hand. Everybody walked past them and did not notice it at all. These things are a way of life in this little war.

"This is Nutcracker 91 to Navy Jet Flight 42," the pilot of the forward air controller's plane said. "Do you have me in sight yet?"

"Ah, this is Navy Jet Flight 42. I have a sighting of a large town with canal flowing east to west."

"Roger, 42, follow canal east to coordinates WQ 960-963, until you see canal empty into river. I'm at 1800 feet. Ah, there are choppers at 1500. Come in at 3000."

"Roger, following canal," the Navy jet pilot said over the radio. "Should see you in two minutes."

The forward air controller's plane, an observation plane called an L-19 circled the area, which was green, watery land. His job was to spot targets and direct the jet planes to them over the radio.

After a long pause, the Navy pilot's voice came into the forward air controller's headpiece.

"Nutcracker 91, have you in sight," the Navy pilot's voice said.

"Roger, there is target at left of canal. Hit tree line on west side of canal, repeat canal, for about 100 yards. Church out about 1000 yards to left of tree line." The forward air controller was speaking easily as he directed the jet, which was over him in the sky some place. "Do not hit church," the air controller said. "Repeat, do not hit church at 1000 yards to left of tree line. Church is out of bounds. Repeat, church is out of bounds." The pilot of the jet plane did not hear anything after the words "tree line." A crackle on the radio, confusion in the words he heard through the crackle. But he thought he had heard it all.

"Roger, Nutcracker 91," the jet pilot's voice said into the forward air controller's earphones.

The jet came out of the sky, came low over the ground, and a long white cyclinder dropped from under it and disappeared into the trees and the trees exploded in smoke that had fire in its middle. The plane kept going. It went right at the church and something came out from under the plane's wings and went up against the church and part of the wall of the church became smoke. The little girl and her mother who were on their knees praying in the church were killed.

THE RUSTING RAILS

Phan Thiet

The railroad which runs beside the sea from Phan Thiet to Nha Trang is a long, rusting strip of 1-meter-gauge track. Green and yellow painted 900-horse-power Diesel engines pull trains along these tracks whenever the people in charge of the railroad can find an engineer with guts to take a train out. The Vietnamese, who do not like to show any emotion at all, weep openly whenever a train is scheduled to leave. Just outside of Phan Thiet, the Viet Cong like to sit on the railroad tracks and have their lunch and they become very angry if a train comes along and disturbs them. This situation bothers Lieutenant Colonel Dinh Van De, province chief of Phan Thiet. He takes it as a personal insult whenever anybody tries to blow up one of his railroad trains.

"We catch some of these people trying to do this and all we give to them is a month, two month, three month in prison," Dinh Van De was saying yesterday. "This is not enough. I have asked the commanding officer of the Second Corps Area if, with all my conscience, with all my responsibility, I can do something else to them."

What Dinh Van De wants to do is exciting. As stated in writing, he wants to capture a couple of Viet Cong trying to put a mine under his railroad tracks. Then he wants to order a whole town out to the railroad tracks to be witnesses. Dinh Van De then would make one of the Viet Cong sit down on top of a mine. The other Viet Cong would stand off to the side and push down hard on the plunger that makes the mine go off.

"That's a beautiful idea," Dinh Van De was told recently.

"Thank you," he said. "It very necessary."

"It's too bad your railroad isn't electrified," he was told.

"Why is this?" he said.

"Because then you could make them kneel down on the tracks and stick their tongues onto the third rail."

"Oh, I see," Dinh Van De said. His eyes gleamed.

After this exchange of ideas, Dinh Van De picked up an attaché case and said he had to go to Nha Trang.

A railroad train was scheduled to depart in the afternoon. Dinh Van De went out to the landing strip and waited for a plane.

The railroad station was at the end of a row of alleys of sand which run between long rows of yellow cement huts where women sit and sell black-market Cokes while they nurse their babies.

The engineer of the train was standing alongside the Diesel. His name was Lai Chong Duong. He wore black pajamas. His assistant, Chu Van Chich, wore gray pajamas. Another man, probably the conductor, stood with them. All three were so afraid they were holding onto each other's hands.

The train consisted of an engine, two flat cars loaded with lumber poles and crates of nuoc mam. Nuoc mam is a sauce made of rotted fish and it is the most popular thing in all of Viet Nam, which is why you never should invite a Vietnamese into the house. After the flat cars there were one passenger car and then three cabooses loaded with Vietnamese soldiers who already had their guns sticking out the windows. The train had not moved an inch yet, but they were ready to fight for their lives. The war is going very well in this district.

The passengers clustered about the one car. They were women in brown shirts and black pants who carried long poles with live ducks and chickens hanging by their feet from the poles. And old men carrying packing cases which were so heavy the men staggered as they walked. They immediately put their cases down and started shoving the women. They wanted to get a choice location, which is a spot down on the floor so the head doesn't show in the window.

Finally Lai Chon Duong went up the metal steps to the engineer's seat. He went up the steps as if he were going to jail. Chu Van Chich, his assistant, followed him. Chu Van Chich followed because two policemen stood behind him and made him go. The conductor said he was sick and wanted to go home. The policemen took him and stuffed him onto the train. With a loud sob, Lai Chon Duong started the train and inched out of the station.

Through the town of Phan Thiet, all five blocks of it, Lai Chong Duong and Chu Van Chich stood erect in the cab of the Diesel engine. The train passed through a wall of rolled barbed wire and sandbag bunkers. Past this, the train was out in the countryside. Lai Chon Duong bent over a little bit. Chu Van Chich took something out of his pocket and dropped it onto the floor. He bent down to pick it up. The train moved through rice fields, with the breeze from the ocean making the rice seem to be waving good-by to the train. The rice fields slipped away and now the real countryside began.

Mr. Lai Chon Duong did a knee-bend. He ran his train by reaching up. His assistant, Mr. Chu Van Chich, squatted down and put his hands on top of his head. Every few seconds or so, Chu Van Chich would jump up to look out the window to see if the tracks were still there. Then he would come back down into his crouch. The countryside became wild and hills overlooked the train tracks and the train moved along with Lai Chon Duong flat on his stomach now and Chu Van Chich jumping up and down to look out the window.

When the shooting started, it was tremendous. Nobody knows who shot first, the Vietnamese soldiers in the cabooses or the Viet Cong up in the hills. But everybody certainly fired a gun. Now it could be seen that Lai Chon Duong was not afraid after all. He was smart. He was stretched out on his stomach. Chu Van Chich was beside him, bouncing up and down so quickly the sweat poured off him. The train went through heavy shooting. It ended. Only snipers would be aiming at the train for a while. The next concentration of Viet Cong undoubtedly would have a big cannon set up on the side of the tracks, and they would blow the train into the next province.

Finally, on one leap, Chu Van Chich let out a howl of glee. He began running in place. Up ahead, where the train had to cross a wooden bridge, he could see that the bridge had been tampered with. During the night the Viet Cong's great 400 HQ section, sapper platoon, had come with two water buffalo and sixteen old ladies and moved the railroad tracks and the bridge three feet to the right. It would take the government a week and a million dollars' worth of equipment to fix it.

A great smile came onto Lai Chon Duong's face when he got off the floor and saw the trouble on the tracks. He quickly placed his railroad train in reverse and, with a minimum of gunfire, backed it through the hills and into Phan Thiet again. In a week or so, when the bridge was fixed, the train would be ready to run again. Two weeks after that, when the search party finally caught up with Lai Chon Duong and Chu Van Chich, they could schedule a trip.

So there was no train ride to Nha Trang this time. And there is no train ride to any place in Viet Nam. The fighting has gone so well that a railroad train, even an armored train, can't go more than six miles out of Saigon. The last time a train tried it, the Viet Cong stole the engine, turned it around, and ran it at the Saigon station at top speed.

THE DAY I COMPANY GOT KILLED

Chu Lai

Eighteen rifles, stuck in the hot sand by their bayonets, stood in a semicircle in front of a tent. A camouflaged helmet rested on each rifle butt.

The rifles were symbols of the men of the 3rd Battalion of the 3rd United States Marine Regiment killed at Van Tuong last week in the biggest American battle of the Viet Nam war.

Inside the tent, the battalion commander, Lieutenant Colonel Joseph Muir, knelt with his men at memorial services. Colonel Muir appeared to be holding back tears. Some of the Marines sobbed.

"They did not come back," said the chaplain. "O God, for those who fell in battle, we know you are with them. And for those who are here, we give you thanks."

The black mountains of Chu Lai come down to the sea with rice paddies in front of them and then a wide area of orange sand that is covered by lifeless bushes that are shoulder-high. The South China Sea, flat and lukewarm, begins where the land ends.

It was here, on the sand and in the bushes, and under a terrible sun, that the United States Marines fought a battle for the first time in this place in Asia called Viet Nam.

They fought all day Wednesday and into the night, and they fought again on Thursday. Their big American tanks and armored vehicles were useless to them. The enemy, these little Asians in black shirts, knocked the armor out right away.

The Marines were hit with shots coming out of the bushes in the sand. They fought with rifles and machine guns. When the Viet Cong were not on the sand any more, the Marines went into the mud of the paddies after them. The fighting was continuous and the dead were everywhere and now everybody knows that America is in a war.

The Marines say they killed 564 Viet Cong. The Marines do not give their own casualties because this is a war. But their dead were in the sand Wednesday and Thursday, waiting to be put in boxes and sent home to America. The broken bodies of the wounded were being taken to field hospitals. And the rest of them, the kids of eighteen, nineteen, and their early twenties, have had their lives changed forever by this day on the sands and in the mud in front of the black mountains of Chu Lai.

"A lot of boys came off that ship," Daniel Kendall, nineteen, a lance corporal, was saying, "and a lot of men are going back."

Kendell is from Boston and he is in I Company. He thinks I Company is the best company in the Marines and when it was put together in October, back at Camp Pendleton, San Diego, they go to know each other right away because they all knew they had thirty months to live together. And on Tuesday afternoon, when they were taken out of their tents at Da Nang and put on a cramped troop ship without being told where they were going, nobody in I Company was worried.

"We all know what we're doing," Terry Hunter, twenty-two, a corporal, said.

"We got the smartest officers and the best noncoms and the best men," George Kendlers, who is twenty, called out.

"India Company is the best in the Marines," another one of them called out.

"Yeah, we're the best," the kids started to yell, and the gray ship pulled out of Da Nang and went into the sea. They were given chili and rice and cold milk. They liked the cold milk. It was the first they had had since coming to Viet Nam.

"They give us this, they must have some wild operation planned for us," Kendlers said.

None of them had been in action before, outside of having a few stray shots thrown at their camp. After dinner, they were told where they were going. They were going to land on the beach twelve miles to the south of the town of Chu Lai.

"Intelligence says a lot of Viet Cong are dug in in the area," one of the officers said. "But this is one of those things. You may not fire a round. Or you might get your behinds shot off."

"Just remember what you've been taught," Bruce Webb, the company captain, told them. "When you're fired on, go down, then come up and shoot. Don't just lay there. After you shoot, move. Move even if bullets are all around you. You run up less casualties when you move."

They went to bed at 9 p.m. and were up at 4 a.m. and had eggs and pancakes for breakfast. At 6:50 a.m., with the sun breaking over the black mountains in the distance, I Company came through the water and onto the sand and bushes, and it was the first time they ever had been in action.

Walking quietly, with no talk, they went into a small cluster of filthy huts with dirt paths between them. They call these places villages here. The village was empty. On the paths leading from the village to the sand and bushes, they found women and children hiding. The women held their children and looked at the Marines and said nothing. The women knew where the Viet Cong were. But they would not tell the Marines. The Marines were the enemy.

A second village was approached. To get to it, they had to go over a small bridge. The front of the village was lined with bushes and shrubbery. I Company moved up to the bridge. They started to go across it when one of the bushes in front of the village moved and a machine gun began firing from a trench under the leaves.

The Marines and mortars dropped into the village. They called for an air strike. Armed helicopters lumbered in. Swept-wing jets dove at the village after the helicopters moved away. When the air strike stopped, all the bushes began to move and there was firing both ways and then black shirts were climbing out of the trenches under the bushes and running back through the village. I Company came after them. They came across the bridge and into the village and Captain Webb was talking with two corporals, a radio man and a runner, and they were going along one of the trenches with the bushes over it when the booby trap exploded. It killed the three of them. I Company now knew what war is.

"He's not dead," another officer kept telling them. "They're taking him out by helicopter. He's all right." The officer didn't want the men to know that their commander had been killed in the first half-hour of the first action of their lives.

Now they were out into this sand with the bushes and the fire was coming at them. Not concentrated fire. But a shot here, a shot here, a machine gun from somewhere else, and all of it coming from holes and bunkers as they came through this sand, with the bushes tearing at their hands. Every few minutes, Michaels, who was carrying the radio, would hear something on it and he'd call over to those around him.

"Smith got hit. He's dead."

"Smith," the one near him would say. He'd turn to somebody else. "Smith got killed." It would go down the line.

They moved over three Viet Cong bodies killed by their machine guns. A helicopter was downed in one of the rice paddies in front of them. A line of tanks and armored carriers was going in to get out the helicopter pilots. I Company was to go with them. There was a line of eight armored vehicles. The tanks went first. The first tank pitched through the sand and into the mud of the paddy and nothing happened to it.

The Viet Cong fired at the second vehicle. It was an armored carrier, and they tried to get it with a .57-millimeter recoilless rifle. The shot missed. The I Company Marines in the carrier were climbing out to fight. The second shot from the .57 hit and covered the carrier with black smoke and the bodies fell out of the black smoke and into the mud.

The water ran out at noon. Fire was too heavy for helicopters to land with supplies. The Marines of I Company went through the sand with the sun glaring at them and the shots trying to kill them and they were licking their lips and trying to forget about water while they fought. These should be stories from a book about 1944. They are about 1965.

In the afternoon, a young boy popped up in front of them. He had crawled out of a hole which had an opening so small you could walk by it and not notice it. He pointed down into the hole. The boy started running. A small hand came out of the hole. Then a black shirt-sleeve. Then a rifle. The Viet Cong pulled himself out and started running. The I Com-

pany machine-gunners caught him in the middle and his body fell in two parts.

I Company dug in for the night. There was firing all night and all morning and Michaels, the radioman, kept calling out to the ones near him the name of buddies who were killed.

Friday, their faces orange from the sand, their lips encrusted with it, their eyes bloodshot, Terry Hunter, Daniel Kendall, and George Kendlers sat in a foxhole with their rifles and a 3.5 rocket-launcher and they were in with another outfit because I Company was not in the battle any more. I Company had been blown apart. The others who were left had been taken back to the beach.

"It's still the best company in the Marines," Kendlers said in the foxhole. "We just had bad luck. Up on the hill, when the captain got killed, I wanted to go right in. When they started shooting at me later, I felt good. I didn't want to be the only one who didn't get shot at."

"We're all real good buddies," Kendall said.

"We always went to the Pike together. Back in Long Beach. I Company always was together."

"The Pike? Is that a gin mill?"

"Gin mill? No. It's an amusement park. It's got rides," Hunter said.

"Dancing," Kendall said. "You know, an amusement park."

Somewhere close, artillery was going off. Jets screamed in the sun overhead. They sat with their chins down so the sand wouldn't blow into their eyes. They talked about an amusement park in Long Beach where young kids go. Then Kendall's eyes came up and he saw a guy walking toward them from another hole.

"What are you, soft?" he yelled. "You'll get shot right through the ass doing that."

The other two looked up. They all looked the same. Three kids in a foxhole with faces that are very old.

NUMBER WAN

Saigon

Cruz had a sling made out of radio wire hanging from the top of the open doorway on his side of the helicopter. He stuck the black grillwork barrel of an M-60 machine gun through the sling and out into the air. He pushed sunglasses over his eyes and looked down the barrel of the gun at the colorless land under him. The land, the Mekong Delta, went for miles.

Flat, with lines cutting it into domino-shaped fields; nothing seemed to be growing in it. Then a cloud moved across the sky and it reflected on each piece of land as it went over and now you could see that the whole place was olive-drab water. Canals ran through the watery land at intervals.

Cruz, his hands on the gun, kept looking for motion. There was none. Then his head moved. "There you go," he said. "Look at that."

Straight down, a string of sticks hugged the bank of a canal.

"Sampans. Sitting all by themselves," he said. "Nobody's around here any place and all of a sudden we got sampans. The VC travels by sampan around here. Damn. Look at them."

He kept looking down his gun at them, and the helicopter went straight down and the sampans went out of view.

"What can you do?" Cruz said. "We don't know who they are, so we can't shoot at them."

He let go of the machine gun and fumbled under his flak jacket to get at a cigar. He unwrapped it, lit it, and sat back in his seat.

The helicopter landed at Ca Tho, where a company of Vietnamese troops filed up the tail ramp and into the belly of a four-engine C-124 transport. They sat on red canvas bucket seats along the sides. Two lines of them sat back to back down the middle of the plane. When they took off their helmets, black straggly hair fell onto their foreheads. They began to lean on each other, their feet sprawled into the aisle. Most of them were asleep before the ramp was pulled up.

A thin-faced American master sergeant carrying two carbines came in and sat by the door. "Look at this," he said. "They just walked off and left them out there standing against a wall."

The back of his neck was red and crisscrossed with wrinkles. The fatigue cap was pulled down over his eyes. Little veins broken by whisky bottles stood out on his .cheeks. This one was an old soldier.

"I'll say one thing for them," he said. "They sure as hell can sleep a lot."

"Are they yours for good?"

"Hell, no. Trainees. We've had them for fourteen weeks. We've got some more work to do, then they get sent into companies. They don't go as a unit."

"How are they?"

"I don't know. Half of them must have disappeared. Already AWOL, like nothing. So many of them have gone off I'm worried about it gettin' to me. I'll wake up some night and run away myself."

"How do they run away?"

"Like nothing. Every time they get dismissed and they start walkin' around and goin' places I get worried. You see them walkin'. They may never come back."

"Are they all like this?"

"You can never say that. I've been with them around here for almost a year. I've seen plenty of them stand right up there and aim and squeeze one off in spots where a lot of guys I know would keep their head in the mud.

"You know," he said, "this is the third one of these things I've played in—Europe, Korea. To get things done in this one just drives you crazy."

"How did you get stuck for this with all that service?"

"I didn't get stuck, I volunteered."

"Why?"

"Because I'm a soldier."

"That's a good answer."

"You say that now. It takes a war to make a people say that. Otherwise a soldier's a bum. I was on East Baltimore Street one night and a guy says to me, 'You're living off the country. You're just a bum.' That's what a soldier is, just an ignorant bum when there's no war. But now! Oh! We love you."

One of the Vietnamese soldiers was up from his seat. His thick lips parted into a smile when he saw the sergeant take out cigarettes.

"Ah." The kid smiled.

"Here," the sergeant said.

The kid came over, took a cigarette, and leaned over for a light. He straightened up. "Number wan."

He said this is an army saying meaning "very good."

"You got a girl?" the kid was asked.

"Ah." He smiled. "Number wan Saigon."

He smiled and went back to his seat.

"What can you say about them?" the sergeant said. "Half the time they don't even get paid. Then they give their money to some guy who gets sent to the post office to mail it home for them. And the guy comes back and says he lost it or something. And the government says it isn't responsible. What can you do if they don't even get paid?"

"Is their food any good?"

He made a face. "Our captain was in talking to their officers about it the other day. These kids were getting pork every day for weeks. Lumps of fat pork. You can't feed troops like that, but what can you do? Somebody's stealing the money for the food."

He leaned over and spat on the floor.

"They steal the money and feed them crap and then one of us has to go out with them and risk his life."

The plane landed at Tan Son Nhut field outside of Saigon. It came to a halt. The engines shut down and the ramp in the back of the plane came down. Outside, the afternoon rain was a wall of white water.

"We'll sit here for an hour waiting for transportation," the sergeant said. "They're taking this company to a barracks some place."

The kid who had taken the cigarette from the sergeant got up and walked to the head of the ramp. He looked out at the rain; then he took off his helmet and put it on the floor. He pulled a fatigue cap out of his hip pocket and put it on. He did not turn around to see if the Vietnamese captain was looking at him. The kid walked straight down the ramp and he was running when he was at the bottom. He disappeared in the rain.

While he ran away from the plane and went to his girl, the sergeant stared at the two carbines the kid had left against the wall.

"Why did they have to pick this place for a war?" he said.

A DAY AT THE RACES

Saigon

The sergeant was with his fat girl friend. He said that her name was Lind and that he liked her the first time he saw her, which was the night before. She was the only girl in the bar who didn't have gold teeth. After introducing his girl, the sergeant did not introduce himself by name because he said his wife in Georgia would get very mad if she ever knew about him going to the racetrack in Viet Nam with a fat girl friend.

The sergeant and his girl were sitting at the small bar in the clubhouse of the Course de Saigon, which the Vietnamese think is a racetrack. It is a place that is overgrown with weeds and has a gloomy wine-colored cement grand-stand. The sergeant and his fat girl friend were drinking Scotch out of dusty glasses. The bar-maid was an old toothless woman who had her hair pulled straight back in a knot. She was short, and only her face showed over the top of the bar.

"A couple of old buddies of mine are down-stairs," the sergeant said. "They know this chink from Hong Kong and the chink knows his way around here. Stick around, we'll get our hands on some money here."

He ordered another drink and the toothless old lady bartender reached between two seltzer bottles to get the sergeant's glass. The old lady picked up the glass, pushed a cockroach the size of a dollar bill off the bar, and then splashed Scotch into the dusty glass.

The sergeant was thirty-four and in the Special Forces. He is a professional soldier. His fat girl friend also was a professional. The sergeant had on a blue polo shirt and dark slacks. He said it was the first time he had been out of fatigues in weeks. His girl friend wore Vietnamese national dress, a white high-collared thing which splits at the waist and goes down to the ground, flowing white trousers, dirty feet sticking out from under them, and the right hand held out for money.

"Maw-ney," she said.

"That's all you know," the sergeant said.

"The chevaux," she said, meaning the hors-es.

"No, you don't bet now," the sergeant said. "You bet when this chink from Hong Kong tells us what to bet. He knows his way around here.

"I got about 7000 piastres left," the sergeant said. This was about $70.00. "I've been down around Mito four straight weeks now. I'm look-ing to have some fun. But I'm not looking to give my money away to my girl friend here.

It's bad enough she robs me all night, she does-n't have to do it in the daylight."

This made great sense. Around Mito, where the sergeant stays, the Viet Cong have a nag-ging habit of shooting guns off at all hours of the day and night. It is particularly hard on eardrums. If a person's job conditions are of this sort, the least he should be able to do is get a little help at the racetrack from a chink from Hong Kong.

The man was downstairs. He was talking to the sergeant's buddies, three regular Army men. The man from Hong Kong was a heavy-set Chinese in sunglasses. He wore a white long-sleeved shirt and tan slacks that were sharply pressed. Field glasses were around his neck and a racing form, printed in Vietnamese, was in his hands. One of the Army men, an old sergeant named Fred Bruder, who comes out of racetrack country, Laurel, Maryland, was going over the form with the man from Hong Kong.

"These two bastards here never run before," he said. "They must be gonna do somethin' here."

"Aho." The Chinese smiled.

"You see?" Bruder said to the ones with him. "I told you this place was a joke. This place isn't for horse racing. It's for embezzling."

The horses were numbered 10 and 3. To win a bet in Saigon, a man must pick the finish one-two.

Bruder and the other two went up the stairs to the bar, where the sergeant was holding hands with his fat girl friend. Bruder informed the sergeant they were betting 10 and 3 in the race.

"Did the chink tell you?" the sergeant said.

"He give it to us," Bruder said. "Hell, you know I don't listen to touts. But they fix so many races around here that a legitimate hand-icapper like me is wasting his time unless he gets in on the larceny."

"Maw-ney," the fat girl said. She held out her hand.

"All right," the sergeant said. He pulled out a thick wad of Vietnamese money and handed her 1000 piastres, which is a huge bet in the Course de Saigon. It amounts to $10 American. In Viet Nam, they will rechannel a river for that kind of money.

The sergeant watched his girl walk to bet the money. "This one, at least she's got teeth," he said.

He was right. Much probably has been said about the beautiful almond-eyed Vietnamese girl. She does not exist. It takes a major talent search to find a girl here with good teeth in her head. Clean feet is too much to ask.

The horses for the day's racing were in a long line of stalls in back of the grandstand. A wooden fence separated the racing fans from the horses. This was to keep any honest people away from the horses. Two Chinese men in sunglasses were directing the grooms. A bucket of water before a race is the finest way there is to make sure a horse will not run so fast.

The jockeys' room, a cement building with a scale out on the porch, was crowded with young kids in pajamas who jammed around the jockeys. The jockey who was to ride No. 10 was found. He was a miniature boy in red silks who was fifteen and weighed 30 kilograms, 66.6 pounds, and gave his name as Phuoc.

"How much does he get if he wins the race?" an official was asked.

"Two thousand piastres," the man said.

"How much does he make if his horse doesn't win the race?"

The official said he didn't understand the question. The jockey, who of course knew no English, smirked. His friends giggled. The jockey got off the scale and walked away. Jockey Phuoc would steal from a candy store.

Back in the stands, the sergeant watched through field glasses when the horses came on the track. "I just bet another thousand piastres on the 10 and 3," he said. "I need some money."

Across the track, the horses lined up for the start. They lined up in a pack, with little men in pajamas standing in front of them and running at a horse when it would try to start. Then with no noise from the stands the race began. It began with the men in pajamas letting one horse run out by himself. The horse got a six-length lead. Then another horse followed. When this one had a real good jump, they let the others come on. The first horse out was No. 8. The second horse out was No. 5. It was suspected that these were the horses they wanted to win.

The sergeant dropped his girl friend's hand. "I'm a sonofabitch," he said. "You can't do this when the sun is still out."

The No. 8 horse led all the way through the weeds. The No. 5 horse received a serious challenge from No. 2. The jockey on No. 2 immediately corrected this by standing up on his horse and yanking the reins so far back he nearly dislocated the horse's neck. Jockey Phuoc, on No. 10, was, as ascertained early, the world's smallest thief. His horse tried to run a little on the turn and Jockey Phuoc immediately stood up in the stirrups. This is a common thing in Saigon. A week ago there was a riot at the track when the jockey on the horse leading in the stretch pulled the horse to a complete stop. Another jockey rode his horse through a hole in the fence. The people ran onto the track and tried to kill both of them. All money was refunded. Of all the characteristics which make up the Vietnamese, the only worth admiring, and the one never mentioned by Henry Cabot Lodge, is their magnificent regard for stealing. It should be protected at all costs. The government should use night raids by B-52s to save larceny in Viet Nam.

Downstairs, in front of the cages where they pay off, a line of kids and grooms and jockeys pushed against each other. They had formed up during the race with their tickets on the two horses they knew would win. There wasn't an American in on the thing. The payoff was 160 for each two piastres put up, and the Chinese from Hong Kong stood at the back with two others. They were waiting until the line cleared so they could cash in their tickets. Then go upstairs and tout the Americans into betting on wrong horses so the price could be built up.

It was evening when the sergeant and his fat girl friend were seen again. They were drunk in a bar on Tu Do Street that had brown rats running across the floor, and the sergeant said he had been robbed all day at the racetrack and now he was going to finish what was left and leave.

"I got to get a helicopter back to Mito," he said.

He left at 5:30 a.m. and flew back for another month of being shot at.

WAR AND RIOTS

Saigon

The radios sit on bunks and on boxes in the mess halls, and out in the field they are on top of the sandbags and every hour the music stops and the news announcer begins: "Rioting in a section of Los Angeles . . ."

And the Negro soldiers stand and listen. And they talk. But they talk with uniforms over their black skins. Yesterday morning two of them, wearing fatigues, were standing in the sun and dirt of Bien Hoa, where the 1st Division troops stay, and they talked about this news which had just gone off the radio in the tent behind them.

"They ask you why you're here, you can't be straight at home," a tall one, smoking a cigar, said. He comes out of St. Louis.

"Why shouldn't they?" the other one said.

"How can you come over here and say to the people, we going to liberate you, when you got to go out in the streets and riot to liberate yourself at home?" This one talking was from Paterson, New Jersey.

"It's none of our business," the one with the cigar said. "They got us here as soldiers, not a race. We got to be soldiers and just walk right by anything else."

"Lemuel Penn," the one from Paterson said. "What about him? He was a lieutenant colonel and he's coming home from camp in Georgia and the Ku Klux Klan shot him. Nobody do anything about it. They got us over here defendin' Georgia. Next thing you know they'll have us fightin' for South Africa."

"That's just you talking," the one with the cigar said. "When you in the Army, anything you say is just talk. It got nothin' to do with what's going on."

"That's all it is," the other one said. "When you finished talking you go right back to what you got to do."

"And you do it or you got trouble, black, white, or any other color," the one with the cigar said. They laughed.

In the USO club in Saigon, which is in a building on a wide, filthy street which has a flower market in the middle, two Negroes from a communications outfit sat down with green mugs of coffee and right away one of them began talking about it.

"Sixteen dead," he said. "What a scene that thing must be."

"This is the custom," the other one, who had a mustache, said.

Whenever there are one or more colored soldiers any place they start talking about the riot in Los Angeles. "If you're alone, do you talk to yourself about it?" they were asked.

"I think it's fine," the one with the mustache said. "Makes me feel good."

"Them easy credit places," the one with him

said. "Boy, they must be catching hell right about now."

"What does it mean to you, right here, as soldiers?" they were asked.

"Nothing," the one with the mustache said. "You can be a rooter. But you just a rooter in the stands and that's all. And you don't get into any conversations with any Vietnamese about it. All that does is get you all raveled up."

"Sure," the one with him said. "How can you sit in a bar some place and explain to somebody why you're here and they got these riots going on? So what you do is just concentrate on being a soldier. There gonna be no civil rights marches in Saigon, I can guarantee you that."

In another room, a Negro in the Air Force sat at a piano. "I don't bother getting into it," he said. "You know, you go into a bar and the girl sits down next to you and she points at her skin and then she points at mine. That's supposed to mean we're all the same. Hell, I know she's trying to con me out of my money. I'm colored to her, same as I'm colored to anybody else."

Outside, the street was jammed and little children wearing only dirty pajama shirts went to the bathroom in the gutter. Saigon is a low-class Harlem and the skin of the people runs from yellow to cocoa, but the minute a Negro serviceman comes into Saigon he heads for bars that are crowded with other Negroes. They are down by the docks.

For years Negro merchant seamen coming into Saigon found themselves comfortable only in these places. No whites go in them. Neither do many Vietnamese, outside of girls looking for payday. The Vietnamese, even the Viet Cong who scream of the race riots in Los Angeles, do not want very much to do with Negroes.

Reuben Simmons was talking about this later in the day. Simmons, a Negro, is an agricultural expert for the United States Mission to Viet Nam. He was sitting in the screened-in-front row of the house he is renting here.

"The Vietnamese?" he said. "They are more color-conscious than we are in the United States. You don't find any of them out taking sunbaths if they can help it. He's death on sunburns, a Vietnamese.

"Then at the same time one of them will say to me, 'Your riots in Los Angeles? How do you feel being here helping us, with all this racial trouble you have at home?' How can I talk to them? There is no way that I can explain Los Angeles to them. They wouldn't believe me. I would tell them what it was like in 1941. I was working for the government and I had to stand in the street in Sixtin, Missouri, and watch them pour gasoline from a truck over a Negro's body and then burn it up. I could tell them how far we have come since then. And how far we are going to go."

"In the Bombay paper," a friend of his said, "they run marriage ads which say: 'Single civil servant wants to meet girl with wheatish complexion.' The whole Orient has its color problems."

What about the effect of the riots on the Negro soldiers here? Simmons was asked.

"None," he said. "This is a controlled situation. They're in the Army. They happen to be Negroes. They can listen to the news on the radio and have their feelings about it. And that's all."

PAID TO BE HERE

Pleiku

We have had so much of it that now it has become a business. In 1917 and then in 1942 people went away to fight for their country with tears and glamour, and everybody cheered at the movies and mooned over love songs about war and slogans for children became the property of adults. The next time, in 1951, it all came up flat. Korea depressed everybody, and soldiers fought because they were drafted. And now, in this place in Asia called Viet Nam, we have reached back into ancient history. Now we have men who fight a war because they get paid for it.

"The government's been paying me for seven years getting ready for a thing like this," Don Fenton, a captain in the Army, was saying. "It's my job. This is the busy season. I've been taking the money for doing nothing. Now I'm earning it. What do I get? I get $850 a month while I'm here. That's not bad? Hell, it should be better. It's about time people learned that they have to pay a soldier."

Fenton is thirty. He came into the Army five days after he graduated from the University of Connecticut in 1957. He had no military backgound in his family. His father worked for the gas company in Hartford, Connecticut. Fenton took a job in the Army because he thought it was a better one than the others he could get. After eight months in Viet Nam, Fenton still thinks he has a good job. There are a lot of people in Viet Nam who think as he does. To them, making war is an occupation.

Fenton was standing in the compound at Pleiku. It is a cluster of old red tile-roofed French buildings and newer white cement ones put up by Americans. And then tents heavy with the smell of waterproofing oil and huts made of sandbags and rolls of barbed wire and sentries who are not put out for show. Fenton was back in Pleiku from his station in a place called Tan Canh, which is out in the jungle-covered hills.

While he talked, Fenton kept fumbling for a cigarette. His fingers kept jabbing onto the side of the package instead of going inside it. Nobody walks away from Tan Canh with the same nerves he brought with him.

"I found it interesting," Fenton was saying, "interesting, worthwhile, and necessary. The only bad thing with it is that I'm married. I had to write my wife about some of it. She knows where I was stationed and she's read the names of villages in the newspapers. Finally she wrote me and said she'd rather know all about it than keep getting these 'everything fine' notes. So I just started to write her and say that there was an operation in such and such a place and that I was there. I'd leave it at that.

"Oh, I don't like being away from her. That kills you. But she understands. My career depends on how well I do over here. How could you be in the Army and want a future in it and not come to Viet Nam?"

The Army used a careful process to put Fenton in Viet Nam. There were no middle-of-the-night orders and a hurried telephone call to home or a last kiss in a crowded waiting room some place. Fenton went to Viet Nam the way Wall Street banks send representatives to the Far East. He received his orders last April. In September he was in school at Fort Bragg. After that he attended a language school in Oakland, California. On January 18, trained for the jungles, able to speak Vietnamese, his wife and new daughter home with her mother in Hartford, he flew to Viet Nam as a professional soldier. Fighting was a clinical thing, his living.

Once they wrote mystically of soldiers thinking about how they would react the first time they came under fire. This is of the forties. The professionals of 1965 step out and go to work with a gun. "Scared," Fenton was saying, "scared as hell. But that doesn't get in the way. You're paid for being here."

In July, a place called Dak To was overrun. Fenton led a group of Vietnamese in to relieve it. They were caught on a road in an ambush and fifteen were killed. When Fenton talks about it, he draws diagrams of the L-shaped ambushes the Viet Cong set, and he describes it flatly.

"I have 125 days to go here," he was saying.

"When I go home I'd like to be assigned some place near a college so I could go for a master's degree. What do I want it for? Why shouldn't I want to get one? Education never hurts you in any business. And that's all the Army is. A business."

An hour away, on the edge of the landing runways at Da Nang, Pappy Hilbert sat on a packing case and smoked a cigarette in the Marine helicopter he flies in. Pappy is not a captain. He is a sergent in the Marine Corps. He looks at it from a working man's viewpoint, not an executive's. But he has been in the service for eighteen years and he intends to stay until he's too old.

"I'd have to get me a job payin' me four dollars an hour to make the equivalent of what I'm making' now," he was saying. "I understand in the States it can get pretty hard to get a job you like. Here, I know anything happens to my wife or family, they just go to the hospital on the base in the States. And I know the kids are gettin' a good schoolin'. Like today. It's raining, it's miserable. I can just set over here and know everything's taken care of.

"Hell, I tried it the other way. I went out and I was a truckdriver, then I hired myself out as a fry cook. I went into a union and got me a job as a second chef. At this place in Santa Ana. I got no satisfaction out of it. What the hell, cookin' for people. At least here I'm gettin' satisfactions."

"Out of what?"

"Out of keepin' them alive. A man gets a lot of satisfaction pickin' up these kids in hills gettin' hit and gettin' them back here."

Pappy is out of Jacksonville, North Carolina. He has a wife and three kids living there, near Camp Le Jeune. It is his second tour in Viet Nam. He spent thirteen months the first time. Of his eighteen years of marriage he has been separated from his wife eleven of them.

"It's all right," he said. "Rather be here than hire me out as a fry cook."

"Fry cooks don't get shot at."

"That's their life. Second day I'm here this time, we land on the hill up there to get this kid. Two of them are bringin' him over to us. Bing! One of 'em goes down and now I got two instead of one. Then a whole load of these bastards come runnin' out of the woods toward us. We shot the hell out of them. We grabbed the two kids and took off. So I got shot at. But I saved a couple of kids. No fry cook can say that to himself."

He sat and looked out at the rain. "Hell, man don't need much here. Appreciate things more. Like last night. Got me a good cold beer last night. Never had one that tasted better."

He closed his eyes and put his head against the side of the ship and took a nap. He felt good. He'd wake up when the pilots came out to take off. He'd wake up and go right to work. Pappy Hilbert likes his job.

THE FLIGHT DECK

The *Independence* was 120 miles out through darkness and rain squalls which began when the plane left the drab coastline and ended when the plane flew out of towering clouds and into the bright sun over the carrier which was moving at 16 knots in 240 feet of light green water.

The gray, angle-decked carrier went into a turn, walking its 80,000 tons through water and into the wind. The fighter planes, darts in the sky overhead, need a 32-knot wind blowing at them when they come onto the deck, their noses pointing to the sky, for landings. Two destroyers, white fountains of water at their bows, followed in file in the wake of the *Independence*. It was, from the window of a plane coming in to land, the picture of the Navy that has been hanging on the sidewalk outside post offices for twenty-five years.

The *Independence* pulled out of Norfolk, Virginia, last May with 4500 men and 90 planes aboard. Now, 11,000 miles away, it moves through the South China Sea as a reminder of things that are gone.

The *Independence* was put together at the foot of Sands Street in Brooklyn from 1955 to 1958. At that time it was common to say that Brooklyn was the only place of its size in the nation that did not have a daily newspaper, a railroad station, and a left fielder. Now Brooklyn does not have a Navy yard either. The men who built the *Independence* have moved to Philadelphia and Boston. And the way of life which the carrier represents seems to be gone too. The *Independence* is a ship that was built to fight in a war that could be seen and found and somehow understood and then fought to a conclusion. Here in the summer and fall of 1965, the *Independence* is part of a grimy little thing where six men coming out of the water in a rice paddy somewhere constitute an attack.

The *Independence* sends long-nosed, exciting planes called F-4B Phantoms exploding off its deck. The planes race away at 1500 miles an hour and bomb little bridges we would spit at in ordinary war. The *Independence* sends planes known as Skyhawks roaring into the night. They dive from 15,000 feet to fire rockets into fields where a handful of men in black shirts and pants may or may not be hiding. There are no enemy carriers for the *Independence* to destroy, no big factories as we know them, no major bases for its planes to dive from the sky at. There are only clusters of nothing in Viet Nam.

The drip of Asian war comes down on the *Independence*. The carrier has lost four planes. Two of its pilots are prisoners in North Viet Nam. Anti-aircraft fire, modern anti-aircraft fire, high and accurate and heavy, meets the planes over North Viet Nam. When the planes return to hit the gun emplacements, they cannot find them. Or the fire is so heavy it isn't worth the price to go in. Surface-to-air missiles

come up from the ground at them. At night, when the rocket boosters look like streetlights, the missiles can be evaded. But in the daytime the missiles are impossible to see. When sites finally are spotted and planes come back to hit them, the planes find only empty ground.

The *Independence* drips down on the Viet Cong too. The carrier planes fly thirteen hours a day, bombing and rocketing, and in North Viet Nam the war is different from what the people there were told it would be. In the South the Viet Cong must remain in small groups and must always be moving and digging holes and getting into them. They are afraid to light fires much of the time. Apparently, malaria sweeps through them. Everybody expected them to come like water under a door in July and August. The jet attacks prevented this. But it all is small. This is a war where you spend a million dollars to fight ten people.

So here is the *Independence,* magnificent and incongruous, lying off the coast of Viet Nam for forty days at a time. The aircraft carrier moves through the light green water as the only way of first-class living and fighting there is.

The captain, John E. Kennedy, was sitting in a high-backed leather chair on the left side of the nearly silent glass-enclosed bridge of the ship. Kennedy was in sunglasses, a blue baseball cap on his square face. His khakis were unwrinkled. He smoked a cigar and had a mug of coffee in front of him.

He asked quietly for another mug and a Marine who had on a white belt with a wide, highly polished brass buckle brought the mug over. A young sailor in denim work clothes ran a waxing machine over the green tiled floor.

Three sailors in white stood in the middle of the bridge, one of them turning the brass wheel of the helm when ordered. Officers in pressed khakis stood at the windows and spoke into intercoms.

A small television receiver was in front of

Kennedy. "It shows landings live and then it plays them back on tape," he said. "It cuts out a lot of arguments about whether the pilot landed right or not. See those little registers on the top of the screen? They show the plane's speed while it is landing. Now if a pilot starts arguing, they just play back the tape for him. We've made a business out of this. Take a look at the planes. Go on any carrier and you won't see paintings of naked girls and nicknames and the like on the planes. That's all gone. The whole attitude here is that it's a business."

An Admiral, James Reedy, a thickset man with gray in his crew-cut hair, was a flight down, sitting in a paneled room that had tan carpeting, easy chairs, and a long brown walnut table with blue chairs at it. The room was set up for President Kennedy, who once used it for a week. Reedy is with the Seventh Fleet. He is in charge of carriers.

"We've lost planes," Reedy said, "too many planes. The anti-aircraft fire can get pretty damn good. And the North Vietnamese are learning how to handle electronics pretty well. Their missiles ride a radar beam to the plane. You've got to read their radar. Then we had one operation accident right on this ship. An officer whose career I've followed since he was on the *Princeton* with me. He came in to land and the ship got out of control and he and the copilot went over the side. We got the bodies. That's all. I watched it right in here on television. I just had to sit here and watch them go right over the side on me. Men I knew."

Through the endless hallways of the carrier, men were going to the dentist, going for religious instructions, going into a carpeted library, or they could be found in paneled sitting rooms, watching the movie *Cleopatra* on a television screen. A lieutenant, Louis Viscomi, who was last seen tending bar in a place called Harvey's in Broad Channel, Long Island, was standing in front of the legal office talking to a seaman who is in trouble with finance com-

panies. The finance companies have been writing the captain of the *Independence* about the sailor. Viscomi, whose bartending got him a law degree, helps advise the sailors.

"Only a rat bastard would try and collect money off of you when you're away to a war," the sailor was saying.

"Why don't we sit down and go over the thing? It's always easier to pay," Viscomi said.

The sailor said a very bad word.

Out on the deck, crews in yellow, brown, blue, green, and red sweatshirts clustered around the blacknosed jet planes. All the crew workers had cuts and scars on their hands. The blast from the jets knocks people off their feet and onto the flight deck, which is covered with rough cement-like coating to prevent skidding.

The carrier has three catapults. The planes were wheeled onto the catapult tracks. The first one, a Phantom, sucked in air through two nostrils on its sides and burned it out the back in a stream of fire.

The head of the crew bent down and touched a button. With a crash and with steam billowing up from the catapult tracks and with red flames coming out of the jet's afterburners, the plane disappeared down the deck and into the air. Then they started to go from all sides. In seven minutes, the carrier had fifteen planes out in the sky. As the last one was off, the crew turned around and the first plane of an incoming group approached the deck and dropped down onto it, and its hook caught the third of four cables stretched across the deck. The cable pulled the plane to a stop.

Bright jerseys dove under the plane and got the cable off the hook. The plane taxied to the front of the deck as another one landed. When the stopped, the pilot got out and took off his helmet and ran a hand through his wet hair. We walked to a doorway and went downstairs for a cup of coffee in a dining room where white-jacketed Filipino waiters served.

Off in a corner, a bald man in a white shirt

and brown slacks sat over coffee. His name is Ellis Bolton. He is a technical representative of North American Aviation. There are twenty others like him on the ship. If something goes wrong with one of his company's planes, he goes twenty-four hours and more with the project until he likes what he sees. They play a whole game on the *Independence*.

Downstairs, red lights in the dimness of the hangar deck showed white 1000-pound bombs hanging in ceiling racks. Rock-and-roll music screamed out of loudspeakers in the twenty-four-hour cafeterias where non-officers eat whenever they want. Music from hi-fi sets ran through the cubicles where the men sleep in three-decked cots, the gray nozzle of an air-conditioner sticking out over the cot on top. Down another corridor, in a room with high-backed leather chairs, Robert Gormley, a tall,

balding man, stood at a lectern and spoke to the pilots in his squadron. They sat in the chairs and drank root beer out of cans. Gormley is a commander. The Navy sent him to Harvard for a year of political-science studies. They seem to have everything handled here. The *Independence* can stay out in the ocean and take care of itself for months.

Its people know what to do. Its planes can knock out a city. But there are no cities to knock out in Viet Nam. There are only these little people moving across empty land who live on cold rice which they carry in a plastic bag. The aircraft carrier does the only job that can be done against them right now. But it is not the kind of war they were thinking of in Brooklyn when they came to work every morning to build the *Independence*.

"The Whole Thing Was a Lie!"
Donald Duncan

Donald Duncan was drafted into the U.S. Army in December 1954. After serving in Germany, he transferred to Special Forces in 1961 and was sent to Vietnam in 1964. There he specialized in operations and intelligence, formulating tactics for operations in War Zone D and the An Lao Valley. Nominated for the Silver Star and the Legion of Merit, he resigned in September 1965, having turned down a field commission to the rank of captain the previous March. He spoke out strongly against United States policy in Vietnam and became the military editor for *Ramparts* magazine. He is the author of *The New Legions*.

When I was drafted into the Army, ten years ago, I was a militant anti-Communist. Like most Americans, I couldn't conceive of anybody choosing communism over democracy. The depths of my aversion to this ideology was, I suppose, due in part to my being Roman Catholic, in part to the stories in the news media about communism, and in part to the fact that my stepfather was born in Budapest,

Hungary. Although he had come to the United States as a young man, most of his family had stayed in Europe. From time to time, I would be given examples of the horrors of life under communism. Shortly after Basic Training, I was sent to Germany. I was there at the time of the Soviet suppression of the Hungarian revolt. Everything I had heard about communism was verified. Like my fellow soldiers I felt frustrated and cheated that the United States would not go to the aid of the Hungarians. Angrily, I followed the action of the brute force being used against people who were armed with sticks, stolen weapons, and a desire for independence.

While serving in Germany, I ran across the Special Forces. I was so impressed by their dedication and élan that I decided to volunteer for duty with this group. By 1959 I had been accepted into the Special Forces and underwent training at Fort Bragg. I was soon to learn much about the outfit and the men in it. A good percentage of them were Lodge Act people—men who had come out from Iron Curtain countries. Their anti-comunism bordered on fanaticism. Many of them who, like me, had joined Special Forces to do something positive, were to leave because "things" weren't happening fast enough. They were to show up later in Africa and Latin America in the employ of others or as independent agents for the CIA.

Initially, training was aimed at having United States teams organize guerrilla movements in foreign countries. Emphasis was placed on the fact that guerrillas can't take prisoners. We were continuously told "you don't have to kill them yourself—let your indigenous counterpart do that." In a course entitled, "Countermeasures to Hostile Interrogation," we were taught NKVD (Soviet Security) methods of torture to extract information. It became obvious that the title was only camouflage for teaching us "other" means of interrogation when time did not permit more sophisticated methods, for example, the old cold water-hot water treatment, or the delicate operation of lowering a man's testicles into a jeweler's vise. When we asked directly if we were being told to use these methods the answer was, "We can't tell you that. The Mothers of America wouldn't approve." This sarcastic hypocrisy was greeted with laughs. Our own military

teaches these and even worse things to American soldiers. They then condemn the Viet Cong guerrillas for supposedly doing those very things. I was later to witness firsthand the practice of turning prisoners over to ARVN for "interrogation" and the atrocities which ensued.

Throughout the training there was an exciting aura of mystery. Hints were continually being dropped that "at this very moment" Special Forces men were in various Latin American and Asian countries on secret missions. The anti-Communist theme was woven throughout. Recommended reading would invariably turn out to be books on "brainwashing" and atrocity tales—life under communism. The enemy was THE ENEMY. There was no doubt that THE ENEMY was communism and Communist countries. There never was a suggestion that Special Forces would be used to set up guerrilla warfare against the government in a Fascist-controlled country.

It would be a long time before I would look back and realize that this conditioning about the Communist conspiracy and THE ENEMY was taking place. Like most of the men who volunteered for Special Forces, I wasn't hard to sell. We were ready for it. Artur Fisers, my classmate and roommate, was living for the day when he would "lead the first 'stick' of the first team to go into Latvia." "How about Vietnam, Art?" "To hell with Vietnam. I wouldn't blend. There are not many blue-eyed gooks." This was to be only the first of many contradictions of the theory that Special Forces men cannot be prejudiced about the color or religion of other people.

After graduation, I was chosen to be a Procurement NCO for Special Forces in California. The joke was made that I was now a procurer. After seeing how we were prostituted, the analogy doesn't seem a bad one. General Yarborough's instructions were simple: "I want good, dedicated men who will graduate. If you want him, take him. Just remember, he may be on your team someday." Our final instructions from the captain directly in charge of the program had some succinct points. I stood in shocked disbelief to hear, "Don't send me any niggers. Be careful, however, not to give the impression that we are prejudiced in Special Forces. You won't find it hard to find an excuse to reject them. Most will be too dumb to pass the written test. If they luck out on that and get by the physical testing, you'll find that they have some sort of a criminal record." The third man I sent to Fort Bragg was a "nigger." And I didn't forget that someday he might be on my team.

My impressions of Vietnam were gained from the window of the jet while flying over Saigon and its outlying areas. As I looked down I thought, "Why, those could be farms anywhere and that could be a city anywhere." The ride from Tan Son Nhut to the center of town destroyed the initial illusion.

My impressions weren't unique for a new arrival in Saigon. I was appalled by the heat and humidity which made my worsted uniform feel like a fur coat. Smells. Exhaust fumes from the hundreds of blue and white Renault taxis and military vehicles. Human excrement; the foul, stagnant, black mud and water as we passed over the river on Cong Ly Street; and, overriding all the others, the very pungent and rancid smell of what I later found out was *nuoc mam,* a sauce made much in the same manner as sauerkraut, with fish substituted for cabbage. No Vietnamese meal is complete without it. People—masses of them! The smallest children, with the dirty faces of all children of their age, standing on the sidewalk unshod and with no clothing other than a shirtwaist that never quite reached the navel on the protruding belly. Those a little older wearing overall-type trousers with the crotch seam torn out—a practical alteration that eliminates the need for diapers. Young grade school girls in

their blue butterfly sun hats, and boys of the same age with hands out saying, "OK—Salem," thereby exhausting their English vocabulary. The women in *ao dais* of all colors, all looking beautiful and graceful. The slim, hipless men, many walking hand-in-hand with other men, and so misunderstood by the newcomer. Old men with straggly Fu Man Chu beards staring impassively, wearing widelegged, pajama-like trousers.

Bars by the hundreds—with American-style names (Playboy, Hungry i, Flamingo) and faced with grenade-proof screening. Houses made from packing cases, accommodating three or four families, stand alongside spacious villas complete with military guard. American GI's abound in sport shirts, slacks, and cameras; motorcycles, screaming to make room for a speeding official in a large, shiny sedan, pass over an intersection that has hundreds of horseshoes impressed in the soft asphalt tar. Confusion, noise, smells, people—almost overwhelming.

My initial assignment was in Saigon as an Area Specialist for III and IV Corps Tactical Zone in the Special Forces Tactical Operations Center. And my education began here. The officers and NCOs were unanimous in their contempt of the Vietnamese.

There was a continual putdown of Saigon officials, the Saigon government, ARVN (Army Republic of Vietnam), the LLDB (Luc Luong Dac Biet-Vietnamese Special Forces) and the Vietnamese man-in-the-street. The government was rotten, the officials corrupt, ARVN cowardly, the LLDB all three, and the man-in-the-street an ignorant thief. (LLDB also qualified under "thief.")

I was shocked. I was working with what were probably some of the most dedicated Americans in Vietnam. They were supposedly in Vietnam to help "our Vietnamese friends" in their fight for a democratic way of life. Obviously, the attitude didn't fit.

It occurred to me that if the people on "our side" were all these things, why were we then supporting them and spending $1.5 million dollars a day in their country? The answer was always the same: "They are anti-Communists," and this was supposed to explain everything.

As a result of this insulation, my initial observations of everything and everyone Vietnamese were colored. I almost fell into the habit, or mental laziness, of evaluating Vietnam not on the basis of what I saw and heard, but on what I was told by other biased Americans. When you see something contradictory, there is always a fellow countryman willing to interpret the significance of it, and it won't be favorable to the Vietnamese. This is due partially to the type of Vietnamese that the typical American meets, coupled with typical American prejudices. During his working hours, the American soldier deals primarily with the Vietnamese military. Many (or most) of the higher-ranking officers attained their status through family position, as a reward for political assistance, and through wealth. Most of the ranking civilians attained their positions in the same manner. They use their offices primarily as a means of adding to their personal wealth. There is hardly any social rapport between GI Joe and his Vietnamese counterpart.

Most contact between Americans and Vietnamese civilians is restricted to taxi drivers, laborers, secretaries, contractors, and bar girls. All these people have one thing in common: They are dependent on Americans for a living. The last three have something else in common. In addition to speaking varying degrees of English, they will tell Americans anything they want to hear as long as the money rolls in. Neither the civilian nor military with whom the American usually has contact is representative of the Vietnamese people.

Many of our military, officers and enlisted, have exported the color prejudice, referring to Vietnamese as "slopes" and "gooks"—two words of endearment left over from Korea. Other fine examples of American Democracy in action are the segregated bars. Although there are exceptions, in Saigon, Nha Trang, and Da Nang and some of the other larger towns, Negroes do not go into white bars except at the risk of being ejected. I have seen more than one incident where a Negro newcomer has made a "mistake" and walked into the wrong bar. If insulting catcalls weren't enough to make him leave, he was thrown out bodily. There are cases where this sort of thing has led to near-riots.

It is obvious that the Vietnamese resent us as well. We are making many of the same mistakes that the French did, and in some instances our mistakes are worse. Arrogance, disrespect, rudeness, prejudice, and our own speical brand of ignorance, are not designed to win friends. This resentment runs all the way from stiff politeness to obvious hatred. It is so common that if a Vietnamese working with or for Americans is found to be sincerely cooperative, energetic, conscientious, and honest, it automatically makes him suspect as a Viet Cong agent.

After my initial assignment in Saigon, which lasted two and one-half months, I volunteered for a new program called Project Delta. This was a classified project wherein specially selected men in Special Forces were to train and organize small teams to be infiltrated into Laos. The primary purpose of dropping these teams into Laos was to try and find the Ho Chi Minh trail and gather information on traffic, troops, weapons, etc. This was purely a reconnaissance intelligence mission, but the possibility of forming guerrilla bases later was considered. There was some talk of going into North Vietnam, but not by Project Delta. Another outfit, Speical Operations Group (SOG) was already doing just that. SOG was a combined forces effort. The CIA, Air Force (US), Navy, Army and detached Special Forces personnel were all in on the act.

Project Delta was paid for by Uncle Sam from CIDG funds. We had to feed, billet and clothe the Vietnamese. Free beer was supplied and lump sums of money were agreed on, money to be paid after completion of training and more to be paid when the teams returned.

Here we are in South Vietnam to help these people "preserve their freedom, etc.," willing to risk our lives to that end and here we are paying them to help themselves. These were men already being paid their regular pay in the Vietnamese Army and we actually had to pay a bonus each time they went to the field on training missions or made a parachute jump, all of which was supposed to be a normal part of their duties.

Originally, it was thought that the teams would be composed of four Vietnamese and two Americans. Although many of the people we were training had natural aptitudes for the area of operations, strong and effective leadership was lacking. It was emphasized constantly to the Pentagon and to the ambassador by those intimately involved in the training program, that if any degree of success was to be realized it was imperative that Americans must accompany the teams.

When at the last minute we received a firm "No Go" for the United States personnel, we asked, "Why?" The answer was that it was an election year and it would cause great embarrassment if Americans were captured in Laos. Anything of that nature would have to wait until after the election. The reaction of this decision on the part of the Americans was one of anger, disappointment and disgust.

The one thing that made it possible to accomplish the things we did was the relationship we had established with the Vietnamese. Each man took it upon himself to establish a friendly relationship with the men on the teams. We

ate the same food, wore the same clothes, lived in the same tents, shared the same hardships. We worked more hours and carried the same loads. We made ourselves the guinea pigs in experiments. The pitch was, "We don't ask you to do anything we won't do ourselves." It worked. We had dedicated teams.

After the decision to eliminate Americans from the drops, the Vietnamese felt that they had been cheated. Petty complaints became rampant; e.g., if we do not get wool sweaters and better watches we will not go. They felt this was one more example of Americans standing back advising Vietnamese on how to get killed without risk to themselves. We started getting an increase in A.W.O.L.s. The Americans had to watch their teams board the infiltration aircraft without them. Hands were shaken but with eyes averted. "Good lucks" were said but with bent heads. We felt guilty. We had strongly advised that the teams not be sent until the Americans could go, but to no avail.

Like everyone, I was disappointed. This was the one thing, if I had to single one out, that made me really start questioning our role in Vietnam. It suddenly occurred to me that the denial of American participation was not based on whether it was right or wrong for us to be going to Laos. The primary concern was the possible embarrassment to President Johnson during an election campaign. Toward this end we sent people on a mission that had little or no chance of success. It became apparent that we were not interested in the welfare of the Vietnamese but, rather, in how we could best promote our own interests. We sent 40 men who had become our friends. These were exceptionally dedicated people, all volunteers, and their CO showed up drunk at the plane to bid the troops farewell—just all boozed up. Six returned, the rest were killed or captured.

As it turned out, the mission found damned little. Most teams didn't last long enough to report what, if anything, they saw. The six survivors came completely through the areas and observed no troop movements, no concentrations of troops, and little vehicle traffic, day or night. In the final stages, two of the project helicopters flew two missions a day for four days, looking for the teams. They saw nothing and were not fired at. As for the highway from Tchepone to Muong Nong, one helicopter flew the highway, taking pictures with a hand-held 35mm camera. It was low enough to take straight-on shots of people standing in doorways.

To many in Vietnam this mission confirmed that the Ho Chi Minh trail, so called, and the traffic on it, was grossly exaggerated, and that the Viet Cong were getting the bulk of their weapons from ARVN and by sea. It also was one more piece of evidence that the Viet Cong were primarily South Vietnamese, not imported troops from the North. One more thing was added to my growing lists of doubts of the "official" stories about Vietnam.

When the project shifted to in-country operations Americans went on drops throughout the Viet Cong-held areas of South Vietnam. One such trip was into War Zone D north of Dong Xoi, near the Michelin plantation. There is no such thing as a typical mission. Each one is different. But this one revealed some startling things. Later I was to brief Secretary of Defense McNamara and General Westmoreland on the limited military value of the bombing, as witnessed on this mission.

As usual we went in at dusk—this time in a heavy rain squall. We moved only a nominal distance, perhaps 300 meters, through the thick, tangled growth and stopped. Without moonlight we were making too much noise. It rained all night so we had to wait until first light to move without crashing around. Moving very cautiously for about an hour, we discovered a deserted company headquarters position, complete with crude tables, stools,

and sleeping racks. After reporting this by radio, we continued on our way. The area was crisscrossed with well-traveled trails under the canopy. A few hours later we reached the edge of a large rubber plantation without incident. Keeping to the thick growth surrounding the plantation, we skirted the perimeter. We discovered that it was completely surrounded by deserted gun positions and fox holes, all with beautiful fields-of-fire down the even rows of rubber trees. None gave evidence of having been occupied for at least three or four days. We transmitted this information to the Tactical Operations Center (TOC) and then the team proceeded across the plantation, heading for the headquarters and housing area in the center.

When we arrived at a point 100 meters from our destination, the team leader and I went forward, leaving the team in a covering position. As we got closer, we could hear sounds from the houses, but assumed these were only workers. The briefing had neglected to tell us that the plantation was supposed to be deserted. Crawling, we stopped about 25 meters from the first line of houses. Lifting our heads, we received a rude shock. These weren't plantation workers. These were Viet Cong soldiers, complete with blue uniforms, webbing, and many with the new Soviet bloc weapons. The atmosphere seemed to be one of relaxation. We could even hear a transistor radio playing music. After 30 or 40 minutes we drew back to the team position. We reported our find to the TOC and estimated the number of Viet Cong to be at least one company. The whole team then retraced the two kilometers to the jungle and moved into it. Crawling into the thickest part, we settled down just as darkness and the rain closed in on us.

Underneath ponchos, to prevent light from our flashlights escaping, the Vietnamese team leader and I, after closely pouring over our maps, drafted a detailed message for TOC. In the morning we sent the message, which gave map coordinates of a number of small Landing Zones (LZs) around the area. We also gave them a plan for exploiting our find. It was fairly simple. Make simultaneous landings at all LZs and have the troops move quickly to the deserted Viet Cong gun positions and man them. At the sight of bombers approaching, the Viet Cong would leave the housing area for the jungle. This would involve them having to travel across two kilometers of open plantation into prepared positions. We told TOC that we were going to try and get back to the housing area so we could tell them if the Viet Cong were still there. If they didn't hear from us on the next scheduled contact, they were to assume that we had been hit and hadn't made it. If this occurred it would be verification of the Viet Cong presence and they were to follow through with the plan. We would stay in the area and join the Rangers when they came in.

This time, we were more cautious in our trip across the plantation. On the way, we found a gasoline cache of 55-gallon drums. We took pictures and proceeded. Again the Vietnamese team leader and I crawled forward to within 25 meters of the houses. It was unbelievable. There they were and still with no perimeter security. Now, however, there was much activity and what seemed like more of them. We inched our way around the house area. This wasn't a company. There were at least 300 armed men in front of us. We had found a battalion, and all in one tight spot—unique in itself. We got back to the team, made our radio contact, and asked if the submitted plan would be implemented. We were told, yes, and that we were to move back to the edge of the jungle. There would be a small delay while coordination was made to get the troops and helicopters. At 1000 hours (10:00 a.m.) planes of all descriptions started crisscrossing this small area. I contacted one plane (there were so many I couldn't tell which one) on the Prick 10 (AN/PRC-10 transmitter-receiver for air-ground communications). I was told that they were reconning the area for an operation. What stupidity. No less than 40 overflights in 45 minutes. As usual, we were alerting the Viet Cong of impending action by letting all the armchair commandos take a look-see. For about 30 minutes all was quiet, and then we started to notice movement. The Viet Cong were moving out from the center of the plantation. Where were the troops? At 1400 hours Skyraiders showed up and started bombing the center of the plantation. Was it possible that the troops had moved in without our knowing it? TOC wouldn't tell us anything. The bombing continued throughout the afternoon with never more than a 15-minute letup. Now we had much company in the jungle with us. Everywhere we turned there were Viet Cong. I had to agree that, in spite of the rain, it was a much better place to be than in the housing center. Why didn't we hear our troops firing?

Finally the bombing ended with the daylight, and we crouched in the wet darkness within hearing distance of Viet Cong elements. Darkness was our fortress. About 2030 (8:30 p.m.) we heard the drone of a heavy aircraft in the rainy sky. We paid little attention to it. Then, without warning, the whole world lit up, leaving us feeling exposed and naked. Two huge flares were swinging gently to earth on their parachutes, one on each side of us. At about the same time, our radio contact plane could be heard above the clouds. I grabbed the radio and demanded to know, "Who the hell is calling for those flares and why?"

"What flares?"

"Damn it, find *out* what flares and tell whoever is calling for them that they're putting us in bad trouble." I could hear the operator trying to call the TOC. I figured that friendly troops in the area had called for the flares to light their perimeter. Crack—crump. I was lifted from the ground, only to be slammed down again. I broke in on the radio. "Forget that transmission. I know why the flares are being dropped."

"Why?"

"They're being used as markers for jets dropping what sounds like 750-pounders. Tell TOC thanks for the warning. Also tell them two of the markers bracketed our position. I hope to hell they knew where we are." A long pause.

"TOC says they don't know anything about flares or jet bombers."

Another screwup. "Well how about somebody finding out something and when they find out, how about telling us unimportant folks? In the meantime, I hope that 'gooniebird' (C-47 plane) has its running lights on."

"Why?"

"Because any moment now the pilot is going to find he is dawdling around in a bomb run pattern. Come back early in the morning and give me the hot skinny."

"Roger—we're leaving—out."

I was mad, a pretty good sign that I was scared. The bombing continued through the night. Sometimes it was "crump" and sometimes it was "crack," depending on how close the bombs fell. When it finally stopped sometime before dawn, I realized that it was a dazzling exhibition of flying—worthless—but impressive. The flare ship had to fly so low because of the cloud cover that its flares were burning out on the ground instead of in the air. The orbiting jets would then dive down through the clouds, break through, spot the markers, make split-second corrections, and release their bombs. However, while it was going on, considering what a small error became at jet speeds, a small error would wipe us out. Should this happen, I could see a bad case of *"C'est la guerre"* next day at air opera-

tions. I couldn't help wondering also how "Charlie" was feeling about all this—specifically the ones only 25 or 30 meters away. It didn't seem possible, but I wondered if the shrapnel tearing through the tree tops was terrifying him as much as us.

First thing in the morning, my Vietnamese counterpart made contact on the big radio (HC-162D). After some talk into the mike, he turned to me with a helpless look:

"They say we must cross plantation to housing area again."

"What? It's impossible—tell them so."

More talk. "They say we must go. They want to talk to you."

When the hollow voice came through on the side band, I couldn't believe it—it was the same order. I told them it was impossible and that we were not going to go.

"You must go. That is an order from way up."

That figures. The Saigon wheels smelling glory have taken over our TOC. "My answer is, Will Not Comply; I say again, Will Not Comply. Tell those people to stop trying to outguess the man on the ground. If they want someone to assess damage on the housing area send a plane with a camera. Better yet, have the Rangers look at it, there's more of them."

"There are no other friendly troops in the area. You are the only ones that can do it. You must go. There will be a plane in your area shortly. Out."

Up to this point we had assumed friendly troops were in the area and that if we got in trouble, maybe we could hold out until they could help us. No troops. Little wonder the Viet Cong are roaming all over the place not caring who hears them.

Soon a plane arrived and I received: "We must know how many Viet Cong are still in the housing area. You must go and look. It is imperative. The whole success of this mission depends on your report. Over."

"I say again, Will Not Comply. Over." (Hello court martial.) I looked at the Vietnamese team leader. He was tense and grim, but silently cheering me on. While waiting for the plane I asked him what he was going to do. He replied:

"We go, we die. Order say we must go, so we go. We will die."

Tell me Vietnamese have no guts. Another transmission from the plane:

"Why won't you comply? Over."

These type questions aren't normally answered. I knew, however, that the poor bastard up there had to take an answer back to the wheels. Well, he got one: "Because we can't. One step out of this jungle and it's all over. I'm not going to have this team wiped out for nothing. There are no Viet Cong in the village; not since 1400 yesterday. The mission was screwed up when you started the bombing without sending in troops yesterday. As for the mission depending on us, you should have thought of that yesterday before you scrapped the plans and didn't bother to tell us. Over."

"Where are the Viet Cong now? Over."

"Which ones? The ones 25 meters from us, or the ones 35 meters from us? They're in the jungle all around us. Over."

"Roger. Understand Viet Cong have left houses—now in jungle—have information necessary—you do not have to go across Plantation."

This was unbelievable. On TV it would be a comedy—a bad one.

Shortly after this uplifting exchange, the bombers returned, and we spent the remainder of the day moving from one Viet Cong group to another. We would come upon them, pull back, and then an A1-E (bomber) would come whining down, machine-gunning or dropping bombs.

I discovered that the old prop fighter bombers were more terrifying than the jets. The jets came in so fast that the man on the ground couldn't hear them until the bombs were dropped and they were climbing away. The props were something else. First the droning noise while in orbit. Then they would peel off and the drone would change to a growl, increasing steadily in pitch until they were a screaming whine. Under the jungle canopy, this noise grabbed at the heart of every man. And every man knew that the plane was pointed directly at him. The crack of the bomb exploding was almost a relief. Many of these bombs landed 25 to 35 meters from where we were lying on the ground. The closest any of us came to being hurt was when a glowing piece of shrapnel lodged in the pack on my back. I couldn't help thinking, "These are our planes. They know where we are. What must it be like for a woman or child to hear that inhuman, impersonal whine directed at them in their open villages? How they must hate us!" I looked around at my team. Others were thinking. Each of us died a little that day in the jungle.

At 1730 (5:30 P.M) the last bomb was dropped. A great day for humanity. Almost 28 hours of bombing in this small area with barely a break.

On the next afternoon we were told by radio to quickly find an LZ and prepare to leave the area. We knew of only one within reasonable distance and headed for it. A short distance from the LZ we could hear voices. Viet Cong around the opening. We were now an equal distance between two groups of the Viet Cong.

Finally they allowed the pick-up ship to come in. Just as the plane touched down and we started toward it, two machine gun positions opened up—one from each side of the clearing. The bullets sounded like gravel hitting the aluminum skin of the chopper. An American assistant took one position under fire and I started firing at the other. Our backs were to the aircraft and our eyes on the jungle. The rest of the team started climbing aboard.

The machine guns were still firing, but we had made them less accurate. I was still firing when two strong hands picked me up and plumped me on the floor of the plane. Maximum power and we still couldn't make the trees at the end of the clearing, but had to make a half-circle over the machine guns. All of a sudden something slapped me in the buttock, lifting me from the floor. A bullet had come through the bottom of the plane, through the gas tank and the floor. When it ripped through the floor it turned sideways. The slug left an eight-inch bruise but did not penetrate. Through some miracle, we were on our way to base—all of us. We would all get drunk tonight. It was the only way we would sleep without reliving the past days. It would be at least three days before anybody would unwind. That much is typical.

I had seen the effect of the bombing at close range. These bombs would land and go for about 15 yards and tear off a lot of foliage from the trees, but that was it. Unless you drop these things in somebody's hip pocket they don't do any good. For 28 hours they bombed that area. And it was rather amusing because, when I came out, it was estimated that they had killed about 250 Viet Cong in the first day. They asked me how many Viet Cong did I think they had killed and I said maybe six, and I was giving them the benefit of the doubt at that. The bombing had no real military significance. It would only work if aimed at concentrated targets such as villages.

One of the first axioms one learns about unconventional warfare is that no insurgent or guerrilla movement can endure without the support of the people. While doing research in my job as an Area Specialist, I found that, in province after province, the Viet Cong guerrillas had started as small teams. They were now in battalion and regimental strength. Before I left, the Viet Cong could put troops in the field in division strength in almost any province. Such growth is not only impossible without popular support, it actually requires an overwhelming mandate.

We were still being told, both by our own government and the Saigon government, that the vast majority of the people of South Vietnam were opposed to the Viet Cong. When I questioned this contradiction, I was always told that the people only helped the Viet Cong through fear. Supposedly, the Viet Cong held the people in the grip of terror by assassination and torture. This argument was also against doctrine. Special Forces are taught that reliable support can be gained only through friendship and trust. History denied the "terror" argument. The people feared and hated the French, and they rose up against them. It became quite obvious that a minority movement could not keep tabs on a hostile majority. South Vietnam is a relatively small country, dotted with thousands of small villages. In this very restricted area companies and battalions of Viet Cong can maneuver and live under the very noses of government troops; but the people don't betray these movements, even though it is a relatively simple thing to pass the word. On the other hand, government troop movements are always reported. In an action against the Viet Cong, the only hope for surprise is for the government to move the troops by helicopters. Even this is no guarantee. General Nguyen Khan, while still head of the Saigon government, acknowledged that Viet Cong sympathizers and agents were everywhere—even in the inner councils—when he made the statement: "Any operation that lets more than four hours elapse between conception and implementation is doomed to failure." He made these remarks in the last days of his regime, right after a personally directed operation north of Saigon ended in disaster.

To back up the terror theory, the killing of

village chiefs and their families were pointed out to me. Those that were quick to point at these murders ignored certain facts. Province, district, village and hamlet chiefs are appointed, not elected. Too often petty officials are not even people from the area but outsiders being rewarded for political favors. Those that are from the area are thought of as quislings because they have gone against their own by cooperating with Saigon. Guerrillas or partisans who killed quislings in World War II were made heros in American movies. Those who look on the Viet Cong killings of these people with horror and use them as justification for our having to beat them, don't realize that our own military consider such actions good strategy when the tables are reversed. When teaching Special Forces how to set up guerrilla warfare in an enemy country, killing unpopular officials is pointed out as one method of gaining friends among the populace. It is recommended that special assassination teams be set up for this purpose.

I know a couple of cases where it was suggested by Special Forces officers that Viet Cong prisoners be killed. In one case in which I was involved, we had picked up prisoners in the valley around An Khe. We didn't want prisoners but they walked into our hands. We were supposed to stay in the area four more days, and there were only eight of us and four of them, and we didn't know what the hell to do with them. You can't carry them. Food is limited, and the way the transmission went with the base camp you knew what they wanted you to do—get rid of them. I wouldn't do that, and when I got back to operation base a major told me, "You know we almost told you right over the phone to do them in." I said that I was glad he didn't, because it would have been embarrassing to refuse to do it. I knew goddamn well I wasn't going to kill them. In a fight it's one thing, but with guys with their hands bound it's another. And I wouldn't have been able to

shoot them because of the noise. It would have had to be a very personal thing, like sticking a knife into them. The major said, "Oh, you wouldn't have had to do it; all you had to do was give them over to the Vietnamese." Of course, this is supposed to absolve you of any responsibility. This is the general attitude. It's really a left-handed morality. Very few of the Special Forces guys had any qualms about this. Damn few.

Little by little, as all these facts made their impact on me. I had to accept the fact that, Communist or not, the vast majority of the people were pro-Viet Cong and anti-Saigon. I had to accept also that the position, "We are in Vietnam because we are in sympathy with the aspirations and desires of the Vietnamese people," was a lie. If this is a lie, how many others are there?

I suppose that one of the things that bothered me from the very beginning in Vietnam was the condemnation of ARVN as a fighting force: "the Vietnamese are cowardly . . . the Vietnamese can't be disciplined . . . the Vietnamese just can't understand tactics and strategy . . . etc., etc." But the Viet Cong are Vietnamese. United States military files in Saigon document time and again a Viet Cong company surrounding two or even three ARVN companies and annihilating them. These same files document instances of a Viet Cong company, surrounded by ARVN battalions, mounting a ferocious fight and breaking loose. I have seen evidence of the Viet Cong attacking machinegun positions across open terrain with terrible losses. This can't be done with undisciplined bandits. For many years now the tactics and strategy of the Viet Cong have been so successful that massive fire power and air support on our side is the only thing that has prevented a Viet Cong victory. These are all Vietnamese. What makes the difference? Major "Charging Charlie" Beckwith, the Special Forces commander at Plei Me, used the words "dedicated", "tough", "disciplined", "well-trained", and "brave" to describe the Viet Cong—and, almost in the same breath, condemned the Vietnamese on our side.

It became obvious that motivation is the prime factor in this problem. The Viet Cong soldier believes in his cause. He believes he is fighting for national independence. He has faith in his leaders, whose obvious dedication is probably greater than his own. His officers live in the same huts and eat the same food. His government counterpart knows that his leaders are in their positions because of family, money or reward for political favors. He knows his officers' primary concern is gaining wealth and favor. Their captains and majors eat in French restaurants and pay as much for one meal as they make in a week. They sleep in guarded villas with their mistresses. They find many excuses for not being with their men in battle. They see the officers lie about their roles in battle. The soldier knows that he will be cheated out of his pay if possible. He knows equipment he may need is being sold downtown. His only motivation is the knowledge that he is fighting only to perpetuate a system that has kept him uneducated and in poverty. He has had so many promises made to him, only to be broken, that now he believes nothing from his government.

I have seen the South Vietnamese soldier fight well, and at times ferociously, but usually only when in a position where there is no choice. At those times he is fighting for survival. On Project Delta there were many brave Vietnamese. When I knew them well enough to discuss such things, I asked them, "Why do you go on these missions time and again? You are volunteers. Why do you not quit and do less dangerous work?" The answer was always the same: "We are friends. We fight well together. If we quit, it will make the project bad." Never, "We are fighting for democracy . . .

freedom . . . the people . . . " or any cause. The "enemy" he was fighting had become an abstraction. He was fighting, and fighting well, to sustain the brotherhood of his friends. The project had created a mystique of individualism and eliteness. He felt important. Trust and faith was put in him and he returned it in kind. The Americans didn't condescend to him. The life of every American on the team was dependent on the Vietnamese, and we let them know we were aware of it. We found out early that appealing to them on the basis of patriotism was a waste of time. They felt that they were nothing more than tools of the scheming Saigon politicians.

ARVN troops and their commanders know that if they don't bother the Viet Cong they will be safe from Viet Cong attacks. I'll never forget what a shock it was to find out that various troop commanders and District Chiefs were actually making personal deals with "the enemy." The files in Saigon record instances where government troops with American advisors were told by the Viet Cong to lay down their weapons and walk away from the Americans. The troops did just that and the Viet Cong promises of safety to the troops were honored.

In an effort to show waning popularity for the Viet Cong, great emphasis was placed on figures of Viet Cong defections. Even if the unlikely possibility of the correctness of these figures is accepted, they are worthless when compared to ARVN desertions. The admitted desertion rate and incidents of draft dodging, although deflated, was staggering. Usually, only those caught are reported. Reading OPSUMS (Operational Summaries) and newspapers while in Vietnam, I repeatedly saw references made to hundreds of ARVN listed as missing after the major battles. The reader is supposed to conclude that these hundreds, which by now total thousands, are prisoners of the Viet Cong. They are defintely not listed as deserters. If this were true, half of the Viet Cong would be tied down as guards in POW compounds—which, of course, is ridiculous.

This lack of enthusiasm and reluctance to join in battle wasn't difficult to figure. The majority of the people are either anti-Saigon or pro-Viet Cong, or both, and ARVN is drafted from the people.

I was not unique among my contemporaries in knowing most of these things. However, whenever anybody questioned our being in Vietnam—in light of the facts—the old rationale was always presented: "We have to stop the spread of communism somewhere . . . if we don't fight the commies here, we'll have to fight them at home . . . if we pull out, the rest of Asia will go Red . . . these are uneducated people who have been duped; they don't understand the difference between democracy and communism. . . ."

Being extremely anti-Communist myself, these "arguments" satisfied me for a long time. In fact, I guess it was saying these very same things to myself over and over again that made it possible for me to participate in the things I did in Vietnam. But were we stopping communism? Even during the short period I had been in Vietnam, the Viet Cong had obviously gained in strength; the government controlled less and less of the country every day. The more troops and money we poured in, the more people hated us. Countries all over the world were losing sympathy with our stand in Vietnam. Countries which up to now had preserved a neutral position were becoming vehemently anti-American. A village near Tay Ninh in which I had slept in safety six months earlier was the center of a Viet Cong operation that cost the lives of two American friends. A Special Force team operating in the area was almost decimated over a period of four months. United States Operations Mission (USOM), civilian representatives, who had been able to travel by vehicle in relative safety throughout the countryside, were being kidnapped and killed. Like the military, they now had to travel by air.

The real question was, whether communism is spreading in spite of our involvement or because of it.

The attitude that the uneducated peasant lacked the political maturity to decide between communism and democracy and ". . . we are only doing this for your own good," although it had a familiar colonialistic ring, at first seemed to have merit. Then I remembered that most of the villages would be under Viet Cong control for some of the time and under government control at other times. How many Americans had such a close look at both sides of the cloth? The more often government troops passed through an area, the more surely it would become sympathetic to the Viet Cong. The Viet Cong might sleep in the houses, but the government troops ransacked them. More often than not, the Viet Cong helped plant and harvest the crops; but invariably government troops in an area razed them. Rape is severely punished among the Viet Cong. It is so common among the ARVN that it is seldom reported for fear of even worse atrocities.

I saw the Airborne Brigade come into Nha Trang. Nha Trang is a government town and the Vietnamese Airborne Brigade are government troops. They were originally, in fact, trained by Special Forces, and they actually had the town in a grip of terror for three days. Merchants were collecting money to get them out of town; cafes and bars shut down.

The troops were accosting women on the streets. They would go into a place—a bar or cafe—and order varieties of food. When the checks came they wouldn't pay them. Instead they would simply wreck the place, dumping over the tables and smashing dishes. While these men were accosting women, the police would just stand by, powerless or unwilling to help. In fact, the situation is so difficult that American troops, if in town at the same time as the Vietnamese Airborne Brigade, are told to stay off the streets at night to avoid coming to harm.

The whole thing was a lie. We weren't preserving freedom in South Vietnam. There was no freedom to preserve. To voice opposition to the government meant jail or death. Neutralism was forbidden and punished. Newspapers that didn't say the *right* thing were closed down. People are not even free to leave and Vietnam is one of those rare countries that doesn't fill its American visa quota. It's all there to see once the Red film is removed from the eyes. We aren't the freedom fighters. We are the Russian tanks blasting the hopes of an Asian Hungary.

It's not democracy we brought to Vietnam— it's anti-communism. This is the only choice the people in the village have. This is why most of them have embraced the Viet Cong and shunned the alternative. The people remember that when they were fighting the French for their national independence it was the Americans who helped the French. It's the American anti-Communist bombs that kill their children. It's American anti-communism that has supported one dictator after another in Saigon. When anti-Communist napalm burns their children it matters little that an anti-Communist Special Forces medic comes later to apply bandages.

One day I asked one of our Vietnamese helicopter pilots what he thought of the last bomb raid. "I think maybe today we make many Viet Cong." In July, when Mr. McNamara asked me how effective the bombing was in War Zone D I told him. "It's an expensive defoliant. Unless dropped in a hip pocket it was only effective in housing areas." He didn't seem surprised. In fact, his only comment after my recital of my team's ex-

periences in War Zone D, was when he turned to General Westmoreland who was sitting on my right, "I guess we still have a small reaction problem." Ambassador Taylor said nothing.

While I was in Vietnam the American and/or Saigon government was forever carping about North Vietnam breaking the Geneva Accords. Yet my own outfit, Special Forces, had first come to Vietnam in civilian clothes traveling on civilian passports for the specific purpose of training and arming the ethnic groups for the CIA, a violation of the Accords. The Saigon respect for the Accords was best symbolized by a political cartoon in the Saigon Post. It showed a man urinating on a scroll labeled Geneva Accords 1954. When the troops of Project Delta uncovered the arms cache at Vung Ro Bay, General Nguyen Khan pointing at the weapons, happily presented them to the three ICC men as proof to the world that Hanoi was breaking the Accords. Evidently they were too polite to point out that they had been found by men wearing American-supplied uniforms, carrying American weapons; men who had been trained by Americans and were being paid by Americans. Neither did they mention that the General flew to this spot in an American helicopter and that the weapons were being loaded onto an American-made ship manned by American-trained sailors.

It had taken a long time and a mountain of evidence but I had finally found some truths. The world is not just good guys and bad guys. Anti-communism is a lousy substitute for democracy. I know now that there are many types of communism but there are none that appeal to me. In the long run, I don't think Vietnam will be better off under Ho's brand of communism. But it's not for me or my government to decide. That decision is for the Vietnamese. I also know that we have allowed the creation of a military monster that will lie to our elected officials; and that both of them will lie to the American people.

To those people who, while deploring the war and bombings, defend it on the basis that it is stopping communism, remember the words of the Vietnamese pilot, "I think maybe today we make many Viet Cong." The Nazi bombing of London didn't make the Londoners quit. We have no monopoly on feelings for the underdog. People of other nations will continue to be increasingly sympathetic to this small agrarian country that is being pounded by the richest and most powerful nation in the world.

When I returned from Vietnam I was asked, "Do you resent young people who have never been in Vietnam, or in any war, protesting it?" On the contrary, I am relieved. I think they should be commended. I had to wait until I was 35 years old, after spending 10 years in the Army and 18 months personally witnessing the stupidity of the war, before I could figure it out. That these young people were able to figure it out so quickly and so accurately is not only a credit to their intelligence but a great personal triumph over a lifetime of conditioning and indoctrination. I only hope that the picture I have tried to create will help other people come to the truth without wasting 10 years. Those people protesting the war in Vietnam are not against our boys in Vietnam. On the contrary. What they are against is our boys *being* in Vietnam. They are not unpatriotic. Again the opposite is true. They are opposed to people, our own and others, dying for a lie, thereby corrupting the very word democracy.

There are those who will believe that I only started to feel these things after I returned from Vietnam. In my final weeks in that country I was putting out a very small information paper for Special Forces. The masthead of the paper was a flaming torch. I tried in my own way to bring a little light to the men with whom I worked. On the last page of the first issue were the names of four men—all friends of mine—reported killed in action on the same day. Among them was Sgt. Horner, one of the men I "procured" for Special Forces when he was stationed at the Army Presidio in San Francisco.

To those friends I wrote this dedication:

"We can best immortalize our fallen members by striving for an enlightened future where Man has found another solution to his problems rather than resorting to the futility and stupidity of war."

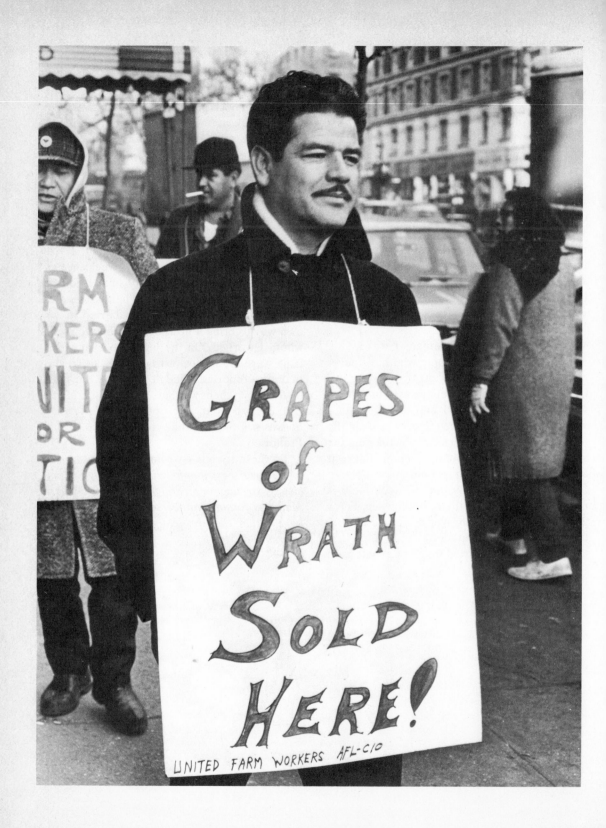

Section Three

Organizing the Unorganized: The California Grape Boycott

For both field workers and family farmers, making a living from the land has always been difficult in California. As early as 1888, the English critic James Bryce wrote in his *American Commonwealth:*

> When California was ceded to the United States, land speculators bought up large tracts under Spanish title, and others, foreseeing the coming prosperity, subsequently acquired great domains by purchase, land grants, or directly from the government. . . . Thus the land system of California presents features both peculiar and dangerous, a contrast between great properties, often appearing to conflict with the general weal, and the sometimes hard pressed small farmer, together with a mass of unsettled labor, thrown without work into the towns at certain times of the year.

Eighty years later, Harrison Williams, Chairman of the Senate Subcommittee on Migratory Labor, noted the same pattern of inequities in California agriculture. "Both small family farmers and field workers are at a competitive disadvantage vis-à-vis the huge agribusiness concerns in selling their labor and their products," he observed. "In California . . . 10 percent of

the farms employ 80 percent of the farmworkers. 6.0 percent of California's farms own 75 percent of the land, and 5.2 percent of California's
farms pay 60.2 percent of the farm labor wages."

For farm workers, who earn low wages and often move from job to job
to keep up with the picking season, the power of the growers with whom
they must bargain has been only the first of the problems they faced. Farm
labor in California has traditionally been thought of as work suited for
"foreigners." Chinese, Japanese, Filipinos, Mexicans have all gone through
periods of being hired at subsistence wages and fired as soon as they demanded changes in their work and pay. In the past, nothing in California
has been considered more un-American than trying to organize agricultural workers. State officials have a tradition of union busting that includes
such episodes as a general roundup of Wobbly (I.W.W.) organizers in the
years before World War I, and the mass arrest during the depression of the
leaders of the Cannery and Agricultural Workers Union (two years later
their conviction under the Criminal Syndicalism Law was reversed, but the
Union had been ruined).

In the early 1960s, when organizing among California farm workers began again, agricultural unions in the state were still looked upon with great
suspicion. Federal and state law worked against them. The *bracero* law,
which was not repealed until 1964, allowed growers to depress wages by
hiring Mexican nationals for the season. Then, as now, farm workers received a lower minimum wage than industrial workers, were in most cases
excluded from social security and unemployment coverage, and as a group
were unprotected by New Deal Legislation as basic as the National Labor
Relations Act.

It was with these conditions in mind that Cesar Chavez left the Com-
munity Services Organization founded by Saul Alinsky and moved to
Delano, California, where in 1962 he began the National Farm Workers
Association (NFWA). Three years later, when Filipino workers from the
Agricultural Workers Organizing Committee (AWOC) struck a series of
Delano grape growers, the NFWA joined them. The California grape strike
and boycott had begun. In 1966 AWOC and the NFWA merged to form the
United Farm Workers Organizing Committee, and a national boycott of
Schenley Liquors and DiGiorgio S&W brands unionized the fields these
companies owned. A year later, in August 1967, a strike and boycott
started against the Giumarra Corporation and soon spread to the remaining unsigned grape growers in California.

The four reports in this section cover the California grape boycott from
its start in 1965 to its conclusion in 1970. It is the tactical success of the
United Farm Workers, their ability to win a 1930s struggle in the 1960s, that
these accounts concern themselves with in particular. They also describe
an equally important matter, the underlying spirit of a union in whose
offices posters of Gandhi and Zapata can be found on the same wall.

The chapters included here from John Gregory Dunne's book *Delano: The Story of the California Grape Strike,* provide an overview of the grape boycott. Dunne has chosen to focus on the town of Delano and to give an account of the contrasts between the growers and the farm workers. Thus, he moves from a picture of the "Anglo" side of Delano to one of the Mexican and Filipino side, from the Farm Workers offices to the DiGiorgio ranch, from a grower talking about his problems to a field hand complaining about being charged for drinking water. Dunne, who arrived in Delano during the summer of 1966, sees both sides deadlocked against each other in a "holding phase, somewhat akin to the trench warfare of World War I." There is rarely any resolution that comes from the contrasts he presents, only antagonisms that draw more and more people into opposing camps.

The other three accounts in this section are different from Dunne's in that they provide more of an insider's view of the United Farm Workers. In the case of Edgar Friedenberg, whose "Another America" was written prior to the merger of AWOC and NFWA, the emphasis is on the difficulties the farm workers faced at the start of their strike. Although sympathetic to the aims of the strike, Friedenberg is not confident it will be successful. In his account of an early morning picket line or the problem of reaching a worker isolated in company housing, he continually stresses the difficulties facing the Union. In the end it is the sense of selfhood the grape strike gave the farm workers that Friedenberg finds most important.

By contrast, my account of the Farm Workers, "The Whip and the Bee: Diary from the Grape Strike" is preoccupied with the matter of winning. The diary is an organizer's notebook that begins with my arrival in Delano prior to the 1967 strike against the Guimarra Corporation and concludes with the end of the grape boycott three years later. The order of events in the diary is the order of events in the Guimarra strike. The diary builds from the period when the Union quietly gathered worker support, to the time when it began planning for a strike vote, to the strike itself. The concern with selfhood that Friedenberg finds so important is not forgotten, but at the heart of the diary lies my belief that for the Farm Workers the crucial problem was proving they could defeat the growers.

Peter Matthiessen, in the section included from his book *Sal Si Puedes: Cesar Chavez and the New American Revolution,* focuses on the relationship between Chavez and the United Farm Workers. (*Sal Si Puedes,* a Spanish expression meaning "Escape if you can," is the name given the area in San Jose where Chavez once lived.) It is Chavez's nonviolence that most interests Matthiessen, and the central event in his account is the 25-day fast Chavez began on February 14, 1968, to protest the violence he saw threatening the grape boycott. Matthiessen explores both Chavez's commitment to nonviolence and the relationship his nonviolence has to the United Farm Workers' organizing. The result is a narrative that moves between the very practical and the intensely personal and climaxes with the speech Chavez used to explain his fast:

> When we are really honest with ourselves, we must admit that our lives are all that really belong to us. So it is how we use our lives that determines what kind of men we are. It is my deepest belief that only by giving our lives do we find life. I am convinced that the truest act of courage, the strongest act of manliness, is to sacrifice ourselves for others in a totally nonviolent struggle for justice.

Delano:
The Story of the California Grape Strike
John Gregory Dunne

John Gregory Dunne, now living in Los Angeles, worked for eight years as a magazine writer in New York City. His articles have appeared in the *Saturday Review, Holiday, Life, Venture, National Review,* and the *New Republic.* He is the author of *Delano: The Story of the California Grape Strike* and *Studio,* a book about the movie industry.

"HUNGRY? TIRED? CAR TROUBLE? NEED GAS?" the road sign beckons from the shoulder of Highway 99. "STOP IN DELANO." Until the strike began in September, 1965, there were few other reasons to stop in Delano.

Geographically, Delano (pronounced Del-*ay*no) is located in the San Joaquin Valley, that part of the Great Central Valley drained by the San Joaquin River. It was founded by the Southern Pacific Railroad in 1873 and the SP, its eye characteristically trained on favors from Washington, named its new rail site after Christopher Delano, Secretary of the Interior under Ulysses S. Grant. For nearly fifty years the town languished in the semidesert of northern Kern County, just south of the Tulare County line. It was not until after the turn of the century, when land was becoming scarce in California, that farmers saw the possibilities in tapping the reservoirs of underground water beneath Delano. With irrigation, Delano began to flourish. The climate was perfect for grapes, and with the added water from the state and federally sponsored Central Valley Project, the town was gradually enclosed in a 37,000 acre vise of Ribiers, Parlettes, Muscats, Almerias, Emperors, and Thompsons.

It is not the grapes, however, but the grape growers that make Delano unique in the Valley. In the 1920's, the climate and fertility of the local vineyards attracted to Delano a contingent of Yugoslavian emigrants who had tended grapes for generations along the Adriatic. Today these Yugoslavians, mostly second generation with a smattering of first-generation patriarchs, set the social tone of Delano. The signs on the packing sheds and along the county roads tell the story—Gutunich, Radovich, Pandol, Caratan; in the Delano telephone book, there are twenty-three "Zaninovich" listings alone. The Yugoslavians have intermarried and crossbred and made a world unto themselves. This is not that part of the Valley where the growers belong to the country club and their daughters to the Junior League. There is no country club at all in Delano; the social life of the growers revolves around the Elks Club and the Slav Hall.

Today the population of Delano is approximately 14,000 and it is split almost evenly between the "Anglos," who live east of the freeway, and the Mexicans, the Filipinos, and the few Negroes who live west of Highway 99. (The term "Anglo," as it is used in the Valley, encompasses all whites, save Mexicans, whether they be Christian or Jew, of eastern or southern European origin.) The town has twenty-eight churches, four elementary schools, one high school, a general hospital with forty beds, a twice-weekly newspaper, four banks, eight doctors, four dentists, three optometrists, and two chiropractors. The East Side is somnolent and well-kept and no different from any one of a dozen other Valley towns. Most of Delano's businesses are located here, the kind whose owners attend the Lions Club or Rotary International luncheons once a week in the Blue Room at the Stardust Motel. There is an International Harvester franchise, a Bank of America branch, two movie theaters (one of which shows Mexican films twice a week), several motels, a Fosters' Freeze, Marshall's Pharmacy, Mulligan's Furniture Store, but no bookstore; the nearest is in Bakersfield, thirty miles to the south. Little distinguishes one East Side residential street from another; block succeeds block of pastel ranch-style bungalows, their exteriors already faded and pockmarked from falling plaster. And then there is The Terrace, the crescent-shaped silk-stocking district of Delano, where the houses are a little bigger, the lots a little larger, and the sunflowers a little taller. Some of the children of the big growers live on The Terrace, as does the president of the local bank, in a mock colonial house which is the only conventional two-story dwelling in view.

At first impression, the West Side looks little different from the East Side. But slowly it becomes apparent that Highway 99 is a social as well as a geographical line of demarcation between the two Delanos. It is not just that the skins of the people on the West Side are darker. The bungalows are shabbier and the cars are older. Occasionally a drainage ditch is exposed, and there are more potholes in the streets. Just west of the Southern Pacific tracks is a strip of lo-ball and draw-poker parlors with names like Divina's Four Deuces, the Monte Carlo, the Guadalajara. Every night, old Mexicans in stained straw field hats and faded work shirts sit stolidly around the tables watching the cards passed to them. It was in this area that Delano's once flourishing red-light district was located. One night in the Four Deuces I asked an old field worker what he thought of the situation in Delano, and he answered, "This used to be a good town before." It turned out that he meant before the construction of the freeway leveled the red-light district; the strike, in his opinion, was only a further and somewhat anticlimactic step in the decline of Delano.

The headquarters of Cesar Chavez's National Farm Workers' Association at 102 Albany Street is no more nor less seedy than the rest of the West Side. The building itself has had a checkered history. Before the NFWA moved in, it had been at various times a grocery and a Jehovah's Witnesses Hall. At almost any hour of the day or night, the NFWA's rolling stock—decrepit automobiles which seem glued together with spit and baling wire from the discards of some manic used-car lot—are parked outside. The cars are easily identifiable in Delano and are at times handy targets. A few days before my arrival in town, a Rambler driven by Chavez's administrative assistant; the Reverend James Drake of the California Migrant Ministry, which has been intimately involved with the strike since its outset, was shot up by assailants unknown, who peppered its chassis and blew out its windows with shotgun pellets while it stood empty outside 102 Albany.

The interior of NFWA headquartsers is a dusty, chaotic shambles of plywood partitions, mimeograph machines, and battered desks. Pasted in the window are paper reproductions of the NFWA's splendidly barbaric coat of arms—a black eagle on a scarlet field on which is printed the Spanish word for strike, HUELGA. The coat of arms is strongly reminiscent of the symbol for the New Deal's National Recovery Administration, but among the townspeople of Delano it is invariably spoken of as "Chavez's Trotsky flag." On every available inch of wall, there is a profusion of maps, telephone numbers, picket instructions, and cartoons which unfailingly depict the growers in planter's hats and sunglasses, smoking fat cigars and carrying bullwhips. Strewn around the outer office are copies of the *Butterick Home Catalogue* and back issues of *Coed* magazine. (One day I came upon a hefty Mexican woman, with most of her teeth missing, engrossed in a *Coed* article entitled "How to Act on a Double Date" and containing such instructions as: "Bring your coat to the table. Tipping is expensive.") The only thing in repose in the whole office is a statue of the Virgin of Guadalupe, patron saint of the NFWA and of the strike.

Tacked to the back wall is a single sheet of paper which, though a joke, attests more than anything else in the room to what life has been like in Delano for the past year. On it are listed the recipients of "The Order of the Purple Grape—the official decoration of the NFWA for injury in action." Among the recipients were a volunteer who had had a shotgun fired over his head by a security guard at one of the ranches, a striker narrowly missed by another shotgun blast, and a one-armed NFWA supporter who had been beaten up by a grower. Perhaps the most illuminating example was that of the Reverend David Havens of the Migrant Ministry. A month or so after the strike started, when the growers had begun bringing in workers from other parts of California and out of state to replace those who had walked out, Havens went out on the picket line one day and, in defiance of deputies from the Kern County sheriff's office, began reading Jack London's famous "Definition of a Strikebreaker":

> After God had finished the rattlesnake, the toad and the vampire, He had some awful substance left with which he made a strikebreaker. A strikebreaker is a two-legged animal with a corkscrew soul, a waterlogged brain and a combination backbone made of jelly and glue. When a strikebreaker comes down the street, men turn their backs and angels weep in Heaven and the devil shuts the gates of Hell to keep him out. Judas Iscariot was a gentleman compared to the strikebreaker. The modern strikebreaker sells his birthright, his country, his wife, his children and his fellow men for an unfulfilled promise from his employer, trust or corporation. There is nothing lower than a strikebreaker.

No sooner had Havens finished than he was arrested by the sheriff's deputies for disturbing the peace. The case was later dismissed in court.

I knew little about the care and cultivation of grapes when I arrived in Delano in the summer of 1966, save for the fact that table grapes presented a greater opportunity for union organizers than any other seasonal crops. Unlike lettuce or asparagus, grapes require attention for some ten months a year. They must be sprayed, trimmed, and girdled. Each process takes a certain degree of skill. As a result, the labor force is relatively stable. There are few migrants, except during the harvest, and since the residents can put in nearly a full year's work, their income levels are accordingly higher. As the richest of the poor, they are less apathetic than migrants whose overriding considerations are the next job, the next meal, and hence more susceptible to an organizing effort.

A day or so after I checked into the Stardust Motel, I drove down to the DiGiorgio Corporation's ranch in Arvin, some thirty miles south of Delano, to see how grapes are grown and how a huge corporation ranch is run. The Arvin ranch has 9,000 acres, slightly less than half planted in grapes, the rest in plums, potatoes, asparagus, cotton, peanuts, wheat, barley, and black-eyed beans. Unlike DiGiorgio's 4,400-acre Sierra Vista ranch in Delano, it was not then being struck. I was met by Joseph A. DiGiorgio, a vice president of the DiGiorgio Corporation and head of its farming operation. (Farming accounts for less than ten percent of DiGiorgio's annual sales of

$230 million; the bulk of its income derives from food processing and grocery wholesaling.) Joseph DiGiorgio is a short, tanned, muscular man in late middle age, with the classic profile of a Renaissance pope. He wore a straw planter's hat with a madras band, a neatly pressed blue buttoned-down sport shirt and work shoes so brightly polished that they would have done credit to a member of a military drill team. He suggested that the best way to see the ranch operate was to drive around with him for the rest of the day, and so I got into his car. There was a two-way radio in the car, and periodically through the morning and afternoon he would call back instructions to his office and receive reports from field foremen.

DiGiorgio explained that the grape season is progressive, proceeding from Coachella and Borrego over to the high desert in Arizona, then back to Arvin, up to Delano, and on up the Valley. In the best of years, the seasons do not overlap and there is no price break, but when they do, as they did in 1965, so many grapes hit the market at the same time that the price plummets. Thus, though 1965 was a vintage year in quality and quantity, many grape ranchers took a serious beating. We passed through vineyards of Cardinals, Thompsons, Ribiers, Red Malagas, Emperors, Almerias, Calmerias, and Muscats, and at each we stopped to sample the grapes. Some were quite tart and not yet ready for picking. I was told that it takes five years to bring a vine into full production and that the productive life of a quality vine ranges from twenty-five to thirty years. Then the vines are pulled out and the land reworked for several years with other crops, such as cotton or potatoes. Throughout the year, there is constant cultural work to be done. Girdling is one example. A strip, or girdle, of bark is cut out of the vine, disrupting its natural water intake and outflow and thus forcing the moisture already in the vine up into the berries, swelling their size. Girdling is

done strictly on a piecework basis, the workers making two or three cents a vine.

We drove down a dirt lane and stopped by a picking stand. There was a sunshade over the stand, and a radio playing Mexican music. DiGiorgio showed me the tally sheet for one crew of field workers. The day before, the crew had picked 117 lugs of grapes, an average of 2.17 boxes an hour, giving the workers an hourly wage of $1.73. "It's hard work," he said. It was an understatement. The workers hunch under the vines like ducks. There is no air, making the intense heat all but unbearable. Gnats and bugs swarm out from under the leaves. Some workers wear face masks; others, handkerchiefs knotted around their heads to catch the sweat. I asked if there were not some way to automate the picking process. He shook his head and brought me under a vine to explain why. "If it were just a matter of picking, it might be feasible," he said. "You could do it for raisins or for wine grapes, but there are too many quality checks for table grapes." He clipped a bunch of grapes and handed it to me. "A picker has got to check color, the size of the berry, the size of the bunch, and trim bad berries before a bunch can be packed," he went on. "How are you going to mechanize these functions?" He examined the bunch and threw it away. "That one would never pass muster."

On the way back to lunch, we passed a plum orchard where a bulldozer was neatly uprooting trees and laying them in symmetrical rows. The trees had been planted in 1947, I was told, but they were no longer economically productive because of poor root stock. I asked if I could see one of the labor camps before lunch. Arvin employs Mexicans, Filipinos, Puerto Ricans, Negroes, and Anglos, and, as they are at every large ranch, the workers are segregated by nationality. At the height of the harvest, the work force runs to a peak of between 1,200 and 1,400 men, dropping to between 400 and 500 during slack periods. "Our basic concept here is to have enough crop diversification so that we'll be harvesting ten months a year," DiGiorgio said. "That gives greater employment."

He chose to show me a Mexican camp. The mess hall reminded me of the army. In the kitchen, cooks were preparing a lunch of steak, corn, and tortillas. (A machine stamps out over three thousand tortillas a day in the Mexican camp.) "This is just a normal meal," he said. "Nothing special." Outside, I saw a cluster of older living quarters with pipe chimneys, but I was steered into a newer building which still smelled of wet paint. The building was air-conditioned and accommodated forty-eight men. In the bathroom there were four toilets, six showers, and eight sinks. Four men live in a room. They sleep on cots and have their own wardrobes and shelves. Room and board costs $2.25 a day, which is deducted from their pay. There was nothing shabby about the building, but it was as cold and as impersonal as a barracks. I asked one of the workers how he liked living there. "It's like any place else," he said. "Some of the people are real clean and some are hogs."

We ate lunch in the supervisors' dining room, which was separated by a plywood wall from the Anglo mess hall. Lunch was cold cuts, a hot vegetable, Jello, and iced tea. We sat at a large table with six or eight ranch department heads who talked shop all through the meal — titration tests, irrigating plans, and crop yields. Someone made a joke about sour grapes and there was a good deal of mechanical laughter. Many of the ranch supervisors, DiGiorgio told me later, were the sons of Dust Bowl Okies who had begun working for the company as pickers. They averaged eighteen years with DiGiorgio. "It's hard to get good young people from Davis and the other agricultural colleges these days," he said. "They all want too much money and think they should start off with my

job. They know all the answers, so maybe they're better off working as county agents."

After lunch, DiGiorgio showed me Arvin's family housing, which, depending on the size of the unit, rents for five dollars, seven-fifty, or ten dollars a month. There was a playground with a baseball field and a tennis court. "We fix up the tennis court every couple of years," he said, "but they never use it except to play basketball on." We then drove to the packing house. It is an enormous building, roughly the size of two football fields. Trailer trucks were backed up along the side of the shed. On the second floor, there were rooms where the truckers could sleep while their trailers were being loaded. We watched the packing from a balcony outside the shed office. The packers were women and most were the wives and daughters of field help. They packed each box of plums and grapes by size and quality of the fruit, picking it off a conveyor belt, examining it, and then placing it in the appropriate box. It seemed a tedious, exacting job. Bunches of grapes that did not meet the quality standards for table grapes were culled and sent down another conveyor, which transported them outside, where they were dumped into gondolas for transport to the winery. Once boxed, the good fruit was placed in huge pre-cooling storage areas where the field heat could fade, giving the fruit longer transit and shelf life.

Before I left Arvin, Joseph DiGiorgio drove me out to see what the land looked like when his uncle, the founder of the company, bought it nearly fifty years ago. We were at the edge of the ranch property line. There was nothing but sand, sagebrush, and cactus. With some pride, DiGiorgio told me he had helped level the land himself. As we drove back to my car, we passed an arbor of blackberry bushes. It was a biological control project. Parasites lived in the bushes during the winter and then spread out from the arbor in the summer, laying their eggs on the eggs of harmful insects, thus acting as a natural pesticide. I remarked that farming was certainly complicated, that it took a combination scientist, engineer, and agronomist to keep a ranch running.

"Nobody stops to think of the farmer's problems," DiGiorgio said. "We have a tremendous capital investment in packing and boxmaking and storing and mechanical equipment, in trucks and cooling systems. Rain can spoil an entire crop, and when a crop overlaps, as it did last year in grapes, the price breaks because of overproduction. Our profit margin is at the mercy of the elements. We've got to know when to plant, what to plant, when to irrigate, when to rotate, when to pick. Five years from now, is the public going to go for a certain type grape we plant today?" The question was rhetorical, and as we shook hands he answered himself. "It's a gamble, that's all it is."

So indeed was the strike. By the time I got to Delano, ten months after the first walkout, it had gone into a holding phase, somewhat akin to the trench warfare of World War I. Except for occasional forays into violence, both sides held fast, hurling little more than a constant stream of epithets at each other. The mood of the town was sullen and suspicious, especially toward outsiders. One day after I had been there for nearly two weeks, I was stopped on the street by a leader of Citizens for Facts from Delano, a local group formed to counteract what they considered prejudiced, inaccurate, and pro-Chavez strike publicity. "I hear you're going to write a slanted story," he said. When I asked how he had come to this conclusion, he replied, "Well, you've been seeing Chavez, haven't you?" He gave me a look of impassive disbelief when I told him that some of the people at NFWA headquarters thought I was committing treason by even venturing over to the East Side.

In both camps there was a morbid fascination with what the other side was thinking and doing, and at times I felt almost like a Red Cross emissary passing between the lines under a flag of truce with parcels of quite meaningless information. Gradually, I grew inured to and versed in the demonology of Delano. There was, to begin with, a local *lingua franca.* Any reference to the strike on the part of the growers was prefaced by the phrase "so-called." A request for reportorial objectivity meant don't-cross-the-freeway. There were also various articles of faith. Not only his supporters but Chavez himself swore the organized opposition on the East Side was led by ex-prostitutes. This was matched by the town's conviction that the various Protestant ministers who had come to town to aid Chavez had "turned their collars around" to masquerade as Catholic priests among the predominantly Catholic Mexicans.

It had taken ten months of attrition for Delano to arrive at this state of paranoia. At the beginning of the strike, Delano, with some forebearance, had looked at Chavez merely as an upstart. His first grievance was economic and the town conceded he had a case. At that time, the average wage in the Valley was $1.20 an hour, plus a piece-rate of ten cents a lug of grapes picked. Chavez demanded $1.40 and twenty-five cents a basket, plus enforcement of the standard working conditions prescribed by state law. These laws were mainly concerned with adequate field sanitation facilities and were in many cases quite casually broken. At one Valley ranch, according to a woman worker, the field boss charged his hands twenty-five cents for a cup of water, and at a farm in the Delano area, sixty-seven workers were forced to drink from one cup, which was an empty beer can. Nor did this second ranch have the portable field toilets required by state law. Here the women workers were forced to squat down several rows over from where they were picking. They also maintained that their foreman used to sneak after them and watch them.

These were grievances that some quarters in Delano were willing to consider legitimate—until Chavez also demanded that the growers recognize the NFWA as bargaining agent for all the field workers in the area. The growers flatly refused. Only a handful of the thirty-eight growers in the Delano area even bothered to open the registered letters Chavez sent out on the eve of the strike asking for negotiations. When later I asked one of them why he had not acknowledged Chavez's letter, he answered, "Why, hell, I didn't get that letter until 12:30 and that meeting was supposed to be at eleven o'clock in the morning. Now you tell me, how can I get to a meeting that began an hour and a half before?" Certain that they held all the cards, the growers pretended that neither Chavez nor the strike existed.

At any other time, this tactic might have prevailed. But the civil-rights movement in other parts of the country had pricked the national conscience. Whatever one felt about the movement itself, few would deny that a vast body of the American public were second-class citizens, none more so than the Mexican-American farm workers. The movement had evolved a methodology of protest perfectly suited to conditions in Delano, as well as a cadre of workers willing to come there to put their special skills to work. They were mostly white college students for whom Delano was the only game in town; the civil-rights movement in the South had been taken over by Negroes grown increasingly sensitive to the fact of white domination, and the anti-Vietnam struggle was an abstraction with relatively few opportunities for confrontation.

Recognizing the need for outside support, Chavez, late in September of 1965, went to Stanford and Berkeley to drum up backing from student activists and invited workers from the Congress of Racial Equality and the Student Nonviolent Coordinating Committee to come to Delano to help organize the picket lines. Most of the picket captains in the early days of the strike were SNCC and CORE volunteers. "You just couldn't have someone who had never been on a picket line before," one of the NFWA leaders told me. "We needed somebody who could talk to the cops—or who had the confidence to talk to the cops. The Mexicans couldn't handle it at first. They had to be trained into the job." The logistics of picketing over thirty ranches were staggering. "It's like striking an industrial plant that has a thousand entrance gates and is four hundred square miles large," one SNCC worker said. "And if that isn't bad enough, you don't know each morning where the plant will be, or where the gates are, or whether it will be open or closed, or what wages will be offered that day."

With two-way radios lent by SNCC and CORE, scout cars would spread out around Delano before dawn, looking for evidence that certain vineyards would be worked that day. The signs were packing boxes stacked by the side of the road or a foreman's pickup parked down a lane. Information also came from inside the camps and from a few friendly truck drivers who told the NFWA where they were taking the crews. "Scouting you never did by yourself," I was told by Wendy Goepel, a limpid, childlike young woman who was one of the first volunteers to arrive in Delano. "I was driven off the road one day, someone just forced me off. After that, I never went out by myself." When a field looked promising, word was radioed back to NFWA headquarters and a caravan of roving pickets would be dispatched to the appointed rendezvous. Often the growers, in the early weeks of the strike, would see them coming and take their workers out of that particular field. One grower cruised over Delano in his private plane on the lookout for the picket caravan, and when he spotted it from the air he would radio its location to his crew on the ground. Some growers would move their workers from the roadside to the middle of a vineyard so that they would not see the pickets. Others drove down the edge of their property line with spraying machines, shooting insecticide and fertilizer on the pickets, or gunned over the roadside in tractors, raising dust to choke the strikers. Growers played car radios at top volume to drown out the pickets' shouts of *"Huelga"* or else placed a line of automobiles between the picket line and their workers so that the strikers could not see the field help.

The pickets were bound by an oath of non-violence, and at times it was sorely tried. Growers walked up and down the picket line, stamping on the toes of the strikers, tripping them up, or elbowing them in the ribs. Augustin Lira, one of the pickets, told me that a grower seemed to have singled him out as his own special project. "He'd come up to me and say, nice like, 'What are you doing here, boy?' and then he'd kick me." On the first day of the strike, a grower's son-in-law wrenched a sign from one picket, stood it against a fence, and calmly blew it apart with his rifle. One day James Drake of the Migrant Ministry was walking in town when a grower stopped his car in front of him, got out, and began pummeling him in the middle of the street. I asked Drake what he had done to protect himself and he answered, "Nothing, he was just a little guy."

Despite the NFWA's oath, however, the violence was not all that one-sided. "The strike is a farce," one nonstriking woman worker said. "It's a phony and a hoax. Those of us who have resisted the union organizing efforts have been beaten, shot at, deliberately run down by cars driven by so-called strikers. Twelve hoodlums forced my husband to go to the union hall, where he was told we had better cooperate or else. The union knew we had been to the authorities. With no other means of protecting ourselves, we were forced to obtain a

restraining order. This cost us our savings." One NFWA supporter aimed his car at three growers standing in the road, scattering them like tenpins, with the result that one grower had his leg broken. Piles of packing boxes were mysteriously put to the torch in the night and the Kern County sheriff's office discovered that Chavez supporters had purchased 4,000 marbles, which they were firing with slingshots at strikebreakers in the field. Rocks were thrown through windows in strikebreakers' houses, and picket signs set up on lawns reading "A SCAB LIVES HERE." One nine-year-old girl was told that unless her father came out of the fields her house would be burned down.

The attitude of the Kern and Tulare county law-enforcement agencies during those early days of the strike was, in the words of one observer, "scrupulously ambivalent." Growers had little difficulty obtaining restraining orders against picketing from friendly local authorities, even though these orders were usually vacated at the next level of appeal. Shortly after the Reverend Havens was arrested for reading Jack London's "Definition of A Strikebreaker," an injunction was issued against the shouting of the word *"Huelga"* on the picket line. Almost immediately, Chavez supporters informed the Kern County sheriff's office that they were going to make a test case of the ruling.

The following morning, the protesters held a meeting at NFWA headquarters to map out details. One of the NFWA staff informed the sheriff's office where the demonstration was to be held, so that deputies would be on hand to make the test arrests. Then the caravan started out. There were no workers at the first stop, and scout cars fanned out over the nearby roads until one reported a crew working at a ranch owned by W. B. Camp. The procession to the Camp ranch had a carnival atmosphere. The workers were followed by reporters, sheriff's cars, and a paddy wagon. At the ranch, a picket line was set up and the demonstrators began to chant, *"Huelga, huelga, huelga."* For nearly a half hour, the deputies took pictures of the pickets. Finally Sergeant Gerald Dodd took over a loudspeaker and told the pickets that they were engaged in unlawful assembly and ordered them to disperse. He issued the same warning personally to each demonstrator and then had it read in Spanish. At last, the arrests began. Almost jokingly, the pickets allowed themselves to be packed into the paddy wagon. They did not lie down or go limp. There was standing room only in the van, and several demonstrators were put in squad cars for the trip to the county jail. Only fifteen of the forty-four pickets arrested were from the Delano area, bolstering Delano's charges of "outside agitators." But the NFWA won its point. The case was dismissed and pickets were allowed to go on shouting *"Huelga."*

One day Chavez and a Catholic priest from Sacramento flew over the vineyards trying to make contact, via a bullhorn, with workers out of range of roadside pickets; they were both arrested for violating the grower's air space. In some cases, the police seemed to go out of their way to harass the roving pickets. "I'd drive a different way every day, but the cops would always stop me," Augustin Lira told me. "They'd tell me my lights weren't working or my signals were out of order or that I didn't make a signal when I turned. The cops always had tape recorders and cameras. I'd tell the people in the fields, 'These tape recorders, these cameras, they don't scare me, they shouldn't scare you.'"

Cameras, in fact, seemed to be indispensable artifacts of keeping the peace in Delano. Police photographed everyone who walked on a picket line, and took down the license number of every car parked in front of NFWA headquarters. The numbers were checked out with the California Department of Motor Vehicles in Sacramento, and the names were then sent to state and federal authorities to see if the owner had a record. With this information, the Kern County sheriff's office was able to make up a card file of 5,000 suspected strike supporters. Each card showed the supporter's name, criminal record if there was one, association with civil-rights groups if known, and a mug shot from the dossier of picket pictures if name and photo could be matched up. In one case, pickets were threatened by workers still in the fields and, instead of arresting the workers who made the threats, the Kern County Sheriff's office arrested the pickets. It was this legal concept which precipitated the following exchange between United States Senator Robert Kennedy and Kern County Sheriff Roy Galyen when the United States Senate Subcommittee on Migratory Labor, in March, 1966, held hearings in Delano on the strike situation:

Kennedy: "What did you charge them with?"

Galyen: "Violation of—unlawful assembly."

Kennedy: "I think that's most interesting. Who told you that they were going to riot?"

Galyen: "The men right out in the field that they were talking to said, 'If you don't get them out of here, we're going to cut their hearts out.' So rather than let them get cut, we removed the cause."

Kennedy: "This is the most interesting concept, I think. How can you arrest somebody if they haven't violated the law?"

Galyen: "They're ready to violate the law."

Kennedy: "Can I suggest that the sheriff read the Constitution of the United States?"

Another America

Edgar Z. Friedenberg

Edgar Z. Friedenberg is professor of education at Dalhousie University, Nova Scotia. He has taught at the University of California at Davis, the University of Chicago, and Brooklyn College. He is the author of *Coming of Age in America,* a study of American adolescence in the secondary school, *The Vanishing Adolescent,* and *The Anti-American Generation.*

In September, 1965, there began in California, a strike whose impact on the evolution of labor relations in this country, and on the quality of American democracy, is likely to be out of all proportion to the number of people, strategic importance of the industry, or bread-and-butter issues involved. This is the strike called against the local grape growers by the independent National Farm Workers Association, and the AFL-CIO Agricultural Workers Organizing Committee. Both are new organizations. Though the most active leaders of AWOC have grown old in the labor movement, AWOC itself was founded in 1959; NFWA was started in 1962 by Cesar Chavez, a native Californian from Brawley, in the Imperial Valley, whose childhood and youth were spent in a series of agricultural labor camps.

Agricultural workers are today the most helpless and deprived labor force in the country, and by a margin that readers accustomed to present-day industrial conditions can hardly imagine. These workers have never been effectively unionized. Partly for this reason, they have been excluded from nearly all legislation that guarantees the rights of workers and establishes collective bargaining machinery in industry. Agricultural workers are still treated under law as if they worked on family farms, under the genial supervision of the farmer and his bountiful wife. This is not justifiable in any part of America today; in California, where agriculture has been big business since long before Steinbeck wrote *The Grapes of Wrath* and Carey McWilliams reported on *Factories in the Field,* it is absurd.

Added to their legal disabilities are those imposed on agricultural labor by the way it is recruited, administered, and housed—limitations which, however, are less applicable to the grape industry than to the "stoop-labor" crops of truck gardens like melons or lettuce. In these crops, which are highly seasonal, workers are usually not employed directly by the grower at all, but by labor contractors who recruit them through publicly operated employment offices, or simply hire them off the streets of Skid Row at dawn and load them into trucks or old school buses for the trip to the fields. For longer or more remote jobs the workers are lodged in camps located on company property and inaccessible except by trespass or the owner's permission.

The difficulties of organizing agricultural workers and getting them into a position to improve their lot are therefore enormous. They are usually disfranchised and virtually unschooled—Chavez, who got as far as the eighth grade by heroic efforts, attended forty schools to do it.[1] Organizers cannot approach them either at work or afterwards, since the camp may be their only home. They are politically powerless and often apathetic; the

---

[1] Truman E. Moore, *The Slaves We Rent* (Random House, 1965), p. 130.

growers have great political influence at all levels.

Administratively, too, the problems are overwhelming. As Henry Anderson, Chairman of Citizens for Farm Labor—an organization including labor and civil rights leaders, university professors, and other Californians—observed in a broadcast on KPFA last December 3rd:

> . . . a strike presupposes the existence of some sort of framework, some sort of ground rules, for negotiation. It presupposes the existence of collective bargaining machinery. There is no such machinery in agriculture. Not more than one in a hundred California farm workers is represented by anyone, in any meaningful sense. There is no way to find by whom farm workers would like to be represented, if anyone. No one has a list of workers who are "attached" to the grape industry; where they live; or anything which needs to be known if there is to be any sort of contract covering them. These are some of the consequences of the fact that agriculture is excluded from the Labor-Management Relations Act of 1947 (Taft-Hartley) and from the jurisdiction of the National Labor Relations Board.

The grape industry, however, presents several features that make it a promising place to begin trying to organize agricultural workers. Grapes are not quite as seasonal as most truck garden crops. Like all crops, they have to be harvested; but they also have to be pruned, and sprayed, and sprayed, and sprayed throughout the growing season. Even the six vines I have in my back yard have become impossibly demanding, and I have about let them go to seed. This means that grape-production relies, in part, on a comparatively stable, less migratory labor force, with potential political power if the workers can be got to register. The grape industry makes little use of labor contractors; growers hire directly, which means that negotiations will be that much simpler if they can ever be got under way. Grape-tending, by and large, requires skill and dependability. It is not a job for casual laborers; "winos" may depend on the grape industry to keep them going, but the industry cannot depend on them to keep it going. This makes workers who strike more difficult to replace.

Striking under these conditions amounts primarily then to trying to persuade grape-workers not to work for the struck growers. This task has two main aspects. First, it is necessary to build *esprit de corps* among local groups of workers and potential workers; then, it is necessary to picket the fields in order to try to dissuade new recruits, or old employees who have decided to remain loyal to the employer, from scabbing. Building group spirit, however, requires great resourcefulness when dealing with a labor force as ethnically varied as grape-workers, who are primarily of Mexican and Filipino stock, but who also include more exotic elements, like one camp full of Yemenites I observed, whose quarters were festooned with highly decorative signs in Arabic.

Picketing is likewise difficult when the workers are brought directly to the employer's property in his own trucks and lodged in its midst; and when the growers find it comparatively easy to obtain restraining orders from familiar and understanding local authorities, even though these orders may be vacated at the next level of appeal. I observed one such picket; and found it an extremely moving experience but not, I should judge, a particularly effective one in getting anybody to quit pruning grapes. Picketing begins at dawn, when workers move out into the fields; but the pickets move in motorcades from one operation to another. At the location I observed, two miles or so out of Delano, about a dozen picketers were drawn up on the far side of a narrow county road while workers' and growers' automobiles were parked on the field side. This picket had been dispatched from Chavez's organization, and bore NFWA's splendid barbaric device—a black eagle on a scarlet ground, with the single word HUELGA (strike). There were some banners, but most of these were circular, wooden signs on long rods which looked like the emblems carried in the grand procession in *Aida*. The young men who composed the picket marched slowly and with great dignity; while a stout and forceful young woman addressed the fields across the road in Spanish through a portable loudhailer.

But only three or four pruners were visible in the field—whether because the strike was succeeding there, or because the field-bosses had moved the pruners back onto the land and out of earshot, as they often do when a roving picket arrives, I do not know. The growers' representative, a young man in a black sombrero, paced up and down the roadside opposite and tended his own public address system, which was being run from the battery of his car and played light music. The intent was to drown out the speech the young woman was giving; but the effect, I thought—since I couldn't understand it anyway—was rather to set it off, like the musical portion of the sound track of a foreign movie. But what contributed most to the emotional impact of the scene was its saturation by police. To protect the peace of Tulare County (Delano is in Kern County, but this was just over the line) from these ten or twelve people who glowed with composure, restraint, and determination, there was a deputy sheriff in his paddy wagon—which here, as is usual in California, is an ordinary station wagon made sinister by removing the inside handles of the rear doors and erecting a heavy metal screen above the front seat—and two cruising patrol cars that drove back and forth along this tiny stretch of road. They were accompanied by two little

unmarked red trucks which the picket captain told me belonged to the grape corporation, whose function I cannot grasp unless it was to remind the police to do their duty impartially. The deputy sheriff, an unusual civil servant, did walk over and bid the pickets a genial good morning, observing that it was going to be a nice day, which it was, in many respects. (On other occasions, several of the pickets informed me, the day had been marred by considerably more aggressive behavior by some of the sheriff's colleagues.)

To plan and conduct this complex enterprise, making the most of limited resources and avoiding the continual danger of internal conflict, requires leadership of a very high order, and self-discipline among a great many hard-pressed people. This is particularly true because of the severely contrasting styles of the NFWA and AWOC. Both are chaired locally by impressive and able men. But Cesar Chavez designed and built his own organization, and its approach is something new to American labor. Larry Itliong, the courtly regional director of AWOC, bears the burden, and occasionally receives the support, of the entire structure of American organized labor. So far, organized labor has behaved rather ambiguously about the grape strike. Walter Reuther has delivered $10,000 to the Delano strike fund, and pledged to support it in the future at the rate of $5,000 per month. Longshoremen have immensely heartened the Delano leaders by refusing to load grapes from struck vineyards on ships for export. But the Teamster's Union would have given the strike far more decisive support if it had refused to truck the grapes out of Delano; and it hasn't. Drivers sometimes observe the picket line *pro forma,* parking outside it and leaving the actual crossing of the line to be done by employers of the grower who bring the grapes out to the truck. And, indeed, there is a question whether such refusal by the Teamsters would be illegal under the Taft-Hartley Act, complicated by the fact that agricultural workers are excluded from it.

What the AFL-CIO has provided unstintingly is a procession of dignitaries giving speeches. AWOC's headquarters are in the Filipino Hall, a shabby, battleship-clean building with an auditorium, a few offices, and a soup kitchen. During the day, idle workers sit around watching television or chatting; there are grave, curious children; and a crew of women preparing delicious and abundant food which they graciously invited a friend and myself to share. The atmosphere is precisely that of a church social; even the sign at the entrance to the chow line advising that "none will be turned away," though active pickets have precedence, is written in gothic script. The hall fills for the evening meal, with gentle, dignified Filipino farm workers. Then, at six-thirty, the meeting begins, and goes on till nine o'clock—and, suddenly, the audience, though addressed by Mr. Itliong from the chairs as "Brother—" or "Sister—," finds itself at the equivalent atmospherically of a Democratic rally in the Bronx. Inspirational greetings are given by the heads of Ethnic-American Associations, down from San Francisco on a visit, along with an official from the SNCC office, or a young civil-rights lawyer, in blue-jeans. Mr. Itliong's superior in AWOC, Al Green, also down from the city, comes on as the horny-handed veteran of the labor movement that he genuinely is, reminding one how times have changed. The favorite daughter of the Delano strike, Mrs. Anne Draper, Regional Director of the Union Label Department of the Amalgamated Clothing Workers of America, AFL-CIO, speaks unabashedly to the workers as her children—"the best children any mother could have"—and they are utterly delighted. No one has worked more devotedly for *La Huelga* than Mrs. Draper, and

she is both indefatigable and very bright. To an ex-Brooklynite like myself, her style suggests rich chicken-soup in an inexhaustible cauldron of tough, shiny, stainless steel. This sort of meeting goes on nearly every night, and most of the distinguished guests tell the workers they can't lose. The effect is of watching a new play of Bertholt Brecht, more ironical than most.

At 102 Albany Street, in a little grocery store converted to offices at the corner of two dirt roads southwest of town, Cesar Chavez has established the very different headquarters of the National Farm Workers Association. The address will, I think, be a historic one; any reader who wishes to be sure to retain it might do well to write it down in some secure place, like his checkbook. NFWA also runs a meal service for its pickets, and pays those on actual duty; stockpiles food and clothing for them and their families, and pays rent and, when it can, car payments. It runs a credit union for its members, who pay $3.50 a month and publishes, for $2 a year, a sprightly illustrated fortnightly called *El Malcriado* in two editions, Spanish and English. It supports a satirical troupe called *El Teatro Campesino,* which puts on sketches and playlets. But its most notable accomplishment was to obtain from the Office of Economic Opportunity a grant of $267,887 for "a plan for sending out cadres of trained workers to collect basic facts about farm workers' lives and also to instruct the marginal workers in better money management and developing their communities."[2] Chavez, on being informed of the grant, immediately requested that the money be withheld until the strike had been settled, so that NFWA could not be accused of using it as a war chest; and this has been done. Nevertheless, the Delano City Council has officially complained

[2] San Francisco Sunday *Examiner and Chronicle,* sec. 1, p. 7, October 17, 1965.

of the grant, characterizing Chavez in a resolution as "... well known in this city, having
spent various periods of his life in this community, including attendance at public schools,
and it is the opinion of this Council that he
does not merit the trust of the Council with
regard to the administration of the grant."[3]

This opinion of the Delano City Council
differs, apparently, from that of Stephen
Spender. On a bulletin board in the barren
outer office at 102 Albany there is pinned,
along with maps and instructions to pickets,
and a list of grocery and laundry items needed
for the striker's depot, a holograph copy of a
poem by Spender inscribed "for Cesar Chavez"
and reading, familiarly;

> *I think continually of those who were truly great*
> *Who from the womb remembered the soul's*
> *history ...*

It is strange that the Delano City Council
should have advanced an argument that tends
to establish Chavez as a home-town boy, since
real resentment of the strike centers, as with
the Civil Rights Movement in the South, on the
issue of outside intervention. Thus, the *Delano
Record* for January 11, 1966 has two headlines:
DEMAND FOR DELANO GRAPES JUMPS
("Delano area grape grower Jack Pandol says
national publicity from union efforts has
helped to boost the sale of Delano grape products. . . .") and CATHOLIC BISHOP
SCORES PRIEST FOR "PERFORMANCE"
HERE—an account of the condemnation by
the Bishop of Monterey-Fresno of the Reverend James Vizzard, S.J., Director of the Washington, D.C. office of the National Catholic
Rural Life Conference "and his intrusive
associates" for coming to Delano and speaking
in support of the strike. A broadside sheet
entitled FACTS FROM DELANO, bearing

no date or attribution, which was given me
by a grower on my request for publications
expressing their viewpoint, features a statement signed by the Delano Ministerial Association and even Protestant ministers individually stating that the Association ... has not
fostered nor does it encourage any ecclesias-
tical demonstration or interference in the
farm labor situation." This sheet also repro-
duces a report from the *Delano Record* that
the Delano chapter of Community Service
Organization:

> ... deplores sincerely the civil rights movement
> that has become the prevailing issue in the former
> local labor dispute in our community. We sym-
> pathize with the plight of the farm worker or any
> other worker in those areas where poverty exists
> and where they are exploited, but we feel that
> these conditions are not prevalent in the Delano
> area. Delano CSO through experience knows that
> living conditions of farm workers in our area are
> far more adequate than those of the poor living
> in the ghetos [*sic*] of our large cities.
>
> We feel that the outside elements invading our
> city are performing a dis-service to the well-being
> of our community by creating adverse conditions
> and feelings of animosity among the citizenry
> that have not existed in our city for the past 25
> to 30 years.

This statement created a hassle when it was
published; for Cesar Chavez was trained in
various CSO operations, and left the organization amicably when he felt that it was emphasizing urban problems too much to provide
scope for his interests in farm labor. CSO is
primarily a Mexican-American social action
group that functions in California along the
self-directing lines laid down by Saul Alinsky;
and at a special meeting in Fresno,[4] the organization repudiated the action of its Delano
chapter by endorsing the grape strike. Never-

---

[3] *The Movement* (published by SNCC of California), Boycott Supplement.

[4] *El Malcriado,* 25, p. 4.

theless, the Delano chapter's statement about working conditions in the area seems to be justified. Chavez's choice of Delano as a proving ground for his approach to the organization of agricultural labor follows the highly sophisticated revolutionary principle that successful revolt starts with the richest of the poor — the poorest are too abject, vulnerable, and apathetic. Even around AWOC I heard few expressions of discontent with the money grape-workers were now earning, which comes close to the $1.40 per hour they want — though there was widespread belief that wages would immediately fall if the strike failed.

On my way north from Delano, I stopped in the neighboring community of Earlimart to interview Mark Zaninovich, Jr., who, two years earlier, had been vice-president of the student body at the University of California, Davis, and who is some twenty years my junior, but who recently took over from his father the management of one of the major grape companies in the state, which is regarded as a leading opponent of the strike. I had not previously met Mr. Zaninovich, and he clearly perceived that I was sympathetic to *La Huelga*. But he received me with flawless, though formal, courtesy and spent more than two hours at the close of an exceptionally busy day driving me over grape fields — his own, and those of other growers — showing me anything I cared to see. He was plainly torn between his conviction that I would be suspicious of anything he selected to point out and his shrewd hunch that I was too ignorant to know what to ask him to show me. But once I got used to the idea of riding over unmarked dirt roads in a beat-up pick-up truck with a mobile telephone in it and a sticker reading "I fight poverty; I work" on the bumper, we got along well enough.

What I wanted to see was the camps the workers are lodged in; and Mr. Zaninovich showed me three, all different, with different owners. I found them appalling; but not because they were physically squalid. None was that. And none suggested any form of oppression — though one did bear on its woodwork the marks of a recent firebomb which had rendered two bedrooms uninhabitable.

What was appalling was the conception of the kind of life that is good enough for a human being, which underlies the very design of these camps. The first one Mr. Zaninovich showed me belonged to his own company; and he apologized for its age and shabbiness. As soon as his company could afford it — and, despite the strike, they were running a little ahead of schedule on their operations — they planned to build one like the next camp he would take me to; his company didn't own it, but it was brand-new and a model of what such a camp might be.

It was a horrible place. The Zaninovich camp had not been bad; it was weathered, but clean, and rather suggested an old-fashioned tourist court of the early days of motoring. The new place was air-conditioned and centrally heated; steam burst aggressively out through the doors of its ample shower rooms. But it was still a long, concrete building whose central corridor was lined with doors that do not reach the floor. Each little room houses two men. Nobody had turned on the electric light in the corridor, which was illuminated only by the light of dusk coming under the stall-like doors. This is not, in the ordinary sense, a temporary dwelling. Migrant workers move from one such camp to another, following the crops; many have no other home than such a camp all their adult working lives. This, as Mr. Zaninovich truly said, was one of the best in the country; but nobody accustomed to an ordinary America life — even a poor man's life — could design such a structure for the use of other human beings unless he believed that they ought to accept a pattern of life so impoverished as to suggest a different species. In the next, and last, camp that we stopped at, Mr. Zaninovich asked one of the workers he knew and was on friendly terms with if he would mind showing me his room. The man at first demurred with a giggle because he had "awful things" in it; then flung the door open. The walls were lined with commonplace nude pin-ups and the bed had a cheap scarf on it with a similar design. The only awful thing was that the man was in his thirties, and this was the best he had, except when he made a visit to his home, in Yemen. Meanwhile, he was saving his money to retire there ultimately, a wealthy man. It was, as Mr. Zaninovich said, a classic example of a man bettering himself economically by his own efforts.

I thought of this man; comparing him to the people I had been with earlier on the picket line; and it occurred to me that they seemed the only people I had seen in months who seemed positively happy and free from self-pity. In their response to me, they had been friendlier and more open, by far, than most of the people I meet; though my speech and manner must have struck them as very unlike their own. I wondered why they had trusted me; then I realized that, of course, they hadn't. It was themselves they had trusted; such people do not fear strangers. Whether he wins *La Huelga* or not, this Cesar Chavez has done; or rather, has taught his people to do for themselves. Nothing I know of in the history of labor in America shows as much sheer creativity as NFWA, as much respect for what people, however poor, might make of their own lives once they understood the dynamics of their society. The cardinal sin of labor leaders, indeed—their special form of *accidia,* not of pride—is pomposity. If NFWA becomes sinful, it will be in quite a different way. I don't know the exact title of this sin; but an example of it would be restoring to all of us our common speech, and reconstructing the Tower of Babel.

The Whip and the Bee:
Diary from the Grape Strike

Nicolaus Mills

Nicolaus Mills previously worked as an organizer for the United Farm Workers. "Diary from the Grape Strike" is from an autobiography he is writing. He is currently a member of the literature department at Sarah Lawrence College. His articles have appeared in the *Nation, New Republic, Dissent,* and *New Leader.* Mr. Mills is also the author of *Comparisons: A Short Story Anthology, American and English Fiction in the Nineteenth Century,* and *The Great School Bus Controversy.*

LOS ANGELES: 1967

I pronounce it like FDR's middle name, and the man at the Greyhound ticket window stares at me. "The bus don't stop at no place like that!"

"But it's on the map."

"I don't care what it's on. The bus don't stop there!"

"You sure?" He nods, and then I spell it out, "D E L A N O!"

"De-*lay*-no. That's different. Sure, we got a 6:30 bus goin' there."

I buy a one-way ticket and start looking for a place to sit. It is close to midnight, but the bus station is still crowded. There is no room on the wooden benches for stretching out, so I prop my feet on my duffle bag and hunch down in a corner. I am half-asleep when two cops come by and ask to see my ticket. They barely look at it once I take it out. They are checking to make sure no one is using the bus station as a flop house, and they go up and down the rows of benches like armed railroad conductors, prodding those who are sleeping with their billy clubs. Only rarely do they touch anyone with their hands. It's as if they were worried about infection. The police who ask for my identification when the bus stops at Bakersfield are the same way. I am asked to show my driver's license, but the minute it is out of my wallet, they nod and move on to the man across the aisle from me. We are the only two on the Greyhound they bother with, and they address us both in Spanish.

THE PINK HOUSE

The bus trip to Delano is made up of sprints down freeways, then sudden turn-offs for small towns, and more freeway driving. The foothills along the way are one gray-brown mound after another. Their monotony is broken only by an occasional orange or lemon grove, and I sleep most of the time. I am tired when we reach Delano, but all I want to do is walk. A man outside the bus station gives me directions for the Farm Worker offices, and I start out for them. His directions, I soon realize, are almost unnecessary. Delano is as racially divided as any Southern city, and after a few blocks it becomes clear which part of town is for Anglos and which part for everyone else.

I head west, past a cluster of stores and cafés and across the overpass which lets Route 99 cut through the center of town. I am surprised by the heat. It is not just that the sun is hot but that everything around me is. It feels as if there were radiators hidden in the trees and telephone poles. I am twenty minutes outside of town when a car pulls up. I wave it on. My instincts, this first morning in Delano, are to refuse a ride from anyone white.

The man in the car ignores my wave and asks, "You going to the Union offices?" I laugh and get in. He is, it turns out, Jim Drake, Cesar's administrative assistant. He drives me to the Union's main office, a stucco bungalow with pink paint coming off all four sides. The dirt road in front of the Pink House is lined with beat-up cars, and a half-dozen people are sitting under a nearby tree. I am introduced to the people under the tree, most of whom have also just come to Delano, and then taken to Filipino Hall for breakfast. It is three days before I am assigned to work with the organizers who are laying the groundwork for a strike against the Guimarra Corporation, the principal grape grower in the area. I have been fearful of getting an office or a research assignment, and now the worst seems over. There is a shortage of sleeping spaces in the houses the Union rents, and so with two others, I move into the back room of *El Malcriado,* the Farm Worker newspaper.

CARD CHECKS

The organizers' meetings begin at eleven in the morning. They start this late because most organizing is done in the evening after the workers come home from the fields, and Bakersfield, where the majority of Guimarra workers live, is an hour from Delano. 10:30 is usually the earliest an organizer can get back home. The only exception is Friday night, when organizing is cut short so that everyone can be at the Union's general meeting. Friday is also special because it is the day on which the Union's $5 a week salary is paid. After the general meeting, most of the organizers end up drinking beer at People's Café, where prices are cheap and nearly all the customers are farm workers.

The organizers' meetings are run by Fred Ross, a tall, gaunt man, somewhere in his middle fifties. It is Ross, who, when he was working for Saul Alinsky's Community Service Organization, started Cesar organizing, and the two have been close ever since. Ross introduces me and another new organizer to the group, but that is it as far as our newness goes. We are assigned older organizers to work with, but there is no theorizing, no special explanations for our benefit. It is assumed we will learn what needs to be done by having to do it ourselves.

The first organizers' meeting I attend begins with Ross asking for newly signed union cards. He is like a school teacher who has consciously decided to put his students in competition with each other. For those who have brought in only a few cards, there is very close questioning, sometimes sarcasm. For those who have brought in a good many cards, there is praise and usually a much greater willingness to hear out their stories. Most of the teams of organizers have brought in between five and eight cards. The exception is a pair who have brought in nineteen. The cards represent commitments by the workers at Guimarra to have the United Farm Workers as their union, and they put the Union in a position to call for a card check election and know that it has the support to win. Still, this is not the main value of the cards. For it is clear that the Guimarras, who insist that their workers don't want a union, will never voluntarily agree to an election. What the cards do is prepare the way for a strike at Guimarra. They give the workers a chance to express their feelings and the Union

a chance to make plans: to know the names and addresses of workers, to begin calculating who is or isn't likely to leave the fields when that time comes.

After the card check Ross asks, "Any more new crews?"

"Two more back in the mountains," one of the organizers answers.

There is a groan, and then a decision on who should make the first contact. This will happen at least three more times in the next weeks. Crews we never knew existed will be reported working on some remote part of the Guimarra vineyards. It is this kind of isolation that has made it difficult for the men to know their own strength or numbers, and when I drive to Bakersfield the next night to meet with a family who has not yet signed with the Union, I am immediately confronted with this situation. We meet with a father and his two sons, and most of our time is spent answering questions they put to us about the Union. It isn't that they don't hate the Guimarras but that they don't know how many other workers are willing to sign union cards and they fear being blacklisted. They are also new enough to be afraid of their crew leader, and so even when no one from the company is around, they keep to themselves during the day.

HOUSE MEETINGS

By the end of June, I have gotten used to the pattern of organizing. Eleven o'clock meetings, late afternoon dinner at Filipino Hall, into Bakersfield by 5:30. There are still only about twenty of us doing full-time organizing, but it is going much faster now. We are no longer finding new crews, and more and more help is being given us by the workers themselves. They are bringing in as many cards as we are. We feel sure we already have the signatures of at least 80 percent of the workers eligible to vote in a union election. We are weak only among the Anglo workers. They are suspicious of a union in which the leadership is Mexican-American and Filipino, aware that at the very least they can no longer expect to monopolize the higher paying jobs, like trucker and irrigator. Many of these men are from families that came to California during the depression years, and they leave me with a vision of John Steinbeck's Joads accepting everything they once fought against.

With one other organizer, I share responsibility for five different crews. With three of them, we meet with the crew leader himself. With the other two, we concentrate on a group of men who rent the same house. We are in contact with each crew at least several times a week, sometimes to get new names, other times just to talk about how the grapes are ripening. From our point of view the ideal time for a strike is when the seedless Thompsons, the Guimarra's biggest cash crop, are ready for picking.

Early in July, Fred Ross makes a decision to hold a house meeting for the crew leaders we absolutely trust. It is a crucial step. So far, the workers have committed themselves only to wanting union representation. They have said nothing about a strike, and our problem is to see how many are willing to leave the fields when it comes to a showdown with the Guimarras. The meeting takes place early in the evening at a farm house just outside Bakersfield. Some of the men arrive in their own cars, others in the trucks they use to take their workers into the fields. We have to introduce at least half the crew leaders to each other, although many of them have been working at Guimarra for more than a dozen years. There is much joking about the need for introductions, but they set the tone for the meeting. The men don't feel anonymous.

When Cesar speaks, it is not to rouse the men but to ask questions. "Do you want a strike? Will your crews stay out? Who else is to

be trusted?" The questions are ones which all of us have been asking, but now it is possible to compare replies and have the men judge one another's accuracy. Most of the crew leaders have never seen Cesar before, and he moves among them slowly, listening, asking questions, nodding in sympathy. Although there is nothing striking in anything he does or says, he sets off reactions we have not gotten in the last month. At the end of the evening Fred Ross asks the crew leaders if they are willing to help us arrange house meetings with their men. They say they are, and the stage is set for the most crucial part of the organizing.

EL MOSQUITO

We try to hold the house meetings early enough in the evening so that we can remain outside and not have to turn on lights and be bothered with bugs. Occasionally we bring beer or soft drinks but usually not very much. We worry that if the meetings seem like a party, people will think the Union is trying to trick them. The questions we get asked are nearly always the same. No one believes the company will allow a union without a fight. What they want to know is how they can endure a strike. "Will the Union help with money? What if the Guimarras find out about the strike ahead of time? What about strikebreakers?" We make no promises. We talk about the Union giving support, but only to those who come to work for it full time. And we insist the strike must be nonviolent. It is slow going, and often we have a second or third meeting with workers from the same crew.

It is at this time that we also begin to publish *El Mosquito Zumbador* (the buzzing mosquito). It is a one-page paper, written in Spanish and English. We take it to the crew leaders at night, or deliver it ourselves in the morning by riding the trucks carrying workers to the fields. Sometimes *El Mosquito* does nothing more than list the Union's demands and compare them to the wages the Guimarras are paying. Other times it explains new benefits, like health and accident insurance. But always it lives up to its name, and whenever there is a rumor or an incident, it appears in *El Mosquito*. At first *El Mosquito* circulates like an underground newspaper, with workers afraid to read it on the job. Then it breaks into the open. We distribute it one morning in front of the Guimarra packing sheds at Edison. Some of the office employees refuse copies, but virtually everyone else takes a paper. One of the Guimarra brothers drives by in a yellow Cadillac and tears up the *El Mosquito* he is offered. It is hard to think of anything more helpful he could do.

FIESTA

By the end of the month we have gone as far as we can with house meetings. It is necessary to see if the workers feel confident enough to turn out in mass for a Union gathering at which they know there will almost certainly be company spies. We decide on a fiesta. It will have free food and *mariachi* bands, and anyone can use these as an excuse for coming, although it is obvious that the fiesta will be for something more. We are worried that not enough workers will come, but we plan for 2,000 anyway and spend the ten days before the fiesta urging our crews to come. Other problems in managing the fiesta become comic, especially the matter of what to serve. Cesar wants brains as the main dish and says he knows just the man to cook them. Everyone else groans, and for days the organizers' meetings open with someone asking if Cesar has given in on the brains. Finally, it turns out that the man who is supposed to cook them can't be gotten, and we settle on lamb instead.

Our fears about attendance prove wrong. We have more than 2,000 as farm workers who have nothing to do with Guimarra also

come. We run out of lamb after several hours of serving, and by the time the speeches begin, we are serving only rice and beans and salad. It is hot inside the arena in Bakersfield where we are meeting, and the crowd is restless at the start, wanting the Union to prove itself, not really believing that they hold the key to a showdown with Guimarra. Only five people have been scheduled to speak, but it is still too many, and when Cesar's turn comes, the crowd is uneasy. He begins in a low voice, not moving his arms, barely moving his feet. He talks the whole time in Spanish, not doing as he usually does, stopping every few sentences and translating into English. I have a hard time following him, but the man next to me translates whenever I ask him a word, and I keep up that way.

It is the Union, much more than the Guimarras, which Cesar wants to talk about. "I want to tell a story about a man with a whip," he says. "This man was an expert with a whip. He could flick the ashes off a man's cigarette while he smoked it . . . even pull a handkerchief out of a pocket with the whip. He could also kill a man with this whip, and because of his temper and his reputation, everyone was afraid of him. His workers always did what he told them, no matter how much they hated it, and his wife and his children were very quiet when he was around the house. . . . After a while, it got so that nobody would stand up to this man, and to keep in practice he began using his whip on anything that bothered him. A stray dog, a cat, even flies. He was so good, he could take the whip and kill a fly while it was still in midair.

"All this went on for many years, and then one day, as the man was sitting on his porch, a bee came buzzing around him. It flew in his hair and around his ears and didn't pay any attention when he tried to brush it away. One of the man's workers was passing by at the time, and when he noticed what was happening, he was very surprised. 'Why don't you use your whip on the bee?' he asked. 'It's no bigger than any of the other things you've gone after.' But the man with the whip just smiled. 'You don't understand,' he said. 'I can kill the bee all right. That would be easy for someone like me. But bees are different from anything I've whipped before. If you go after one, they all come after you. So if I took my whip to this bee, there would be the whole hive to fight, I'd get stung for sure. . . .'" Cesar stops at this point. There is no sound, no movement, just waiting. Then he begins again. "That is what the Union means. The Union is like the bees, and the man with the whip is like the grower. He cannot do anything to one of us without having all of us come after him."

It could not have been more than a few seconds between when Cesar stopped speaking and when people began shouting. But it seemed to take forever, and I remember feeling that silence as important as everything that came after it.

STRIKE VOTE

We call for a strike vote the first week in August on the night after the men get their paychecks. We want to make sure no one has a reason for going to work the next day. The strike vote is unanimous, and the tension is so great after it that speeches are unnecessary. The meeting ends with the singing of *Nosotros Venceremos,* and for a brief moment I feel as if I were in Mississippi again, leaving a civil rights meeting. In less than half an hour we are back in the office the Union has rented in Bakersfield, planning for the next morning. So far, everything is going better than expected, but we still worry about workers we have not seen at the fiesta or the strike meeting. What will they do? How much influence will they have on their friends? Is it just fear that keeps them away?

The next morning all of us are up by three. Four of the five crews I share responsibility for have said they will join the strike. We go to the fifth crew leader's house before he is up, and when he leaves, we follow his truck. At each house that he stops, we get out and ask the men who are up to stay away from work. More than half do, and by the time the truck gets to its last stop—an ice store—it is carrying only a dozen men. We get out and begin talking with the men, but this time less about the Union than who they are loyal to: those who have joined the strike or the Guimarras. Just as I think we have failed, the man sitting nearest me climbs down from the truck, then two more follow, then everyone else climbs down. We promise them rides back home, and they start heading for our station wagon. Suddenly, we realize we will never fit everyone into it, and it is not until their crew leader (who has been opposing us) says that he will drive everyone home that our problem is solved. We follow his truck to make sure everyone gets back home all right, and then we go out to the fields.

The sun is up, and it is still cool, the ideal time in the day for picking grapes. But the Guimarra fields are empty. The only people at the gates I go to are pickets and police. Later we learn that, except for the Anglo workers, only two crews have broken the strike. Despite the number of men involved, our strategy has been kept a secret and the Guimarras caught by surprise. It is not until the following week that they realize most of their workers are not coming back, and they start breaking the strike by bringing in crews from Texas and Arizona or border cities like Calexico.

The crews are bused in late at night so they can avoid our picket lines, but they cannot be kept under cover for more than a day or two. Most of the new workers were not told a strike was going on, and getting them to leave the fields is difficult. Roving picket lines, equipped with bull horns, speak to the workers whenever they get close to the road, and sometimes whole crews will throw down their boxes of grapes and leave the job. But most of the new workers are a long way from home and feel trapped. They have no money or transportation, and they don't know where else to look for a job. As the week goes on, new workers are brought in at a much faster rate than we can turn them away. The Guimarras also begin radio advertisements saying the strike is over, and before we can get the advertisements stopped, they have done us enormous harm.

BOYCOTT

We ask the Department of Labor and Department of Immigration to check on what the Guimarras are doing (the men in a number of crews do not have legal work permits, and it is a violation of the law for the Guimarras not to inform anyone they hire that a strike is going on). But the government officials we speak to are of no help. Unprotected by the National Labor Relations Act, we are as handicapped as any union was before the New Deal. Even with a strike, we have no legal right to a representation election. We can only have one if the company agrees to it. Another week goes by, and it becomes clear that, if the strike is going to be successful and nonviolent, we must move to a national boycott of Guimarra grapes (we later include all California-Arizona grapes when other growers start letting the Guimarras use their labels). Organizers are sent out to key cities, and we begin cutting down on our work in California. Still, we maintain a picket line in front of the Guimarra packing sheds, and when word comes that some Teamster locals are prepared to honor the line, we run it around the clock. Along with a crew of five workers, I have a midnight to eight shift. Our one compensation is that it is cool at night. Not cool enough to wear a jacket but cool enough so that we don't sweat.

Most of our time is spent trying to keep awake. We get threats from some of the white packing shed workers and from some of the high school boys who have been hired to break the strike, but while I am there, nothing happens. I will be in Cambridge, doing research of my own and working part time for the Boston boycott, when I will learn that the men I have been picketing with were beaten up so badly they had to be hospitalized. Two of the men were in their sixties. It is enough to make me stop imagining in more detail.

WINNING: 1970

I am in the office of the Ladies Garment Workers Union in New York when word comes in that the Guimarras are about to sign a contract and that the other Delano growers are ready to follow their lead. There has been talk of victory for weeks, and now when it is official, the news seems flat. I look around me at the office the Garment Workers let the New York Grape Boycott Committee share. We have a picture of Cesar and some *Huelga* posters on the wall, but basically the typewriters and the telephones and the florescent lights belong here most of all. How different from the Pink House or Filipino Hall, where you never stop running into children. I cannot believe we would take the news about the Guimarras so calmly there. But then I wonder. Somewhere along the way, our organizing has come to take on a life of its own. The satisfaction it provides lies in the effort itself. When it is over and we win, there is a feeling of relief, above all, purpose, but the intensity is gone. Perhaps we are punchdrunk in a way? I can imagine an outsider seeing us in that light. And then I stop thinking about it. A lettuce strike has begun in Salinas, and I have calls to make.

Sal Si Puedes:
Cesar Chavez and the New American Revolution

Peter Matthiessen

Peter Matthiessen is well known as a naturalist and explorer whose many publications include *Wildlife in America, The Cloud Forest,* and *Under the Mountain Wall.* He is also the author of several novels, one of which—*At Play in the Fields of the Lord*—was nominated for the National Book Award in 1965. His book *Sal Si Puedes* is a personal journalistic account of the Delano grape boycott.

Before leaving for California I had expected that I would be impressed by Cesar Chavez, but I had not expected to be startled. It was not the "charisma" that is often ascribed to him; most charisma is in the eye of the beholder. The people who have known him longest agree that before the strike, Chavez's presence was so nondescript that he passed unnoticed; he is as unobtrusive as a rabbit, moving quietly wherever he finds himself as if he had always belonged there. The "charisma" is something that has been acquired, an intensification of natural grace which he uses, not always unconsciously, as an organizing tool, turning it on like a blowtorch as the job requires. Once somebody whom he had just enlisted expressed surprise that Chavez had spent so little time in proselytizing. "All he did for three whole days was make me laugh," the new convert said, still unaware that he'd been organized.

Since Chavez knows better than anyone else what his appeals to public sentiment have accomplished for *la causa,* I had no doubt that as a writer I would be skillfully organized myself; but warmth and intelligence and courage, even in combination, did not account for what I felt at the end of the four-hour walk on that first Sunday morning.

Talking of leadership during the walk, Chavez said, "It is like taking a road over hills and down into the valley: you must stay with the people. If you go ahead too fast, then they lose sight of you and you lose sight of them." And at the church he was a man among his neighbors, kneeling among them, joining them to receive holy communion, conversing eagerly in the bright morning of the churchyard, by the white stucco wall. What welled out of him was a phenomenon much spoken of in a society afraid of its own hate, but one that I had never seen before—or not, at least, in anyone unswayed by drugs or aching youth: the simple love of man that accompanies some ultimate acceptance of oneself.

It is this love in Chavez that one sees and resists naming, because to name it is to cheapen it; not the addled love that hides self-pity but a love that does not distinguish between oneself and others, a love so clear in its intensity that it is monastic, even mystical. This intensity in Chavez has burned all his defenses away. Taking the workers' hands at church, his face was as fresh as the face of a man reborn. "These workers are really beautiful," he says, and when he says it, he is beautiful himself. He is entirely with the people, open to them, one with them, and at the same time that he makes them laugh, his gaze sees beyond them to something else. "Without laying a cross on him," Jim Drake says, "Cesar is, in theological terms, as nearly 'a man for

others' as you can find. In spite of all his personal problems—a very bad back, poverty,
a large family—he does not allow his own life
to get in the way."

We sat for an hour or more in the adobe
shade outside the small room where he had
spent his fast, and as he spoke of the old
missions and his childhood and the fast, I
grew conscious of the great Sunday silence and
the serenity that flowed from the man beside
me, gazing out with such equanimity upon the
city dump. What emerges when Chavez talks
seriously of his aim is simplicity, and what is
striking in his gentle voice is its lack of man-
nerisms; it comes as naturally as bird song.
For the same reason, it is a pleasure to watch
him move. He has what the Japanese call *hara,*
or "belly"—that is, he is centered in himself, he
is not fragmented, he sits simply, like a Zen
master.

For most of us, to quote Dostoevsky, "to
love the universal man is to despise and at
times to hate the real man standing at your
side." This is not true of Chavez. But he is
super human, not superhuman. He acknowl-
edges that his reactions are not entirely un-
affected by the humiliations and pain of his
early life, so that even his commitment to non-
violence is stronger in his head than in his
heart. And like many people who are totally
dedicated, he is intolerant of those who are
less so. I asked him once for the names of the
best volunteers no longer with the Union, and
he said flatly, "The best ones are still here."
I dropped the subject. As his leadership inevitably extends to the more than four million
Mexican-Americans in the Southwest, Cesar
will necessarily become more lonely, more cut
off in a symbolic destiny. Already, sensing this,
he puts great emphasis on loyalty, as if to allay
a nagging fear of being abandoned, and people
who are not at the Union's disposal at almost
any hour of the day or night do not stay close
to him for very long. It has been said that he

is suspicious of Anglos, but it would be more
accurate to say that he is suspicious of everybody, in the way of people with a tendency to
trust too much. He is swift and stubborn in
his judgments, yet warm and confiding once
he commits his faith, which he is apt to do
intuitively, in a few moments. The very com-
pleteness of this trust, which makes him vulnerable, may also have made him wary of betrayal.

The closer people are to Chavez, the greater
the dedication he expects. If they can't or
won't perform effectively, he does their job
himself ("It's a lot easier to do that than keep
after them"), or if they are going about it the
wrong way, he may let them persist in a mistake until failure teaches them a lesson. Some
of these lessons seem more expensive to the
Union than they are worth, but Chavez is
determined that his people be self-sufficient—
that they could, if need be, get along without
him.

His staff has also learned to sacrifice ego to
political expedience within the Union. Watching Chavez conduct a meeting, large or small,
is fascinating: his sly humor and shy manner,
his deceptive use of "we," leave his own position flexible; he directs with a sure hand, yet
rarely is he caught in an embarrassing commitment. Most of his aides have had to take responsibility for unpolitic decisions initiated by
Cesar himself, and may experience his apparent disfavor, and even banishment to the
sidelines, for circumstances that were not
their fault. The veterans do not take this
personally. In private, Cesar will be as warm as
ever, and they know that their banishment will
last no longer than the internal crisis. They
know, too, that he never uses people to dodge
personal responsibility, but only to circumvent
obstruction from the board or from the membership that would impede *la causa's* progress;
he is selfless, and expects them to be the same.

"Sometimes he seems so *damned* unfair, so
stubborn, so irrational—oh, he can be a sonofa-

bitch! But later on, maybe months later, we find ourselves remembering what he did, and every damned time we have to say, 'You know something? He was right.' That edge of irrationality—that's his greatness."

Because he is so human, Cesar's greatness is forgiven; he is beloved, not merely adored. "Often he says, 'Have you got a minute?' but what he means is, 'Talk to me,' and he doesn't really mean *that;* he just has to have somebody close to him all the time, it doesn't matter who, just someone who isn't a yes-man, who will bounce his ideas back at him. We all take turns at it, and he knows we're always there."

Jim Drake recalls a day sometime ago when he and Cesar and Marshall Ganz drove north to a hospital in Kingsbury, near Fresno, to visit Dave Fishlow, the editor of *El Malcriado,* who had been badly burned in a car accident. Although they had come one hundred and twenty miles, the supervisor would not let them in because they arrived after visiting hours. "Just a typical Valley cluck, you know. He says, 'Now what's going *on* out here, don't you know you can't break regulations? Absolutely not!' So I said, 'How about letting me see him? I'm his minister.' So he agreed, and then I said, 'Well, since you're letting somebody go in, it might as well be Cesar, since he's the one that would do your patient the most good.' But he said no, so I went in, and Dave suggested to me that Cesar come around under the window, just to say hello. But Cesar refused. You know how he hates discrimination of any kind; well, he thought he'd been discriminated against. I didn't but he did. He said he had gone to the back door all his life, and he wasn't going to do it any more. He was almost childish about it. That's the only time I've ever seen him that mad—so stubborn, I mean, that he wouldn't say hello to a friend. Most of the time that Cesar's mad, he's *acting* mad; he loves to act mad. But this time he was *really* mad."

On another occasion Drake himself got angry when Al Green, the AFL-CIO man, referred to Chavez as "that beady-eyed little Mex," and was astonished when Chavez, hearing this, burst out laughing. "He does very strange things, you can't anticipate him. When we had that conference at St. Anthony's Mission, he was very anxious to have everybody get to work and everything, and then he just disappeared. Later we found out that he and Richard and Manuel had been scooting around taking pictures of the nearby missions."

"In public, he's simple in his manner," Dolores Huerta says, "and when things are tense, he can make everyone relax by acting silly. When he used to drink a little, he was a real clown at parties; there were always games and dancing, and he would dance on the table." She laughed, remembering. "But I find him a very complicated person." In truth, Dolores finds Chavez difficult, but Dolores can be difficult herself, and anyway, her openness about him is a sign of faith, not disaffection.

One person in the Union with reservations about Chavez remarked to me of his own accord that in the creation of the United Farm Workers, Chavez had done something that "no one else has ever done. What can I say? I disagree with him on a lot of things, but I work for him for nothing."

This last sentence is eloquent because it says just what it means. Applied to the Chavez of *la causa,* ordinary judgments seem beside the point; a man with no interest in private gain who will starve himself for twenty-five days and expose his life daily to the threat of assassination, who takes serious risks, both spiritual and physical, for others, may be hated as well as adored, but he cannot be judged in the same terms as a man of ordinary ambitions.

The fast began on February 14, 1968, just after his return from a fund-raising journey around the country. Everywhere he went, the militant groups which supported him or sought his support were ranting about the violence planned for the summer of 1968. In the background, like a pall, was the destruction of Vietnam, which was still seen by its perpetrators as a tactical problem, not a moral one, and in the foreground, in Delano, his own people were rivaling the growers in loose talk of quick solutions. It was winter, in the hungry time between the pruning and girdling of vines, and the strike had drained the workers' nerves for two and a half years, and some were muttering that they had waited long enough. Many were still concerned with their *machismo,* or manliness, which sometimes emerges in oblique ways, as one worker says, "the women get afraid. The growers say they goin to call the law, and we don't know no law. So the women, they get afraid." They felt they were being cowardly in permitting the growers to continue exploiting them; anyway, wasn't violence traditional to labor movements? Hadn't violence gotten results in the ghetto riots of 1967? Perhaps a little burning in Delano, an explosion or two, might force the growers to negotiate. (Chavez doesn't deny this. "If we had used violence," he once told me, "we would have won contracts long ago, but they wouldn't be lasting, because we wouldn't have won respect.") Depressed, Chavez decided on the fast as a kind of penitence for the belligerence that had developed in his own union, and a commitment to nonviolence everywhere.

From every point of view, the twenty-five-day fast was the most serious risk that Chavez had ever taken, and it placed the hard work of six years in the balance. Chavez himself speaks mildly of the fast, but his people don't feel mild about it, even now; it split the Union down the middle. Helen, Richard and Manuel knew that Cesar had been fasting before he

made it known, but they were stunned by his intention to prolong the fast indefinitely. So were Leroy Chatfield, who still speaks of Chavez's announcement speech with awe, and Marion Moses, a volunteer Union nurse now on the boycott in New York, who has lent me some notes that she set down at the time.

Chavez called a special meeting for twelve noon on Monday, February 19, assembling the strikers as well as the office staff and families, and talked for an hour and a half about nonviolence. He discussed Vietnam, wondering aloud how so many of his listeners could deplore the violence in Asia, yet promote it in the United States. He said that the Mexican tradition of *machismo*—of manliness proved through violence—was in error: *la causa* must not risk a single life on either side, because it was a cause, not just a union, dealing with people not as green cards or social security numbers but as human beings, one by one.

"Cesar took a very hard line," Leroy Chatfield says. "We were falling back on violence because we weren't creative enough or imaginative enough to find another solution, because we didn't *work* hard enough. One of the things that he said in the speech was that he felt we had lost our will to win, by which he meant that acting violently or advocating violence or even thinking that maybe violence wasn't such a bad thing—that is really losing your will to win, your commitment to win. A cop-out. This seems like a very idealistic position, but there's truth in it. Anarchy leads to chaos, and out of chaos rises the demagogue. That's one of the reasons he is so upset about *la raza.* The same Mexicans that ten years ago were talking about themselves as Spaniards are coming on real strong these days as Mexicans. Everyone should be proud of what they are, of course, but race is only skin-deep. It's phony, and it comes out of frustration; the *la raza* people are not secure. They look upon Cesar as their 'dumb Mexican' leader; he's become their saint. But he doesn't want any part of it. He said to me just the other day, 'Can't they understand that that's just the way Hitler started?' A few months ago the Ford Foundation funded a *la raza* group and Cesar really told them off. The foundation liked the outfit's sense of pride or something, and Cesar tried to explain to them what the origin of the word was, that it's related to Hitler's concept. He feels that *la raza* will destroy our union faster than anything else, that it plays right into the growers' hands; if they can keep the minorities fighting, pitting one race against another, one group against another . . . We needed that Ford money too, but he spoke right out. Ford had asked him if he wouldn't be part of that Southwest Council for *La Raza,* or whatever it is, and he flatly refused. I mean, where would Mack Lyons be if we had that kind of nonsense? Or where would *I* be? Or the Filipinos?"

In his speech on February 19, 1968, Chavez discussed the civil rights movement and how its recourse to violence had made black people suffer; black homes, not white, were being burned, and black sons killed. The Union, he said, had raised the hopes of many poor people; it had a responsibility to those people, whose hopes, along with all the Union gains, would be destroyed after the first cheap victories of violence. Finally, he announced the fast. It was not a hunger strike, because its purpose was not strategic; it was an act of prayer and love for the Union members because as their leader he felt responsible for their acts as individuals. There would be no vote on the fast, which would continue for an indefinite period, and had in fact begun the week before. He was not going into seclusion, and would continue his work as best he could;

he asked that his hearers keep the news entirely to themselves. Since it was difficult to fast at home, and since the Forty Acres was the spiritual home of the Union, he would walk there as soon as he had finished speaking, and remain there until the fast was done. Throughout the speech Chavez quoted Gandhi and the Epistles of St. Paul. "His act was intensely personal," Leroy recalls, "and the whole theme of his speech was love. In fact, his last words to us before he left the room and started that long walk to the Forty Acres were something like 'I am doing this because I love you.'"

Helen Chavez followed Cesar from the hall, and everyone sat for some time in stunned silence. After that, as Marion Moses notes, "A lot was said, most of which, as far as I am concerned, had little or nothing to do with what Cesar was really saying to us." The meeting was taken over by Larry Itliong, who said straight out that Brother Chavez should be persuaded to come off the fast. Manuel Chavez then declared that Cesar was an Indian and therefore stubborn, and that once he had made up his mind to do something, nothing anyone could say was going to stop him. In that case, Leroy Chatfield said, in the most impassioned speech of all, every precaution must be taken to guard Cesar's health—good bed, blankets, and so forth—and to insure quiet, no cars were to be permitted on the Forty Acres until the fast was over.

Tony Orendain said sourly that the meeting need not concern itself with Cesar's blankets; the brothers should get back to work. Other members made many other comments. Epifanio Camacho, for example, dismissed the whole business of striker violence as grower propaganda, and therefore saw no reason for the fast. Camacho, as well as other Protestants and agnostics, white and brown, still resented the Catholic aura of the Sacramento march and now felt offended all over again. They were supported by those Catholics who felt that the Church was being exploited, and also by most of the white volunteers, and the Jews especially, who disliked any religious overtone whatsoever.

For the first week after the announcement, before the press arrived, almost the whole board of directors, led by Orendain, were boycotting the fast and refused to attend mass at the Forty Acres. On the other hand, the membership, largely Catholic, accepted the fast in apprehensive faith. "If Cesar thought it was right," Richard says, "then they did too." Fred Ross, like Chatfield, was worried that Cesar might be damaging his health, but they soon realized that nothing was going to stop him.

The Franciscan priest, Mark Day, later announced that he would offer mass at the Forty Acres every night of the fast, and Marion Moses went there after the meeting to help clear out the storeroom for the service. "Nick and Virginia Jones," she wrote, "pitched a little pup tent and stayed there the first night, and gradually there were more and more tents at the Forty Acres. It looked like a mining settlement in the Old West. We built a fireplace and we had chocolate every night. The masses were beautiful. On the first night Leroy and Bonnie made an offering of a picture of JFK, and Tony Mendez gave a crucifix. About 100 people came to the first mass and probably 200 will come tonight. It really looks good— the huge banner of the Union is against the wall, and the offerings the people make are attached to the banner: pictures of Christ from Mexico, two crucifixes, a large picture of Our Lady of Guadalupe—the whole wall is covered with offerings. There is a permanent altar there (a card table) with votive lights, almost like a shrine. It's impossible to describe the spirit of what is happening."

The people obeyed Cesar's request that no one try a fast of sympathy on their own, but he learned later, from the open annoyance of their wives, that three young men had taken a vow of chastity for the duration of the fast, and held to it. He speaks of this sacrifice with regret, but it seemed to him a convincing proof of the farm workers' new spirit.

The resentment of the young wives was not the only obstacle Chavez had to deal with: many other people had serious doubts right to the end. "When we visited Cesar in his little room at the Forty Acres," Leroy says, "he would point at the wall and say, 'See that white wall? Well, imagine ten different-colored balls, all jumping up and down. One ball is called religion, another propaganda, another organizing, another law, and so forth. When people look at that wall and see those balls, different people look at different balls; each person keeps his eye on his own ball. For each person the balls mean many different things, but for everyone they can mean something!' My ball was propaganda, and I kept my eye on that; I could therefore be perfectly comfortable, and understand the fast completely in those terms, and not negate the other nine balls—organization, say. And as matter of fact, we never organized so many people in such a short time, before or since. The fast gave the lie to the growers' claim that we have no following. Some people came every night to that mass at the Forty Acres, came sixty-five, eighty-five miles every night. People stood in line for an hour, two hours, to talk to him. He saw it as a fantastic opportunity to talk to one man, one family at a time. When that person left, he went away with something; he's no longer a member, he's an organizer. At the Sunday mass we had as many as two thousand people. That's what the growers don't understand; we're all over the state. In fact, there's nowhere in this state or anywhere in the Southwest where the people don't know about Cesar Chavez and the United Farm Workers. And they say, 'When is he coming? Are we next?'"

People close to Chavez like to envision a national farm workers union, but if Chavez has any such idea, he keeps it to himself. UFWOC now has offices in Texas, with sympathetic organizations in Arizona, Oregon, Washington, Ohio, New York, New Mexico, Wisconsin and Michigan. The Texas strikes, led by Gilbert Padilla, operate mostly in Starr County, which echoes Kern and Tulare counties in its cries of outraged patriotism. Although Texas can claim more paupers than any state in the nation, and although Starr County residents, mostly Mexican-Americans, had an average per capita income of $1,568 in 1966, a Starr County grand jury has called the strike effort "unlawful and un-American . . . abusive of rights and freedoms granted them as citizens . . . contrary to everything we know in our American and lawful way of life." It is just this spluttering hypocrisy, of course, in a country that is surely the most violent and unlawful on earth, that has alienated the best of the nation's young people and a growing minority of their parents. How much closer to what we were taught was the true spirit of America is the spirit of an elderly migrant, one of the objects of Starr County's righteous wrath: "I have lived in poverty and misery all my life and I live in poverty during the strike . . . but now I can walk with dignity."

The fast was also a warning to the growers that after a century of exploitation—the first anti-Mexican vigilantism occurred in 1859— the brown community was as explosive as the black, and that Chavez could not control his people indefinitely. If his nonviolent tactics failed, he would be replaced by more militant leaders, and there would be sabotage and bloodshed. Already minor violence had been committed by Union people or their sym-

pathizers, and the threat of further violence was the main reason for the fast. Without question, the fast worked. It taught the farm workers that Chavez was serious about nonviolence, that it wasn't just a tactic to win public support; and it taught them what nonviolence meant.

Chavez spoke a lot about the fast during the Sunday walk. Although he had fasted twice before, for periods of four days and ten, he had had no idea, when he began, how long this one would last. "I told everybody that it should be kept as secret as possible, but that the people could come to see me day or night, and the strike should go on as usual. But it didn't; there was a lot of confusion.

"When I disappeared, there was a rumor that I had been shot, and then everybody said that I was very sick, and finally we had to tell the press the truth, but we still said we didn't want any interviews or pictures or anything. I didn't talk to the newsmen, didn't want to, I just wanted to continue working." He laughed. "I did more organizing out of this bed than I did anywhere. It was really a rest, though; to me, it was a vacation.

"As soon as the word got out, the members began to come. Just people! From all over the state! We estimated that ten thousand people came here during the fast—we never turned anybody away. Anyway, everything went beautifully. The Filipinos came and began to paint these windows, and all kinds of little things began to appear. They weren't artists, but the things looked *beautiful*"—he spoke this last word with real intensity, turning to look at me. "I think the fast was a sort of rest for the people, too. You know? Oh, I could go on for days about the things that happened in the fast that were really great! I guess one time I thought about becoming a priest, but I did this instead, and I'm happy to be a part of it. For me, this work is fun, it's really fun! It's so great when people participate. Mexico is such a poor country, and I could never understand how, after the Revolution, they could produce all that beautiful art. But now I see it in our own strike, it's only a very small revolution, but we see this art beginning to come forth. When people discover themselves like this, they begin to appreciate some of the other things in life. I didn't understand this at first, but now I see that art begins in a very simple way. It's very simple—they just go out and *do* things.

"Then they began to bring things. Offerings, you know, religious pictures, mostly. Some people brought a hundred-and-fifty-year-old Christ of the Miners, handmade out of silver down in Mexico, and there were some other real valuable pieces. We've got everything safe, and we'll put it on display one day here at the Forty Acres.

"Something else very beautiful happened. For years and years the Mexican Catholics have been very discriminatory against the minority Mexican Protestants. They didn't know anything about them, they were just against them. Well, we used to hold mass every day in the store across from my room, we made it into a kind of chapel. And about the fifth day a preacher came, he works out there at Schenley and he has a little church in Earlimart. And I said, 'How would you like to come and preach at our mass?' He said, 'Gee . . . no . . .'" Chavez shrank back, imitating his voice. "'Sure!' I said. I told him this was a wonderful time to begin to repair some of the damage that had been done, the bad feeling, but he said, 'I can't preach here, I'll get thrown out.' I said, 'No, if that happens, I'll go out with you.' So he said, 'All right, fine.' And when he came, I introduced him, gave the full name of his church and everything so there would be no room for doubt about where he came from. And he did it in great form, and the people

accepted him. There was a great spirit; they just took him in. So three days later I asked another one to come, and he came, and he was also great, and then a Negro minister came—it was beautiful. So then the first one came again with his whole group, and they sang some real great Mexican Protestant music that we're not familiar with because of that prejudice. And now our Franciscan priest has gone and preached out there, in that little Protestant church in Earlimart!"

I asked him if his concept of the fast derived from Gandhi.

"Well, partly. In India, fasting is part of the tradition—there's an Indian engineer here who is a friend and comes to see us, and he says that in India almost everybody fasts. But Mexicans have the Catholic concept of sacrifice; the *penitencia* is part of our history. In Mexico, a lot of people will get on their knees and travel for five miles.

"I didn't know much about it, so I read everything I could get my hands on, Gandhi, and I read some of the things that he had read, and I read Thoreau, which I liked very much. But I couldn't really understand Gandhi until I was actually in the fast; then the book became much more clear. Things I understood but didn't feel—well, in the fast I *felt* them, and there were some real insights. There wasn't a day or a night that I lost. I slept in the day when I could, and at night, and I read. I slept on a very thin mattress, with a board—soft mattresses are no good. And I had the peace of mind that is so important; the fasting part is secondary."

During the fast Chavez subsisted on plain water, but his cousin Manuel, who often guarded him and helped him to the bathroom, was fond of responding to knocks on the door by crying out, "Go away, he's eating!" I asked if, in the fast, he had had any kind of hallucinations.

"No, I was wide awake. But there are certain

things that happened, about the third or fourth day—and this has happened to me every time I've fasted—it's like all of a sudden when you're up at a high altitude, and you clear your ears; in the same way, my mind clears, it is open to everything. After a long conversation, for example, I could repeat word for word what had been said. That's one of the sensations of the fast; it's beautiful. And usually I can't concentrate on music very well, but in the fast, I could see the whole orchestra and everything, that music was so clear.

"That room, you know, is fireproof, and almost soundproof—not quite, but almost. It's a ten-inch wall, with six inches of poured concrete. There were some Mexican guitars around, this was about the nineteenth day, and I turned to Helen and my brother Richard and some of my kids, and said, 'I hear some singing.' So everybody stopped talking and looked around: 'We don't hear anything.' So I said, 'I'll bet you I hear singing!' This time they stopped for about forty seconds: 'But we don't here anything!' 'Well,' I said, 'I still hear singing.' Then my sister-in-law glanced at Richard, her expression was kind of funny, so I said, 'We'd better investigate this right now, because either I'm hearing things or it's happening.' They said it was just my imagination, and I said, 'Richard, please investigate for me, right now, because I won't feel right if you don't.' So Richard went outside, and there were some guys there across the yard having a drink, and they were singing." He laughed. "Then, toward the end, I began to notice people eating. I'd never really noticed people *eat*. It was so . . . so . . ."—he struggled for words to express fascination and horror—"well, to use what we call in Spanish a *mala comparación*, like animals in a zoo! I couldn't take my eyes off them!"

I asked Chavez what had persuaded him to end the fast.

"Well, the pressure kept building, especially from the doctor. He was getting very concerned about the acids and things that I didn't know anything about—a kind of cannibalism occurs, you know, the acid begins to eat your fat, and you have to have a lot of water to clear your kidneys. First of all, I wouldn't let him test me. I said, 'If you declared me physically able to begin the fast, then it's not a sacrifice. If you find out that I'm ill, there will be too much pressure not to do it. So let me begin, and after I've started, *then* we'll worry about what's wrong with me.' But I forgot that the doctor was responsible for me, that if something went wrong with me, he would get it. So I argued, and he worried. Finally, after the twelfth day, I let him check my urine, and about the seventeenth day I let him check my heart, and he said, 'Well, you're fit.' And I said, 'I known I'm fit, I knew it when I got into this.' And after the fast they gave me a complete analysis, blood and all that stuff, and do you know something?" He smiled his wide-eyed smile, shaking his head. "I was perfect!"

On the twenty-first day of the fast, Dr. James McKnight had insisted that Chavez take medication, and also a few ounces of bouillon and unsweetened grapefruit juice. Dr. McKnight and many others felt that Chavez might be doing himself permanent harm, and subsequent events seem to bear them out; the worsening of what was thought to be a degenerative lumbar-disc condition that was to incapacitate him for three months in the fall of 1968 was generally attributed to protein deficiency, not only in the fast but in the ascetic diet that he has adopted since. Chavez himself does not agree. His bad back gave him less trouble during the fast than at any time since 1957, when it first began to bother him, and chronic headaches and sinusitis also disappeared; he never felt better.

Remembering something, Chavez began to smile. "Usually there was somebody around to guard me, give me water or help me out if I had to go to the rest room, but one time, about two o'clock in the morning, they were singing out there, and then they fell asleep, and the door was open. This worker came in who had come all the way from Merced, about fifty miles from here, and he'd been drinking. He represented some workers committee, and his job was to make me eat, and break my fast." He began to laugh. "And he had tacos, you know, with meat, and all kinds of tempting things. I tried to explain to him, but he opens up this lunch pail and gets out a taco, still warm, a big one, and tries to force me. And I don't want to have my lips touch the food— I mean, at that point, food is no temptation. I just thought that if it touched my lips, I was breaking the fast, you see, and I was too weak to fight him off. This guy was drunk, and he was pretty big, and so he sits on top of me, he's wrestling with me, and I'm going like this"—Chavez twisted and groaned with horror, rolling his eyes and screwing up his mouth in a perfect imitation of a man trying to avoid a big warm taco, crying "Oh! Ow!"—"like a girl who doesn't want to get kissed, you know. I began to shout for help, but this guy really meant business. He had told his committee, 'Look, you pay my gas and I'll go down there and make him eat; he'll eat because I'll *make* him eat, and I won't leave there *until* he eats.' So he didn't want to go back to Merced without results. First he gave me a lecture and that didn't work; then he played it tough and that didn't work. Then he cried and it didn't work, and then we prayed together, and that didn't work, either."

I asked if the man was still sitting on him while they prayed, and Chavez said that he was. By this time we were laughing so hard that we had to stop on the highway shoulder. Chavez's expression of wide-eyed wonderment at human behavior is truly comic; reliving the experience, he pantomimed both parts. "He

got my arms, like this"—he gestured—"and then he got my hands like *this*"—he gestured again—"in a nice way, you know, but he's hurting me because he's so heavy. I'm screaming for help, and finally somebody, I think it was Manuel, opens the door and sees this guy on top of me; Manuel thinks he's killing me, but he's so surprised he doesn't know what to do, you know, so he stands there in the door for at least thirty seconds while I'm yelling, "Get him off me!" Then about fifty guys rush in and pull him out of there; I thought they were going to kill him because they thought be was attacking me. I can hardly speak, but I try to cry out, 'Don't do anything to him, bring him back!' 'No!' they yell. 'Bring him back!' 'No!' they yell. I'm shouting, you know. 'Bring him back, I have to talk to him, don't hurt him!'" Chavez's voice, describing this scene, was quavering piteously. "So finally they brought him back." He sighed with relief, quite out of breath. "He wasn't hurt, he was too drunk. So I said, 'Sit down, let me explain it,' and I explained it, step by step, and the guy's crying, he's feeling very dejected and hurt." Chavez laughed quietly at the memory, in genuine sympathy with the emissary from Merced.

On the seventeenth day, Chavez asked Richard to construct the cheap and simple cross that was later destroyed by vandals. The cross was the ultimate affront to at least two volunteers. One dismissed the entire fast as a "cheap publicity stunt"; the other, who had once been a priest, accused Chavez of having a messiah complex. Both soon quit the United Farm Workers for good. The messiah charge, which has been made before and since, does not ring true to my own experience of Chavez. His account of the taco man from Merced, to cite just one example, is not a parable constructed by a man who takes himself too seriously; perhaps what the ex-priest was threatened by was not an aspirant messiah but a truly religious man.

"Anyway, the kids began to feel the pressure, and my father and mother. My dad began to lose his sleep—he's fantastic, he'll never talk about himself—but he's over eighty, you know, so I got a little worried. He has fasted a couple of times himself. Once he had dysentery and he couldn't clear it up, and he was dying. And one of those hobos on his way through—this was in the Depression, and they were white Okies, mostly—learned about my father and said he could take care of it. He was an old guy with a beard, he had books in his bindle, you know, and my sister translated for him into Spanish, and he said, 'I'll either save you or I'll kill you, and I'll be back in three days, so you think it over.' Well, my dad had been to a specialist and everything, and nobody could help him, but he said, 'Hell, how can I stop eating, I can't stop eating for even half a day!' And the hobo said, 'No, you can go for twenty days, maybe thirty days.' Anyway, when the hobo came back, my dad said he would try it. So he stopped eating, and in three days he got rid of the dysentery, there was nothing to feed it. He went on for twenty days. I said to him, 'Dad, you fasted for twenty days,' and he said, 'Yes, but that was different.'

"I had no set date in mind, but a combination of things made me end it on March eleventh. I could have gone a few days more. I broke the fast on a Sunday, it must have been about one or two o'clock. I ate a small piece of bread, but actually, I kept on fasting for the next four days, because you can't eat right away. So really I felt weaker *after* the fast was over."

The fast continued four days longer than Gandhi's famous hunger strike in 1924 (or so I've read; Chavez would be the last to make this claim). As it wore on through February and into March, many of the farm workers became apprehensive, and a number of strikers came to Manuel and swore that they would never be violent again if he could just persuade Cesar to quit; like the emissary from Merced with his bag of tacos, they were terrified that the leader of *la causa* would be harmed.

During the fast Chavez received a wire from Senator Robert Kennedy (I WANT YOU TO KNOW THAT I FULLY AND UNSWERVINGLY SUPPORT THE PRINCIPLES WHICH LED YOU TO UNDERTAKE YOUR FAST . . . YOUR WORK AND YOUR BELIEF HAVE ALWAYS BEEN BASED SOLELY UPON PRINCIPLES OF NONVIOLENCE . . . YOU HAVE MY BEST WISHES AND MY DEEPEST CONCERN IN THESE DIFFICULT HOURS) and the senator, with a phalanx of the press, appeared in person on the epochal Sunday when the fast ended.

In early 1960, while in the CSO, Chavez had met Robert Kennedy in Los Angeles, in a brief early-morning meeting that concerned a voter-registration drive for John Kennedy's presidential campaign; when he saw him next, he was Senator Kennedy, attending the hearings of the Senate Subcommittee on Migratory Labor in 1966. Apparently Kennedy had seen no point in going to Delano, but was finally persuaded by an aide that endorsement of Chavez and the minority-group Mexican-American cause could not hurt him politically and might be a very good investment; the investment was to win him the California primary two years later. And Chavez took Kennedy's commitment at face value. "Even then, I had an idea he was going to be a candidate for the Presidency, and I was concerned for him because he endorsed us so straightforwardly, without straddling the line. This was a time when everybody was against us; the only people for us were ourselves. I was sitting next to Dolores Huerta, and we both had the same thought—that he didn't have to go that far. Instead of that awful feeling against politicians who don't commit themselves, we felt protective. He said we had the right to form a union and that he endorsed our right, and not only endorsed us but joined us. I was amazed at how quickly he grasped the whole picture. Then the hearings started and they began to call the witnesses, and he immediately asked very pointed questions of the growers; he had a way of disintegrating their arguments by picking at the very simple questions. He had to leave just before the hearings ended, but he told the press that the workers were eventually going to be organized, that the sooner the employers recognized this, the sooner it was going to be over. And when reporters asked him if we weren't Communists, he said, 'No, they are not Communists, they're struggling for their rights.' So he really helped us, and things began to change."

On March 11, 1968, while in Los Angeles, Kennedy was notified that the fast was ending; he chartered a plane and flew to Delano with the United Auto Workers' Paul Schrade. At first, according to Chavez's aides, Kennedy seemed rather cold. "He felt kind of uneasy," Chavez told me, "and one of our people heard him ask Paul Schrade or somebody, 'What do you say to a guy who's on a fast?' He was only in the room with me about thirty seconds. He looked at me"—Chavez grinned mischievously—"and he says, 'How are you, Cé-zar?' I said, 'Very well, thank you. And I thank you for coming.' He said, 'It's my pleasure,' or something. So then we kind of changed the subject." Chavez laughed. "I was very weak, and I did not know what to say either; I think I introduced him to Paul Schrade.

"The TV people were there, and one poor cameraman got blocked out, the monitors wouldn't let him by. I saw he was frantic, and I was too weak to shout, but finally I signaled Leroy Chatfield, and Leroy got him in. The poor guy was really pale. And he said, 'Senator, this is probably the most ridiculous request I ever made in my life, but would you mind giving him a piece of bread,' and the senator gave it to me, and the camera rolled, and the man said, 'Thank you very, very much.'"

Chavez, who used to be stocky, had dropped from one hundred and seventy-five pounds to one hundred and forty during the fast; bundled up in a dark-checked hooded parka against the March cold, he was half carried to the Mass of Thanksgiving held in a Delano park where an altar had been set up on the flatbed of a truck.

The mass began with a prayer in Hebrew: the sermon was Protestant, and Catholic ritual preceded the breaking of the poor man's bread, *semita*. After Chavez and Kennedy had shared bread, priests passed through the thousands of witnesses, distributing the loaves. Because Chavez was too weak—he could scarcely keep his head erect during the ceremony—others read his speech for him, both in English and Spanish. In it, he told the gathering that his body was too weak and his heart too full for him to speak. He thanked everyone for being there, then told them that the strict water fast had been broken with liquids on the twenty-first day. He touched on the purpose of the fast, and concluded as follows: "When we are really honest with ourselves, we must admit that our lives are all that really belong to us. So it is how we use our lives that determines what kind of men we are. It is my deepest belief that only by giving our lives do we find life. I am convinced that the truest act of courage, the strongest act of manliness, is to sacrifice ourselves for others in a totally nonviolent struggle for justice. To be a man is to suffer for others. God help us be men."

Chavez's concept of the meaning of life being based in service to mankind is like that of Tolstoi and Hesse; his love is philosophical, not just religious. "How many people do you know," Dolores Huerta inquired one day, "who *really* love people, good and bad, enough to lay down their lives for them?" She meant that last part literally.

Robert Kennedy, who recognized Chavez's uncommon qualities, declared that he was present out of respect "for one of the heroic figures of our time—Cesar Chavez!" After taking communion with Chavez, he began his speech in a Spanish so awful that he stopped with good grace to laugh at himself. "Am I murdering the language?" he inquired, and was widly cheered. "*Hool*-ga!" he cried, in an effort to pronounce the strike slogan. "*Hool*-ga!" During the offertory, on behalf of his auto workers, Paul Schrade presented the Union with $50,000 for the construction of the new headquarters at the Forty Acres. After a feast of thanksgiving contributed by numerous families and committees, the meeting concluded with a fiery speech by Reies Lopez Tijerina, the leader of New Mexico's Mexican-Americans, who was later mentioned as a possible Vice-Presidential candidate for the Peace and Freedom party. Tijerina is an old-style Latin demagogue, full of shout and menaace, but he failed to excite the *campesinos* of Delano. "The trouble is," one staff member says, "that you get spoiled working for Cesar. When I see a person ranting and raving, I don't feel there's much substance there. It turns me off."

The mass was attended by from four to ten thousand people, depending on the source of the estimate: about eight thousand is probably right. "I told the senator that we could do most everything in Delano except control crowds, and he said that that didn't matter so long as the crowds were there. But he had a heck of a time getting from where we were sitting to the car. The crowd was pushing and surging, and when he got there, he didn't get in; the way the people were reacting, he wanted to stand there and shake their hands and talk to them. Everybody was afraid of so many people pushing like that, and when Jim Drake got him inside, the people were saying through the windows, 'Aren't you going to run?' 'Why don't you run?' 'Please run!' Then Jim got the car moving, and Kennedy turned to the people in the car and said, 'Maybe I will. Yes, I think I will.' So when he announced his candidacy a week later, it was no surprise to us. Everybody had suggested that I leave Delano for a little while after the fast, to rest, so Helen and I were on the coast near the Santa Ynez Mission. Helen got a paper and brought it back to the farm where we were staying, and I was excited, but I knew he was going to do it all along.

"On March 19, when Paul Schrade called to ask if I would endorse him and be a delegate, I knew it would not be honorable to ask for something in return. With most politicians, this would have been all right, but not with this man, who had already helped us so much. After a three-hour discussion, our members voted unanimously that I should be a delegate, and we immediately began a voter-registration drive.

"We worked right up to the last minute, we had a beautiful time, and the drive was a tremendous success. Some precincts went out one hundred percent for Kennedy! But I was very tired, and I felt embarrassed when my name was called at the rally at the Ambassador, and so I left early, before the senator came downstairs. The last time I ever talked to him was when he gave me that piece of bread."

In the voter-registration drive for Kennedy, Chavez's CSO experience, combined with his great gifts as an organizer, were very effective; the Mexican-American vote in June was virtually unanimous, and few people doubt that it was Chavez who won for Kennedy the primary that Kennedy had to win in order to be nominated. Possibly the task was made more urgent by the murder of Martin Luther King, soon after the voter-registration drive began; there was a growing fear among the poor that all their champions were to be assassinated. Although King and Chavez had never met, only corresponded, the loss of King was personal for Chavez. "That was one time I came very close to losing my cool. I was at a rally in Sacramento, and I really resented the press, you know, resented their questions." Still, he had not lost hope. In a telegram to Mrs. King he said: "DESPITE THE TRAGIC VIOLENCE THAT TOOK YOUR HUSBAND, THERE IS MUCH THAT IS GOOD ABOUT OUR NATION. IT WAS TO THAT GOODNESS THAT YOUR HUSBAND APPEALED. . . ." In his opinon, King's kind of nonviolence, like Gandhi's, was the practicing of what Christ preached, but generated violence on the other side because it wasn't passive. Since Chavez's nonviolence is also of this kind, he has had to live with the possibility of his own assassination; fear of death was one of the problems that he dealt with in the fast.

"No one accepts death, I think," he has said, "but what is the alternative? If you lock yourself in or give up, it's a living death, that's no alternative. Death is not enough to stop you. You're really too busy to think of it. Unimportant, day-to-day things get your attention, which is just as well."

Between the King and Kennedy assassinations, the following document was widely circulated in the Valley:

BAKERSFIELD, CALIFORNIA

THE NEW CATHOLIC CHURCH "APOSTLES CREED"

I believe in CESAR CHAVEZ, creator of all the TROUBBBBLE, and HELL, and the "UNITED FARMERS ORGANIZATION COMMITTEE." I believe in SAINT MARK DAY (the 2 bit politician priest of Delano) that "FOXXES" THE POOR FARMERS THE "CATHOLIC WAY" . . . I believe [Chavez] is the NEW POPE HOLY . . . I believe that he is SAINT CESAR CHAVEZ . . . I believe in WALTER REUTHER, HIS MENTOR. I believe in the $$$$$50,000 FIFTY GRAND CHECK donated by Walter Reuther to Chavez so Saint Cesar could HARRASS THE POOR FARMERS AND NON UNION WORKERS

IN POOR CALIFORNIA . . . I believe HE will be SHOT "a la KENNEDY STYLE" (oh happy day). . . .

I believe LBJ-HHH-and MACNAMARA, did all their best to give all us poor Americans a GOOD FOXXING with VIETNAM, NORTH KOREA, LA FRANCE, THE ARABS, THE JEWS, THE CUBANS, THE NEEGAHS AND THE CIVIL RIGHTERS. I believe that ALL THE CATHOLIC BISHOPS in HEAH-U.S.A. are for CESAR CHAVEZ, CIVIL RIGHTERS, CARD BURNERS, DRAFT DODGERS, RAPERS, THIEVES, MURDERERS AND THE NIGGERS.

I believe BISHOP TIMOTHY MANNING OF FRESNO will "RENOUNCE" HIS IRISH BLOOD AND ANCESTORSHIP and will claim to be (like Chavez) a real COOL MEXICAN and half NEGRO. (He is a NIGGERS LOVER).

. . . I believe GEORGE C. WALLACE WILL SCARE THE SHEETS OUT OF ALL THE NEEGAHS (neeegers to you) by being ELECTED PRESIDENT OF THE U.S.A. I believe FATHER GROPPIE THE S.O.B. OF MILWAUKEE WILL REST IN HELL NEXT TO A BELOVED FRIEND OF HIS, (REV.) M.L.K. (Beautiful News.)

I believe that MARTIN LUCIFER KING is also resting in . . . HE . . . (how do you spell it?) we got it; in he///hea///ven; their NEW BLACKIE SAINT (whose dead MARTYRDOM) Oh yeah? the Catholic Church BLAMES ON US POOR CATHOLICS . . . I believe that VERY SOON WE (You and I) WILL ATTEND A JOYFUL FUNERAL FOR OUR HONORABLE GUEST??????? AND NEW SAINT. (Can you name him?) GLORY BE, GLORY BE, AMEN, AMEN, amen, ALELUYA, ALELUYA; Pax bobis. PAXXX BOBIS? Pax bobis my eye. PAXXXXXX FOXXXIS US ALL.

Section Four

Students in Revolt: Crisis at Columbia

At the end of E. L. Doctorow's novel *The Book of Daniel,* Doctorow's central character, a Columbia University graduate student, is sitting alone in the library, when suddenly he is told:

> "Time to leave, man, they're closing the school down. Kirk must go! We're doin' it, we're bringing the whole motherfucking university to its knees!"
> "You mean I have to get out?"
> "That's right, man, move your ass, this building is officially closed."
> "Wait—"
> "No wait, man, the time is now. The water's shut off. The lights are going out. Close the book, man, what's the matter with you, don't you know you're liberated?"
>   I have to smile. It has not been unexpected. I will walk out to the Sundial and see what's going down.*

The new journalism in this section attempts to evaluate what "did go down" at the Sundial and throughout Columbia during its 1968 student strike. Above all, it tries to answer the kinds of questions implicit in the passage just quoted from *The Book of Daniel:* Who was liberated during the Co-

* E. L. Doctorow, *The Book of Daniel,* Random House, Inc., 1971, p. 302. Copyright 1971 by E. L. Doctorow.

lumbia strike? And who were the liberators? To what degree was the strike
a result of pent-up frustrations with the University? To what degree did
it depend on such broader issues as the construction, without community
approval, of a Columbia gym in a Harlem park?

These are questions important in their own right but made even more so
by the relationship the Columbia strike bears to the student revolts that
after 1964 spread across the United States and Western Europe. Within
this wider context, a veteran activist like Tom Hayden could call for "two,
three, many Columbias" and insist, "Columbia opened a new tactical stage
in the resistance movement which began last fall: from the overnight
occupation of buildings to permanent occupation . . . from symbolic civil
disobedience to barricaded resistance." In contrast to the 1964 Free
Speech Movement at Berkeley, which gave rise to the first campus upheaval, the Columbia strike brought to the fore a student movement demanding not just a liberalization of the rules by which universities were run
but a change in basic university policy. At Northwestern, at San Francisco
State, at City College of New York the issue would be racism. At Stanford,
at Harvard, at Kent State it would be the university's relationship to the
war. Not until May, 1970, would the protests peak, and by that time they
would involve a National Student Strike with demonstrations on an estimated 700 campuses.

In the Columbia strike both the war and racism were important. But
more than that, they were issues on a campus and in a community ready to
explode. Opposition to the gym Columbia proposed to build in Morningside Park had been voiced as early as 1965 by, among others, Thomas
Hoving, New York Parks Commissioner. In 1966 Columbia CORE and
Student Council came out against the gym, and in 1967 the West Harlem
Morningside Park Committee was formed to bring together neighborhood
opposition to the gym. By early 1968, when gym construction began, police
were needed to keep demonstrators from halting work. A similar pattern
of opposition had developed with regard to Columbia and the war in Vietnam. Beginning in 1966, there were protests against representatives from
the CIA, the Marines, and Dow Chemical appearing on campus, and in
March 1968, growing opposition to Columbia's involvement with the
Institute of Defense Analyses reached a peak, with a protest held in defiance of a University ban on indoor demonstrations.

All of these forces came to a head on Tuesday, April 23, when SDS and
SAS (Students Afro-American Society) held a joint rally at the Columbia
Sundial. The result was a week-long strike that took the following scenario:

Tuesday, April 23: Rally at Sundial. March to gym after an attempt to enter Low
Library thwarted. Confrontation with police at gym. One student arrested. Re-
turn to Sundial. A decision made to take a hostage in retaliation for arrest. Dean
Coleman held in his office at Hamilton Hall, which is then taken over by pro-

testors. Later in the evening, racial divisions among protestors. Early Wednesday morning, blacks expel whites from Hamilton Hall.

Wednesday, April 24: Expelled whites take over Low Library and President Kirk's office. Avery Hall seized by architecture students. Dean Coleman released. President Kirk makes effort to reach terms with black students. Strike Coordinating Committee established in Low.

Thursday, April 25: Fayerweather seized early in the morning. Ad Hoc Faculty Group (AHFG) forms and suggests more conciliatory position than President Kirk. AHFG favors stopping gym construction, promises to stand in front of halls to prevent police from entering.

Friday, Saturday, Sunday, April 26 to 28: Tension builds. Some fighting between students and police, and between protestors and Majority Coalition, heavily composed of athletes. Campus march by Charles 37X Kenyatta narrowly avoids clash.

Monday, April 29: President Kirk makes final offer without any firm commitment on gym. Students refuse to leave buildings.

Tuesday, April 30: The Bust. (Poll taken earlier of students and faculty not in building shows: 74 percent favor halting gym, 66 percent favor cutting ties with IDA.) Blacks leave Hamilton peacefully and are taken away. Resistance in other halls with bloody, early morning clashes. 692 arrests.

Richard Goldstein's "Groovy Revolution: Fold, Spindle, Mutilate" seeks to capture the mood of a student strike that in Goldstein's words was "one part dogma to four parts joy." As his title indicates, Goldstein sees the key factor in the Columbia uprising the students' belief that to the University they were little more than punch cards. "There were issues involved in the insurrection which paralyzed Columbia this past week," he writes. "But beyond these specifics the radicals were trying to capture the imagination of their campus by giving vent to some of its unique frustrations. In short, they had raised the crucial question of who was to control Columbia?" For Goldstein, the posters that went up, the classrooms that got rearranged, the omnipresent rock music were not just sidelights of the Columbia strike but serious indicators of the strikers' desire to humanize the University, to make it more like a home. In the end, when all that is left from the strike is litter, Goldstein notes how the "revolution had begun and ended in trash." It is an observation that points directly to the University's failure to distinguish between the new order created by students and the disorder created by the police bust.

The next two accounts, "The Shit Hits the Fan," a chapter from James Simon Kunen's book *The Strawberry Statement,* and F. W. Dupee's "Uprising at Columbia" are the reports of active participants, one a student, the other a senior member of the English department. Both reports are structured in terms of a chronology of events, and provide a yardstick for judging the momentum of the strike. But what makes these reports especially valuable is that they suggest that for those involved in the strike there was often a greater closeness, a greater sense of Columbia as a community than ever before. As Dupee observes just before the police bust begins:

> Something now occurred to me that had occurred earlier during the crisis but never before with such force. Just about everything on campus was being thoroughly *put to use* or would probably soon be put to use, although not for the purposes for which the things were intended. Blankets, sheets, ledges, window sills, lawns, walks, tunnels, the trees students perched in to see better. . . . All were blithely liberated—the word was *true*—from their usual functions. What had been University or individual property was now almost anyone's property to make of what he liked in this charmed circle of pure improvisation. It was exhilarating.

The concluding report, Jack Newfield's "Pre-Fitting the News at the Paper of Record," levels one of the major charges new journalists have made against established journalism: namely, that under the guise of objectivity, it has traditionally defended the status quo. Newfield's charge is that in its coverage of the police bust at Columbia, the New York Times, whose publisher is a trustee of Columbia, deliberately slanted the news against the students. Newfield has in mind not simply poor coverage by the Times, but such actions as: changing an article sharply critical of the police; refusing to print an account of police brutality by a *Times* reporter, deciding in advance not to tell certain *Times* reporters that a police raid was coming. The saddest part of Newfield's account is, however, the observation with which it ends. For instead of seeing the new journalist's version of Columbia becoming history, he sees the *Times* interpretation prevailing: "Five years from now, when *Newsweek,* or CBS, or some curious author wants to research what really happened during the great bust at Columbia, these yellowed *Times* clippings will be their only resource. The distortions and slanting will be institutionalized as truth by then."

The Groovy Revolution:
Fold, Spindle, Mutilate

Richard Goldstein

Richard Goldstein, editor of the underground magazine *US*, has written for the *Village Voice*, the *New York Times Magazine*, and *New York* magazine. He is the author of two books on rock music, *The Poetry of Rock* and *Goldstein's Greatest Hits*.

FOLD

You could tell something more than springtime was brewing at Columbia by the crowds around the local Chock Full, jumping and gesturing with more than coffee in their veins. You could sense insurrection in the squads of police surrounding the campus like a Navy picket fence. You could see rebellion in the eyes peering from windows where they didn't belong. And you knew it was revolution for sure, from the trash.

Don't underestimate the relationship between litter and liberty at Columbia. Until last Tuesday, April 23, the university was a clean dorm, where students paid rent, kept the house rules, and took exams. Then the rebels arrived, in an uneasy coalition of hip, black, and leftist militants. They wanted to make Columbia more like home. So they ransacked files, shoved furniture around, plastered walls with paint and placards. They scrawled on blackboards and doodled on desks. They raided the administration's offices (the psychological equivalent of robbing your mother's purse) and they claim to have found cigars, sherry, and a dirty book (the psychological equivalent of finding condoms in your father's wallet).

Of course this is a simplification. There were issues involved in the insurrection which paralyzed Columbia this past week. Like the gymnasium in Morningside Park, or the university's ties to the Institute for Defense Analysis. But

beyond these specifics, the radicals were trying to capture the imagination of their campus by giving vent to some of its unique frustrations. In short, they had raised the crucial question of who was to control Columbia? Four buildings had been "liberated" and occupied by students. The traditional quietism that had been the pride of straight Columbia was giving way to a mood of cautious confrontation. The groovy revolution—one part dogma to four parts joy—had been declared.

The rebels totaled upward of 900 during peak hours. They were ensconced behind sofa-barricades. You entered Fayerweather Hall through a ground floor window. Inside, you saw blackboards filled with "strike bulletins," a kitchen stocked with sandwiches and cauldrons of spaghetti, and a lounge filled with squatters. There was some pot and a little petting in the corridors. But on Friday, the rebellion had the air of a college bar at 2 a.m. In nearby Avery Hall, the top two floors were occupied by architecture students, unaffiliated with SDS, but sympathetic to their demands. They sat at their drawing boards, creating plans for a humanistic city and taping their finished designs across the windows. In Low Library, the strike steering committee and visiting radicals occupied the offices of President Grayson Kirk. On the other side of the campus, the mathematics building was seized late Friday afternoon. The rebels set about festooning walls and making sandwiches. Jimi Hendrix blared from a phonograph. Mao mixed with Montesquieu, "The Wretched of the Earth" mingled with "Valley of the Dolls."

It was a most eclectic uprising, and a most forensic one as well. The debates on and around the campus were endless. Outside Ferris Booth Hall, two policemen in high boots took on a phalanx of SDS supporters. Near Low Library, a leftist in a lumberjack shirt met a rightist in a London Fog. "You've got to keep your people away from here. We don't want any violence," said the leftist. "We have been using the utmost restraint," answered his adversary. "But," insisted the lumberjack shirt, letting his round glasses slide down his nose, "this gentleman here says he was shoved."

In its early stages, at least, it was a convivial affair, a spring carnival without a queen. One student, who manned a tree outside Hamilton Hall, had the right idea when he shouted for all to hear: "This is a liberated tree. And I won't come down until my demands have been met."

SPINDLE

Ray Brown stood in the lobby of Hamilton Hall, reading a statement to the press. His followers stood around him, all black and all angry. It was 7:30 p.m. Sunday, and the press had been escorted across a barricade of tabletops to stand in the lobby while Brown read his group's demands. By now, there were dozens of committees and coalitions on the campus, and students could choose from five colors of armbands to express their sympathies (red indicated prostrike militancy, green meant peace with amnesty, pale blue meant an end to demonstrations, white stood for faculty, and black indicated support for force).

But no faction worried Columbia's administrators more than the blacks. They had become a political entity at 5 a.m. Wednesday morning when 300 white radicals filed dutifully from

Hamilton Hall at the request of the blacks. From that moment, the deserted building became Malcolm X University christened by a sign over the main door. In the lobby were two huge posters of Stokely Carmichael and Malcolm X. That was all whites were allowed to see of Hamilton Hall. The blacks insisted on holding out alone, but by joining the demands of the people in Harlem and the kids in Low, they added immeasurable power to the student coalition. This is easier explained by considering the University's alternatives. To discharge the students from Hamilton meant risking charges of racism, and that meant turning Morningside Park into a rather vulnerable DMZ. To eject only the whites would leave the University with the blame for arbitrarily deciding who was to be clubbed and who spared.

In short, the blacks made the administration think twice. And Ray Brown knew it. He read his statement to the press, and after it was over, looked down at those of us taking notes and muttered, "Clear the hall." We left.

There was a second factor in the stalemate and its protraction. The issue of university control raised by the radicals had stirred some of the more vocal faculty members into action. They arrived in force on Friday night, when it became known that police were preparing to move. When the administration issued a one hour ultimatum to the strikers early Saturday morning, concerned faculty members formed an ad hoc committee and placed themselves between the students and the police. This line was defied only once—at 3 a.m. Saturday by two dozen plainclothesmen. A young French instructor was led away with a bleeding head. The administration backed down, again licked its wounds, and waited. It played for time, and allowed the more militant faculty members to expend their energies on futile negotiations. All weekend, the campus radio station, WKCR, broadcast offers for settlement and their eventual rejection. While the Board of Trustees voted to suspend construction of the gymnasium pending further study, they made it clear that their decision was taken at the Mayor's request, and that they were not acceding to any of the striker's demands. Over the weekend, factions multiplied and confusion grew on campus. This too played into the administration's hands. Vice-president David B. Truman blamed the violence, the inconvenience, and the intransigence on the demonstrators. When a line of conservative students formed around Low Library to prevent food from being brought to the protesters, the administration ordered food for the anti-picket line at the school's expense.

Finally, it called the first formal faculty meeting in anyone's memory for Sunday morning. But it made certain that only assistant, associate, and full professors were present. With this qualification, the administration assured itself a resolution that would seem to signify faculty support. Alone and unofficial, the ad hoc committee persisted in its demands, never quite grasping its impotence until late Monday night, when word began to reach the campus that the cops would move.

MUTILATE

At 2:30 Tuesday morning 100 policemen poured on campus. The students were warned of the impending assault when the University cut off telephone lines in all occupied buildings. One by one, the liberated houses voted to respond non-violently.

While plainclothesmen were being transported up Amsterdam Avenue in city busses marked "special," the uniformed force moved first on Hamilton Hall. The students there marched quietly from their sanctuary after police reached them via the school's tunnels. There were no visible injuries as they boarded a bus to be led away, and this tranquil surrender spurred rumors that a mutual cooperation pact of sorts had been negotiated between police and black demonstrators.

Things were certainly different in the other buildings. Outside Low Memorial Library, police rushed a crowd of students, clubbing some with blackjacks and pulling others by the hair. "There's gonna be a lot of bald heads tonight," one student said.

Uniformed police were soon joined by plainclothesmen, identifiable only by the tiny orange buttons in their lapels. Many were dressed to resemble students. Some carried books, others wore Coptic crosses around their necks. You couldn't tell, until they started to operate, that they were cops.

At Mathematics Hall, police broke through the ground floor windows and smashed the barricade at the front door. Students who agreed to surrender peacefully were allowed to do so with little interference. They walked between rows of police, through Low Plaza, and into vans that lined College Walk. In the glare of the floodlights which normally light that part of the campus at night, it looked like a bizarre pogrom. Platoons of prisoners appeared, waving their hands in victory signs and singing "We Shall Overcome." A large crowd of sympathizers were separated from the prisoners by a line of police, but their shouts of "Kirk Must Go" rocked the campus. Police estimated that at least 628 students were jailed, 100 of them women. Officials at nearby Saint Luke's Hospital reported that 74 students were admitted for treatment. This figure did not include those who were more seriously injured, since these were removed to Knickerbocker Hospital by ambulance. Three faculty members were reportedly hurt.

Many of the injuries occurred among those students who refused to leave the buildings. Police entered Fayerweather and Mathematics Halls and dragged limp students down the stairs. The sound of thumping bodies was plainly audible at times (demonstrators had waxed the floors to hamper police). Many emerged in masks of vaseline, applied to ward off the effects of Mace. Police made no attempt to gas the demonstrators. But some of those who had barricaded themselves in classrooms reported that teams of police freely pummeled them. A line heard by more than one protester, as the police moved to dislodge groups linking arms, was "Up against the wall, mother-fuckers."

There was no example of incredible police brutality visible at Columbia on Tuesday morning. It was all credible brutality. Plainclothesmen occasionally kicked limp demonstrators, often with quick jabs in the stomach. I saw students pulled away by the hair, scraped against broken glass, and when they proved difficult to carry, beaten repeatedly. Outside Mathematics Hall, a male student in a leather jacket was thrown to the ground when he refused to walk and beaten by half a dozen officers while plainclothesmen kept reporters at a distance. When he was finally led away, his jacket and shirt had been ripped from his back.

The lounge at Philosophy Hall, which had been used by the ad hoc faculty committee as an informal senate, became a field hospital. Badly injured students lay on beds and sofas while stunned faculty members passed coffee, took statements, and supplied bandages. The most violent incidents had occurred nearby, in Fayerweather Hall, where many students who refused to leave were dragged away bleeding from the face and scalp. Medical aides who had moved the injured to a nearby lawn trailed the police searching for bleeding heads. "Don't take him, he's bleeding," you heard them shout. Or: "Pick her up, stop dragging her."

The cries of the injured echoed off the surrounding buildings and the small quad looked like a battlefield. Those who were awaiting arrest formed an impromptu line.

Facing the police, they sang a new verse to an old song:

> "Harlem shall awake,
> Harlem shall awake,
> Harlem shall awake someday . . ."

Though two of Mayor Lindsay's top aides, Sid Davidoff and Barry Gottehrer, had been present throughout the night, neither was seen to make any restraining move toward the police. Commisioner Leary congratulated his men. And University President Grayson Kirk regretted that even such minimal violence was necessary.

By dawn, the rebellion had ended. Police cleared the campus of remaining protesters by charging, nightsticks swinging, into a large crowd which had gathered around the sundial. Now, the cops stood in a vast line across Low Library Plaza. Their boots and helmets gleamed in the floodlights. Later in the morning, a reporter for WKCR would encounter some of these arresting officers at the Tombs, where the prisoners were being held. He would hear them singing "We Shall Overcome," and shouting, "victory."

At present, it is difficult to measure the immediate effects Tuesday's police intervention will have on the university. Most students are too stunned to consider the future. On Tuesday morning they stood in small knots along Broadway, stepping around the horse manure and watching the remaining policemen leave. Their campus lay scarred and littered. Walks were innundated by newspapers, beer cans, broken glass, blankets, and even discarded shoes. Flowerbeds had been trampled and hedges mowed down in some places. Windows were broken in at least three buildings and whole classrooms had been demolished.

It would take a while to make Columbia beautiful again. That, most students agreed.

And some insisted that it would take much longer before the university would seem a plausible place to teach or study in again.

The revolution had begun and ended in trash, and that litter would persist to haunt Columbia, and especially its President, Grayson Kirk.

The Shit Hits the Fan
James Simon Kunen

James Simon Kunen is the author of *The Strawberry Statement*, a journal of the Columbia University strike of 1968. It is a significant documentation of student revolution and its participants in which Kunen shares his life style and personal views. His most recent book is *Standard Operating Procedures.*

Columbia used to be called King's College. They changed the name in 1784 because they wanted to be patriotic and *Columbia* means *America*. This week we've been finding out what America means.

Every morning now when I wake up I have to run through the whole thing in my mind. I have to do that because I wake up in a familiar place that isn't what it was. I wake up and I see blue coats and brass buttons all over the campus, ("Brass buttons, blue coat, can't catch a nanny goat" goes the Harlem nursery rhyme.) I start to go off the campus but then remember to turn and walk two blocks uptown to get to the only open gate. There I squeeze through the three-foot "out" opening in the police barricade, and I feel for my wallet to be sure I've got the two I.D.'s necessary to get back into my college. I stare at the cops. They stare back and see a red armband and long hair and they perhaps tap their night sticks on the barricade. They're looking at a radical leftist.

I wasn't always a radical leftist. Although not altogether straight, I'm not a hair person either, and ten days ago I was writing letters to Kokomo, Indiana, for Senator McCarthy;

my principal association with the left was that I rowed port on crew. But then I got involved in this movement and one thing led to another. I am not a leader, you understand. But leaders cannot seize and occupy buildings. It takes great numbers of people to do that. I am one of those great numbers. What follows is the chronicle of a single revolutionary digit.

Monday, April 22: A mimeograph has appeared around the campus charging SDS with using coercion to gain its political ends. SDS is for free speech for itself only, it is charged. SDS physically threatens the administration. SDS breaks rules with impunity while we (undefined) are subject to dismissal for tossing a paper airplane out a dorm window. Aren't you TIRED, TIRED, TIRED of this? Will Mark Rudd be our next dean? Do something about it. Come to the SDS rally tomorrow and *be prepared.* At first anonymous, the leaflet reappears in a second edition signed Students for a Free Campus. The jocks have done it again. As with the demonstrations against Marine campus recruiting in the spring of '67, threats of violence from the right will bring hundreds of the usually moderate to the SDS ranks just to align themselves against jock violence. I personally plan to be there, but I'm not up tight about it. At the boat house, a guy says he's for the jock position. Don't get me wrong, I say, I'm not against beating up on a few pukes, I just don't think you should stoop to their level by mimeographing stuff. We both go out and kill ourselves trying to row a boat faster than eight students from MIT will be able to.

Tuesday, April 23: Noon. At the sundial are 500 people ready to follow Mark Rudd (whom they don't particularly like because he always refers to President Kirk as "that shithead") into the Low Library administration building to demand severance from IDA, an end to gym construction, and to defy Kirk's recent edict prohibiting indoor demonstrations. There are around 100 counter-demonstrators. They are what Trustee Arthur Ochs Sulzberger's newspapers refers to as "burly white youths" or "students of considerable athletic attainment"—jocks. Various deans and other father surrogates separate the two factions. Low Library is locked. For lack of a better place to go we head for the site of the gym in Morningside Park, chanting "Gym Crow must go." I do not chant because I don't like chanting.

I have been noncommittal to vaguely against the gym, but now I see the site for the first time. There is excavation cutting across the whole park. It's really ugly. And there's a chain link fence all around the hole. I don't like fences anyway so I am one of the first to jump on it and tear it down. Enter the New York Police Department. One of them grabs the fence gate and tries to shut it. Some demonstrators grab him. I yell "Let that cop go," partly because I feel sorry for the cop and partly because I know that the night sticks will start to

flagellate on our heads, which they proceed to do. One of my friends goes down and I pull him out. He's on adrenaline now and tries to get back at the cops but I hold him, because I hit a cop at Whitehall and I wished I hadn't very shortly thereafter.* After the usual hassle, order is restored and the cops let Rudd mount a dirt pile to address us. As soon as he starts to talk he is drowned out by jackhammers but, at the request of the police, they are turned off. Rudd suggests we go back to the sundial and join with 300 demonstrators there, but we know that he couldn't possibly know whether there are 300 demonstrators there and we don't want to leave. He persists and we defer.

Back at the sundial there is a large crowd. It's clear we've got something going. An offer comes from Vice-President Truman to talk with us in McMillin Theatre but Rudd, after some indecision, refuses. It seems we have the initiative and Truman just wants to get us in some room and bullshit till we all go back to sleep. Someone suggests we go sit down for awhile in Hamilton, the main college classroom building, and we go there. Sitting down turns to sitting-in, although we do not block classes. Rudd asks, "Is this a demonstration?" "Yes!" we answer, all together. "Is it indoors?" "Yes!"

An immediate demand is the release of the one student arrested at the park, Mike Smith, who might as well be named John Everyman, because nobody knows him. To reciprocate for Mike's detention, Dean Coleman is detained.

---

*In October of 1967, there was a series of "Stop the Draft Week" demonstrations at Whitehall, the Army Induction Center for Manhattan. At about 6 A.M. on a Thursday morning a blue cossack rode his lumbering steed at me on the sidewalk. It was just too early in the morning to get run over by a horse. I slugged him (the cop) in the thigh, which was as high as I could reach, and was immediately brought to bay and apprehended by a detective, who smashed me in the knee with a movie camera, and later let me go when he deduced from my name that I was Irish, which I'm not.

At four o'clock, like Pavlov's dog, I go to crew, assuring a long-hair at the door that I'll be back. At practice it is pointed out to me that the crew does not have as many WASPS as it should have according to the population percentage of WASPS in the nation, so don't I think that crew should be shut down? I answer no, I don't think crew should be shut down.

Back at school at eight I prepared to spend the night at Hamilton. My friend Rock is there. We decide that we are absolutely bound to meet some girls or at least boys since there are 300 of them in the lobby. Every ten minutes he yells to me, "Hey, did you make any friends yet?" I say no each time, and he says that he hasn't either, but he's bound to soon.

I go upstairs to reconnoiter and there is none other than Peter Behr of Linda LeClair fame* chalking on the wall, "'Up against the wall, motherfucker, . . .'" from a poem by LeRoi Jones. I get some chalk and write "I am sorry about defacing the walls, but babies are being burned and men are dying, and this University is at fault quite directly." Also I draw some SANE symbols and then at 2:30 A.M. go to sleep.

Wednesday, April 24, 5:30 A.M.: Someone just won't stop yelling that we've got to get up, that we're leaving, that the blacks occupying Hamilton with us have asked us to leave. I get up and leave. The column of evicted whites shuffles over to Low Library. A guy in front rams a wooden sign through the security office side doors and about 200 of us rush in. Another 150 hang around outside because the breaking glass was such a bad sound. They become the first "sundial people." Inside we rush up to Kirk's office and someone breaks the lock. I am not at all enthusiastic about this and suggest

_____

* Two students who became a cause célèbre after admitting they were sharing an apartment.

that perhaps we ought to break up all the Ming Dynasty art that's on display while we're at it. A kid turns on me and says in a really ugly way that the exit is right over there. I reply that I am staying, but that I am not a sheep and he is.

Rudd calls us all together. He looks very strained. He elicits promises from the *Spectator* reporters in the crowd not to report what he is about to say. Then he says that the blacks told us to leave Hamilton because they do not feel that we are willing to make the sacrifices they are willing to make. He says that they have carbines and grenades and that they're not leaving. I think that's really quite amazing.

We all go into Kirk's office and divide into three groups, one in each room. We expect the cops to come any moment. After an hour's discussion my room votes 29–16 to refuse to leave, to make the cops carry us out. The losing alternative is to escape through the windows and then go organize a strike. The feeling is that if we get busted, *then* there will be something to organize a strike about. The man chairing the discussion is standing on a small wooden table and I am very concerned lest he break it. We collect water in wastebaskets in case of tear gas. Some of it gets spilled and I spend my time trying to wipe it up. I don't want to leave somebody else's office all messy.

We check to see what other rooms have decided. One room is embroiled in a political discussion, and in the other everyone is busy playing with the office machines.

At about 8:30 A.M. we hear that the cops are coming. One hundred seventy-three people jump out the window. (I don't jump because I've been reading *Lord Jim.*) That leaves twenty-seven of us sitting on the floor, waiting to be arrested. In stroll an inspector and two cops. We link arms and grit our teeth. After about five minutes of gritting our teeth it dawns on us that the cops aren't doing anything. We relax a little and they tell us they have neither the desire nor the orders to arrest us. In answer to a question they say they haven't got MACE, either.

In through the window like Batman climbs Professor Orest Ranum, liberal, his academic robes billowing in the wind. We laugh at his appearance. He tells us that our action will precipitate a massive right-wing reaction in the faculty. He confides that the faculty had been nudging Kirk toward resignation, but now we've blown everything; the faculty will flock to support the President. We'll all be arrested, he says, and we'll all be expelled. He urges us to leave. We say no. One of us points out that Sorel said only violent action changes things. Ranum says that Sorel is dead. He gets on the phone to Truman and offers us trial by a tri-partite committee if we'll leave. We discuss it and vote no. Enter Mark Rudd, through the window. He says that twenty-seven people can't exert any pressure, and the best thing we could do would be to leave and join a big sit-in in front of Hamilton. We say no, we're not leaving until our demands on the gym, IDA, and amnesty for demonstrators are met. Rudd goes out and comes back and asks us to leave again, and we say no again. He leaves to get reinforcements. Ranum leaves. Someone comes in to take pictures. We all cover our faces with different photographs of Grayson Kirk.

It's raining out, and the people who are climbing back in are marked by their wetness. Offered a towel by one of the new people, a girl pointedly says "No, thank you, I haven't been out." Rationally, we twenty-seven are glad that there are now 150 people in the office, but emotionally we resent them. As people dry out, the old and new become less differentiable, and I am trying for a field pro-motion in the movement so that I will not fade into the masses who jumped and might jump again.

The phone continues to ring and we inform the callers that we are sorry, but Dr. Kirk will not be in today because Columbia is under new management. After noon, all the phones are cut off by the administration.

At 3:45 I smoke my first cigarette in four months and wonder if Lenin smoked. I don't go to crew. I grab a typewriter and, though preoccupied by its electricness, manage to write:

The time has come to pass the time.

I am not having good times here. I do not know many people who are here, and I have doubts about why they are here. Worse, I have doubts about why I am here. (Note the frequency of the word *here*. The place I am is the salient charac-teristic of my situation.) It's possible that I'm here to be cool or to meet people or to meet girls (as distinct from people) or to get out of crew or to be arrested. Of course the possibility exists that I am here to precipitate some change at the University. I am willing to accept the latter as true or, rather, I am willing, even anxious, not to think about it any more. If you think too much on the second tier (think about why you are thinking what you think) you can be paralyzed.

I really made the conflicting-imperative scene today. I have never let down the crew before, I think. Let down seven guys. I am one-eighth of the crew. I am one-fiftieth of this demonstration. And I am not even sure that this demonstration is right. But I multiplied these figures by an absolute im-portance constant. I hate to hamper the hobby of my friends (and maybe screw, *probably* screw, my own future in it), I am sorry about that, but death is being done by this University and I would rather fight it than row a boat.

But then I may, they say, be causing a right-wing reaction and hurting the cause. Certainly it isn't conscionable to hold Dean Coleman cap-tive. But attention is being gotten. Steps will be taken in one direction or another. The polls will fluctuate and the market quiver. Our being here is the cause of an effect. We're trying to make it good; I don't know what else to say or do. That is, I have no further statement to make at this time, gentlemen.

The news comes in that Avery Hall, the architecture school, has been liberated. We mark it as such on Grayson's map. At about 8 P.M. we break into Kirk's inner office, which had been relocked by security when we gathered into one room when the cops came in the morning. The $450,000 Rembrandt and the TV have gone with the cops.

We explore. The temptation to loot is tremendous, middleclass morality notwithstanding, but there is no looting. I am particularly attracted by a framed diploma from American Airlines declaring Grayson Kirk a V.I.P., but I restrict myself to a few Grayson Kirk introduction cards. Someone finds a book on masochism behind a book on government. Someone else finds what he claims is Grayson's draft card and preparations are made to mail it back to the Selective Service. On his desk is an American Airlines jigsaw puzzle which has apparently been much played with.

We have a meeting to discuss politics and defense, but I sit at the door as a guard. A campus guard appears and, before I can do anything, surprises me by saying, "As long as you think you're right, fuck'em." He hopes something good for him might come out of the whole thing. He makes eighty-six dollars a week after twenty years at the job.

I go down to the basement of Low, where the New York City Police have set up shop. There are approximately forty of them; there is precisely one of me. I ask one for the score of the Red Sox game. He seems stunned that a hippie faggot could be interested in such things, but he looks it up for me. Rained out.

I use the pay-phone to call a girl at Sarah Lawrence. I tell her how isolated I feel and how lonely I am and hungry and tired and she says oh. I explain that I'll be busted any minute and she says she knows that.

I return upstairs. One of these people who knows how to do things has reconnected a phone, but he needs someone to hold the two wires together while he talks. I do it. I'll do anything to feel like I'm doing something.

Thursday, April 25: I get up and shave with Grayson Kirk's razor, use his toothpaste, splash on his after-shave, grooving on it all. I need something morale-building like this, because my revolutionary fervor takes about half an hour longer than the rest of me to wake up.

Someone asks if anyone knows how to fix a Xerox 3000, and I say yes, lying through my teeth. Another man and I proceed to take it apart and put it back together. To test it I draw a pierced heart with "Mother" in the middle and feed it to the machine. The machine gives back three of the same. Much rejoicing. Now we can get to work on Kirk's files. My favorite documents are a gym letter which ends with the sentence "Bring on the bulldozers!" and a note to a Columbia representative to the land negotiations telling him to be careful *not* to mention to Parks Commissioner Hoving that the date for digging has been moved up. ("We don't want him to know that we decided on this over a year ago," the note explains.)

Since a bust does not seem imminent, I climb out the window and go to crew at four. I talk to the coach and we agree that I will sleep in Low but will show up for the bus to Cambridge the next morning if I'm not in jail.

When I get back from crew I have to run a police cordon and leap for the second-story ledge. A cop, much to my surprise, bothers to grab me and tries to pull me down, but some people inside grab me and pull me up.

A meeting is going on discussing defense. J. J. wants to pile art treasures on the windows so the cops will have to break them to get in. I'm for that. But he also wants to take poles and push cops off the ledge. When this is criticized he tries to make it clear that it will be done in a nonviolent way. A friend whispers to me that J. J. is SDS's answer to the jock. A guy in a red crash helmet begins to say that maybe we won't fight because we're not as manly as the blacks, but it is well known that he is loony as hell and he is shouted down in a rare violation of the democratic process. After two hours' debate it is decided to man the barricades and resist passively. A motion to take off all our clothes when the police arrive is passed, with most girls abstaining.

I get back to the Xerox and copy seventy-three documents, including clippings from *The New York Times.* I hear over the radio that Charles 37X Kenyatta and the Mau Maus are on campus. This does not surprise me.

J. J. is recruiting volunteers to liberate another building. He has thirty, male and female, and at 2 A.M. he's ready to move. I go out on the ledge to check for cops. There are only three, so we climb down and sprint to Mathematics Hall. There we are joined by twenty radicals who could no longer stand the Establishment-liberal atmosphere of the previously liberated Fayerweather Hall. We get inside and immediately pile up about 2000 pounds of furniture at the front door. Only then do we discover two housekeepers still in the building. They are quite scared but only say "Why didn't you tell us you were coming?" and laugh. We help them out a window and along a ledge with the aid of the just-arrived-press movie lights.

We hold the standard two-hour meeting to decide how to deal with the cops, whom we understand to be on their way. The meeting is chaired by Tom Hayden, who is an Outside Agitator. Reverend Starr, the Protestant counselor, tells us the best positions for firehoses and so on. Dean Alexander B. Platt is allowed in through the window. He looks completely dead. We consider capturing him, but no one has the energy, so we let him go after thanking him for coming. Professor Allen Westin, liberal, comes and offers us a tripartite committee which he has no authority to constitute and which we don't want. He is thanked and escorted to the window.

At 6 A.M. I go to sleep.

Friday, April 26: I wake up at 8:55 and run to the crew bus and leave for MIT. From Cambridge I call my home in Marlboro. My mother asks me, "Are you on the side of the law-breakers in this thing?" For ten minutes we exchange mother talk and revolutionary rhetoric. She points out that neither Gandhi nor Thoreau would have asked for amnesty. I admit I haven't read them. But Gandhi had no Gandhi to read and Thoreau hadn't read Thoreau. They had to reach their own conclusions and so will I.

Saturday, April 27: I row a boat race and split. That wraps up the crew season—for me. On the MTA to Logan Airport a middle-aged man starts winking and smiling and gesticulating at my right lapel. Looking down, I see that I am wearing a broken rifle pin, symbol of the War Resisters' League. I tell him that it so happens I am on my way back to Columbia right now to carry on a Revolution. He thinks that's fine.

I get back to Math around 4:30 and sit down on the public-relations ledge over Broadway. People from a peace demonstration downtown are depositing money and food in a bucket at the bottom of a rope. Each time we haul it up and re-lower it we include I.D.'s for people who want to get into the campus. A remarkable number of cars toot their support, and when a bus driver pulls over to wave us a victory sign, ten people nearly fall off the ledge.

In the evening I discover that the electricity to the kitchen is cut off. I run downstairs and almost call for "someone important" but somehow I am unwilling to accept that kind of status relation. I tell several of my peers and one of them finds the fuse box and sets things right.

I volunteer for shopping. We buy twenty dollars of food for eighteen dollars (the merchants earlier had contributed food outright) and on the way back to meet a gentleman who seems to belong to Drunken Faculty to Forget the Whole Mess. Someone whom I think of as a friend threatens to punch me because I am carrying food.

As the evening wears on I feel less useful and more alienated, so I assign myself the task of keeping the mayonnaise covered. After covering it twelve times I give up and decide to write home. I wonder whether the Paris Commune was this boring.

In the letter I try to justify rebelling on my father's money. I point out that one of the dangers of going to college is that you learn things, and that my present actions are much influenced by my Contemporary Civilization (C1001y) readings. After sealing the letter I realize that my conception of the philosophy of law comes not so much from Rousseau as from Fess Parker and Davy Crockett. I remember his saying that you should decide what you think is right and then go ahead and do it. Walt Disney really bagged that one; the old fascist inadvertently created a whole generation of radicals.

I discover a phone which has not been cut off and call my brother. As I am talking someone puts a piece of paper beside me and writes "This . . . phone . . . is . . . tapped." I address myself briefly to the third party and go on talking. It feels good to talk to someone on the outside, although it is disappointing to find out that the outside world is going on as usual.

Sunday, April 28: Four hours of meetings about tactical matters, politics, and reports from Strike Central. I begin to long for a benevolent dictator. It is announced that we are spending as much money on cigarettes as food. I wonder, as I look about me, whether Lenin was as concerned with the breast size of his revolutionary cohorts as I am. It is now daylight-saving time; under all the clocks are signs saying "It's later than you think."

I spend the day sunning and reading *Lord Jim* on the ledge. At 3 P.M. four fire trucks scream up and men go running onto the campus with axes. Some people think this is the bust, but it seems like the wrong public agency to me. It turns out to be a false alarm.

The neighborhood little kids are anxious and able to squeeze through the fences. I talk to some of them and they are all conversant with the issues and on our side. I conduct an informal class in peace graffiti and distribute chalk.

The older brothers of these same kids are in the middle of Broadway throwing eggs at us. This action—one of them tells me later—is completely apolitical.

We have red flags flying from the roof. I explain to a cop on the sidewalk below that these stand for revolution, not for communism. He says yes, he remembers reading something about that. I hope he is not referring to the *Daily News*. The *News* charges us with vandalism and alcoholism. (Actually we voted to bar both grass and liquor, and there was only one dissident, named Melvin.) One cartoon, titled "Dancing to the Red Tune," shows a beatnik and some sort of cave girl dancing as a band sings "Louse up the campuses, yeah, yeah, yeah."

In the evening I walk into a room where

there is a poetry reading. I don't want to be rude so I stay. A med student who looks like Dr. Kildare reads a poem entitled "Ode to Mickey Mantle's Five-hundredth HR."

Mutiny on the Bounty (Gable) is on TV and I find it inspirational, or at least amusing.

The student radio station, WKCR, announces that a clergyman is wanted in Fayerweather; a couple wants to get married. This does not surprise me. Reverend Starr performs the ceremony and says, "I pronounce you children of the new age." Shortly after we hear it, we see a candlelight procession approaching. The bride is carrying roses. She hands them to me and I pass them inside. The demonstration peaks for me as I touch the roses—I am stoned on revolutionary zeal. The newlyweds call themselves Mr. and Mrs. Fayerweather.

I volunteer for jock-watch from 2:00 to 3:00 but do not wake up the next man and stay out on the entrance window ledge until five. I am to let no one in as we now have a population of 150 and we want a stable commune— no tourists. We even consider a Stalinist purge to reduce the mouths to feed. Only tonight does my roommate decide to occupy a building. I have about seven degrees of disdain and contempt for him, but he got in before my watch. I stamp "Rush" on the hand of anyone who leaves. This allows them to get back in.

During my watch five guys in black cowls come by dragging a coffin and murmuring in Latin.

Monday, April 29: The Majority Coalition (read: jocks) have cordoned off Low and are trying to starve the demonstrators out. We decide to break the blockade. We plan tactics on a blackboard and go, shaking hands with those staying behind as though we might not be back. There are thirty of us with three cartons of food. We march around Low, making our presence known. Spontaneously, and at

the wrong tactical place, the blacks in front jump into the jock line. I go charging through the gap with my box of grapefruit and quickly become upon the ground, or, more accurately, on top of two layers of people and beneath two. I manage to throw three grapefruit, two of which make it. Then I become back where I started. Some blood is visible on both sides. Back at Math, some of our people say that the jocks they were fighting had handcuffs on their belts. Band-Aided noses abound and are a mark of distinction. We discuss alternative plans for feeding Low and someone suggests blockading the jocks—"If they run out of beer they're through." In the meantime, we can see hundreds of green armbands (for amnesty) throwing food up to the Low windows. We decide on a rope-and-pulley system between a tree and the Low windows, but there is some question about how to get the line up to the people in Low without the jocks grabbing it. When one kid suggests tying an end to a broom handle and throwing it like a harpoon, John (Outside Agitator) suggests we train a bird. A helicopter has already been looked into by Strike Central, but the FAA won't allow it. Finally we agree on shooting in a leader line with a bow and arrow.

A girl and myself are dispatched to get a bow. We go to the roof of the Barnard Library where the phys. ed. archery range is. We are in the midst of discovering how incredibly locked the cabinet is when a guard comes out on the roof. We crouch. He walks right past us. It would be just like TV were I not so preoccupied with it being just like TV. After ten minutes he finds us. The girl laughs coyly and alleges that oh, we just came up to spend the night. I am rather taken with the idea, but the guard is unmoved and demands our I.D.'s. This is our first bust.

Our second bust, the real one, begins to take shape at 2:30 A.M. We hear over WBAI that there are busloads of TPF (Tactical Police

Force, Gestapo) at 156th and at 125th and that patrol cars are arriving from all precincts with four helmeted cops per auto. I am unimpressed. So many times now we've been going to be busted. It just doesn't touch me anymore. I assume that the cops are there to keep the Mau Maus out.

A girl comes up to me with some paper towels. Take these, she says, so you can wipe the vaseline (slows tear-gas penetration) off your face when you're in jail. I haven't got vaseline on my face. I am thinking that vaseline is a big petroleum interest, probably makes napalm, and anyway it's too greasy. I hear over the walky talky that Hamilton has been busted and that the sundial people are moving to Low and Fayerweather to obstruct the police. I put vaseline on my face. I also put vaseline on my hands and arms and legs above the socks and a cigarette filter in each nostril and carefully refold my plastic-bag gas mask so I'll be able to put it on quickly with the holes at the back of my head so my hair will absorb the gas and I'll be able to breathe long enough to cool the cannister with a CO_2 fire extinguisher and pick it up with my asbestos gloves and throw it back at the cops. Someone tells me that he can't get busted or he'll miss his shrink again.

I take my place with seven others at the front barricade. All along the stairs our people are lined up, ready to hole up in the many lockable-from-within rooms on the three floors above me. We sing "We Shall Not Be Moved" and realize that something is ending. The cops arrive. The officer bullhorns us: "On behalf of the Trustees of Columbia University and with the authority vested in me. . ." That's as far as he is able to get, as we answer his question and all others with our commune motto— "Up against the wall, motherfuckers." We can't hold the barricade because the doors open out and the cops simply pull the stuff out. They have to cut through ropes and hoses and it

takes them fifteen minutes before they can come through. All the while they're not more than thirty feet from me, but all I can do is watch their green-helmeted heads working. I shine a light in their eyes but Tom tells me not to and he's head of the defense committee so I stop.

At 4:00 A.M. the cops come in. The eight of us sit down on the stairs (which we've made slippery with green soap and water) and lock arms. The big cop says "Don't make it hard for us or you're gonna get hurt." We do not move. We want to make it clear that the police have to step over more than chairs to get our people out. They pull us apart and carry us out, stacking us like cord wood under a tree. The press is here so we are not beaten. As I sit under the tree I can see kids looking down at us from every window in the building. We exchange the "V" sign. The police will have to ax every door to get them out of those offices. They do. Tom Hayden is out now. He yells "Keep the radio on! Peking will instruct you!" When they have sixty of us out they take us to the paddy wagons at mid-campus. I want to make them carry us, but the consensus is that it's a long, dark walk and we'll be killed if we don't cooperate, so I walk. At the paddy wagons there are at least a thousand people cheering us and chanting "Strike! Strike! Strike!" We are loaded in a wagon and the doors shut. John tells a story about how a cop grabbed the cop that grabbed him and then said "Excuse me." We all laugh raucously to show an indomitable spirit and freak out the cops outside.

We are taken to the 24th precinct to be booked. "Up against the wall," we are told. I can't get over how they really do use the term. We turn and lean on the wall with our hands high, because that's what we've seen in the movies. We are told to can that shit and sit down. Booking takes two hours. Lieutenant Dave Bender is the plainclothesman in charge. He seems sternly unhappy that college turns out people like us. He asks John if he thinks he could be a policeman and John says no; he doesn't think he's cut out for it.

We are allowed three calls each. A fat officer makes them for us and he is a really funny and good man. He is only mildly displeased when he is duped into calling Dial-a-Demonstration. He expresses interest in meeting a girl named Janice when three of us give him her number, one as his sister, one as his girl friend, and one as his ex-wife.

We go downstairs to await transportation to court. A TPF man comes in escorting Angus Davis, who was on the sixth floor of Math and refused to walk down. He has been dragged down four flights of marble stairs and kicked and clubbed all the way. A two-inch square patch of his hair has been pulled out. Ben, Outside Agitator, yells, "You're pretty brave when you've got that club." The officer comes over and dares him to say that again. He says it again. The cop kicks for Ben's groin, but Ben knows karate and blocks it. John says to the cop, "Thank you, you have just proved Ben's point." This is sufficiently subtle not to further arouse the cop, and he leaves. A caged bus takes us all the way downtown to the tombs (the courthouse). The kid beside me keeps asking me what bridge is this and what building is that. Finally he recognizes something and declares that we are going to pass his grandmother's house. I am busy trying to work a cigarette butt through the window grate so that I can litter from a police bus. Arriving, we drive right into the building; a garage door clamps down behind us.

Our combs and keys are confiscated to that we won't be able to commit suicide. In the elevator to the cells a white cop tells us we look like a fine bunch of men—we ought to be put on the front lines in Vietnam. Someone says that Vietnam is here, now. As we get out I look at the black cop running the elevator for some sort of reaction. He says "Keep the faith."

He said "Keep the faith," I say, and everyone is pleased. We walk by five empty cells and then are jammed into one, thirty-four of us in a 12x15 room. We haven't slept in twenty-four hours and there isn't even space for all of us to sit down at one time.

Some of our cellmates are from Avery. They tell us how they were handcuffed and dragged downstairs on their stomachs. Their shirts are bloody.

After a couple of hours we start to perk up. We bang and shout until a guard comes, and then tell him that the door seems to be stuck. Someone screams "All right, all right, I'll talk." It is pointed out that you don't need tickets to get to policemen's balls. We sing folk songs and "The Star-Spangled Banner." They allowed one of us to bring in a recorder and he plays Israeli folk music.

A court officer comes and calls a name. "He left," we say. Finally he finds the right list.

We are arraigned before a judge. The Outsiders are afraid they will be held for bail, but they are released on their own recognizance, like the rest of us, except they have some form of loitering charge tacked on to the standard second-degree criminal trespassing.

Back at school I eat in a restaurant full of police. As audibly as possible I compose a poem entitled "Ode to the TPF." It extolls the beauty of rich wood billies, the sheen of handcuffs, the feel of a boot on your face.

Meeting a cellmate, I extend my hand to him and he slaps it. I have to remember that— handslaps, not shakes, in the Revolution.

Tom Hayden is in Chicago now. As an Outside Agitator, he has a lot of outsides to agitate in. Like the Lone Ranger, he didn't even wave good-bye, but quietly slipped away, taking his silver protest button to another beleaguered campus.

Everyone is organizing now—moderates, independent radicals, Liberated Artists, librarians. And the Yippies are trying to sue the

University for evicting us from our homes which we owned by virtue of squatters' rights. You can hardly move for the leaflets here. Except at Barnard. The Barnard girls are typing their papers and getting ready to go to Yale for the weekend.

We are on strike, of course, There are "liberation classes" but the scene is essentially no more pencils, no more books.

I saw a cellist math major in Chock Full O' Nuts looking alone. Liberation classes won't help him. He is screwed. Every Revolution leaves a trail of screwed drifting in its wake.

The campus is still locked, although I think you could get in with a Raleigh coupon as an I.D. today. That's our latest issue; a liberated campus should be open. We want free access by June so we can open the summer school under our own aegis.

A particularly thick swatch of air pollution drifted by today and a lot of people thought the gym site was burning. That did not surprise me. Nothing surprises me any more.

The Uprising at Columbia

F. W. Dupee

F. W. Dupee, critic and scholar, was editor of *Partisan Review* during its early years. A professor of English at Columbia University, he is the editor of *Great Short French Novels* and *The Selected Letters of Charles Dickens.* Mr. Dupee has also authored *Henry James* in the *American Men of Letters* series and the book *The King of the Cats.*

These are some impressions and reflections occasioned by the *first phase* of the Columbia University crisis of 1968 as that crisis was experienced at first hand by a veteran member of the faculty. The phase in question began with the student demonstrations of Tuesday, April 23. It ended with the big police action during the early hours of Tuesday, April 30, when the demonstrators were forcibly evacuated from the occupied buildings. After that, the crisis continued in the form of a student strike, ending in an uneasy peace at the close of the spring semester, June 4. The impressions and reflections reported here are peculiarly, though I think not uniquely, my own. For if the Columbia ordeal was primarily a vast collective shake-up, it also involved an intense individual shake-up for most of us who participated in the experience—an experience which, in its duration and its bitterness, its capacity to absorb every major issue then dividing the nation, was probably without precedent in the history of American universities at that time. (It may be significant that Martin Luther King was assassinated shortly before, and Robert Kennedy immediately after, the Columbia events.) I say "at that time," because of course the Columbia crisis was followed by further, and in several cases far more violent and shattering, crises in other American universities as well as in, for example, the universities of Paris, Berlin, and Mexico City. For publication in this volume, I have slightly revised the original text of this article, correcting a few factual errors and clarifying a few details.

I

During the early hours of Wednesday, April 24th, I was preparing for my Shakespeare class at 11 a.m. The subject that day was *The*

Winter's Tale; Coriolanus had gotten its final touches at the preceding session—"Just in time for the *local* mob scenes," a student remarked later. I wasn't happy about meeting any class that day. The show must go on, but I wished it could go on without me. For there was trouble on campus and I was by self-election a teacher and not a campus politician or a "trouble shooter."

It was one of Columbia's great virtues that it allowed its teachers this freedom of election, together with plenty of intellectual and social freedom and plenty of good students. It is true that my habitual detachment from campus politics had recently broken down as I saw the students growing more and more desperate under the pressures of the War. The War's large evil was written small in the misery with which they pondered hour by hour the pitiful little list of *their* options: Vietnam or Canada or graduate school or jail! Naturally they were edgy, staying away from classes in droves and staging noisy demonstrations on campus. To all this, the Columbia Administration added further tension. Increasingly capricious in the exercise of its authority, it alternated, in the familiar American way, between the permissive gesture and the threatened crackdown.

So little unchallenged authority survives anywhere at present, even in the Vatican, that those who think they have authority tend to get "hung up" on it. Many of my fellow teachers shared the Administration's "hang-up." One of them said to me of the defiant students, "As with children, there comes a time when you have to say no to them." But the defiant students weren't children, and saying no meant exposing them to much more than "a good spanking." The War was doing far more violence to the University than they were. Altogether, Columbia (especially the undergraduate College where I teach and where the big April disturbances began) had been grim throughout the school year. And

while nobody—not even the student radicals—expected any such explosion as actually occurred, I would not have been surprised if the year had ended with an epidemic of nervous breakdowns. On that Wednesday morning I was tired of the routines of teaching. I wanted neither to lecture on *The Winter's Tale* nor cope with a student riot.

But I must go back a day. The disturbances began at noon on Tuesday, April 23. That morning a College dean phoned and asked me, in a slightly anxious voice, to join him and others at a noonday rally called by the Students for a Democratic Society (SDS) at the Sundial. It was hoped, the dean said, that the demonstrators might be persuaded to adjourn to McMillin Theatre where they could discuss their grievances peacefully with David Truman, the former dean of Columbia College, now [as of 1968] the University's Vice-President. If persuasion worked, would I sit on the McMillin stage with other senior professors? I said I would attend the rally and see what happened.

It seemed doubtful that persuasion *would* work in this case. On March 27 the SDS had staged an indoor demonstration in open defiance of a ban on such demonstrations issued by President Grayson Kirk still earlier in the year. In itself the ban was acceptable to a majority of students and faculty, including myself—indoor demonstrations *are* disruptive—even though many of us thought it impolitic of the President (to put it mildly) to have made this important move without consulting formally any faculty or student body. Six student leaders who had participated in the March event were now subject to University discipline. The SDS claimed, first, that the six had been invidiously singled out; and second, that only a public trial conducted with due process could properly dispense justice in such cases. The Administration had denied both claims, in particular the second. The demand for a public trial challenged the right of this private university to conduct its disciplinary affairs by the *in loco parentis* principle that governed most of its relations with its students. Thus the issues behind the present rally combined, just as the issues presented by the demonstrators in the coming crisis were to do, a relatively superficial one (the disciplining of the six) with an absolutely fundamental one: the theory and practice of the University *vis-à-vis* its student body. "The University is *not* a democracy," its officials announced, with a candor which, in the present state of unrest, was the opposite of disarming.

I went to the rally; access to the campus is quick and easy from my apartment on West 116th Street, a short half block from the Amsterdam Avenue gate to College Walk. The rally, I found, was already in progress on and around the Sundial. Columbia's chief landmark, this squat cylinder of granite is capable of seating a dozen or so persons around its rim. It can also serve as a rostrum for a speaker and several associates if they all cling together. As rostrum, the Sundial was now occupied by a speaker and three or four associates, including (briefly) a couple of what I guessed were Barnard girls. The boys tended to be quite tall with hair wild, eyes haunted, lower jaws protruded, shoulders hunched; the SDS look; while the girls were short, dark, stern-faced, and had their hair pulled tight into knots at the back. The group didn't look as scary to me as they were reputed to be, perhaps because a couple of them were students of mine—the family quarrel aspect of the coming crisis was already present. In the bright Spring sunlight, squinting watchfully across the expanses of the campus, the SDSers made a familiar, storybook or TV Western impression—that of an embattled cluster of frontiersmen and their women in Indian country. This image fitted in—too

conveniently, I was to find—with what I knew of their ideology (or anti-ideology) which, despite its debts to Marcuse, Sorel, Camus, Mao, etc., seemed to me in essence radically American and populist, with Cuba as the latest frontier and Che Guevara as the tragic hero.

Now one of the taller youths—Mark Rudd, the SDS chairman—was making a speech to a crowd thickly gathered around the Sundial. Farther off, on Low Plaza, where I was standing, the crowd was more fluid. Unaffiliated students, faculty members, University officials, we moved around easily, exchanging campus pleasantries while keeping eyes and ears on the Sundial speaker. Beyond us, at the foot of the Low Library steps, was a line of picketers shouting "Stop SDS!" They were some of the Students for a Free Campus, a faction whose numbers were soon to multiply, and with them its own potential for violence.

Something now went on at the Sundial which I couldn't follow at that distance but learned about later. A College dean handed the speaker David Truman's letter inviting the group to McMillin. The speaker read the letter aloud, went into a huddle with his associates, and then told the dean that they would go to McMillin if the meeting there were converted into a public trial of the six students under discipline. To this demand the dean is said to have replied, "Unthinkable." A famous last word if there ever was one.

With that, the Sundial crowd broke and ran for the security entrance. One of the four smallish ground floor entrances to the bulky granite pile of Low Memorial Library, which houses the university's administrative offices, this entrance owes its name to the presence just inside of the campus police headquarters. The security entrance was locked. So, I believe, were the rest of the building's doors. The SDSers were being thwarted in their attempt to stage an indoor demonstration and thus provoke a confrontation which the Administration couldn't overlook, as it had overlooked others on various pretexts, hesitating to enforce a ban which it had imposed too rashly. What the authorities expected to accomplish by the present maneuver, at once so provocative and so petty, remains obscure. But for a few moments the lockout looked effective. The SDSers paused, consulted; and Mark Rudd, less impulsive at that moment than many of his followers, continued to ponder Truman's letter as if hoping to find in it some negotiable item. Finally, without Rudd, the others rushed off in the direction of Morningside Park. There, ominously overlooking black Harlem, construction of a gymnasium was under way in defiance of opinion not only in City Hall but in the University and among the militant elements of Harlem itself. At the gymnasium site, the demonstrators tore down a section of fence and briefly battled some patrolmen, who arrested one demonstrator.

I saw the start of the rush to the Park and later in the day, when I went to Hamilton Hall, headquarters of Columbia College (where many of us have our classrooms and our offices), for a 2 p.m. office hour, a sort of sit-in seemed to be developing in the lobby. At that moment the affair looked insignificant. However, coming down about 3:30 I found the crowd much larger and louder. Its spirit was still festive, though: there were guitars, far-out costumes, acrobatics. The walls were hung with posters of Che Guevara, etc. This quick transformation of the lobby's drab expanses was remarkable. Compared to the radicals of the Thirties, so stodgy and uninventive, these youths seemed to unite the politics of a guerrilla chieftain with the aesthetic flair of a costumer and an interior decorator. Of course they could draw, as Depression radicals could not, on an affluent and elaborate popular culture which was more or less the exclusive property of their generation.

In the crowd were students I knew. They were excited, talkative, unapologetic, even rather proud of the show. About one feature of it they were, nevertheless, somewhat uneasy. This was the confinement of Dean Harry Coleman in his office about an hour earlier. One of the students maintained that Coleman had been forcibly detained, a bad deal. Another disputed this, saying that Coleman was free to leave at any time and that if he chose to stay that was his business.

Once out of Hamilton Hall I didn't go back till the following day (Wednesday the 24th). But the radio had brought news of Hamilton's occupation by student blacks and of the seizure of President Kirk's offices in Low Library by student whites. Hence my reluctance to go to the Shakespeare class—the classroom had been changed to Teachers College. Nevertheless I went, found about a third of the students present, asked some questions about *The Winter's Tale* and got some answers, collected the term papers, which were due on that date, called the class off early, and on my way to Hamilton walked past the west wall of Low Library. Several large windows form a stately row along the second story of that wall. An incredible number of rebel students stood or sat in those windows, while others were climbing up to them, or down from them, by the wrought iron grilles conveniently fixed to the smaller windows on the ground floor. Some of the students, again, I recognized. All of them looked fatigued, bedraggled, and a little ghostly, as if they might be washed away by the rain that was beginning to fall. So that's where Kirk's office is, I thought, and only later wondered why, after some twenty-five years on the Columbia faculty, I had never known this before, or even cared enough to inquire. A while later, I learned that some patrolmen had entered the President's office earlier, not to remove the rebel students, as might have been expected, but to salvage a Rembrandt painting that hung in those offices.

So it turned out that our art-impoverished University secreted a Rembrandt. The things one didn't know!

I went on to the entrance of Hamilton Hall, where much of my academic existence has centered. The life-size bronze of the youthful Alexander Hamilton, a graduate of the college, in front of the building had had his shoes painted red several days earlier—possibly a portent. They were still red; and he now supported a red flag, a placard, and an empty coke bottle. The three glass doors that form the entrance to Hamilton were blocked from within by benches, tables, stacks of mailboxes—familiar schoolhouse objects now converted to the uses of a barricade. Two very young, very serious blacks perched on the uncomfortable pile behind the center door. They were guards.

What was going on farther inside could be seen by cupping one's hands to the glass of the doors and unabashedly spying on one's former domain. The lobby swarmed with busy blacks. Our entire schoolhouse was now definitely their hive. While I watched, several more were let in: mostly adults, evidently members of the Harlem community. Loaded with shopping bags, blankets, towels, and bulky packages intended for the occupants, they were as casual about this traffic as if delivering provisions to the victims of a flood or fire, or helping a friend to stock his new home.

Rumors multiplied in the circle of watching whites. These packages might hold guns, grenades, ammunition, cans of gasoline! But the calm presence of all these blacks might, I thought, argue something different from "Burn, baby, burn." It could mean that Columbia's student blacks had completed their self-taught course in racial separatism and now, with the aid of Harlem brothers and sisters, were settling in, not for good, but for long enough to set the precedent for some lasting take-over in the future. It wouldn't necessarily, or even probably, be a *violent* take-over. It

was conceivable that Columbia, half or more of whose income derives from public funds of one kind or another, *could* have its charter revoked by the State of New York, in which case it *could* become the Harlem branch of the State University system. In such a transformation there would be a certain rough justice. But would a preponderantly black Columbia be any better, educationally, humanly, than the present preponderantly white Columbia? I didn't think so.

Watching outside Hamilton I saw a professor approach the two guards with a grin and a "Hello!" He probably needed something in his office. Luckily I didn't urgently need anything in mine: classes had been officially suspended for the rest of the week. The guards ignored the professor. No campus pleasantries or amenities for them. No visible reaction of any kind. And was it that day or later that a banner appeared over the entrance saying MALCOLM X UNIVERSITY? This message seemed a mixture of put-on and—again—portent, especially if one remembered that angry shouts of "To Columbia!" had been heard during the disturbances in Harlem following Martin Luther King's death three weeks earlier.

It was clear that the blacks dominated the situation at Columbia. There were only about seventy active student blacks at the University. But, organized into the Students Afro-American Society (SAS), and supported by Harlem CORE, SNCC, and the Mau Mau Society, the strength of each was as the strength of, say a hundred whites. This weird imbalance of forces had been dramatized the night before in the muted power struggle between the SAS and the SDS-oriented whites in Hamilton. Some of the story of this struggle was in Wednesday's *Spectator,* the undergraduate-edited newspaper; and the rest of it could be heard over WKCR, the student-run radio station. (These two local media were more reliable than the city media, and they

continued to function admirably throughout
the crisis.) What happened in Hamilton during
the long, unseasonably hot, sleepless night of
Tuesday-Wednesday was, in its political essence, very much what had happened the year
before at the Chicago Conference for a New
Politics—a decisive black–white split engineered by the blacks, greatly to their advantage. But this time the split occurred, not
only on the parliamentary level as at Chicago,
but also on the level of *action,* intense, confused, beset by immediate perils for both
factions. I doubt that American students had
ever before, even at Berkeley in 1964, found
themselves engaged in decisions and actions
of such moment, locally and nationally.

The all-white demonstration in Hamilton
had been gradually infiltrated by blacks,
including the professional outside organizers.
"The black community is taking over," a
SNCC man announced. Two separate caucuses developed. Those in the white caucus
debated whether they should leave the building or stay and risk involvement with the
blacks, some of them reportedly armed, in an
action of indeterminate magnitude and violence. Those whites who wanted to stay hoped
for some limited form of action carried out on
the basis of black-white solidarity. At dawn,
the blacks settled the matter by asking—ordering—the divided whites to leave in a body.
They did, very unhappily, their dreams of
interracial solidarity disappointed.

There they were, some 300 of them, outside
in the dawn light, shaken, exhausted, confused, the doors of Hamilton barricaded behind them. What then came into play among
them was a kind of "challenge and response"
psychology which was to operate throughout
the entire crisis of the next few weeks. Some
people have dismissed this mental state as the
low-grade "chicken" psychology of gang warfare. But I think it is more accurately described
as a system of competitive militancy. Their

militancy challenged by that of the blacks, the
whites could only respond as militantly as
possible. They were soon streaming across
campus to the formidable bulk of Low Library,
from which they had been locked out the day
before. There they smashed through the
Security Entrance and occupied the President's
suite. In doing so they incurred large temporary losses. About half of them fled at the noise
of the door being smashed; a lot more leapt
from the windows when the police arrived for
the Rembrandt. But some forty-seven stayed,
and many others returned later. Why did their
occupancy of Low survive the removal of the
Rembrandt? Because, as I understand it, the
Administration feared that to evacuate the
whites in Low would have been to invite re-
prisals from Hamilton and from a Harlem still
smouldering in the aftermath of the King
murder. Besides, Dean Coleman was still a
Hamilton hostage.

By Wednesday afternoon the group in Low
felt secure enough to act as if this were no mere
sit-in demonstration but a take-over demonstration. So, by way of making themselves at
home, they went about doing all those things—
daring, ingenious, outrageous—that everybody
in the world was soon to hear about. They
re-connected lights and phones; explored the
President's files for tell-tale documents, found
his Xerox machine out of order and repaired
it to copy the documents, reportedly discovered his World War II draft card and sent
it back to his draft board; smoked his cigars,
drank his sherry, worked at his desk, lined up
to use his bathroom, inspected the books on
his shelves, vacuumed the rugs, slept wherever
a surface offered, held interminable meetings,
climbed in and out of windows, and received
guests. The guests included a distinguished
professor of history. Wearing the academic
robe in which he, uniquely at Columbia, con-
ducts his classes, he arrived "like Batman" by
the grille-and-windowsill route to urge their

departure. But it was the brave, conscientious professor who did the departing.

They had—in their word—"liberated" the President's office and everything usable in it. By doing so they had also released in themselves latent energies of all kinds, from the creative to the euphoric to the malicious. Euphoric, it seemed to me, was the impulse that led them to read, copy, and publicize portions of the President's correspondence. In the long run this procedure was self-defeating. It indulged the revolutionary delusions of the fanatical few in their own ranks, while submitting too many others to a test of political sophistication which they were glad to flunk.

The euphoria, I must add, was no overnight phenomenon. It persisted beyond the first dramatic hours in Low, consolidated itself as a political force on campus, became a contagion, spread to large numbers of students and younger teachers who, I would guess, by normal temper and conviction, were scarcely to be identified with the fanatical few. In other words, what had originated as a demonstration began to assume in their minds the stature of a revolution—a power seizure effected within a single institution which they regarded as a microcosm of the whole society. True, this delusion—as I fear it must be called—was unwittingly encouraged by the grim intransigence of the central Administration, which, becoming virtually invisible, refusing to negotiate with the rebels "under coercion," threatening police action, was like an embattled government-in-exile. Their fear of the consequences of the demonstration seems to have amounted to sheer physical repugnance toward meeting its leaders in person. David Truman confided to a *Newsweek* interviewer that it made him "uncomfortable to be in the same room with" Mark Rudd. (It is reported, however, that David Truman did on at least one occasion try, with-

out success, to make personal contact with the rebels in the President's office.)

Still, the delusion remained a delusion, whatever its causes. And although industrious rebel researchers were able to come up with historical precedents for their "liberation" of the President's letters (for example, Benjamin Franklin's interception of the Governor Hutcheson letters in 1775), these precedents had the effect of further confusing the issue. The issue, as I saw it, was the precise function of demonstrations in the realm of radical politics. The leftist English critic, John Berger, writing in *New Society* (May 28, 1968), observes that "the aims of a demonstration are symbolic." They are "rehearsals . . . of revolutionary awareness. . . . The demonstrators' view of the city surrounding their stage changes. By demonstrating, they manifest a greater freedom and independence—a greater creativity even, although the product is only symbolic—than they can ever achieve individually or collectively when pursuing their regular lives. In their regular pursuits they only modify circumstances; by demonstrating they symbolically oppose their very existence to circumstances." Up to a point "the rehearsal of revolutionary awareness" at Columbia was the more effective in its symbolic character, the richer in "creativity," because, unlike average street demonstrations—which, as Berger says, symbolize the revolutionary seizure of whole cities—the Columbia event took place almost entirely on the confined territory formed by the University's walled-in Morningside campus. This territory became a kind of articial city, but *only* an artificial one. To assume, as the extremists assumed, that the University could be subverted, as a city state or a national state can be subverted by large-scale revolutionary action, was to mistake the symbol for the reality, and thus to threaten the future of the University under any conceivable management. To my mind, the rifling and publicizing of the letters was a symbol more of revolutionary hubris, than of revolutionary consciousness.

For the rest, the inventive zeal let loose by the Low demonstrators was to be a powerful force on campus for many days and nights. Columbia became the setting for a continuous "Happening," in which the political content was fused with the generally antic form, and the meaning of the whole act was—or seemed to be—in the act itself. Reporters and photographers flocked to Morningside to record the scandalous comedy of it all. With raggle-taggle students draped all over its classic facades, the University's austerely monumental campus, in neo-Renaissance brick and stone, had never before been so photogenic. But the actions were not *always* antic and their meaning was not *wholly* in the actions themselves. On the contrary they attracted many formerly uncommitted students to the cause of the demonstrators.

Being "where the action is" had acquired political status. Meanwhile many other students were driven to extremes of opposition, an opposition which soon consolidated itself in the quasi-vigilante group known as the Majority Coalition replacing the Students for a Free Campus mentioned above. By Wednesday afternoon, moreover, the demonstrators were ready with a list of demands, duly mimeographed and distributed on campus. The demands boiled down to three: no gym in Morningside Park, no ties with the Pentagon-related Institute for Defense Analysis, and amnesty for all the demonstrators in the present action as well as in that of March 27. But the amnesty demand was declared to be non-negotiable: Acceptance of it by the Administration was a condition for any transactions at all. Similarly, the Administration had announced itself to be opposed to amnesty as firmly as the demonstrators were for it. So the

list of demands looked like a bid for further confrontations from both parties, culminating sooner or later in the supreme confrontation of a police raid.

It was, however, only the fearsome presence of the Hamilton blacks that enabled the whites to hold out in Low, at least through the first day (Wednesday) of their occupancy. After Wednesday—since nothing succeeds like success or, in political terms, nothing makes for *de facto* legitimacy like staying put—they collected, as I said, enough moderate support to survive in Low more or less on their own, and presently to add three more buildings to their empire. With three entire buildings and a presidential suite for whites, and one entire building for blacks, the rebels had, one sardonic professor noted, the makings of an independent "university complex," duly separatist, and lacking nothing toward the inauguration of intramural sports—except a gymnasium. Something like this possibility was to occur retrospectively to Archibald Cox of the Harvard Law School, who became the chairman of a fact-finding commission set up after the April 30 police raid. Questioning a witness, Cox asked: "Did it ever occur to the Administration to just *leave* the demonstrators in the buildings and go on with the university's business?" "No," replied the witness, "that was unthinkable."

So a tenuous solidarity did actually exist between the two racial groups until the police raid. The declared demands of the blacks coincided with those of the whites. After the raid the blacks, making their own deal with the Administration, agreed to a peaceful evacuation of Hamilton under the auspices of the police, a couple of watchful city officials, and an elder statesman of the black movement, Kenneth Clark. In the month-long student strike that ensued, the blacks took no active part. Presumably, they decided—or it was decided for them—that their point had been sufficiently made by their occupying Hamilton for a week and leaving it neat as a pin. I mention the neatness because the University authorities made so much of it in their propaganda, possibly by way of trying to justify their separate treatment of the blacks. If so, their defense was logically vulnerable. It was as if the illegal occupation of buildings were somehow less illegal if the occupiers were good housekeepers. In any case, there was to be no special treatment for the whites, and no guard of honor to preside over their final dragging-out on April 30. If the authorities were less afraid of the whites, they were also, it seems, more determined to punish them, or at least to make certain of punishing their leaders. "Whatever happens, *you'll* be expelled!" one high official impulsively shouted at Mark Rudd on a public occasion.

II

The official propaganda was one thing. The tightness of the spot the officials were on was another: fearful, pitiable, grotesque, disastrous. Physically they were confined to substitute quarters on the ground floor of Low where they communed endlessly with representatives of the Trustees, of City Hall, of Harlem, of the police, of the faculty, of the moderate student body, etc. Emotionally and politically they were confined by less tangible but more serious considerations. Among these *may* have been: personal anger, understandable but unstatesmanly, at the invasion of presidential privacy by the demonstrators upstairs; belief that the rebellion was merely an extreme symptom of a debilitated and overly "permissive" society against which President Kirk had inveighed in certain public addresses; inefficient operation of the Complex Trustees-Kirk-Truman chain of command (three days notice was required to convene a meeting of the Trustees); refusal to appoint an emergency

committee of faculty and students to advise Administration members, mediate between them and the demonstrators, keep them posted on campus affairs, above all on the rapidly swelling ranks of student protestors. The authorities' lack of information on this last point, their persistence in the belief that only "a small disruptive minority" was involved, made great trouble for all, including the undermanned police contingent, when the April 30 raid occurred. Testifying weeks later to the Cox Commission, the Dean of the Graduate Faculties, who is third in command among Administration members, admitted that he had been "flabbergasted" at the multitude of demonstrators found in the buildings by the police. Instead of the estimated total of 350, he said, there had been 300 in Fayerweather Hall alone.

Contributing crucially to the tightness of the spot the Administration was on was the urgency of the time element. This element, however, the Administration itself clearly introduced into the situation from the start. Early Wednesday, one official said, "There's going to be a limit" on the time allowed the demonstrators; while another made the situation still clearer by saying "We are making every effort to reach a solution without *resorting to police action*" (my italics). Only as the end approached did the active faculty— and, I think, many of the demonstrators— suspect that it had been more or less predetermined, both as to the date and to the means (i.e., police action). Meanwhile, faculty members and demonstrators had been consulting together in mediation sessions and, seemingly, in good faith, as if the end were *not* fully determined, as to either date or means.

What no one outside the Administration quite knew at the time, however, was the exact extent and nature of the outside pressure being exerted upon it to act quickly and firmly. The authorities did, it is true, make a great deal of the numerous letters and phone calls they received from other schools urging upon Columbia the kind of prompt and decisive action which would keep the infection of student revolt from spreading to their own premises. Out of these appeals, which no one doubts were many and impassioned, the authorities constructed for Columbia a messianic role. Columbia alone could save academic America! This was a terrible error. Columbia could best have helped to save academic America by first saving itself. Doing this required that the authorities move with all *deliberate* speed. They did the opposite, and by resorting to speed without sufficient deliberation they imperiled Columbia's own future.

The severest pressure on the Administration seems to have come directly from the alumni—or rather from four members of the Board of Directors of the College Alumni Association who delegated to themselves the privilege of speaking for a total membership of about 25,000.

This point can be documented. Copies of a letter of April 27 addressed to President Kirk by the four alumni have circulated on campus. The letter formed a part of a document issued several weeks later by a group of sixteen athletes (including the all-star basketball players, David Newmark and James Mc-Millian). The sixteen had been invited to attend an official alumni dinner to receive awards. But they were subsequently *disinvited* when, hearing about the alumni's high-handed communications to Kirk, the athletes asked permission to read at the dinner a statement of their own position on the crisis. The letter of April 27 to President Kirk from the four alumni read, in part:

The take-over of Hamilton Hall and other University buildings, students ransacking and vandalizing your office, the complete disruption of the

University—this is anarchy and mob rule and cannot and must not be tolerated.

Accordingly, we urge upon you the following considerations:

1 The ultimatum of the demonstrators must be rejected;

2 The Administration must retain the right to discipline and that right should not be surrendered or delegated in this situation;

3 Discipline must be invoked and it must be swift, strong and appropriate to the circumstances.

We commend you and Dr. Truman for the firmness which you have shown in not capitulating to mob rule. We urge you to remain steadfast.

Any action short of the foregoing will, in our view, result in an invitation for further trouble of a higher order; further, the affection and *support* (my italics) which you have from the alumni will be lost.

It was only natural and decent for the alumni to express solidarity with the President in his distress. But to mingle threats with the sentiments of solidarity, and actually to specify, in their three points, the precise procedures he should use in settling the crisis, was to stage a "confrontation" of their own, and one which, as the word "support" probably implies, had important financial implications. But the fact is that the President, resentful though he may well have been at this rude intrusion into University affairs, accepted, for whatever reasons of his own, the alumni ultimatum. He eventually acted in a manner that was "appropriate to the circumstances," namely, called in the police.

The sixteen athletes refused to be excluded from the alumni dinner. While the alumni were drinking and dining inside the Columbia Club the sixteen picketed the building outside, wearing their C jackets, in a rainstorm—to be grudgingly admitted after considerable delay on the insistence of younger alumni at the dinner. Another lockout of students had been enacted, this time not of radical students but of just ordinary ones. A *New York Times* sportswriter made out of this incident an ironic little story worthy of Charles Dickens.

But the sixteen were not a band of helpless Dickensian waifs shut out in a storm by a lot of Mr. Podsnaps. They had had a Columbia education!—and on top of that a month-long extra-curricular course in crisis politics. The statement they had prepared for the alumni is headed WHY WE ARE HERE and is better formulated than most such documents issued during the Troubles by other groups, student or faculty or Administration. It has the further advantage, for me as the author of this article, that it documents fully the general state of opinion prevailing among those many students whom I have vaguely called the "moderates" and who were, and still are, a very effective force for good on campus. For all these reasons I include the important part of their statement *in toto*.

1 The "fundamental rights of free speech and assembly" were abrogated by the University Administration. President Kirk had issued an arbitrary ban on indoor demonstrations. But far more important than this, free speech is meaningless at Columbia when it exists in a vacuum and is unheeded by Administration officials.

2 One cannot divorce the issues from the events at Columbia. The issues here *are* the Institute for Defense Analysis, the gymnasium, and the restructuring of the University. The occupation of buildings by the demonstrators came after many attempts by students, faculty, and community members to oppose I.D.A. and the gym through legitimate channels. The Administration was repeatedly unresponsive to the demands of these groups.

3 The Administration must *now* delegate disciplinary powers to the students and faculty. Those most involved in student life are the most qualified to pass judgment on disciplinary affairs.

4 An overwhelming majority of students supported the demands of the demonstrators in a university-wide referendum conducted by the Ted Kremer Society and the Van Am Society (two undergraduate honor societies). The Strike Committee now represents 5,000 students. The demonstrators and their supporters were never a "small militant minority."

5 We find it deplorable that in the statement issued directly after the police action on campus, there was *no* mention whatsoever of the brutal and terrifying violence committed by the police who were called onto this campus by the Columbia Administration. By resorting to this police action the University once again displayed its intransigence and unwillingness to negotiate. This action inevitably resulted in the aggravation of the situation. In addition, many people, including faculty and innocent bystanders, were injured by the police. Do the members of the Alumni Association actually support police intervention on campus?

6 The Board of Directors of the Alumni Association has claimed to speak for 25,000 alumni. Do they represent your views accurately enough to threaten the Administration with loss of alumni support? This coercion may well have contributed to President Kirk's decision to bring the police on campus.

Our Proposals

1 We believe that the University exists for its faculty and its students. The University also exists within a community. These groups must play a *significant role* in the decision-making process of the University. The ultimate role of the Administration should be to implement and co-ordinate the will of students, faculty, and community.

2 Civil and criminal charges must be dropped against all demonstrators; discipline should be handled within the University by faculty and students.

3 The gym and I.D.A. are urgent and pressing considerations and action must be taken on them immediately. We do not want these issues to be submerged in committees for yet another year.

Considering the powerful and unique position occupied by the Alumni, we strongly urge you to help us to implement the necessary reforms in our University.

The sixteen signatures that follow I omit.

III

Because the Administration refused to negotiate "under coercion"—while, that is, the rebels remained in the buildings—the only other permanent University body with any claims to authority, and hence with any grounds for attempting negotiations, was the faculty. But the authority of the Columbia faculty is clearly defined only in respect to academic affairs. It is particularly amorphous in respect to administrative affairs. Moreover, the total Columbia faculty is actually made up of a number of individual and quite separate faculties (of Medicine, Law, Business, Engineering, etc.) which until the crisis had never been convened as a single body. Further, these several faculties have widely divergent interests and include members with differing ideas of their roles and responsibilities as teachers. In addition, the members of Columbia's faculty system have recently been subjected to a complication of loyalties which if not peculiar to Columbia has become exceptionally acute here. On the one hand, our Vietnam-fevered students have been expecting—and getting—more sympathetic attention from us individually and as a body than ever before—attention which, on the war issue, can amount to outright identification. On the other hand, we have—or had— equally personal affinities with the Administration which, from the Vice President down to the local deans, is now packed with men who recently belonged to the faculty and who, as in the prime case of David Truman—

elevated to his present rank only last year—we think of as colleagues still. Finally, as I have said, Columbia has had no faculty-administration committee or all-University senate, such as exists in certain other universities, to act in emergencies.

In the present Columbia emergency, the gap was filled by a self-appointed body that came to be known as the Ad Hoc Faculty Group (AHFG). The nucleus of the AHFG met informally on Wednesday morning the 24th. Those present were greatly alarmed by the possibilities of destruction and bloodshed which seemed to be implicit in the blacks' occupation of Hamilton and the confinement of Dean Coleman. The discussion was agitated. Out of it emerged, in embryonic form, two considerations that were to become major issues in the later deliberations of the AHFG. One was the strongly felt necessity of forestalling police action. The other was the necessity of setting up some kind of body—students, faculty, administrators—to decide methods of disciplining the offenders in the present demonstration. Without such a body, disciplinary action would rest in the hands of the President, in whom all final powers—legislative, executive, *and* judicial—are vested by our 150-year-old statutes.

Both of these concerns were embodied in a resolution introduced by Daniel Bell (Sociology) to an emergency meeting of the *College* faculty Wednesday afternoon. The meeting was a curiously casual affair. At the start, more than a half hour was spent debating the first clause of the Bell resolution, which of necessity had been composed in haste. The first clause read: "A university exists as a community dedicated to rational discourse, and the use of communication and persuasion as the means of furthering discourse."

Such an abstract appeal to first principles would be a luxury at any time. It was an absurdity just then, when the necessary corollary to it—the recognition that a university is also a *social institution*—was being luridly dramatized in several ways: by the fact that we were meeting in a science classroom instead of in our usual quarters, the elegant Faculty Room adjacent to the President's now "liberated" offices; by the shouts of mutually hostile student groups outside; by the sudden arrival of Dean Coleman, just released from his round-the-clock confinement in a Hamilton Hall threatened—as it appeared—by an outbreak of fires and gun battles. Some "community"! Some "discourse"! The meeting did nonetheless pass the Bell resolution with several modifications. These represented compromises appropriate to a faculty now clearly divided into, roughly, right, left, and center contingents. In the resolution the demonstrators were condemned; amnesty was tacitly refused them; opposition to police action was cautiously affirmed; suspension of further work on the present gym site was urged pending the approval of "a group of community spokesmen to be appointed by the Mayor"; and the disciplinary body proposed at the morning meeting was voted in, having acquired the name of a "tripartite committee," to include faculty, student, and administration representatives.

President Kirk, who briefly chaired the meeting, took occasion to remind us that "under the present statutes of the University, its role (that of the tripartite committee) would be purely advisory." He made no mention at this time of any disposition to have the statutes changed by the Trustees, whose "property" they are; although later on, when the general situation was much worse, he did give vague indications of such a disposition. When, however, the tripartite committee was finally established (as the Joint Committee on Disciplinary Affairs), after the April 30 police

raid, the President harassed its feeble infant existence to such an extent that the committee members made reluctant concessions which proved unfortunate all round.

Indeed, I have come to think that the whole tripartite committee issue as developed by the AHFG, which took it over from the College faculty meeting, was a mistake. For one thing, the motives behind it were mixed, or at least confused, in our minds at the time. On the one hand, the motives were both humane and politic. We wanted to make it as certain as possible that the disciplining of the demonstrators would not be so severe as to make for further strife on campus. On the other hand, we capitalized on the general emergency to attempt a cautious power play of our own by way of the proposed Tripartite Committee. It didn't work, owing to Kirk's stubborn shrewdness in defending the prerogatives of his office. Meanwhile the President's qualified acceptance of the committee bred illusions among the membership concerning the reality of our little power. Further, those members of the AHFG who set about holding mediation sessions with the demonstrators were in the awkward position of using, however cautiously, this and other merely *projected* reforms as a bargaining point.

On Thursday, April 25, the AHFG acquired its name, together with a steering committee of sixteen professors, many of them specialists in the relevant disciplines of government, law, history, and sociology. The AHFG also acquired a general membership composed of the approximately 200 professors (junior staff was later admitted) who signed the AHFG statement Wednesday afternoon. The statement's contents approximated those of the College faculty resolution voted Wednesday afternoon, but the severity of the crisis was described in terms far more emphatic and authoritative. Point 4 read: "Until this crisis is settled, we will stand before the occupied buildings to prevent forcible entry by the police or others." Finally, the AHFG acquired a regular place of meeting: the Graduate Students Lounge in 301 Philosophy Hall where the students are normally served tea and cookies and provided with other much needed forms of assistance. With its comfortable chairs and sofas in green leather, its immensely tall, heavily draped, windows extending around three sides, 301 Philosophy became our political clubroom throughout the April days. It was the scene of crowded gatherings; of reports from the members of the steering committee who were carrying on mediation sessions with the demonstrators; of endless speeches; of disputes which in a few cases (extreme left and extreme right) resulted in walk-outs; of rumors; of excited announcements of sudden emergencies on campus. In the long run, the AHFG's efforts toward conciliation were a failure—or, as an original member of the Group, Professor of Anthropology Marvin Harris, has asserted in a brilliant and indispensable article (*Nation,* June 10, 1968), in effect a sell-out and a disaster because the faculty as a whole failed to act independently and decisively. In any case, mediation between the intransigent Administration and the intransigent "hard core" demonstrators proved futile in the circumstances. Amnesty remained non-negotiable for both sides. Hostility toward the mediators increased on both sides. On Saturday the 27th Mark Rudd rushed panting into 301 Philosophy to shout that the whole procedure was "bullshit."

For me, however, the Group meetings were at least vastly instructive. While Marvin Harris's drastic conclusions seem to rest on the assumption that Columbia's faculty was capable of instant "politicalization," my own reaction was the opposite. I was amazed at the extent to which we *were* "politicalized,"

and within a single week. With this in mind, I believed that concerted and independent faculty action would be an achievement of the future, and despite many disappointments thus far, I cling to that belief, if only by my thumbs.

Listening to the chief speakers of the AHFG, I occasionally asked myself if they constituted any kind of an intellectually cohesive group which might be said to form a Columbia "elite." Elite, yes, I decided, but without the overtones of exclusiveness attached to that word. No faculty group is so cohesive at Columbia as to constitute itself a ruling circle, even if it wanted to. Indeed, it is not unusual for an exceptional individual, such as the late Andrew Chiappe (English), to be thought of as an elite of one. Still, most of the Ad Hoc leaders shared enough intellectual common ground to cause, not the deliberate exclusion of others, but the necessity on the part of certain others to exclude themselves, to go their own way. One of these was the great mathematician and pioneer Columbia reformer, the lean gentle quixotic Serge Lang. Another was Marvin Harris, a powerful speaker, whose logic never lapsed, whose syntax never wavered, even when his face went literally black with passion. No, in the leaders' eyes Lang and Harris were not politically "reliable." From the start they were for granting amnesty or some rhetorical simulacrum of it. So was I (and so were many others) after about the third day. In the past my own differences with the "elite" had been a matter more of temperament than of fully formulated or expressed dissent on my part. From their point of view amnesty wasn't a reliable position, politically; it was too simple to be arguable in an intellectual milieu where only the arguable was the possible. The mere thought of amnesty annihilated that universe of logics, structures, processes, continuities, compromises, pragmatic realism, anti-ideology "discourse," and "dialogue" which most of the leaders inhabited by reason partly of the subjects they taught, partly of the generation they belonged to.

So I have, after all, characterized the Ad Hoc leaders, or a majority of them, as an intellectually cohesive group: the post New Deal, post World War II intelligentsia. Naturally, their own talents and good will, with a little help from the *Zeitgeist,* had made them influential—but, again, not wholly dominant—at Columbia. And naturally they chose to exercise their special talents and temperaments in those strenuous, and well-meaning, efforts at mediation with the radical students, even at the risk of their turning out to be—as in fact they were—as quixotic as Serge Lang. In any case it was a pleasure to study their several styles as speakers and thinkers, together with their efforts, in some cases, to *preserve* their styles amid the terrible identity-devouring convulsions of the crisis: Allan Westin (Public Law and Government), with his man-of-destiny manner, his powerful compact figure, an artist of parliamentary procedure to the extent of audaciously violating procedure when he saw fit; Immanuel Wallerstein (Sociology), with his affecting wailing-wall rhetoric and gesticulation; Allen Silver (Sociology), quiet, concentrated, intense, suffering, his considerable wit sounding as if it, too, were wrung from world anguish; and Robert Belknap (Russian) whose perfect logic and selfless adherence to principle make him a one-man vindicator of classic liberalism.

If the mediation efforts were quixotic, so was another specialty of the AHFG: the patrols we organized, partly to keep the peace between the demonstrators and the Majority Coalitionists (or "jocks"), partly to manifest our opposition to the use of police in the crisis. This passionate opposition to the police was, I think, the one great stabilizing and unifying element in the AHFG. The impulse behind it would probably bear extensive analysis—

legal, psychological, and phenomenological. On our parts, however, it was just a matter of instinct, but the instinct proved right. The police action resorted to by the authorities on April 30—and again, on a smaller scale but with more vicious effects on May 22–23—was catastrophic for the cause of peace and unity at Columbia.

When, as a patrol member, you weren't attending meetings in 301 Philosophy you were on the patrol line alongside some occupied building, wearing a white armband made out of a rolled up handkerchief like an improvised tourniquet to identify you. You worked in daily and nightly shifts. And between your attendance at meetings and your presence on the patrol line there was little time for sleep, reading, food, reflection. Memory failed; all happenings seemed somehow simultaneous in the mind. The passing days added up to a single unit of time, unbroken and seemingly endless.

The increasingly hallucinatory atmosphere of our lives was intensified by the unpredictableness of happenings on campus. There were continual emergencies that required your hasty departure from your apartment or from 301 Philosophy to the scene of action. Once it is the sudden arrival at the Broadway gate of some fifty members of the Mau Mau Society led by Charles X Kenyatta, many of them in jungle dress, the kids swinging bicycle chains, the whole band demanding entry to College Walk, while the jocks, a couple of hundred strong, demand their exclusion from campus, and Dean Coleman with the aid of the faculty patrol seeks to "cool it"—and finally does. Again, at about 10 p.m. on Thursday the 25th, it is the jocks again, this time moving on Fayerweather, determined to drag out the rebels who had earlier added this fourth building to the university-complex. No city police or campus police are on hand to intercede. So 301 Philosophy is largely emptied of Ad Hocs to serve as riot police. There is no bull-horn, but Seymour Melman (Industrial Engineering) has a voice (and spirit) of roughly equivalent carrying power. He uses it. The jocks hesitate, listen. An exchange of witticisms between Westin and a boy in the crowd relaxes things. Belknap—calm, sensible, teacherly—says, "I am Robert Belknap of the Russian Department, chairman of freshman humanities. You've read all those books by Plato and Aristotle and Thucydides. You know that violence is no good." The crowd attends, but one youth slips around the corner to climb unseen on to a windowsill. "If you go inside you'll have the blood on your mind for a lifetime," somebody sternly warns him. The youth climbs down. The jocks are invited to send a delegation to the AHFG meeting. They agree to do so and the crowd disperses—for the time being.

Actual violence does briefly erupt early Friday, this time from the police. It is about 1 a.m. and I am just leaving Philosophy for some reason when I see David Truman striding into the building with a very grim face, and naturally I follow him back inside. Taking his stand at the rear of the crowd, he says, "Gentlemen, you're not going to like what I have to tell you. Five minutes ago President Kirk was on the phone to call for the police." Since the police call defies AHFG sentiment, Truman may have felt that he owed it to his old colleagues to at least warn them, at whatever cost to his dignity. If so, this is decent of him and the cost is great. He promptly leaves amid cries of "Shame," "Liar," and "I resign." The meeting is in an uproar. Most of us rush outdoors, I to patrol Hamilton with about fifty others. There on the steps we form lines three deep, locking arms for warmth as well as solidarity. Inside Hamilton, the blacks show no awareness of our presence. In front of us a crowd of student sympathizers masses, some of them passing us containers of coffee. Occasional hoots of derision and menace come

out the windows of Hartley, the residence hall adjacent to Hamilton. The hooters are jocks, evidently. A cherry bomb explodes in the narrow court between the buildings, making loud reverberations. Out of the darkness, one by one, come several eminent visitors to pass along our line, reviewing the troops; City Hall men, an unidentified Harlemite, the sympathetic politician Paul O'Dwyer, shaking our hands as he passes. After a couple of very tense hours somebody announces that the raid has been called off and work on the gym site temporarily suspended.

So at Hamilton our heroism went unrewarded that night, except that our presence there, and the presence of faculty lines at other occupied buildings, notably at Low, where plainclothesmen did attack the line and injure at least one man, made the Administration call off the raid. Meanwhile, several AHFG members had gone inside Low to join Lindsay's aides in urging restraint on the Administration. They report of finding Truman in a torment of indecision. One cause of his indecision may have been communicated to him by police officials: if the police were not used that night they would be unavailable in sufficient numbers until Sunday night at the earliest, because so many of them would be needed to control the Peace demonstrations and counter-demonstrations scheduled for the weekend (Saturday and Sunday the 27th and 28th) in several parts of the city.

The Administration seems to have tried to turn this delay to advantage. About noon on Friday a College dean remarked to me in a confidential tone, "We are educating the faculty." He meant, I think, that the Administration was granting us time to exhaust our mediation efforts, with the expectation that we would then become reconciled to police action. By Saturday, when Rudd made his historic cry of "Bullshit," the attempts at mediation, conducted as they were without substantial support from the administration, *had* failed. A number of perfectly conscientious professors *were* reconciled to police action. But a good many others were *not* reconciled to it. Communication between the AHFG and the Administration became increasingly strained. There were intemperate public outbursts from high University officials and members of the Board of Trustees. These were taken by many to mean that the few conciliatory gestures made by the University authorities were bluff. A fifth domain was added to the rebel empire: Mathematics Hall, with a red flag flying from the roof, and the professional SDS organizer, Tom Hayden, more or less in charge. By Saturday some 600 police were on and around the campus, despite the Peace demonstrations.

The meetings in 301 Philosophy became wilder and stranger, especially at night, with the room's expanses taxed to capacity, the air dim with tobacco smoke. Outside, watchers pressed against the tall windows in spectral masses. Along the north wall the row of windows is cut by a diagonal line made by the ramp leading up to Revlon Plaza outside. The watchers strung upwards along the ramp diminished in size till, at the top, only their faces were visible, floating in air like disembodied cherubs or gargoyles. (The watchers at the top were sitting or lying on the ramp in order to see in.) Fingers slyly inserted themselves under the window frames to raise the frames so that our orations could be heard as well as seen. "Shut the windows, please," Westin the chairman repeatedly and patiently directed. As public figures we commanded vaster and more excited audiences than any of us could ever have had, or wanted, as mere teachers!

When we were outside on patrol the fantastic nature of our operations became unmistakable. Politically, this patrolling was a delicate business. We could be—and were—accused of, on the one hand, protecting the demonstrators and, on the other hand, of sealing them off. In fact our platonic neutrality was almost impossible to maintain. Physical nearness to the rebels brought us closer to them in sympathy, hardship for hardship, danger for danger. And qualm for qualm, too (assuming *they* felt any), because their illegal acts were forcing us to engage in acts which if not illegal were certainly unconventional, turning teachers into cop watchers. And just as the demonstrators constantly improvised, so did we. Indeed certain highly politicized members of Columbia's religious counseling staff excelled at showy improvisations, verbal, acrobatic and ceremonial, one of them solemnizing the marriage of a rebel couple in an occupied building. As a result, some of us wished that God *hadn't* died. So, day and night, as violence threatened and the number of cops on campus steadily multiplied, and my block of West 116th Street filled up with squad cars, mobil information units, busloads of bored and waiting patrolmen, limousines bearing policewomen in chic uniforms and high-heels, splendidly mounted police from (presumably) the theater district, our ambiguous patrolling went on.

IV

Along the west wall of Low, on Sunday and Monday, real action threatened. Several hundred members of the Majority Coalition, their original ranks increased by the arrival of girl friends and of graduate recruits from the professional schools, moved in to block further deliveries of food to the demonstrators occupying the President's offices. The Ad Hoc patrol was strung along a narrow ledge (an architectural not a geological ledge) beneath the demonstrators' windows. A twelve-foot strip of turf separated us from a low-clipped privet hedge bordering a brick walk where the Coalitionists first gathered. On this accidental playground a heady three-cornered game commenced at close quarters. It got tougher when, after several impatient hours, the Coalitionists suddenly leaped the hedge *en masse* and gathered on the turf between ledge and hedge, within grabbing distance of the patrol—if either party, patrol or Coalitionists, had wished to do any grabbing. How the Ad Hoc group tried—and failed—to set up rules for this game may be seen from the following instructions, drafted and mimeographed at about 3 a.m. Sunday the 28th.

Policy On Patrolling Low Library
28 April, 1968

1. Faculty will not permit ingress of persons (i.e. demonstrators and sympathizers) except for specially designated couriers accompanied by a mediator or a member of the Steering Committee of the Ad Hoc Faculty Group.

2. If an individual reaches the ledge with food, he may hand it up; however, he may not approach the ledge via the steps.

3. Faculty will not assist individuals to run a blockade at the hedge.

4. Blockaders at the hedge will not be permitted on the ledge.

5. Faculty will aid the ingress of required medical supplies.

The hedge-ledge affair has become historic at Columbia. It epitomized, among other things, the eccentric uses to which our exuberant neo-Renaissance architecture (as full of inviting surfaces, ascents, and footholds as a jungle gym) and not so exuberant landscaping were being put, not to mention the eccentric roles now adopted by faculty members *vis-à-vis* the fiercely polarized bands of their students.

The game got still gamier as Sunday passed into Monday. Then rebels from the Math commune started tossing groceries to rebels in Low over the heads of the Coalitionists and the faculty patrol, while the athletic Coalitionists—

barehanded or with bats, tennis rackets, and food trays from the dining hall—sought to intercept the groceries in their flight. Fights broke out—which members of the patrol or other peace-makers usually cooled. For a while my post was at one end of the ledge, adjoining a ground floor entrance to Low which some of the jocks were impatient to enter. From there I stared down into the leaders' imploring or defiant faces. "If they ever caught Rudd they'd tear him to pieces," another patrol member said in my ear. Though unbelieving, I knew that his remark was definitely in the bleaker mood of the moment.

Other moods were grotesquely orchestrated with that one. The weather—that weekend as throughout most of the crisis—was ideally the weather for a ball game, a sail, a picnic, a wedding—the sky deeply blue, the spring sunlight inexhaustibly benign. Below me the strip between hedge and ledge was full of sturdy pink tulips, and "Don't step on the tulips!" was one slogan everybody took up. The tulips stayed intact until two very little black boys sneaked onto the ledge from somewhere. Could they pick some flowers? So they pulled several up by the bulbous roots, shouting, "Look, they got *onions* on them!" Just above me, a student I knew settled in an open window of the President's office and began to thumb a guitar. In the other windows other rebels began to sing "Solidarity Forever." Briefly, the yearning innocence of the oldtime Labor song, and of the singers' voices, silenced the crowd below. For me, momentarily, hedge, ledge, jocks, rebels, faculty, tulips, little blacks, newsmen, and sunlight all resolved themselves into the constituents of a painted scene, unforgettable.

The scene inside the occupied buildings was, we knew, less idyllic during that weekend. The occupants were getting ready for the police raid that was generally thought imminent. Barricades were strengthened. Precautions were taken against possible assaults with chemical MACE. Individually each demonstrator pondered where he (or she) would take his stand and whether he would accept or resist arrest, or maybe "split" beforehand. A Fayerweather student writing in *Rat* (May 3–16) says, "each liberated area was different, ours being wracked with political debate, wrangling and tensions. . . . Anyone who wanted could have left." The Fayerweather tensions came about because many occupants wanted, *primarily,* not a reformed world, but a reformed Columbia, one in which more self-determination would be possible for all, including workers in the University cafeterias.

In Fayerweather, too, a faction questioned the wisdom of the total amnesty demand and showed some willingness to consider an alternative—uniform, or collective, discipline—proposed by Ad Hoc mediators. Similar differences were possible, even in militant Math, where the commune spirit was especially exalted. But the several liberated areas finally stuck together, thanks chiefly to the persistence of the competitive militancy I have mentioned, with the supremely cohesive Hamilton blacks setting the pace for all the liberated areas, from Low to Math, to Avery, to Fayerweather.

At dawn on Sunday the 28th a Western Union operator waked me to read on the phone the text of a telegram from President Kirk that was sent to all members of the Morningside faculties. The convening of these traditionally separate entities in a joint meeting was unprecedented. President Kirk evidently wished to explore the sentiment and/or solicit the approval of faculties (Law, Business, Journalism, Engineering) whose members were not so likely to be found among the liberal arts activists who made up the Ad Hoc group's majority. There had been advance knowledge of this joint meeting. For presentation to it, the Ad Hoc steering committee had drafted a document known formally as The April 28th Resolution and informally as the "bitter pill" because it proposed solutions to the crisis which exacted hard sacrifices from all parties, not excluding the Administration. The heart of the resolution was in the first and fourth of the clauses.

I. . . . We believe that the dimensions and complexity of the current crisis demand that a new approach of collective responsibility be adopted, and in this light insist that uniform penalties be applied to all violators of the discipline of the University.

IV. These proposals being in our judgment a just solution to the crisis our University is presently undergoing, we pledge that

a. If the President will not adopt these proposals, we shall take all measures within our several consciences to prevent the use of force to vacate these buildings.

b. If the President does accept our proposals but the students in the buildings refuse to evacuate these buildings, we shall refuse further to interpose ourselves between the Administration and the students.

The resolution was accepted by a huge majority of the Ad Hoc membership meeting, at 9 a.m. on that same Sunday. It was then introduced into the Joint Faculties meeting at 10 a.m., with rhetorical skill and passion, by Allan Westin in conjunction with Immanuel Wallerstein (Sociology) and Dankwart Rustow (International Forces). The clause advocating collective punishment was debated pro and con on the floor. There appeared to be an increase in sentiment favorable to this promising compromise between, on the one hand, blanket amnesty, and on the other, a policy of graded individual punishments. The latter would require many separate trials for which acceptable evidence might be hard to produce. It would also thicken the punitive atmosphere on campus. Nonetheless Westin & Co. failed to bring our resolution to a vote. They decided, as I understand it, that a vote taken in this heterogeneous body might result in present cleavages which would lessen the chances of greater unity in the future. Instead, a substitute resolution was introduced by another group. Conciliatory toward all parties except the demonstrators, empty of any positive proposals, it was passed by a huge majority. I should add, the "greater unity" was never to materialize, the students eventually facing trials were to number some 900, and the punitive atmosphere on campus was to thicken and thicken.

The Ad Hoc resolution was not buried. It went to President Kirk with a request for a prompt reply. On Monday the 29th the reply came, in graciously phrased prose. Examined carefully, however, the phrasing was seen to be full of possible legal quibbles. There followed an agitated meeting of the Ad Hoc general membership that went on almost continuously until Monday midnight. One speaker, well known to all, urged us to trust in the President's good intentions. He seemed to be in the President's confidence. He suggested that the President's reply was as candid as possible under the circumstances. The President could not have said more without violating the University's statutes and exceeding the authority vested in him by the Trustees. In itself this appeal to trust was moving. But to go along with it meant trusting not only the President, whose conduct thus far was not reassuring. It also meant trusting the speaker's *impressions* of the President's mind. Finally it meant our asking the students to trust our impressions of the speaker's impressions of the President's mind. It all sounded like some improbable argument out of *Alice in Wonderland*. The President's reply was, in effect, rejected.

Later, as the evening wore on to midnight, our immediate concern was with the probable imminence of a police raid. Nobody seemed to know for certain that a raid would or wouldn't occur that night. It *was* known that the President had appointed a three-man "notification committee" to act if and when the Administration decided to call the police—a decision which, it was also known, required giving Police Commissioner Leary at least five hours to collect and deploy his forces. But the notification committee's function was, evidently, to advise the Administration and not to notify us. We had to rely on news brought us by members of the patrol coming off duty. Some reported that the number of police on campus was increasing. One man rushed in to announce that they were already in the tunnels, Columbia's far-flung network of underground passages created for the innocent purpose of housing cables, heating pipes, and other utilities. The announcement was premature, but only by a couple of hours!

In the meeting we could only try to dream up last-ditch solutions. The room was more packed than ever, the air dimmer with smoke, the watchers outside the windows a spectral multitude. Should we immediately appeal to the Trustees to stop the raid? Yes, but did anybody *know* a trustee? Somebody knew Trustee Butterwieser's *son*. How about Mayor Lindsay? No, he had probably washed his hands of the Columbia mess.[1] Or Governor Rockefeller— for after all Columbia was chartered by the State of New York? A telegram to the Governor was actually drafted, offstage so to speak. But whether it was ever sent I don't know, and it didn't matter.

Around midnight many of us left 301 Philosophy to join various patrol lines or simply to wander and look around. The appear-

---

[1] A telegram to Mayor Lindsay, dated April 29 and urging his intervention, *was* drafted by six officers of established student organizations, and copies were distributed to us and to members of the Administration. The telegram read: "Entire Columbia University student body would reject police presence on Campus. Widespread physical opposition certain. We strongly urge you to mediate between the administration and the demonstrators."

ance of the night-bound campus differed little from its appearance the night before, when predictions of a bust had proved false. For an hour or so I managed to hold in suspension the certainty that tonight was the night and the certainty that tonight wasn't the night. This divided state probably registered some deeper tension in me between dread and desire—desire, I truly confess, that my suspicions of the Administration would be confirmed by a raid. But if they *were* confirmed, should I, aged sixty-three, really "interpose" myself between the students and the police, as, in a way, our patrol duties thus far, and clause III B of the Bitter Pill Resolution, prescribed that we should do? I wavered, and even when the decision came, it did so through a conjunction of impulse and accident.

As I see it now, the intervening hours intensified the impulse. Such a lot of things were going on everywhere. You felt quite lost, as when you go alone to a movie in the afternoon and emerge afterwards, blinking, confused, and anonymous in the glare and racket of the city. It was as if I were two distinct persons, one of them almost stifling in the blackout of his usual "style," character, profession, identity; the other vaguely exulting in the strange feeling of freedom consequent upon the same feeling of loss.

This was a panic reaction and soon subsided. Joining the patrol on the crowded ledge at Low I found a couple of lively English instructors at the far end. They had got hold of a telephone connected to a long extension cord that snaked mysteriously through a half-open window into whatever dark office was inside. Neither of them knew how the phone got out there on the ledge, but one of them was calling his wife to tell her not to worry. We thought it amusing that the University's "facilities" were available to us in this outlandish situation. Below us were the milling jocks and their girls who, in the course of a couple of days and

nights, had become fixtures on the scene. Farther off, in the dark gaps between Lewisohn and Earl, and Earl and Math, battalions of patrolmen moved in and took stands under the tall trees in that quarter of the campus. Perhaps, we said, they were only changing guard again. They too had become fixtures within the artificial eternity of the past few days. Above us, however, the windows of the presidential suite were completely black and there was no sign or sound from the demonstrators within. So one feature of the scene appeared to be absent. (I learned later that they had decided to wait for the police in darkness.) It was disturbing.

I was cold. The Low patrol was more than adequately staffed. I left to go home for a sweater. On College Walk, however, I stopped for a time. From there much of the whole campus spectacle could be seen in its sinister grandeur. It held me: the glare of klieglights coming from the television crews who were setting up their equipment in front of Low; the winking of flashlights at several points in the dark reaches of South Field; the fluttering of the little candles, sheltered in cups, among the sprawl of students who had come to be known as the Sundial People; the stars that spattered the high, cold New York sky. A police lieutenant passed, unconcernedly checking with a pencil something attached to a clipboard—surely a map of the campus. I joined a couple of English department friends on the fringes of the Sundial crowd. The Sundial People were neither for God nor for his enemies (the Kirkites or the Ruddites), only against the police. Boys and girls, they lay around on dormitory blankets making talk and music. "It would be a good night to get laid," said one of my English department friends. Another reported the news from 301 Philosophy. There the band of faithful departmental secretaries, who for days had been supplying us with coffee and sandwiches, was about to set up an emergency First Aid station, since there was no sign that the University had itself made any provision for treating the injured. The secretaries were tearing up sheets for bandages—sheets commandeered, I believe, from one of the dormitories.

Something now occurred to me that had occurred earlier during the crisis but never before with such force. Just about everything on campus was being thoroughly *put to use* or would probably soon be put to use, although not for the purposes for which the things were intended. Blankets, sheets, ledges, window sills, lawns, walks, tunnels, the trees students perched in to see better, the roofs lined with watching students—or were they police? All were blithely liberated—the word was *true*—from their usual functions. What had been University or individual property was now almost anyone's property to make of what he liked in this charmed circle of pure improvisation. It was exhilarating.

I went home for a sweater. The warmth of the apartment was inviting. I hesitated whether to stay there or return to duty on campus. Suddenly the phone rang and my wife, calling from the country, said she had heard on the radio that the Bust was about to begin. I rushed out and, wearing a bulky ski sweater, was able to pass as one of fifty or so bulky sweatered plainclothesmen who were just then piling out of a bus and filing through the Administration gate, which I heard banging shut behind me, or should I, considering my latest disguise, say "us"? The big bust of April 30 was started.

The following Friday (May 3) I met my Shakespeare students for the first time in ten days. About half of the class (forty) was present. Several wore bandages, one was on crutches, one had his arm in a sling, and the teacher had a black eye. A well-organized student strike was strongly in force. There was great resentment of the police and still more resentment of an Administration which had been unable to solve the University's problems without resorting to force. The strike was supported—or in the prevailing euphemism— "respected" by large numbers of faculty members. Respecting the strike meant primarily holding class meetings in off-campus buildings, or on the lawn, or in the apartments of faculty members—anywhere except in regularly scheduled classrooms. This I, like many others, was delighted to do, and I asked the Shakespeare students to scribble down notes on what they wanted to do in class and where they wanted to do it. They were told that they could sign their notes or not as they pleased. All signed and with only two exceptions seemed to be pro-strike. Here are some representative responses:

No formal classes, nothing under University auspices. Off-campus meetings.

Classes: pure, unliberated Shakespeare.

Shakespeare is relevant to nearly everything, even the past week. I feel we should meet in any way possible—but without opposing or violating the strike.

Class should be kept as much as possible on Shakespeare. My saturation point for police and Trustee invective is very near.

After six days in the liberated building, which seems like two years ago, I would like to re-connect with Western Civilization's past, after a rather exhausting vision of the future.

The only studying I have been able to do in the past ten days has been to read *The Tempest* and *The Winter's Tale*. Classes *off-campus!*

Concluding note: Following the 1968 crisis, the University underwent a number of changes and reforms. President Kirk retired and Vice President Truman resigned his post. The gymnasium project in Morningside Park was abandoned. Under several legal guises, "amnesty" was granted the large majority of demonstrators who had been arrested and charged with various offenses. The University's connection with the Institute for Defense Analysis was formally severed. An all-University senate was instituted, with representatives from the faculty, the student body, and the administration. The curriculum was subjected to intensive scrutiny, and in some cases to useful innovation, by numerous student-faculty committees. Opposition to the Vietnam War became far more open and pronounced on campus, extending even to certain members of the high administration. It may therefore be concluded that the immediate objectives of the demonstrators, at least the more moderate faction among them, were in one way or another attained. But the extent to which all this activity made for a significantly better University is still a matter of debate.

Pre-Fitting the News At the Paper of Record
Jack Newfield

Jack Newfield, author of *Bread and Roses Too,* a collection of his articles written for the *Village Voice,* has been an editor for the *Voice* since 1965. His articles have also appeared in the *Nation, Life, Partisan Review,* and *Commonweal.* He worked for the Students for a Democratic Society at the time of its founding, was editor of a Manhattan community weekly, and later was a reporter for the *New York Post.* His other books include *A Populist Manifesto, A Prophetic Minority,* and *Robert Kennedy: A Memoir.*

It was 2 a.m. last Tuesday morning, outside Hamilton Hall, a few minutes before 1000 police and plainclothesmen began to charge the barricaded Columbia University student rebels. I turned to a tense and exhausted Human Rights Commissioner, William Booth, and asked, "What are your thoughts at this moment?"

"That the publisher of the New York Times and the District Attorney of Manhattan are trustees of Columbia," Booth replied.

It proved to be a prophetic comment in light of the way the Times reported the events at Columbia the next two days. Almost every story this planet's official "newspaper of record" published was inept, dishonest, and slanted against the student demonstrators.

Police brutality was downplayed. President Kirk was romanticized into a Lincolnesque victim. The fact that the police department's display of force unified the students for the first time was ignored. The questions why plainclothesmen were used in the raid, and why no ambulances were present, were never asked.

But before analyzing the stories published by the Times, two background facts must be established, First, that there actually was brutality, and second, that the Times itself was unethically implicated in the planning of the police raid.

The fact of brutality seems self-evident. Almost 100 injured students treated at two

hospitals. Bloody newsreel footage on television. The savage beating of one of the Time's
own reporters, Robert Thomas. The testimony
of Dr. June Finer in the New York Post that
the police sadism exceeded anything she had
witnessed in Alabama or Mississippi.

Now to the mysterious complicity of the
Times. On the day of the bust, the Times city
editor Arthur Gelb had lunch with Police
Commissioner Howard Leary. At lunch, or a
few hours later, Leary gave Gelb a copy of a
mimeographed memorandum detailing the
logistics of the police department's plans for
mass arrests that night. The memo included
details down to the minute, like "At 1.30 a.m.,
mounted police to move on campus."

Later in the day, the memo was passed dis-
creetly to several reporters who would be
assigned to cover the police raid. It was in-
tentionally NOT shown to certain reporters,
including Richard Reeves, who covers Mayor
Lindsay, because the Times editors feared they
would tip off the students about the timing of
the bust. One cannot help but wonder at this
point what the Times editors would have done
if they were told the students planned to
liberate other campus buildings. Would they
not tip off the police and administration? But
the more important question is why did the
police department brief the Times so thoroughly about their plans? For protection? Because
the Times's publisher is a Columbia trustee?

The police briefing was so complete that
the Times's story of the raid was written several
hours before it actually took place, and was
in type by midnight. Only a few facts had to
be added when reporters called in with the
actual details. The next day, A. M. Rosenthal
was bragging how 500,000 copies of the Times's
last edition contained the story of the 2 a.m.
raid, while only 50,000 copies of the last edition of the News had the story. At 1 a.m., on
the Columbia campus, Jules Feiffer and I

accidentally saw Rosenthal emerge from a
secret meeting of top police brass. Rosenthal,
a little embarrassed, claimed he did not know
if a police raid on the students was imminent.

Now to analysis of Times coverage of the
police raid, the only background necessary to
recall that all the "think pieces" and editor-
ials published by the Times since the revolt
began at Columbia have been stridently anti-
SDS. One editorial, in fact, on April 25, was
titled, "Hoodlumism at Columbia."

The four-column lead story in most copies
of the late city edition of the April 30 New
York Times, written in advance by Sylvan
Fox, a former New York City police department press officer, began: "A handpicked
force of 1000 policemen moved onto the
Columbia University campus early today and
began ordering student demonstrators out of
the five buildings the students have occupied
in a tense week-long protest.

"The police moved with stunning suddenness at 2.30 a.m. . . . ."

The police did not "order" students out of
the buildings; they dragged them out. And
what "stunning suddenness"? The Times had
the minute by minute details of the operation
more than 12 hours in advance.

The next day, May 1, the Times printed one
major lead story on Columbia and eight subsidiary stories. The afternoon before, the lead
story in the New York Post was that the police
brutality had created a new campus majority
against the administration. That crucial insight was totally missing from the Times coverage the next day. And not until the 23rd paragraph of Sylvan Fox's lead story were "charges"
of police brutality even mentioned.

The major side-bar story was by Rosenthal.
It began on the front page and was intended
as a mood piece about the campus. It focused
on the anguish of President Kirk and the van-

dalism of the students who occupied his office. It did not describe a single act of police brutality. But Rosenthal, remember, was with Commissioner Leary while the raid was being planned.

(Student leaders who rifled the files in President Kirk's office say they have a memo indicating that on at least one occasion Columbia officials used Rosenthal when they wanted a friendly story in the Times.)

The subsidiary story, on page 35, that dealt with police brutality, was not written by Times reporter Thomas, who needed 12 stitches in his scalp, but by Martin Arnold.

Arnold is one of the brightest and fairest reporters on the Times, and his city room friends say the editors "changed" and "toned down" his copy. Nevertheless, he wrote a story worthy of textual analysis in all journalism schools.

In his third paragraph, Arnold wrote:

"To an experienced anti-war or civil rights demonstrator, yesterday morning's police action on the Columbia campus was, for the most part, relatively gentle."

Now there is some truth to that. The police were not quite as systematically brutal as they were during the anti-draft demonstrations last December, or even in Washington Square Park April 27. But the point is, on those occasions, the Times ALSO failed to report any police brutality. Times reporter John Kifner was a witness to the police brutality in Washington Square Park two weeks ago, and offered to write a lengthy story about it, but was rebuffed by his editors. (Four paragraphs of his copy was inserted into the main story, however.)

But after satisfying his desk by describing the police action as "relatively gentle," Arnold goes on to describe for persevering readers what actually went on in the darkness at Columbia:

"On a small green plot dividing Avery and Fayerweather Halls two uniformed policemen grabbed a young woman and as each officer held her by an arm they spun her about and flung her into a tree.

"Nearby two other officers were seen flinging a man to the ground. When he tried to get up, they grabbed him and threw him down again. A plainclothesman rushed up and stomped the fallen man.

"At one point, Prof. Sidney Morgenbesser was standing on the north steps of Fayerweather shouting loudly to about 125 students and 30 faculty members who had gathered, some in blankets against the chill, to block the two double door entrances. 'You ought to very carefully observe what transpires. Watch carefully.'

"Plainclothesmen and uniformed officers formed a wedge and, without any attempt to pick up or even push aside the people, charged through the faculty and student line, stomping on hands and feet and arms and flinging bodies to the ground. John F. Khanlian, an undergraduate, said, 'I was hit with a club in the head. I was punched in the nose.' He could hardly see because blood was running down the side of his face.

"In Avery Hall, Robert McG. Thomas Jr., a New York Times reporter, was struck on the head by a policeman using handcuffs as brass knuckles. He required 12 stitches to close the wound. Steve Shapiro, a Life magazine photographer, was punched in the eye by a policeman and one of his cameras was smashed after, he said, he had shown the officer his press identification."

Finally, there is the case of John Kifner. Kifner, a first-rate investigative reporter, was the only daily journalist to be inside any of the "liberated" buildings when the police attacked; he had gotten into the Math Building at 11.30 p.m. Monday. But when Kifner volunteered to write an exclusive story for the

Times on what it was like inside the beseiged Math Building in the hours before the bust, the desk inexplicably told him they weren't interested. Instead, the editors assigned Kifner to write a piece on the vandalism committed by the students. The fact that most of the property damage, especially in the Math Building, was caused by the police, did not appear in the printed version of Kifner's copy. I saw police storm into the Math Building with crowbars and axes. At one point, an officer came out and exclaimed, "The creeps have burrowed into the walls. We need more axes." But Kifner's story only described the vandalism of the rebels, which was, in fact, merely piggyness and sloppiness, probably causing only a fraction of the actual property damage. The students did not break windows and chop up walls the way the police did.

Five years from now, when Newsweek, or CBS, or some curious author wants to research what really happened during the great bust at Columbia, these yellowed Times clippings will be their only resource. The distortions and slanting will be institutionalized as truth by then. That is the real tragedy, that the Times's reputation for objectivity will endure, despite any bitter words in The Village Voice.

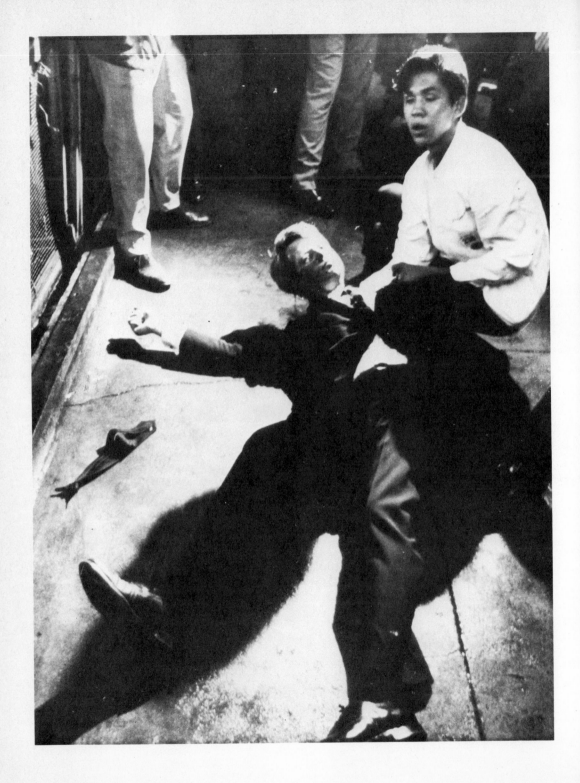

The Politics of Assassination: The Death of Robert Kennedy

Medgar Evers, John Kennedy, Malcolm X, Martin Luther King, Robert Kennedy. All men in their thirties and forties. All murdered at key points in their careers. The list is long enough to numb us with sorrow and anger. But more than that, it reminds us that in the 1960s the unthinkable came true in American politics. There was a leveling of political leadership that no election could have accomplished. Looking back at the decade, it is difficult to see where Marshall Frady exaggerates when he writes, "In retrospect, the sixties seem a decade in the life of this country during which some cellar door was left ajar. Suddenly loose and rampant in the house were all manner of trolls and intruders, manic apparitions, a dark ransacking berserkness from the chaos of the old night outside. . . . Ten years passed like a malarial dream in which the unthinkable became the familiar, the surreal became the commonplace."*

The reportage in this section focuses on Robert Kennedy's death and its

*Marshall Frady, "My Dream Came True, I Was Mr. Maddox," *New York Review of Books,* April 6, 1972, p. 13. Copyright © 1972 Nyrev, Inc. Reprinted by permission of the New York Review of Books.

relationship to the series of political assassinations preceding it. In some cases the accounts of Kennedy's death are intensely personal. In others, they concentrate on the political milieu of 1968: specifically, the anti-war movement in the Democratic party, the efforts of Eugene McCarthy and Robert Kennedy to defeat the Johnson-Humphrey forces, the coalition Kennedy put together in the California primary, and the Senator's chances for winning the Democratic nomination in Chicago. In each account, however, the overriding question remains the one Robert Lowell poses in his poem "RFK" when he asks of the murdered Robert Kennedy, "What can I catch from you now?"

Pete Hamill's "Two Minutes to Midnight: The Very Last Hurrah" offers a deeply personal view of Robert Kennedy's death. Hamill, who was covering the Democratic primary in California in June 1968, was standing near Kennedy in the pantry of the Ambassador Hotel in Los Angeles when Sirhan Sirhan opened fire. "The shots went pap-pap pap-pap-pap, small sharp noises like a distant firefight or the sound of firecrackers in a backyard," he writes. "I saw Kennedy lurch against the ice machine, and then sag, and then fall forward slowly to be grabbed by someone, and I knew then that he was dead." Hamill's first instinct is to strike out against Sirhan. "I wanted to damage that insane little bastard they were holding. . . . Just one punch. Just one for Dallas. Just one for Medgar Evers, just one for Martin Luther King. Just one punch. Just one." But his desire for revenge is almost immediately absorbed by much deeper feelings of disgust for a nation he describes as "America the Beautiful: with crumby little mini-John Waynes carrying guns to the woods like surrogate penises." In the end Hamill finds that he cannot shake off the emptiness he feels. "I had learned that I knew nothing finally. . . . I sat there drinking rum until I was drunk enough to forget that pimpled face cracking off rounds into the body of a man who was a friend of mine."

In very different fashion, the personal impact of Robert Kennedy's death is the subject of Malcom Muggeridge's "The Elevation of Senator Robert Kennedy." Muggeridge is most concerned with the transformation of Kennedy into instant legend. "Within 24 hours after his assassination," Muggeridge writes, Kennedy "was fully equipped with a halo, a hagiography, and all the other trappings of martyrdom in preparation for Instant Canonization." Muggeridge's interest in demythologizing Kennedy is not motivated by the desire to supply an uncomplimentary picture of him however. On the contrary. Muggeridge finds the idea of Robert Kennedy as political saint highly destructive to Kennedy's reputation. "Instant Legend," he argues, "is in the same category as Instant Coffee or LSD-generated Instant Ecstasy—convenient and expeditious, but soon liable to pall. . . . Instant Legend only enshrines the moment's passing fancy, and so quickly disperses."

David McReynolds in his "Notes on Another Death—And Our Shadowed

Future" is also preoccupied with moving beyond the legend of Robert Kennedy. But in McReynolds's case he is grimly insistent that the Kennedy assassination, like the other political murders of the 1960s, be understood as a reflection of American life. "Notes on Another Death" cuts through the standard political explanations for Kennedy's assassination to focus on the violence that McReynolds, himself a pacifist, sees as pervasive. Mc-Reynolds asks, "Is there one among us who did not want to cry out, as we caught the first news of the attack on Kennedy, 'Oh God, why don't they kill those who deserve it' . . . or who did not want in the baffled rage and confusion and sorrow of those moments to scream, 'Kill the killers, murder the assassins!'" In the end McReynolds offers no soothing answer to his own question; he only insists that it will not be easy to stop the cycle of assassinations that afflict American life. "One has the feeling there may be little hope for us as a nation," he writes. "But if there is hope it will lie in the courage we have rarely demonstrated—the courage to admit, as a people and a nation, that we have been wrong. The courage to admit that our violence at home is in part a reflection of our barbarism abroad."

The final selection, Elizabeth Kaye's article "The Man Who Held RFK in his Arms," was written four years after the assassination. It is the story of Juan Romero, the bus boy in the Ambassador Hotel who gave the dying Robert Kennedy a rosary. Kaye's account moves from the immediate shock of the assassination on Juan Romero, to how it turned him into a celebrity at school, to the doubts it raised in him about his own motives in rushing to Kennedy's aid. As her story develops, we come to realize both the dimension of Juan Romero's feelings and the way these feelings have prevented him from being understood. "Talking to the doctor helped [Juan] a little, though not much. The doctor advised him to try not to think about the murder, or Kennedy, when he was alone, and when he was with people who asked him about either, to try, if he could, to answer them." It's as if on one end of a scale there existed Juan Romero's desperate need to come to terms with Robert Kennedy's death, whatever the cost; and on the other end of the scale, an equally desperate, collective need to confine Kennedy's murder to some ordered framework.

Two Minutes to Midnight: The Very Last Hurrah
Pete Hamill

Pete Hamill, who has been a columnist for the *New York Post* and a contributing editor to *New York* magazine, describes himself as "a free man, a New Yorker, a Democrat, and an American—in that order. And I would gladly give up the last three descriptions to retain the first." His reportage of the Vietnam War in 1966 grasped the tragedy this country did not feel until several years later. He is the author of *Irrational Ravings* and most recently a novel, *The Gift.*

Los Angeles—It was, of course, two minutes to midnight and the Embassy Room of the Ambassador Hotel was rowdy with triumph. Red and blue balloons drifted up through three golden chandeliers to bump against a gilded ceiling. Young girls with plastic Kennedy boaters chanted like some lost reedy chorus from an old Ray Charles record. The crowd was squashed against the bandstand, a smear of black faces and Mexican-American faces and bearded faces and Beverly Hills faces crowned with purple hair. Eleven tv cameras were turning, their bright blue arclights changing the crowd into a sweaty stew. Up on the bandstand, with his wife standing just behind him, was Robert Kennedy.

"I'd like to express my high regard for Don Drysdale," Kennedy said. Drysdale had just won his sixth straight shutout. "I hope we have his support in this campaign." There was a loud cheer. He thanked Rafer Johnson and Rosey Grier (cheers) and Jesse Unruh (timid cheer) and Cesar Chavez (very loud cheers), and he thanked the staff and the volunteers and the voters, and the crowd hollered after every sentence. It was the sort of scene that Kennedys have gone through a hundred times and more: on this night, at least, it did not appear that there would be a last hurrah. Kennedy had not scored a knockout over Eugene McCarthy; but a points decision at least would keep his campaign going.

"I thank all of you," Kennedy was saying. "Mayor Yorty has just sent a message that we have been here too long already" (laughter). "So my thanks to all of you, and now it's on to Chicago. . . ."

I was at the rear of the stand, next to George Plimpton. Kennedy put his thumb up to the audience, brushed his hair, made a small V with his right hand, and turned to leave. The crowd started shouting: "We want Bobby! We want Bobby!" Plimpton and I went down three steps, and turned left through a gauntlet of Kennedy volunteers and private cops in brown uniforms.

We found ourselves in a long grubby area called the pantry. It was the sort of place where Puerto Ricans, blacks and Mexican-Americans usually work to fill white stomachs. There were high bluish fluorescent lights strung across the ceiling, a floor of raw sandy-colored concrete, pale dirty walls.   On the right were a rusty ice machine and shelves filled with dirty glasses. On the left, an archway led into the main kitchen and under the arch a crowd of Mexican American cooks and busboys waited to see Kennedy. Against the left wall, three table-sized serving carts stood end to end, and at the far end were two doors leading to the press room where Kennedy was going to talk to reporters.

Kennedy moved slowly into the area, shaking hands, smiling, heading a platoon of reporters, photographers, staffers, the curious, tv men. I was in front of him, walking backward. I saw him turn to his left and shake the hand of a small Mexican cook. We could still hear the chants of "We want Bobby!" from the Embassy Room. The cook was smiling and pleased.

Then a pimply messenger arrived from the secret filthy heart of America. He was curly haired, wearing a pale blue sweatshirt and bluejeans, and he was planted with his right foot forward and his right arm straight out and he was firing a gun.

The scene assumed a kind of insane fury, all jump cuts, screams, noise, hurtling bodies, blood. The shots went pap-pap, pap-pap-pap, small sharp noises like a distant firefight or the sound of firecrackers in a back-yard. Rosey Grier of the Los Angeles Rams came from nowhere and slammed his great bulk into the gunman, crunching him against a serving table. George Plimpton grabbed for the guy's arm and Rafer Johnson moved to him, right behind Bill Barry, Kennedy's friend and security chief, and they were all making deep animal sounds and still the bullets came.

"Get the gun, get the gun."

"Rafer, get the gun!"

"Get the fucking gun!"

"No," someone said. And you could hear the stunned horror in the voice, the replay of old scenes, the muffle of drums. "No. No. Noooooooooooo!"

We knew then that America had struck again. In this slimy little indoor alley in the back of a gaudy ballroom, in this shabby reality behind the glittering facade, Americans were doing what they do best: killing and dying, and cursing because hope doesn't last very long among us.

I saw Kennedy lurch against the ice machine, and then sag, and then fall forward slowly, to be grabbed by someone, and I knew then that he was dead. He might linger a few hours, or a few days; but his face reminded me somehow of Benny Paret the night Emile Griffith hammered him into unconsciousness. Kennedy's face had a kind of sweet acceptance to it, the eyes understanding that it had come to him, the way it had come to so many others before him. The price of the attempt at excellence was death. You saw a flicker of that understanding on his face, as his life seeped out of a hole in the back of his skull to spread like a spilled wine across the scummy concrete floor.

It was as if all of us there went simultaneously insane: a cook was screaming, "Kill him, kill him now, kill him, kill him!" I tried to get past Grier, Johnson, Plimpton, and Barry to get at the gunman. The Jack Ruby in me was rising up, white, bright, with a high singing sound in the ears, and I wanted to damage that insane little bastard they were holding, I wanted to break his face, to rip away flesh, to hear bone break as I pumped punches into that pimpled skin. Budd Schulberg was next to me; I suppose he was trying to do the same. Just one punch. Just one for Dallas. Just one for Medgar Evers, just one for Martin Luther King. Just one punch. Just one. One.

Kennedy was lying on the floor, with black rosary beads in his hand, and blood on his fingers, His eyes were still open, and as his wife Ethel reached him, to kneel in an orange-and-white dress, his lips were moving. We heard nothing. Ethel smoothed his face, running ice cubes along his cheeks. There was a lot of shouting, and a strange chorus of high screaming. My notes showed that Kennedy was shot at 12.10, and was taken out of that grubby hole at 12.32. It seemed terribly longer.

I don't remember how it fits into the sequence, but I do have one picture of Rosey Grier holding the gunman by the neck, choking the life out of him.

"Rosey, Rosey, don't kill him. We want him alive. Don't kill him, Rosey, don't kill him."

"Kill the bastard, kill that sum of a bitch bastard," a Mexican busboy yelled.

"Don't kill him, Rosey."

"Where's the doctor? Where in Christ's name is the doctor?"

Grier decided not to kill the gunman. They had him up on a serving table at the far end of the pantry, as far as they could get him from Kennedy. Jimmy Breslin and I were standing up on the table, peering into the gunman's face. His eyes were rolling around, and then stopping, and then rolling around again. The eyes contained pain, flight, entrapment, and a strange kind of bitter endurance. I didn't want to hit him anymore.

"Where the fuck is the doctor? Can't they get a fucking doctor?"

"Move back."

"Here comes a doctor, here's a doctor."

"MOVE BACK!"

Kennedy was very still now. There was a thin film of blood on his brow. They had his shoes off and his shirt open. The stretcher finally arrived, and he trembled as they lifted him, his lips moved, and the flashbulbs blinked off one final salvo and he was gone.

The rest was rote: I ran out into the lobby and picked up my brother Brian and we rushed to the front entrance. A huge black man, sick with grief and anger and bitterness, was throwing chairs around. Most landed in the pool. The young Kennedy girls were crying and wailing, knowing, I suppose, what the guys my age discovered in Dallas: youth was over. "Sick," one girl kept saying. "Sick. Sick. What kind of country is this? Sick. Sick." Outside, there were cops everywhere, and sirens. The cops were trying to get one of the wounded into a taxi. The cabbie didn't want to take him, afraid, I suppose, that blood would sully his nice plastic upholstery.

When we got through the police barricades, we drove without talk to the Hospital of the Good Samaritan, listening to the news on the radio. The unspoken thought was loudest: the country's gone. Medgar Evers was dead, Malcolm X was dead, Martin Luther King was dead, Jack Kennedy was dead, and now Robert Kennedy was dying. The hell with it. The hatred was now general. I hated that pimpled kid in that squalid cellar enough to want to kill him. He hated Kennedy the same way. That kid and the bitter Kennedy haters were the same. All those people in New York who hated Kennedy's guts, who said "eccch" when his name was mentioned, the ones who creamed over Murray Kempton's vicious diatribes these past few months: they were the same. When Evers died, when King died, when Jack Kennedy died, all the bland pundits said that some good would come of it in some way, that the nation would go through a catharsis, that somehow the bitterness, the hatred, the bigotry, the evil of racism, the glib violence would be erased. That was bullshit. We will have our four-day televised orgy of remorse about Robert Kennedy and then it will be business as usual.

You could feel that as we drove through the empty L. A. streets, listening to the sirens screaming in the night. Nothing would change. Kennedy's death would mean nothing. It was just another digit in the great historical pageant that includes the slaughter of Indians, the plundering of Mexico, the enslavement of black people, the humiliation of Puerto Ricans. Just another digit. Nothing would come of it. While Kennedy's life was ebbing out of him, Americans were dropping bombs and flaming jelly on Orientals. While the cops fingerprinted the gunmen, Senator Eastland's Negro subjects were starving. While the cops made chalk marks on the floor of the pantry, the brave members of the National Rifle Association were already explaining that people commit crimes, guns don't (as if Willie Mays could hit a home run without a bat). These cowardly bums claim Constitutional rights to kill fierce deer in the forests, and besides, suppose the niggers come to the house and we don't have anything to shoot them with? Suppose we have to fight a nigger man-to-man?

America the Beautiful: with crumby little mini-John Waynes carrying guns to the woods like surrogate penises. Yes: the kid I saw shoot Kennedy was from Jordan, was diseased with some fierce hatred for Jews. Sam Yorty, who hated Kennedy, now calls Kennedy a great American and blames the Communists. Hey Sam: you killed him too. The gun that kid carried was American. The city where he shot down a good man was run by Sam Yorty. How about keeping your fat pigstink mouth shut.

At the approach to the Good Samaritan Hospital the cops had strung red flares across the gutter, and were stopping everyone. A crowd of about 75 people were on the corner when we arrived, about a third of them black. I went in, past those black people who must have felt that there was no white man at all with whom they could talk. A mob of reporters was assembled at the hospital entrance. The cops were polite, almost gentle, as if they sensed that something really bad had happened, and that many of these reporters were friends of the dying man.

Most of the hospital windows were dark, and somewhere up there Robert Kennedy was lying on a table while strangers stuck things into his brain looking for a killer's bullet. We were friends, and I didn't want him to die but if he were to be a vegetable, I didn't want him to live either.

We drove home, through the wastelands around L.A. and the canyons through the mountains to the south. When I got home, my wife was asleep, the tv still playing out its record of the death watch. Frank Reynolds of ABC, a fine reporter and a compassionate man, was so upset he could barely control his anger. I called some friends and poured a drink. Later I talked to my old man, who

came to this country from Ireland in flight from the Protestant bigots of Belfast 40 years ago. I suppose he loved John Kennedy even more than I did and he has never really been the same since Dallas. Now it had happened again.

"If you see Teddy," he said, "tell him to get out of politics. The Kennedys are too good for this country."

I remembered the night in 1964, in that bitter winter after John Kennedy's murder, when Robert Kennedy appeared at a St. Patrick's Day dinner in Scranton, Pennsylvania. He talked about the Irish, and the long journey that started on the quays of Wexford and ended in Parkland Hospital. He reminded them of the days when there were signs that said "No Irish Need Apply" (and it was always to his greatest dismay that so many sons of Irishmen he came across in New York were bigots and haters). Bob told them about Owen O'Neill, an Irish patriot whose ideals had survived his martyrdom. Men were crying as he read the old Irish ballad:

Oh, why did you leave us, Owen?
Why did you die? . . .
We're sheep without a shepherd,
When the snow shuts out the sky.
Oh, why did you leave us, Owen?
Why did you lie?

I didn't know. There was some sort of answer for John Kennedy, and another for Robert Kennedy. But I had learned that I knew nothing finally, that when my two young daughters present the bill to me in another 10 years, I won't have much to say. I sat there drinking rum until I was drunk enough to forget that pimpled face cracking off the rounds into the body of a man who was a friend of mine. Finally, easily, with the sun up, I fell asleep on the couch. I didn't have any tears left for America, but I suppose not many other Americans did either.

The Elevation of Senator Robert F. Kennedy

Malcolm Muggeridge

Malcolm Muggeridge was a university lecturer in Cairo before taking up journalism. He has worked for the *Guardian, Calcutta Statesman,* the *Evening Standard,* and the *Daily Telegraph.* In 1953 he became the editor of *Punch.* As a broadcaster on television and radio, Muggeridge has done a series of documentaries for BBC. He is the author of *Something Beautiful for God: Mother Teresa of Calcutta.* A collection of his journalism appears in *The Most of Malcolm Muggeridge.*

Why do we make martyrs out of ordinary men and ordinary men out of martyrs?

Mass-communication media, especially television, facilitate the Instant Legend. One might even, greatly daring, modify the famous saying of Marshall McLuhan to read: The Medium is the Legend. Never has this been more clearly and dramatically demonstrated than in the case of the late Senator Robert F. Kennedy. Within twenty-four hours of his assassination he was fully equipped with a halo, a hagiography and all the other trappings of martyrdom in preparation for Instant Canonization. It was, admittedly, an off-the-peg rather than a custom-built Calvary; in view of the time factor, it had to be. Nonetheless, it served its purpose well. Overnight, the Senator was transformed from a Presidential candidate avidly seeking votes wherever and however he could find them into a martyred saint who had lain down his life for the poor and the oppressed. His whistle-stop tours became a Via Dolorosa; his bruised flesh from too much handshaking before too many cameras became stigmata, and the spurious promises so profusely and unscrupulously scattered were little candles bravely and brightly shining in a dark world—all, be it noted, achieved in a matter of hours, not years or centuries.

The role of a latter-day Christ had already been allotted to the Reverend Martin Luther King, and in any case would scarcely have been appropriate for Senator Kennedy, the younger brother of a martyred President, and himself only at the beginning of the long haul to the White House. His martyrdom, therefore, was conceived in political, rather than moral or spiritual, terms. He died, Mr. Harold Wilson, our Prime Minister, told us, for democracy. Curiously enough, and, I am sure, all unbeknownst to Mr. Wilson, this was in a sense true. It appears to have been Senator Kennedy's advocacy of arms to Israel—a bone thrown to the important Jewish vote in New York—which inflamed his assassin's mind. If such devices are to be identified with democracy (as common practice would suggest), then the Senator may be said to have died for it. Thus his martyrdom may more appropriately be compared with Byron's than Christ's, or even Martin Luther King's, though it is significant that it has taken nearly a century and a half since Byron's death in 1824 to transform this sick, perverse, ill-tempered Scottish snob into a radical saint of our time. Only just recently have the Dean and Chapter of Westminster Abbey agreed to accept a Byron Memorial in the Poets' Corner; Senator Kennedy stepped straight into his country's pantheon.

In the remoter past, legends were constructed, like Chartres Cathedral, over long periods of time. Now they can be hoisted, prefabricated, into position in the twinkling of an eye. Equally, they can be as quickly demolished, and tend to rise and fall as rapidly as buildings on Park Avenue. Instant Legend is in the same category as Instant Coffee or LSD-generated Instant Ecstasy—convenient and expeditious, but soon liable to pall. More than a thousand years passed between the Crucifixion and the miraculous liquefaction of the Holy Blood in Bruges. If the two happenings had occurred in continuity, as did Senator Kennedy's murder, obsequies and canonization, would the legend of the Holy Blood have been as acceptable as it proved to be after the passage of ten centuries? I doubt it. Instant Legend, in other words, will not keep, and we need a durable variety. Legends built up over the years enshrine the collective experience and wisdom of mankind, whereas Instant Legend only enshrines the moment's passing fancy, and so quickly disperses. Who will remember Robert Kennedy a thousand years, or even a century, from now? Few, if any, but St. Francis of Assisi, or even a Robin Hood, is never forgotten. We need legends to protect us against the great fraud and mumbo jumbo of the twentieth century—facts. La Belle Dame Sans Merci is a sanctuary from Dr. Kinsey, as the Holy Grail is from Fort Knox.

One may even without irreverence ruminate on whether the Crucifixion itself would have had the same fabulous impact, providing, as it has, the basis for two thousand years of the greatest civilization so far known, if it had been projected "live" and in "living color" to all and sundry as, for instance, the Vietnam war is today. It was too obscure and seemingly insignificant as a mere happening to appeal to contemporary legend makers—then known as historians. Only Josephus, in one dubious passage, so much as noted it. But supposing the death of Christ had been given the same

sort of treatment as the death of Robert Kennedy. The film cameras clustered round the Cross, the lugubriously solemn commentary intoned into a microphone, the close-ups of Mary the Mother of Christ and Mary Magdalen in the hope of catching them weeping, the candid-camera shots of Pilate and Caiaphas with a fleeting glimpse of Pilate's wife at an upstairs window, the zoom lenses out for the final agony. Great excitement when the Roman soldier lifted the sponge of vinegar up to Christ's dying lips: "Hold it, Mr. Centurion; oh, hold it!" Then, in the failing light, the death pangs filmed, and the last despairing cry recorded. It's finished, for the film crew as well as the Man on the Cross. Cut!

The result might well have momentarily held the attention of the pagan world, but the impression, we may be sure, would soon have passed when some new thrill was devised at the games—the Roman's television, providing them, as our TV does, with vicarious excitement in the shape of violence and eroticism viewed in the arena instead of on a screen. Legends, that is to say, if they are to endure must be stored away like port wine, and then after a decent interval brought out to delight and refresh, cleansing the mouth of the bitter, dusty taste of daily living. Instant Legend, on the other hand, is like new wine which soon makes one tipsy, and brings in its train a hangover of gruesome proportions. How wise of the Roman Catholic Church to fix a statutory period of delay in canonization, however saintly the subject! Joan of Arc must assuredly have seemed to many of her contemporaries a troublesome, tiresome female, rather in the style of our woman M.P.'s—loquacious, aggressive and opinionated. Centuries later when at last her canonization took place the qualities of heroism and vision with which she was credited were readily acceptable. In Senator Kennedy's case, the canonization has come too soon; the old image of the pushing, power-hungry politician is still too lively to be quite overlaid by the new one of the dedicated lover of peace and mankind.

It is often contended that nowadays, thanks to our mass-communication media, especially television, people are better informed than ever before, and so harder to deceive. They can see for themselves what is going on in the world, we are told. Up to a point, this is true enough. They saw with their own eyes Senator Kennedy immediately after he had been assassinated, clutching a rosary, his grief-stricken family and associates gathered round him, just as they saw Ruby kill Oswald; saw it all in "living color," with the blood redder than red and the grass greener than green. In this connection, it is interesting that within a stone's throw of where Senator Kennedy was struck down in Los Angeles there must have been several studios where shots were similarly ringing out and bodies slumping to the ground precisely as his did. The only difference was that in his case, instead of getting up when the scene had been shot, he stayed where he was. Whereas the others could wash away the blood with a little soap and water, his blood continued to flow. It was real blood, though in "living color" indistinguishable from the other. Surely the most perfect comment on the whole episode was a small newspaper paragraph giving our Top Ten television programs for that week according to TAM ratings. This showed that *The Saint* and the assassination of Robert Kennedy tied for ninth place.

Against those who claim that seeing Senator Kennedy die on television makes his death more actual, I propound the opposite proposition—that it removes his death from actuality altogether, taking it into a world of fantasy where *Peyton Place,* advertisements, news and all the other offerings form a sort of stewpot of visual images as Muzak does of musical sounds. All the world's a stage, Garrick said.

Now all the world's a screen whose "living color" makes the earth's actual ones—blue of sky, gold of sunset, yellow of daffodil and white of sea spray—drab by comparison; whose drama is for the living room, not for living; whose loves, like those on Keat's *Grecian Urn,* are "For ever warm and still to be enjoyed/For ever panting and for ever young." In the end fantasy takes over. There is no longer any distinction between life and the screen. The Dallas assassination drew a big crowd, so let's have another; that young-looking guy who's been killed and is holding the rosary—what a shame! Pity the poor widow—Jackie? No, it can't be her; look! she's strewing flowers on the other grave. That other veiled lady, then. No, she's black; it must be Mrs. King. There she is, poor soul, and that's her kid helping to lift the coffin. What a great funeral! What a turnout, what music! And Mr. Cronkite there—he speaks some lovely words.

Yes, sir, I'll be watching at the same time tomorrow.

I surely will.

I have long been of the opinion that the camera is the most significant, and probably the most destructive, invention of our time. Whereas nuclear power can only reduce us and our world to a cinder, the camera grinds us down to spiritual dust so fine that a puff of wind scatters it, leaving nothing behind. It is the ego's very focus, with all the narcissism of the human race concentrated into its tiny aperture; it advances upon one in a television studio like some ferocious monster, ravening and bloodshot-eyed. They ever must believe a lie, Blake wrote, who see with, not through, the eye. The camera is par excellence an instrument for seeing with rather than through, and has certainly, in fulfillment of Blake's prophecy, caused many lies to be believed. Our great ones must live in it, as fish in an aquarium, showing their silver fins and flashing colors, diving and swimming and leaping, all in the public gaze. The Kennedys more than any other public family have fallen in with the camera's exigencies; Instant Legend has claimed them for its own, even unto death.

Notes on Another Death—And Our Shadowed Future

David McReynolds

David McReynolds, a former editorial secretary for *Liberation* magazine, is currently a full-time staff member of the War Resisters League. He campaigned for Congress in 1968 along with Eldridge Cleaver, was a leader in the Socialist Party, and has traveled widely for the cause of peace. Mr. McReynolds is the author of *We Have Been Invaded by the 21st Century.*

Medgar Evers, John F. Kennedy, Lee Harvey Oswald, Malcolm X, George Lincoln Rockwell, Martin Luther King, Robert F. Kennedy. Black, white, left, right. Politics by assassination.

It is impossible just now to arrange the events of the past week into order for some profound analysis. Too much is hurting us. If there were no riots this time it was because we were, all of us, too exhausted from the assassination of Martin Luther King. Is there one among us who did not want to cry out, as we caught the first news of the attack on Kennedy, "Oh God, why don't they kill those who deserve it—why King, why Kennedy," or who did not want in the baffled rage and confusion and sorrow of those moments to scream "Kill the killers, murder the assassins!"

I realize, looking at the question I've just posed, that none of us can speak for others on this matter. We have each had our private thoughts this past week. These are, therefore, simply my own thoughts, notes to myself on a death.

. . . I did not support Robert F. Kennedy for President. I could not share the political enthusiasm for him of Jack Newfield and Mike Harrington and Mike Macdonald. But his death touched me more deeply than that of John F. Kennedy. Bobby may have been ruthless but I cannot believe he was cold. He had those small shy gestures of his hands, those constricted and almost mechanical movements of his hands and arms when he spoke and yet, to balance that, he had a smile that lighted his face, making him look younger than his years, and making it impossible to believe he was simply ruthless or simply ambitious. There was a radiance, a humanity, and a vitality to him that made the news of his death not only painful but almost literally impossible to accept.

. . . His death made me aware of how the Kennedy family has become for us all, whether or not we wish it, the "first family" of the land, giving us the pattern of genuine contemporary aristocracy. At his death the jets roared off from Paris and London and New York bearing the brightest members of this aristocracy to Los Angeles. Imagine, if you will, the murder of any other contemporary American political leader and you will fail to conjure up the same image of a special class of people moving together to comfort one another. Robert Kennedy had close friends from a remarkable range of social groupings, rich, poor, white, black, politicians, artists, intellectuals. The late John F. Kennedy was not a secure aristocrat, there was in his Camelot something a bit brittle. But the very suffering and shock of the Kennedy family and friends following the murder of the President somehow deepened the group and, one felt, Robert Kennedy in particular. What had been a myth became a reality. There were many who argued that Robert Kennedy "was not the man his brother was." In fact I think Robert Kennedy was more impressive. The Kennedy family casts a long shadow over our future. As I looked at the front page of the June 7 New York Post, with its photo of Robert F. Kennedy, Jr., at the bier of his father, I felt I was looking at one of the earliest photos of our once and future President.

. . . I was unexpectedly sorry for Lyndon Johnson, a man whose impeachment I have urged and with whose political views I could not be in greater disagreement. Yet Johnson, despite his massive personal faults and political sins, is human and there is something as terrible about the suspicions to which he has been subjected and against which he cannot defend himself as there is about the suffering to which the Kennedys have been subjected.

. . . America will not live down the events of the past five years for at least a generation to come. Even if we ourselves could forget the horror of these years the world as a whole cannot. To them the events here will appear as something like a blood purge of political opposition. The civilized world has not seen anything like the series of murders we have endured since Japanese extreme nationalists employed assassination as a political weapon in the years just before World War Two.

. . . We have been lucky in our assassins.

Blacks, not whites, cut down Malcolm X. No Jews have been involved, no deranged leftists. (Think what would have happened if Robert Kennedy had been killed by a hippie, or some ultra-militant Maoist student.)

. . . Now is the time for gun control. Everyone talks about this but no one discusses it in practical terms. The National Rifle Association is well organized and well financed. They can pour letters into Washington. If every reader would write both senators and his congressman and demand (don't ask—demand) strong and very tight gun control laws we have a chance to get them now. Let the lobby of the American people be heard above the lobby of the NRA.

. . . One thinks of the Egyptians, whose first born of every household had to be struck down before they would finally let the children of Israel go out of bondage—the gun that was used to murder Robert F. Kennedy was purchased at a sporting goods store during the Watts riot by an old and fearful white man who thought to protect himself and who, instead, started that particular gun on a journey toward an assassin's hand. We armed ourselves against the blacks but the bullets struck Kennedy.

. . . There are those (including the President) who insist that we are not all sick, that the society as a whole is not deranged. But we are. We are sick and we aren't going to get better by pretending we've only got a few crackpots loose. If Congress really wanted "law and order" it would long ago have passed a stiff gun control law. If we were not sick as a society a movie like "Scorpio Rising" (trash as art, sado-masochism as culture) would not be considered avantgarde. Leather wouldn't be in as high fashion. We would be less worried about words like "fuck" and more concerned with words like "kill." We would be deeply worried about the violence in our films, on our tv, in our daily papers, and even in the toys we buy our children. Politically we wouldn't have let ourselves get boxed into a Johnson-Goldwater race in 1964, we wouldn't have a governor like Reagan, and we wouldn't have George Wallace as a serious minor party candidate.

. . . As a native of Los Angeles I am certain I speak for many—perhaps a majority—of the residents of that city when I express my shame at the behavior of the mayor of Los Angeles, Sam Yorty, in seeking publicity at the risk of making a fair trial impossible, and in seeking to invent a Communist plot out of the murder.

. . . The words "manly" and "unmanly" are often used loosely but I felt as I watched tv that while Yorty's appearances were a genuine example of an unmanly performance, the brief statement by Senator Eugene McCarthy was an equally genuine example of a manly reaction to a national tragedy. His face was not a mask, his words were not glib, his shock and grief were not feigned. The depth of the tragedy could be read in his face, as well as his own personal sense of shock.

. . . When I noted earlier that we are all sick, I meant all of us, not simply reactionaries or racists. I know myself how I have felt a morbid satisfaction that the President could not move safely through our streets, and that if we could not keep him from sending men abroad we had at least succeeded in making it impossible for him to travel freely at home. How much better if we had met Johnson's tours with black armbands and silence rather than with juvenile chants of "Hey, hey, LBJ, how many kids did you kill today?" And the students at Columbia, in most ways so correct and courageous, did not dignify their cause by adopting the chant "Up Against the Wall Motherfucker." It is time now for all of us on the left to recognize how close we are to losing what is left of our democracy, and to grasp how profound is the threat to the republic. It is impossible to ask that politics be conducted without passion or that we approach our domestic and foreign

policy without rage, but it is not impossible to remind the left that if we would in fact lead, rather than simply give vent to our own alienation, then we must prove ourselves not only more militant but also more compassionate and more responsible than our opposition. Anger is one thing and hatred is another, rage is legitimate and necessary but violence is destructive for all of us. The commandment against violence is as close to an absolute as we have and we must not let ourselves be tricked into violence even by the violence of our opposition. Police violence does not justify mob violence. Our goal may well be the "destruction" of society as it now exists but we also seek the creation of a new society. Nihilists are neither radical nor revolutionary. Even on those rare occasions when men may feel, with some reason, that violence is necessary it remains an evil even if it becomes a necessary one. If we weep for the killing of Che then let us also weep for the fact that he killed others.

. . . Finally, let us for God's sake be honest with ourselves. When politicians speak of the need for law and order in the wake of this assassination it is clear they demand action against the blacks, the poor, the peace movement, the students, the hippies—in short, they are against flowers and beads as much as against guns and bombs. Would to God that this cry for law and order meant a demand that the State itself return to the rule of law, and that it meant a recognition that without justice there cannot be "order."

When President Johnson tells us that "we must not permit men that are filled with hatred and carelessness—and careless of innocent lives—to dominate our streets and fill our homes with fear" one must ask what threatens the man in the street more—random violence or the military draft? Are mothers more fearful that their sons will be knifed at school or killed in Vietnam?

I am raising what are for me fundamental

questions and they are directed not only to Johnson but to us all. Who can believe the CIA was not aware of plans to assassinate Diem and yet who on the left protested against this exercise of murder? Who can believe the CIA was not implicated in the killing of Che and yet who on the right protested that action? Did we think we could play this game abroad and not legitimize it here at home? When 500,000 Indonesians were slaughtered in the purge of Communists did the President or the State Department express concern, dismay, and horror—or quiet satisfaction? How many of those who now oppose the war in Vietnam waited to cry out against it only when it became clear that it was not simply immoral and unjust but also unsuccessful? Our hearts must surely go out to the Kennedy family in this moment of their private grief—yet how many of us are aware of the number of Vietnamese families which have suffered losses as great and greater?

One has the feeling there may be little hope for us as a nation. We have not seen the last assassination—there will be more. But if there is hope it will lie in a courage we have rarely demonstrated—the courage to admit, as a people and a nation, that we have been wrong.

The courage to realize that our violence at home is in part a reflection of our barbarism abroad. The courage to simply admit we have been wrong in Vietnam and to begin withdrawing our troops now. The courage to admit that we have imposed violence on the blacks of this land for hundreds of years and that we shall choose to pay higher taxes to reconstruct our society rather than to pay higher taxes to police it. The "lawless rioting" of blacks is a result of our policy and we cannot not say to the restless sea "be still." The "lawless rioting" of our students is a consequence of building a society in which they can find no place of human worth. Indeed, the healthiest aspect of our society is the alienation of our students and we should welcome that and be grateful for it.

Law and order are reflections of justice and compassion. We must resolutely oppose, without exception, all violence. But we must first of all oppose the violence of the State, of the white majority. We must take the President at his word—and hold him to his word—when he says "There is never—and I say never—any justification for the violence that tears at the fabric of our national life."

June 4, 1968: The Man Who Held RFK in His Arms

Elizabeth Kaye

Elizabeth Kaye is a freelance writer whose articles have appeared in the *Village Voice, Los Angeles Times,* and *Redbook.* She has had short films on various subjects produced, and previously worked as a production assistant and reader for David Merrick in New York.

Los Angeles, California—A very big sign in red, white and blue says "Kennedy." It is nailed across the front of a building three blocks from another building with another, smaller sign. This second sign is a map marked with numbers, and what I want to tell you begins where it is, at a place an arrow designates as "You Are Here."

What I am looking for is not shown on the key to this map. There is, however, a spot marked number eight called "Ballroom" and, marked number nine, another room called "Colonial." In between, unnumbered, are two small rectangles; in the middle of one is the word "stage," in the middle of the other it says "pantry." And those places are why I am here, standing outside the Ambassador Hotel, where four years ago, Robert Kennedy was murdered somewhere in that still unnumbered area, somewhere between the spaces marked eight and nine.

I follow the map and end up where I thought I wanted to be, next to a cold and dripping ice machine where something I told myself I would never get over happened four full years ago. It is a ridiculous place for a requiem and I leave quickly because I want very badly now to make a connection with someone whose name is Juan Romero.

Perhaps you don't remember him. He is the young man who reached the Senator just after he was shot, gave him his rosary, and was photographed as he gently held Robert Kennedy in his arms. Juan Romero is a name I just happen to remember. I do not think of him often and would not be thinking of him now if I were not in this place; but I am here, recovered enough from that event to stand in the pantry of the Ambassador Hotel, haunted enough by it still to want to talk with this young man, because on that night his face was full of the loss and horror I felt.

Juan Romero does not work at the Ambassador now. But after an hour I finally meet someone who tells me where I can find him and suggests that after 6 p. m. I call the number he writes out for me on a paper napkin. I do, and when the telephone is answered I ask if we might meet. We agree on the day after tomorrow.

It is four years later and Juan is 21 years old. He is a very handsome young man. Tall and thin, he seems much older than he is, perhaps because of a gentleness in his face, an attitude of quiet in his bearing. His mother wanted him to get a hair cut before our meeting, but by the standards of 1972 his hair is extremely neat and not terribly long. He is living at home again, with his mother, stepfather, sisters, and brothers, two of whom are lying of the floor watching "Get Smart" on color tv. After the assassination Juan moved away for a while, partly because of family problems, partly because he sensed the management of the Ambassador was becoming annoyed by the vast number of guests who wanted to talk to him about that night. He was becoming upset by it too, and so, in the last week of June 1968, he quit his busboy job. He has not been back to the Ambassador since.

On the night of June 4, 1968, Juan Romero was the busboy in attendance at a dinner for four in room 514. The diners were Mr. and Mrs. Andy Williams, guests of Senator and Mrs. Robert Kennedy. Juan was excited to be that close to Kennedy for that long; his whole family liked the Senator and would, several weeks later, hang a photograph of him in the living room next to an oil painting of his brother. "I'm not trying to be prejudiced," Juan says, "but they done a lot of good for us people, you know, for the ghettos. I really believe people like that would help poor people, try to straighten out people, like the kids."

So when Kennedy won the California and South Dakota primaries that night, Juan was happy, and he stayed in the kitchen to see the Senator pass through on the way to his victory speech in the ballroom. As Kennedy passed him, they shook hands.

On an ordinary night, Juan would have been on duty at the time of the murder. But that night the hotel was expecting orders for champagne, not food, so Juan Romero was let off early and decided to go and get another look at Robert Kennedy.

When the shooting began, Juan and everyone else thought the sound was firecrackers. Then the Senator fell, and Juan thought it must be a joke, a stunt "for publicity," a game of some kind. Though he remembers what he thought, he cannot recall what he did. Another kitchen worker, standing near him at the time, does: "Everybody runs in that moment, everybody ducks or runs away, but Romero runs to him. Remember, we didn't know then if there was more guns, more people shooting. But Romero didn't thought about it. He went right away to give help to him."

Juan was kneeling on the floor, holding Robert Kennedy's head, when he felt something warm and odd, like water flowing, on his hands. "I wasn't sure what it was, if it was the emotion I felt touching him or something. I wasn't sure of myself, so I moved my hand, to look at it, and saw there was blood on it." It was then that Juan reached into his pocket and placed the rosary in Kennedy's hand. Then he started shouting for a doctor. Juan does not always carry a rosary with him. He does not know what happened to the one he had with him that night—it was never returned to him and he did not attempt to get it back. Some people told him he should try to find it because he could sell it for a lot of money.

The rest of that night he remembers only in disconnected flashes, though he does clearly remember the photographers asking him to hold up his hands so they could take pictures of the blood still dripping on them, and he remembers that for the next three days he did not sleep at all. He also remembers what happened when he went to school Wednesday morning, the day after the assassination.

The students barely mentioned the shooting. These children of the families thought to be Robert Kennedy's truest constituency were not at all sad, but happily excited because of what Juan had done. For the first time in his life Juan Romero was treated as someone important, someone who mattered, whose name and picture got in the newspapers. His classmates asked for his autograph, and though Juan thought that was "real silly" he liked being the eye of this storm of attention, liked the way they gathered around him to hear him tell what had happened so they could later say, casually, to someone less fortunate, that they had "spoken to Juan." He liked it until he got home, where he heard on the television that Kennedy was probably going to die. He didn't go back to school for the next two weeks.

The first thing he did when he finally returned was drop out of his ROTC course which he was taking because he thought, and still thinks, the only way he will get a good education is through the Army. "It might have been stupid to drop it," he says now, "but I said to myself, I just won't touch a gun. The teachers understood." But in those two weeks when he'd stayed home from school his family life, which had been difficult anyway, got worse; and so before the school year was over, he quit both school and his job, left home, and Los Angeles, and went to work in Santa Barbara.

It was there that Juan Romero found out, at the age of 17, that to run away means to take oneself along too, and so six months later he came home, back to where a problem had begun to form in his mind on June 5, 1968, a problem that was far from solved and still growing. "After the thing was over, people started saying I was a celebrity, and then I started to think, celebrity for what . . . why a celebrity? Is it because a person is dying and you try to help them . . . is it because a person is shot and you were there?"

This "you were there" marks the psychic place where Juan's troubles begin, for while letters congratulating him on his behavior that night were being sent to him from all over the country and from as far away as England and Spain, he knew something these people who wrote him did not know, something that frightened him all the more because it seemed no one even suspected it—simply, Juan wished that on that night, when the shots were fired, he had been "stacking tables, picking up an order, anywhere but there." And if it was somehow unavoidable for him to have been someplace other than that pantry, his actions seem to him useless, and after-the-fact response that helped no one, certainly nothing to be "celebrated." To be congratulated for what he did does not make sense to him, because he believes there is something else he might have done, ought to have done; and did not do—it occurred to him that he must have been standing, waiting for Kennedy, quite near Sirhan Sirhan, perhaps even next to him. "If I could have had split-second reactions, you know, to either get the gun, or knock it from his hand, or stand in front of him, I could have saved his life, anything. . . ." When I ask if what he means by "stand in front of him" is he would rather have taken the bullet himself, he answers very quietly. "I think I would prefer that to the way the situation is now. He's dead, and I'm still living and can't stop thinking about it. He could have done so much good for so many people, and I'm just alive, sitting here."

To further complicate the contradictions of wishing he hadn't been there, and a sense that he might have prevented the tragedy, was a new, exceedingly uncomfortable factor—for Juan Romero, by doing a small though decent thing, began to receive attention from people who previously might not even have tipped him. These people sought him out, offered him jobs, scholarships, even money. And as Juan saw how easily the murder of Robert Kennedy might benefit him, he wondered if somehow, on some dark level of his mind, he might have known this all along, might have known this when he ran to Kennedy, might even have tried to help Kennedy because he somehow sensed that act could later help

him. He is sure it all happened too fast for such thoughts to have occurred, but wanting to make very, very sure no one else would doubt his action, he did not accept any of the offers.

His feelings were exacerbated by the fact that he could tell no one about them; certainly he could not explain how he felt to people who were congratulating him, who thought of him as a "celebrity," sometimes even as a hero." He could not say how meaningless he though his action was, or that he questioned not only its validity but its motivation as well. Finally, needing to talk to someone, he did what very few people with very little money do—he went to a psychiatrist.

Mexican-Americans do not generally go to psychiatrists—for reasons that are as much religious as financial. Most are devout Catholics with problems that can, hopefully, be faced and dealt with in a confessional. It was a very big step for Juan to go to this doctor, and he did it because he thought it was something he had better do "before it was too late."

Talking to the doctor helped a little, though not much. The doctor advised him to try not to think about the murder, or Kennedy, when he was alone, and when he was with people who asked him about either to try, if he could, to answer them. And, when Juan told him he wished he was "in one of those fantasy machines, like in science fiction, that could take me back in time, to just before it happened," the doctor said that in spite of that wish, in spite of everything, Juan's life must, and will go on.

Which, of course, it has.

This year, Juan went back to finish high school; he was surprised to learn he is too old for regular high school classes, that he would have to go at night now. Each morning he gets up at 5, goes to work in a laundromat at 6; most evenings, before school, he plays basketball. He hopes to graduate before his brother, who is five years younger. If he does, he will be the first member of his family to get a high school diploma. Then, maybe college, maybe the army. He would like to be a mechanic, but that is unlikely because "it takes too long." Someday, he knows he will want a wife and children, so he is trying hard to improve himself: he says he can "use a lot of improving."

Though he has tried to follow the doctor's advice and not think about Kennedy, he still dreams of him, dreams in which, for example, they are flying together in an airplane, the only passengers. Something goes wrong, he does not know what, and then they are floating together, supported by parachutes, through the blue blue sky, descending slowly down down to the sea which at the very last moment turns out to be made not of water, but of popcorn.

When he has these dreams they come back to him slowly the next day, in pieces, so that while he is working at the laundromat he will remember another, and then another instance of his being alone with Robert Kennedy, both of them laughing, both unhurt. Those days, he says, the days he is remembering his dreams, are happy for him.

When I left Romero's house, I drove back to the Ambassador, as if the physical going from the one place to the other could close the gap between where we have been where we are, and where we may be headed.

Juan had told me he will not vote in this year's Presidential election unless one of the candidates is Edward Kennedy. Juan is hoping he will run "so his brothers will not have died in vain."

That hope of Juan's was as close as I may ever come to finding that link between then and now; it is what I was thinking about when I drove past the Ambassador and first saw that sign, the red, white, and blue one with the name "Kennedy." I looked at it and wondered how it could be that in all these years no one had bothered to take it down. Then the light changed and, moving the car forward, I saw that the sign was wrapped around a building that curves, so that all the words on it could not be seen, from a distance, at once.

What the sign said was "Ted Kennedy . . . 1972."

Conquest of Space: The Apollo 11 Moon Landing

In terms of announced goals, few government projects begun in the 1960s succeeded so well as the Apollo Space Program. Apollo got a man to the moon ahead of the Russians, opened up vast fields for scientific study with the 594 pounds of lunar rock the astronauts retrieved, and produced technological spin-offs ranging from the development of fuel cells to miniature computers. Yet justification for the Apollo Space Program, for its $26.5 billion cost, for the talent it absorbed, and the astronaut deaths it caused was never a basically utilitarian issue. Apollo always involved the more complicated motives of national pride and the conquest of the unknown. The country did not just treat the astronauts as returning heroes. The National Aeronautics and Space Administration (NASA) made sure the astronauts were presented as heroes before they went into space.

The new journalism that follows offers a look at America's space effort through reports on the most significant of the 17 Apollo flights—Apollo 11, the first landing on the moon. The flight, which began on July 16, 1969, and concluded eight days later when the astronauts splashed down in the Pacific and were greeted by the President aboard the U.S.S. Hornet, proved that America could get a man to the moon and *safely* back. Indeed, from

NASA's point of view, Apollo 11 was an ideal combination of human drama and technological brilliance. Following a perfect lift-off from Cape Kennedy, the space capsule needed few midcourse adjustments to get within range of the moon by July 19. Orbiting procedure went equally well, and on July 20 astronauts Armstrong and Aldrin began the landing maneuvers that would bring the lunar module Eagle to rest on the moon. This was the most dangerous part of the flight, and significantly, it was the point at which the astronauts' skill was most evident. As the Eagle got within range of the moon's surface, a computer overload made it necessary for the astronauts to switch to a semiautomatic landing procedure and bring the Eagle down manually for a dramatic soft landing in the Sea of Tranquillity. Only after this point could the accomplishments of Apollo 11, particularly a 2½-hour moon walk, be savored. There would be some shaky moments when the Eagle and the command ship *Columbia* docked, and the astronauts would be kept in quarantine for 18 days to make sure they had not brought back any new strains of bacteria. But following the moon landing, the tension in the flight of Apollo 11 would fall within the "acceptable levels" planned by the Manned Spacecraft Center in Houston.

In the accounts of Apollo 11 collected here, it is the human rather than the scientific implications of the moon shot that receive the most attention. The result is, however, less often a celebration of space venture than doubts as foreboding as the concluding lines of James Merrill's poem "Pieces of History":

> There on the moon, her meaning now one swift
> Footprint, a man my age with a glass face
> Empty of insight signals back through space
> To the beclouded cortex which impelled his drift.*

The initial account, "An Expression of Man's Self-Determination," is from *First on the Moon: A Voyage with Neil Armstrong, Michael Collins, and Edwin E. Aldrin, Jr.,* written in conjunction with Gene Farmer and Dora Jane Hamblin. The structure and point of view in *First on the Moon* are explained by Hamblin and Farmer as follows: "Some of the writing is in the third person, partly because this was the easiest way to explain the immediate historical background which was relevant to the flight of Apollo 11, and partly because it was impossible for Armstrong, Collins, and Aldrin to be everywhere at once. Yet in a very real sense this *is* the Apollo 11 astronauts' personal book; it represents their view of the grandest voyage yet in history." Certainly it is difficult to imagine a book placing the Apollo 11 voyage in a more favorable light. The title of the chapter included here comes from a sermon by "Buzz" Aldrin's minister in which he spoke of the moon landing as "an expression of man's ability—of

---

* From *Braving the Elements,* Atheneum, New York, 1972, p. 8. Copyright 1972 by James Merrill.

man's determination . . . the concretizing of man's potential," and the chapter, like its title, emphasizes the role of the astronauts in getting the Eagle down safely. Despite long sections of technical dialogue between Mission Control and the astronauts, nothing is allowed to obscure the point with which the chapter concludes: "The lunar module of Apollo 11 had soft-landed successfully on the moon because men like Neil Armstrong and Buzz Aldrin were on board."

In contrast to *First on the Moon,* the view of Apollo 11 advanced in the next three reports is highly critical. William Honan's Le Mot Juste for the Moon," which was published before the moon shot, is at once a facetious and a serious essay on the remarks the first man on the moon should make. "Future generations," Honan notes, "will be able to relive all that was said and done at that moment as never before in the history of exploration. The stupendous magnitude and unprecedented visibility of what Commander Armstrong is about to do, therefore, combine to pose the question: when the astronaut takes that first step on the moon, what should he *say?*" Honan reviews the statements of other explorers and inventors on their great occasions and finds their observations in general anticlimactic. The Apollo 11 astronauts, he fears, are not likely to get away from the American tradition of dullness, epitomized by such exclamations as Alexander Graham Bell's, "Watson, come here—I need you," and Charles Lindbergh's, "Well, I made it." When he reviews the comments of previous astronauts, Honan finds them confined to technical jargon, outmoded slang, or vapid expressions of rapture like, "Beautiful sight!" Only rarely does Honan cease being humorous, but he does stop long enough to make us ask: What is the relationship between events like the moon shot and the language used to describe them? Is the deadness of expression that so often results a reflection of strain, or does it reveal an underlying deadness of purpose? And how, under these circumstances, are we to judge Neil Armstrong's "That's one small step for a man, one giant leap for mankind"?

In "Apollo 11: The Time Machine" Peter Collier is also concerned with analyzing the language of the astronauts and judging them in the light of past heroes. But irony and sarcasm, rather than humor, dominate his treatment of the astronauts. "They were sent to outer space to rejuvenate America and to provide flowered slipcovers for a system of values which is in a state of chaos," Collier writes. "They were to be our Galahad, on a quest to recover the national purpose; our Aeneas, removing America's household gods—a flag and a television set—to a foreign clime." Collier compares the blandness and boy-scout heroism he sees in Neil Armstrong to that of Jack Armstrong, the "all-American boy," a character in a radio program he listened to as a child, and finds the similarity between them indicative of the "forces which have allowed this culture to pull the wings off flies and yet retain the illusion of childlike experimentation rather than adult evil." For Collier, the moon shot is in the final analysis "America flexing muscles that had almost atrophied in Viet Nam."

In "A Sleep on the Moon," a chapter from his book, *Of a Fire on the Moon,* Norman Mailer's judgments are often as harsh as Collier's. Of NASA, for example, Mailer writes, "Somewhere in the center of NASA was the American disease. Focus on one problem to the exclusion of every other. When Communism had been the problem, nothing had existed for national policy but anti-Communism. Now, ever since the fire of Apollo 204, there had been only one idea at NASA. Get men to the moon by the end of the decade and get them back. If drama had to be sacrificed, rid the situation of drama. If scientific investigations would hamper a smooth flight, restrict scientific investigations." Mailer is unwilling, however, to limit his criticism to the technological-political implications of Apollo 11. He is most concerned with what new perspective, if any, the moon shot can give us of ourselves, and he sees the astronauts themselves as the key to this knowledge. His speculations on the astronauts' dreams, on what it would be like for them to be stranded on the moon are part of an overriding interest in discovering whether the strains of Apollo 11 have made it impossible for the astronauts to be the bearers of new insight or even stay in touch with themselves. "A Sleep on the Moon" ends with the following passage: "They have been as far as Achilles and Odysseus, as far as Jason who sailed to meet the argonauts, as far as Magellan and Columbus, they have been far. And their fingertips are smooth from plastic, their lungs are leather from days of bottled gas. What does an astronaut give up of the ultimate tastes to travel so far?"

An Expression of Man's Self-Determination

Neil Armstrong, Michael Collins, and Edwin E. Aldrin, Jr., with Gene Farmer and Dora Jane Hamblin

Neil A. Armstrong, Edwin E. Aldrin, Jr., and Michael Collins were the astronauts of Apollo 11, which landed the first man on the moon on July 20, 1969. Armstrong, a former Navy pilot and the pilot of Gemini 8, was the first to set foot on the moon's surface, followed by "Buzz" Aldrin, who had previously walked in space for 5½ hours during the flight of Gemini 12. While the two men made tests and collected rock samples, Michael Collins, a former Air Force test pilot and an astronaut with Gemini 10, orbited the moon in the lunar module. Their book *First on the Moon* is their story of the Apollo 11 mission, told with the help of Dora Jane Hamblin, a staff worker for *Life,* and Gene Farmer, a senior editor on *Life.*

We go into space because whatever mankind must undertake, free men must fully share—
JOHN F. KENNEDY

*What, indeed, is man? Having witnessed this symbolic event, how shall we interpret our lives and our accomplishments?—*THE REVEREND DEAN WOODRUFF

It was a few minutes past midnight in Houston when Apollo 11 went "over the hill" for the seventh time; that was about the time Neil Armstrong and Buzz Aldrin went to sleep. Mike Collins stayed awake a little longer, finally dozing off about the time Apollo 11 went around the back side of the moon for the eighth time. *Should have acquisition again at 90 hours and 25 minutes through Honeysuckle Creek, Australia. . . . Three hours and 57 minutes remaining in the sleep period. Crew heart rates running in the forties. Apollo 11 in lunar orbit with a pericynthion of 55 nautical miles, apocynthion 64.4 nautical miles. Still just right. Velocity 5,363 feet per second. 3,656.5 statute mph. . . . Ninety-one hours and 36 minutes, less than one minute remaining until loss of signal as Apollo 11 goes onto* the lunar far side for the eighth time. *Two hours remaining in the crew rest period. Four o'clock in the morning Houston time, Sunday, July 20. . . . Spacecraft systems looking good. Forty-five minutes and 28 seconds to next acquisition of signal. All asleep at 91 hours and 37 minutes GET. . . .*

All asleep—the astronauts and their wives, yes; but not quite all. There was Mission Control, where it always looked so calm on the television screen. At four rows of lighted consoles, casually attired young men sat quietly, their eyes flicking back and forth across instruments and dials, pausing to study the changing numbers on a centrally mounted video screen, jotting down quick notes, reaching out to press a button or two. Most of them were around thirty-five years of age. They were all imperturbable—cool, unruffled and definitely not nervous. Those who might have become nervous in a tight situation—the shaky souls—had been weeded out and had not made it to this room. The ones who had made it had to make important decisions, not just decisions that would mean a few hundred million dollars blown one way or another, but decisions that could mean life or death for three men in the spacecraft of Apollo 11. Christopher Columbus Kraft Jr., director of Flight Operations, had built this team, then moved upstairs to let his key people take command and perspire in the limelight of public attention. He said, "I'm like an orchestra conductor. I don't write the music. I just make sure it comes out right."

Between two and six o'clock in the morning of July 20, Houston time, there was not much to do except monitor the consoles and "make sure it comes out right." Occasionally one of the men, or two or three at once, would leave their positions to gather around the small console in the middle for a quiet conference with the man they called FLIGHT—in this case Flight Director Glynn Lunney, head of the "black team." (Head Flight Director Cliff Kranz the "white team," Milt Windler the "maroon team.") With Lunney were BOOSTER (Booster Systems Engineer Don H. Townsend); RETRO (Retro-fire Officer Charles F. Dieterich); FIDO (Flight Dynamics Officers Jay H. Greene and Philip C. Shaffer, monitoring and evaluating flight trajectories, verifying maneuver times and results); GUIDO (Guidance Officers William E. Fenner and Stephen G. Bales); SURGEON (Flight Surgeon Kenneth Beers, counting the white dots that blipped across his screen from left to right; they represented the heart and respiration rates of the astronauts, and he had to be ready at all times to diagnose an illness or prescribe a medication); EECOM (Electrical and Communications Systems Officer Seymour Liebergot, assisted by Thomas L. Hatchett from North American Rockwell and James R. Fucci from Philco); TELCOM (Telemetry and Communications Officer Jack Knight Jr., concentrating on the lunar module); OPS (Operations and Procedures Officer Granvil A. Pennington); CAPCOM (Spacecraft Communicator Ron Evans); NETWORK (Network Controller Ernest L. Randall, in liaison with the worldwide tracking network, passing on instructions and talking to his friends in Australia and Spain; AFD (Assistant Flight Directors Harold M. Draughon and David E. Nicholson); PAO (Public Affairs Officer Robert White, known as "Terry"), and about a dozen others—perhaps twenty-five in all.

But Mission Control, for all its complexity and specialization, was only the tip of the iceberg, the central strand of a web that stretched across the nation. There was a staff support room down the hall, manned around the clock by a dozen or more experts. The major contractors (North American Rockwell for the command and service module, Grumman for the lunar module) also were set up in support rooms, maintaining their own "hot lines" to major subcontractors and keeping updated lists of the whereabouts of some forty thousand key scientists and engineers associated with Apollo. Suppose there was a "glitch" involving a component deep inside the command and service module? The problem would be relayed instantly to North American Rockwell's staff support room, and possibly the hot line to Downey, California, would hum. It might even be necessary to find the man who had designed the balky component, get him on the telephone and get his ideas on what to do. Few Apollo problems had had to be taken that far, but—as at Cape Kennedy on the morning of July 16—there did seem to be a special pressure-cooker atmosphere in Mission Control as the time for the lunar touchdown drew near. "I've never seen things so tense around here." George Low said.

Houston (PAO Terry White): This is Apollo Control, 93 hours 29 minutes Ground Elapsed Time. Some five minutes away from loss of signal on this revolution. . . . Present orbital velocity around the moon 5,370 feet per second [3,661.3 statute mph]. . . . Standing by for Ron Evans's big moment as he makes his call to the spacecraft. . . . Here we go.

Capcom (Evans): Apollo 11. Apollo 11. Good morning from the black team.

Collins: Good morning Houston.

Capcom (Evans): Good morning. Got about two minutes to LOS here, Mike.

Collins: Oh my, you guys wake up early.

Capcom (Evans): Yes, you're about two minutes early on the wake-up. Looks like you were really sawing them away.

Collins: You're right.

Capcom (Evans): Eleven, Houston. For planning purposes, you can go ahead and take the monocular into the LM with you.

Collins: Okay. I'll tell them. How are all the CSM systems working?

Capcom (Evans): Eleven, Houston. Looks like the command module's in good shape. Black team has been watching it real closely for you.

Collins: We sure appreciate that because I sure haven't.

Capcom (Evans): Apollo 11. Thirty seconds. AOS will be 94 plus 21. [*Loss of signal at 93 hours and 36 minutes GET. . . . Apollo 11 over the hill for the ninth time. . . . Ninety-four hours and 21 minutes, standing by for acquisition of signal. . . . AOS is confirmed. . . .*]

Houston (White): The descent orbit insertion burn is now scheduled at 101 hours 36 minutes 13.5 seconds. Powered descent initiation at 102 hours 32 minutes 5.1 seconds. . . . Still in the middle of their breakfast period. . . . Members of the white team of flight controllers headed up by Eugene Kranz are drifting into the control room now to relieve the night watch.

Aldrin: Houston, Apollo 11. We just had a very good view of the landing site. We can pick out almost all of the features we've identified previously.

Capcom (Evans): Eleven, Houston. Roger, sounds real fine. And eleven, I have your maneuver PAD and consumables update whenever you want them.

Aldrin: Stand by a little, please. . . .

Collins: Ready to copy.

Capcom (Evans): SPS G&N 36 639 your NOUN 48 minus 072 plus 051. . . .

Collins: Okay, thank you.

Capcom (Evans): Apollo 11, Houston. I have your baseline altitude update now if Buzz is ready to copy.

Collins: Go ahead.

Capcom (Evans): Roger. Alpha One is 500, that's 500 feet above the landing site.

Collins: Houston, Apollo 11. Our crew status report for sleep: commander 5.5 [hours], command module pilot 6.0, lunar module pilot 5.0. Over.

Capcom (Evans): The Black Bugle just arrived with some morning news briefs if you're ready. . . . Church services around the world today are mentioning Apollo 11 in their prayers. President Nixon's worship service at the White House is also dedicated to the mission, and our fellow astronaut Frank Borman is still in there pitching and will read the passage from Genesis which was read on Apollo 8 last Christmas. The Cabinet and members of Congress, with emphasis on the Senate and House space committees, have been invited along with a number of other guests. Buzz, your son Andy got a tour of MSC yesterday. Your Uncle Bob Moon accompanied him on his visit which included the LRL [lunar receiving laboratory, in which the astronauts were to be quarantined following their return from the moon.]

Aldrin: Thank you.

Capcom (Evans): Roger. Among the large headlines concerning Apollo, this morning there's one asking that you watch for a lovely girl with a big rabbit. An ancient legend says that a beautiful Chinese girl called Chango has been living there [on the moon] for four thousand years. It seems she was banished to the moon because she stole the pill of immortality from her husband. You might also look for her companion, a large Chinese rabbit, who is easy to spot since he is always standing on his hind feet in the shade of a cinnamon tree. The name of the rabbit is not recorded.

Aldrin: Okay, we'll keep a close eye for the bunny girl.

Capcom (Evans): While you're on your way back Tuesday night the American and National League all-stars will be playing ball in Washington. Mel Stottlemyre of the Yankees is expected to be the American League's first pitcher. . . . Even though research has certainly paid off in the space program, research doesn't pay off, it seems. The Woodstream Corporation, parent company of the Animal Trap Company of America, which has made more than a billion wooden spring mousetraps, reports that it built a better mousetrap but the world didn't beat a door to its path—didn't beat a path to its door. As a matter of fact, the company had to go back to the old-fashioned kind. They said, "We should have spent more time researching housewives and less time researching mice." And the Black Bugle is all completed for the morning.

Armstrong: Thank you very much. We appreciate the news.

Eight o'clock, Sunday morning, Houston time, lunar landing a little more than seven hours away. . . . Ninety-five hours and 25 minutes into the flight, three minutes to loss of signal, AOS at 96 hours 20 minutes. . . . Loss of signal, behind the moon for the tenth time.

About a month before Apollo 11 was due to fly, Buzz Aldrin asked his minister, the Reverend Dean Woodruff of Webster Presbyterian Church, "to research what he had available, to come up with some symbol which meant a little bit more than what most people might be thinking of. What we were looking for—what I was interested in—was something that transcended modern times. Somehow we weren't quite able to work this into something that would have an appeal." Mr. Woodruff did prepare a paper which he called "The Myth of Apollo 11: The Effects of the Lunar Landing on the Mythic Dimension of Man." He concluded:

Since myth and symbols are so pervasive in the psyche of man, a fairly dramatic and meaningful event is required to have any effect on this dimension of man. The Apollo event will be the kind of occurrence that will reach down to this level in man because this flight will change our view of the world. After Copernicus man could no longer see himself as the center of the world and had to adjust to the new knowledge that things had not been designed especially for him and that he was no longer the center of the universe. And after Darwin man had to make a similar adjustment in understanding himself as a part of nature rather than specially created. Events with such an impact do have an effect on man's self-understanding.

One of the most ancient motifs found in mythology is called "the magic flight." Professor Eliade comments: ". . . It is found everywhere, and in the most archaic of cultural strata . . . the longing to break the ties that hold him in bondage to the earth is not a result of cosmic pressures or of economic insecurity—it is constitutive of man. . . . Such a desire to free himself from his limitation, which he feels to be a kind of degradation . . . must be ranked among the specific marks of man."

Apollo 11 will have the effect of saying to man that he can stand outside his world and view it as a whole. Science, as the achievement of man, has created a worldwide technical civilization and, as yet, has not given birth to any cultural symbols by which man can live. The Apollo event comes at a time when we need a symbol, and need to tap a myth that will graphically express the unending journey outward. Perhaps when those pioneers step on another planet and view the earth from a physically transcendent stance, we can sense its symbolism and feel a new breath of freedom from our current cultural claustrophobia and be awakened once again to the mythic dimension of man.

Nearly nine o'clock in the morning, Houston time, Sunday morning, July 20. . . . Ninety-six hours and 19 minutes into the mission, less than one minute from reacquisition of signal. . . . Buzz Aldrin in the LM beginning the LM power up and checkout, soon to be joined by Neil Armstrong. . . . Stand by for the call to the crew. . . .

Houston (Duke): Hello, Columbia, this is Houston. Do you read? Over. . . . Eagle, did you call me? Over.

Eagle (Aldrin): Roger, how do you read? Over.

Houston (Duke): Roger . . . a lot of noise on the loop. We think it's coming in from Columbia, but we can't tell. We're unable to raise voice with him. Would he please go to high gain? Over.

Eagle (Aldrin): Okay. I'll have him go to high gain. . . . I'm up to the point where I turn on the IMU.

Houston (Duke): Roger, stand by. Did you get your high gain to work?

Columbia (Collins): Houston, Columbia. Reading you loud and clear. How me?

Houston (Duke): Roger, about three by [medium clarity and volume]. Mike, we've got a lot of noise in the background. It's clearing up now. Eagle, Houston. Do you read? Over.

Eagle (Aldrin): Houston, Eagle. About four by four, go ahead.

Columbia (Collins): Houston, Columbia, we have Poo and ACCEPT, and how are you reading me now?

Houston (Duke): Roger, understand. We have Poo and ACCEPT. You're about three by in — on the voice, Mike, over.

Columbia (Collins): Okay, you're coming in loud and clear, and I'm configured for normal voice. If you've got any switch changes, let me know.

Houston (Duke): Roger, we've got the noise somewhere in the system down here, I think. We're working on it. And I've got a 130 landmark update for you, and also a DAP load whenever you're ready to copy. Over. [*"We*

copy" had better carrying power than "We understand." . . .]

Columbia (Collins): Stand by. . . . Go ahead.

Houston (Duke): Roger, Mike. Coming at you with the 130,P one is niner 8 37⌐35, P2 niner 8 42 44, 4 miles north, over. [*"I get my kicks out of those niners," Joan Aldrin had said; "niner" had better carrying power than "nine."* . . .]

Houston (Duke): Columbia, Houston. Did you hit the command reset around after LOS on the last pass? Over.

Columbia (Collins): That's affirmative. When we were having difficulty getting you, Charlie, I pushed the command reset to make sure I had control of high gain.

Houston (Duke): Roger. Thank you much. We're in good shape now. Over.

Eagle (Aldrin): Houston, Eagle. Can you tell me if you're picking up biomed [medical data] on the commander now? Over.

Houston (Duke): Eagle, Houston. We're not getting any biomed on the commander now. . . . Eagle, Houston. We got the biomed on the commander now. Over.

Eagle (Aldrin): Very good. Thank you. . . . Houston, Eagle. We're ready for an E-memory dump if you are. Over. [*Armstrong now in the lunar module. . . . LM activation and checkout going well, somewhat ahead of schedule.*]

Houston (Duke): Eagle, Houston. Could you give us a hack on the time that you switched to LM power and also verify that we're on glycol pump one? Over.

Eagle (Armstrong): This is Eagle. We're on pump one, stand by for the switchover time. . . . The switch time to LM power is 95:54:00 [GET].

Houston (Duke): Roger, copy, Neil. Is Buzz back in the Columbia now? Over.

Eagle (Armstrong): Yes, he is. [*Thirty-three minutes before loss of signal, Aldrin back in the command module to don his pressure garment before rejoining Armstrong in Eagle.*]

Eagle (Armstrong): Did you get the time? We're 97:14:20.

Houston (Duke): Roger, copy. . . . Columbia and Eagle, LOS for both spacecraft 97:32, AOS 98:18. . . . Eagle, Houston. We have your gryo torquing angles if you're ready to copy . . . .

Eagle (Aldrin): Houston, Eagle. Lunar module pilot. How do your read? Over. [*Aldrin now back in Eagle.* . . .]

Houston (Duke): Roger, five by five, Buzz [perfect]. How me? Over.

Eagle (Aldrin): Oh, loud and clear. I'm going to be going through an ascent battery check. You want to check my biomed briefly? Over.

Houston (Duke): Eagle, Houston. We got a biomed on you, Buzz. . . . When we go LOS, we'd like you to go OFF on the biomed. [*Four minutes to loss of signal.* . . .]

Columbia (Collins): The capture latch is in the probe engaged in the drogue. Would you like to check them from your side?

Eagle (Armstrong): Mike, the capture latches look good. [*Thirty seconds to loss of signal, both spacecraft looking good as they go over the hill for the eleventh time. . . . Loss of signal. . . . Another forty-five minutes of silence.* . . .]

Houston (Ward): This is Apollo Control at 98 hours 16 minutes. We are now less than two minutes from reacquiring the spacecraft. At this time Armstrong and Aldrin should be completing pressure checks on their space suits. Coming up in this revolution, they will be running checks on the guidance platform of their LM guidance system. They will also be running checks on the reaction control system thrusters and their descent propulsion system, as well as the rendezvous radar. We will also be giving them the go/no go for undocking in the following revolution. All systems performing well. . . . Now about forty-five seconds from reacquiring. . . . CAPCOM Charlie Duke putting in a call to the crew. . . .

(Columbia (Collins): Houston, Columbia. Down-voice backup, do you read?

Houston (Duke): Roger, we read you. Columbia, did you call, over?

Columbia (Collins): Affirmative. Calling you on down-voice backup. How do you read me?

Houston (Duke): Roger, better, Mike. . . . We're satisfied with this COMM configuration. Let's stay with where we are. Over.

Eleven in the morning. Houston time; and it was Sunday. . . .

Jan Armstrong spent the morning in her El Lago home, just waiting for the coming afternoon. In Nassau Bay the Collins daughters, Kate and Ann, served their mother breakfast in bed; their father had always brought Pat her breakfast on Sunday when he was home. Then Pat Collins, the three children and Pat's sister, Ellie Golden, attended the ten-thirty Mass at St. Paul's Roman Catholic Church.

The service had begun an hour earlier at the Webster Presbyterian Church, of which Buzz Aldrin was an elder. Joan Aldrin, along with Michael, Jan, Andy and Bob and Audrey Moon, arrived in a NASA station wagon driven by Bill Der Bing. Microphones were thrust into Joan's face as she entered the church. "Let's do this later," she suggested. The church was attractive, light and airy—rather stark and simple. It was also jammed tight with people; ushers were setting out folding chairs to acommodate the overflow. A girl said, to nobody in particular, "I've never seen it so full. I should have stayed home and watched it on television. I just didn't think." The atmosphere was charged with the same kind of emotion which George Low had noted around the consoles of Mission Control. There was tension in the face and in the manner of the Reverend Dean Woodruff; this was not a day for a long sermon, but he had given considerable thought to the form of the service. The scripture reading, in which the congregation joined, was printed on a folding sheet, white words on a black background which showed color pictures (taken by Apollo 8) of the earth as seen from just above the lunar surface. Then there were the words of the opening hymn, No. 84 in the Presbyterian hymnal:

I sing the mighty power of God,
That made the mountains rise;
That spread the flowing seas abroad,
And built the lofty skies.
I sing the Wisdom that ordained
The sun to rule the day;
The moon shines full at His command,
And all the stars obey.

The text of the sermon took up less than three pages of double-spaced typescript, but Mr. Woodruff had gone over every word many times:

Today we witness the epitome of the creative ability of man—and we, here in this place, are not only witnesses but also unique participants. How is it we come to this place at this time to be a part of this event?

What happens today is an expression of man's ability—of man's self-determination. It is the molding of knowledge and theory; it is the channeling of human resources in solving problems; it is dreaming dreams and having visions; it is the concretizing of man's potential. . . .

Self-determination is our way of surviving in the mundane and through the spectacular; it is our existence—our fight with failure, our impetus toward achievement, our struggles with demonic forces; it is the grit of man.

Self-fulfillment is "oughtness" and "givenness" —what we "ought to be" and "what it is given us to be." Fulfillment is the heart and soul of determination. Fulfillment is the meaning and purpose of self-determination.

When these two are put together perfectly we are what we are meant to be. This is what Nietzsche developed in his idea of the "superman." It is not a new biological species but a new kind of man who realizes his capacity for self-transcendence and self-fulfillment. This is what Nietzsche meant when he spoke through Zarathustra: "Bless the cup which is about to overflow, so that the water, golden flowing out of it, may carry everywhere the reflection of thy rapture. Lo! this cup is about to empty itself again, and Zarathustra will once more become a man."

Apollo 11 is the sharply focused symbol of man's power to accomplish—of self-determination. Today Armstrong, Aldrin and Collins will take us to the threshold of the possibility of self-fulfillment. They, as "representative man," will implicitly ask the question, "What is man . . . thou hast made him little less than God, and dost crown him with glory and honor."

As I have said before to this congregation, since World War II we are in the advent of the modern worldwide civilization that is based upon science —for the language and technique of science is the same in every country. If we are, in fact, in the midst of this new worldwide civilization, then the first symbolic event of that civilization is "the bomb." The second symbolic event of that civilization is Apollo 11, the first and most imaginative nondestructive event of a new civilization.

From the back of the church a young soprano sang the anthem, "Let Us Break Bread Together." The service concluded with Communion. As Mr. Woodruff broke the loaf of bread and held it up for view, he pointed out that the loaf was not whole; he did not say what had happened to the missing piece, but the congregation understood that, symbolically, it had gone with Buzz.

There was no formal benediction; Mr. Woodruff suggested that each member of the congregation say his own benediction later on this day, the day of the lunar landing. He did repeat the prayer he had used at the earlier private Communion: "Even as the door to the universe is being opened by this flight, this crew, this man, deliver us all from pride and arrogance and all unrighteousness which make men the enemies of one another. We dedicate unto Thee, Thy servant and our brother, Edwin Aldrin, to represent the Body of Christ, our nation, and all mankind on the first expedition to another planet."

Joan Aldrin waited in line to shake hands with the minister, then ran into a cluster of photographers and had to be escorted to Bill Der Bing's station wagon. By half-past eleven she was home, and the Archers left to attend Mass. When she came back Rosalind Archer said, "I said my Hail Marys for Buzz. I've said so many for him in the last few months and lit so many candles for him. But they didn't have any candles down there today."

Houston (Duke): Eagle, Houston, could you give us an idea where you are in the activation? Over.

Eagle (Aldrin): Roger, we're just sitting around waiting for something to do. We need a state vector and a REFSMMAT.

Houston (Duke): Roger, Eagle, we'll have the state vectors and the REFSMMAT for you as soon as we get the high gain. Over. [*Communications noisy. . . . Mike Collins preparing to take marks on a landmark near the prime landing site. . . .*]

Eagle (Aldrin): Houston, Eagle.

Houston (Duke): Go ahead, Eagle. Over.

Eagle (Aldrin): Roger. In the first of—on page 47 [of the flight plan], step one, we had the guidance control in PGNCS and mode control PGNCS AUTO and of course the circuit breakers are not in on the thrusters yet. So when we started through the DAP and proceeded on NOUN 46 and we're looking at NOUN 47 now, so we've got an RCS TCA light and we've got four out of the eight other bright colored red flags. I think that this is explained by the fact that we are in PGNCS and AUTO and unable to fire the thrusters. Over.

Houston (Duke): Roger, stand by. . . . You are correct. The lights are there and the flags because we haven't closed the breakers yet. Over.

Eagle (Armstrong): And Houston, Eagle. Are you going to need the high gain before you can look at our GDA position indicator?

Houston (Duke): Stand by. . . . We can see all the throttle data.

Eagle (Aldrin): I could give you high bit rate on the OMNI if that would help any.

Houston (Duke): Negative. We have all the throttle data we need. You can stay low bit rate. You can proceed through the throttle test, but do not do the gimbal trim, over. Repeat, do not do the gimbal trim.

Columbia (Collins): Boy, you just can't mess with the check point. . . . Auto optics are pointed just a little bit north of crater 130.

Houston (Duke): And Eagle, Houston. Have you deployed the landing gear yet? Over.

Eagle (Armstrong): That's affirmative.

Columbia (Collins): Houston, Columbia. I've completed my marks. [*Landmark tracking job completed. . . .*]

Eagle (Aldrin): Houston, Eagle. I believe I've got you on the high gain antenna now.

Houston (Duke): Columbia, Houston. If you go to REACQ on the high gain we can acquire you now. Over. . . . Eagle, Houston. We got some loads for you. . . . We've got both of you on the high gains now. It sounds great now. Over.

Columbia (Collins): Houston, Columbia. Comment on P22. Worked just fine. The target I marked on is a small crater down inside crater 130 as described by John Young.

Columbia (Collins): Eagle, Columbia. Let me know when you come to your RCS hot fire checks so I can disable my ROLL.

Eagle (Aldrin): Roger, we're right there now. . . . We'd like wide dead-band ATT HOLD [attitude hold]

Columbia (Collins): You got it. Are you going to do your hot fire now?

Eagle (Aldrin): Roger.

Columbia (Collins): Okay, I'm disabling my ROLL. ROLL is disabled.

[*Less than ten minutes before loss of signal. . . . Flight Director Gene Kranz talking to his flight controllers about the go/no go decision for undocking. . . . Lunar landing a little more than three hours away. . . .*]

Columbia (Collins): Would you believe you've got thrusters onboard that vehicle?

Eagle (Aldrin): Houston, Eagle. The RCS hot fire is complete. How do you observe it? Over.

Houston (Duke): Stand by. Eagle, Houston. The RCS hot fire looks super to us. We're all go. . . . Apollo 11, Houston. We're go for undocking. Over.

Columbia (Collins): Roger. There will be no television of the undocking. . . . I'm busy with other things. [*Loss of signal, around the far side of the moon for the twelfth time, 99 hours and 31 minutes into the mission. . . . One hundred hours and 14 minutes. Less than two minutes from reacquisition of signal. . . .*]

Houston (Ward): When next we hear from them the lunar module should have undocked from the command and service module. We're presently about twenty-five minutes away from the separation burn which will be performed by Mike Collins in the command module. . . . The separation maneuver is scheduled to occur at a Ground Elapsed Time of 100 hours 39 minutes 50 seconds; the descent orbit insertion maneuver, which will be performed on the back side of the moon, set for 101 hours 36 minutes 14 seconds, and the beginnings of the powered descent at 102 hours 33 minutes 4 seconds. We're now fifty-five seconds from reacquiring Apollo 11. . . .

Houston (Duke): Hello, Eagle, Houston. We're standing by. Over. . . . Eagle, Houston. We see you on the steerable. Over.

Eagle (Armstrong): Roger. Eagle's undocked.

Houston (Duke): Roger. How does it look?

Eagle (Armstrong): The Eagle has wings.

Nassau Bay, Texas

The women of the Webster Presbyterian Church brought a cold lunch for the Aldrin family; the frosting of a cake carried an American flag and the legend "We came in peace for all mankind." Joan Aldrin said, very graciously, "I can't thank you enough—you don't know how much it means to me." Andy Aldrin asked his mother, "Do you think we'll all get to go to the White House this year?" Joan said she hoped so, "unless they ask us to dinner at night." Andy had had the idea that an extra satellite might establish spacecraft communications from behind the moon, and Bob Moon got out a map to explain why the suggestion was not really practical. Waiting for reacquisition of signal, Joan grew increasingly restless. A television commentator reported that another baby had just been named Apollo. *"Another* one of them!" Joan exclaimed, fiddling nervously with the TV set. Still waiting for the signal, Andy asked plaintively, "What can I do?" His mother answered quietly, "There's nothing to do." Then she caught Buzz's voice on the squawk box. "That was a good readback, Buzz," she said, and settled back on the couch once more. The Reverend Dean Woodruff came; suddenly the room was once again full of people and bubbling with conversation. Mike Aldrin burst in from the back porch in great excitement: "Mom, do you have a coffee can?" He had a small water snake clutched in one fist; he and Kurt Henize had just caught it. Mr. Woodruff exclaimed, "That's all we want now!" Joan urged Mike to "get out of here with that," and Mike and Kurt went to look for a coffee can in the kitchen.

Eagle (Aldrin): Go ahead, Houston, Eagle is ready to copy.

Houston (Duke): Eagle. Coming at you with a DOI pad. . . . Stand by on your readback. If you are ready to copy the PDI data, I have it for you. Over.

Eagle (Aldrin): Go ahead.

Houston (Duke): PDI pad. . . . Ready for your readbacks. Over.

Columbia (Collins): Neil, I'm maneuvering in ROLL.

Eagle (Armstrong): Roger, I see you.

Houston (Duke): Columbia, Houston. How do you read?

Columbia (Collins): I've been reading you loud and clear, Houston. How me?

Houston (Duke): Roger, Mike, five by. On my mark seven minutes to ignition. MARK seven minutes.

Eagle (Aldin): I got you. Everything's looking real good.

Houston (Duke): You are looking good for separation. You are go for separation, Columbia. Over.

In Nassau Bay Mary Engle, wife of astronaut Joe Engle, had come into the Collins home to supervise the peanut butter and jelly sandwiches for the children's lunch. Waiting for confirmation that the undocking had been accomplished behind the moon, Pat Collins updated her record of which astronaut's wife had sent or brought which casserole or cake. She also made a note to call her brother David in Boston; David's son, two weeks old, was being christened this afternoon—Michael Collins Finnegan. Then voice contact was made, and the inevitable numbers came pouring out of the squawk box. "What are the numbers for?" Kate Collins asked. "They're updating in case they lose contact," her mother answered. "They'll have the numbers on the pad. This makes me nervous." Checking off times in her copy of the flight plan, Pat was interrupted by young Michael: "Mommy, can we have some candy?" Still concentrating on the flight plan, Pat said "Yes, but don't forget to brush your teeth, children. You know I'm not checking you very well. . . . That's Charlie Duke speaking. Doen't he have a nice clear voice? Pat's sister Ellie replied, "That's because he went to school in Massachusetts"—everyone within earshot had been teasing Ellie Golden about her "vodker and tawnic" Boston accent. They were still reading the numbers and suddenly

Pat Collins shouted to the children: "Hey, listen! Did you hear Daddy's 0073's?" Ellie insisted that Pat have some lunch: "Quiet, child. It's crucial."

Columbia (Collins): We're really stabilized, Neil. I haven't fired a thruster in five minutes . . . . I made a small trim maneuver.

Eagle (Armstrong): Mike, what's going to be your pitch angle at sep [separation]?

Columbia (Collins): Zero zero seven degrees . . . . Is that close enough for you or do you want it to a couple of decimal places?

Eagle (Armstrong): No, that's good.

Columbia (Collins): I think you've got a fine looking flying machine there, Eagle, despite the fact you're upside down.

Eagle (Aldrin): Somebody's upside down. [*One minute to the separation burn.* . . .]

Columbia (Collins): Okay, Eagle. . . . You guys take care.

Eagle (Armstrong): See you later.

El Lago, Texas
When Columbia and Eagle came around following the twelfth trip "over the hill," Jan Armstrong said it again: "Hot dog!" The next item of business was separation—the burn.
Jan tapped the flight plan with her pencil and said, "Come on, LM! Make it a good one!" Ken Danneberg, a Denver oilman who had served with Neil Armstrong in Korea, was there. He asked, "How do they know which numbers go VERB and which go NOUN?

"They know," Jan said.

When Neil said "See you later," Jan's sister Carolyn Trude said. "It must be burn time."

It was.

Columbia (Collins): Houston, Columbia. My DSKY is reading 4.9, in X, 5.0, make it and EMS 105.4. Over. [*Separation performed as scheduled.* . . . *Separation about eleven hun-*

dred feet at the beginning of descent orbit insertion, coming up on the thirteenth trip over the hill. . . . Lunar landing a little more than two hours away. . . .]

Eagle (Armstrong): Going right down U.S. One, Mike.

In El Lago Jan was explaining to Carolyn, "It's a maneuver operation." Bill Anders dropped in, and so did Marilyn Lovell. Anders pointed to a lunar strip map on the bed and said, "This is the famous Mount Marilyn." Jan leaned over the map with Anders and pointed to the center.

"Are they right on this line or not?" she asked. She was pointing at the lunar equatorial line.

"It's my opinion that they are," Anders said. "Maybe a little bit off, but I can't tell you which side they'll be on." *Forty-five minutes from DOI, descent orbit insertion, on the back side of the moon, the two spacecraft about half a mile apart. . . .*

Jan Armstrong had another question: "What are the prime mission rules about touchdown? What can go wrong and they can still go?"

"They wouldn't leap right off immediately," Anders said. "They have a two-minute look around. Then it depends on what went wrong."

"Like things they had backups for?" Jan asked.

"Like things they didn't have backups for," Anders answered. "Like, say, your oxygen system blew up. . . ."

Astronaut Ron Evans, one of the CAPCOMs, came in, and Jan asked him, "What can they lose and still land?"

"It gets pretty complicated," Evans said.

Houston (Ward): We're coming up on fifteen minutes now until loss of signal with the lunar module. Flight director Gene Kranz has advised his flight controllers to review all their data, take a good close look at the spacecraft,

and in preparation for a go/no go decision on the descent orbit insertion. . . . .

Houston (Duke): Columbia, Houston. We'll have LOS at 101:28. AOS for you 102:15. Over.

Columbia (Collins): Thank you.

Houston (Duke): Eagle, Houston. You are go for DOI. Over.

Eagle (Aldrin): Roger, go for DOI. Do you have LOS and AOS times?

Houston (Duke): Roger, for you, LOS at 101:28. AOS 102:15. Over. [*Three minutes to loss of signal, both spacecraft looking good going over the hill for the thirteenth time. . . . Loss of signal. . . . Silence. . . .*]

Houston (Ward): We've had loss of signal, and spacecraft Eagle has been given a go for descent orbit insertion. That maneuver to occur in 7 minutes 40 seconds. . . . The burn duration 29.8 seconds, and the resulting orbit for the LM will be 57.2 by 8.5 nautical miles. When next we acquire the lunar module, it should be at an altitude of about eighteen nautical miles on its way down to a low point of about fifty thousand feet, from where the powered descent to the lunar surface will begin. [*One hundred one hours and twenty-nine minutes into the flight, six minutes to DOI, lunar landing a little more than an hour away. . . .*]

Houston (Ward): This is Apollo Control at 101 hours 35 minutes. We're now less than one minute from the scheduled time for the descent orbit insertion maneuver performed by the lunar module on the back side of the moon. Of course, we don't have radio contact with the spacecraft. . . . Flight controllers standing around in little groups. Not much that we can do at this point. . . . We're now twenty minutes—or twenty seconds, rather—from ignition. . . . It will be a 29.8 second burn, first at ten percent and then forty percent thrust, of the ninety-eight hundred pound thrust descent propulsion system. We should be burning at this time. . . . We should have a cutoff by this time. We would expect to re-acquire the command module first. . . .

Charlie Duke was the Houston CAPCOM waiting for reacquisition of signal at 102 hours GET; it was a little more than half an hour to lunar touchdown. The CAPCOM was really the crew's representative in Mission Control; as Duke said: "We're supposed to know how the crew responds, and whether this is good from an operational standpoint or not. So our inputs into the total decision-making process are of an operational nature. To be a good CAPCOM, you've got to know the procedures used by the crew and also the software—in other words, the operational details of how they're flying the spacecraft and also the flow of information to the crew. That's the software, the program in the computer. Or the *programs*—plural." Duke had known since the flight of Apollo 10 that he would have this shift as CAPCOM on Apollo 11. Tom Stafford had asked him to be the prime CAP-COM of Apollo 10, and had got him; therefore, on that flight, he had helped put together the "timeline" for the checkout of the lunar module in lunar orbit. Because of that experience, and because of the knowledge of lunar rendezvous he had acquired during the Apollo 10 mission, Neil Armstrong asked Duke to be the CAPCOM for the lunar orbit phase in which the Apollo 11 lunar module would be checked out, and the normal cycling of Mission Control crews would then make Duke the CAPCOM at lunar landing time. Neil Armstrong recalled having said, "I want you to do it for me, because you probably have a better knowledge of this than anybody that's not flying." Duke himself recalled ruefully that "I would have liked to say that I was on a crew and wouldn't have time to do it. But I wasn't on a crew." Duke was one of those Annapolis graduated astronauts (like Bill Anders, Tom Stafford, Donn Eisele and Jim Irwin) who had gone into the Air Force and then decided to try for the space program. Duke decided to opt for the Air Force after his second Navy cruise ("I got seasick"). He applied to become an astronaut rather late—in 1965, when it became apparent to him at Edwards Air Force Base that there would be no place for him very soon in the program which was flying the rocket-powered X–15. Somewhat to his surprise, getting into the space program turned out to be easier than getting an assignment to fly the X–15, and he was accepted in the spring of 1966. At the time of Apollo 11 Duke was thirty-three years old and had been an astronaut for three years. He was still waiting for a crew assignment, and he sometimes wondered if he would be the first rookie astronaut to fly at the age of fifty. But on the afternoon of Sunday, July 20, he was—from the standpoint of the Apollo 11 astronauts—just about the most important man on the ground at Mission Control. *Acquisition signal. . . . There they were, dead on time. . . .*

Houston (Duke): Eagle, Houston. If you read, you're a go for powered descent. Over.
Collins: Eagle, this is Columbia. They just gave you a go for powered descent.
Houston (Duke): Columbia, Houston. We've lost them again on the high gain. Would you please—we recommend they yaw right ten degrees and then try for high gain again.
Collins: Eagle, you read Columbia?
Houston (Duke): Eagle, Houston. We read you now. You're go for PDI. Over. . . . MARK, 3:30 until ignition.

Charlie Duke was beginning to get a little upset. It was an easy afternoon to get upset: "It always happens that when we have the critical revolution or the critical pass, we have lousy communications. It just seems like that's our luck. The data kept dropping out. I said to myself, 'Oh, no, here we go again,' because we had a mission rule that said we needed adequate communications and data from the spacecraft before we would commit to powered descent. We had telemetry data in spurts. It was dropping out along with the voice. The high gain for some reason was dithering around up there, and as the signal strength would fall down we'd lose the telemetry.

"Pete Conrad made a suggestion. He was sitting down in the front row, and he came up to the front console and said, 'Hey, how about letting them yaw?' So we let them yaw right and it did help. We were getting just enough data to give all the systems people a warm feeling about—well, the spacecraft's ready to go and the guidance looks good. So we committed to descent, although it was an uneasy feeling to know that you were going into the critical phase of the mission with marginal communications.

"We had good communications at ignition when we really needed them, right at the start of the powered descent. We kept communications for a couple of minutes, and then they dropped out again on us. About that time Neil made his big yaw maneuver of a hundred and eighty degrees, yawing around to place the lunar module in an upright, forward-facing position."

Forty thousand feet above the lunar surface now, about ten minutes to go. . . . Time for the lunar module's landing radar to lock on. . . .

San Diego, California
T. Claude Ryan was seventy-one years old and about to retire as chairman of the Ryan Aeronautical Company. As the lunar module hit the forty thousand-foot mark he felt a special thrill, for the landing radar which had to work, starting right now, had been made by Ryan

Aeronautical. He had felt the same thrill a little over forty-two years ago when a primitive high-wing monoplane, built by little Ryan Airlines and piloted by a quietly confident young man named Lindbergh, flew nonstop from New York to Paris. The relative simplicity of that flight by *The Spirit of St. Louis,* risky as it appeared at the time, stood in stark contrast to the complexity of this mission. Mr. Ryan had seen it all and remembered it all. He remembered getting that telegram in 1927: "It asked if we could build a plane capable of flying from New York to Paris, nonstop, with a Wright Whirlwind engine. It was very short, that's about all there was to it. And signed, however, by Robertson Aircraft Company. I know why Lindbergh signed it that way. He was thinking that we would know the name Robertson, which we did, and that we would pay a little more attention to it and not think that it was just some crackpot. And we did.

"I happened to be alone in the office at the time with our sole secretary—we had thirty-five or forty employees. My partner, Franklin Mahoney, was in town, and I got hold of Don Hall, who was our one and only full-time engineer. Don and I figured out that maybe this could be done." *(In 1961 John F. Kennedy would figure out, more or less by instinct, that something could be done—time for a great new American enterprise. . . .)*

At the time it seemed to T. Claude Ryan "a rather ambitious thing" to build a little two-hundred-h.p. airplane which would carry enough fuel to go farther than any airplane had gone before: "However, it did look possible. Franklin Mahoney came back and we talked about it. He was not quite so enthusiastic about giving a favorable answer as I was. But I thought, what harm could it do to tell him yes, we could do it? So we answered in the affirmative."

In his own book, General Charles A. Lindbergh dated the return telegram from Ryan Airlines February 4, 1927: "CAN BUILD PLANE SIMILAR M ONE BUT LARGER WINGS CAPABLE OF MAKING FLIGHT COST ABOUT SIX THOUSAND WITHOUT MOTOR AND INSTRUMENTS DELIVERY ABOUT THREE MONTHS RYAN AIRLINES." Forty-two years later Mr. Ryan remembered the quotation price as being something like ten thousand dollars: "We gave them a price without the engine, without instruments, just the bare airplane."

Then Lindbergh came out—by train. Mr. Ryan did not meet him: "I had flown up to Los Angeles to try to run down an airplane we had sold and had not collected the money for. Mahoney met him at the Santa Fe station and brought him out here. We had some M-1's under construction. The airplanes were made one at a time. There was no production line. And with this one fuselage, it was to be the B-1, the Brougham, we expected to tap a new market and get into the passenger-carrying field for charter work. This first airplane—we had an order for it from Frank Hawks. He was quite a famous pilot and he wanted to fly the first one. He had a deposit on it. We persuaded Frank to forego delivery and let us use the fuselage to convert over and use for Lindbergh's plane.

Lindbergh wanted the airplane delivered in sixty days, not ninety; he had competition. Other people, mostly better financed than he, were trying to fly the Atlantic. Could Ryan Airlines deliver it? Forty-two years later Mr. Ryan answered that question: "You betcha we did! We talked it over with our people, a pretty compact group of people; almost every workman in the plant was taken into the decision. . . . Of course, Lindbergh added a lot to morale because it got to be a challenge to everybody. He went around the plant all the time. He had such a nice personality, was just such a young boyish fellow. They all fell for

him. They liked him very much." Mr. Ryan liked Lindbergh too: "He had a very pleasing personality. Not very forward, a little bit bashful in a way, but he was just another pilot as far as I was concerned. I knew he was qualified and knew what he was talking about. I never once thought that he was going about the thing in a foolhardy way. I thought he had an awful lot of nerve, and that he was a brave man, because many times I was talking to him and we discussed and compared notes as to what the percentage of risk had been in making the flight. I had asked him at the time, 'What do you think the percentage of your chance is of success in making it?' I knew that he had a single engine that could stop. He had the weather, which could be impossible, and all these things that could be beyond his control. He turned the question to me and said, 'What do you think the percentage is?' Well, I made it a little better than I really believed, not to be discouraging. I said, 'I think you've got a seventy-five–twenty-five chance of making it.' He said, 'That's just about what I figured.' So he knowingly took his life in his hands on that basis." Many years later Neil Armstrong would say, with a parallel professionalism: "I'm not going to say there's no risk concerned, personal risk. Certainly there are risks, and they occur periodically, but they're not overwhelming risks, and they are far disproportionate to the gain. They are of no significant consideration with respect to the gainful objectives that we're working for. I suspect that on a risk-gain ratio this project would look very favorable compared to those projects that I've been used to in the past twenty years. It's fact that most people feel the urge to do what they think they're able to do. They would rather work in the area that they feel comfortable in. We feel that we can do this job. We feel comfortable doing it. It's the kind of thing we like to do and want to do."

Mr. Ryan thought the young Charles Lindbergh an outstandingly good pilot: "He could fly an airplane. He had a perfect feel in an airplane, and he had good judgment. He was a master pilot, really. Then, in 1967, he met the astronaut Neil Armstrong. Until then he had never thought about Lindbergh and the astronauts having anything in common; but Lindbergh and Armstrong: "They had quite a bit in common. They both were just completely running over with enthusiasm about what they were doing. They had great self-confidence. And Neil Armstrong had a magnetic personality. Just marvelous. When he went through our electronics plant and saw the working people making the actual landing radars that were going to be so important in landing on the moon, he shook hands with and smiled at them and those people—they would go the limit to do a good job, personally knowing him. Of course, they didn't know he was going to be *the* man, the first man to put his foot on the moon. But they were full of pride that they actually knew him, and I was too. Forty-two years—and we had the privilege of being aboard in this wonderful scientific industry. We had a lot of dreams then, and we had a lot of confidence, but none of us could have visualized that a man would be flying to the moon. That was science fiction, with emphasis on the word fiction."

But not anymore. . . . That landing radar on the lunar module was Ryan's, and this was for real. . . .

In all types of wave motion there is something called the Doppler effect. Discovered by an Austrian physicist named Christian J. Doppler, it is created by the phenomenon of light waves and the color spectrum. The electromagnetic waves which make up a beam of light are all of a specific wave length; each color relates to a different wave length, and all the wave lengths together make up the spectrum. The same effect exists in terrestrial sound motion. As a sound recedes, it has a longer wave length and a lower pitch; as a sound approaches its wave length is shorter and its pitch higher. What was important in all this to the astronauts was the fact that a color could be changed by the movement of the source of light; in fact the slight change in color was proportional to the speed of an object. Ryan Aeronautical had done some pioneering in Doppler type radar. . . .

"We developed it mainly for navigation equipment," Mr. Ryan recalled. "We developed our Ryan Radar Doppler Navigation Systems which were used on a large number of Navy airplanes and some other planes. The development of this technique, and the acquisition of that rather broad and extensive experience gave us the capability of developing the Doppler radar control for the lunar landing. There was a little parallel here with that M-1 monoplane which was designed for public transport and which was modified to become *The Spirit of St. Louis.* When we were developing our Doppler radar we had no idea that it was the precursor of the system which would help make possible a landing on the moon. But so often that's the way scientific progress is made. You can't see where it's going to lead and you're often surprised about where it does lead.

"But the romance of space travel still has something in common with the romance of flight in the barnstorming era of the 1920's and some of the revolutionary flights of the 1930's. Despite automation and computerization, the individualism has not gone out of the experience. What the astronauts have to know and what they have to do show that it hasn't. The astronauts are still important. The pilot has to be a trained engineer and scientist himself in order to know all this. Lots of these things are automated, but the pilot is there. He understands what is going on and can take over if necessary; in some operations the automated part is just a standby. There is still an awful lot of romance in it, in the combined human brains of all these people. All these computers are just their servants. As in Lindbergh's case in 1927, it seems to me that among the astronauts there is that feeling of wanting to do what's never been done before—an identical spirit."

"12 02, 12 02. . . ." *The voice was Neil Armstong's.* Charlie Duke felt as if he had been kicked in the stomach: "This alarm, the 12 02, is called an executive overflow. The computer is informing the crew that it is too busy and saying 'I'm going to restart the program.' And MIT coined a phrase called 'bail-out.' The computer just bails out and starts over at the top but drops off the things at the bottom which are not important. But we had had this powered descent simulation in June with a 12 02 alarm due to a hardware failure. The people who had written the script for the simulation had programmed the landing radar to fail. This caused the computer to look at the landing radar for information, but the information wasn't available. So the computer kept saying, 'I want it, I'm just going to keep looking for it.' The crew had no control over eliminating this problem between the computer and the landing radar. After it issued the alarm, the computer stopped doing guidance equations; it just kept looking at the landing radar. So the crew kept getting 12 02, 12 02, and they could not get the computer out of this lockup. So we had to abort during the simulation.

"After that failure Gene Kranz did a brilliant thing. He called a meeting of all the flight controllers who were involved in this area, the FIDOs and the GUIDOs, and all the MIT and support room people. We spent all day going over every possible program alarm that we could get during the descent. Some of them were mundane little things that you knew could

not possibly happen, but it wasn't possible to get a 12 02 alarm either—or so we had thought. A guy named Jack Garman, who is *the* program expert, worked up a presentation on all the program alarms. As he came up with each alarm he'd say, 'Okay, we *can* get this one, and what are you going to do?' We finally decided that if we had those alarms and they did not recur constantly, we were go. If the computer caught up right away every time it got too busy and then started over, we were go for landing. But if the alarms kept recurring, then the computer couldn't perform its other routines and we would have to abort. And Steve Bales, the guidance officer [GUIDO] on this shift at Mission Control, was the one who had to make the go/no go decision. He was in the trench—the first row of Mission Control. He had been following the descent part of the mission for a couple of years and had developed the displays they were looking at.

"As I recall we got five 12 02 alarms and one 12 01 alarm during the powered descent. [As it turned out, the rendezvous radar, not the landing radar, was overloading the computer.] But the computer always fixed itself. However we were concerned, very concerned, at the time. Suppose we had to lift off a couple of hours after touchdown? The computer is busier during ascent than it is during descent! So here we are with a computer that seems to be saturated during descent and my gosh, we might be asking it to perform a more complicated task during ascent. But the alarms were not recurring often enough, *not quite often enough,* to make Steve Bales order an abort. Thank God we had had that meeting after the simulation abort in June. When I heard Neil say '12 02' for the first time, I tell you my heart hit the floor. But there was Steve Bales coming back with the answer instantaneously—we were a go flight. [Bales was "believing" the landing radar.] And Neil was doing a beautiful job of manually directing the landing. I think he's the greatest pilot in the whole world."

Neil and Buzz Aldrin were both rather busy while this was going on. Armstrong said later. . . .

Supposedly, in this time period, the crew member is supposed to look out and see the landing area, and if any small changes where the automatic system is taking him are required, he initiates those himself manually by putting control inputs into the stick. This was the area where we failed: we got tied up with computer alarms and were obliged to keep our heads inside the cockpit to assure ourselves that we could continue flying safely. So all those good pictures Tom Stafford took for me on Apollo 10, in order to pick out where I was going and to know precisely where I was, were to no avail. I just didn't get a chance to look out the window. In fact, when the problems were less important and I did get a chance to look out about three thousand feet, we had already passed most of the landmarks I had memorized.

When Mount Marilyn went by, before the alarms began, and our ignition occurred at the proper time, we knew that we were going to be approximately right; that is, we weren't going to land on the wrong side of the moon or something like that. The ignition was smooth; the engine's start-up power is only ten percent of thrust, somewhat like an idling motor engine. You can neither feel nor hear that, but you can observe on the instruments that the engine appears to be operating properly. After twenty-six seconds the engine begins to operate at full throttle, and there's no question at that point that you do have a good engine. When we made our final downrange position check, over Maskelyne W., that crater Tom Stafford called 'a big rascal,' we were quite certain that we would land a little long. The old rule is when in doubt, land long. Had we been able to look out the window at five or ten thousand feet I think we would have been able to identify our

location more specifically. But then there were those alarms, and there was some difficulty in getting them cleared. But we were able to continue because we had memorized the descent reasonably well, and we could go on the instrument readings even though the computer information was not being displayed to us on the lunar module's DSKY.

When I was finally able to look out we were so low that we couldn't see far enough to identify any significant landmarks. There was a large, impressive crater which turned out to be West Crater, but we couldn't be sure of that at the time. As we neared the surface we considered landing short of that crater, and that seemed to be where the automatic system was taking us. But as we dropped below a thousand feet, it was quite obvious that the system was attempting to land in an undesirable area in a boulder field surrounding the crater. I was surprised by the size of those boulders; some of them were as big as small motorcars. And it seemed at the time that we were coming up on them pretty fast; of course the clock runs at about triple speed in such a situation.

I was tempted to land, but my better judgment took over. We pitched over to a level attitude which would allow us to maintain our horizontal velocity and just skim along over the top of the boulder field. That is, we pitched over to standing straight up. Then the automatic throttle was still giving us a descent rate that was too high, and it was going to get us down to an altitude where we would be unable to look out ahead far enough.

That was when I took command of the throttle to fly the LM manually the rest of the way. I was being absolutely adamant about my right to be wishy-washy about where I was going to land, and the only way I could buy time was to slow down the descent rate.

There are three kinds of throttle control on the LM; I chose the semiautomatic version in which I controlled the attitude and the horizontal velocity and let my commands, in conjunction with computer commands, operate the throttle. I changed my mind a couple of times again, looking for a parking place. Something would look good, and then as we got closer it really wasn't good. Finally we found an area ringed on one side by fairly good sized craters and on the other side by a boulder field. It was not a particularly big area, only a couple of hundred square feet, about the size of a big house lot. But it looked satisfactory. And I was quite concerned about the fuel level, although we apparently had a little bit more than our gauge had indicated. It's always nice to have a gallon left when you read empty. But we had to get on the surface very soon or fire the ascent engine and abort.

Neil Armstrong had noted, as Eagle went by Makelyne W, that the "rascal" crater was passing underneath two seconds early: "If you applied that same two seconds to the point where ignition took place, when the velocity had been on the order of a mile per second—why, then this would tend to put us about two miles long. Anyway we had had good indications from visual observations, up to three and one-half minutes from ignition, that we were going to be a little bit long. Then we lengthened our trajectory to miss that West Crater, the one we were headed for, and that made us further long. We actually landed about four miles long."

But they landed. . . . Buzz Aldrin's voice came through: *Contact light. . . . Engine stop . . . . Engine arm, off. . . .* Then Neil Armstrong: *Tranquility Base here. . . .*

Tranquility Base! That was not in the flight plan; nobody in Mission Control had known that Neil Armstrong would call it that, although the expression was logical enough. What was more important was the fact that Eagle had landed. Inside Eagle Buzz Aldrin, the man Neil Armstrong once called "my most competent critic," stuck out his gloved hand and shook—hard—with his commander. *Yes,* Neil Armstrong conceded, *there certainly was a sense of relief there. . . .*

. . . And on the ground as well. Among those who had gone unnoticed by Douglas Ward at Mission Control was Dr. John Houbolt, who had argued through the lunar orbit concept which had made it necessary to create the LM. The quiet at Mission Control reminded him of a well-ordered public library. He thought, "By golly, the world ought to stop right at this moment." Then he wondered how many people were not watching at all; it was Sunday, and how many people were playing golf? The method of getting to the moon had been Dr. Houbolt's idea, but he still felt a sense of incredulity; it seemed unbelievable that this was actually taking place, "within the time we had our sights set on it." He had complete faith that the LM's legs would not sink too deeply into the lunar surface, as some had feared; he was convinced that the subsurface would be hard. (It was.)

Charlie Duke, who had been agonizing over those 12 02 alarms, also found it hard to comprehend: "When I heard Buzz say 'Engine stop' it was hard for me to believe that they were there. Later Chris Kraft told me, 'Boy, Charlie, I thought we were gone when they had those things' [the 12 02 alarms]. On my way home I was saying, 'Well, they've actually done it.' But it sort of boggled the mind to think that the thing had been accomplished. There had been no time to react."

In North Amityville, Long Island, Herman Clark, the quality control inspector who had checked out the ascent engine of Apollo 11's lunar module, found that his own emotional reaction had just begun. Armstrong and Aldrin were on the moon, but the engine he had checked out still had to get them off. And if it failed. . . .

But man had landed on the moon. It had not been easy. All those problems during the descent; all those 12 02 alarms that had nearly driven Charlie Duke and Steve Bales out of their minds; could they have been managed had not men like Neil Armstrong and Buzz Aldrin, with minds of their own, been abroad the lunar module—two trained, intelligent, thinking human beings? The question brought up the whole scientist-engineer argument, the manned *vs.* unmanned argument. Nearly four months later Robert Jastrow, director of the Institute for Space Studies of NASA's Goddard Space Flight Center, addressed himself to this question and came out with a tough answer. With the capability now achieved, he argued, it was cheaper, not dearer, to carry out scientific research on the moon by man rather than with robot instruments. And, "The short history of space flight is filled with examples of manned missions that would have failed without men on board—and of unmanned missions that did fail for want of a fix that could easily have been supplied by man."

In short, lunar module No. 5, the lunar module of Apollo 11, had soft-landed successfully on the moon because men like Neil Armstrong and Buzz Aldrin were on board.

Le Mot Juste for the Moon
William H. Honan

William H. Honan, formerly the managing editor of the *Saturday Review of Society,* is a senior Sunday editor of the *New York Times.* He has also been a national affairs editor of *Newsweek* and an assistant editor of the *New Yorker.* His publications include the book *Ted Kennedy: Profile of a Survivor* and numerous magazine articles for *Esquire, The New Republic,* and *The New York Times Magazine.*

We, the human race, hereby request that the first man on the moon, destined to speak on our behalf, pause for a moment and give some consideration to what he intends to say.

When Neil H. Armstrong, a blond, blue-eyed, thirty-eight-year-old civilian astronaut from Wapakoneta, Ohio, steps out of the lunar landing module this summer and plants his size eleven space boot on the surface of the moon, the event will eclipse in historic importance the landing of Christopher Columbus in the New World. Commander Armstrong's step will not immediately affect the nature or quality of life on earth, of course (neither did Columbus'), but it will mark the departure point of a fantastic new adventure in the saga of man. For that step onto the moon will signal a readiness to travel throughout the solar system, even the universe—in flights that will lead not merely to new worlds, new substances, new conceptions about the nature of matter and of life itself, but, it can scarcely be doubted, to contact with new beings as well. Moreover, Armstrong's will be the first such epic stride to be recorded in detail by the microphone and the television camera. Future generations will be able to relive all that was said and done at that moment as never before in the history of exploration. The stupendous magnitude and unprecedented visbility of what Commander Armstrong is about to do, therefore, combine to pose the question: when the astronaut takes that first step on the moon, what should he *say?*

At the great moments of discovery and invention in the past, men have risen, or stumbled, to the occasion with everything from instant eloquence to stupefied silence. But whatever they have said, or left unsaid, has been handed down to posterity. It was meticulously noted, for example, by a sailor who kept the logbook during Columbus' first voyage to the New World, that it was not the Admiral and commander of the expedition who first set eyes on the New World, but a lookout aboard the *Pinta* named Rodrigo de Triana who drew the watch early on the morning of October 12, 1492. At approximately two a.m., de Triana saw a white sand cliff gleaming in the moonlight and sang out: *"Tierra! Tierra!"* ("Land! Land!"). The captain of the *Pinta,* Martin Alonso Pinzon, rushed up on deck, confirmed the sighting, and fired a gun as a signal to Columbus, aboard the flagship *Santa Maria* which lay behind. The *Pinta* then permitted the *Santa Maria* to overtake her, and, as she did so, Columbus, too, must have seen land for he called across to Pinzon: "Senor Martin Alonso, you have found land! I give you five thousand maravedis as a present!" The *Pinta's* logbook noted that when Columbus led a small party ashore the next morning, he knelt on the beach to offer prayers of thanks and then rose and gave the island the name San Salvador (Holy Savior).

After Magellan had circumnavigated the globe in 1522, his fleet cast anchor off the quay of Seville and, according to a crewman, "discharged all our artillery." Then the ragged sailors went, "in shirts and barefoot, each holding a candle," to offer thanks at the shrines of Santa Maria de la Victoria and Santa Maria de l'Antiqua. When Marco Polo met the great Kublai Khan in China he "made obeisance with the utmost humility." The Khan was flattered and so entertained him "with good cheer." When the Portuguese navigator Vasco da Gama sighted the New World—if we are to

believe Meyerbeer's L'Africane—he burst into song, twittering: "Ooooo! Pa-aa-ra-di-so!" Captain Cook was tongue-tied when he came upon Tahiti; evidently he just ogled at the girls. And Commodore Perry, on stepping ashore in Japan, also kept his thoughts to himself but had a Marine band play *Hail! Columbia!,* which caused the samurai warriors standing alongside their troops to scowl ferociously. Stanley, of course, said, "Dr. Livingstone, I presume?" when he found the famous British explorer starving almost to the point of death in Ujiji after having vainly sought the headwaters of the Nile. Livingstone's reply—less well-known, although not bad for keeping his sangfroid under the circumstances—was' "Yes." Admiral Peary, after he discovered the North Pole, wrote home: "Northern trip entirely satisfactory." Lindbergh, after flying the Atlantic and landing in Paris, peered out of his cockpit groggily and said, with a faint smile, "Well, I made it." He was hauled off to be formally greeted by the American Ambassador and several French dignitaries. "Thank you," he told them. "I am awfully happy." And then, according to a reporter who was standing nearby, "his fatigue could be fought off no longer and he seemed to go to sleep standing there on his feet." When Admiral Byrd flew over the South Pole two years later in his boxy Ford trimotor monoplane, he must have come under Lindbergh's spell because the first words he radioed home were: "Well, it's done." And Sir Edmund Hillary, when returning to his base camp from the summit of Mount Everest, "shouted the good news," according to his own account, "in rough New Zealand slang."

Ever since the cry "Eureka!" rang out from the baths at Syracuse when Archimedes figured out the principle of flotation, scientists and inventors have also contributed to the literature of famous first words. A good many, no doubt, have merely exclaimed in their laboratories or workshops, "Aha!" or "By jove!", yet others have been a great deal more self-conscious about what they were doing and recognized that classy language might add luster to their accomplishments. One so wordly wise was Samuel F. B. Morse, the American painter who began tinkering with electromagnets in the early 1840's and invented the telegraph. When Morse was later granted an appropriation by Congress to set up the first large-scale test of his invention, between the Supreme Court chamber in Washington and a hotel room in Baltimore some sixty miles away, he invited Annie Ellsworth, the bright and attractive daughter of the U.S. Commissioner of Patents, to think up a suitably lofty first message for him to send. Miss Ellsworth suggested a Biblical quotation—"What hath God wrought!"—and when the wire was finally strung and all preparations ready, Morse tapped it out letter by letter and so into history as the world's first intercity telegram.

Alexander Graham Bell, the Scottish-American professor of vocal physiology who invented the telephone a generation later, was much impressed by Morse's first message. When Bell realized he was on the verge of having his gadget operational, therefore, he began to declaim Shakespeare into it—usually the "To be or not to be" soliloquy from *Hamlet*— in testing an improvement or a new piece of equipment. On March 10, 1876, Bell and his assistant Thomas Watson were trying out a new transmitter. Watson strolled off to his receiving station in a room just outside the laboratory and Bell prepared to recite. Just then Bell accidentally sloshed battery acid over his chothes and cried out anxiously: "Watson, come here—I need you!" Watson heard him over the telephone! And came running. Bell, in his joy at Watson's having heard his summons, forgot about the acid spreading over his clothes and the two men took turns rhapsodically declaiming verse, pithy quotations and finally "God save the Queen!" over the world's first telephone. When Bell demonstrated his invention at the Philadelphia Centennial Exhibition later that year, and in subsequent trials, he boomingly recited "To be or not to be. . . ." But telephonic Shakespeare made little impression on the public; the rhetoric of accident and chance remark seemed more relevant to that increasingly technology-conscious era. Accordingly, on January 25, 1915, when Bell was called upon to inaugurate the opening of the first transcontinental telephone line, nothing would do but to have Bell in New York tell Watson in San Francisco, "Watson, come here—I need you!"

Unfortunately, no one knows what Thomas A. Edison said when he invented the electric light bulb, but in 1877 when he tested his first crude phonograph he simply bellowed a utilitarian "Halloo!" into the instrument and then waited breathlessly for it to replay a whisperish and warbling "Ha-ha-loo-oh-oo." A quarter of a century later, in 1901, when Guglielmo Marconi was pecking out the world's first transatlantic radio signal, it surprised no one that he had selected to send—not a glittering *terza rima* from the immortal Dante but merely the letter "S" in Morse code, repeated over and over again until the team at St. Johns, Newfoundland, finally picked up a faint "dit-dit-dit, dit-dit-dit. . . ." That was the new rhetoric of technology in its purest form.

Two years after, the Wright brothers also expressed themselves in the new fashion. Following the first success with their flying machine, Wilbur and Orville hiked a few miles to the government wireless station at Kitty Hawk and Orville telegraphed to his father a message that now seems almost prophetic of the staccato gauge-reading one hears from the astronauts while in space: "SUCCESS FOUR FLIGHTS THURSDAY MORNING ALL AGAINST TWENTY ONE MILE WIND STARTED FROM LEVEL WITH ENGINE POWER ALONE AVERAGE SPEED THROUGH AIR THIRTY ONE MILES LONGEST

FIFTY NINE SECONDS INFORM PRESS HOME CHRIST-
MAS."

Prophetic or not, the astronauts have carried
on in the same cryptic style. The technical
chatter they banter back and forth with the
ground is simply unintelligible to the layman.
Sometimes, in fact, it is unintelligible to the
astronauts. During the flight of Apollo 9, for
instance, at one point Mission Control told the
men in space: "We'd like to have a P.R.D.
readout from each of you. And we'll see you
over Tananarive at about 24:25." To this, the
spacecraft replied, a little sleepily: "Uh . . .
Roger and thank you. We'll get a P.R.D. report as soon as we figure out what it is."

But technical jargon, and its attendant con-
fusions, are to be expected when the business
at hand is a highly sophisticated feat of engineering. What is distressing about the messages
the astronauts have sent crackling back from
space, however, is that when attempting to
express themselves on nontechnical subjects,
as they quite often do, words fail them. Indeed,
the astronauts have shown themselves to be so
inarticulate, so crippled in their speech, it must
now be stated, with no little alarm, that when
they land on the moon this summer the clear
indication is they will follow the worst, not the
best, of the historic precedents set for them—
mumbling and fumbling like Captain Cook and
Lindbergh rather than soaring and swelling like
Vasco da Gama and Samuel F. B. Morse.

Consider the astronauts' record. February
20, 1962, dawns cloudy and grey. Suddenly the
sun breaks through, the sky clears, and from
that little-known pancake flat off the Florida
coast—a belch of orange flame, the roar of
horsepower loosed. Up, up and away! Colonel
John H. Glenn Jr. rides the great, shimmering
Atlas booster up toward the limitless reaches
of space and then arches gracefully into orbit.
What a day for America! It was Step One to
the moon; the door to the universe flung open!

Amidst all this, what did Colonel Glenn have to
say?

"Smoothing out real fine. We're doing real
fine up here. . . . This is very comfortable . . .
I have nothing but a very fine feeling. It feels
very normal and very good. My status is excellent. I feel fine. Over . . . We're doing real fine
up here. Everything is going well. Over. Roger.
That sure was a short day. . . . Yes, sir!
Roger. . . . Negative ..I feel fine. . . . Man, this
is beautiful. Hey, Gordo, I want you to send a
message to the Commandant of the U.S. Marine Corps in Washington. Tell him I have my
four hours required flight time this month, and
request a flight chit be made out for me. . . .
Roger. . . . Affirmative. . . . Negative. . . . I
feel real good, Wally. . . . Chute is out. Beautiful chute. Chute looks good. Chute looks very
good. The chute looks very good."

The newspapers ballyhooed Glenn's spatial
effusions; radio and TV commentators played
and replayed the tapes, yet now that all the
patriotic beating of breasts is over with, it
seems clear that whatever else he may have
added to the Saga of Man, John Glenn filled
the first chapter in the Book of Space with five
hours of unrelieved drivel—much of it on a par
with the McGuffey Reader ("I see the ball. The
ball is red"). If the transcript of Glenn's flight
was a warning that the first man in space might
be some kind of a linguistic throwback, proof
came the following year during the flight of
Major Leroy Gordon ("Gordo") Cooper Jr. in
Faith 7. Cooper's flight was seven times as
long as Glenn's and it contained roughly seven
times as many muffed opportunities to describe
space or express the sensations of a space
traveler, and about seven times as much of the
sort of Smilin' Jack jargon ("Rog. I read you
loud and clear. Affirmative. . . . Negative. . . .
Over") that schoolchildren had already begun
to pick up from Glenn. A few phrases of particular significance, however, cropped up in the

colloquy between the astronaut in space and Commander Walter M. Schirra Jr. who served as the capsule communicator on the ground. At the moment Cooper was successfully injected into orbit, Schirra told him, "You're right smack dab in the middle of the plot." *Smack dab?* No American had used such an expression, except in jest, for more than a generation. And then, hours later, when Cooper landed Faith 7 only seven thousand yards from the aircraft carrier *Kearsarge*— a bull's-eye for a vehicle reentering from space—he exclaimed joyously that he had come down "right on the old bazoo!" Had Cooper said "right on the money" it would have sounded at least vaguely contemporary. Even "right on the old gazola"—a World War II expression—would have called less attention to itself. But *bazoo?* That sounded more like Granny on *The Beverly Hillbillies* than a daring young man flashing around the globe at 17,000 miles per hour.

And Granny was not far from the mark. Both "smack dab" and "old bazoo" came into vogue at the turn of the century through the popular novels of Will N. Harben, a now completely forgotten literary artist who specialized in tales of small-town life in northern Georgia. Harben had an absolute genius—unrivaled before or since—for phony colloquialism. He could cram more "By crackeys," "Tarnations," "Looky heres," "Gee whillikins" and "Jumpin' Jehoshaphats" on a page than Shakespeare could images or Alexander Pope rhymes. And the public ate it up. So successful in fact, was Harben that it is almost impossible for present-day philologists to determine whether anyone ever really said "Looky here" or "Gee whillikins" before Harben popularized such expressions in his novels, claiming, of course, that the people down in northern Georgia really talked that way. In any case, it now appears that Harben was a sort of rhetorical Robert God-

dard of the space program. Both "smack dab" and "bazoo" appear in Harben's novel *Abner Daniel*—a tale about a kindly old Georgian Mr. Chips—published in 1902. "A railroad is goin' to be run from Blue Lick Junction to Darley," says one of Harben's characters. "It'll be started inside of the next yeer an' 'll run *smack dab* through my property." Later on, another character says, "Don't shoot off yore *bazoo* on one side or t'other." The book is a veritable glossary of space terms.

As the American moon program topped the feats of Glenn and Cooper, new astronauts with equally curious manners of speech became known to the public. For instance, on September 12, 1966, as Commander Charles Conrad Jr. aboard Gemini 11 was closing his range to an Agena rocket in order to perform a docking maneuver, he said: "Whoop-de-doo!" In 1968, when Captain Schirra was maneuvering his Apollo 7, he cried: "Rub-a-dub-a-doo!" And five months later, when Russell L. Schweickart stepped out on the "front porch" of Apollo 9 and became the first self-contained human spacecraft, he was asked by a fellow astronaut to look toward the TV cameras and say something. Schweickart mugged, and remarked: "Hello, dere." These expressions also, it can scarcely be doubted, originated in the unexpectedly influential works of Will N. Harben.

What is disturbing about all this is not just that our space rhetoric appears to have been informed by a hack Victorian novelist—that comes as a lump to our national pride—but that the language the astronauts use is resolutely, almost defiantly, uncommunicative. Never, in all those hours they have bobbed around up there, have they managed to convey what space really looks like or feels like. All they ever tell us is that it is "beautiful." They use that word, like a Boy Scout jackknife, for every imaginable task.

As with much else about orbital space flight, it was Colonel John H. Glenn Jr. who conducted the first experiments with the word "beautiful." It was during that maiden orbit of the earth in 1962 when Glenn peeked out the window of Friendship 7 to take a look at the cloud-dappled state of Florida that he exclaimed, "Beautiful sight!" Three months later, as Captain Scott Carpenter was flying the U.S.'s second orbital mission, he tried to describe the succession of sunrises and sunsets that he saw. "Boy!" Carpenter said, "They are more beautiful than anything I have ever seen on earth!" And five months after that, Captain Schirra was making six revolutions of the earth. "How's your spacecraft handle?" asked Ground Control. "Beautifully," said Schirra.

If the peninsula of Florida, the effects of sunlight and the performance of American spaceships were all "beautiful," so indeed was space itself. This discovery was made on March 23, 1965 when the late Major Virgil I. ("Gus") Grissom and Lieutenant Commander John W. Young were making the first orbital maneuvers in space. One could almost feel Young straining to escape the practically gravitational pull of that word upon astronauts, only to be drawn at last into its clutches. "You can't take your eyes away from the window at first," he radioed back to earth. "It is incredible. [That, at least, was original.] There aren't words in the English language to describe it. [The first danger signal.] It was . . . [now falling helplessly] bee-*yoot*-iful!"

The space journey of Majors James McDivitt and Edward H. White in June, 1965, aboard Gemini 4 is memorable not only because it was the first time man took a "space walk," but because it added a new word to the astronaut's lexicon. The new term emerged, like many a great leap of the imagination, casually and unheralded. It popped out of McDivitt's mouth as his Gemini capsule was separating from its booster. McDivitt happened to turn around just at that moment and saw the gleaming, stainless-steel rocket canister sailing away behind him—*E'en like the passage of an angel's tear / That falls through the clear ether silently.*

Unquestionably, the scene looked beautiful to him, yet McDivitt did not call upon that adjective which had been so faithful a companion of man's timid first steps into the great great beyond. Instead, McDivitt said: "It looks pretty."

That was, as Mission Control would say, another first. A new word was in orbit. And for months thereafter everything that swam into our astronauts' ken was pronounced "pretty." In August, 1965, for example, when Lieutenant Colonel Cooper was making the first extended flight in space, he said in his slow Oklahoma drawl: "Space is the purtiest thing I ever have seen."

It was Commander Eugene A. Cernan who rediscovered the beauty of space, and thereby got the astronauts back in the groove again. On the morning of June 3, 1966, Cernan opened the hatch of his Gemini spaceship and stepped out into the void. "It sure is beautiful out here, Tom," he radioed to his copilot, Captain Thomas Stafford. And then, turning around and looking back at the capsule, Cernan made yet another discovery: "Oh, what a beautiful spacecraft!" he said. And from that moment on the astronauts were never again in space without the word "beautiful." They clung to it, like a parachute pack, secure in the knowledge that whenever tormented with doubts about what to say, whenever some new sight or sensation might cause the amber light of wonderment to flicker, "beautiful" was always there to bail them out. Take for example, the flight of Lieutenant Commander Richard F. Gordon Jr. in September, 1966. After Gordon rendezvoused and docked his Gemini 11 capsule with an Agena rocket, he took a space walk to inspect this unearthly copulation of robots in the lonely void. "How's it look?" he was asked from the ground. Quick as a flash, Gordon shot back: "Beautiful day!" Two months later, Major Edwin E. Aldrin opened the hatch of Gemini 12 in order to photograph an eclipse of the moon—the first eclipse witnessed in space unimpaired by any wafting of the earth's atmosphere. It was, said Aldrin, transfixed by the glorious sight, "a beautiful view." Last year, just after Captain Schirra throttled up the Apollo spacecraft's great rocket motor for its first manned test in space, commanding enought thrust to fling himself to the moon and back, he was asked how the motor performed. "Beautifully," he said. And when Colonel Frank Borman and his crew were circumnavigating the moon last Christmas, Borman looked out the window at one point and glimpsed the green earth as a distant planet looming up over the barren horizon of the moon, and, sure enough, he reported, it was something "beautiful" to see.

Because of the fairly widespread feeling that the astronauts ought to increase their word power if they were to continue to enjoy the interest and support of their public, Julian Scheer, N.A.S.A.'s Chief Public Affairs Officer, suggested to Colonel Borman that while he and his crew were nipping around the moon last Christmas, it might not be a bad idea to broadcast to earth something appropriate for a change. Borman took the suggestion, and, being a lay reader in the Episcopal church, hit upon the device of reciting from the Book of Genesis. He presented his plan to the rest of the crew and they, naturally, thought it a beautiful idea. Accordingly, Major William Anders began with, "In the beginning, God created the heavens and earth . . ."; Captain James A. Lovell Jr. took over at "And God called the light Day. . . ." And Borman was the anchor man coming in with "And God called the dry land Earth. . . ." Their renditions proved a little stiff, and of course the whole concept was vividly stippled with anachro-

nism—reading Genesis while circumnavigating the moon was a little like using an advanced digital computer to work out horoscopes. Nevertheless, one could only wish well those cramped and rather forlorn wayfarers on that cold Christmas Eve, and so the public good-naturedly accepted this Scriptural lesson in the hope that it was bolstering the spirits of the astronauts themselves if not, especially, anyone else. Now that they are safe at home, however, it must be said that since Borman, Anders and Lovell did not compose Genesis, the recitation did little to dispel the notion that the astronauts as a group tend to share, among other things, a pronounced verbal dysfunction.

Indeed, it is now perfectly clear—it would be folly to deny it longer—that while the space program is poised on the brink of a truly epoch-making triumph of engineering, it is also headed for a rhetorical wreck. The principal danger is not that we will lose the life of an astronaut on the moon, but that the astronauts will murder English up there; not that we run the risk of biologically contaminating space, but that they are likely to litter the intergalactic void with gibberish and twaddle, despoil the written record of man's reach for the stars with the sentiments of squares, and very likely cause the long, pointed ears of those who may be awaiting our arrival to droop with disappointment when the astronauts open their mouths.

Some weeks ago, at the suggestion of this magazine, I resolved to do what I could to help Commander Armstrong and his fellow moon-landers by issuing a call the world over to poets and philosophers, scientists and politicians, novelists, judges, scholars, entertainers and others of distinction, asking them: What would *you* like to hear the astronaut say when he takes that historic first step on the moon? All told, I received sixty-one answers. They came from such a varied lot of persons as U Thant, George Plimpton, Hubert Humphrey, Truman

Capote, John Lindsay, Timothy Leary, Muhammad Ali, John Kenneth Galbraith and Tiny Tim. I fervently hope the astronauts can find the time, amid the rigors of their training program, to read and contemplate their suggestions.

Not all of my respondents took the question seriously. And yet, considering the temper of the times, a witty remark should not be automatically ruled out. A good quip might be better than a thousand meandering words. For example, Dan Rowan of *Laugh-In* hinted in his contribution that Armstrong might not be the first man on the moon after all, and might exclaim: "We finally found Judge Crater!" With airliner hijacking in the headlines, Bob Hope was prepared to say: "Well, at least I didn't end up in Havana." Mrs. Yetta Bronstein, last year's "Jewish Mother" candidate for President of the United States, imagined herself glowering at the desolate, forbidding moonscape through jewel-framed sunglasses and muttering: "Miami Beach, it isn't." And Art Buchwald seemed preoccupied about the sex life of the astronauts when he proposed: "Instead of reading from the Bible, they might try *Portnoy's Complaint.*" The Madison Avenue admen I queried were bubbling with gags. William Bernbach, chairman of the board of Doyle Dane Bernbach, the ad agency, gave me four alternatives as if he were making a presentation to Volkswagen or Polaroid, ranging from anti-moon: "Nice place to visit, but I wouldn't want to live here," to pro-moon: "This neighborhood is never going to be the same again." Rosser Reeves, former chairman of the board of Ted Bates & Company and father of the "hard sell" in radio and TV commercials, dug into his *Mother Goose* to come up with: "You now have proof positive that the moon *isn't* made of green cheese." At least one of my experts, however, was wary of all efforts to be funny in outer space, no doubt recalling some of the lame attempts the astro-

nauts have already made. When my cable caught up with Vladimir Nabokov at the Palace Hotel in Montreux, Switzerland, the author of *Lolita* shot back: "You want a lump in his throat to obstruct the wisecrack."

Three others (Norman Cousins, Peter De Vries and Joseph Heller) agreed with Nabokov that the occasion called for silence, or "perhaps even meditation" as Cousins put it, and two (Marya Mannes and General Anthony C. McAuliffe) said the ones who should keep mum are us kibitzers. "It ought to be spontaneous," General McAuliffe told me when I reached him at his home in Washington, D.C., "—just the way it was when I said 'Nuts!'" (in response to a German surrender ultimatum when he was trapped at Bastogne in 1944).

Some of the most with-it intellectuals on my list responded wryly. While their replies may not be of any direct assistance to Commander Armstrong and his crew, they nevertheless illuminate a problem the astronauts may wish to cope with in whatever they decide to say on the moon; namely, that an influential segment of the American intelligentsia is profoundly alienated from the space program. Many intellectuals simply look on the plan to put a man on the moon as a distraction from more pressing needs here on earth—a "Moon-doggle" as Amitai Etzioni, the Columbia sociologist, has called it in the title of a recent book. John Kenneth Galbraith pretty clearly felt this way when I reached him at his ski chalet in Gstaad, Switzerland. He retorted, perhaps after a good swig of hot mulled *glüh,* "We will hafta *pave* the damn thing!" Similarly provoked by all the effort (and billions) expended by N.A.S.A. was Marshall McLuhan, who gave the undertaking the back of his hand with two replies: "The thickest mud that was ever heard dumped" and "Spitz on the iern while it's hot." Buckminster Fuller's proposal, too, seemed disdainfully frivolous: "Wish you were here." And George Plimpton thought he ought to say, "It's real beautiful," since "that's what he's going to say anyway."

Other intellectuals were downright suspicious of the moon program. When I asked W. H. Auden what he would like to hear Armstrong say, he replied at first with a mischievous chuckle: "I've never *done* this before!" adding, "What else *should* he say? It would be a true statement." But when I went on to ask if he would not prefer something more elevating, perhaps about world peace, he grew sober. "Well, that's a little different," Auden said. "We all know that the chief reason for their going there is military, so I don't think you should ask them to say much about that!" Auden's fear that the moon will become a military base, whether justified or not, is widely shared. His fellow poet, Robert Graves, touched on that concern when he cabled darkly from Majorca suggesting a tactful propitiation of the Moon Goddess: "Forgive the intrusion, Ma'am. Don't smile so bitter at good Yanks tidying up your Sputnik litter." Timothy Learly suggested that the first astronaut on the moon would be a kind of Shore Patrol sergeant, saying: "Eldridge Cleaver, you are under arrest for trespassing on a military reservation."

Going even beyond the fear of moon militarism was Father Malcom Boyd, the Episcopal priest who wrote *Are You Running With Me, Jesus?*, now a fellow at Yale, who was worked up about lunar colonialism. His answer was: "I baptize thee in the name of the Father, and of the Son and of the Holy Ghost. Amen. All right, you guys, whoever you are standing behind that rock over there, come out with your hands up!" As he explained to me: "That's been the history of missionary-oriented colonialism—a great deal of self-righteousness about one's mission coupled with a great deal of pragmatic self-interest."

The political leaders, in contrast to the foregoing men of letters, tended toward idealistic statements, perhaps in the hope that a pitch for peace would steer the development of the moon in the right direction. One such suggestion came from U Thant. "When I greeted Colonel Frank Borman . . . at U.N. headquarters . . . the Secretary-General told me through his assistant, Ramses Nassif, "he responded by saying: 'We saw the earth the size of a quarter and we recognized then that there really is one world. We are all brothers.' So I would like the first astronaut to land on the moon to remind us again of this fact so that we may all have a new sense of perspective to enable us, in the language of the Charter of the United Nations, to practice tolerance and live together in peace with one another as good neighbors." Hubert Humphrey also sounded a characteristically up-beat note: "May the conflicts and troubles of man never find a home here. May the moon be a symbol of peace and cooperation among the nations of the earth." Senator George McGovern added a novel touch to the internationalist theme, saying that in the manner of the polar explorers a flag should be planted in the crust of the moon —the U.N. flag, naturally. "I raise the Flag of the United Nations to claim this planet for all mankind and to signal a new era of understanding and cooperation among nations—both on the Moon and on Earth," wrote Senator McGovern. More parochial (and less serious) was Mayor John V. Lindsay's proposal: "I claim all moon mineral rights in the name of the government of New York City—they need the money the most!" Another interesting notion came along from Congressman Edward Koch, who represents Mayor Lindsay's old "silk-stocking" congressional district in Manhattan. Congressman Koch, a member of the House Committee on Science and Astronautics, said he would like to hear the astronaut proclaim the moon "an international scientific laboratory."

President Nixon neglected to answer my question, but William Safire, one of his chief speechwriters during the campaign and now a Special Assistant to the President, liked the words: "Free at last." They were, Safire told me, "a reprise of a Martin Luther King line, applied to the emancipation of earthbound men." Then, just to keep things politically balanced, I got in touch with Richard Goodwin in Boston, a long-time Kennedy speechwriter. Goodwin puzzled over the question for a few days and then remarked: "I would have to be there on the moon myself to know what to say."

If politicians contributed some fresh thought to the exercise, not surprisingly poets (aside from Auden and Graves) expressed the feeling of emotional uplift that might come over the first man to realize the age-old dream of treading the lunar surface. Marianne Moore, now eighty-two and dowager queen of the poets of America, embroidered lyrically on a line she drew from a song by Harry Belafonte: "Just got here and I have to look around. / Sit down. I can't sit down. I've just got to Heaven and I have to look around."

By contrast, Lawrence Ferlinghetti, the San Francisco beat poet and proselytizer of underground causes, came on with a statement that clanks as if with heavy armor: "We Roman emperors of space have hereby proved that heaven doesn't exist and that the only god is consciousness itself."

Stanley Kunitz, the New York poet who has won both a Pulitzer prize and the 1968 American Poets Fellowship Award, wrote of the moon as a mere steppingstone into the starry firmament in his contribution: "I shall never escape from strangeness or complete my jour-

ney. . . ." he wrote exultantly. "I am your man on the moon, a speck of megalomania, restless for the leap towards island universes pulsing beyond where the constellations set. . . . Forward my mail to Mars. What news from the Great Spiral Nebula in Andromeda and the Magellanic Clouds?" And Sun-Ra, the jazz musician who describes himself as a "cosmic space musician/poet," would have the astronaut chirp with joy: "Happy Space Age to You. . . ." Brother Antoninus, the Dominican lay brother who is a leading exponent of the school of poetry known as erotic mysticism, seemed intrigued by what men might make of the moon in his suggestion: "Bone cold. An immense Golgotha. Out of this tomb, what resurrection? Out of this dust, what weird rebirth?"

Two other poets preferred to think of the moon as a vantage point from which to contemplate the earth. Theodore Weiss, currently Professor in Creative Arts at Princeton who has just completed his fifth volume of poetry, *The Last Day and the First,* put it this way: "Moon that we have for thousands of years looked up to, now help us to see the earth in its true light, as whole and one." And David Slavitt, playwright and poet whose *Day Sailing and Other Poems* will be published later this year, wrote: "We have realized an ancient dream, and it is rock and dust; now we must look back to earth, imagine what it ought to be, and hope that dream turns out better." Slavitt then asked his five-year-son, Joshua, what he would like to hear Commander Armstrong say, and out of the mouth of the babe popped: "Hi there, nobody!"

Apollo 11:
The Time Machine

Peter Collier

Peter Collier has been a teacher and the editor of *Ramparts* magazine. He is the author of a book on the Cherokee Indians entitled *When Shall They Rest?* and is the editor of two anthologies: *Crisis: A Contemporary Reader* and *Justice Denied.* His latest book (forthcoming, Spring 1974) is a portrait of the Rockefeller dynasty.

For on that day many men of the Achaians and Trojans lay sprawled in the dust face down beside one another. (Iliad, Book IV)

IN AMERICA, national events are usually merely awkward and embarrassing. The recent voyage of Apollo 11, however, was to be no routine state occasion. It was to be an overwhelming experience, the happening of the century, a genuine American epic unfolding before the wondering eyes of the world. It came at a time when the country was in a particularly ugly and vindictive mood and was reasserting its damaged potency like an old ram in rut. All things considered, the moon shot was best watched in a spirit of self-preservation.

Despite the gossip about rock samples and moon dust and the talk about man's unquenchable desire for new horizons, one was never offered any very good reason for Apollo to take place. It was happening because it was necessary; it was necessary because it was happening. Every tentative rationale for the flight only made it seem more like a fateful, bureaucratic syllogism, the final working out of a process begun years ago in a fit of Cold War pique. That it had no special identity did not distinguish the moon shot from other national enterprises; but it meant that the flight would be easily co-opted by the patriotic

revival sweeping the country. It would be in space what the vogue of the flag decal and the cult of the frightened, tax-obsessed middle class had become on earth: a vision of America resurgent. Apollo would be a ritual celebration for a people whose sensibilities had been extended to the limit and were now snapping back.

Those who criticized the mission as an example of expensively confused priorities mistook its character. The social orbit out of which the spaceship erupted was indeed divided and brutalized; but this did not mean that the journey could be viewed as just another appropriation. Apollo had become a fantasy, not an item in the budget, and it was as fantasy that it had to be appreciated. That the whole expedition could just as easily have been acted out on the back lot of Universal Studios only increased one's regard for those sitting in the producer's chair. They wanted realism and were willing to shoot on location.

These were the strongest generation of earth born mortals—the strongest, and they fought against the strongest, the beast men, living within the mountains, and terribly destroyed them. (Book I)

The astronauts were the cornerstone on which the fantasy of Apollo was laid. Even so, it was hard to have anything very definite against them: they were bland and efficient, unassuming and God-fearing. One would finally see their defects and virtues crowded together in a widely circulated close-up taken of Aldrin on the moon. It showed no face at all, only the impermeable depth of a brown face-mask reflecting a miniature scene of the moon-ship's glittering hardware. The photograph was proposed as a classy middlebrow work of art, but it was more a classical statement about man and machine, as eerie as the purported lunar winds.

It seemed a paradox: the astronauts were faceless, yet they were put forth as our cultural heroes, as America's finest product in its finest hour. But if Armstrong and Co. had no personality, it was so much the better for those whose job it was to supply them with one. The three men were the proper human stuff to plug the credibility gap. This was evident in the biographical portfolios that pictured lives of nice modesty, but linear dedication, unstinting accomplishment, solid families, and in the official portraits staring out in semi-bewilderment from every magazine rack. Larger-than-life, unpimpled, composed beyond a disquieting thought, these craggy faces no longer belonged to the three explorers—they belonged to the country. They had been remade by hands familiar with the old masters of Soviet socialist realism. If Joseph Stalin could be transformed into a benign, ruddy-cheeked partiarch standing guard over his people on some remote battlement, couldn't Neil Armstrong become the representative American?

Of, by, and for middle-class America, the astronauts were its revenge against all the scruffy third worlders and long-haired deviants who had stolen arrogantly onto the center stage. It was for this reason that the faces in the NASA photographs stuck in one's mind. They were WASPer than thou; they were composed of that utter, Melvillean whiteness which

is lack of color. These faces were meant to negate the domestic history of the last ten years—the long, unsuccessful struggle to get color and diversity into the face of America. Every citizen was conscripted into the public relations legions working ant-like around these men. As they labored, one got another view of something that had already begun to take an ominous shape: the last decade had been too complex and demanding; the questions that had been raised threatened insights into the national character that would be too painful. The country was now turning its back on that history, on a part of itself. American technology would dare anything, it seemed, even making us into a collective schizophrenic and returning us to where we had left off in the Fifties—in the middle of a midwestern idyll of simplicity and moral cretinism.

The role assigned to Armstrong, Aldrin and Collins was far more demanding than simply going to the moon, loping about on the grainy blacks and whites of the lunar surface, doing the make-work tasks that kept their transmission from looking like the most expensive test pattern ever, and then returning to decontamination and a barrage of ticker-tape parades. They were sent to outer space to rejuvenate America and to provide flowered slipcovers for a system of values which is in a state of chaos. They were to be our Galahad, on a quest to recover the national purpose; our Aeneas, removing America's household gods— a flag and a television set—to a foreign clime.

As is the generation of leaves, so is that of humanity. The wind scatters the leaves on the ground, but the live timber burgeons with leaves again in the season of Spring returning. (Book XIV)

In the flight of Apollo, we were insisting— as we often do in times of social upheaval— that the one enduring national trait is innocence. As the going gets rough, we scurry for safety into the monolithic mythology of the frontier, that state of mind where the questions are clear, the answers easy, and the youthfulness perpetual. The frontier has always been the place where we discovered new supplies of spiritual naiveté, the place which gave us our sense of power. In the moon shot, this simple, grinding, and very American need for new space and all that it symbolizes could be met again. It gave new hope to the forces which have allowed this culture to pull the wings off flies and yet retain the illusion of engaging in child-like experimentation rather than adult evil. Just as the West has been for the 19th century, outer space would be the place where the American myth was reformed in our time. We were not landlocked after all, not stuck with ourselves and where we live.

But this recurrent, enforced vision of innocence has never itself been innocent. Apollo was not the open-handed offering to the world that it pretended to be. As much as anything else, the moon shot was a naked show off of technological force, simultaneously a threat and a boast. It was America flexing muscles that had almost atrophied in Viet-Nam.

History was being made and unmade in this flight, the clock was being rolled forward and back with a dizzying disregard for one's attachment to cause and effect. It was a frivolous thought, but just after the first foot had stepped down on the lunar surface and the first rehearsed words had been spoken, I found myself remembering vaguely that I had spent hours in front of an old console radio when I was a boy, listening to the exploits of a character named Jack Armstrong. I don't remember the exploits; I only remember that they were fantastic and seemed well within the reach of any American boy. That was more than 25 years ago, when a boy's imagination was necessarily filled with images of war and

visits to the army surplus store—with the possibility of one American machine-gunning thousands of Japs before being martyred by a bullet aimed at his back by slant-eyes. The innocence syndrome was more plausible then, not only for the innocent young, but for an adult world still unaware that it was littering the visions of its children, and its history, with corpses.

Now, after all the intervening years, the name Armstrong had come bobbing to the surface again. It was only an association, but couldn't Neil—as we were given him—be an engineering school version of Jack? He was about the right age. The all American boy grown up into an all American boy-man doing his tight-lipped duty, having his exploits inflated beyond any semblance of their reality, ready to suffocate for his country if the Eagle failed to burn its way out of the moon's gravity. The name was there, still being used to harden a flaccid mythology of limitless power without responsibility. When his giggling President appeared on the split screen to congratulate him, Armstrong replied, "It was an honor for us to be able to participate here today." *Participate?* The only thing missing was the heavy-booted foot scuffing the moon dust, and the aw-shucks-'twarnt'-nuthin' muttered under the breath.

Boy scouts, even good ones, could be heroes for the national epic of no other country but this one.

And the games broke up, and the people scattered to go away, each man to this fast-running ship, and the rest of them took thought of their dinner, and of sweet sleep and its enjoyment. (Book XXIV)

There were many vectors of force at work in Apollo, all of them pulling on the psyche simultaneously. It finally became an exercise in subjectivity; it was, as in other things, your vision against theirs. Finally one could not forget that he was watching television, and that without the medium there would be no message. At Apollo's most confusing moments, one could retreat into one's own solipsistic fantasy: kicking at the set and muttering, as Sam Johnson might have, "Thus do I refute thee, Dr. Von Braun."

A Sleep on the Moon
Norman Mailer

Norman Mailer helped found the *Village Voice* in 1955 when it was the only true underground newspaper in the United States. He wrote for *Esquire* in the early 1960s and won the Pulitzer Prize in 1968 for *Armies of the Night*, a personal account of the four-day antiwar protest that took place in Washington, D.C., in 1967. He ran unsuccessfully for mayor of New York City in 1968 and later told the story of his campaign in *Running Against the Machine*. A series of articles written in 1969 for *Life* magazine on the United States space program appear in *Of a Fire on the Moon*, from which this article was taken. Mailer's most recent book is a biography of Marilyn Monroe.

I

They were down, they had landed—the decade in which the project had been conceived was the decade in which it was achieved. What an achievement! Hannibal had taken his legions across the Alps, Cortez had conquered the mighty armies of the Aztecs with less than a thousand conquistadors, Castro landed in Cuba with eighty-two men, lost seventy in ambush on the beach, and five days later, hiding in the jungle, said to the survivors: "the days of the dictatorship are numbered." Now Apollo 12 had landed on the moon, for if Apollo 11 was down, Apollo 12 could not be far behind. A new age of man had probably begun: just conceive of those purifications of discipline and cooperation that ordinary technicians working for most ordinary if immense corporations had shown. What an abstention from intrigue, treachery and betrayal had been forged in the million links of the chain.

Yet the question remained. Apollo was the god of the sun, so NASA did not fail to use his name for the expedition to the moon. Was the voyage of Apollo 11 the noblest expression of a technological age, or the best evidence of its utter insanity? It was the question which would dog Aquarius into the tenderest roots of his brain. So any spirit of impatience which would now have the astronauts open the hatch may as well burn its fumes—six hours are to go by before a man's boot comes off the Lem and puts the mark of sneaker cleats on the moon. In the meantime, moon conceivably all quivering in its finest registers from the four landing feet of the Lem, the question persists—are we witness to grandeur or madness? So the mind casts back to the source of Project Apollo and the birth of NASA, back into the warlock's pot of high politics in that hour after American prestige drooped in the eyes of the world because the Russians had put Sputnik into orbit and Soviet technology was in some ways at least superior to American. Eisenhower complained. If he had signed the bill which created NASA in 1958, he still did not know, he would announce, why everyone was thus inflamed about space. And in 1961, on the way out, in his last message to Congress a few days in January before John F. Kennedy would be inaugurated, Ike gave the word that he would not advise any extension of space flight after Mercury, no, not unless—and here came Elixir of Eisenhower—not unless "further experiment and testing" gave go to good reason. Can we be certain it was altogether out of Eisenhower's reach to realize that a vain young President from an opposing party, consumed with the large desire to do things his way, was not going to take the ex-President's advice? But then we never give credit to Eisenhower for being so sly a man he was not even aware of it himself.

If it is natural to assume Kennedy was sympathetic to a moon shot when Eisenhower was publicly opposed, Kennedy was also a man with a regard for consensus; a national poll showed fifty-eight percent of the public sample were opposed to spending forty billion dollars in a race against the Russians to the lunar sphere. Kennedy was therefore not about to make a push. Not then. After the Bay of Pigs, however, the national desire may have moved up to the stars; certainly, after Alan Shepard's flight in Mercury-Redstone 3, public opinion took a full shift. It shifted with a rush. All the while, Johnson had not been chairman of the Senate Space Committee and head of the National Aeronautics and Space Council for nothing, no, and had not personally picked James E. Webb to be head of NASA for no reason, nor looked upon fast-expanding Houston without plans for even more rapid expansion. It is not hard to conceive of how fast the tip of his tongue could flicker in and out of Kennedy's ear when public opinion began to turn. Indeed the President had to agree with

the Vice President about something. And Space was congenial to Kennedy, congenial to the metaphor of a new frontier, congenial to his love of doughty ships and mysterious seas; besides, the brightest of his economists were fond of the absurdity of space. The most advanced of them had come to the conclusion that economics was a phenomenon which resisted planning—the Soviet Union had been giving its unwilling demonstration of this point for thirty years: yes, economies were most interesting when they developed off the target. It was as if one did not achieve a career in the theater by studying how to act but by mountain-climbing or road racing. The effort, not the technique, seemed to prepare the result, or if not the intended result, another equally desirable. The voyage to the moon came to be seen by many of Kennedy's liberal advisers as the most imaginative way to prime an economic pump in a time of relative prosperity and no war. Who cared if it succeeded? When the decade was out, there might be no moon rocks in the hand, but a new kind of prefabricated housing could well have been discovered instead, or some new fuel for automobiles. Plastics were bound to accelerate themselves into products and industries not yet conceived. Advances in metallurgy and electronics would inspire huge new plants of higher education, boom them up from swamps newly filled by the exudations of the cities. The technological age, bloated with waiting, was ready to burst on the landscape of America. That technological age would solve all the old problems—so declared the confidence of Kennedy's elite. What better for the symbol of a new age than a landing on the moon before the decade was out? It was a blind push, equal to the hot sobs of the Oklahoma land grabber who plunked down his marker and said, "Mah land runs from this stone to that tree," before he even knew if he had bottom lands or water. Before the decade was out. Why? Because the trip to the moon had to serve as the embodiment of a new vision and visions are obliged to be neat. Kennedy, like many an enterprising young man before him, knew the best approach to large and complex mysteries was to plunge your hands into the short hair. "This is a new ocean," he said, "and I believe the United States must sail upon it."

II

So Project Apollo was born. On a landscape of machination, economic cynicism, warlockery, the maneuvers of Lyndon Johnson's gravyboat navy, and out of John F. Kennedy's profound respect for the dynamics and mechanics of new romantic ages, was Project Apollo born. She would prime a pump for the Government until the war in Vietnam would rip the handle out of her grasp, she would gild the balance sheet of many a corporation until the war in Vietnam would cause a crisis of priorities for the work of corporations, she would give work to hundreds of thousands, and did, until she had to let many of them go; she would create towns and counties; she would be handmaiden, then wife, to the computer; and her spin-offs had hardly begun, she would still change the age; but she had failed until now to become a vision of technology which would put light in the eyes of every poor man. She had failed to become a church for the new age. She was only a chalice for the wounded bewildered heart of the Wasp, a code of honor for corporation executives hitherto bereft of pride. She set electronic engineers and computer programmers to dreaming of ways to attack the problems of society as well as they had attacked the problems of putting men on the moon. But she had not unified nor purged that accompanying world of feverish development and pollution which had kept pace with her pure endeavor.

In this hour they landed on the moon, America was applauding Armstrong and Aldrin, and the world would cheer America for a day, but something was lacking, some joy, some outrageous sense of adventure. Strong men did not weep in the street nor ladies copulate with strangers. Any armistice to any petty war had occasioned wilder celebrations. It was almost as if a sense of woe sat in the center of the heart. For the shot to the moon was a mirror to our condition—most terrifying mirror; one looked into it and saw intimations of a final disease. But probably it will take the rest of the trip to absorb the remark.

Armstrong and Aldrin were to do an EVA that night. EVA stood for Extravehicular Activity, and that was presumably a way to describe the most curious steps ever taken. It is one thing to murder the language of Shakespeare—another to be unaware how rich was the victim. Future murders stood in the shadow of the acronyms. It was as if on the largest stage ever created, before an audience of half the earth, a man of modest appearance would walk to the center, smile tentatively at the footlights, and read a page from a data card. The audience would groan and Beckett and Warhol give their sweet smiles.

So, now, on that moon (whose name was *Mond* in German, even if *monde* was the word for "world" in French, now on that moon called *maan* and *maane* in Dutch and Danish) a set of television activities would soon begin. The astronauts would go out from the Lem and set up a TV camera and the American flag, they would lay out three experiments, obtain two tubes of moon soil, fill two boxes of rocks, speak to the President, take photographs, and go back to their Lem. Never would they be more than a hundred feet from the ship. Out of the variety of activities available, they would go through a schedule about as attractive to watch as an afternoon of qualitative analysis in a college lab. Fact, they would not even perform the experiments—they would merely lay them out.

Somewhere in the center of NASA was the American disease: Focus on one problem to the exclusion of every other. When Communism had been the problem, nothing had existed for national policy but anti-Communism. Now, ever since the fire of Apollo 204, there had been only one idea at NASA. Get men to the moon by the end of the decade and get them back. If drama had to be sacrificed, rid the situation of drama. If scientific investigations would hamper a smooth flight, restrict scientific investigations. A narrowness of vision, constricted by the panic which followed the Apollo fire, lost all register of the true complexity of the event. Propriety had always been the natural soup of any engineering society; now NASA propriety spoke of supercongelations of moral lard. No curse, omen, oath, scar or smell could intrude on the landscape, no revel, no voice, and no unnecessary chancing of human life. It was not that anybody wanted the blood of astronauts any more than they desired the death of bullfighters, auto racers or boxers, it was that NASA had come to believe that if Apollo 11 resulted in death, all space investigation was gone, whereas in fact the irony was that the world, first sacrifices in outer space paid, would have begun to watch future flights with pain and concern. It was not that anybody was about to argue for the taking of unnecessary chances, it was more as if some of the precautions became absurd and so expensive that the mind had to engage in brute thoughts of what the money would mean in all the other places one could name.

Say, it was even that the most necessary experiments were not made. The most cumbersome element in all the flight was the Pressure Garment Assembly, the bulky-wham suit. It was a danger in itself, for it was all too easy, as Aldrin had noted, to press against a whole bank of buttons. It had been designed to protect the astronauts in the vacuums of space, and it consisted of fifteen layers of plastic material, a suit as hard as the material on a fire hose—it took prodigies of strength to move it and intricate adjustments of grace and balance—it is yet worth describing in detail—and this suit, which left the astronauts about as much coordination as a two-year-old in three sets of diapers, was designed to protect them against puncture. Yet no one knew what puncture might mean in space. It was uncertain whether exposure of the flesh to a vacuum would result in quick death or supportable injury. Still, no canary was brought along to be partially exposed, its death or its ability to survive for a time carefully noted. It is a horror, of course, to let a bird die on the moon—ecology hard upon us, who can jeer at the claim of the antivivisectionists that something divine might not also die, but animals are used everywhere in every closet of behavioral psychology labs, rabbits go out of their minds in electrode-laden harnesses before they are finally fed to the town dump, so what would it have cost NASA except an incision in their hypocrisy if the first critical experiments had been taken to see if partial or temporary exposure to a vacuum was feasible. If so, the suits could be made more agreeable—the explorations more adept.

Well, such experiments were for other occasions. The astronauts, in preparation for the EVA, had been garbed in EMU, the Extravehicular Mobility Unit, or moon-walk space suit complete. EMU consisted first of three envelopes, a liquid cooling garment, a pressure garment, a thermal-and-micrometeoroid garment, plus a Portable Life Support System for oxygen, plus a backup system, a radio, a waste-management system, a maintenance kit (to work on their own life-supporting machinery), a set of special visors for their helmets, and the ubiquitous biomedical belt. The total weight was one hundred eighty-three pounds—on earth the astronauts staggered around in the EMU when they were able to move at all. On the moon, weight of the suit and pack would be more like thirty pounds, but it still had to feel as much like a spaceship as a space suit, and indeed with a quadrant of rocket thrusters, a computer, and a bag of food-injector, there would have been little to keep the astronauts from going into orbit for a revolution or two. Six hundred pounds of fuel weighing only one hundred pounds on the moon might have done the job!

That was a joke which in another year or two could prove less of a joke. In any case, the EMU was designed to provide an environment in which a man might live while walking through the vacuum of space and the radiations of the solar wind plus the cosmic rays—a suit designed to be bulletproof as well against the occasional micrometeoroid. Most meteoroids were smaller than buckshot, but they traveled at a speed of forty-five thousand miles an hour. (Still, the chance of getting hit was only one in ten thousand—no army was going to be stopped by that.) More to the point: the EMU would also protect against the heat of the sun in the full lunar day when temperatures rose clear above boiling to 243 degrees Fahrenheit on the moon soil. So the suit had to be insulated against the heat of a fall on the seared ground.

We can imagine what a construction was involved. Early that morning, over nine hours before their landing, back in the Command Module, they had taken off their constant-wear garments, been naked for once after all these days, and as quickly had put on the liquid cooling garment, which was a long-sleeved pair of long johns with two layers of Beta cloth, one on either side of a network of tubing through which cooled water would pass—the liquid cooling garment was not dissimilar in appearance to a scuba diver's rubber formfitting suit. It was estimated that their labor on the moon pushing the total EMU around would be equal to the exertions of a man shoveling sand, or snow, or sawing wood. So cooling was critical. In that sealed envelope, that man-shaped spaceship surrounding their skin, even a little too much overheating could fog their visor, overload all purge systems.

Next came the Pressure Garment Assembly, a submarine chamber complete in itself. Putting that on over the liquid cooling garment, they would be safe in flight if there were any leaks or punctures in the Lem. The Pressure Garment Assembly was in fact a true space suit itself, the one indeed they wore for the launch; the PGA consisted of a helmet, gloves, and the torso-and-limb suit. PGA had a "comfort" layer of nomex, then a neoprene-coated pressure bladder, finally a nylon restraint layer. The bladder pressed against the skin of the astronaut, pressed all over their bodies with a pressure about a quarter of the earth's normal atmosphere. Without this bladder, it was assumed that blood might boil in the veins or skin pop open from the internal pressure of the body, which from birth had been stressed to maintain itself against normal atmospheres on earth—in fact no one knew exactly what would happen if a few square inches of skin were suddenly exposed by a tear in the suit to the moon vacuum, no one could even be certain whether the skin would burn, for the heat of the sun might be less than 243 degrees Fahrenheit even a foot above the moon soil since there would be no air to trap the heat. In any case, once in the pressure garment suit, the effect was equivalent to moving about in a man-shaped ballon. There were restraints on the bladder of course, subtle hoops and rings at all the joints, not altogether unlike the joints in armor; the gloves, in fact, to enable bending of the knuckles, were reminiscent of jouster's gauntlets, but a balloon it was still, and movements were necessarily deliberate in order not to work at further compressing air already overcompressed in a joint. Needless to say the Pressure Garment Assembly had a plenitude of valves, faucets, plugs, taps, and redundancies. There were four gas connectors, two for oxygen in, two for oxygen out, a water interface between the Portable Life Support System (PLSS) which was worn on the back and the liquid cooling garment underneath, an electrical connector to provide communications, instrumentation and power interface from PLSS to PGA. There was also a urine transfer collector (with valve) to avoid depressurizing the pressure garment. Also pressure gauges, pressure relief valves and seven pockets for data cards, penlight, sunglasses, lanyard, scissors, checklist and utility.

This was the space suit for wear inside the cabin of the Command Module or Lem during launch, docking, undocking or through any period when the hatch door had to be open. For the walk itself, they would add still another covering, the Integrated Thermal Micrometeoroid Garment, formfitting cover which was laced over the pressure garment and consisted of a plastic armor, proof against heat and meteoroids, composed of two layers of nylon, seven layers of Beta Kapton space laminate, and an outer cloth of Teflon-coated Beta, Teflon being the synthetic with which nonchar frying pans are coated.

The helmet was a transparent polycarbonate shell of Lexan with a sealing ring for attachment to the collar of the suit. For the moon walk two extra visors were attached, a lightly tinted inner visor to reduce glare and fog, and an outer visor in appearance like a fencer's mask with a gold film on its surface to reflect solar radiation. When lowered, one could not see the face, but the gold film obstructed no vision from within and altered no colors.

Finally, there was the PLSS and the Oxygen

Purge System, which had a half hour of oxygen supply as backup for the PLSS. Both were packs, the Oxygen Purge sitting on the PLSS, and both were hefted in a special fiber-glass shell molded to fit the back. The PLSS contained four hours of oxygen supply and a VHF transmitter and receiver to enable the astronauts to address each other, or by relay to connect themselves to the S-band on the Lem and thereby be able to speak to the ground. There were batteries in the PLSS, and oxygen supply, and ventilation, and a cooling system for the water in the liquid cooling garment, also a remote control system worn on the chest with a camera attached. It had a fan switch, a pump switch, a space suit communicator switch, a volume control for voice, an oxygen quantity indicator, five status indicators, and an interface to switch over to the oxygen purge system. Slung around the neck just beneath the helmet, it was as if a slab of the instrument panel on the Lem had been brought along.

So equipped, in an outfit bulkier than a diving suit, an enormous pack on their back, and heavy lunar overshoes, they were ready to go out on the moon. But we have leaped over their activities in the hours between; it will come without surprise that the astronauts have hardly been idle.

III

They had landed, there was jubilation in Mission Control, and a moment of fraternization between Armstrong and Aldrin, but in fact they were actually at work in the next instant. No one knew what would await them—there were even theories that most of the surface of the moon was as fragile as icing on a cake. If they landed, and the moon ground began to collapse, they were ready to blast off with the ascent stage even as the descent stage was sinking beneath. But no sound of crumbling came up through the pipes of the legs, no shudder of collapse. A minute passed. They received the order to Stay. The second Stay—No Stay would be on them nine minutes later, and they rushed through a checklist, testing specific instruments to make certain they were intact from the landing. The thirty-odd seconds of fuel they still had left when they touched down was vented from the descent stage, a hissing and steaming beneath the legs like a steed loosing water on icy ground. Verbs and Nouns were punched into the DSKY. Now came the second Stay. There would not be another Stay—No Stay until the Command Module had made a complete revolution of the moon and would be coming back toward them in good position for rendezvous. So, unless some mishap were suddenly to appear, they had at least another two hours on the satellite. It was time to unscrew their gloves at the wrist and take them off, time to unscrew their helmets at the neck, lift them off.

They gave their first description of the landing, and made a few general remarks about the view through the window, the variety of rocks. But there was too much work to look for long. After a few comments on the agreeableness of lunar gravity, after a conversation with Columbia and mutual congratulations, they were back at the computer. Now, in the time before the next Stay—No Stay, they had to simulate a countdown for a planned ascent and realign the Inertial Measurement Unit, that is, determine the vertical line of moon gravity, and install its index into the Inertial Measurement Unit, then level the table and gyroscope from which all navigation was computed. Star checks were taken. Meanwhile, Armstrong was readying the cameras and snapping photographs through the window. Now Aldrin aligned the Abort Guidance Section. Armstrong laid in the data for Program 12, the Powered Ascent Guidance. The Command Module came around again. The simulated countdown was over. They had another Stay. They powered down their systems.

In the transcript the work continues minute after minute, familiar talk of stars and Nouns, acronyms, E-memory dumps, and returns to POO where Pings may idle. They are at rest on the moon, but the dialogue is not unencumbered of pads, updata link switches and noise suppression devices on the Manned Space Flight Network relay.

Then in what is virtually their first pause in better than an hour on the moon, they request permission to do their EVA early, begin in fact in the next few hours rather than take a halt to sleep. For days there had been discussion in every newspaper of the world whether the astronauts could land on the moon and a few hours later go to sleep before they even stepped out of the Lem; now the question has been answered—they are impatient to go.

CAPCOM: *We will support it.*
ALDRIN: *Roger.*
CAPCOM: *You guys are getting prime time TV there.*
ARMSTRONG: *Hope that little TV set works, but we'll see.*

Now the astronauts stopped to eat and to relax. Over the radio came the dialogue of Mission Control talking to Collins in orbit overhead. Around them, through each pinched small window, were tantalizing views of the moon. They could feel themselves in one-sixth gravity. How light were their bodies. Yet they were not weightless. There was gravity beneath them, a faint sensuous tug at their limbs. If they dropped a pencil, it did not float before drifting slowly away. Rather, it dropped. Slowly it dropped, dropped indeed at the same leisurely speed with which Apollo-Saturn had risen off its launching pad four and a half days ago. What a balm for the muscles of the eye! One-sixth of earth gravity was agreeable, it was attractive, it was, said Aldrin, "less *lonesome*" than weightlessness. He had, at last, "a distinct feeling of being somewhere." Yes, the moon was beneath them, hardly more than the height of a ten-foot diving board beneath them—they were in the domain of a presence again. How much like magnetism must lunar gravity have felt.

ALDRIN: *This is the Lem pilot. I'd like to take this opportunity to ask every person listening in, whoever and wherever they may be, to pause for a moment and contemplate the events of the past few hours, and to give thanks in his or her way.*

In the silence, Aldrin took out the bread, the wine, and the chalice he had brought in his Personal Preference Kit, and he put them on the little table in front of the Abort Guidance Section computer. Then he read some passages from the Bible and celebrated Communion.

A strange picture of religious intensity: there is of course no clue in Aldrin's immediate words—they are by now tuned to precisely what one would expect.

"I would like to have observed just how the wine poured in that environment, but it wasn't pertinent at that particular time. It wasn't important how it got in the cup. It was important only to get it there"—and not spill, we may assume, this most special blood of the Lord. "I offered some private prayers, but I find now that thoughts, feelings, come into my memory instead of words. I was not so selfish as to include my family in those prayers at the moment, nor so spacious as to include the fate of the world. I was thinking more about our particular task, and the challenge and the opportunity that had been given us. I asked people to offer thanks in their own way, and it is my hope that people will keep this whole event in their minds and see beyond minor details and technical achievements to a deeper meaning behind it all, challenge, a quest, the human need to do these things and the need to recognize that we are all one mankind under God."

Yes, his recollections are near to comic in their banality, but one gets a picture of this strong-nosed strong-armed gymnast in his space suit, deep in prayer in the crowded closet space of the Lem, while Armstrong the mystic (with the statue of Buddha on his living room table) is next to him in who knows what partial or unwilling communion, Armstrong so private in his mind that when a stranger tried to talk to him one day on a bus, he picked up a book to read. There, before his partner, Aldrin prayed, light lunar gravity new in his limbs, eyes closed. Can we assume the brain of his inner vision expanded to the dimensions of a church, the loft of a cathedral, Aldrin, man of passions and disciplines, fatalist, all but open believer in predestination, agent of God's will, Aldrin, prodigy of effort on Gemini 12, whose pulse after hours of work in space had shot up only when he read a Veteran's Day message to the ground. Patriotism had the power of a stroke for Aldrin and invocation was his harmony. Tribal chief, first noble savage on the moon, he prayed to the powers who had brought him there, whose will he would fulfill—God, the earth, the moon and himself all for this instant part of the lofty engine of the universe, and in that eccentric giant of character, that conservative of all the roots in all the family trees, who now was ripping up the roots of the ages, that man whose mother's name was Moon, was there a single question whose lament might suggest that if the mission were ill-conceived or even a work of art designed by the Devil, then all the prayers of all good men were nothing but a burden upon the Lord, who in order to reply would be forced to work in the mills of Satan, or leave the prayers of his flock in space. Not likely. Aldrin did not seem a man for thoughts like that, but then his mind was a mystery wrapped in the winding-sheet of a computer with billions of bits.

IV

Later, Armstrong would say, "That first hour on the moon was hardly the time for long thoughts; we had specific jobs to do. Of course the sights were simply magnificent, beyond any visual experience that I had ever been exposed to," and Aldrin would describe it as "a unique, almost mystical environment." In fact, there is an edge of the unexplained to their reactions. Their characteristic matter-of-fact response is overcome occasionally by swoops of hyperbole. And to everyone's slight surprise, they were almost two hours late for their EVA. Their estimate of time was off by close to fifty percent. For astronauts that was an error comparable to a carpenter mistaking an eight-foot stud for a twelve-foot piece. If a carpenter can look at a piece of wood and guess its length to the nearest quarter-inch, it is because he has been working with lengths all his life. Equally, people in some occupations have a close ability to estimate time.

With astronauts, whose every day in a simulator was a day laid out on the measure of a time-line, the estimate of time elapsed had to become acute. Armstrong and Aldrin had consistently fulfilled their tasks in less time than was allotted. Now, curiously, they fell behind, then further behind. There were unexpected problems of course—it took longer to bleed the pressure out of the Lunar Module than had been anticipated, and the cooling units in the backpacks were sluggish at first in operation, but whether from natural excitement and natural anxiety, or an unconscious preoccupation with lunar phenomena so subtle that it is just at the edge of their senses, any extract from the transcript at this point where they are helping to adjust the Portable Life Support System on each others' backs shows real lack of enunciation. Nowhere else do the NASA stenographers have as much difficulty with where one voice ends and another begins.

TRANQUILITY: *Got it (garbled) prime rows in.*
TRANQUILITY: *Okay.*
TRANQUILITY: *(garbled)*

TRANQUILITY: *Let me do that for you.*
TRANQUILITY: *(Inaudible)*
TRANQUILITY: *Mark I*
TRANQUILITY: *(garbled) valves*
TRANQUILITY: *(garbled)*
TRANQUILITY: *Okay*
TRANQUILITY: *All of the (garbled)*
TRANQUILITY: *(garbled) locked and lock locked.*
TRANQUILITY: *Did you put it—*
TRANQUILITY: *Oh, wait a minute*
TRANQUILITY: *Should be (garbled)*
TRANQUILITY: *(garbled)*
TRANQUILITY: *Roger. (garbled)*
TRANQUILITY: *I'll try it on the middle*
TRANQUILITY: *All right, check my (garbled) valves vertical*
TRANQUILITY: *Both vertical*
TRANQUILITY: *That's two vertical*
TRANQUILITY: *Okay*
TRANQUILITY: *(garbled)*
TRANQUILITY: *Locked and double-locked*
TRANQUILITY: *Okay*
TRANQUILITY: *Miss marked*
TRANQUILITY: *Sure wish I would have shaved last night.*
PAO: *That was a Buzz Aldrin comment.*

The hint is faint enough, but the hint exists—something was conceivably interfering with their sense of order. Could it have been the lunar gravity? Clock-time was a measure which derived from pendulums and spiral springs, clock-time was anchored right into the tooth of earth gravity—so a time might yet be coming when psychologists, not geologists, would be conducting experiments on the moon. Did lunar gravity have power like a drug to shift the sense of time?

Armstrong was connected at last to his PLSS. He was drawing oxygen from the pack he carried on his back. But the hatch door would not open. The pressure would not go low enough in the Lem. Down near a level of one pound per square inch, the last bit of man-created atmosphere in Eagle seemed to cling to its constituency, reluctant to enter the vacuums of the moon. But they did not know if they could get the hatch door open with a vacuum on one side and even a small pressure on the other. It was taking longer than they thought. While it was not a large concern since there would be other means to open it—redundancies pervaded throughout—nonetheless, a concern must have intruded: how intolerably comic they would appear if they came all the way and then were blocked before a door they could not crack. That thought had to put one drop of perspiration on the back of the neck. Besides, it must have been embarrassing to begin so late. The world of television was watching, and the astronauts had exhibited as much sensitivity to an audience as any bride on her way down the aisle.

It was not until nine-forty at night, Houston time, that they got the hatch open at last. In the heat of running almost two hours late, ensconced in the armor of a man-sized spaceship, could they still have felt an instant of awe as they looked out that open hatch at a panorama of theater: the sky is black, but the ground is brightly lit, bright as footlights on the floor of a dark theater. A black and midnight sky, yet on the moon ground, "you could almost go out in your shirt-sleeves and get a suntan," Aldrin would say. "I remember thinking, 'Gee, if I didn't know where I was, I could believe that somebody had created this environment somewhere out in the West and given us another simulation to work in.'" Everywhere on that pitted flat were shadows dark as the sky above, shadows dark as mine shafts.

What a struggle to push out from that congested cabin, now twice congested in their bulky-wham suits, no feeling of obstacle against their flesh, their sense of touch dead and numb, spaceman body manipulated out into the moon world like an upright piano turned by movers on the corner of the stairs. "You're lined up on the platform. Put your

left foot to the right a little bit. Okay, that's good. Roll left."

Armstrong was finally on the porch. Could it be with any sense of an alien atmosphere receiving the fifteen-layer encapsulations of the pack and suit on his back? Slowly, he climbed down the ladder. Archetypal, he must have felt, a boy descending the rungs in the wall of an abandoned well, or was it Jack down the stalk? And there he was on the bottom, on the footpad of the leg of the Lem, a metal plate perhaps three feet across. Inches away was the soil of the moon. But first he jumped up again to the lowest rung of the ladder. A couple of hours later, at the end of the EVA, conceivably exhausted, the jump from the ground to the rung, three feet up, might be difficult in that stiff and heavy space suit, so he tested it now. "It takes," said Armstrong, "a pretty good little jump."

Now, with television working, and some fraction of the world peering at the murky image of this instant, poised betweeen the end of one history and the beginning of another, he said quietly, "I'm at the foot of the ladder. The Lem footpads are only depressed in the surface about one or two inches, although the surface appears to be very very fine-grained as you get close to it. It's almost like a powder." One of Armstrong's rare confessions of uneasiness is focused later on this moment. "I don't recall any particular emotion or feeling other than a little caution, a desire to be sure it was safe to put my weight on that surface outside Eagle's footpad."

Did his foot tingle in the heavy lunar overshoe? "I'm going to step off the Lem now."

Did something in him shudder at the touch of the new ground? Or did he draw a sweet strength from the balls of his feet? Nobody was necessarily going ever to know.

"That's one small step for a man," said Armstrong, "one giant leap for mankind." He had joined the ranks of the forever quoted.

Patrick Henry, Henry Stanley and Admiral Dewey moved over for him.

V

Now he was out there, one foot on the moon, then the other foot on the moon, the powder like velvet underfoot. With one hand still on the ladder, he comments, "The surface is fine and powdery. I can . . . I can pick it up loosely with my toe." And as he releases his catch, the grains fall back slowly to the soil, a fan of feathers gliding to the floor. "It does adhere in fine layers like powdered charcoal to the sole and sides of my boots. I only go in a small fraction of an inch. Maybe an eighth of an inch. But I can see the footprints of my boots and the treads in the fine sand particles."

Capcom: "Neil, this is Houston. We're copying."

Yes, they would copy. He was like a man who goes into a wrecked building to defuse a new kind of bomb. He talks into a microphone as he works, for if a mistake is made, and the bomb goes off, it will be easier for the next man if every detail of his activities has been mentioned as he performed them. Now, he released his grip on the ladder and pushed off for a few steps on the moon, odd loping steps, almost thrust into motion like a horse trotting up a steep slope. It could have been a moment equivalent to the first steps he took as an infant for there was nothing to hold onto and he he did not dare to fall—the ground was too hot, the rocks might tear his suit. Yet if he stumbled, he could easily go over for he could not raise his arms above his head nor reach to his knees, his arms in the pressure bladder stood out before him like sausages; so, if he tottered, the weight of the pack could twist him around, or drop him. They had tried to shape up simulations of lunar gravity while weighted in scuba suits at the bottom of a pool, but water was not a vacuum through which to move; so they had also flown in planes carrying two hundred pounds of equipment on their backs. The pilot would take the plane through a parabolic trajectory. There would be a period of twenty-two seconds at the top of the curve when a simulation of one-sixth gravity would be present, and the two hundred pounds of equipment would weigh no more than on the moon, no more than thirty-plus pounds, and one could take loping steps down the aisle of the plane, staggering through unforeseen wobbles or turbulence. Then the parabolic trajectory was done, the plane was diving, and it would have to pull out of the dive. That created the reverse of one-sixth gravity— it multiplied gravity by two and a half times. The two hundred pounds of equipment now weighed five hundred pounds and the astronauts had to be supported by other men straining to help them bear the weight. So simulations gave them time for hardly more than a clue before heavy punishment was upon them. But now he was out in the open endless lunar gravity, his body and the reflexes of his life obliged to adopt a new rhythm and schedule of effort, a new disclosure of grace.

Still, he seemed pleased after the first few steps. "There seems to be no difficulty in moving around as we suspected. It's even perhaps easier than the simulations . . ." He would run a few steps and stop, run a few steps and stop. Perhaps it was not unlike directing the Lem when it hovered over the ground. One moved faster than on earth and with less effort, but it was harder to stop—one had to pick the place to halt from several yards ahead. Yes, it was easier once moving, but awkward at the beginning and the end because of the obdurate plastic bendings of the suit. And once standing at rest, the sense of the vertical was sly. One could be leaning further forward than one knew. Or leaning backward. Like a needle on a dial one would have to oscillate from side to side of the vertical to find position. Conceivably the sensation was not unlike skiing with a child on one's back.

It was time for Aldrin to descend the ladder from the Lem to the ground, and Armstrong's turn to give directions. "The shoes are about to come over the sill. Okay, now drop your PLSS down. There you go. You're clear. . . . About an inch clearance on top of your PLSS."

Aldrin spoke for future astronauts: "Okay, you need a little bit of arching of the back to come down . . ."

When he reached the ground, Aldrin took a big and exuberant leap up the ladder again, as if to taste the pleasures of one-sixth gravity all at once. "Beautiful, beautiful," he exclaimed.

Armstrong: "Isn't that something. Magnificent sight out here."

Aldrin: "Magnificent desolation."

They were looking at a terrain which lived in a clarity of focus unlike anything they had ever seen on earth. There was no air, of course, and so no wind, nor clouds, nor dust, nor even the finest scattering of light from the smallest dispersal of microscopic particles on a clear day on earth, no, nothing visible or invisible moved in the vacuum before them. All light was pure. No haze was present, not even the invisible haze of the finest day—therefore objects did not go out of focus as they receded into the distance. If one's eyes were good enough, an object at a hundred yards was as distinct as a rock at a few feet. And their eyes were good enough. Just as one could not determine one's altitude above the moon, not from fifty miles up nor five, so now along the ground before them no distance was real, for all distances had the faculty to appear equally near if one peered at them through blinders and could not see the intervening details. Again the sense of being on a stage or on the lighted floor of a room so large one could not see where the dark ceiling began must have come upon them, for there were no hints of gathering evanes-

cence in ridge beyond ridge; rather each outline was as severe as the one in front of it, and since the ground was filled with small craters of every size, from antholes to potholes to empty pools, and the horizon was near, four times nearer than on earth and sharp as the line drawn by a pencil, the moon ground seemed to slope and drop in all directions "like swimming in an ocean with six-foot or eight-foot swells and waves," Armstrong said later. "In that condition, you never can see very far away from where you are." But what they could see, they could see entirely—to the depth of their field of view at any instant their focus was complete. And as they swayed from side to side, so a sense of the vertical kept eluding them, the slopes of the craters about them seeming to tilt a few degrees to one side of the horizontal, then the other. On earth, one had only to incline one's body an inch or two and a sense of the vertical was gone, but on the moon they could lean over, then further over, lean considerably further over without beginning to fall. So verticals slid and oscillated. Rolling from side to side, they could as well have been on water, indeed their sense of the vertical was probably equal to the subtle uncertainty of the body when a ship is rolling on a quiet sea. "I say," said Aldrin, "the rocks are rather slippery."

They were discovering the powder of the moon soil was curious indeed, comparable in firmness and traction to some matter between sand and snow. While the Lem looked light as a kite, for its pads hardly rested on the ground and it appeared ready to lift off and blow away, yet their own feet sometimes sank for two or three inches into the soft powder on the slope of very small craters, and their soles would slip as the powder gave way under their boots. In other places the ground was firm and harder than sand, yet all of these variations were to be found in an area not a hundred feet out from the legs of the Lem. As he explored his footing,

Aldrin sent back comments to Mission Control, reporting in the rapt professional tones of a coach instructing his team on the conditions of the turf in a new plastic football field.

Meanwhile Armstrong was transporting the television camera away from the Lem to a position where it could cover most of their activities. Once properly installed, he revolved it through a full panorama of their view in order that audiences on earth might have a clue to what he saw. But in fact the transmission was too rudimentary to give any sense of what was about them, that desert sea of rocks, rubble, small boulders, and crater lips.

Aldrin was now working to set up the solar wind experiment, a sheet of aluminum foil hung on a stand. For the next hour and a half, the foil would be exposed to the solar wind, an invisible, unfelt, but high-velocity flow of noble gases from the sun like argon, krypton, neon and helium. For the astronauts, it was the simplest of procedures, no more difficult than setting up a piece of sheet music on a music stand. At the end of the EVA, however, the aluminum foil would be rolled up, inserted in the rock box, and delivered eventually to a laboratory in Switzerland uniquely equipped for the purpose. There any noble gases which had been trapped in the atomic lattice of the aluminum would be baked out in virtuoso procedures of quantitative analysis, and a closer knowledge of the components of the solar wind would be gained. Since the solar wind, it may be recalled, was diverted by the magnetosphere away from the earth it had not hitherto been available for casual study.

That was the simplest experiment to set up; the other two would be deployed about an hour later. One was a passive seismometer to measure erratic disturbances and any periodic vibrations, as well as moonquakes, and the impact of meteors in the weeks and months to follow; it was equipped to radio this information to earth, the energy for trans-

mission derived from solar panels which extended out to either side, and thereby gave it the look of one of those spaceships of the future with thin extended paperlike wings which one sees in science fiction drawings. In any case it was so sensitive that the steps of the astronauts were recorded as they walked by. Finally there was a Laser Ranging Retro-Reflector, an LRRR (or LRQ, for L R-cubed), and that was a mirror whose face was a hundred quartz crystals, black as coal, cut to a precision never obtained before in glass—one-third of an arc/sec. Since each quartz crystal was a corner of a rectangle, any ray of light striking one of the three faces in each crystal would bounce off the other two in such a way that the light would return in exactly the same direction it had been received. A laser beam sent up from earth would therefore reflect back to the place from which it was sent. The time it required to travel this half-million miles from earth to moon round trip, a journey of less than three seconds, could be measured so accurately that physicists might then discern whether the moon was drifting away from the earth a few centimeters a year, or (by using two lasers) whether Europe and America might be drifting apart some comparable distance, or even if the Pacific Ocean were contracting. These measurements could then be entered into the caverns of Einstein's General Theory of Relativity, and new proof or disproof of the great thesis could be obtained.

We may be certain the equipment was remarkable. Still, its packaging and its ease of deployment had probably done as much to advance its presence on the ship as any clear priority over other scientific equipment; the beauty of these items from the point of view of NASA was that the astronauts could set them up in a few minutes while working in their space suits, even set them up with inflated gloves so insensitive that special silicone pads had to be inserted at the fingertips in order to leave the astronauts not altogether numb-fingered in their manipulations. Yet these marvels of measurement would soon be installed on the moon with less effort than it takes to remove a vacuum cleaner from its carton and get it operating.

It was at this point that patriotism, the corporation, and the national taste all came to occupy the same head of a pin, for the astronauts next proceeded to set up the flag. But that operation, as always, presented its exquisite problems. There was, we remind ourselves, no atmosphere for the flag to wave in. Any flag made of cloth would droop, indeed it would dangle. Therefore, a species of starched plastic flag had to be employed, a flag which would stand out, there, out to the nonexistent breeze, flat as a slab of plywood. No, that would not do either. The flag was better crinkled and curled. Waves and billows were bent into it, and a full corkscrew of a curl at the end. There it stands for posterity, photographed in the twists of a high gale on the windless moon, curled up tin flag, numb as a pickled pepper.

Aldrin would hardly agree. "Being able to salute that flag was one of the more humble yet proud experiences I've ever had. To be able to look at the American flag and know how much so many people had put of themselves and their work into getting it where it was. We sensed—we really did—this almost mystical identification of all the people in the world at that instant."

Two minutes after the flag was up, the President of the United States put in his phone call. Let us listen one more time:

"Because of what you have done," said Nixon, "the heavens have become a part of man's world. And as you talk to us from the Sea of Tranquility, it inspires us to redouble our efforts to bring peace and tranquility to earth . . ."

"Thank you, Mr. President. It's a great honor and privilege for us to be here representing not only the United States, but men of peace of all nations . . ."

In such piety is the schizophrenia of the ages.

Immediately afterward, Aldrin practiced kicking moon dust, but he was somewhat broken up. Either reception was garbled, or Aldrin was temporarily incoherent. "They seem to leave," he said to the Capcom, referring to the particles, "and most of them have about the same angle of departure and velocity. From where I stand, a large portion of them will impact at a certain distance out. Several—the percentage is, of course, that will impact . . ."

Capcom: "Buzz, this is Houston. You're cutting out on the end of your transmissions. Can you speak a little more forward into your microphone. Over."

Aldrin: "Roger. I'll try that."

Capcom: "Beautiful."

Aldrin: "Now I had that one inside my mouth that time."

Capcom: "It sounded a little wet."

And on earth, a handful of young scientists were screaming, "Stop wasting time with flags and presidents—collect some rocks!"

VI

There were as many as one hundred and fifty laboratories waiting for rocks. Five hundred of the world's best selenologists and geologists were preparing experiments to measure the age of the moon, its trace elements, stable isotopes, rare gases and particle tracks. The mineralogy of the satellite would be studied and its magnetic and electrical properties; the thermoluminescence, compressibility and elastic wave of lunar material would be examined as well; the soil mechanics, the solar radiation, the analysis of organic compounds, even the simple search for paleontological traces of once-living material were all going to be explored in the products of the two boxes of rocks the astronauts would bring back. There was a time line on the EVA — they had hardly more than two hours on the moon, and a string of chores to complete, duties sufficiently numerous for them to keep plastic cards with a list of reminders taped to the wrist of their suits. Now, after almost an hour of Armstrong's oxygen supply had already been used up, now sensing that they have once again fallen behind in their sense of time, Armstrong began to work at filling the first rock box. Using a scoop, he picked up those rocks and fragments he thought most unusual or most significant, a gross collection selected as quickly as possible and inserted and packed in the rock box, which was immediately sealed with a vacuum-type seal. Later, they hoped to have time to fill the other box. There were plans to document the second collection of rocks, photograph them with a stereoscopic camera as they were picked up, for the position of rocks could offer significant clues to a trained geological eye. But they were already half an hour beind, and the Lem had still to be given a thorough photographic examination, the seismometer and the LRQ had yet to be deployed, and the core samples of moon dirt were still waiting to be obtained. The careful documentation of the rock gathering finally suffered. We might assume there was finally too much stimulation, too much near-familiar and subtly unfamiliar phenomena to be absorbed. The rocks themselves were full of unexpected variation. Some were as ordinary as cinders in an ash dump, others seen in the spectroscopic photographs are without dimension. One does not know if it is a photograph of a three-inch fold of rock or the full study of a ledge and a cave.

So they hopped around, prodigies of discipline, soldiers of caution. Standing on the edge of craters even six feet deep, the shadow was so dark they could have been looking down an air shaft to the cellar of the moon. Such phenomena must have teased the powerful fortifications of their common sense. Armstrong was to repeat over and over that the moon was friendly, the moon was hospitable. They were to say it again and again. It was presumably to the advantage of NASA that the moon be friendly to justify the outlay of those billions of bucks; never spend money on an ingrate! although in fact, the assumption was about as deep in real knowledge of public opinion as any thought the colored races of the world would be soothed by Muzak. How much more the world might have honored the exploit if the moon aroused anguish, awe and terror. No matter! It was friendly, it was beguiling. Afterward, Armstrong found himself describing again and again the mysterious properties of color on the moon. The terrain, by his description, was tan if one looked along it in the direction of the sun; it was the same tan if one turned completely around and stared at the land beyond one's shadow. But to right and left, at either side, the colors were darker, not tan but brown. Directly beneath one's feet, or looking at soil in one's hand, the color was dark gray, sometimes even black.

Then there were other phenomena. One is mentioned by Armstrong only once. He looks at his shadow on the ground and . . . "Downsun through a very, very light gray, light gray color, a halo around my own shadow, around the shadow of my helmet." Yes, immediately after they had landed, they had spoken of how interesting were the colors. Twenty minutes later, immersed in routine, the colors were matter-of-factly described as tan and gray. Yet later there are halos, and color has become a function of the vector along which one looks. Aldrin, in turn, was having his troubles with soil mechanics. Aldrin, familiar with shovel and pick, was driving core tubes into the ground, but the resistance was a phenomenon. To drive the tube down even six inches, he had to use his hammer with such force that the top of the core tube was dented. The soil may have been loose to the touch of his foot, but it was almost as firm as rock just a few inches down. Still, it supported nothing. Difficult as it was to drive a tube into the ground, yet the tube would not stand. "It was a unique, almost mystical environment." Yes, soil mechanics like light, altered its properties with a change in direction. Perhaps the friendliness of the moon was also a matter of the direction in which one faced. A turn of the body in a dream can drop us into the long slide of a nightmare.

But now the time had come for them to pick up the rock boxes, pick up the foil of the solar wind, pick themselves up and the tendrils of their attention and reenter the Lem. Their EVA—it is now just after midnight—is done. They climb up the ladder, they close the hatch, bring up the pressure in the cabin. Now they take off their PLSS and their overshoes, and remove their helmets. They sniff. There is a pronounced odor in the cabin. The moon dust they have brought back on their suits now smells like gunpowder to Aldrin, and like wet ashes to Armstrong. The moon has a smell.

VII

Still, the EVA has been a gross disappointment. With every effort by Aquarius to find an edge of the sinister in his first expedition to the peculiar soil of the moon, the astronauts are obviously as equally determined—they must certainly be employed by NASA!—to make the moon a playground of the future. Tranquility Base! "The moon was a very natural and very pleasant environment in which to work." Aldrin reports after what excessive expenditure of BTU's it has taken a strong man like himself to drive a narrow pipe all of six or eight inches into the ground when the flight plan had called for twelve. Then the dented hard-smacked stick wouldn't even stand up.

"I was sure," said Armstrong, "it would be a hospitable host. It had been awaiting its first visitors for a long time." The logic was impeccable. "Come into my house, Joey Namath," said the eighty-year-old spinster, "We got a welcome for you, my sister and I." No, sentiments conceived in buildings with windowless walls were pushing upon the very perceptions of the explorers. They could not help but like the moon—cold curse of their employers if they did not. Still, they were now back in the Lem; their EVA was done. They had only to open the hatch one more time, throw out some pieces of equipment, lock up again, go to sleep, and in the morning they would be ready to depart, perhaps never to return again. Can they conceivably have felt cheated? They would be a mirror to the sentiments of the world. If the moon was not sinister, then NASA was heir to a chilling disease, for they had succeeded in making the moon dull, the moon, that planet of lunacy and harvest lovers, satellite unlike any other moon in the solar system, the plane of its orbit even canted at an angle to the plane of the earth and the sun—no other moon could make such a claim—and besides the moon had properties of light so mysterious as to suggest that a shift of direction might be its equivalent for a passage of time, since a turn of the head could alter the mood of its colors from the look of a morning on earth to the mood of a late afternoon. A step into shadow was a visit to night.

They were, however, not near to contemplation for this hour, nor for the next. Duties pressed to check over the systems on Eagle and prepare for the jettisoning of extra equipment. There was film still left in the magazines and additional pictures to take through the windows. It was the middle of the night in Houston but still young in the two-week-long day of the moon. The sun glared on the ground like the sun of the Southwest on desert wastes. Programs 8 to 13, relating to the ascent from the moon, were sent up from earth, and the Environmental Control Canister was changed. Their heart rates during the EVA were reported. Aldrin had reached a peak of 125, Armstrong had gone as high as 160 at the end, a very high rate, even higher than the rate at which his heart was beating during the descent.

But languor, or disorientation, or some intoxication of the moon kept delaying progress. The time-line in the flight plan called for them to jettison the Portable Life Support System packs an hour and fifteen minutes after they first closed the hatch, but now two and a half hours had gone by and still they were not ready to depress cabin pressure and open the hatch, get rid of the packs. Fatigue or some indifference to time had slowed them up again. Capcom asked, "Do you have a time estimate for us until you're ready to start cabin depress? Over."

"Fifteen minutes maybe?"

That would put them seriously back of the latest revision on schedule. They had been almost two hours late starting the EVA, they had lost an additional half hour during the EVA. Altogether, it was astonishing. Men who were never late had somehow consumed four extra hours in the last nine.

Deke Slayton was on the mike at Mission Control, "I guess you guys know that since you're an hour and a half over the time-line, and we're all taking a day off tomorrow, we're going to leave you. See you later."

Armstrong: "I don't blame you a bit."

Slayton: "That's a real great . . . I really enjoyed it."

Armstrong: "Thank you. You couldn't have enjoyed it as much as we did."

Slayton: "Roger. It sure was great. Sure wish you'd hurry up and get that trash out of there, though."

Now they sped up. It took them seven minutes instead of the estimated fifteen to begin depressurization of the cabin, and almost immediately the PLSS, the lithium hydroxide canisters, and the armrests from the Lem were thrown out. Fatigue, bemusement, and the rest, they must still have watched in fascination as the objects sailed away on a long lazy throw to the ground. Even the PLSS, which on earth would have dropped like a loaded barrel, floated off as far as a diver arching out from the high board.

Capcom: "We observe your equipment jettison on TV and the passive seismic experiment reported shocks when each PLSS hit the surface. Over."

Armstrong: "You can't get away with anything anymore, can you?"

Yes, this was the year in which for the first time a naked couple had fornicated on the New York stage in a play called *Che!* and man had landed on the moon. If hippies had fantasies of being measured and taped during extraordinary experiences, it was in fact the astronauts whom it was done to.

Capcom: ". . . a magnificent job up there today."

Aldrin: "Thank you very much. It has been a long day."

Capcom: "Yes, indeed. Get some rest there, and have at it tomorrow."

The faintest trace of the Elizabethan had at last entered the language of the event. "Have at it tomorrow." It was almost three in the morning, but Aldrin responded, "Did you-all come up with any other solution that we might try to the mission-timer problem?"

That was worked out in the next ten minutes, then there was a consumables update, then a list of ten questions relating to observations they had made on the moon that day. "We can either discuss it," said the Capcom, "a little later on this evening, or sometime later in the mission. It's your option. How do you feel?"

"I guess we can pick them up now."

So for the next fifteen minutes, at the end of

this twenty-one-hour day in which they had entered the Lem, prepared it, separated from the Command Module, gone into a separate orbit, landed, and done a first walk on the moon, they were still in harness, still looking for more work. The ten detailed questions they chose to answer at three in the morning were on the position of their Lem, the depth of their digging, the rays beneath the descent-engine bell, the driving of the core tubes, the stroke of the landing struts and the possible existence of hills on the horizon which might block the solar rays during sunset, those questions and others. It was almost three-thirty in the morning when the astronauts finally prepared for sleep. They pulled down the shades and Aldrin stretched out on the floor, his nose near the moon dust. Armstrong sat on the cover of the ascent engine, his back leaning against one of the walls, his legs supported in a strap he had tied around a vertical bar. In front of his face was the eyepiece of the telescope. The earth was in its field of view, and the earth "like a big blue eyeball" stared back at him. They could not sleep. Like the eye of a victim just murdered, the earth stared back at him.

VIII

It used to be said that men in the hour of their triumph knew the sleep of the just, but a modern view might argue that men sleep in order to dream, sleep in order to invoke that mysterious theater where regions of the unconscious reach into communication with one another, and charts and portraits of the soul and the world outside are subtly retouched from the experience of the day. If this is so, what a gargantuan job of ingestion had fallen upon the unconscious mind of the two astronauts, for the experience of their world would not include the moon. Deep in a state of exaltation and exhaustion, tonight—it is now

four in the morning—was hardly the time to embark upon the huge work of a dream which could begin to feed into the wisdom of the unconscious those huge productions of the day behind. If their senses had been witness to sights and sensations never experienced before, their egos were also in total perturbation, for on the previous day their names had been transported to the eternal moonlight of the ego—they were now immortal. It is not so easy for men to sleep on such a night, for they know their lives have been altered forever—what a dislocation of the character's firm sense of itself; in fact it is precisely in the character of strong egos that they are firmly rooted. Now, they are uprooted and in a state of glory. What confusion! A disorientation of the senses and coronation of the ego are the problems to be approached this night by the dream, and that while lying in the most uncomfortable positions possible in the foreign skin of a pressure garment while the temperature grew chilly inside that stiff sack, for even with water circulation down to a minimum, the suits insisted on cooling their tired heat-depleted bodies. How indeed to go past the threshold and enter the great chamber where the kingdoms of sleep will greet them with a revel equal to the hour, no, no man in a state of exhaustion would dare to change the rigors of a powerful night of dreams, for important decisions which may shape the future can be decided on bad nights by the poor artwork of dreams not sufficiently energetic or well enough conceived to offer the unconscious a real depth of answer—which is why perhaps insomnia is self-cycling, for, too tired or fearful to engage in serious dreams one night, we are even more exhausted for the next, and do not dare to sleep. Who will be the first to swear that deep contracts of the soul are never sworn to in the darkest exchanges of slumber, or failure too quickly accepted in the once ambitious hearts of exhausted men? No, the astronauts were in no shape to sleep. Just so quickly ask a computer to work when its power supply is erratic, its mechanical parts need oiling, and it has just been instructed to compute all further trajectories as if earth gravity did not exist and the moon were motionless before the sun!

Yet, all of this—this kaleidoscope of impressions, this happiness of the heart, sore and tender and merry in the very pumping of its walls, these thrifty ducts of aviator's love for family, children and mate open now if ever open, the patriotic incandescence of a dialogue with the President, the delivery of a job promised to the team—these tributaries of happiness carrying the uprooted tree of the ego and the mysterious house of the moon downstream in full flood are still only half of their inability to sleep. Few men could sleep with such happiness flowing unaccustomed in them, but now add a fear which has been kept in the vaults, a firm well-regulated natural concern of the executive mind, yet a fear not even primitive, but primeval in its uncharted depths: are they going to be able to ascend from the moon? It is one thing to shatter a taboo, it is another to escape the retribution which follows the sacrilege—where is the savage society whose folklore is not crowded with tales of the subtlety of every outraged curse? It is a fear which still lives in many an athlete and celebrity, in many an excessive modesty in any poor man who has found at last some luck, it is in the groveling of a dog at what comes next after he has won a fierce fight. The danger is always greatest just beyond victory—in some men that is a deeper belief than any other, for not yet at climax they can see themselves as deserving; once triumphant their balance has shifted, they know guilt, they are now not deserving. Well, whether the astronauts were deeply superstitious in this fashion or barely superstitious at all, we can be certain that any residual of this prime and hallowed fear would be awake in them to-night, for they were not by any measure yet free of the moon. In the morning, after all preparations were taken, a moment would still come when they would have to fire up their engines and lift off in the upper half of the Lem from the descent stage left behind. The ascent stage would rise if the ascent motor functioned—they were doomed if it did not, for all the redundancies of the equipment passed here through the bottleneck of one and only one piece of mechanism. There was no substitute for the ascent engine. Double tanks of fuel, and double tanks of oxidizer; double containers of helium to put pressure on fuel and oxygen; valves and cutoff valves in a plenitude of substitutions and alternate paths; but, finally, there was only one motor with only one throat and one bell, and that motor would have to flame up to 90 percent of its full thrust in the first three-tenths of a second after it ignited so that the ascent stage would lift and not settle back—no refinements to blast-off here!

There had been tests beyond measure on that motor, tests in vacuums and tests in fast-descending elevators to simulate lunar gravity; there had been refinements inserted within refinements to make certain that when a fuel spray of hydrazine and unsymmetrical dimethylhydrazine came through the injectors to meet a spray of nitrogen tetroxide the combustion would take place.

Since it had been designed for ignition in a lunar vacuum, so there was no air to feed the fires of the fuel. The equivalent of air was supplied by the nitrogen tetroxide, whose oxygen would sustain the burning hydrogen, whose oxygen would indeed ignite the hydrogen by merely meeting it. The very elements of water were here the elements of a fire so contagious it needed no match, merely the mating of the gases, a fire so explosive that a motor with a nozzle only two and a half feet across could lift the ascent stage and the men inside, lift them and fling them into orbit, all ten thousand pounds and more.

Still, this motor had never been fired before on the moon. It had been fired in vacuums, yes, but they were artificial vacuums on earth and not the pure vacuum of the moon where who knew what subtleties atomic particles, subparticles, and cosmic rays could present upon ignition? Nothing in any theory or working hypothesis of physics even began to suggest there was any reason why a moon vacuum should not prove the practical equal of an earth vacuum, but nobody could be certain, nobody could swear there were not unforeseen conditions which could inhibit the flame or cause it to flame out. Who knew the dispositions of fire on the moon when the air we breathed was also the stuff of fire, and hydrogen and oxygen could make water or electricity or fire? Yes, the real explanation of the flames remain as much a mystery as man's first hour in a forest after lightning struck a tree.

Primeval fears inspire primeval thoughts. There in the Lem, one body on a floor, the other with his heroic posterior carefully spotted on the very cover of that ascent engine which would lift them off in the morning, how they must have drifted on runs of happiness and rills of deep-veined fear. How easily they must have passed into large sleep-deprived inchoate thoughts of a world of men and women back on earth secretly wishing them well or ill, intervening in the long connected night of the world's sleep with whatever gods or powers were sitting upon the ignition of the engine in the morning. So scourged and exalted, hovering on that ultimate edge of moral balance where one wonders if the sum of one's life has been for good or ill and if the morning will return a fair and just verdict, fingers crossed, ready fair enough to laugh or cry, dopey, exhausted, chilled, feverish no doubt with desire for morning to come, alert, high on the empty holes of the numbers they would punch into the computer in the morning, ears alert to the quiet pumps of the nocturnal Lem whose skin was baking in the moon morning heat, there in a cave of chilly isolation, happy, numb, and full of a fear of dreams, not knowing if their glory was to be doubled by the next night or if they would be at one among the martyred dead yes, how were they to sleep and dare to dream when the future must look either to a transformation of the psyche, or a trip down the underground river of them all? Yet, if they were to die on the moon—was there an underground river there? or would they be forced, full strangers, to wander together, a queer last place for the mortal bones. Who, indeed, could sleep?

IX

Collins was listening to the pumps. He had been alone in space for fifteen hours, more than enough to go around the moon seven times, and for seven times he had been alone on the far side, which was seven more times than any other man had ever been alone there. Even the Public Affairs Officer was ready to use superlatives for the occasion. "Not since Adam has any human known such solitude as Mike Collins is experiencing during this forty-one minutes of each lunar revolution when he's behind the moon with no one to talk to except his tape recorder aboard Columbia." Shades of Krapp's Last Tape, one had another facet of Beckett's vision of the apocalyptic loneliness of the end; why, even the near side of the moon was civilization in comparison to the far side. There, out of contact with any voice on radio, alone in his Command Module, rattling around in his new commodious dimensions with the center couch removed and no other astronauts to break into his peace, Collins and his machine were like a coin on edge in the universe, the acme of technology, the acme of uprooted existence.

Yet later Collins spoke warmly of what he had come to call his "mini-cathedral." The tunnel which connected up to the Lem was now like a bell tower; with the couch removed, he had a center aisle; the instrument panel could serve as nave and transept. Later he would protest that he was not lonely in Columbia. "I've been flying airplanes by myself for about seventeen years, and the idea of being in a flying vehicle alone was in no way alarming. In fact sometimes I prefer to be by myself." Still, it is a protest. He was obviously filled with uneasiness much of the time; his later comments give more than one evidence of it. "I figured that any chain as long and tenuous as this had to have a weak link. Believe me, I spent a lot of time worrying about that link. Could I be it? Could my training have neglected some vital bit of information? Or had I been properly exposed but simply forgetful?" A phrase later, he is stating that by launch day he had convinced himself he had taken all the steps to prepare himself, at least within reason, but it is a remark without logical substance against the larger fear of something loose and unknown in the material, or something treacherous in himself. He had a curious job in the morning. If the Lem lifted without difficulty and came into its proper orbit, the rendezvous would be simple. The Lem in fact would fire all the moves and do all the work to join him. He need merely stay in his orbit. If something went wrong with the Lem's ascent, however, and it went into odd orbit or low orbit or if it had to fire off prematurely and therefore might be half the circumference of the moon away from him, why then he would have to make the maneuvers. Some might be difficult. Rendezvous could always prove deceptive, for one was able to approach another spaceship by accelerating one's speed but also by braking it. A reduction of speed reduced one's orbit and so reduced the time it took to circumnavigate a planet—one could thereby catch another

spaceship. It was also possible, however, to catch up with the other spaceship by accelerating, provided one was certain of the rendezvous. If you missed the other ship, however, the price was to go rocketing off into a long and wasteful orbit; the amount of fuel they could spend in such maneuvers was limited. Moreover, rendezvous, if the circumstances were unusual enough, might have to be independent of Mission Control. Suppose immediate maneuvers were necessary on the far side of the moon. Then there would not be time to come around from Loss of Signal and get detailed programs from the ground—Collins might have to work out the computations on his own computer, or in a deteriorating situation make rough estimates without a computer and hope he could sight the Lem. It was an uneasy situation, reminiscent of the favorable odds on the ascent engine. By any logical or practical measure those odds had to be 100 to 1 or 1000 to 1 in favor of a good ascent; yet in those unspoken fears where wonder resides about the real nature of the universe, the unspoken odds were nearer to even.

So, too, with rendezvous was nothing likely to go wrong, yet Collins was obliged to live in the readiness for everything to go wrong. But if any disaster occurred to the others, how could he be certain afterward that some envy in himself had not triggered the result? It was not a happy position to be in, and Collins was the chief worrier of the three astronauts. Over and over the transcript is filled with his finicky insertions on the difficulties and small discrepancies of the equipment. Less of an engineer than Aldrin, less of a pilot than Armstrong, and in a flicker of doubt about his own body after an operation had been necessary to remove a growth from his spine (which if uncorrected could have left him paralyzed) Collins was one of those men who nibbled on the details of routine programs and data loads the way people who are bored at a party nibble peanuts. Rare was the astronaut who could be happy as the pilot of the Command Module; Collins with his quiet but wholly intent competitiveness was not going to be the first. Besides Collins had suffered an added tension in the day which had just passed. The Lem, during the excitement of the 1202 alarms, had failed to land in any place Mission Control could locate precisely on the map. Collins had spent the day searching the moon ground from sixty miles up for some glint of the Lunar Module, but in five passes had had no luck, not even in a painful eye-screwing search over one grid square after another. While that was not great cause for anxiety since the Lem could orient itself quickly enough once up in orbit, it was like a bad augury. He was out of touch with the men he must meet tomorrow in rendezvous.

Besides, there had been hordes of proper deportment required of him throughout the day, bountiful copious congratulations to offer the other astronauts for their glory. Oversweet may have been the recollection of his voice.

CAPCOM: *Columbia, this is Houston. Say something. They should be able to hear something. Over.*

COLUMBIA: *Roger. Tranquility Base, it sure sounded great from up here. You guys did a fantastic job.*

ARMSTRONG: *Thank you. Just keep that orbiting base ready for us up there now.*

What formal relations! It is as if the winning captain is patronizing the losing captain. Collins' loyalties were certainly not tenuous—no man could remain an astronaut without a strong sense of responsibility—but Collins was being tried in a court of highest pressure. If there was any joy to be alone in the Command Module, alone with himself in the incommunicable regions of the far side of the moon,

nearer then to the messages of the outer galaxies than ever before, if Collins was free to bathe in the pleasure of lonely thoughts like no man ever had before, if Collins could even indulge the legitimate narcissism of the pilot who lives in a machine which is an exquisite extension of his will, well, Collins also had all the anxiety of listening to every tick in the murmur of the pipes, every slip and minuscule clutch of sound in that machine which transported him, and if ever a man felt the anxiety to think cheerful rather than evil thoughts for fear he would spring a glitch in the labyrinthine conjunctions of his machine, Collins had to be that man. There were unhappy precedents for being too long alone in space. Collins had to be aware, as all the astronauts were, of what had happened to Bonny, the monkey who had gone up in orbit around the earth on Biosatellite 3 and had come down nine days later, three weeks ahead of schedule, in an emergency splashdown. Bonny had been ill and died twelve hours later from causes which could not be determined. An unpleasant business. Bonny's death had been but a week before their own launch. Now, as much alone as Bonny, did Collins think for an instant of that trained fourteen-pound space animal who had become sluggish in weightlessness and ceased to perform his tasks? Did Collins wonder if the animal had sickened out of boredom, or out of the misery of its pure animal heart being unable to pick up a clue to where it might now be located in its weightless cage, or did Bonny begin to sicken and die because of some drear but most recognizable message its animal senses had received from space, some message too fine for the insulated nerves of man to receive? Yes, did Collins brood on Bonny? It was a long seven revolutions and then some more.

Yet Collins, at least, was able to sleep. Did he dream of Ags and Pings, of REFSMMAT, IMU and EMU? Did he descend to the first disorder of the dream with DSKY in hand and DAP and POO? To bore with one's brain into the hard-stuffed methods and modes of technology did one not also go back to those chaos-holds, those ledges of meaning that meaningless words provided in infancy as a set of arbitrary stations of sound which were somehow better and less chaotic than no sound? Acronyms! Collins slept.

X

And in Mission Control down on earth in the black reaches of the night, the Black team would normally have been clowning around. They were the Blacks, they were the lonely, they were the youngest engineers with the lowest seniority, who invariably worked the consoles while the astronauts were asleep. Theirs was the job with the least to do. Whether called Black because they worked through the night, or Black out of some brimming class humor at NASA, their job had the pleasure of frequent breaks for coffee and wild technological discussions about how much it would cost to build an actual and real superhighway U.S. Moon 1—how many thousands or millions of Apollo-Saturns to send up to do it brute and direct, as opposed to how many if factories were built over lunar ground. On quiet nights they could put the question into an unoccupied computer and get back answers which opened other games. The computer on such nights was their farm animal washed and ready for picnic.

But the coffee was chilly coffee tonight, as cold and dank with anxiety as the plastic of their consoles. There were dungeons in the liberty of this moon-conquered night. The vault of silence in the Mission Operations Control Room (display for Eagle at rest; display for Columbia slowly crossing the screen) was there to offer a rebuke to any levity. In fact, the Black team was not even on. They

would do work for the rendezvous later, on assignment out of turn—it was the plum which had been given them, even if the astronauts were to do most of the work.

XI

Two hours of sleep. One hour to sleep. And no real sleep for Armstrong and Aldrin. They are heroes, they are first among their peers, the knights of the silent majority, but they are suffering from insomnia. They have finally emerged onto the landscape of the modern novel. They emerge incidentally as promotion men as well.

> PAO: *This is Apollo Control. Let's join the call to Tranquility Base.*
> CAPCOM: *How is the resting, standing up there? Or did you get a chance to curl up on the engine can?*
> ALDRIN: *Roger. Neil has rigged himself a really good hammock with a waist tether, and he's been lying on the hatch and engine cover, and I curled up on the floor.*

XII

At 12:53 on Monday morning, July 21, not twenty-two hours after they landed, with rendezvous radar put most carefully in Off position to avoid new program alarms, with hearts beating, fair to assume, and with minds wondering for the last occasion whether fire might not lose a vital property or two in the immediate domain of the moon—time, after all, was known to alter at the speed of light; with Pings loaded with every bit of data for Program 12, the Powered Ascent Guidance; with the simple ascent motor incapable of being run at anything other than full throttle they now put the master arm on, gave a last count to Mission Control, "Forward 8, 7, 6, 5, Abort Stage! Engine Arm Ascent! Proceed!" and fired off from the moon.

The detonator cartridges exploded on time to separate the thorax of the Lem from the sac; the ascent stage rose, the descent stage remained. Just before that separation, all signal and electrical power between the two was sundered. Then the nuts and bolts joining the stages were also exploded. In the same fraction of a second, an explosive guillotine severed the connecting spine of wires, cables, and water lines between the two stages. The ascent motor flamed up to 90 percent of full thrust in three-tenths of a second, and with hardly more than a big jerk and a blast! and a Proceed! they rose off the moon in a wobbling climb, oscillating from side to side as their fuel sloshed in the tanks.

Aldrin: "That was beautiful. 26 feet, 36 feet per second up. Be advised of the pitchover. Very smooth . . . very quiet ride. There's that one crater down there."

PAO: "1000 feet high, 80 feet per second vertical rise."

Later Armstrong would say, "a beautiful fleeting final view of Tranquility Base as we lifted up and away from it." Did they have the recognition at this instant that on another day there might be lunar cities under domes, and moondromes with their names? On climbed the ascent, up half a mile in the first minute, its direction no longer vertical, but tipping out, then pitching over toward the eventual curve of its orbit. Behind them was the memory of the blastoff, the Kapton and all the other loose-wrapped plastic insulations of the descent stage being blown in all directions, far out in the bulletlike trajectories of the moon, all that plastic, silver and gold debris, and behind them—first refuse of the first moon city—was already the handle of the rock contingency sample, the TV camera and its tripod, the staff for the solar wind experiment, the passive seismometer, the closeup camera, the Laser Ranging Retro-Reflector and its packing materials and brackets—there had been over a hundred brackets and they were now strewn on the moon ground—and there were two backpacks of the PLSS also left behind and overshoes, and tramped ground for a hundred feet around the descent stage, ten thousand prints of the marks of their boots on top of other marks of their boots, messy as a bivouac where troops have been milling in the rain. If men never came back, those marks might remain for millions of years. And the motionless waving of the flag.

But that was behind them, and their little wobbling ascent stage climbed up through its oscillations and out into the sea of space.

ALDRIN: *We're at 3000, 170 up, beautiful . . . 1500 185.*

CAPCOM: *You are GO at 3 minutes.*

ARMSTRONG: *We're going right down U.S. 1.*

Rising right out of their dread; they were leaving the loneliest death in the world. If that ascent engine had not worked—there were no suicide capsules on the Eagle. They would not have needed them. When the frustration of being trapped on the moon proved too great, they would only have had to open the hatch, and remove their helmets. That could not have felt much worse than being a drowning man. But now they slung themselves down that track, pouches of fuel tanks carried like chaws of tobacco, one for each cheek of the ascent stage. On they came up into orbit.

CAPCOM: *Eagle, Houston, 4 minutes . . . everything's great.*

PAO: *Horizontal velocity approaching 2500 feet per second.*

ALDRIN: *Now we got—got Sabine off to the right now. . . . There's Ritter out there. There it is right there. Man, that's impressive-looking isn't it?*

CAPCOM: *Eagle, Houston, you're looking good.*

PAO: *One minute to go in the burn. 4,482 feet per second horizontal velocity.*

ALDRIN: *About 800 to go. 700 to go. Okay I'm opening up on the main shutoffs. Ascent feed closed. Pressure's holding good. Crossfeed on. 350 to go. Stand by on this engine arm. 90. Okay, off. 50, Shutdown . . .*

PAO: *Showing a perilune of 9.4 nautical miles, apolune of 46.7 nautical miles on the PNGCS. Shutoff velocity showing about 5,537 feet per second.*

In seven minutes and eighteen seconds after fires had been lit, they had consumed their fuel, turned off their ascent engine, and were coasting over a mile a second in an eccentric orbit around the moon, something like forty-seven miles from the surface at farthest point and nine and a half miles up at the nearest or perilune, at which point they had just arrived.

Capcom: "Eagle, Houston. . . . The whole world is proud of you."

Armstrong: "We had a lot of help down there."

PAO: "Flight Operations Director Chris Kraft commented that he felt like some five hundred million people around the world are helping push Eagle off the moon and back into orbit."

During the ascent, they had monitored the heart rates. Armstrong had been hardly above normal, pegged at 90, a low figure for him. Aldrin had been up at 120. It was the only time in the flight that his heartbeat had been higher than Armstrong's. Is it possible that Aldrin was feeling a new sense of dread at the oncoming rendezvous? It would be a curious state to find oneself in after the worst technological moment has just been passed in a flying test.

XIII

To hold a gyroscope in the hand is to obtain an inkling of orbit. There is a sense of energy revolving in a powerful pattern, of rapid movement in some alliance with rest, for a gyroscope offers to the palm a sensation of high speed and high stability, as if all its activity is devoted to being precisely where it is.

So, now at high speed and yet in no more than a fast-moving corollary of the state of rest, the Lem is in orbit and the Command Module is in orbit, each traveling in elliptical rings around the moon, Columbia in the outer ring, which is close to a circle of sixty nautical miles in diameter, while Eagle is in the ellipse we have described of 46.7 by 9.4 nautical miles. It has taken a burn of 438 seconds in its ascent motor to reach this stage and it has consumed two thousand pounds of fuel and three thousand pounds of oxidizer in four tanks whose volume was each thirty-six cubic feet. Now it would go the rest of the way to joining the Command Module on small increments of velocity or small braking burns offered it by its four quadrants of thrusters and they are fed by two tanks of fuel and two tanks of oxidizer whose volume is no more than two cubic feet each, or taken all together, the four thruster tanks could fit into a cube with two-foot sides. The amount of energy capable of being released under fire by that much hydrogen and oxygen will be sufficient to close the gap which remains between Eagle and Columbia.

In a sense, the critical part of rendezvous has been finished already. The Eagle was only obliged to get into some kind of orbit. If its ascent motor had failed any time in the last sixty seconds of ascent, its thrusters would have been able to drive it the rest of the way into that first planned ellipse, and then the Command Module could have descended for rescue. Indeed, once Eagle succeeded in getting into any kind of orbit at all, the Command Module would be able to come down for it, but all orbits below six miles of altitude were dangerous indeed, for then Eagle would have no ability to clear mountains. Rendezvous maneuvers might have had to be speeded up. One could even conceive of a cinematic rescue with Columbia accelerating down toward the moon, slowing just long enough only for Armstrong and Aldrin to open the hatch, crawl outside, get a handhold on a quadrant of Columbia's thrusters and Sput! Sput! Columbia would be on her way up again as the Lem coasted into a lunar peak.

That was hardly the operation today. It proceeded smoothly. A little while after Eagle coasted up to her apolune of 46.7 miles above the moon, she fired her thrusters for a little more speed and was inserted into Concentric Sequence Initiation, a rough circle forty-five miles in diameter which was situated within the rough sixty-mile circle of the Command Module. Almost an hour later, halfway around from that position, came another burn, called the Constant Differential Height, whose purpose was to make certain that if both ships were traveling in concentric ellipses, the distances between them did not vary. (All this, well planned in advance, was readjusted in flight by measurements taken from the Inertial Measurement Unit, then calculated by the guidance computer, as well as by checks obtained from rendezvous radar.)

About thirty-eight minutes later, Eagle was ready to begin Terminal Phase Initiation. That was at a point where Columbia was thirty miles in front of her and seventeen miles overhead. Driving forward at a small increase of velocity, which closed distance at about a nautical mile a minute, on an angle 27 degrees above her local horizontal, Eagle swallowed the last gap in something less than forty-five minutes. The two ships came within view of each other in less than four hours and less than two revolutions from the time lift-off had occurred. Collins reported a great feeling of relief at seeing them come up toward him. "I really got excited then because for the first time, it was clear they had done it. They had landed on the moon and got off again." They had in fact come up all the way on their own power, with Columbia— power available not only in her thrusters but in

her main propulsion motor—maintaining all the tools and options in reserve. It was more elegant to solve the problem with the lesser means. Besides, it left Columbia in possession of more fuel for the trip back.

Now came the last maneuvers. Little braking burns to put their velocity equal to one another were done in an operation called stationkeeping: now they could wheel through lunar space close enough to take photographs of one another. Let us listen to the transcript as they approach. It is very calm. What has happened to Aldrin's anxiety of a few hours ago?

ARMSTRONG: *Okay, Mike. I'll get—I'll try to get in position here, then you got it . . . I'm not going to do a thing, Mike. I'm just letting her hold in attitude HOLD.*

COLUMBIA: *Okay.*

ARMSTRONG: *Okay, we're all yours.*

COLUMBIA: *Okay. Okay, I have thrusters D3 and D4 safetied.*

ARMSTRONG: *Okay.*

COLUMBIA: *I'm pumping up cabin pressures.*

The docking took place with a light touch. Collins never even felt the two ships meet. The probe of the Command Module slid into the Eagle's drogue. "They're held together then," Collins said, "by three tiny capture latches, and it's almost like tiny little paper clips holding together two vehicles, one of which weighs thirty thousand pounds, the other five thousand. It's a tenuous grasp. To make the combination rigid you fire a little gas bottle that activates a plunger which literally sucks the two vehicles together. At this point the twelve capture latches fire mechanically and you are held together very strongly. That's the hard dock."

Just before that moment "all hell broke loose." It was Collins' remark, there on the transcript, but he has no recollection of saying it. As he fired the charges, there was an abrupt, shocking and "abnormal" oscillation. The ships began to yaw from side to side at a rapid rate. What an instant for Armstrong—did the memory of the sun flashing through the window of Gemini 8 come back to him? What a thunder for Aldrin after the mishaps with the computer on the day before, what a stroke of doubt for Collins at where the mistake could be. "All hell broke loose." Hell was when the unforeseen insisted on emerging. Shivering and quivering, the ships slapped from side to side.

Well, it lasted for "eight or ten rather dubious seconds," while Collins and Armstrong worked to get back in line with one another, and all the while the automatic retract was working and they finally came together with a big bang and were docked "and it was all over."

It was essentially all over. The chores were done, the suits were vacuumed of moon dust, the tunnel was opened, and they met and shook hands, no comment recorded for posterity, and then passed the rock boxes through to Collins who handled them "as if they were absolutely jam-packed with rare jewels which" he adds, "in a sense they are." Now the hours were spent on the details of final housekeeping aboard the Lem, in the final transfer to the Command Module, the repositioning of the probe and the drogue. Soon the Lem would be jettisoned. The two ships would separate and Eagle would ebb away at a few feet a second. Once it was out of sight, it would never be seen again. Still, an essential part of it would certainly expire in full view of their recording instruments for the primary cooling system, which kept the computer from overheating, was disconnected before they left. As the hours passed, the computer on the Eagle kept sending data, but the signal became weaker and weaker. Finally it died. Pings with her sneak circuits, Executive Overflows, and DSKY was dead. Long before that, they had fired up their Service Propulsion Motor on the back of

the moon, and the Command and Service Module had come over the hill with velocity sufficient to throw her out of lunar gravity and out on her long way home. Pings on the Lem was not in fact to die until after midnight when thousands of miles away the crew was settling in for a real sleep.

The trip back had begun. They had sixty hours to spend in modest work, in a repetition of chores, and in a great deal of thought. It is doubtful if they brooded too long on the wild gyrations before the hard dock. Possibly there had been more concern at Houston. For the Lem was a machine of machines, a beauty of a beast which had never seen work on earth. She had habits like a horse who was crazy once a year. She had taken off on Cernan for a rampant little trip, she had dipped this crew toward the moon, then, as if magnetized by magnetisms never quite measured before, charged with some sense of person from the remarkable components of her crew, or by her contact with the moon, charged perhaps by some sensitivity to the difference between the men in herself, and the man in the Command Module she soon would meet, she had quivered, or the Command Module had quivered, or both had quivered, space machine to moon machine, quivered like magnets which approach and gyrate when suspended on a string. Something happened up there which no one could explain, something once again had stirred the hairs in the secret cave. The psychology of machines was a whisper in the dark and sultry Houston night.

XIV

It is almost sixty hours before reentry for the astronauts, and their return will be without events of the largest scope. Collins will grow a mustache, and Mission Control will report that the crime rate in Italy was at a low for the year on the night they walked the moon. A

girl will be born in Memphis who is christened
Module McGhee, and a boy named Greg
Force will fix a bearing on the huge antenna
in Guam because he is the only one whose arm
is small enough to reach into the hole. The
Capcom on duty the following night will mistake the moon for the earth on a murky television screen and the astronauts will have the
experience of seeing the earth and moon looking equal in size out opposite windows. Slowly
the earth will grow in the window. Blue she
will gleam and brown and gray and silver and
rose and red. Her clouds will cover her like
curls of white hair, her clouds will turn dark
as smoky pearls and the lavender of orchid,
her clouds will be brown and green like marsh
grass wet by the sea, and the sea will appear
beneath like pools of water in the marsh grass.
The earth will look like a precious stone, blue
as sapphire, blue as diamond, the earth will
be an eye to look at them in curious welcome
as they return. They have been as far as Achilles and Odysseus, as far as Jason who sailed
to meet the argonauts, far as Magellan and
Columbus, they have been far. And their
fingertips are smooth from plastic, their lungs
are leather from days of bottled gas. What does
an astronaut give up of the ultimate tastes to
travel so far? We are back to Aquarius molder-
ing on flatlands not far from the sea.

The Counter Culture in Action: Woodstock

At the time it was being organized, it seemed like any other music festival. Big-name rock bands. Expensive tickets. A place in the country. But once it began on August 15, 1969, the Woodstock Music and Art Fair at Max Yasgur's 600-acre farm in Bethel, New York, took on a life of its own. It became an attempt to establish a new community, a counterculture in action, not just a hipper Newport Folk Festival or a second Monterey Pops. In three days' time Woodstock became one of the largest cities in the country, with a population estimated at 450,000.

It is difficult to think of a parallel for Woodstock. In American history probably only the revivals Jonathan Edwards led during the Great Awakening of the 1740s can be said to equal Woodstock for their psychological impact on a whole generation of the young. In terms of the sixties and seventies the implications of Woodstock are not at all obscure, however. They are those Theodore Roszak describes when he observes in *The Making of a Counter Culture*:

> Ironically, it is the American young, with their underdeveloped radical background, who seem to have grasped most clearly the fact that, while such immediate emergencies as the Vietnam war, racial injustice, and hard-core poverty de-

mand a deal of old-style politicking, the paramount struggle of our day is against a far more formidable, because far less obvious, opponent, to which I will give the name "the technocracy". . . . The American young have been somewhat quicker to sense that in the struggle against *this* enemy, the conventional tactics of political resistence have only a marginal place, largely limited to meeting immediate life-and-death crises. Beyond such front-line issues, however, there lies the greater task of altering the total cultural context within which our daily politics takes place.*

It is a short transition from Roszak's observations to Abbie Hoffman's response to Woodstock:

I emerged exhausted, broke, and bleeding from the WOODSTOCK NATION. It was an awesome experience but one that made me have a clearer picture of myself as a cultural revolutionary—not a cultural nationalist, for that would embrace a concept of hip capitalism which I reject—and not a political revolutionary either. Political revolution leads people into support for other revolutions rather than having them get involved in making their own. Cultural revolution requires people to change the way they live and act in the revolution rather than passing judgments on how the other folks are proceeding.†

The accounts of Woodstock that follow focus on its cultural implications: particularly, the question of how seriously Woodstock is to be taken. The analyses they offer are in general toughminded, but interestingly there is one possibility they barely consider—a Woodstock-like venture turning into a disaster. Reading the descriptions of Woodstock in this section, we get no premonition of an event like the Rolling Stones' Altamont Raceway Concert four months later, where Hell's Angels, who had been hired as security for $500 worth of beer, beat spectators with pool cues and killed a man in full view of the stage.

Unlike the other reports in this section, Al Aronowitz's were written to meet a daily newspaper deadline. As a result they are especially sensitive to the changing mood of Woodstock. Aronowitz captures the way each day, and sometimes each hour, brought the festival a new crisis—too many cars, too few doctors, not enough food, drenching rain—and how, as each crisis was overcome, the spirit of Woodstock grew. "It has been there for three days now, this monster benign, magnificent, sometimes larger, sometimes smaller, roosting on the hillside where alfalfa once grew, drowning in mud, thirsting for water, chilled by rain, unsheltered, unfed, yet kept alive by something on that stage that can't be explained except in terms of

---

*Theodore Roszak, *The Making of a Counter Culture,* Doubleday & Company, Inc., New York, 1968, pp. 4–5. Copyright 1968, 1969 by Theodore Roszak.

†Abbie Hoffman, *Woodstock Nation,* Random House, Inc., New York, 1969, p. 7. Copyright © 1969, 1971 by Abbie Hoffman.

magic." Even when all that remains of the festival is a soggy cow pasture filled with garbage, Aronowitz sees the improvisational spirit of Woodstock overshadowing everything else. Observing one of the festival's organizers "emptying the papers out of his desk like a general whose command post is about to be overrun," he concludes, "You are inside his trailer office behind the big stage . . . and you shudder when you learn they improvised it as they went along, only guessing it would hold all the weight. . . . Is the enemy at the gates? They are only the bill collectors."

The next three reports also provide an extended description of Woodstock, but they may be distinguished from Aronowitz's writing by the degree to which they are concerned with making a cultural and political judgment of Woodstock.

In contrast to Al Aronowitz, Richard Reeves went to Woodstock with little sense of what it would be like. At one point in his "Mike Lang (groovy kid from Brooklyn) plus John Roberts (unlimited capital) equals Woodstock," he confesses how it finally sank into "my 32-year-old mind" that "almost every person there was using marijuana, at least." But despite such admissions of naiveté, Reeves's observations on Woodstock are penetrating. His description of the manager of The Who telling one of the Woodstock organizers, "'Cash or a certified check, or we don't go on,'" like his analysis of a Woodstock organizer who is "willing to work hard within the system" but wants freedom rather than a suburban home, is part of a picture in which the hip-capitalist quality of Woodstock is captured with murderous accuracy.

A far more accepting view of the cultural and political implications of Woodstock is provided in the concluding *Rolling Stone* accounts, Greil Marcus's "Woodstock Festival" and Andrew Kopkind's "Woodstock Music and Art Fair." For Marcus, the significance of Woodstock is the emotional freedom it made possible. "Janis Joplin and Creedence Clearwater are more important than most would have guessed not because they carry some arcane political message, but because when people hear them they get excited and ecstatic and feel more alive." It is the fact that Woodstock provided a social context in which it was unnecessary to be in revolt that Marcus finds crucial. "There was no sense of cheating the cops out of a bust," he writes. "Kids who had their first taste of dope or sex or nudity at Woodstock might remember later that these were acts that at least *somebody* thought were wrong, but at the festival it was as natural as cruising Main Street or catching a subway." In the end Marcus has few doubts about the value of Woodstock. It is the problem of arranging for more Woodstocks—free to all who come—that concerns him.

Andrew Kopkind is equally enthusiastic about the spirit of Woodstock, but he is far more preoccupied with the tensions between Woodstock and American society as a whole. "What is not illusionary is the reality of a new culture of opposition," he writes. "It grows out of the disintegration of the old forms, the vinyl and aerosol institutions that carry all the inane and destructive values of privatism, competition, commercialism, profitability and elitism." For Kopkind, the difficulty with the new culture is that it lacks its own institutions, and the great task he sees for the future is giving this culture social viability. "Political radicals have to see the cultural revolution as a sea in which they can swim," he argues in conclusion. He is confident that they will be diving into fresh rather than polluted water.

Woodstock

Alfred G. Aronowitz

Alfred G. Aronowitz formerly wrote a rock column for the *New York Post.* He has been a reporter for the *Newark News* and pop music critic for the *New York Times* and *Life* magazine, and contributes articles to numerous magazines. He is the author, with Pete Hamill, of *Ernest Hemingway: The Life and Death of a Man,* and is the manager for David Bromberg, a Columbia recording artist. Mr. Aronowitz is also the producer for the Country in New York concert series.

THE GREAT ROCK PILEUP—FANS JAM ROADS TO WOODSTOCK FAIR

The Woodstock Music and Art Fair, described by its incorporators as probably the largest gathering of this generation, didn't begin until 4 p.m. this afternoon. But by 4 this morning every road leading to the big stage at the bottom of a sloping alfalfa field was clogged for miles.

"It took us an hour and 20 minutes to drive the three miles from the stage to our rooms," said John Morris, the managing director of the production. With him was 24-year-old Mike Lang, a quarter-owner of the enterprise and the man who thought it up. Even if they had been able to get to their accommodations for some sleep, what dreams could Lang possibly have left?

"Our biggest problem," said one spokesman "is the traffic. It's tied up for miles. There are over 100,000 persons here now and the festival didn't even start yet."

Highway route 17B, he said, "is completely blocked. They're just sitting along the road, wondering where they'll find places to park."

The festival has sold close to 200,000 tickets in advance and by the time it ends with a climactic performance by Jimi Hendrix close to 1 a.m. Monday an estimated 400,000 persons are expected to pass through the two main gates in the cyclone fence surrounding the alfalfa.

Eight dollars a seat? Bring your own chair. The attraction has already surpassed the Monterey Pop Festival, drawing crew-cut college students as well as pilgrims bearing the colors of the freak scene.

By yesterday, most of the campsites on the 600-acre farm leased from dairyman Max Yasgur had filled up and Lang and Morris had to rush through this Catskill vacationland buying up parking rights on another 600 to 800 acres.

But dozens of music lovers didn't make the scene immediately. Twenty were busted as they crossed the bridge from Canada to Buffalo and charged with possession of narcotics.

Five Californians ran afoul of the law on similar charges at Wellsville, when state troopers stopped their car for a routine check and said they not only possessed narcotics, but a loaded pistol.

Six teenagers from Torrington, Conn., were critically injured when their small bus went off the road near Yorktown, N.Y., a seventh was treated at the scene and continued to the festival.

Earlier, there were at least 51 arrests on drug charges.

Meanwhile, the 346 off-duty New York City policemen who yesterday were forbidden to moonlight as $50-a-day "ushers" in the festival's own security force were said to be showing up anyway. In an unexplained last-minute move, Police Commissioner Leary issued a reminder to all precincts of the department's 1967 regulations against such off-duty employment, but the cops apparently were reporting to the festival under assumed names.

They were immediately issued red jackets and bell-bottom trousers and badges that said "Peace" instead of "Police."

The stars of tonight's show will be Richie Havens and Joan Baez. Tomorrow night's performance will feature the San Francisco sound of the Grateful Dead and the Jefferson Airplane. There also will be sideshows of arts, crafts, ceremonial Indian dances and a folksinger named Rosalie Sorrels.

There were no signs of rain in the skies and the only clouds to cast an early pall over the festival came from marijuana smoke. State police and Sullivan County Sheriffs officials reported at least 51 arrests for possession of hashish and marijuana by this morning.

Most of those taken into custody were found smoking pot on the festival grounds. Others were picked up on the highway after being observed smoking in cars stuck in the traffic tie-ups. Especially vulnerable to arrest were the growing number of hitch-hikers. Hitch-hiking is illegal in New York State, and police were quick to search offenders.

"But mostly," a state police spokesman said, "we're getting the obvious ones."

Previous music festivals in Los Angeles and Denver had come under the pall of mace with riots that resulted in extensive property damage and numerous arrests. Otherwise, everybody was all smiles in the festival area.

And Mike Lang's smile was as wide as Route 17B. That doesn't allow for many lanes of automobiles, but then how bad could Mike Lang feel to be stuck in a traffic jam when every car that got past his happy face was actually headed for his pocket?

CRISIS

The head of medical services at the Woodstock Music and Art Fair warned today that if the crowd continued to grow "a medical disaster" would be imminent.

Dr. William Abruzzi said that "from a medical point of view it's not an emergency yet, but we're almost at the breaking point."

"We simply can't cope with the medical needs of what amounts to a large city packed into a field," he said.

He said that 15 doctors were being flown in from New York today to bolster the staff of 20 on hand. There are also about 50 nurses, he said.

State and nearby Monticello police, however, said that as far as they knew no such disaster was likely.

Abruzzi, of Wappingers Falls, said that 50,000 to 100,000 persons had been anticipated, but that the crowd "now numbers 330,000 to 350,000 people."

Abruzzi said that "we've seen just about

everything" in the way of medical problems. A number of persons have been evacuated to area hospitals, including a young woman with a fractured spine.

A State Police spokesman in Liberty said that the overcrowding, coupled with last night's rains, had turned the field into a muddy shambles.

"It's a disaster area in the sense that it's flooded, you've got about 500 people on every acre and the sanitation facilities have broken down," he said.

He said that many of the persons taken to hospitals were suffering from drug overdoses.

Abruzzi said that his staff had treated diabetics in comas as well as epileptics.

Monticello Police Chief Lou Yank said "most of these kids just seem to be exhausted."

Meanwhile, law enforcement authorities reported another 60 arrests for drugs.

When singer Richie Havens opened the festival shortly after 4 yesterday, the state police estimated there were still perhaps a million persons on the highways trying to get to the sloping alfalfa field that looks down on the festival's 60-by-70-foot temporary stage. With some 200,000—the police estimate—already inside the cyclone fence that surrounds the field, there wasn't room for anyone else.

There also wasn't any way to collect admissions.

"This," said John Morris, managing director of production, "has turned out to be the greatest freebee of all times."

Attendance at this festival is expected by its promoters to total more that 600,000 before it ends with the space ship blues of Jimi Hendrix shortly after 1 a.m. Monday.

Those who thought themselves lucky enough to get here early found themselves snowed in by people. The festival management had to make an emergency expenditure of $10,000 to hire helicopters to fly in food for sold-out concessionaires and hungry staff workers. The only reason Richie Havens opened the show was because Sweetwater, the group originally scheduled as the curtain-raiser, was marooned in traffic—with all its heavy equipment—three miles from the stage.

Even with a police escort, Sweetwater, Tim Hardin and the cherubic female chanteuse Melanie had to be rescued by helicopters which plopped down by the side of the road and carried them the rest of the way to the festival site.

Meanwhile, with entertainers pouring in from all parts of the world, the festival also had to run a helicopter shuttle service from Sullivan County's landing strips, including the one at Grossinger's, noted more for its rye bread than its affection for musicians carrying hippie colors.

With only 150,000 admissions paid in advance, festival executives faced the possibility that the more who showed up the more they'd lose. "We may have to forget about trying to sell any more tickets," said 24-year-old Mike Lang, an entrepreneur who seems to care as much about raising dust as cash.

Besides the 200,000 inside the gates, police estimated there were another 100,000 camped outside. Cars blocked the country roads where owners had abandoned them to walk the rest of the way.

Someone who started out for the festival site from Liberty, only 12 miles away, didn't arrive until five hours later—even though he left at 4 a.m.

The trip back to Liberty after last night's session of the festival was averaging nearly six hours.

"Yes," said Ravi Shankar, India's celebrated sitar virtuoso "this is definitely larger than the pop festival at Monterey. But that is what is so frightening about it. I am frightened in case something goes wrong with so many people."

Shankar was in the midst of his performance when the rain began falling, accompanied by a few lightning bolts, and it was the water that proved to be the most frightening. The rain began collecting in the canopy atop the stage and threatened to collapse it.

At another point, festival guards expressed the fear that the stage, built on scaffolding, was beginning to slide in the mud. The harder the rain fell, however, the more determined the crowd seemed to stay. Huddled around bonfires, most of the audience waited an hour while the music was interrupted because the water threatened to short the electrical equipment. But even in the rain the crowd gave standing ovations to Shanker, Melanie, Arlo Guthrie and Joan Baez, who closed last night's installment of the festival.

BENIGN MONSTER DEVOURED MUSIC

You sat on the big stage watered by the blue spotlights while the Big Pink Band plays Bob Dylan's "I Shall Be Released" and you look out into the eyes of the monster.

It has been there for three days now, this monster, benign, magnificent, sometimes larger, sometimes smaller, roosting on a hillside where alfalfa once gvxrew, drowning in mud, thirsting for water, chilled by rain, unsheltered, unfed, yet kept alive by something on stage that can't be explained except in terms of magic. Is music alone miracle enough to sate the appetites of 45,000 people?

You sit on the big stage listening to the sweet plea of innocence of a singer who tells you that every distance is not near, and on the ground 20 feet below a state trooper is chasing a bunch of kids off their perch on a heavy construction crane while a bearded acid head stands next to him stark naked.

The rain has left an early morning chill that is warping the piano strings out of tune and there is no excuse to be walking around without clothes on, but the state trooper ignores the acid head and instead turns his attention to getting permission for a 15-year-old boy to sit on the stage. When you learn that the 15-year-old boy is the state trooper's son you realize where the monster comes from. It is America's child.

Your feet are puffed with the blisters of no-other-way-to-get-there and your head tilts to one side with the weight of your eyelids and you wonder why the monster doesn't just go home. But out there on the rain-sogged hillside it lives, reminding you of its existence every now and then with a full-throated roar that also tells you how terrifying a monster can be. There are bonfires on the hillside and you can smell the marijuana smoke on the monster's breath and you wonder what dreams it sees when it looks down at the stage you're standing on. Is it music that dreams are made of?

There were two births reported at the Woodstock Music and Art Fair, called an Aquarian Exposition because we are at the end of the Age of Pisces and the 2000 years of the Christian era and the promoters thought they could earn a few dollars by capitalizing on an underground which fancies itself the secret early Christians of a new religion.

Woodstock? It's an hour and a half away in light traffic, but then listen to the testimony of Artie Kornfeld, who is one of the promoters of the fair and who now feels absolved of all guilt because he stands to lose a fortune.

"From now on," he says, "when people hear the name Woodstock they won't think of the town, they'll think of our festival." Has Kornfeld found a new religion? "This weekend turned me around so much," he says, his eyes burning with the passion of some unknown fuel, "that I could never go back to what I was doing." Artie Kornfeld was a commercial record producer whose greatest credit was the Cowsills, but now he's going to spend more time with his wife and daughter.

Meet Mike Lang, host to his generation. At 24, Mike dreamed up the Woodstock Music and Art Fair, and his plans were so thorough that when you sat down for bologna and cheese snacks in the performers' pavillion, there were boxes of Wash N' Dry on the tables. But yesterday morning, the 800 portable toilets on the festival site were filling up.

Is it an indictable offense to underestimate your power? If the promoters didn't realize how easy it was to get so many kids in one place, then perhaps they shouldn't have tried to get any.

When you first came over the hill in a helicopter three days ago, the site was breathtaking. Only the Pope could draw a crowd like that. The monster came dressed for a picnic, but it would have worn a shirt and tie if it had to.

Wilted collars? First it rained, then the sun shone too brightly. The crowds walking on the temporary plastic water pipes caused leaks, and then the wells didn't deliver as promised. The showers and drinking fountains which had been placed so thoughtfully throughout the festival site turned out to be as useful as the tickets that had been sold to get into the place: Not at all.

The 150,000 who bought advance admissions ended up subsidizing the whole show. By the time the festival management was ready to open its gates, the monster was already inside. With close to 200,000 on the alfalfa field, another 100,000 milling throughout the nearby campsites, and as many as a million waiting in long lines of traffic trying to get there, Max Yasgur's 600-acre dairy farm had become one of the most populous cities in the state. All told an estimated 450,000 made it there. By yesterday morning Max was on the great stage greeting the monster with a peace sign.

Is the freakout scene over? More than 40 kids had to be carried away, flipping out from bad trips. One of them reportedly died in Middletown Hospital. Still another was run over by a tractor.

Most of the LSD cases were treated by members of the Hog Farm, long experienced with acid. "The cops like that," said Hugh Romney, who patrolled the festival site, as Police Chief, with his front teeth missing, carrying a staff stuck through a tiny drum, wearing a 10-gallon hat, consciously doing the work of the Lord and giving lessons in gentleness.

By this morning, the monster was almost gone. Jimi Hendrix, the biggest star of the festival, had to play to the smallest crowd of the weekend. When you left by helicopter you looked down at the mud and the exhaustion and wondered which would you remember more, the monster or his footprint.

AFTERMATH AT BETHEL: GARBAGE AND CREDITORS

For three days it had been a position of honor, this soggy cow pasture, a place of status for that horde who had managed to beat out nearly a million others for a seat in the rain, the wind, the night and the glory of having been part of a miracle.

Now it was a city dump. The flies clumped on your arms. The stink attacked your stomach. Long-haired volunteers and professional garbage men kept trying to sweep it into piles while girls in see-through maxis picked through the debris. There were cans and blankets and containers and hot dogs, ponchos and wrappers and towels and utensils, and there were trousers. On the long hillside and in the surrounding roads, mud-caked and trampled, some ragged, some new, some from boys, some from girls, some abandoned with their belts still in them, there were trousers. Could the people of Sullivan County ever allow this again?

"The thing that scares me now," says John Morris, managing director of production of the Woodstock Music and Art Fair, "is that the schlocks will try to do it. Somewhere, somehow, some great brainy schlock is going to look at what we've done here and get the bright idea that he's going to try to put 300,000 people in a field again."

And what about the promoters of the Woodstock Music and Art Fair? Will they do it again? "They'll do it," he answers. Even though they now claim to be losing as much as a million on this one? "Oh, sure," he says, "They'll do it."

You are inside his trailer office behind the big stage, lonely and quiet now beneath rigging that reminds you of a circus tent without the big top, and you shudder when you learn how they improvised it as they went along, only guessing it would hold all the weight. John Morris is emptying the papers out of his desk like a general whose command post is about to be overrun. Is the enemy at the gates? They are only the bill collectors.

There is, for example, Harvey Rosen, the manager of the Howard Johnson's motel in Liberty, who says he went for $7200 to hire helicopters just because the festival needed them and just because the promoters asked him to. He is 25 and self-conscious about his corpulence, so he walks to the site, where Mike Lang, still smiling at the miracle, asks him to wait until Thursday.

Harvey says OK and then walks the seven miles to White Lake, where he meets four kids trying to hitchhike home from the festival. They are broke, so Harvey reaches into his pocket and pulls out his last $22 to pay their bus fair to New York. When he gets back to Liberty, he bursts into laughter.

"Let me tell you," says Harvey's boss, Mrs. Mildred Blanks, "it's been quite an experience, but it's been a pleasure. My own kids came home yesterday looking like drowned rats, after a while couldn't stand smelling each other, but they had a great time. If we had 500 rabbis and priests here, let me tell you some of them would have been arrested.

"Last night a bunch of kids came in on motorcycles soaked to the skin. We had no room for them, but I put them in the laundry room and made them take their clothes off and I put their clothes, you know, in the dryer." Mrs. Blanks is 45. Sullivan County always treats its guests as if it's a Jewish mother.

You wonder where the four kids who promoted this thing are going to get the money, and Mike Lang smiles and tells you how happy he is. Meanwhile, back in New York, his partner 24-year-old John Roberts, is busy transferring several hundred thousand dollars from one account to another. It was Roberts' personal fortune that was used to underwrite the venture, with the liability divided four ways.

"John," says Mike Lang, wearing the same Indian leather vest he has worn all week, "is very happy with the success of this thing," and he tells you how the town and the county and Max Yasgur, who owns this stinking cow pasture, have asked the festival to return next year. The banks have promised to hold all festival checks until Thursday, and some of the construction bosses are busy paying off their key help with their own money. You ask why you haven't seen John Roberts all weekend.

"Oh," says Mike, "John didn't come. He was too nervous."

Mike Lang (Groovy Kid from Brooklyn) Plus John Roberts (Unlimited Capital) Equals Woodstock

Richard Reeves

Richard Reeves, a contributing editor to *New York* magazine, has written numerous articles for major magazines. Formerly an engineer, he has been an editor with *Phillipsburg Free Press* and a reporter for the *Newark News,* the *New York Herald Tribune,* and the *New York Times.* Mr. Reeves has also been an adjunct professor in the Columbia University Graduate School of Journalism and a lecturer at Hunter College. He is presently the cohost of "Sunday" on WNBC-TV.

Here comes Mike Lang! He's rolling along the New Jersey Turnpike in a U-Haul truck filled with a few thousand psychedelic posters and some other salable stuff. The kid from Brooklyn is coming home from Florida, 23 years old, curly brown hair down to his shoulders, Indian vest and dungarees. Groovy! February, 1968. Look out, New York! Look out, America! Look out, John Roberts!

There's John Roberts in his apartment on East 85th Street. Same age as Mike, horn-rimmed glasses, Rogers Peet suit. At 25 he'll inherit the first million dollars from the Polident trust fund. Outasight! A year ago he and a friend put that advertisement in The New York Times: "Young men with unlimited capital looking for interesting and legitimate business enterprises."

Beautiful! There were 1,400 replies, including one from the man with the flying car and another from the lady with a formula for watermelon-flavored Popsicles.

Mike and John were meant for each other, poet and patron. Sorry, Popsicle lovers, but Mike got most of that unlimited capital. He had an idea, the greatest happening in history—The Woodstock Music and Art Fair. Wow!

"I knew it was going to happen," Mike said the other day as his white Porsche stopped in front of the Plaza. "Even before I found the money, I knew it was going down. I have this sense of time."

"Mike's from another planet," said the lank redhead with him as men stopped to watch her climb up out of the little car. "He has these two bumps on his head, like horns. And funny leprechaun ears and eyes that slant up."

Maybe she's right. Maybe Mike, who describes himself as a nice Jewish boy from Benson-hurst, was sent from another world to turn this one on. He turned on about 400,000 young earthlings for three days—Aug. 15–17—in tiny Bethel, N.Y. Then he looked happily over the kids, the mud, the drugs, the sharing, the ecstasy and the anarchy and proclaimed: "The world is a little less uptight because of what we did here."

Of course, John Roberts was a little *more* uptight. He spent the weekend far from the madding crowd writing $600,000 in bad checks to pay the groups, feed the kids, fly medicine in and generally to prevent a riot—by the kids or by angry creditors.

At one point, a few of those creditors, un-impressed by the slogan, "Three Days of Peace and Music," managed to get into Mike's trailer behind the throbbing one-acre stage and began hassling him for their bread.

"We don't have cash right now," Mike said softly, smiling; no one can remember ever hearing him raise his voice. "We didn't plan it this way, but this is a free concert. There is no gate. There's no cash. It's a beautiful thing. Have some faith."

"Bull—!" screamed the manager of one of the 30 top groups that played at Bethel. "You say you have $40-million behind you. Then get up $5,000 cash—now!" Another group man-ager, John Wolff of The Who, knifed in with, "Cash or a certified check, or we don't go on."

"Oh," said Joyce Mitchell, the trailer's office manager. "Where is my lucky hat? I don't like to talk about money without my hat." She found it, a floppy brown great-white-hunter's hat, on a desk where a staff member named Terry had been slowly popping a row of multi-colored pills and capsules, washing them down with a can of Fresca. With each pill she pressed the heel of her right hand against her fore-head and gazed at the ceiling like someone using eyedrops.

A man in a green shirt and a crewcut wandered through the arguing group, telling everyone: "I'm from Wells Fargo. We're here to pick up the receipts." Someone finally no-ticed him and said, "I can personally assure you that there are no receipts to pick up." Wells Fargo seemed satisfied and excused himself through the crowd and out of the trailer.

It all ended, as usual, when Mike said, "Call John." Joyce or somebody telephoned John Roberts who was working—signing checks, that is—in an office seven miles away in the village of White Lake.

"It was a nightmare—I wrote a lot of bad paper that weekend," Roberts said later as he sipped a Seven 'n' Seven (that's 7-Up and Sea-gram's 7 Crown) in the Cavendish, a private club his father belongs to on Central Park South. "My family is scurrying around getting the collateral to make the checks good. Every-one will be paid within 60 days."

Young Mr. Roberts chain-smoked Marlboros as he talked about the festival's financial his-tory, which Business Week compared to the script of a nineteen-forties Mickey Rooney movie. The expenses totalled $2.7-million and revenues were $1.4-million, although he hopes a movie of the festival will make up the loss over the next couple of years.

For now, the $1.3-million deficit has driven him to the wall, or rather to the National Bank of North America, where his family has a $3-million credit line.

With the size of the crowd and the ticket price of $18 for the three days, Woodstock Ventures, Inc., should have made a fortune. But Woodstock was not your average up-tight corporation. Staff meetings tended to be inconclusive, with half the executives smoking marijuana and the other half sipping the champagne (Piper-Heidsieck) that always seemed to be around. New employees were asked their signs—Aquarius and Gemini rated higher than Harvard and Yale, Company cars, like Lang's, were sometimes Porsches. And the two changes in sites (Woodstock to Wallkill to Bethel) left the promoters in such panic that they were unmercifully overcharged. One Bethel farmer, for example, got $5,000 for a three-day lease on 10 acres that had been *for sale* at $8,000.

Most of all, no one knew that something like a half-million kids would come, and no one seemed to be in charge of blocking off the gates to the music area. On Friday morning, 12 hours before the music was supposed to start, Lang woke up and found 30,000 kids without tickets sleeping in front of the stage. He asked them to leave; they smiled and cheered, and he decided a free concert was better than a riot. The corporation was left with the advance sale of $1.4-million.

"I think you could say that from the beginning we were plagued by a certain amount of disorganization," Roberts said as he nodded to friends at his father's club and accepted congratulations because one of his horses—Egomaniac—had won the first at Belmont Park.

"We" is Woodstock Ventures, four people: Lang and his friend, Artie Kornfeld, 26, who was a successful young "contemporary music" executive at Capitol Records; Roberts and his friend, Joel Rosenman, 26, a Yale Law School graduate who wants to be a singer.

Roberts put up all the money—$500,000 to start and finally the $2.7-million. As he talked

about what has gone on during the past year, two things he said stuck with me:

1 "Michael and Artie are tremendously good salesmen, I think."
2 "The theory was that Michael and Artie would put up the *expertise* and I would put up the money. I thought that was about right, 50 per cent for *expertise,* 50 per cent for money. My father told me that was hare-brained."

John's father is Alfred Roberts, president of Lydia O'Leary, Inc., a cosmetics firm that makes Covermark and Spotstik. His mother was Elizabeth Block, whose family owned Block Drug Co., Inc., which makes things like Polident and Pycopay toothbrushes. John's mother died in 1953, leaving him a trust fund that will provide him with at least $4-million to be paid in three installments on his 25th, 30th and 35th birthdays.

After the right schools—St. Bernard's, Deerfield Academy and the University of Pennsylvania—Roberts worked as a reporter for a small news service that provides features for European newspapers. He was, he says, a poor little rich boy—rich because he could borrow against the trust fund, and poor because he was lonely, bored and a lousy writer.

He met Joel Rosenman, a Long Island dentist's son, on New Year's Day in 1967. Within a month they were roommates, in John's apartment. No one involved in the festival got to know Rosenman too well, and that may have something to do with the unkind things they have to say about him—particularly his habit of pushing publicity people to "get my name in the papers; it will help my social position." Generally, he is dismissed as "a guy who saw a good thing in Roberts and moved in."

Six weeks after John and Joel met, they were writing the ad in The Times to find ways of spending John's money. They rejected Popsicles and other schemes, though they did prepare for a big-time future, incorporating themselves as Challenge International, Ltd. Joel's musical ambitions led them to establish a recording studio in Manhattan, which has been moderately successful. Then one day Joel's singing teacher's lawyer sent them "two young men with an idea."

The two young men, of course, were Mike and Artie. They had met while Artie was at Capitol and Mike stopped in there with a group he was managing, The Train. Both had sidelines. Kornfeld, president of the class of 1964 at Adelphi University, had made a name for himself as the producer and lyricist of a big-money group, The Cowsills. Lang, a New York University drop-out, who had run a Miami "head shop" (posters, Zig-Zag papers, pipes and other drug paraphernalia), was dealing in posters and more profitable stuff in the East Village.

Their idea, born during a pot party around Christmas of 1968, had two parts, both to be set in Woodstock, a Hudson River village fabled for its beauty, its artists' colony and Bob Dylan, who lives there. Part I: a recording studio. Part II: a giant music festival.

The four young men met for the first time a month later, and after Roberts got over Lang's hair—"It was the first time I'd seen anything like that close up"—they got along very well. Basically, they still do. Some men might be bitter, but not John Roberts.

"Yes, it was all my money," he says. "But my partners have equally guaranteed any loss. Of course, they don't really have any money, and I certainly wouldn't want to bankrupt them.

"I hope we can make up the losses on the film. We're making a deal with Warner Brothers—I haven't seen it; Mike's taking care of that—but I think that if it grosses $10-million, that will give us enough to cover the $1.3-million my family has borrowed.

Shortly after their first meeting, the four young men decided to form Woodstock Ventures as a partnership. Challenge International put up $500,000 for the festival and studio. Of that amount, $55,000 was used to purchase a 26-acre estate in Woodstock for the retreat-studio, a sylvan setting for rock groups to live and record in. The festival, though, would be the first order of business—the studio has yet to be built.

The day after the papers were signed, Lang called Roberts to assure him that the festival was going to draw the biggest crowds in history, bigger than the 40,000 to 100,000 that profitable festivals drew in Atlanta, Atlantic City, Los Angeles and Newport, R.I. "I have begun to spread the word," Mike told his new partner. "The word is spreading throughout the underground."

Starting in the spring, the word-spreading took on a more professional look. Some $200,000 was spent to advertise the event, not just in underground papers but in The Village Voice and The Times and for nonstop commercials on radio stations.

Problems came along with fame. Lang almost found a site for the festival in Woodstock, but the owner backed out of the deal when the papers were delivered. After marching over dozens of fields in the foothills of the Catskill Mountains with a blank check in the bearskin medicine bag he wears, Mike picked a farm in Wallkill.

He signed the check—"I'm fantastic at spending bread," Mike says with a laugh—but he neglected to get all the right signatures from the town fathers. After Woodstock had invested hundreds of thousands of dollars in Wallkill—things like $18,000 for telephone lines—the angry Wallkill Concerned Citizens Committee finally drove the festival out. What the citizens were concerned enough to go to court about was an "invasion by 60,000 hippies." Little did they know.

On to Bethel and the 600-acre farm of Max Yasgur, a dairy farmer who has become a folk hero among youth simply because he was not hungup about long hair, weird clothes and young freaks. Yasgur got $50,000 for the use of his land but he, like John Roberts, thinks there was more to it all than cash—they both did something that made a lot of kids happy.

The move to Bethel, 70 miles northwest of New York City, began just four weeks before Aug. 15. The young promoters were desperate: They paid $65,000 for a $5-million insurance policy to cover local damage, and they lost at least $500,000 in duplicated expenses (it cost $20,000 for the Bethel telephone lines). They were hard hit by the inflated prices of Catskill bandits. The farmer who rented his $8,000 land for $5,000 and the grocer who charged $1 for a can of Pepsi are two local residents who want the festival back next year.

By then, late July, Woodstock and John Roberts were in a mudslide of trouble. Even with 1,000 paid employees, the stage was never finished—it had no roof. Two trailer trucks crammed with lighting equipment were parked alongside the stage, but their doors never opened. The New York Police Department ordered 350 officers hired as security guards not to work at Bethel. Although some cops ignored the order (festival officials swear the patrolmen who came were perpetually high on marijuana or whiskey), the chief security forces were 50 teen-age ushers from the Fillmore East, a Manhattan rock club, and 100 members of the Hog Farm, a New Mexico commune flown East in an airliner chartered for $16,000.

Although the Hog Farmers provided an oasis of organization in the gentle chaos of Bethel—they handed out free food to thousands and expertly "talked down" kids on bad LSD trips—some festival aides were dubious about calling them security officers. "They stole everything that wasn't nailed down," one man said. Roberts has no idea of who took what, but

he does say: "Everything was taken. The jackets we planned to sell, our walkie-talkies. Even the jeeps disappeared."

The lack of real security was one of the reasons that Roberts and others worried constantly about the potential for riot. Some of the production people on stage looked in awe at the crowd out there as a sleeping monster. "Those kids are going to snap," someone said. "They're going to realize that it's not really fun to slap, slap, slap through the mud; then they're going to rise up and kill us all."

But neither rain, nor garbage, nor Students for a Democratic Society could provoke the kids. S.D.S. and other radical groups, however, were paid well not to start trouble. Yippie leader Abbie Hoffman got $10,000 from Woodstock to set up a big tent as headquarters for assorted radicals. The one fistfight that almost started was stopped when people all around started talking about love and peace. One fighter, who thought his girl had been insulted, reacted to the talk by yelling, "Bull—." But he put down his fists when the crowd around him started chanting: "Bull—, bull—, bull—. . . ."

It's easy to imagine what this would have been like 10 years ago—it would have been impossible; youth wasn't a tribe then—the beer, the brawls, the retching, maybe even some rape. In 1969, there was none of that. The kids really wanted peace, their music and drugs. As long as the helicopters, some costing Roberts $500 an hour, could bring in the $250,000 worth of rocking talent, and as long as the dealers were selling ("Grass. Hash. Acid. Get your dope here"), there was no hassling.

Was it luck, love or drugs? Is this generation really different? Or are they the pioneers of Huxley's brave new world—a gram of *soma* is peace? That question came to my 32-year-old mind after I was finally convinced that almost every person there was using marijuana, at least. After the rains, matches were scarce, and I had the feeling that a man with a Zippo could be king of the grass-smokers.

But there was peace and fantastic harmony—a dozen hippies were draped on and in New York State Police Cruiser 6084 while a trooper happily directed traffic 10 feet away. That was one of John Robert's few consolations as he wrote out bad checks totaling $600,000 for the eight helicopters and the food and medicine that may have staved off the disaster he was afraid he had financed.

Roberts, a husky Jewish boy whom everyone calls "a sweetheart," was confused by a lot of what he saw. "To me," he said a week later, "this was a nightmare in many ways. I don't know much about drugs. Could this signal the dawning of some significant sociological change? I think I can understand this lifestyle. I might have done the same thing if I got out of college without money."

Later, he was talking about the possibility that the district attorney of Sullivan County would order a grand-jury investigation of the fair. (State Attorney General Louis J. Lefkowitz is considering whether Woodstock Ventures should be forced to pay refunds to people who bought tickets in advance but couldn't get to Bethel because of the traffic jams.)

"An investigation might be a good thing," Roberts said. "It would clear the air about a lot of what went on."

He is a terribly concerned and honorable young man. After the festival, he drained his personal bank accounts to pay cash to people—diner owners, for example—who had unpaid Woodstock bills and badly needed the money. In an interview with Alfred G. Aronowitz of The New York Post, Roberts talked about the checks he wrote over the weekend and said: "When I was in that office, the most important thing was not the money but those 60 vials of penicillin that the hospital needed

at the time. There's an old saying. You can lose your money a dozen times, but you can lose your name only once."

One thing that has kept Roberts going is the support of his father and family friends like Sonny Werblin, onetime president of MCA-TV and the New York Jets. "Dad came in like a white knight," the son said. "He may call me an idiot later, but now it's: 'What can I do?'" ("John will lose money on this one," Alfred Roberts said. "But he's bright and hardworking. He'll do all right.")

While John Roberts is picking up the pieces, Michael Lang is already moving forward. He's a big man now—the kids would say he's "heavy." He got what he wanted out of Woodstock. First, he got what the kids got: He was together with his tribe, and he found out it was a big tribe, a tribe that might be powerful enough to inherit the nation. He also got to carry John Roberts's checkbook, which he sometimes clutched under his bare arm, and he graciously stood still while N.B.C., C.B.S., Time, Life and Newsweek waited in line to hear him explain what was happening in the world. That's important to Mike, just as having his name listed above Roberts's on the festival program was important enough for him to call the publisher four times to make sure.

The last time I saw him, in front of the Plaza, Lang had just come from Madison Square Garden where he wants to produce a Thanksgiving Day rock concert with Roberts's backing. Then he started talking about next summer:

"I can't speak for the corporation. But I can personally guarantee that there will be another Woodstock festival. We'll have a bigger site next time—it's called America. I get excited when an idea is fresh." He added, "I get hits."

What's to be his next hit? "Television," he

answered. "I want to do a couple of television documentaries that really communicate."

Lang is, as Roberts said, a tremendously good salesman. He's been hustling since he was 16, when he left home—Avenue "P" in Bensonhurst, where his father is a heating contractor—to live in Greenwich Village.

What makes Mike run? His motivation, at least as some friends understand it, is almost super-American: He wants the freedom of the rich, freedom never again to worry about money, to have any luxury including Porches and Piper-Heidsieck, to hire your friends to work on a music festival. Part of that freedom is the privilege of giving. Lang made money in Florida (friends say his shop grossed at least $50,000 in six months) but he spent most of it buying food, clothes and lawyers for kids who got in trouble—sometimes drug trouble—around the shop. And people who know him are convinced that he was happy when Woodstock collapsed into a free concert—and that he never considered that the collapse might hurt Roberts or anyone else.

Lang's attitudes are significant because they are probably shared by many of the affluent white college kids who made up the bulk of the festival crowd. They're willing to work hard within the system—they go to Harvard, Lang works 20 hours a day—and they want the rewards, but they don't want the reward to be a suburban home. They want the freedom Lang has hustled for himself.

The kids wanted to sit in the mud like poor and pure savages so someone would notice them and say they were different, but they also wanted those 1969 cars they left strewn all over the Catskills. They want both. Maybe the rock musicians the kids watched were important because *they* have both—they would be picked up as vagrants in most American towns, but they make enough money to fly first class to Las Vegas or the Virgin Islands whenever the whim strikes.

That's the life-style of Mike Lang from Brooklyn. He had an idea—Woodstock—and probably a million kids tried to get there and share it with him. Now he was walking through the lobby of the Plaza Hotel in his muddy Indian suit, talking about what was happening, and I was writing it all down: "We're giving people a new head. . . . This generation, I hope, won't be pushed out by the next. We'll flow. . . . What we showed is that peace can't be enforced, it has to be allowed. . . . You can do it without drugs, but why should you?"

As he strolled through the lobby, a very small and old Plaza lady stopped in front of him with a little smile. She looked at the hair and the whole thing and said: "That's cute."

Look out, lady!

The Woodstock Festival

Greil Marcus

Greil Marcus, a former editor of *Rolling Stone* from 1969 to 1970, has also written for the *San Francisco Express Times* and the *New York Times.* He presently contributes articles to *Creem* and *Let It Rock.* A forthcoming book (1974) deals with images of America in rock 'n' roll. Mr. Marcus is the editor of the book *Rock and Roll Will Stand* and the coauthor of *Double Feature.*

It was Sunday afternoon and Joe Cocker and the Grease Band had finished their power-house set and suddenly the sky turned black and everyone knew it was going to rain again. It did. The ground on which two or three hundred thousand kids were sitting was begging to be turned back into mud and it got its wish and it couldn't have mattered less to anyone. The wind hit, then, too; it seemed to come from some half-forgotten Biblical apocalypse but no one was ready for the Last Judgment so we turned calamity into celebration.

"Cut the power, cut the power," they shouted on stage, and the kids yelled "Fuck the rain, fuck the rain," but it was really just another chance for a new kind of fun. Odd gifts of the elements, our own latter-day saints appeared out of nowhere. In front of the bandstand a black boy and a white boy took off their clothes and danced in the mud and the rain, round and round in a circle that grew larger as more joined them.

Moon Fire, a kindly warlock, preached to a small crowd that had gathered under the stage for shelter. A tall man with red-brown hair and shining eyes, barefoot and naked under his robes, he had traveled to the festival with his lover, a sheep ("call her 'Sunshine' if you're a vegetarian, 'Chops' if you're not," he said.) Off in a corner was his staff, topped by a human skull, the pole bearing his message: "Don't Eat Animals, Love Them/the

Killing of Animals Creates the Killing of Men." He carefully explained how sheep were blessed with the greatest capacity for love of all animals, how a sheep could actually conceive by a man, though, tragically, perhaps because of some forgotten curse, the offspring was doomed to die at birth. Albert Grossman, his pigtail soaking wet, was standing nearby and Moon Fire ambled over to lay on his blessing. Grossman dug it. Rain simply meant it was a good time to meet new people.

The rain had been coming down for a long time now, but it seemed safe, and the stage crew put on a record. Creedence Clearwater's "Born on the Bayou" went soaring out of the great sound system and over the enormous crowd and suddenly the Battle of the Bands of the night before had turned into American Bandstand. Three hundred thousand people jumped up out of the mud and started to dance. Bopping their bodies and shaking their hair to the beat, hopping over and into the new puddles of garbage and mud.

The crush of more than a quarter of a million people *sitting down* had been some sight, but this was almost more than anyone could believe. Frisbees began to sail out of the crowd toward the stage and the sound men jumped forward to throw them back. Then a football, then oranges, sandwiches, whatever was close at hand and friendly to throw at other people.

Country Joe and the Fish had been scheduled to go on next and Barry Melton cornered the head man and announced that the band wanted to play. "You can't play *now,* you'll all get electrocuted!" "We wanna play, man, we wanna play now, we don't need electricity." "They want to play," said one staffer to another. "*You* tell them they can't. Not me." The Fish played. In pouring down rain, good old never-say-die-and-never-down Country Joe and the Fish got up and pantomimed their music for the crowd that had turned them on. Barry grabbed a mike with no cord and Mark Kapner hoisted his little ukelele and Joe handled the footballs that kept bouncing onto the stage. Greg Dewey, their new drummer, brought out his kit and sat down and pounded out a loud, fast, dancing drum solo that kept the audience moving and grooving. It was certainly the only drum solo I've ever dug, and by the time three or four others had joined Dewey on his cymbals he was into it all the way, a musician making music for the people out front.

A tall fellow jumped on stage and began to dance across the boards while everyone cheered. Then he flashed and pulled off his pants and danced naked in the rain, grinning wildly, holding out his arms in a big gesture of welcome. Someone passed a bottle of champagne into the audience and then all the food that could be found on stage, and the Fish kept on playing and Joe kept on smiling. They reminded me of the brave rodeo clowns that run into the pit when a rider's hurt and the bull's ready to trample him. They came through. But nobody was scared.

THE LAST TRAFFIC JAM

Friday was the first day of the Woodstock Music and Arts Fair, now moved to White Lake near Bethel, N.Y., a hundred miles from New York City and fifty miles from Wood-stock proper. The intrepid ROLLING STONE crew thought it would be bright to beat the traffic, so we left the city early in the morning and headed up. When we got to Monticello, a little town eight miles from the festival, the traffic had been light. Then we hit it. Eight miles of two-lane road jammed with thousands of cars that barely moved. Engines boiling over, people collapsed on the side of the road, everyone smiling in a common bewilderment.

Automotive casualties looked like the skeletons of horses that died on the Oregon Trail. People began to improvise, driving on soft shoulders until they hit the few thousand who'd thought of the same thing, then stopping again. Finally the two lanes were transformed into four and still nothing moved. Fat, bulbous vacationers (for this was Jewishland, the Catskills, laden with chopped liver and bad comedians) stared at the cars and the freaks and the nice kids, their stomachs sticking out into the road. It was a combination of *Weekend* and *Goodbye Columbus.* Here we were, trying to get to the land of Hendrix and the Grateful Dead, all the while under the beady eyes of Montovani fans.

There wasn't any traffic control. We sat still in our car and figured out all sorts of brilliant solutions to the transportation problem, everything from one-way roads to hired buses (a plan that failed at the last minute) but we still weren't getting anywhere and it had been four hours now. This was the road on the map, right? No other way to get there? A lot of kids were pulling over and starting to walk through the fields. Beat-out kids heading back told us nothing moved up ahead and that we had six miles to go. It was a cosmic traffic jam, where all the cars fall into place like pieces in a jigsaw puzzle and stay there forever.

The police estimated that there were a million people on the road that day, trying to get to the festival. A million people. 186,000 tickets had been sold and the promoters figured that maybe 200,000 tops would show. That seemed outlandish, if believable. But no one was prepared for what happened, and no one could have been.

Perhaps a quarter of a million never made it. They gave up and turned back, or parked on the highway and set up tents on the divider strip and stuck it out. Shit, they'd come to camp out for three days and they were gonna do it. Many had walked fifteen miles in the rain and the mud, only to give up a mile or so before the festival and turn back, but they were having fun. Camped on the highway with no idea where White Lake was or what was going on, they were digging it, making friends, dancing to car radios and making their own music on their own guitars.

"Isn't it pretty here, all the trees and the meadows? And whenever it gets too hot it rains and cools everyone off. Wow." "Yeah, sure, but you paid eighteen dollars and drove all the way from Ohio and you can't even get to the festival. Aren't you disappointed? Or pissed off?" "No, man. Everyone is so friendly, it's like being stuck in an elevator with people when the power goes off. But it's much nicer here than in an elevator."

It was an amazing sight, the highway to White Lake: it looked, as someone said, like Napoleon's army retreating from Moscow. It looked like that for three days. Everywhere one saw tents and campfires, cars rolled into ditches, people walking, lying down, drinking, eating, reading, singing. Kids were sleeping, making love, wading in the marshes, trying to milk the local cows and trying to cook the local corn. The army of New York State Quickway 17B was on maneuvers.

A VIEW OF THE SECOND DAY

Thinking back to Saturday, one image sticks in my mind, an image that I doubt is shared by many but one that I will never forget. Friday night the folk music had been played, Joe Baez, Arlo Guthrie, Sweetwater and Ravi Shankar, but by the next morning the future was unclear and rumors that the area had been declared an official disaster seemed quite credible. Many left Saturday morning, oppressed by water shortages and ninety degree heat and ninety-nine percent humidity and the crush of bodies.

"I love all these people," said a young girl, "they're all beautiful, and I never thought I'd be hassled by so many beautiful people, but I am, and I'm going home." Faces were drawn and tired, eyes blank, legs moving slowly on blisters and sore feet. The lack of water, food, and toilets was becoming difficult, though everyone shared, and many simply roamed the area with provisions with the sole purpose of giving them away. But it got hotter and hotter and a boy was running toward the lake in panic, cradling his little puppy in his arms. The dog was unconscious, its tongue out of its mouth but not moving. The boy thought the dog was going to die, and he was scared. He kept running and I stared after him and then I left the festival and decided to go home. I couldn't get a plane and I was lucky to stay, but that dreadful scene was real and it too was part of the festival at White Lake.

CROSBY-STILLS-NASH & YOUNG

Everyone in the country has seen pictures of the crowd. Was it bigger than it looked? Whoever saw so many people in the same spot with the same idea? Well, Hitler did, and General MacArthur, and Mao, but this was a somewhat better occasion. They came to hear the music and they stayed to dig the scene and the people and the countryside, and at any time, no matter who was playing, one could see thousands moving in every direction and more camped on every hill and all through the woods. The music became something that was going on there, and it was terrific, but it was by no means the whole show. The magnificent sound system was clear and audible long past the point at which one could no longer see the bands, and some were discussing the bass player in Janis' band even though they hadn't the slightest idea of what he looked like.

The reader will be spared a careful, critical analysis of the performance of each group and of the validity and impact of their sound, music, stage show, and demeanor. The outstanding thing was the unthinkable weight of the groups that played. Take Saturday night and Sunday morning (the music was scheduled to begin at one in the afternoon and run for twelve hours, but it began at three or four and went until the middle of the next morning). Here's the line-up: Joe Cocker, Country Joe and the Fish, Ten Years After, the Band, Johnny Winter, Blood Sweat & Tears, Crosby-Stills-Nash & Young, the Butterfield Blues Band, Sha Na Na . . . and Jimi Hendrix. It's like watching God perform the Creation, "And, for My next number . . ."

The scene on stage Sunday night was a curious one. Three groups were hanging out there, performing, setting up, digging the other musicians: the Band, Blood Sweat & Tears, and Paul Butterfield. Now there was no doubt that in terms of prestige the Band was king that night, to the other musicians if not to the audience. As Helm, Danko and Robertson sat on amplifiers, listening to Johnny Winter, stars of the past and the present came over to say hello, to introduce themselves, to pay their artistic respects. David Clayton-Thomas, the young Canadian lead singer for BS&T, flashed a big grin and shook hands vigorously—a man on the way up, his group outselling everyone in the country and impressing the audience far more than the Band did that night, but still very much in the shadow of the men from Big Pink who play real music that comes out of real history.

And then Paul Butterfield came over. Regardless of what one may think of the quality or the relevance of Butterfield's music in the year 1969, his impact on rock and roll is incalculable and he is very much a father of the modern scene, as crucial to the emergence of San Francisco or Bob Dylan as anyone in the country. Butterfield's first band and his first records broke down the doors and brought hundreds of musicians that are now famous into the light, and if his star has faded now and his albums sell only moderately, the jovial respect the Band showed him that night was simply more proof of his dignity. He's a dignified fellow—black tie shoes, beat-up jacket, his hair cut in the style of Chicago's hillbilly-ghetto. He was, in fact, the only bluesman on the stage, and the way he carried himself provided a sense of what that word really means.

Some time around four in the morning the stage crew began to assemble the apparatus for the festival's most unknown quantity. Crosby-Stills-Nash & Young. This was not exactly their debut—they'd played once or twice before, but this was a national audience, both in terms of the factual composition of the crowd and the press and because of the amazing musical competition with which they were faced. They followed the Band, Winter, and Blood Sweat & Tears.

It took a very long time to get everything ready, and the people on stage crowded around the amplifiers and the nine or ten guitars and the chairs and mikes and the organ, more excited in anticipation than they'd been for any other group that night. A large semi-circle of equipment protected the musicians from the rest of the people. The band was very nervous—Neil Young stalking around, kissing his wife, trying to tune his guitar off in a corner, kissing his wife again, staring off away from the crowd. Stills and Nash paced back and forth and tested the organ and the mikes and drummer Dallas Taylor fiddled with his kit and kept trying to make it more than perfect. Finally they went on.

Crosby Stills and Nash opened with "Judy Blue Eyes," stretching it out for a long time exploring the figures of the song for the crowd, making their quiet music and flashing grimaces at each other when something went wrong. They strummed and picked their way through other numbers, and then began to shift around, Crosby singing with Stills, then Nash and Crosby, back and forth. They had the crowd all the way. Many have remarked that their music is perfect, but sterile; that night it wasn't quite perfect and it was anything but sterile. They seemed like several bands rather than one.

After perhaps half an hour Neil Young made his way into the band and sat down with Steve Stills, and the two of them combined for an extraordinary acoustic version of "Mr. Soul." Stills pushed stinging blues out of his guitar and Young's singing was as disturbing and compelling as ever. And from that point they just took off. They switched to rock and roll and a grateful electricity—Nash, Stills, Crosby and/or Young on guitar, Young and Stills trading off on organ, and two terrific sidemen, Dallas Taylor on drums and Greg Reeves on bass.

Visually they are one of the most exciting bands I have ever seen, the six of them. David Crosby finally looks exactly like Buffalo Bill, his flowing hair and twisted moustaches twirling in the lights. Steve Stills, from Canada, . . . seemed as Californian as a beach boy, with page-boy blonde hair, a Mexican serape fitting the Baja Peninsula groove he's so fond of. Graham Nash appeared as one of these under-nourished-in-childhood English kids, weighing in at maybe seventy-five pounds, and Neil Young, as usual, looked like a photo from Agee's *Let Us Now Praise Famous Men,* dust bowl gothic, huge bones hung with very little

flesh, all shaped by those odd, piercing eyes that have warmth even as they show fear. And Taylor! This is a drummer. He plays his stuff like P. J. Proby sings, shaking his head wildly, the most cataclysmic drummer I've ever seen. Well, they hit it. Right into "Long Time Gone," a song for a season if there ever was one, Stills on organ, shouting out the choruses, Neil snapping out lead, Crosby aiming his electric twelve-string out over the edge of the stage, biting off his words and stretching them out, those lyrics that are as strong as any we are likely to hear:

> *There's something, something, something*
> *Goin' on arrrround here*
> *That surely, surely, surely*
> *Won't stand*
> *The light of day*
> *Oooohhhh!*
> *And it appears to be a long time . . .*

I have never seen a musician more involved in his music. At one point Crosby nearly fell off the stage in his excitement.

Deep into the New York night they were, early Sunday morning in the dark after three days of chaos and order, and it seemed like the last of a thousand and one American nights. Two hundred thousand people covered the hills of a great natural amphitheatre, campfires burning in the distance, the lights shining down from the enormous towers onto the faces of the band. Crosby Stills Nash & Young were just one of the many at this festival, and perhaps they wouldn't top the bill if paired with Hendrix or the Airplane or Creedence Clearwater or the Who or the Band, but this was their night. Their performance was a scary brilliant proof of the magnificence of music, and I don't believe it could have happened with such power anywhere else. This was a festival that had triumphed over itself, as Crosby and his band led the way toward the end of it.

THE TRANSFIGURATION OF BLIND JOE WOODSTOCK

The big cliché of the festival, heard more before it began than afterwards, came down to this: If Monterey was the beginning, Woodstock was the end. Al Aronowitz, writing in the New York Post, spoke for many when he called the festival "a wake." But Woodstock/ White Lake was not a wake, but rather a confused, chaotic founding of something new, something our world must now find a way to deal with. The limits have changed now, they've been pushed out, the priorities have been re-arranged, and new, "impractical" ideas must be taken seriously. The mind boggles.

The festival constituted the third largest city in the state of New York. To call it *over* was like saying that the entire population of Minneapolis had to pack up and leave, right now. To convey the meaning of it one must chase after ultimately useless metaphors about stars in the sky or the people in China. Well, if you laid 'em all in a line, they'd reach around the equator five times. Got it? But everyone there was a rock and roll fan and knew how to dance and had their favorite groups and called out for their favorite songs. People just like those everyone hangs out with, but this time it seemed as if they were all in one place at one time. They weren't though—not yet.

The logistical problems we will have to face in the coming rock and roll years are at bottom emotional ones. There were hundreds of thousands of people, over-flowing toilets, garbage and not enough food mainly because the music is exciting and because the kind of life one could live for a few days up in the Catskills is more attractive to huge numbers of kids and retreating adults than any other mode of existence.

Janis Joplin and Creedence Clearwater are more important than most would have guessed not because they carry some arcane political message but because when people hear them they get excited and ecstatic and feel more alive. This feeling is one that people *must* have, and to achieve that feeling hundreds of thousands will endure all sorts of privations and sufferings that they would consider intolerable in the ordinary circumstances of city or suburbia. And the music and those who perform for the huge crowds are now so well established, so impressive and so magnificent that those who come to hear and see no longer have to vent their frustrations or their anger on each other, but rather the people can now take the stars as benchmarks and move out to close frontiers and build their own instant communities—for a weekend, for a few days, they can live on their own terms with no thought of rebellion.

I think this is an important point. At the festival thousands were able to do things that would ordinarily be considered rebellious, in the terms of whatever current nonsensical sociological theory one might want to embrace. Selling and using all kinds of dope, balling here, there, and everywhere, swimming, canoeing or running around naked, and, believe it or not, *staying up all night*—one could do all of these things simply because they were fun to do, not because such acts represented scoring points against parents or Richard Nixon or Readers' Digest.

The Woodstock festival provided a setting and a context in which all these things and many more were natural, seductive, and obvious. The now famous Dope Supermarket is a case in point. Off in the woods, on the crossroads of "Groovy Way" and "Gentle Path," right next to an over-priced bead shop, a dozen dope dealers called out for their wares. "Hash? Acid? *Really* good mescaline?" "Who's got opium?" "He does, he does, the cat in the red jacket." "Who's got grass?" "One lid left, man, come an' get it." And on and on and on.

R. Crumb's dream come true. It was an amazing spectacle simply because it made so much sense—lot of people wanted the stuff so a central trading post had been set up where everything was available.

A photographer came by. "Hey," yelled the guy with the opium, "take *my* picture." There was no sense of cheating the cops out of a bust. Kids who had their first taste of dope or sex or nudity at Woodstock might remember later that these were acts that at least *somebody* thought were wrong, but at the festival it was as natural as cruising Main Street or catching a subway.

This is not to say that repression has vanished overnight, or vanished at all, but rather that the festival created and provided a place of freedom. The promoters laid the roads and brought in the music and built a Babylonian hanging garden sound system and the kids did the rest. The problem now is to find a way for such festivals to continue, with a clear knowledge that the audience *cannot* be limited by sales of tickets or by anything else.

We could cut back. We could have festivals with one or two "headliners" instead of festivals where everyone and no one is a headliner; we could categorize it, with "folk festivals" and "jazz festivals" and "blues festivals" and local festivals. All of these possibilities are good ones and all will take place, but after Woodstock they have to be seen, at least to some extent, as mere devices for holding down the number of people who will want to be there. . . .

Woodstock initiated all-night concerts with a staggering line-up of bands—a truly national festival, a hemispheric one, really, since Canada contributed much of the best. Great music from afternoon to morning, just like concerts in India, except here one could see virtually everyone and all at once. One could sit and dig the finest groups in the world, and if Ike and Tina and B. B. King and Aretha and

Sam and Dave and Blind Faith weren't there, they will be, and if Bob Dylan and the Stones and the Beatles weren't there, they will be, if such a festival can be held again, and again.

The logistical problems are the minor ones. Everyone knows by now that the people must be bussed in from satellite parking lots; that the festival should last a week—perhaps two or three days before and after each main concert; that there should be two or three stages instead of one, with entertainment taking place simultaneously on each of them. And garbage and water and food and so on. These problems are minor not because it will not take tremendous effort to deal with them but because they are essentially simple. The true problem is the audience.

All over the nation and the world kids are moving to rock and roll. It's the most important thing in their lives. Janis Joplin's new album is more important than landing on the moon. If two thirds of the country can watch the moon landing then some equivalent production must take place to allow the rockers to hear rock and roll. Plan a festival like Woodstock for 150,000 and you get nearly a million. Plan next year for a million and you'll get ten million. And plan and plan and plan and you'll go deeper and deeper into the hole. Ticket sales will not do it. Getting the bands to play for free will not do it. We are, for better or for worse, beyond those sorts of solutions. We also cannot revert to electrified fences, police dogs, tear gas, and the rest of the contemporary American paraphernalia in an attempt to keep the "legitimate" audience separate from the rest of the rock and roll population.

Probably an attempt will have to be made to get the record companies to finance the next national festival, whether it's held in Woodstock, Mill Valley, or Toronto. It has to be considered in the same light as the Olympic Games, which is exactly what this festival was, yet more like the Games of 2500 years ago than those of today. If we cut back, if we cut back to a festival that is really little more than three bills from the Fillmore East sandwiched together, then we will also be cutting off the greatest possibilities of rock and roll.

Three hundred thousand people taking whatever went down all around them and a new challenge to their guts and their ingenuity,

sitting on a great hill all through the night to hear their favorites play and play and play, working for *them,* making new discoveries about each other and the land day after day, digging it, now Janis! Sly Stone! The Airplane! The Dead! The Who! The Band! Hendrix— this is just the beginning—or the end—and we must now sit down and figure out how to make it work.

The Woodstock Music and Art Fair
Andrew Kopkind

Andrew Kopkind wrote extensively on Vietnam and other topical subjects as an editor for the *New Republic.* He is a founding editor of *Hard Times,* a radical, muckraking journal, originally published under the name *Mayday.*

The Woodstock Music and Art Fair wasn't held in Woodstock; the music was secondarily important and the art was for the most part unproduced; and it was as much of a fair as the French Revolution or the San Francisco earthquake. What went down on Max Yasgur's farm in the low Catskills last weekend defied categories and conventional perceptions. Some monstrous and marvelous metaphor had come alive, revealing itself only in terms of its contradictions: paradise and concentration camp, sharing and profiteering, sky and mud, love and death. The urges of the ten years' generation roamed the woods and pastures, and who could tell whether it was rough beast or speckled bird slouching towards its Day-Glo manger to be born?

The road from the Hudson River west to White Lake runs through hills like green knishes, soft inside with good earth, and crusty with rock and wood on top. What works of man remain are rural expressions of an Other East Village, where the Mothers were little

old ladies with sheitls, not hip radicals with guns. There's Esther Manor and Siegel's Motor Court and Elfenbaum's Grocery: no crash communes or head shops. Along that route, a long march of freaks in micro-buses, shitcars and bikes—or on thumb and foot—passed like movie extras in front of a process screen. On the roadside, holiday-makers from the Bronx looked up from their pinochle games and afghan-knitting and knew that the season of the witch had come.

"Beatniks out to make it rich": Woodstock was, first of all, an environment created by a couple of hip entrepreneurs to consolidate the cultural revolution and (in order?) extract the money of its troops. Michael Lang, a 25-year-old former heavy dealer from Bensonhurst dreamed it up; he then organized the large inheritance of John Roberts, 26, for a financial base, and brought in several more operatives and financiers. Lang does not distinguish between hip culture and hip capital; he vowed to make a million before he was 25, beat his deadline by two years, and didn't stop. With his Village/Durango clothes, a white Porsche and a gleaming BSA he looks, acts, and *is* hip; his interest in capital accumulation is an extension of every hippie's desire to rip off a bunch of stuff from the A&P. It's a gas.

The place-name "Woodstock" was meant only to evoke cultural-revolutionary images of Dylan, whose home base is in that Hudson River village. Woodstock is where the Band hangs out and the culture heroes congregate; it's where Mick Jagger (they say) once ate an acid-infused Baby Ruth right inside the crotch of a famous groupie. A legend like that is good for ticket sales, but the festival was always meant to be held in Wallkill, 40 miles away.

By early summer, Woodstock looked to be the super rock festival of all time, and promoters of a dozen other summertime festivals were feverishly hyping up their own projects to catch the overflow of publicity and enthusiasm: Rock music (al fresco or recorded) is still one of the easiest ways to make money off of the new culture, along with boutique clothes and jewelry, posters, drugs and trip-equipment, Esquire magazine, Zig-Zag papers and Sara Lee cakes. But the Woodstock hype worried the burghers of Wallkill, and the law implemented their fears by kicking the bash out of town. Other communities, however, were either less uptight or more greedy; six hard offers for sites came to the promoters the day Wallkill gave them the boot. With less than a month to get ready, Woodstock Ventures, Inc., chose the 600-acre Yasgur farm (with some other parcels thrown in) at White Lake, N.Y.

Locals there were divided on the idea, and Yasgur was attacked by some neighbors for renting (for a reported $50,000) to Woodstock. But in the end, the profit motive drove the deal home. One townsman wrote to the Monticello newspaper: "It's none of their business how Max uses his land. If they are so worried about Max making a few dollars from his land they should try to take advantage of this chance to make a few dollars themselves. They can rent camping space or even sell water or lemonade." Against fears of hippie horrors, businessmen set promises of rich rewards: "Some of these people are shortsighted and don't understand what these children are doing," one said. "The results will bring an economic boost to the County, without it costing the taxpayer a cent."

The vanguard of freaks started coming a week or more before opening day, and by Wednesday, they were moving steadily down Route 17-B, like a busy day on the Ho Chi Minh Trail. The early-comers were mostly hard-core, permanent dropouts: Their hair or their manner or their rap indicated that they had long ago dug into their communes or radical politics or simply into oppositional life-styles. In the cool and clear night they played music and danced, and sat around fires toasting joints and smoking hashish on a pinpoint. No busts, pigs or hassle; everything cool, together, outasight.

By the end of the next day, Thursday, the ambience had changed from splendor in the grass to explosive urban sprawl. Light and low fences erected to channel the crowds without actually seeming to oppress them were toppled or ignored; cars and trucks bounced over the meadows; tents sprung up between stone outcroppings and cow plop. Construction went on through the night, and already the Johnny-on-the-Spot latrines were smelly and out of toilet paper, the food supply was spotty, and long lines were forming at the water tank. And on Friday morning, when the population explosion was upon us all, a sense of siege took hold: Difficult as it was to get in, it would be almost impossible to leave for days.

From the beginning, the managers of the

festival were faced with the practical problem of control. Berkeley and Chicago and Zap, N.D., were the functional models for youth mobs rampaging at the slightest provocation— or no provocation at all. The promoters interviewed 800 off-duty New York City policemen for a security guard (Sample question: "What would you do if a kid walked up and blew marijuana smoke in your face?" Incorrect answer: "Bust him." Correct answer: "Inhale deeply and smile."), chose 300 or so, and fitted them with mod uniforms. But at the last minute they were withdrawn under pressure from the Police Department, and the managers had to hire camp counselors, phys ed teachers and stray straights from the surrounding area.

The guards had no license to use force or arrest people; they merely were to be "present," in their red Day-Glo shirts emblazoned with the peace symbol, and could direct traffic and help out in emergencies if need be. The real work of keeping order, if not law, was to be done by members of the Hog Farm commune, who had been brought from New Mexico, along with people from other hippie retreats, in a chartered airplane (at $16,000) and psychedelic buses from Kennedy Airport.

Beneath the practical problem of maintaining order, was the principal contradiction of the festival: how to stimulate the energies of the new culture and profit thereby, and at the same time control them. In a way, the Woodstock venture was a test of the ability of avant-garde capitalism at once to profit from and control the insurgencies which its system spawns. "Black capitalism," the media industry, educational technology, and Third World economic development are other models, but more diffuse. Here it was in one field during one weekend: The microcosmic system would "fail" if Woodstock Ventures lost its shirt, or if the control mechanisms broke down.

The promoters must have sensed the responsibility they carried. They tried every aspect of cooptation theory. SDS, Newsreel and underground newspapers were handed thousands of dollars to participate in the festival, and they were given a choice spot for a "Movement City"; the idea was that they would give hip legitimacy to the weekend and channel their activities "within the system." (They bought the idea.) Real cops were specifically barred from the camp grounds, and the word went out that there would be no busts for ordinary tripping, although big dealers were discouraged. There would be free food, water, camping facilities—and, in the end, free music, when attempts at crowd-channeling failed. But the Hog Farmers were the critical element. Hip beyond any doubt, they spread the love/groove ethic throughout the farm, breaking up incipient actions against "the system" with cool, low-key hippie talk about making love not war, the mystical integrity of earth, and the importance of doing your own thing, preferably alone. On the other hand—actually, on the same hand—they were the only good organizers in camp. They ran the free food operation (oats, rice and bulgar), helped acid-freaks through bad trips without Thorazine, and (with Abbie Hoffman) ran the medical system when that became necessary.

The several dozen Movement organizers at the festival had nothing to do. After Friday night's rain there was a theory that revolt was brewing on a mass scale, but the SDS people found themselves unable to organize around the issue of inclement weather. People were objectively trapped; and in that partial aspect, the Yasgur farm was a concentration camp—or a hippie reservation—but almost everyone was stoned and happy. Then the rain stopped, the music blared, food and water arrived, and everyone shared what he had. Dope became plentiful and entirely legitimate; in a soft cool forest, where craftsmen had set up their portable headshops, dealers sat on tree stumps selling their wares: "acid, mesc, psilo-cybin, hash. . . " No one among the half-million could not have turned on if he wanted to; joints were passed from blanket to blanket, lumps of hash materialized like manna, and there was Blue Cheer, Sunshine acid, and pink mescaline to spare.

Seen from any edge or angle, the army strung out against the hillside sloping up from the stage created scenes almost unimaginable in commonplace terms. No day's demonstra-tion or political action had brought these troops together; no congress or cultural event before produced such urgent need for in-gathering and self-inspection. The ambiguities and contradictions of the imposed environment were worrisome; but to miss the exhilaration of a generation's arrival at its own campsite was to define the world in only one dimension.

Although the outside press saw only masses, inside the differentiation was more impressive. Maybe half the crowd was weekend-hip, out from Long Island for a quick dip in the compel-ling sea of freaks. The other half had longer been immersed. It was composed of tribes dedicated to whatever gods now seem effec-tive and whatever myths produce the energy needed to survive: Meher Baba, Mother Earth, street-fighting man, Janis Joplin, Atlantis, Jimi Hendrix, Che.

The hillside was their home. Early Saturday morning, after the long night of rain—from Ravi Shankar through Joan Baez—they still had not abandoned the turf. Twenty or forty thousand people (exactitude lost its mean-ing: it was that sight, not the knowledge of the numbers that was so staggering) sat stonily silent on the muddy ground, staring at a stage where no one played: petrified playgoers in the marble stands at Epidaurus, thousands of years after the chorus had left for the last time.

No one in this country in this century had ever seen a "society" so free of repression. Everyone swam nude in the lake, balling was easier than getting breakfast, and the "pigs" just smiled and passed out the oats. For people who had never glimpsed the intense communi-tarian struggle—People's Park or Paris in the month of May or Cuba—Woodstock must al-ways be their model of how good we will all feel after the revolution.

So it was an illusion and it wasn't. For all but the hard core, the ball and the balling is over; the hassles begin again at Monticello. The repression-free weekend was provided by promoters as a way to increase their take, and it will not be repeated unless future profits are guaranteed (it's almost certain now that Woodstock Ventures lost its wad). The media nonsense about death and O.D.'s has already enraged the guardians of the old culture. The system didn't change; it just accommodated the freaks for the weekend.

What is not illusionary is the reality of a new culture of opposition. It grows out of the disintegration of the old forms, the vinyl and aerosol institutions that carry all the inane and destructive values of privatism, competi-tion, commercialism, profitability and elitism. The new culture has yet to produce its own institutions on a mass scale; it controls none of the resources to do so. For the moment, it must be content—or discontent—to feed the swinging sectors of the old system with new ideas, with rock and dope and love and open-ness. Then it all comes back, from Columbia Records or Hollywood or Bloomingdale's in perverted and degraded forms. But some-thing will survive, because there's no drug on earth to dispel the nausea. It's not a "youth thing" now but a generational event; chrono-logical age is only the current phase. Mass politics, it's clear, can't yet be organized around the nausea; political radicals have to see the cultural revolution as a sea in which they can swim, like black militants in "black culture." But the urges are roaming, and when the dope freaks and nude swimmers and love-niks and ecological cultists and music groovers find out they have to fight for love, all fucking hell will break loose.

The Protest to End Protests: Mayday in Washington

It all began in 1963 with the March on Washington for Jobs and Freedom organized by Bayard Rustin and A. Philip Randolph to gain support for the administration's civil rights bill. From then on, few events in the 1960s were as predictable as a protest march in the Capital. By the end of the decade the marches were occurring at the rate of one a year. 1967: the march on the Pentagon to protest the Vietnam war. 1968: Resurrection City and the Poor People's Solidarity Day March. 1969: Moratorium Day and the March against Death.

In size the marches were impressive. At the first March on Washington an estimated 200,000 people heard Martin Luther King deliver his "I Have a Dream" speech. At the Moratorium Day rally six years later, more than 500,000 gathered to protest the Vietnam War. For those who had never before made their feelings public or who were politically isolated in the communities where they lived, the marches were especially valuable. But they also had an effect on whatever administration was in power. Any politician knew that if thousands of people took the trouble to come to Washington for a day, thousands more shared their views. By the start of the 1970s the impact of the marches on Washington had begun to decline, however. The sight of angry protestors filling the streets of the Capital was now a familiar one, and the marches had become increasingly self-contained with the converted speaking to the converted rather than addressing the "silent majority" they needed to reach.

Against this background the 1971 Mayday demonstrations were called as a protest to end protests. Geared for civil disruption, they were a revolt against past demonstrations and their domination by people whom Russell Baker of the *New York Times* once described as a "vast army of quiet, middle-class Americans who had come in the spirit of a church outing." The organizers of the Mayday protest believed the time for orderly demonstrations was over and that the course the country was following at home and in Vietnam required tactics that did not rely on conventional political protest. As I. F. Stone wrote in his *Weekly,* the question the Mayday organizers sought to pose as dramatically as possible was, "Will you be a good German and look the other way?"

The Mayday protest—its symbol was Gandhi sitting cross-legged with a raised fist—was designed to bring Washington to a halt through nonviolent disruption. Mayday began, however, not in May, but on April 24 with a mass rally, followed by a "People's Lobby" directed by the National Action Group April 26–30. Each day the People's Lobby went to a different government office and tried to persuade federal employees to join the protests scheduled for May 3–5. It was not until Saturday, May 1, that a serious confrontation between the police and the Maydayers occurred. Following a rock concert in West Potomac Park, the police revoked the camping privileges they had extended the Maydayers, and by Sunday more than 30,000 demonstrators had left town. Monday morning it was a thinned-out crowd that began trying to shut down Washington by traveling in small "affinity groups" and blocking bridges and traffic arteries. In general the Maydayers were unsuccessful, but whether they would have had much better results with a larger crowd is difficult to say. The police countered Mayday with dragnet operations that swept anyone off the street who looked as if he were going to cause trouble. By the end of Monday, 8,000 had been arrested. After demonstrations Tuesday at the Justice Department, and Wednesday at the Congress, the figure reached 14,000. Few attempts were made by D.C. police to follow standard arrest procedures, and when the jails became crowded, demonstrators were put in pens set up for the occasion.

The stories that follow detail what it felt like to be caught up in the Mayday events. But more than that, they struggle with the question of whether Mayday—in view of its stated aim of stopping the government if the government didn't stop the war—was a success or a failure. No one pursues this question more strikingly than Nicholas von Hoffman in the three columns he did on Mayday for the *Washington Post.* Von Hoffman's account begins with a description of the Marines at the Washington Monument that reads like a Vietnam dispatch. "The Marines were securing the Washington Monument and turning it into Firebase Martha; there were troops on the bridges across the Potomac," are the first lines of his story. But the parody is a serious one. For von Hoffman finds the government response to Mayday similar to its actions in Vietnam. He is not concerned with the failure of the Maydayers to bring Washington to a halt. What he thinks important is that the demonstrations escalated the level of protest against the Vietnam War. "It is very hard for respectable, working and shaving doves to understand that their real leaders are the freaks and the crazies," he writes. "Yet it is so and has been throughout the development of this most unusual of American social movements. What the freaks say today the respectables will say in about a year."

The next two accounts of Mayday focus on the impact made by specific groups of protestors. For Dotson Rader in his "One Weekend in May" the real heroes of Maydays are "kids who never attended organizational meetings, who did not know Tom Hayden from Tom Jones, who were ignorant of the history and the polemic of the left, but who were . . . on our side." He admits their lack of discipline was one of the reasons the disruptions failed tactically, but he thinks this failure far less significant than the kids' ability to change the antiwar movement from a protest with "vertical command and decision structures" to one with a "highly collectivistic, communalistic yet anarchical attitude which rejects traditional leadership concepts." "It is their incredible energy and glee, the simple-mindedness of their politics . . . that will end this war and the pernicious social, political, and economic arrangement which wages it," Rader concludes.

By contrast, Robin Reisig in her "The Vets and Mayday" pins her hopes on the veterans who came to Washington to protest the war. The time period she describes is the People's Lobby Week, when the Vets staged operation Dewey Canyon III, in which they carried out a simulated "search and destroy" mission among Washington citizens, shouting at them in a strange language (Vietnamese) and pretending to shoot them when they failed to obey an order. Reisig sees the Vets with their bitterness over the war, the willingness of 800 of them to throw their medals in a trash barrel set up in front of the Capitol, and their testimony before the Senate Foreign Relations Committee having a far more powerful effect than protestors without their experience. No passage in her account is more revealing than her description of a demonstration organized by the vets. "There were the usual marchers chanting 'Ho! Ho! Ho Chi Minh! The NLF is gonna win!' Only this time the men chanting were 'Active Duty GIs.' There were the usual hardhat-looking types who in the past have heckled and hit demonstrators. Only this time, the burly, short-haired men in teamsters jackets were parade marshals, guarding the demonstrators." In all the accounts of Mayday, the kind of harmony between disparate groups is rarely present.

The reason why this harmony was so rare is examined in Michael P.

Lerner's "Mayday: Anatomy of the Movement," in which the internal politics of Mayday are discussed. Lerner traces the divisions within the organizational structure of Mayday to the spring of 1970 when the New Mobe implied there would be a civil disobedience in Washington to protest the Cambodian invasion, and then backed off because of a split within its ranks. Lerner sees this schism affecting Mayday 1971; and the first half of his article is devoted to the power struggles within the movement. In Lerner's eyes the consequences of the Mayday divisions were less serious for Washington, however, than for the rest of the country. Divided Mayday demonstrators could, he points out, disrupt the Capital, but they did not have the strength to organize demonstrations across the country, and fell unavoidable victims to "the old dynamic of one-shot national actions." Lerner's criticism of Mayday, despite his approval of its goals, thus turns out to be severe. It is a view that tells us much about his thinking but also suggests that the differences between the four accounts of Mayday in this section may have more to do with the political outlooks their authors brought to Washington than anything they saw there.

Mayday

Nicholas von Hoffman

Nicholas von Hoffman was a staff writer for the *Chicago Daily News* from 1963 to 1966; during that period he wrote *Mississippi Notebook,* a discussion of the civil rights movement, and *The Multiversity,* an account of what happens to students at American universities. In 1966 he joined the *Washington Post* for which he continues to write a column. Lately, Mr. Von Hoffman has been participating in the Point-Counterpoint debates on CBS television's "60 Minutes." He is also the author of *We Are the People Our Parents Warned Us Against* and *Left at the Post.*

WASHINGTON: ON THE ROPES

The Marines were securing the Washington Monument and turning it into Firebase Martha; there were troops on the bridges across the Potomac; the police were zipping and zooping around town in the squad cars chucking tear gas canisters out of the windows, and the Newzak, all-news radio station was reading triumphant official communiques proclaiming the government had been saved, the Republic yet stood and the flag still flew. The President would not be deposed by some 19-year-old college freshman from Teaneck, N.J.

The nature, composition and intent of the freaks making up the foot soldiers in the Army of Peace was widely and wildly misunderstood. The reactionaries were yelling that the shaggy-frizzies were in cahoots with Hanoi, which was true enough but beside the point; the liberals were, as is their wont, being reasonable and complaining how this hadn't changed anyone's mind; while the bums, crumbs, loafers and dirty, permissive ne'er-do-wells of the People's Army were cast down because the system had reacted just as their main people had predicted it would.

What was lost was that in this land where we have to beg people to register to vote, 7,000 persons, count 'em 7,000, had gone out and incurred arrest for something they believe in. In addition, they'd turned this capital city into a simulated Saigon with the choppers flying all over, the armed men everywhere, and the fear that at any moment something worse, something bloody might happen. They'd caused chaos in Georgetown, the opulent gathering place for so many of the powerful and influential people who made this war or failed to oppose it.

The statusquotarians are gloating that the urchins with anti-tear gas rags around their necks didn't overthrow the state. They can't focus in on who their opponents are, although the filthy funkies left signs on the walls that say. Like this one at Freak Central on Vermont Avenue: "Peggy—If and when you get out, please let's get together before I split—Maybe Thursday. I'm staying at a place on the corner of blank and blank street NW. Things will be alright. Don." Or noted on a wall in the Municipal Court zoo: "To Walter Archibald—Your wife is now at the Superior Court lockup. Please get in touch if you can. Grace."

These are the people who kicked Washington in the pants, people with exams to take, jobs to go to, with families to love, with all the same drives that make the rest of us curse politics and the government for absorbing so much of our time, money and energy. They differ only in degree from the government worker in the straight suit and the attache case at 19th and Pennsylvania who couldn't control himself and suddenly began helping the crazy filthies drag trash cans out on the Avenue to block the road.

What's happened in Washington the past few days has been more than to show the intensity of a growing number of people's feelings. It has also demonstrated that if these people come back in yet larger numbers they can paralyze this city, or at least turn it into pancake batter.

They've had it on the ropes, exhausted the police force until it has begun to lose its normally good discipline and indulge in indiscriminate and promiscuous busting of most anybody young looking or different. It's made the judicial system malfunction by showing that when you arrest that many people there's no way on earth of keeping up with the paper work or preparing enough evidence for a trial. The government here has been reduced to sweeping the streets, rumbling through with huge tractor-trailer jail-vans, mobile Bastilles that suck people off the sidewalks into improvised pens and camps where there's no toilet paper but heightened bitterness.

As noteworthy is the change in the internal organization of this demonstration. In times past a few leaders or groups with small memberships have called for an action at a particular place and time and hoped someone would come. That hasn't been the case this time. Instead, in a number of parts of the country there has been intensive prior organizational work.

This is the reason that the charging and rushing of the gendarmerie hasn't had the effect of instantaneously scattering the thousands here. Driven from the parks, driven from the college campuses the naughty nasties have repeatedly reformed, regrouped and gone ahead with their peace-making mischief. Also by working in squads of 10 or so, romantically called affinity groups, the ragamuffin rabble have been able to throttle the impulse to fight back and intensify the violence.

They haven't trashed (torn up) the city, although there are some rough characters in town who are aching to smash the glass of the ruling class. They've kept the violence to the minimum of dragging garbage cans into the street, that kind of thing, when they could have done a lot more.

Not every part of the country is tightly organized, nor has everyone who came here been part of a self-discipline group, but where you get it, in Texas, Michigan, upstate New York, the Boston area, you get stamina and the restraint that put the requirements of tactics above the acting out of anger.

Should this kind of organizational work continue and spread, the activist element of the Peace Movement will be able to carry out a kind of antiwar Tet Offensive in the Capital. They will be in a position to sneak in thousands of people to live in sympathetic local homes and conduct harassing operations over a period of days or weeks in order to bring about a crisis.

A crisis is what they seek, a crisis that will put the government in the kind of bind that will force it to respond in some more important way than arresting people. It is a volatile kind of politics, loaded with potential danger, that thousands of people would play. It is a sign of what Johnson/Nixon have brought us to.

For those of us who want peace but shrink back from such things, we ruminate that the people arrested for blocking traffic here have already spent nearly as much time in jail as Calley has for Mylai.

PEACE FREAKS

A girl had already inked the newest slogan on her work shirt; "Free the D.C. 10,000." She was part of the crowd at St. Stephen's Church, an Episcopalian establishment in a black neighborhood where the invading peace freaks met every night. The groups composing the great antiwar incursion would send delegates to the church to thrash out what kind of funny business they were going to pull the next day.

The meetings were late, long and labored. At this one, Hosea Williams of the Southern Christian Leadership Conference had put a half-nelson on the boy from Gay Lib to get the microphone away from him. The place had a meshugenah atmosphere with balloons being popped and a slightly spaced girl at the mike. She was giving announcements with the janitor standing behind her holding two clusters of brooms: "How many people need housing? . . . Anybody know the brother who just passed out? . . . There are brooms here and the church needs cleaning. How are we going to deal with that? . . . There's a suggestion we break up into small groups. How do people relate to that?"

You almost feel sorry for the police spies who sometime later in the night are going to have to tell their bosses what the Youth Liberation Front is thinking about doing on the morrow. Mostly you feel an irritable sympathy for these dirty freaks with their matted hair and their perverted perseverance to make Nixon stop the killing.

They come around and ask long, impossible questions about how the papers are playing their story. Really just as self-centered as most young persons. They want to involve you in sticky, distended, analytical conversations about abstruse political points that you don't understand much less have an opinion on.

Their brains are as ratted up as their hair, but one thing they got straight: One, two,

three, four, end our you-know-what-kind-of war and they will do anything to accomplish it. Oh, if Westmoreland and Nixon could have had such troops, their one, two, three, four kinda war would have ended long since, but this kind of spirit you don't buy, and you don't conscript.

The grunts in the freaking fag army sleep ten in a closet, stand out in the rain with their paper plates to get their rations of brown rice and salad scooped out of galvanized garbage cans. And then when they go out on the streets they have to play hide and seek with the hippie underground cops. They have these mod squads of cops in beat up VW's dressed to look like freaks. There was a bunch of them at the Trio Bar and Grill the other day, but the freaks caught on to them when they didn't have the smarts not to wink at their uniformed buddies. Anyway, the Peggy Lipton in the Squad was too dike-ish and dressed wrong, like in slacks, with fat high heel sandals and a non-utilitarian maxi-coat. Genuine girl freaks don't dress like that. It's hard for the cops to dress exactly like the freaks, goes too much against their self-image so half the time they end up looking like bikers.

During days like this you think about cops, how it's a strange vocation, how isolated cops get, how they never join the revolution, anybody's revolution. Everybody else quits the government, even, finally, the civil service, but never the cops. They hold with the regime, as it was in Hungary in 1956 when the army went over to the democratic forces but the cops stuck with the commissars, and during those short hours of freedom it was the cops, the political cops, that the people wanted to get at and revenge themselves on.

It's not that bad here, nothing like it. Washington has a lot of good cops who obviously don't like doing John Mitchell's dirt, but you

can also see gratuitous nastiness above and beyond the call of duty: Packing 10 to 14 people
in 5- by 7-foot jail cells and leaving them there
for 24 hours to live on an occasional baloney
sandwich; deliberately slowing the booking
proceedings so that people are serving sentences meted out in accordance with police
chiefs' politics.

David Ifshin, the president of the National
Student Association who was held at the general lockup at police headquarters and also at
the 14th Precinct, recounts the following:

The police boasted that they'd heated the cells to
120 degrees . . . They put 13 guys in a one-man
cell and this was really bad because we had to
have at least four to five guys standing up at any
one time. Nobody could lie down except one man
under the iron bunk . . . It was so bad the guards
couldn't look us in the eye. We had to hang from
the bars in order to sleep.

We had a veteran who was wounded in the leg
at Khesanh in with us, and when the Air National
Guard guys called us cowards he yelled back and
called them a bunch of draft dodgers and asked
where they'd served except IBM.

It was so bad in that station that they had a
peace sign on the bulletin board with the words
'American Chicken Footprint' under it.

There were plenty of acts of what the freaks
call piggery. The busting of Peace Army ambulances. The Medical Committee on Human
Rights alone claims that 250 of its red cross
arm-banded personnel were busted.

That's not surprising, but what is are the
number of accounts of helpful, friendly policemen, especially black cops, and the even larger
number of open sympathizers in the ranks of
the Army. This narrative comes from Robert
Abelson, a 27-year-old ex-SDS member, now
attending the New School for Social Research
in New York. He was arrested at the Justice
Department demonstration on Tuesday and

held that night in the Washington Coliseum:

It was mind blowing. The soldiers were throwing
frisbies and sharing their food with us. Whenever
they'd change guards the MP's would march off
and we'd shout 'Power to the People' and a lot of
the MP's would make the clenched fist.

The soldiers didn't agree on the tactics of disrupting traffic because some of the people held up
might have been private citizens and not government employees, but they thought it was very unfair to arrest us for the Justice Department demonstration where we weren't blocking traffic. They
didn't agree on politics with us but they did on the
human life issue because a lot had lost friends in
Vietnam.

The most mind blowing was that they were collecting bail money for us. I saw them passing a
helmet around to put it in. Some friends of mine
said they saw the cops do it, too, but I didn't see
that.

A lot of the cops were friendly. The black cops
most of all. Some of them had peace buttons
under the lapels of their uniforms. They'd show
them when no other cops were looking. We talked
to them a lot and they told us their bosses had
said that there was going to be a lot of bombing
and arson.

The peace freak experience with the courts
was equally various. Many hundreds had been
arrested without any ticket being made out on
them so that the government had no idea of
who they were or under what circumstances
they'd been taken into custody. The only way
they could be prosecuted would be by perjury,
and this was attempted by a group of Justice
Department lawyers filling out fraudulent
arrest slips in the basement.

At least one black judge, Theodore New-
man, wasn't having any part of it. He sat in the
courtroom finding any technicality to let people go. At one point, when he discharged some
straggly haired young nogoodnik, the other
freaks in the courtroom applauded him.

But many had the bad luck to go before bush league Julius Hoffmans who'd hang you before you could enter a not guilty plea. One such was Nicholas Nunzio who spent the hours of the night hectoring the defendants thusly: "How do you propose to get out of here if bond is set? . . . Are you through demonstrating? You through violating the law? . . . You start walking down to that bus depot and you get on that bus and get out of town."

This is all said to people who haven't been tried and won't be convicted. But that's all right because the Justice Department act is to scare people out of the city, after forcing them to submit to mug shots and finger prints . . . For Big Mother, John Mitchell's main computer.

That's okay with the freaks, too. If that's what it costs to give peace a chance, they'll pay. pay by present uncomfort and dangers and risking future, life-long blackballing.

They do it and the tepid and tardy editorialists, who realized years too late the stupidity of Vietnam, chide them. They chide them for poor organization, as if the funky rascals had taxpayers' money to go out and get it together like the Marines.

They chide them for naivete, for not understanding politics like Muskie and Fulbright and McGovern and the other powerful men who've been so effective in ending the conflict in a timely fashion. They chide them but if peace does ever come, it will be the smelly, obtuse, stridently non-comprehending freaks who will have won it for us.

"NYAAA, NYAAA, WE WON"

The aftershocks from the quaking demonstrations of the last couple of weeks are still registering on the seismographs around here.

The Mitchell/Kleindienst faction is running around saying, "Nyaaa, nyaaa, nyaaa, we won. You said you were going to overthrow the government and ya didn't! Nyaa, nyaa on you." If these politicians have any notion of what these enormous demonstrations must look like to the country and the world they're keeping it to themselves.

They appear to have lost all perspective and to have locked themselves into a vendetta with the weirdo leaders. So Mitchell, who didn't think Fred Hampton and Mark Clark's civil rights were violated when they were rubbed out by the Chicago cops, is going to indict Rennie Davis for conspiring to deprive commuters of their civil rights by tying up traffic. How they think the manufacture of so many martyrs with all the trouble that causes is going to help this increasingly insecure and inept administration surpasses explanation.

While Mitchell angers more and more people to action, Nixon meets with his Washington police chief to prepare for next time. He's assuming that the next demonstrations will be like the last, but he does that with everything—deals with the future by replaying the past.

In truth, with all the dough they spend on spies, snoops and taps, the government had no idea that so many people would be parading around here. Nixon's domestic intelligence is no better than what he gets in Southeast Asia. He'd help himself if he'd stop reading those silly apathy-on-the-campus articles. He won't, so he'll be as surprised and maladroit next time. But that is as it must be for his part in history is to be everybody's foil.

The crew-cut, narrow-lapel doves are also in disarray. They're wringing their hands and asking themselves how much have we lost because of the behavior of the berserker freaks throwing the garbage in the streets and creating dangerously overcrowded and unhealthy conditions in Washington's jails.

It's very hard for the respectable, working and shaving doves to understand that their real leaders are the freaks and the crazies. Yet it is so and has been through out the development of this most unusual of American social movements. What the freaks say today the respectables will say in about a year. A year ago the creeps were telling people that the POW issue was just a crock, now the respectables are saying it too. It's been the same with everything from war crimes to Vietcong flags. The freaks break the ice with some new outrage which gets everyone apoplectic and then people think about it and often agree. So it is that Rennie Davis and the rest of his sordid lot have done more to shape and change American political opinion than the last three presidents.

In 50 years this city of statues will have one of Rennie, but for the time being the liberal hero is John Kerry, the ex-Naval officer who made that moving speech to the Senate Foreign Relations Committee. He's a good boy. He doesn't go too far; he goes instead to fancy Washington dances like The Fivers and plays houseguest at the home of multi-million dollar heiress ladies. Him Washington can relate to for he tickles the emotions without threatening anybody.

The freaks themselves have no idea what they're going to do next. They were bowled over, too, both by their numbers and their successes. There's a great desire to do it again, not only because the need to do something remains but also because they had such a helluva good time. They had an action high from running around on the streets, but the best was the jail . . . girls and boys balling, chanting. "Today's pig is tomorrow's baloney sandwich,"

marvelous fun, all that singing and carrying on, but even the people who were not lucky enough to be in Mitchell's detention pens, but were stuffed 14 to a jail cell under beastly conditions, even these went through an inspiriting experience, as though they'd swallowed the eucharist of fraternity. A movement heavy from Detroit may have summed it up when he said, "Whatever it was we had at Woodstock and lost at Altamont, we found again in D.C.'s jails."

In the meantime, something may be happening at long last in the United States Senate. Sen. Mike Gravel from Alaska says he's going to filibuster the draft bill which must be passed by midnight of June 30 or Nixon's water is cut off.

Gavel swears he's going to do it, that he won't take a dive when the boys lean on him. "We're all talking about ending the war, but THIS IS REALLY GOING TO DO IT. I'm physically younger than most of those guys (he's 40) and I'll stay till I fall over."

You have to be a little suspicious of what senators say they're going to do, particularly if it's going to cause a lot of trouble, but Iron Mike says, "Look, I'm not up again till '74. I'm still in my statesman years. I can do it."

But even with a few of the Southerners giving him lessons on how to hold out on the floor, he'll need help. What he's hoping for is a *Mr. Smith Goes To Washington* kind of outpouring of letters, phone calls, delegations and finally, a huge, silent and very orderly vigil in front of the Capitol.

"There's nothing else but the draft to focus on from now to November, 1972," he says remarking that it's too late to cut off the money. "So let's cut off the people. What's more important, money or people? These other approaches, these resolutions, are just fun and games with the President, but he's got the power to change the rules on you every time.

If you think you're playing on a dry field, he'll switch to a muddy field."

He's right but he's also got to get 34 votes to prevent his filibuster from being shut down. He claims to have Cook of Kentucky, and Proxmire and Hughes of Wisconsin and Iowa, but he needs more, he needs all those senatorial doves to put their votes where their mouths are. When you ask Iron Mike about that, he laughs and says, "If I've heard it once from colleagues, I've heard it six times. They come up to me and say, 'Goddamn you're courageous,' but when the vote comes a lot of these guys are gonna suck air."

One Weekend in May
Dotson Rader

Dotson Rader, a student at Columbia University in 1968, wrote *I Ain't Marchin' Anymore!* about the student strike. A contributing editor to *Evergreen Review* and an editor of *Defiance: A Radical Review,* his other books are *Government Inspected Meat* and *Blood Dues.* Mr. Rader writes for *Esquire, Partisan, Rolling Stone,* and other periodicals, and is currently working on a novel.

It began for me at the 14th Street Bridge with Noam Chomsky of MIT, Howard Zinn, Dave McReynolds of the War Resisters League, Tom Seligson of *Defiance,* and about one hundred and fifty long-haired commie freaks in bellbottoms and beads, under the direction of Hosea Williams of the Southern Christian Leadership Conference, trying to sit down in the street and drive the government ape-shit by blocking the traffic from the lily-white Virginia suburbs into the city. It was a failure.[1]

[1] There was success elsewhere. Two bridges were blocked, as were a good number of intersections. Distributor caps were taken from city buses while drivers (mainly blacks) yelled encouragement. One admiral, trapped on Memorial Bridge, sat behind his sealed windows while a militarist's nightmare, populated by dirty filthy you-fuckers-need-a-bath fag revolutionary hippies, removed his four tires and his engine. And the police, as the police will, misdirected tear-gas canisters and sent Justice Department workers hacking and coughing. And horse manure was thrown by Vietnam Veterans Against the War on the infamous steps of the Pentagon. And the capital of this empire woke to discover that the American people had laid it to siege.

We could not even pull off arrest, and we had with us a good percentage of the few notables who took the time to stand with the kids that day.[2] The police, like half-wit bullies in a school-yard laying into weaker brothers and sisters went at us with clubs and tear gas until our main body was scattered like stampeding sheep across the Washington Monument meadow. Absurd, surreal scenes occurred: Tom Seligson and I, with several small children, huddling in the cherry trees as police cars roared at the edges of the grove, prevented by the gnarled trunks from running over us; stumbling with Jerry Rubin and several friends through the grass in a cruel haze of

[2] I think a wide number of antiwar celebrities are open to legitimate criticism for their failure to act in solidarity with the protesters during the May Day weekend. Where were the rock stars, the actresses, the writers, the professors, the critics, the politicians, who ply the trade of Movement celebrity? At home with Norman Mailer and Jane Fonda and Betty Friedan and Robin Morgan and Carl Oglesby and Gloria Steinem.

tear gas like a poisoned evening fog, direction-less; crowding around soldiers at the Commerce Department as they defied orders and poured their canteen water over our burning eyes. Monday morning was a disaster in many ways. The tactics, the logistics, the planning, the communications of the People's Coalition and the May Day Tribe were a bankruptcy.

However, the significance of the May Day weekend does not rest in the inability of forty thousand kids to stop the government. Rather what granted it its curious dignity and its place in history were the widespread arrests (14,000) and the prison experience suffered by thousands of young demonstrators never arrested before. It produced the radicalization of large numbers of youth, with much the same immediacy and depth in conversion, although strangely lacking the bitterness, as that of the young people in the busts of Columbia and Chicago. The arrests were unexpected, both the Movement leadership and the government were unprepared for the scale of arrests, and they came as a result of a conscious decision on the part of Nixon to implement his policy of preventive detention and terror (later I will recount the terror experienced by those jailed) and, secondly, it was made possible by a conflict in political strategy and tactics between the moderate People's Coalition (WRL, SCLC, Women Strike for Peace, etc.) and the more militant May Day Tribe (non-PL SDS, Weatherman, radical street groupings, etc.).[3]

The People's Coalition did not openly support the traffic stoppages, but, by the sheer weight of events, they were caught up in the

process, for the government did not distinguish between the moderates and the radicals. They arrested the May Day Tribe en masse, and then on the following days at the Justice Department and the Capitol they picked up the more moderate Coalition people. The result was the radicalization of the moderates via a brutalizing prison experience, and the discrediting of peaceful, legal protest as the primary avenue of dissent.

The May Day weekend not only witnessed an escalation in the tactics of the antiwar movement from lawful protest to massive civil disobedience, but also displayed what has become the dominant psychological tendency within the Movement: a highly collectivistic, communalistic yet anarchical attitude which rejects traditional leadership concepts. One of the reasons for the failure of disruption was the refusal on the part of the mass of demonstrators to follow or even recognize the authority of established leadership. Or rather the inability of institutional leadership cadres to organize and control demonstrators in the street. Their authority over events was no more acknowledged than was that of the government. All authority was disregarded. A kind of compelling tribal anarchy reigned in Washington in place of vertical leadership structures. You had the curious phenomenon of Jerry Rubin and Abbie Hoffman, Rennie Davis and Dave McReynolds, and people from SCLC, and others, who would, under normal circumstances, have been in control of the actions of demonstrators, finding themselves without followers. Everyone became the victim of events raging about him over which no one could exercise effective control.

On Monday morning, during the traffic disruptions, you had situations where "leadership cadres" attempted repeatedly, completely without success, to discipline and direct large groups of demonstrating youth. The kids paid them no mind. The leadership figures, in the

---

[3] A note on the April 24 demonstration, which brought four hundred thousand demonstrators to the capitol. The Peace Action Coalition, which sponsored the demonstration, is dominated by the Moratorium-Student Mobilization Committee (SCM), which is in turn dominated by the Socialist Workers' Party, a Trotskyite organization. SWP has about five thousand members and they have moved successfully in the last year and a half to co-opt the leadership of the moderate wing of the peace movement. They were not active in the May Day weekend protest.

end, had to join the ranks and follow the group wherever it collectively determined it was headed. All the mimeographed maps and tactical charts and protest targets chosen by committees in advance were of no avail. The kids plowed over everyone with a kind of delighted, giddy abandon.

This communalistic spirit was also vigorously evident in the jails, where no one leader was able to command jurisdiction over the people. The Coliseum concentration compound was one long, joyous, romping hippie trip, a kind of spontaneous *Hair* production with the genuine cast. The cellblocks, while harrowing, brutal circles, developed the same type of communal character; only there the attitude was bleaker. I will come to the actualities of the jail experience in a moment. To repeat: what the street demonstrations proved was that the old-style leadership (which was deeded to the Movement by the experience of the Old Left), with its vertical command and decision structures, its petty bureaucracies, its status and reward systems, was no longer pertinent to present affairs. Something new existed which was refreshingly, perhaps dangerously, antileadership per se, anti-authority.

It was precisely because of this rampant, at times beautiful, communalism on the part of the kids that there was so little violence. If Mayday had occured a year or two ago, during the period when the Weatherman and the Progressive Labor still had some vitality and the capability of organizing street kids behind what are essentially Stalinist approaches to political structure, there would have been violence. But that time has passed, and with it whatever was politically germane about the overbearing, intolerant, humorless thugs who clustered like armed Methodist missionaries in the Weatherman and PL collectives. For in that period there existed the possibility of convincing numbers of people to act, not only against their own personal interests (we have

learned that that is not a difficult goal to achieve), but against the immediate interests of their own community in the name of an abstract goal. That was untenable in Washington. The Weatherman, who have called for a continuing revolution within the Revolution, have been taken at their word. And that spontaneous revolution has discovered that the Weatherman are dated, their concepts and theoretics, their tactics and presumed martyrdom, their dark, brooding, joyless mentality are of another time. Things have opened up and become gentler and more serious. The community, and the manner in which that community was realized by the young, made actions which placed the community beyond the limits of tolerable peril individually impossible. The day of left-wing adventurism on any significant scale is over. The response in Washington to those who called for suicidal actions imperiling the community was to label the advocates "pig provocateurs."

Tom Seligson and I, and about twenty-five hundred other stoned and dancing protesters, were arrested at the Justice Department on Tuesday afternoon, May 4. We were arrested in the presence of Attorney General John (Martha's john) Mitchell and Jerry Wilson, Chief of Police for the District. We were arrested illegally because we were demonstrating under the protection of a police permit issued to the People's Coalition. Upon arrest we were loaded into police buses and taken to the jail of Precinct 7, Georgetown, a correctional facility which had not been used in eighty years.

We were in high spirits on the bus. We sang "Take Me Out to the Ball Game," for we believed, incorrectly, that we were on our way to join our brothers and sisters in the concentration compound at the Coliseum. Instead we were jammed, twelve to sixteen men to each cell, into cages measuring five by seven feet. We were held for seventeen hours. We were given no food, water or cigarettes. We were allowed no phone calls. We were denied access to an attorney. We were not informed of the charges against us, nor were we advised of our rights.

Unable to sleep (in order for half the boys in my cell to sit, the other half had to stand), we spent the long hours rapping, singing, chanting, telling jokes, talking about sex and health food and baseball. What I learned about my cellmates, beyond the knowledge, once more confirmed, that it is all too easy to love this generation of young Americans and to envy them their enthusiasm and dizzy wit and decency and unlikely gentleness, was that most of them had never participated in a mass demonstration before. Unlike previous ranks of demonstrators, they were not, by and large, college students. They were very young. In three jails I encountered only two youths over twenty-four years of age. They are not bitter. They led me to believe that they have little tolerance for the shrill rhetoric of the left. They do not understand it. They have little patience with political systems. They inhabit a world and are possessed of a consciousness so fundamentally communalistic and noncompetitive, so unacquisitive, that they cannot appreciate traditional leftist concerns. They want the war to end because they do not like people to be killed. It has nothing to do with imperialism. All murder, whether imperialist or socialist, is intolerable. They cannot justify death for any reason. They draw back, like children, before the reality of political murder. They are freedom-crazy. It was impossible to speak to them on a theoretical level. They distrust abstraction. Hunger, illness, war, police, they are evil. That is all. There was nothing more to be said. That alone was sufficient to act. I think if Rudd or J. J. or even Tom Hayden had been in my cell, he would have fallen silent before the sheer indifference of his audience to his theoretics.

We were in cell No. 2. On either side of us were cells with radical feminists in them. Two in one cell. Four in the other. The sisters had room to lie down and sleep. They had working toilets. They were able to purchase Cokes and receive food and make calls and get cigarettes. Initially there was great solidarity between the men and women in the cellblock. It faded after several hours. The men became resentful of the sisters' privileges. And the sisters refused to submit to processing (giving their names and addresses) and, as a result, kept their brothers holed up without food and water or working toilets, standing crushed together like subway riders at rush hour. Only the crowding lasted seventeen hours.

Nine o'clock the following morning we were removed to the central lockup of the Superior Court, near 4th and I Streets in Washington. There I experienced the worst prison conditions I have ever witnessed. The cellblock was without windows and without adequate ventilation. Two hours after our confinement the temperature rose to over one hundred degrees. Four o'clock that morning a guard informed us that the temperature had hit one hundred and twenty degrees. Here again the cells were brutally small (six feet by seven) and crammed with ten to fifteen boys in each cage. There were two bunks, without mattresses, one suspended from chains above the other. The effect of the placement of the bunks was to reduce the actual standing space by half. Again, with the exception of one piece of baloney and two pieces of bread, there was no food or cigarettes or toilet paper or soap or (for half the cells) water. Waterless cells were passed canteens from other cages. The heat, the smell of dirty bodies, the overcrowding, the lack of sanitary facilities, the continual abuse from correctional and police officials, produced a paranoia in us reaching psychotic dimensions.

After the first ten hours or so of standing

up or crouching on the urine-wet floor one's mind began to unravel. Two boys in my cell (cell No. 18) claimed to see cats pacing before the cell door snarling at them. Tom Seligson admitted to seeing the cell bars swaying like branches in a wind. I myself turned into a deadheaded zombie, sitting hunched in a corner by the toilet, someone's head resting on my shoes, my head on my arms, squeezing my eyes to keep the floor from tilting. I was afraid I would fall off the floor, slide toward the bars like a sled on an icy hill.

Late that evening (Wednesday night) a young man in cell No. 20 suffered an asthma attack, went unconscious, and began to turn blue. The entire cellblock shouted for a doctor. None was called. Moments later, a boy in cell No. 4 collapsed from claustrophobia and went into convulsions. We yelled for a doctor. For thirty minutes no guards appeared. And during that time the conviction took root in our minds that the government, the Movement, our parents and friends, everyone had abandoned us here. It is odd how the passage of several hours under certain conditions, under great duress, can reshape one's reality, wipe out the underpinnings of security like so many shingles blown in a storm. A kind of whimpering terror takes hold, completely irrational, but then one's position is utterly inexplicable, for you find yourself suddenly, absolutely without defense and dependent upon people who despise you. We needed favor from the guards. And that was at the same time both demeaning and threatening and yet absurdly erotic. One wished to be regarded by his jailer. Our actions became a combination of rage and seduction.

I think that is understandable. We did not know what we were charged with. We had no news from the outside, no contact, the physical conditions themselves were close to unbearable. That and the fact that, with the exception of myself and a handful of others, none of the six hundred-plus prisoners had ever been arrested before.

A guard (badge No. 4168) came into the cellblock. We shouted that our brothers were sick. Then we quieted down. His response was so exquisitely sadistic that it seems almost funny now. It was too appropriate, too much of a theatrical piece, although at the time it was numbingly frightening. "Let him die. Let all you fucking troublemakers die." His remark sent the cellblock into pandemonium, canteens banged against the bars, walls were kicked, youths screamed obscenities against the guards. We hated America at that moment. For he had become it.

After a time we quieted down. Another guard appeared. "If you fucking hippies don't shut up, we got police outside with gas and we'll gas this fucking place and you can die here. We done it before." We believed him. Looking back it seems silly to have taken him at his word, but then it seemed moments away, the gas.

We fell silent. It had turned unreal for us. What the hell was happening to us, and why? Someone shouted to the guard that we were good boys. I nodded dumbly in agreement that indeed we were.

Shortly after the gas threat, David Lee Denhartigh, a young man in cell No. 2, started shouting obscenities at the guards. An officer named Layton went to his cell and told him to repeat what he had shouted. David repeated it. Layton pulled David from his cell, put David's arm against the wall, and smashed the steel cell door against his arm, breaking his wrist. David screamed. Then Layton (badge No. 4) and another guard took David out and beat him.

Thirty hours later we were taken to the bull pen of the Superior Court. In groups of seven we were arraigned before a judge and released upon posting one hundred dollars bond. So it ended.

Later I ran into some of my cellmates in Franklin Square. "Will you ever do this [demonstrate] again?" They said they would. They had seen the Monster Biggie (the gov) and survived him. They were convinced they could do it again.

What I think the May Day weekend brought to its conclusion was the appeal to legal protest to end the war. It established massive, non-violent disruption as a majoritarian tactic within the Movement. What had been the tactic of the fringe—disruption—was legitimated by May Day. It ended, I think, any further flirtation with constitutional instrumentalities by the protest movement. And it illustrated to all of us in the struggle against the war (and to those outside the struggle) who had come to suspect that the Nixon-proclaimed moratorium on massive antiwar dissent was effective, that a kind of deadman's calm had been produced by Vietnamization and co-option; May Day showed us that the Movement was tougher and broader than we believed; braver, younger, more handsome. And I personally came to respect the guts and toughness of the nowhere kids who appeared one day in Washington and disappeared the next and who would be back again when the call was issued—principled kids who never attended organizational meetings, who did not know Tom Hayden from Tom Jones, who were ignorant of the history and the polemic of the left, but who were, at sixteen, seventeen, and eighteen, by birth, by condition, by right of history, necessarily on our side. Without knowing it, they had renounced the bribes which still tempted us. They were free and clear. Unaware, they had already won the struggle inside themselves which many of us who came to our politics earlier were still fighting. And they had won it without throwing a blow. How stupid all our macho excesses seemed in the face of their simple courage. I could not help but think of Norman Mailer

(the best we got) and his silly, nitty, running battle with Women's Liberation, and with his own disfigured, vanquished manhood. How petty it seemed, for Mailer's battle was mine and Rudd's and Hayden's and maybe Che's, too. And yet, in the context of these kids, it seemed unclean and perverse. Well, we will never be able to organize them. They have slipped back out of history into their private communal pursuits. We will never discipline them nor teach them. We will never draw them from the eager crazy freakass zonked yoyo yipyipyippy trip they are winging their life on. *They* are the exploding plastic inevitable. It is their incredible energy and glee, the simple-mindedness of their politics, the easy, attractive impulse to human justice which lightly fires both their optimism and their passing rage; it is that which will end this war and end the pernicious social, political, and economic arrangement which wages it.

It is plain: I was enthralled by their born-again American character, as free of guile as of any sense of history. Lanky, good-humored, generous, easy-going kids who learned early to cope. In some ways that are not true for me, this unhappy country is familiar to them and unthreatening. They take it in stride. For they come to it without educated notions. They live it without guilt (and those of us in the Movement are crippled by guilt). The Goodies and the Baddies. That is how they size things up. My cellmates were a cross section of this free America. Let me pay them my respect: David Knapp, Kalamazoo, Michigan; Dayton Hanford, Belport, New York; Stanley Reed, Waltham, Massachusetts; James Fred Jones, Bloomington, Illinois; Dana "Tennessee" Carlson, Atlanta, Georgia; Lee Eastman, Orlando, Florida; Tom Elgin, Baltimore, Maryland; Bob Maringo, Burlington, Vermont; Lee Breslow, Wilmington, Delaware; John Crane, Rochester, New York. Power to you.

The Vets & Mayday

Robin Reisig

Robin Reisig has been a reporter for *The Southern Courier,* an Alabama civil rights newspaper. She received the 1972 Don Hollenbeck Award for an article about reporters in conflict-of-interest situations. Her articles have appeared in various magazines including *Ramparts, Life,* and *New Republic,* and she currently writes for the *Village Voice.*

Washington, D.C.—A man in dirty green was shouting at me in a language I didn't understand. "Dung lai!" Someone said he was asking for my identification. I said I didn't have any. So he shot me.

Secretaries ran screaming from soldiers saying *nice* girl" as they thrust their guns into them. Men were shot because they were men. Soldiers "overrule Supreme Court," screamed the headline in the Washington Daily News. One army of police took another army of Americans prisoners, and these American prisoners-of-war shouted in Vietnamese, "Chu hoi! Chu hoi!"—I defect.

There was murder in the heart of the Empire last week, and blood on the steps of the Capitol. The guns were plastic, the bullets toys, the "blood" red goo, and the soldiers acting out "one last mission—to search out and destroy the last vestige of this barbaric war." The Vietnam veterans, the maimed and bitter men our government sent to war, were bringing the bloody war home to Washington.

With an army of veterans camped out under the setting half moon of the Capitol last week, and with the peace movement committing itself next week to using for the first time the tactics of the civil rights movement—civil disobedience and non-violent direct action—this spring's peace offensive is indeed different from all other spring peace offensives.

Even the mass spring rite of exorcism of guilt, the seventh (or is it 17th?) annual spring peace parade, haroo, haroo, the one-day march on an empty Capitol building, struck a new note. There were the usual marchers chanting "Ho! Ho! Ho Chi Minh! The NLF. is gonna win!" Only this time the men chanting were "Active Duty GIs." There were the usual hardhat-looking types who in the past have heckled and hit demonstrators. Only this time, the burly, short-haired men in teamsters jackets were parade marshals, guarding the demonstrators.

As President Abraham Lincoln (and the April 24 march's slogan) put it: "You can fool all the people some of the time; you can even fool some of the people all the time; . . . but you can't fool all of the people all the time."

Or as a march button put it: "Enough."

You can't fool the vets. They've been there.

The war has gone on too long—long enough for them to come home and unmask the lies. They called their operation "Dewey Canyon III." It was named after U. S. operations in "northern South Vietnam," claimed the Washington Star last week. It was named after U.S. operations held "illegally in Laos" in 1969 and now, said the vets.

The Dewey Canyons involved several thousand men who penetrated several thousand meters into Laos, veterans testified before a Senate committee. Were you aware Congress had specifically forbidden this? Senator George McGovern quietly asked. There was no answer.

Other vets told me they had fought deep in Laos and Cambodia in small patrols during all the years when we said we had no ground troops there, and that they had signed statements swearing, under penalty of long prison terms, never to reveal what they had done.

Alan Swann, a former Special Forces lieutenant, explained why he was in Washington: he had been part of long-range reconnaissance patrols operating in Laos and Cambodia in 1968–69, he said. "We were told by our commander that the President was briefed each morning about our operation." Then Swann learned that President Nixon was at the same time publicly swearing we had no troops in Laos, "so either Nixon was lying or the military has gotten grossly out of hand—it has no control by the nation." The duplicity made him distrust America; Richard Nixon had created a rebel.

Paul Withers, a former Special Forces platoon sergeant who said he worked with the CIA in Cambodia and Laos and 15 miles the other side of the "DMZ," pointed to very faint brownish smears on his pants: "See this blood here—it's from a little 12-year-old girl a guy shot to see if his gun worked."

Withers walks with a limp. He had nine purple hearts, a silver star, a bronze star, and a distinguished service cross—symbols, the soldiers' spokesman said, of "dishonor, shame and inhumanity," memories of a "Vietnamese people whose hearts were broken, not won." He threw the lot at the gleaming Capitol building.

Quietly they marched, 800 or so men begging forgiveness for their "medals for murder," which they heaped at the Capitol dome, over a wire fence marked "trash," toward the lap of a statue of former Chief Justice John Marshall, a statue no more deaf, it seemed, than the living Supreme Court Justices—the Supreme Court where more than 100 wounded veterans had come to ask for a ruling on the legality of

the war—and were arrested for "obstructing justice."

The medals flew, the apologies were quietly, painfully said . . . "I'd like to say just one thing: to the people of Vietnam, God, I'm sorry." . . . A man in a wheelchair hurls the medals "They're worthless.". . . "I'm sorry I became part of a hatred so bad I didn't believe mankind was possible of it." . . . A father plays taps for his dead son "for all our wonderful sons, no more, *no more.*" . . . "A silver star: *bullshit.* A bronze star: *cram it up your ass.*" . . . "I'm disgraced that I served in a war like this."

Marines wept and mothers shed their dead sons' medals, soldiers in tears apologized to the wives of Vietnamese soldiers they had killed . . . "Here's my merit badges for murder" . . . "They're *blood*" . . . "Lieutenant Palmer *died* so I got a medal, Sergeant Johnson *died* so I got a medal, I got a silver star, a bronze star, and all the rest of this garbage. It doesn't mean a *thing.*"

The White House reportedly said only 30 per cent of the men were vets. When the 1000 veterans produced their papers, when their wounds and words belied this, White House officials denied making the statement. But no one in the administration visited the encampment.

"We are here to ask, and to ask vehemently, where are the leaders of our country?" John Kerry, a former Navy lieutenant, told the Senate Foreign Relations Committee to ask: Where is the leadership? McNamara, Rostow, Bundy, Gilpatric and so many others, where are they now that we the men they sent to war are returned? These are commanders who have deserted their troops, and there is no more serious crime in the law of war. The army says they never leave their wounded. The Marines never leave even the dead. These men have left all the casualties and retreated behind a pious shield of public rectitude . . . and finally this administration has done us the ultimate dishonor. They have attempted to disown us and the sacrifices we made for this country. In their blindness and fear, they have tried to deny we are veterans, that we served in Nam. We do not need their testimony. Our own scars, and stumps for limbs, are witness enough for others and for ourselves."

Only Senator Stuart Symington broke the silence. "Mr. Kerry," he asked, "will you move your mike a little bit?"

"Which way, sir?"

"This way."

"You have a silver star, have you not?"

"Yes, sir."

"You have a purple heart?"

"Yes, I do."

"How many clusters on it?"

"Two."

"You've been wounded three times?"

"Yes, sir."

"I have no further questions."

On Friday, Attorney General John Mitchell called a press conference with student journalists and warned that there was a "substantial possibility of physical confrontation and a substantial possibility of physical harm" at some time during the next two weeks of demonstrations. Mitchell ought to know. The government does not seem to be playing an innocent role in the initiation of "physical harm."

Charges of "agent provocateurs" are so rampant among the left that I dislike making them without having witnessed the unmasking of the agent myself, but from various reports it seems quite certain that there were government agents attempting to provoke violence among the vets.

For example, when the Maryland delegation was discussing whether to stay awake all night in compliance with the Supreme Court ruling that they could stay in the mall only if they did not sleep, one man seemed suspicious because of his "hard core insistence on violence," re-

ported a medical student who was part of the delegation. "He said the only way to teach the pigs a lesson is to break their heads if they're gonna break our heads," and urged men to keep rocks handy. "Most of our men have been through enough unnecessary violence," said the student, so the vets took the tough-talking "vet" over to their own security detail of men who had been in military intelligence. The man had claimed he was a vet who left the service in 1966. He had identification papers on him, said the vets, showing an active military ID with security clearance and an intelligence classification.

Another agitator was identified by members of a local underground newspaper who showed vets photos of him in their "Pig-ture" column. Another was recognized by Withers as someone in the CIA he had worked with. The man claimed a different background. But the government is good at pretending. That is what Vietnam is all about.

The organizers of the Mayday demonstrations are planning to give "literally every" person who joins them training in *non-violent* civil disobedience. Many of the civil disobedience trainers met last Friday at the DMZ, a GI coffeehouse in Washington, with about 50 active duty GIs from several nearby army bases who were being given riot control training for the coming demonstrations. The GIs tattled on what their commanders were telling them. According to Brian Yaffee, a veteran civil disobedience trainer with the Quaker Project on Community Conflict, the soldiers said the commanders were scaring the troops, telling them the demonstrators would have guns and ammunitions, that an arsenal had been broken into, that the Weatherman were surfacing. (Gas would not be used indiscriminately, it was reported, but helicopters would be used to spray CN gas, like at Berkeley.)

But never has so large a demonstration prepared so carefully for non-violence. The idea of

Mayday is to "*enforce* the people's peace treaty" or "if the government won't stop the war, then the people will stop the government." "It's a time to demonstrate power," said Rennie Davis, "but it's got to be a power of non-violence."

In the workshops, demonstrators acted out the roles of police and demonstrators and learn how it feels to be called a "pig." "As people begin to understand what kinds of things they do to each other," said Carl Zietlow and Sukir Rice, "they see police as persons rather than as stereotyped pigs." "They see them as human beings they can relate to," said Yaffee.

The peace movement is in a time of change, and a time when its members are going divergent ways. So the National Peace Action Coalition held another demonstration on Saturday. It did a splendid job of organizing and turned out a massive crowd. It called charges that Trotskyists were in important positions in NPAC "red-baiting." "Whether the charges are true or untrue is irrelevant," said coordinator Jerry Gordon, who then denied them. Dave McReynolds, a member of the other coalition, the Peoples Coalition for Peace and Justice, wrote in Win "I am a little confused why I

should be called a 'red-baiter' since the whole weight of my attack on the Trotskyists is that they refuse absolutely to break the law. I am really providing a kind of character reference for them."

Saturday's demonstration was a day of sunshine and life and joy, but there is no sun bright enough to penetrate the Capitol dome. The scents of April, all flowers and grass and love and youth, cannot penetrate the thick, aging walls of the White House. And speeches cannot make the rulers see what the people for years have been proclaiming of the President and his war: the clothes have no Emperor.

The veterans and Mayday will be more difficult to hide from, as men use their bodies to say what words have failed to impress on the rulers, and to underscore the duplicity of a government that has called a war of aggression a "defensive" action, that has called Laos "Vietnam" whenever it invaded it, that has called murder "heroism" and imperialism "democracy." The demonstrators are calling for men to choose: either break the law, or hop on the "last train for Nuremberg—all on board."

Mayday: Anatomy of the Movement

Michael P. Lerner

Michael P. Lerner worked with the Mayday collective before the demonstrations in Washington, D.C. He served five weeks in a federal penitentiary on a contempt citation while a defendant in the Seattle conspiracy trial.

The Mayday demonstrations in Washington cannot be understood without recalling the profound effect that the Cambodian protests a year earlier had on the consciousness of movement organizers and on young people

generally. In May 1970, more than 70,000 people came to Washington, D.C., to protest the invasion of Cambodia. The New Mobe had called the demonstration and had implied that there would be civil disobedience.

But at the crucial moment the Mobe failed to lead. It was severely split, with radicals and pacifists on one side (including people like Rennie Davis, Dave Dellinger, and groups like the Fellowship of Reconciliation and War Resisters League), and the Trotskyists of the Socialist Workers Party, Young Socialist Alliance and Student Mobilization Committee (which SWP and YSA dominated) on the other. These Marxist-Leninists firmly opposed civil disobedience. And when the moment of decision came inside the Mobe, it was they who prevailed, because of their superior organizational strength combined with the indecisiveness and division of the radicals. The Trotskyists controlled the marshals for the demonstration, who were under the leadership of chief Marshal Fred Halstead, Socialist Workers Party Presidential candidate in 1968. Halstead gave them strict instructions to prevent civil disobedience, using force if necessary.

The vast majority of people had come to Washington for civil disobedience, and would have acted on it even in open opposition to the marshals if they had been called to do so by the radicals. But an immediate fear of publicly splitting the Mobe made them hesitate, and that hesitation transformed the event into a meaningless march barely noticed around the country and bitterly denounced by many who had participated in it. In the aftermath, Rennie Davis, Dave Dellinger, Syd Peck and many others realized that a golden opportunity had been wasted, and resolved never again to let their actions be undermined by the Trotskyists. Their failure to lead in 1970 became a heavy burden on their consciences, and prepared the way for a complete split with the SWP, the dissolution of the Mobe, and the demonstrations of May 1971.

The dissolution of the Mobe was also made inevitable by the new recognition among large numbers of anti-war demonstrators that the issue of the war was intrinsically linked to other forms of domestic oppression and repression. This recognition had been part of the radicals' political field of vision since early in the anti-war movement; now it was becoming popularized even among groups like the American Friends Service Committee and the Clergy and Laymen Concerned About the War in Vietnam. But such a view was dogmatically opposed by the Trotskyists, who had always argued that mass mobilizations could only be built around single issues, and that protest about the war should not be somehow diluted by raising questions of poverty, racism and the like.

The Trotskyists and their Socialist Workers Party are essentially vestiges of the 1930s, and of the tense struggle between Trotsky and Stalin for the soul of the Russian Revolution. (Trotsky, who is a major and greatly misunderstood figure in the revolutionary tradition, would no more approve the contemporary Trotskyists of the SWP than would Marx and Lenin most of the self-proclaimed Marxist-Leninists running around in the American left these days.)

The SWP is a peculiar organization to be playing a central role in the New Left; like its traditional old left foe, the Communist Party, the SWP is organized as a democratic centralist "combat party" and is committed to old-speak Marxism-Leninism. The SWP and its Young Socialist Alliance emphasize the need to reach "ordinary people" in the United States, to radicalize workers and farmers. It sees itself as the vanguard of the revolution, and tries to channel revolutionary energy into its own organizational designs. "We are not simply a component of the mass revolutionary party," says the SWP. "We are the *essential* component that embodies in living cadres today the programmatic conquests that are essential for molding the kind of mass revolutionary workers party that can win the socialist victory in this country." This organizational chauvinism leads to the most sectarian policies when the SWPYSA engages in domestic political activity. This is evident in its insistence on single-issue mass organizations, like those it has built around the war and women's liberation. By keeping the level of political discussion in its mass organizations simple and at a low level, it is able to attract large numbers. At the same time, when any members in these organizations begin to sense the interrelatedness of issues, they are recruited into the YSA and later into the SWP: "So you want to be a revolutionary: well, here we have a full-scale revolutionary program for you, complete with disciplined cadre and an elaborate ideology." The attraction of such a proposal to many new recruits to the anti-war movement is irresistible. After all, the New Left has nothing comparable to offer—it is organizationally in shambles, flirts with different and contradictory ideologies every other week, and is afraid to provide leadership for itself, much less put forward a vision for other Americans.

But the effect of all this is that the "vanguard" SWP, by its own dogmatism, acts to retard the political growth of the mass movements it has taken over for fear that the fronts would themselves begin to rival the party in providing a locus for serious radical activity. Hence, year after year it fights against broadening its marches to relate the war to poverty, sexism or racism, despite the fact that there is no reason to believe that those marches would diminish in size because of a broadened political perspective.

The split between the Trotskyists and the radicals in the anti-war movement was institutionalized during the summer of 1970 in the formation of an SWP anti-war group called the National Peace Action Coalition and a radical anti-war front called the National Coalition Against War, Racism and Repression. The NCAWRR, which later changed its name to the People's Coalition for Peace and Justice, included not only the traditional anti-war groups, but a variety of others, including Ralph Abernathy's Southern Christian Leadership Conference and the National Welfare Rights Organization. It lacked, however, the support of radical students who felt betrayed by May 9th and who still thought of the People's Coalition as part of the old New Mobe, which had been discredited in their eyes by its failure to do more than engage in another of a series of marches.

Against this background, plans for May Day emerged during the summer of 1970. These plans were linked to another idea: that while the government refused to make peace with the Vietnamese, the people could declare a separate peace directly. The plan was to send a group, representing various segments of the American population, to Vietnam to actually negotiate a peace agreement with the Vietnamese; it emerged at the National Student Association Convention where Rennie Davis had been invited to speak. (Radicals were surprised to find that the NSA, only a few years earlier an integral part of CIA operations, had been markedly radicalized by the invasion into Cambodia.) The NSA adopted an ultimatum to the President saying that if the war in Vietnam was not terminated by May 1970, students would engage in massive non-violent civil disobedience on a regional and national level. The peace treaty idea was similarly endorsed.

The plan was now brought to the National Coalition Against War, Racism and Repression in Milwaukee. A position paper endorsing non-violent civil disobedience beginning May 1 in Washington, D.C., was adopted in principle. In the next months, the plan was brought back to most of the constituency groups and endorsed by them. Fred Halstead sat in on the meeting in Milwaukee as an invited spectator, so there was no doubt that the Trotskyists knew about the plans and the date.

But the Trotskyists had their own plans, which they counterposed to those of the National Coalition. With ritual monotony, they decided to promote a re-run of the mass march on Washington—a tactic that had been used year after year since 1965. Meeting in December, the Trotskyists' new mass organization, NPAC, called for a peace march on April 24, one week *before* the May demonstrations were planned to begin.

The People's Coalition had planned to have a massive peaceful rally on May 2nd, and to start civil disobedience on the 3rd. It was thought that many people who came on the 2nd could be persuaded to stay by the arguments put forth at the rally. The Trotskyists knew that it would be extremely difficult to convince people to stay in Washington for *two* consecutive weekends—another blow aimed at undermining the potential of the May rally.

Unlike the diverse groupings in the Coalition, the Trotskyists were as organized and disciplined as the Communists of old. The unshakeable determination of the Trotskyists to proceed with their demonstration forced the People's Coalition into a dilemma: would it be wise to split the potential strength of a mass assembly between two separate dates, or should they combine into one? While it was clear that the Trotskyists had deliberately created the split and caused the confusion, wouldn't it be destructive for the People's Coalition to proceed with its own plans? While the Coalition worried over this question, other forces were in motion that would provide at least a partial solution.

For radicals, the People's Coalition had never seemed much of an answer to the problems of organization in the movement. While it was true that the Coalition was not a single-issue organization like the New Mobe, it was also true that the various organizations that were its constituents shared no common vision or analysis of American society. Further, though the name and the demands were different, these were for the most part the same people who had fecklessly allowed the New Mobe to channel the dissent of May 1970 into a meaningless march and who even now were agonizing over some way to reconcile activities so as not to come into open conflict with the Trotskyists. Recognizing this problem, a group of radicals resolved to work outside the structure of the Coalition and build an independent youth force committed to the May action. It was recognized that the Coalition's endorsement would be important for support among some constituencies, but since there was very little trust for the Coalition among young people, the youth force would have to have separate organizational status. The Treaty became the focus for building that separate organization (and thus a special target of the Trotskyists' attack).

National Student Association President David Ifshin chose a delegation of college student leaders to go to Hanoi and Saigon to negotiate the treaty. The trip had no financial angels—and the bills are yet to be paid. The delegation that went to Hanoi had no first draft ready, but the proposal it finally came up with seemed reasonable and it was quickly adopted by over 200 colleges when it was brought back in final form following meetings with Madam Binh and Xuan Thuy in Paris. To spur ratification within the U.S., a national conference of "Students and Youth for a People's Peace" was called for Ann Arbor on February 5–7 of this year, and was attended by over 2000 people. The conference endorsed the treaty and the May scenario. An organization was set up, composed of regional structures headed by a national coordinating council (which, however, subsequently failed to play any instrumental role).

Most experienced left people who attended the conference were very enthusiastic about May, but the May Day Collective organized by Rennie Davis which actually planned the demonstration in Washington was composed almost entirely of people who were new to the movement and who had had no previous experience in confrontation activities. People with movement experience gave two main reasons for not going to Washington to work on the action until it had actually begun. First was the fear of conspiracy indictments, following the Chicago and Seattle precedents. The Nixon-Mitchell regime had made quite clear its readiness to indict people for organizing demonstrations, and the absence of any national movement organization meant that people would have to face these indictments basically by themselves. Since there was no guarantee that the demonstration would be successful, it was unclear whether the risks would be worth it. The second obstacle to their participation came from the movement itself. Anti-elitism had reached such a fever pitch that virtually anyone who assumed leadership would risk being denounced for his or her efforts. A female activist, Anselma dell'Olio, described this phenomenon in a letter published in the *Liberated Guardian* in early March: "Productivity seems to be the major crime—but if you have the misfortune of being outspoken, and articulate, you are accused of being power-mad, elitist, racist, and finally the worst epithet of all, a male identifier."

The decision to form a separate youth organization to ensure an action even if the Coalition wavered was justified in the weeks after Ann Arbor. Faced with the inflexible decision by the Trotskyists to go ahead with their march on the 24th, and frightened that it did not have the organizational strength to

compete, the Coalition decided to cancel its own rally on May 2nd and endorse the march instead. At the same time, the Coalition did not want to abandon its endorsement of civil disobedience. It unequivocally urged people to come to Washington on April 24th, and to prepare to stay for what was to come: The week of April 26–30 would be a massive People's Lobby in which government workers would be urged to sign the People's Peace Treaty and join in a government workers' moratorium May 3 to May 5; then, on May 3rd, the Coalition would join the May Day tribe in civil disobedience.

The Coalition's cancellation of the strategically important May 2 rally was a severe blow to May Day. Not only had the Trotskyists offered nothing substantive in exchange, they now used that cancellation as a way of further weakening the May Day demonstrations. Through their rather extensive communications network, the Trotskyists sent out the message that the demonstrations planned for May had been cancelled. A statement issued by the People's Coalition announcing the cancellation of its separate rally was distributed by YSA and SMC members as proof that the Coalition no longer backed anything associated with May. Virtually every public planning meeting for May held in March and early April was attended by squads of YSAers who came to violence-bait the May actions, and, most bizarre of all, to denounce them for being associated with a "liberal" demand—namely, acceptance of the Peace Treaty. (The Peace treaty was denounced as liberal because the Vietnamese who wrote it had called for setting a date for withdrawal rather than for immediate withdrawal.)

Thus the Trotskyists tried to portray the "unauthorized" demonstrations as both violent and liberal. Very often they succeeded in confusing people, which was itself enough to undermine their determination to come to

May. After all, there was some element of risk in the May demonstrations, and in a situation where there appeared to be a split among radicals about the desirability of taking that risk, the path of caution would be likely to win out. (Like their CP forbears, the Trotskyists manage to supply seemingly radical arguments for doing nothing or taking no risks.)

On April 24 at the march, the Trotskyists distributed free copies of their paper, the *Militant,* which purported to give "the truth about May Day." In a gesture that may some-day be used by U.S. prosecutors as evidence that everyone knew that the May Day collective was trying to incite a riot, the *Militant* warns those who might be considering staying for civil disobedience, "Although it mouths niceties about the nonviolent character of its plans the May Day Tribe has been organizing its action in such a way as to almost guarantee a violent attack on the demonstrators." (As it turned out, the demonstrators were almost totally non-violent. This was a direct result of the efforts of the May Day organization, which did everything in its power to ensure the nonviolent character of the demonstrations: from holding classes in non-violent action, to publicly urging people who did not accept the non-violent discipline not to come at all.)

The beginning of the spring offensive came with the arrival of the Vietnam Vets on April 20. The vets' demonstrations made a tremen-dous impression on people, legitimating anti-war protest in the eyes of many who had not understood it previously.

The spirit of defiance among the vets was in marked contrast to the march on April 24th, which was passive and meaningless. Most of the people who came simply marched ritualis-tically a few blocks, then left without listen-ing to the endless round of boring speeches. Dave Dellinger was the only radical speaker permitted on either coast by the Trotskyists

and the only one in Washington scheduled to talk about why people should stay for May. (He failed to do so, primarily because he was in pain from an eye infection which later was to hospitalize him.) The speeches were televised, but when Dellinger seemed to be getting a bit too radical, his speech was interrupted for a few minutes of commercials. The entire rally had the air of a sporting event, and so it must have appeared to the TV audience.

On Sunday, April 25, the drama of May Day finally began to unfold. The government had authorized a permit for use of West Potomac Park. The area was extremely bad from a tactical standpoint, being on an isthmus jutting out onto the water, easily cut off by govern-ment police or troops. But it was all we had that was available, and there was a unanimous feeling among May Day people that there should be no confrontation over turf. The con-frontation must be about the war, and it would not begin in earnest till May 3rd.

The people who set up tents and started camping out at "the land" (also called "Algonquin Peace City") were a strange mix-ture. May Day had urged people to come April 24th and stay, so there were a number of political people. But at least half the crowd was unmistakenly rock-concert lumpen, and many of the men were extremely chauvinis-tic; political people foiled several attempted rapes, and other women were hassled and de-meaned. But at the same time, there was a great deal of community spirit and lots of mutual help. The movement glorifiers of the "new culture" saw in Algonquin City the fusing of politics and culture, because every night there was a town meeting at which political discussions were held and decisions about "the land" were made. But the bad drugs, the strychnine poisonings and the hasslings of women provided some cause for concern about the identification of rock culture with revolu-tion.

The glorification of the culture and the pre-dominance of anti-elitist sentiments reached their peak later that week when the May Day collective accepted an invitation by the Foreign Relations Committee of the Senate. Two of the five representatives chosen were selected on the basis of their being in touch with "the spirit of the land" in West Potomac Park. Rennie Davis, the most experienced, articulate and knowledgeable person in the entire operation, was deliberately excluded because he was a "superstar" and had received too much publicity and because the press had identified him—correctly—as the prime mover of the May Day operation. In a procedure typical of the inward orientation of the move-ment, little thought was given to the best way to bring the message about congressional in-action on Vietnam to the attention of the American people. Instead, the main question was how to present "ourselves"; the result was that of the five people chosen only Jay Craven, Boston University student body presi-dent, had been to Vietnam, and only Chip Mar-shall, a defendant in the Seattle conspiracy trial, had had any experience in the anti-war movement and treated the encounter as an integral part of the May action itself.

Marshall explained why many movement people viewed the senators as war criminals: they had the constitutional responsibility to stop the war, as well as the power to do so, but instead they had only made pious anti-war statements coupled with little effective action. Their function had been to deflect anti-war criticism by making people feel that there were people inside the Establishment who "really cared." Marshall put before the senators the central demand of the May demonstrations: if senators and congressmen are really against the war, they should filibuster against busi-ness-as-usual until the war is ended. May Day held that the minority in Congress—represent-ing the majority in the country—should take decisive action to prevent any legislation or appropriations from passing. The Washington demonstrations were meant to put anti-war liberals on the spot: "No more Presidential campaigns launched on the anti-war move-ment, no more flowery speeches to assure your constituencies that you're in touch—we de-mand decisive action now to stop the war machine," said Marshall.

But other May Day delegates to the Senate Foreign Relations Committee had different concerns. While the senators listened in shocked amazement, a woman calling her-self "Kathy Sister" read a prepared statement discussing "our" experience on "the land": We have had many problems in our encamp-ment on the Potomac, she told the Foreign Relations Committee; the presence of strych-nine in the acid showed that we are not yet able to treat each other as true brothers and sisters, and we have come to realize how far we have to go in transforming ourselves. Then a representative from Gay Liberation talked about the way male characteristics had been manipulated to create "fighting man"; and a woman from a Washington women's collective talked about the gentleness, humanity and beauty of the Vietnamese people as qualities to emulate. The senators picked up on these themes, ignoring the demand that had been put before them to act in accordance with the fact that 73 percent of the American people wanted out. While the ensuing exchanges about acid and personal relations certainly exposed the chauvinism of the senators to the 70 people sitting in the room, they did not do much to advance the struggle against the war.

The decision as to who should testify was made the same way as most of the May decisions: whoever was working on any aspect of a project, from the rock concert to logistics for the land, and happened to be present at the time, participated in the decision. Since there was no formal decision-making apparatus, most such ad hoc groupings felt themselves more or less legitimate depending on the number of people who actually attended the meeting, and then attempted to clear their decisions with Rennie since everyone generally acknowledged his experience and power, at least informally. The only shared politics of these meetings, beyond acceptance of the basic scenario for May, was the spirit of anti-elitism, which usually translated itself into dismissing anyone with competence on the grounds of their competence. If you could demonstrate that you were new to the operation, had no clearly defined politics, no experience in comparable situations, and only a faltering ability to articulate what you thought, then you had an excellent chance of becoming a public spokesman or spokeswoman for the group.

The fiasco at Foreign Relations was not much noticed by the press, since it was largely out-shadowed by the beginning of civil disobedience in Washington. The week of April 25–30 was the week of "People's Lobby," a project directed primarily by the National Action Group. Each day the target shifted: Congress, IRS, HEW, Justice, Selective Service. The tactic was to leaflet government workers and talk to them about the war, urging them not to go to work during the government workers' moratorium on May 3–5. This was coupled with mass blocking of entrances to governmental offices in a non-violent and disciplined way, mostly through massive sitdowns. Each day a few hundred people were arrested and carted away, charged with unlawful assembly, and released on bond. The People's Lobby involved many older pacifists from around the country who did not particularly relate to "Algonquin Peace City."

One Saturday, May 1, a rock concert was held on the northern grounds of West Potomac Park. The crowd was composed mainly of people who had come to Washington for the May actions and only incidentally for the rock concert. The regional representatives who had arrived Thursday and who did not share the May Day collective's enthusiasm for the culture used their power to eliminate the concert scheduled for Sunday evening, when Arlo Guthrie and Johnny Winter were to play. Some of the regional representatives felt the whole concert should be eliminated as well, to give more time for Monday's action. But Rennie Davis and the majority of the May Day collective felt strongly that Saturday's music should go on as scheduled, arguing that without it many people would become angry, since they had expected it, and might begin trashing (which was to be avoided at all costs). As a compromise, there was some attempt to make this rock concert more explicitly political, and several raps were given about Vietnam.

But just as the previous weekend's march had been fitted into the football format for TV, so the politics were fitted into rock-concert-ese by M. C. John Leland, who managed to homogenize everything into the mellifluous tones of "we are all together, we are beautiful, we are all having a good time, because that's what we are here for, a goo-oood time." After Jay Craven gave a moving speech about Vietnam, Leland took the mike and said, "Very important rap. Very important thing. Important things. Here are some more important things: Jennie meet Bill behind the stage. Steven Smith, your wallet has been found." There was almost no discussion of concrete details for the days ahead—Leland argued that that would bum out the crowd—but there were some political presentations of the new lifestyle. In fact, the residual sexism of the crowd almost got completely out of control when a gay brother in a flowing dress gave a speech about being gay. Instead of explaining Gay Liberation's rejection of socially defined roles, and the need for men to learn how to relate to each other as lovers instead of competitors, the spokesman focused on the need for men to "put on the dress," this year's substitution for "pick up the gun." "You recognized your own femininity," the speaker told the rock crowd of some 70,000, "when you started to grow your hair long. You've gone half the way, but now you've got to go all the way—start wearing a dress. Until you do that, you'll never be able to deal with your own sexism." Phil Ochs, standing backstage, said he felt so out of touch with this movement that he could not in good conscience urge people to stay for May: he had little faith in the movement's sanity. Jerry Rubin said, "I'm going to send Rennie a postcard saying, 'Thanks, Rennie, for the greatest trip of my life. (Signed) Jerry.'" At that point, Jerry kissed the ground, threw dirt in the air and exclaimed, "This is better than Woodstock."

The police moved in around 6:00 A.M. after the sound equipment had been removed and ordered people to leave Algonquin Peace City. The permit had been cancelled due to violations. The permit had allowed for only five tents on the land; since the previous Monday there had been countless tents, by Friday over 500. The government had picked its moment to move perfectly. People were exhausted or drugged out after the rock concert; no resistance was possible, though none would have been contemplated anyway, at least by the May Day leadership, which was so solidly committed to non-violence. With hundreds of police in full riot gear and the army's airborne units not far behind, people began to split. The prime destinations were the university campuses in town, although most of the regional groupings had also made arrangements to stay in various churches that had been volunteered as movement centers.

But what the people discovered as they entered town on Sunday was that martial law was in force for them, even though it was never declared. People were told they could not be on streets, or in parks, or together in groups of three, and were herded from place to place by riot-geared police. Under severe pressure from the government, the campuses declared the people were not welcome there, and on Monday police were called in and mass arrests were made at Georgetown. In the chaos of Sunday, the police provided one sure avenue of safety: they urged people to avoid arrest by leaving town. Many did, though some returned the next day, because they were able to stay at the University of Maryland which made available 700 places in the dormitories. There were about 70–75,000 people at the rock concert, at least 30,000 of whom either never intended to stay or left town as a result of the unexpected police raid that morning. About 35,000 people remained and were on the streets Monday morning.

It came off as scheduled. A detailed tactical manual of 20 printed pages included photographs and maps of the targets that were to be hit by the different regional groupings. In the weeks before May 3rd, regions had been urged to send groups of people to Washington to look over their targets and the surrounding areas. The main targets were the bridges leading into town from Virginia, and several key traffic circles leading to the main governmental thoroughfares. The tactics were decided regionally: basically they consisted of either sitting down in front of traffic, stalling cars, or standing in front of traffic and then using mobile tactics, i.e., moving down the block as the police came so that they could block traffic there. The police, of course, had easy access to the tactical manual since it was widely distributed and generally available. By mid-Sunday afternoon each of the targets was completely guarded by thousands of police and regular army armed with M-16s. Police helicopters kept careful surveillance of the movement of demonstrators throughout the next three days. Demonstrators were particularly wary of being trapped in their sleeping places—they feared an encirclement that would prevent them from getting to their targets and disrupting traffic. So they tended to make the opposite mistake of getting to their targets too early.

Demonstrations at most targets began at 6:00 A.M., well before the heaviest rush hour traffic began. The demonstrators were quickly routed from many places, and arrested by the thousands at others. The police tactic of mass arrest was not unexpected. Though the papers played it down, there were many instances of police brutality, as club-swinging cops beat and bloodied many heads. But while on an absolute scale the number of such incidents was high, it was very low on a scale relative to the number of arrests. Most people arrested received little hassle; they were simply placed on buses and shipped off to the prisons and later to the large concentration camp at JFK stadium. The police used much tear gas around the bridges but very little at the traffic circles closer to the downtown areas. Again, martial law, while not declared, was enforced. Anyone who looked vaguely representative of the new life-style was subject to arrest at any moment. Several hundred people who had no intention of relating to the demonstration were thus arrested. You did not need to be in the action to get arrested: as long as you were outside you were a target for the police.

The spirit of the people in the detention camp was very high. Despite the fact that there were almost no sanitary facilities, no blankets, and for a long time no food, the demonstrators were spirited and together. As each new group arrived there was cheering and singing from the crowd inside. A Viet Cong flag was raised over the compound. Most of the people in the compound were not booked or even formally placed under arrest; they were able to keep their belongings. On Tues-

day many of them were released on a federal court order since they had been illegally detained—there was no record for many of them showing why they had been arrested or by whom.

But it was not all pleasant. The police set off tear gas from time to time to keep people "under control." And it was far from pleasant in the crowded Washington jails, where several thousand demonstrators were taken and then often doused with tear gas. By evening the arrests had climbed to 8000, the largest figure for any anti-war demonstration in U.S. history. By Wednesday the figure was to top 13,000. The high number of arrests was particularly important for dispelling the impression the government and press had conveyed on Sunday that almost everyone had left town and that only a small number of demonstrators remained. It showed the commitment of the demonstrators—many people were willing to put their bodies on the line in some meaningful way.

Mass arrests had apparently been decided on by Attorney General Mitchell and communicated to Police Chief Wilson; the Black mayor of the town, Walter Washington, was not consulted about the mass arrests. The reaction from the Black community was immediate. On Tuesday morning an extraordinary press conference of religious and community leaders from the ghetto announced their support for the demonstrators and offered moral and material aid. They announced that the homes of the Black community would be open for those who were being thrown out of university sanctuaries and that they would make a contribution to the bail fund. On Tuesday a march to the Justice Department was led by members of the Black community.

That march and rally were in marked contrast to the march to the Pentagon the day before, also called by the People's Coalition for Peace and Justice. On Monday the Pentagon march had been scheduled at the same time as the May Day actions and the PCPJ found that it had very few constituents, as less than a thousand people participated in three separate march attempts, each of which was stopped and busted. On Tuesday, the PCPJ called its action for late morning, after traffic disruptions had ceased, and many May Day people showed up. About 5000 rallied at the Justice Department. (Rennie was in jail: on Monday afternoon, walking back from a press conference, he was seized by eight FBI agents and arrested on charges of conspiracy to block governmental operations and to interfere with the civil rights of government workers. Fellow Chicago defendant John Froines was named as co-conspirator and arrested at the Justice Department demonstration on Tuesday. On Wednesday night another Chicago defendant, Abbie Hoffman, who had played no organizational role whatever in May Day, was busted at his New York apartment for crossing state lines with intent of inciting to riot. Many more indictments were expected.)

The demonstration at Justice on Tuesday was a massive sit down in front of the building, which was suddenly sealed off and surrounded; 3000 people were arrested. This time the government was more cautious to get everyone's name and the name of the arresting officer. Attorney General Mitchell supervised the arrests from the fifth floor of the building. On Wednesday there were no traffic disruptions planned—instead, the tactic was a mass march to Congress. Government workers held a support rally at Lafayette Park, but the permit allowed only 500 into the park, which was surrounded by police to enforce the limitation. Outside the police lines several thousand more government workers milled around, listening to speeches. From there they marched to the Capitol, where May Day people had gathered on the House steps to listen to several congressmen and congresswomen address the crowd. As one of them spoke, police moved in on orders from Speaker of the House Carl Albert; over 1500 were arrested.

It is interesting that the discipline of non-violence was kept throughout the day-long demonstration, despite considerable provocation from the police and considerable disagreement among some of the demonstrators about the value of non-violence. In this way the demonstration lived up to the claims of its organizers, who had used the symbol of Gandhi sitting cross-legged, with raised fist, as the symbol of the entire May Day protest. It is also important to note that most of the participants in the demonstrations were people with some movement background. It was estimated by many regional representatives that at least 70 percent of the people who came to Washington would have come even if there had been no commitment to non-violence, and that without that commitment there might have been much more sustained disruption.

At a press conference held Monday morning after the roads had been opened by army and police, May Day people were asked to admit that they had failed in their stated goal to stop the government. The May Day tribe was asked to explain its slogan, "If the government won't stop the war, we will stop the government." The spokesmen agreed that from a strictly military standpoint the demonstration had failed, but that no one had ever had a military interpretation of the slogan. It was absurd, of course, to believe that people could both be committed to non-violence and actually physically stop the government from functioning. The government had ordered its key personnel either to come in Sunday night or arrive at work by 5:00 A.M.. It had reserved rooms in downtown hotels for many. And it had a fleet of helicopters ready to assist others.

The May Day objective had been a political one: to set in motion forces that could stop the government and then stop the war. Those political forces might actually have been set in motion if the focus on Congress, as a body with the power and the mandate but without the will to end the war, had been communicated to people around the country. That message will certainly be taken home to the hundreds of communities towards which the tired army of the Potomac, dwindled from its 40,000 strength of Monday, started to make its way on Wednesday.

In terms of shaking people from their apathy, and stopping business-as-usual in the Capitol, the May demonstrations were clearly a success. People may have been at their desks, but it was the demonstration against the war, not their business, that was the main focus of attention, not only on Monday but throughout the week. And the depth of sentiment and urgency about the war had once again been brought to the attention of the country. Whatever other criticism one may have about May, this result surely made the whole effort worthwhile.

Another important success of the May Day demonstrations was the Women's March held on Sunday afternoon. The march had over 1000 participants, who managed to get together despite the attack by the police on Algonquin Peace City earlier in the day. The march was spirited and one of the best actions of the entire series of demonstrations. It reflected a new prominence of women's leadership in anti-imperialist struggles, a prominence confirmed in the regional coordinating council of May Day which was heavily influenced by that leadership. The regional groupings, formed around May Day, were another promising development—they provided much leadership during the demonstrations, and were generally more thoughtful and better experienced than the May Day collective.

Unfortunately the May Day collective tended to guard its power jealously and did not allow the regional groupings much room to grow, but now that the demonstrations are over the regions have indicated a determination to stick together and begin to chart some new directions for the summer.

At least two of the crucial goals, however, of the May Day strategy did not occur: the demonstrations in Washington did not touch off a rash of similar demonstrations around the country; and the organizing for May did not create thousands of collectives that would engage in ongoing organizing at the local level. Both of these goals had originally been taken seriously by Rennie and the May Day collective, but without any real organization to pull off the more grandiose plans, the old dynamic of one-shot national actions took hold again, and all resources were mobilized to ensure that people actually came to Washington. The notion of the D.C. arrests as tinder for an inflammable country would have worked if the movement had had a national organization to take up the cause. Without one, the idea was merely one of a series of hopes that were shattered against the hard rock of present-day political realities. (Of course, a national organization that continued to espouse the inward-oriented ideology of the current movement would have done almost as badly.)

The left could provide the direction for leading people out of the war, just as it once provided the leadership in revealing that the war was wrong. At the same time, it could help people make sense of their increasingly chaotic experience in an American empire in continual internal crisis. But just at the moment when sentiment in the country is opening up these possibilities, the left seems bent on making itself appear irrelevant to the vast majority of the people. When it approached government workers about the war, it did not even mention

the connection between the war and the inflation which had been used a week before as
Nixon's excuse for denying them a salary increase. Issues like inflation, health care, taxes,
transportation, and even work conditions, are
often written off by the organized left as
"liberal." In their place, concern for the quality
of people's relationships becomes an exclusive
center of attention.

But even as the left is about to make a breakthrough around that concern, it stops itself
and decides that it is in no position to talk to
people about their lives, since the lives of
movement people are screwed up too. So the
focus shifts to our own lives: until we are good
exemplifications of the new revolutionary person, we have "no right" to talk to anybody
else. In the process the relationship between
how our own lives have been formed and the
structure of a capitalist society falls by the way-
side, and the movement becomes totally transfixed on itself. Even when, as in May Day, the
inwardness is temporarily overcome, it still
permeates every aspect of the planning and
organizing for the event. Hence we are fighting
against the war not because we oppose American imperialism, but because the Vietnamese
people are beautiful, having supposedly already achieved the changes in social and personal relations that we are striving for. And we
choose our public spokeswomen and spokesmen not because they are good at communicat-
ing to others, but because they show what *we*
are really like. The thought that somehow we
must embody the revolutionary goals before
the revolution takes place is just an extreme
reaction to the earlier doctrine of the Old
Left—that we make the revolution without any
concern for transforming ourselves in the process. Both attitudes are destructive.

The reaction to elitism was certainly an
understandable response to the extreme forms
of male domination, manipulativeness and
chauvinism in the old movement. The syn-

drome of "superstar," which reached its apex
around the Chicago conspiracy trial, was extremely stifling and retarded the political
and personal development of most New Left
activists at the same moment that it was building the egos of the "heavies." The absence of
a national organization to which these heavies
could be held politically responsible increased
the separation between these leaders and their
supposed base. But the extremes to which the
anti-elitist reaction has gone can only be explained by a fuller understanding of the failures
of the movement to break out of its early
isolation. Frustrated by its own powerlessness,
and seeing this less in terms of its inflated
rhetoric and unwillingness to talk to ordinary
people than in terms of its own internal structure and mind sets, the movement began to
turn this frustration inward upon itself. But
while it may be easier (as well as necessary)
to deal with the powerhouses in our own movement, in many ways this has inhibited the
struggle against the real power in America:
the ruling class. The result has been a politics
of spontaneity and personal development that
has intensified the movement's isolation and
inwardness while, paradoxically, strengthening the position of the heavies who, in the absence of a national organization, remain the
only recognizable spokespeople for the entire
movement.

An alternative to this impasse ought to
combine the vitality, creativity and originality
of the New Left with some of the discipline
and organization, and a lot of the outward
orientation, of the old. It ought to be national
in scope in order to be able to develop national
strategies and offer a coherent direction to the
energies that have been unleashed against
American capitalism in the past few years. If
these energies have often developed in a somewhat parochial direction, at least part of the
reason has been the absence of an organiza-

tional structure which would make co-ordinated attacks on the system even conceivable.

Such an organization would have to avoid the major pitfalls of the past. Unlike SDS, which was built around a very undefined politics and spent several years trying to achieve such definition, it would have to start with an explicit set of radical politics. It would have to experience its radicalism not in the outrageousness of its rhetoric or the impenetrability of its jargon, but in the extent to which it mobilized sections of the population into active struggle against the system. It would have to see itself moving beyond campus and youth constituencies: addressing the problems of working people, women, the aged, the poor, and avoiding the tired formulas of Old Left sects or the arrogance and superiority the New Left has sometimes fallen prey to. It would have to reject categorically the anti-intellectualism of the current movement that parades under the banner of anti-elitism, while simultaneously struggling against the chauvinism and manipulativeness that caused the anti-elitist reaction. It would have to see itself as providing leadership, and not just as an instrument for self-development. It would have to be democratically structured to maximize local autonomy and creativity. It would have to encourage and strengthen community organizing projects, but at the same time it would have to overcome the parochialism of current movement organizing projects that always seem to counterpose their own activities to national strategies and actions.

Without the development of this kind of organizational structure, the next year will see the forces of the New Left splitting in equally useless directions: surges of new Marxist-Leninist sectarianism, increased isolationism ultimately ending up in the farmlands of America (the greening movement), and desperate attempts to get back into touch with reality by moving back into the system via the left wing of the McGovern-Kennedy-Bayh-whoever campaigns.

The movement has got to get it together now. It may not get another chance for a long time to come.

Section Nine

The Women's Movement: Birth of a New Feminism

"Again and again, as I read the literature of the women's movement," the poet Adrianne Rich has written, "I am struck by courageous imaginations that are now trying to go further than feminism has gone before: to grapple with immediate political necessities, with the emotional imprintings of the culture . . . and with a sense that time, in the sense of human survival, is running out." The new journalism in this section, all of it written by women deeply concerned with feminism, reflects the feelings of hope and crisis Rich describes.

It is journalism that cannot be separated from the economic and political realities the women's movement has confronted since its resurgence in the middle 1960s. It is related to the kind of job discrimination revealed by Department of Labor figures for earnings in 1967:

White males	$6,704
Nonwhite males	$4,277
White females	$3,991
Nonwhite females	$2,861

Equally important, the articles here continually remind us that, even in areas where women have made progress, the results are often still disappointing: For example, although 20 percent more women were elected to public office in 1972, they held only a little over 5 percent of the total number of offices.

The feminist journalism in this section does not, however, concentrate simply on the social struggles of the women's movement or what NOW in its founding statement describes as the effort "to bring women into full participation in the mainstream of American society." Most often, the reportage collected here reflects the view Susan B. Anthony expressed a century ago when she observed, "The ballot is not even half the loaf; it is only a crust—a crumb." Instead of being apolitical, the feminist journalism that follows is thus broadly political in the sense described by a Redstockings' Manifesto of 1969: "Because we have lived so intimately with our oppressors, in isolation from each other, we have been kept from seeing our personal suffering as a political condition. This creates the illusion that a woman's relationship with her man is a matter of interplay between two unique personalities, and can be worked out individually. In reality . . . the conflicts between individual men and women are *political* conflicts that can only be solved collectively."

From the writing in this section, we do not accordingly get a chronological account of the women's movement from, say, the formation of NOW in 1966 to the 1973 convention of the National Women's Political Caucus, nor do we get reportage on such women's movement victories as abortion reform or Congressional passage of the Equal Rights Amendment. The journalism here explores primarily the process of women realizing collectively and individually the nature of their experiences in a society where "masculine" values pervade everything from psychoanalysis to the ideal of the family.

The first account, Ingrid Bengis's "Heavy Combat in the Erogenous Zone," begins on a deeply personal note with Bengis describing her own experience of trying to talk to her psychiatrist about sexuality. "I am suddenly forced to realize," she writes, "that all the available terms we have are either clinical or male-power-oriented. The English language does not have words to express a 'female view' of sexuality." For Bengis, this limitation is more than a semantic one. It goes "straight to the heart of the problem of female sexuality, which is that women's ideas about it have been explained primarily by men. A female Freud or a female Jung just hasn't appeared yet." Under these conditions Bengis finds the current "sexual revolution" destructive. She believes it has freed men and women for *more* sex rather than *better* sex, and that its preoccupation with techniques and erogenous zones makes it especially reductive for women. What is to be done under these circumstances? Bengis provides no categorical answer. She is only sure "I'd rather make a vow to eternal chastity" than accept the relationships that generally exist between men and women.

Sally Kempton's "Cutting Loose" explores many of the same personal problems as "Heavy Combat," but Kempton writes from the viewpoint of a woman involved in a marriage, and her account ends on a very different note of ambiguity than Bengis's. As she observes, not without self-mockery, "The true dramatic conclusion of this narrative should be the dissolution of my marriage; there is a part of me which believes that you cannot fight a sexist system while acknowledging your need for the love of a man. . . . But in the end my husband and I did not divorce, although it seemed at one time as if we would." The marriage Kempton describes at the end of "Cutting Loose" is, however, radically different from the one she describes at the beginning. It is a marriage based on a change in values ("we are trying to be together as equals, to separate our human needs from the needs imposed on us by our sex roles"), and it is a marriage about which she will not hide her reservations: "I wonder always whether it is possible to define myself as a feminist revolutionary and still remain in any sense a wife. . . . I also fear that no man will ever love me again, that no man could ever love a woman who is angry."

In contrast to "Heavy Combat" and "Cutting Loose," the final pieces in this section are concerned with collective efforts by women to change their lives. Vivian Gornick's "Consciousness♀" centers on the experiences of a consciousness-raising group in New York City. Gornick defines consciousness raising as "the feminist practice of examining one's personal experiences in the light of sexism . . . that theory which explains woman's subordinate position in society as a result of cultural decisions to confer direct power on men and only indirect power on women." She regards consciousness raising as "at one and the same time, both the most celebrated and accessible introduction to the women's movement as well as the most powerful technique for feminist conversion known to the liberationists." The evidence Gornick offers for the value of consciousness raising is the concrete experience of the New York women she describes —not theory. There is, moreover, no effort on her part to portray the women in the Manhattan group she reports on as "committed feminists." Instead, they appear simply as women who have found their meeting together gives them insight into their lives that they did not have before.

Jill Johnston's "March of the Real Women" brings this section to a close with an account of the preparations for the 1972 New York march commemorating the Nineteenth Amendment. Johnston finds it essential to discuss the divisions within the women's movement rather than dwell on the unity, as is usually the case with analyses of marches celebrating the Nineteenth Amendment. The division that most concerns Johnston, herself a feminist and a lesbian, is the one between the "straights" and the lesbians. It is the lesbians, she believes, who now "constitute the revolutionary pivot of the feminist movement," and it is time, she argues, for them to stop accepting a subordinate role for fear of damaging the feminist cause. It is not, however, for political reasons alone that Johnston wants lesbians to occupy what she believes is their rightful place in the women's movement. She sees lesbians giving the women's movement psychological stability at a time when straight feminists cannot because they are "sexually confused sick celebate furious at men" and unsure of "the (still criminal) pleasures of love and sex with their sisters."

Heavy Combat in the Erogenous Zone

Ingrid Bengis

Ingrid Bengis, writer and feminist, has written for the *Village Voice.* Her recent book, *Combat in the Erogenous Zones,* was nominated for the National Book Award in 1973.

A few months ago, I had a dream, what might be thought of as a typically Freudian dream, if we did not live in such questioning times. These days a Women's Liberationist (and deep down there are very few women who aren't) can't afford to assume anything too literally at the risk of undermining her own nascent point of view. The battle for alternative interpretations of role, of identity, of sexuality, has just begun, and we are in delicate areas of combat where each thrust behind the areas leads to the slaughter of an image once thought of as benign and to the opening up of strange unexplored corners of consciousness.

My own symbolic thrust begins in the middle of the night. I am dreaming. I wake up, grab the pencil alongside my bed, and write down what I have "seen." I am walking into my analyst's office (he is a Freudian in the best and most flexible sense of that word), and as I pass the foyer, I bump into him coming out of a closet which doubles as a darkroom. A camera with a telephoto lens is hanging around his neck. I bend to look at it while he explains to me the process he has been using in the darkroom. I am fascinated and ask several questions about technique. Our heads are bent close together, and the feeling of intimacy in the situation comes from this small gesture of closeness. At this point the dream ends.

The anatomical symbology (and whatever other symbology comes naturally to you) seems fairly obvious, but when I talk to *him* about it, he is more interested in the fact that in the

dream it was him teaching me about photography whereas in reality he knows nothing about photography and I am a fairly talented amateur photographer. In fact, just a few weeks before, I had given him a poster-size enlargement of one of my photographs.

"Who's supposed to teach who?" he says.

"Oh," I answer, "I don't know anything about photographic *technique*. I couldn't teach anyone anything. I just have good instincts."

The subject ends there, for the moment at least, but the idea stays with me. "Technique," I think. "And he was teaching me what I knew more about?"

It is several days before we return to the subject of sexuality. I have a hard time finding the right words to say what I mean. Always before I have been somewhat vague, but this time I want to be specific. I am suddenly forced to realize that all the available terms we have are either clinical or else male-power-oriented. The English language simply does not *have* words to express a "female view" of sexuality. We have the language Freud gave us—of libido and penis envy; the words Kinsey gave us—of prone position, vaginal orgasm, coitus interruptus; the words Henry Miller gave us—of fucking and coming. Then we have a few poetic words, mostly borrowed from nature, which speak of storms, of quiet seas, whirlpools and whirlwinds. But do any of these express the way a female thinks about sex? And how in fact, *does* a female think about sex? Is there really any difference between sexuality and sensuality? Does that difference *mean* anything? And what about technique? Do you care? Do I care? Does anyone care?

One of the more blatant examples of how language has tempted us into unconsciously accepting a version of ourselves which is fundamentally degrading is the use of that now common household work "fuck." There was a time when, for me, and I am sure for many other women, the word "fuck" stood as a symbol of liberation, a word which would cut loose another puritanical shackle. I remember that for a long time I was hung up on the brutal vulgar sound of the word, and could feel myself flushing every time I forced myself to say it. "I'm being overly delicate," I thought. "Earthy words are a lot better than romantic ones, so stop this virginal prissiness. Fuck is a perfectly good word, a free word." The inner struggle went on until at last I was able to say "fuck you" and "fuck off" with near-perfect nonchalance. But never to this day have I been able to refer to "whatever the word should be for that thing which two people do together when they are sexually joined" as "fucking." And now, a few mental millennia later, it comes to me that my instincts, which then seemed to me to be backward, were in reality far ahead of my ideas, as is so often the case . . . particularly with women who *are* more instinctive and intuitive (let's not, while trying to expand ourselves, deny what is best in us). This "plateau" I had reached of being able to stab sexual hypocrisy in the back was in fact nothing more than taking on a new and more insidious form of bondage.

Just stop for a second. Who is it who does the fucking? And who gets fucked? And how is the word used in other contexts . . . "fucked up," "fucked over," "fucked off." Do *any* of those expressions point to something besides a damaged or brutalized state? Do they indicate mental or emotional well-being? No. They are words of power and powerlessness, of seducer and seduced, of victim and victim-izer. And for a great many men, perhaps the majority, this is precisely what they mean when they use the word "fuck," only they haven't been clear enough in their own minds to see through their use of language, or perhaps they have and it is *we* who have traipsed along like children following the Piper to their own destruction. It may even be that with our perverse and masochistic inclination to find something attractive in male brutality, we have tacitly agreed with and looked up to that vision of the male as stud. I've had a history of that, and know full well that it is not at all uncommon among women. But recognizing that fatal weakness for self-denigration, that tendency of victims to cooperate in their own execution, is perhaps the first step in freeing ourselves from just one more hang-up. And any woman who uses the word "fuck" comfortably should begin to think about the reasons why . . . and then STOP . . . unless of course it serves as a reminder of where things are at and how far they have to go.

There are those who would respond to this argument by saying, "So what words would you like to use . . . 'making love' or 'sleeping with'?" But that is precisely the point. The words have yet to be invented. "Making love" and "sleeping with" are more than euphemistic expressions for sexual intercourse, they are signposts to wish-fulfillments. Most women say "making love" more easily than they say "fucking," but that's because "making love" is what they think sex *should* be. But even that concept is faulty. One does not "make," i.e., "create" love through the act of sex. Ideally one expresses love which already exists. But in our choice of words, we tacitly acquiesce in the fact that for many men (and let's face it, for many women too, since we have cooperated with things and sold ourselves out at the bargain rate) love's creation comes about *through* sex, not together with it. If language is any barometer, we are confusing what should be with what is, and given the current state of things, men and women rarely enough make love with each other.

In talking with my analyst, I ended up using the clinical words. The male conquest words were quite simply repellent to me (not because I'm a prude but because I don't like to be thought of as an object), and the clinical vocabulary at least had the comparative virtue of being neutral. But in the course of the conversation I was struck with how utterly foreign to my *experience* they seemed, how utterly they betrayed my mobile sense of things. Now what, I ask myself, do I mean by mobile? Well, mobile refers to movement. And what does static refer to? Well, static refers to staying in one place. And how does that fit in? I wasn't sure. I just had the vague sense that I wasn't getting across, that what my analyst was referring to and what *I* was referring to might be two different things.

We were talking about stimulus . . . about "erogenous zones" and also about how I got furious when men on the street whispered obscene comments in my ear. What I resented about that almost as much as the "cruel anonymity, sexual toy" aspect of it was the fact that they made the word "woman" equal to the word breast or the word cunt (womb? crotch? pelvic region? . . . you see the problem). Thinking about that made me remember the time when I modeled for a beginning painting class. One of the boys did a picture of me in which there were two breasts floating in the air in the approximate place where my breasts would be when I was standing up, a pelvic area, and a head with no features, just a lot a hair. The rest of me was simply left out.

"But there *are* areas which are connected with erotic activity," my analyst said. "People in primitive cultures didn't make enormous statues of phalluses for nothing. And your feet are not the same as your breasts."

I had to think about that for a while . . .

for a couple of days in fact. And then I realized what was the matter. Who in primitive cultures was responsible for phallic worship? And in which cultures was it common? The answer was fairly simple, I thought. Phallic worship was fostered in patriarchal societies by men, societies in which the male point of view dominated, in which men had the positions of authority and were concerned with maintaining that authority. If women believe the phallus is something to be *worshipped* (not acknowledged, not thought of as just a part of a whole . . . but *worshipped*) then their dependency upon men is assured.

On the island of Delos in Greece, there are dozens of huge statues of phalluses. To the ancient Greeks (and to the modern Greeks as well) women were property. Good conversation, good sex, good warfare were all to be carried on with other men. Today in Greece, the women of 25 are dressed in black. Their faces are deeply lined. They scrub the floors, work in the fields, take care of the children. And the men? At the age of 60, they're hale and hearty . . . you remember Zorba . . . and they sit all day in cafes drinking coffee and ouzo. Why? Because women are supposed to be inferior. And what is the symbol of their inferiority? The fact that they don't have a phallus, and a phallus is power.

America isn't Greece and women don't look like 50 at the age of 25. But they do try to look like 25 when they're 50. They have cosmetic surgery done on their breasts, dye their hair blonde because Gentlemen Prefer Blondes, and struggle into Junior Dresses. All this because they want to continue to be desirable to a man, and men desire young bodies. (Just for the record, I'm 25.) And what must a man do to continue to be attractive to a woman? He must be capable of having an erection. Doesn't that say something about our social values, about phallic worship, and about how both men and women become distorted through it? Little girls become co-quettes . . . little boys measure the size of each other's penises. Big girls worry if they're too flat-chested or big-breasted, depending on the fashion (also determined largely by men), and big boys worry about coming too fast, too soon.

I thought again of what my analyst had said, and it seemed to me that the difference in our points of view went straight to the heart of female sexuality, which is that women's ideas about it have been primarily explained by men. A female Freud or a female Jung just hasn't appeared yet. Geniuses are rare crea-tures, and despite the current vogue for dis-paraging Freud, especially among women's liberationists, he *was* a genius, popular "syntheses" and distortions of his thinking notwithstanding. He's still light years ahead of us on the question of bisexuality, which we've accepted objectively and have yet to deal with subjectively. But poor Freud just wasn't a woman. As he said to his diary at the age of 77, "What do women want? Dear God! What do they want?" The people who can answer best are women . . . and they should be doing it . . . women psychiatrists, women anthro-pologists, women women. One would hope, after all, that genius, as has so often been as-serted, is not the exclusive province of men.

Not only did I disagree with my analyst about phalluses, but I also disagreed with him about breasts and feet. Not that I was a foot fetish-ist . . . not that I thought that phalluses were horrid . . . not that I was a wrinkled crone whom no man had ever looked at . . . but that the whole notion of categories of anatomy, of erogenous zones, had nothing to do with the way I, as a woman, felt about love-making.

And that brought me right back to the idea of mobility. I was beginning to understand what I had been trying to get at. Specifically . . . that sex was not an engagement in which segments of the body assumed carefully co-ordinated positions . . . it was an activity which

absorbed every inch of you, from your toes to the small of your back to your fingertips. To men though, or at least to most men, sex meant "what you do with your penis" and "how you build up to what you're going to do with your penis." Fucking a woman means coming and, hopefully, by careful manipulation of the proper erogenous zones, getting her to come too.

A familiar pattern of behavior which has never cease to alienate me came to mind. First there was the kiss on the mouth, then the kiss on the ear and/or neck, then a gradual movement toward the breasts and finally . . . ah . . . the holy grail. And that was supposed to be "making love." For me, on the contrary, what had always been beautiful about bodies was the way they moved together, the feel of skin on a belly, the curve of a hipbone, the changing pressure of fingertips, the hollow of a shoulder, the tangle of arms and legs, the sense of moving and growing together like something organic. Sure, having intercourse with someone you *liked* was great, sure or-gasms were great, but in the long run they had less merit per se than the feeling of a warm mobile body, the whole of it, engaged in being physically close, physically responsive. I would even go so far as to say that I would infinitely prefer spending the night with someone who was *impotent,* but warm and affectionate, to spending it with a man I once dated whom I overheard saying in a bar to one of his friends, "She wouldn't fuck, Danny. She just wouldn't fuck." And his friend's words of consolation were, "You should have turned over on your side and waited five minutes . . . then she would have been all over you." Frankly, I could have cheerfully castrated the both of them.

We have all been taught that having an or-gasm is nirvana . . . a vaginal orgasm no less. Well, orgasms, in all their varieties, are nice experiences, but if you haven't had one, it *isn't* a disaster. On the other hand, if you've never spent half an hour in bed with a man who enjoyed exploring your body as if it were a map of the world and every country on it were interesting. . . . If you've never been with a man who, when he said "touch me," was referring to *any* part of his body . . . if you haven't spent an hour talking comfortably with a man about social-political-aesthetic-mathematical-scientific questions, then baby you've got a problem . . . or rather society's got a problem, because we've been taught to think *their* way and that's not where it's at these days. (So as not to be too much of a "ball-crusher," I want to take this opportunity to tell the silent minority of male women's liberationists out there that this verbal assault is *not* aimed at you, there may be fewer of you than you think.)

In Andre Malraux's, "Man's Fate," an apparently uninteresting woman writes a note to her lover in which she says: "Do you know dear that Persian women beat their husbands with their nailed slippers when they are angry . . . and then of course they afterwards return to everyday life, the life in which to weep with a man does not commit you, but in which to go to bed with him makes you a slave, the life in which one *has* women. I am not a woman to be *had,* a stupid body in which you may find your pleasure by telling lies as to children and invalids. You know a good many things, dear, but you will probably die without its ever having occurred to you that a woman is *also* a human being. . . . I have met enough men to know how to regard a passing affair: nothing is without importance the moment it involves his pride, and pleasure allows him to gratify it most quickly and most often. I refuse to be regarded as a body, just as you refuse to be regarded as a checkbook. You act with me as the prostitutes do with you: talk but pay. I am *also* that body which you want me to be *wholly;* I know it. It is not always easy for me to protect myself from the idea people have

of me. Your presence brings me close to my body, with disgust, as springtime brings me close to it with joy. . . ." That is surely as profound a statement as has been made on the right of women to control their bodies, about the right to be simply a person, not a collection of erogenous zones.

For a "traditional" perspective on things, sugar-coated with a little bit of poetics, I turn to the "Kama Sutra" of Vatsayana, which in recent years has become a popular favorite. Here are some entries from the Table of Contents:

Chapter Five. "Love bites and techniques to be used on women from different lands."

Chapter Seven. "The various ways to hit a woman and the accompanying sounds."

Chapter Eight. "Women who play the role of the man."

Part Three, Chapter Two. "How to win the confidence of a virgin."

Part Seven (Seduction), Chapter One. "On seduction and aphrodisiacs."

Part Seven, Chapter Two. "Ways and means of exciting desire. Technique for strengthening the lingam. Experiments and recipes."

Then I turned to the chapter on "A Close Examination of Women": "When a man tries to seduce a woman he should pay particular attention to her mood and humor and act accordingly. . . . A man should take the initiative in regard to women and hold her in deep conversation. He should then allow himself a few amorous advances, and if he feels that she is willing by her response, he should continue without fear until he has achieved his purpose and enjoyed her. . . . It can perhaps generally be stated that all women, whether wise, simple, or trustful, who openly reveal their affection can be easily won." Every woman can be seduced, says the sage. It's only a question of finding the right method.

I felt as if I was going to throw up. I felt as if I could never stop hating the kind of men (and they *are* in the majority) who are Vatsayana's kinsmen. "Goddamn it," I yelled. "I can't be seduced, and what's more I don't want to be." Somebody can care for me and I can care for them and we can make love together, and if we care for each other we'll do things which express that caring, but I *refuse* to be a warmblooded diagram, I refuse to provide the models for any more "profound" works on the "Art of Love-making." Because the real "art of love-making" comes from caring about the person you're making love *with*. Because technique is what you absolutely *must* have when you don't have feeling, when you're trying to "make" a woman. Technique is what the so-called "sexual revolution" has freed women for . . . so they can have sex with a man they don't care about, so they can be free to do it on *his* terms. Nowadays a woman can sleep with anyone she wants. But dare she refuse if she doesn't want to be a cipher, a notch in someone's belt, if she just doesn't care enough about the man? Most of the time the answer is no. The price is too high. It's a buyer's market, and there's plenty of merchandise around. Well, you want to know the truth . . . I'd rather make a vow to eternal chastity than submit to that kind of degradation. And believe me, I don't like chastity any better than any other woman who is genuinely capable of "openly revealing her affections."

But until "technique" and "erogenous zones" can be replaced by the warmly, human sound of "I like you . . . I like all of you . . . yes you're beautiful, your blood and your bones and your heartbeat and your mind and the small of your back and the arch of your foot, yes you're beautiful you're warm and passionate and tender . . . yes you're beautiful even if we *don't* make love," then goddamn it, it's just not worth it.

Cutting Loose: A Private View of the Women's Uprising
Sally Kempton

Sally Kempton has written for *Esquire* magazine, the *New York Times Book Review,* and other periodicals.

Once another woman and I were talking about male resistance to Woman's Liberation, and she said that she didn't understand why men never worry about women taking their jobs away but worry only about the possibility that women may stop making love to them and bearing their children. And once I was arguing with a man I know about Woman's Liberation, and he said he wished he had a motorcycle gang with which to invade a Woman's Liberation meeting and rape everybody in it. There are times when I understand the reason for men's feelings. I have noticed that beyond the feminists' talk about the myth of the vaginal orgasm lies a radical resentment of their position in the sexual act. And I have noticed that when I feel most militantly feminist I am hardly at all interested in sex.

Almost one could generalize from that: the feminist impulse is anti-sexual. The very notion of women gathering in groups is somehow anti-sexual, anti-male, just as the purposely all-male group is anti-female. There is often a sense of genuine cultural rebellion in the atmosphere of a Woman's Liberation meeting. Women sit with their legs apart, carelessly dressed, barely made-up, exhibiting their feelings or the holes at the knees of their jeans with an unprovocative candor which is hardly seen at all in the outside world. Of course, they are demonstrating by their postures that they are in effect off duty, absolved from the compulsion to make themselves attractive, and yet, as the world measures these things, such demonstrations could in themselves be seen as evidence of neurosis: we have all been brought up to believe that a woman who was "whole" would appear feminine even on the barricades.

The fact is that one cannot talk in feminist terms without revealing feelings which have traditionally been regarded as neurotic. One becomes concerned about women's rights, as Simone de Beauvoir noted, only when one perceives that there are few personal advantages to be gained from accepting the traditional women's roles. A woman who is satisfied with her life is not likely to be drawn into the Woman's Liberation movement: there must be advantages for her as a woman in a man's world. To be a feminist one must be to some degree maladjusted to that world, one must be, if you will, neurotic. And sometimes one must be anti-sexual, if only in reaction to masculine expectations. Men do not worry about women taking their jobs because they do not think that women could do their jobs; most men can only be threatened by a woman in bed. A woman who denies her sexuality, if only for an evening, denies her status as an object of male attention, as a supplicant, successful or not, for male favor. For a woman to deny her sexuality is to attack the enemy in his most valuable stronghold, which is her own need for him.

I became a feminist as an alternative to becoming a masochist. Actually, I always was a masochist; I became a feminist because to be a masochist is intolerable. As I get older I recognize more and more that the psychoanalytical idea that women are natural masochists is at least metaphorically correct: my own masochism derived from an almost worshipful respect for masculine power. In my adolescence I screwed a lot of guys I didn't much like, and always felt abused by them, but I never felt free to refuse sex until after the initial encounter. My tactic, if you can call it a tactic, was to Do It once and then to refuse to see the boy again, and I think I succeeded, with my demonstrations of postcoital detachment, in making several of them feel as rejected by my lovemaking as I had felt by their desire to make love to me without love. Yet I felt in those years that I had irretrievably marked myself a sexual rebel, and I was given to making melodramatic statements like "I'm not the kind of girl men marry." Years later I realized that I had been playing a kind of game, the same game boys play at the age of sexual experimentation, except that, unlike a boy, I could not allow myself to choose my partners and admit that I had done so. In fact, I was never comfortable with a lover unless he had, so to speak, wronged me. Once during my senior year in high school I let a boy rape me (that is not, whatever you may think, a contradiction in terms) in the bedroom of his college suite while a party was going on next door; afterward I ran away down the stairs while he followed, shouting apologies which became more and more abject as he realized that my revulsion was genuine, and I felt an exhilaration which I clearly recognized as triumph. By letting him abuse me I had won the right to tell him I hated him; I had won the right to hurt him.

I think most American adolescents hate and fear the opposite sex: in adolescence it seems that only one's lovers can hurt one, and I think that even young people who are entirely secure in other relations recognize and would, if they could, disarm the power the other sex has for them. But for adolescent boys, sexual success is not the sole measure of worth. It is assumed that they will grow up and work, that their most important tests will come in areas whose criteria are extra-sexual. They can fail with girls without failing entirely, for there remains for them the public life, the male life.

But girls have no such comfort. Sex occupies even the economic center of our lives; it is, we have been brought up to feel, our lives' work. Whatever else she may do, a woman is a failure if she fails to please men. The adolescent girl's situation is by definition dependent: she *must* attract, and therefore, however she may disguise it, she must compromise the sticky edges of her personality, she must arrange herself to conform with other people's ideas of what is valuable in a woman.

I was early trained to that position, trained, in the traditional manner, by my father. Like many men who are uncomfortable with adult women, my father saw his daughter as a potential antidote to his disappointment in her sex. I was someone who could be molded into a woman compatible with his needs, and also, unlike my mother, I was too impressionable to talk back. So I became the vessel into which he fed his opinions about novels and politics and sex; he fed me also his most hopeful self-image. It reached a point where I later suspected him of nourishing a sort of eighteenth-century fantasy about our relationship, the one in which the count teaches his daughter to read Virgil and ride like a man, and she grows up to be the perfect feminine companion, parroting him with such subtlety that it is impossible to tell that her thoughts and feelings, so perfectly coincident with his, are not original. I had three brothers, as it happened, and another sort of man might have chosen one

of them to mold. But my father had himself a vast respect for masculine power. Boys grow up and have to kill their fathers, girls can be made to understand their place.

My father in his thirties was an attractive man, he was witty by adult standards and of course doubly so by mine, and he had a verbal facility with which he invariably demolished my mother in arguments. Masculine power in the intellectual classes is exercised verbally: it is the effort of the male supremacist intellectual to make his woman look clumsy and illogical beside him, to render her, as it were, dumb. His tactic is to goad the woman to attack him and then, resorting to rationality, to withdraw himself from the battle. In my childhood experience, subtlety appeared exclusively a masculine weapon. I never saw a woman argue except straightforwardly, and I never saw a woman best a man in a quarrel. My mother tried, but always with the conviction of ultimate failure. She attacked with pinpricks to begin with, in the end, maddened invariably by my father's ostentatious mental absence, she yelled. He was assisted in these struggles by his natural passivity. Withdrawal came easily to him; he hated, as he told us over and over again, scenes. My mother, it seemed to me, was violent, my father cool. And since it also seemed to me that he preferred me, his daughter who never disagreed with him, to his wife who did (that was a fantasy, of course, but one to which my father devoted some effort toward keeping alive), I came to feel that male power, because uncoercible, could only be handled by seduction, and that the most comfortable relation between men and women was the relation between pupil and teacher, between parent and child.

My father taught me some tricks. From him I learned that it is pleasant and useful to get information from men, pleasant because it is easier than getting it for yourself, and useful because it is seductive: men like to give information and sometimes love the inquirer, if she is pretty and asks intelligently. From him I also learned that women are by definition incapable of serious thought. This was a comforting lesson, although it made me feel obscurely doomed, for if I was to be automatically barred from participation in the life of high intellect, there was no reason why I should work to achieve it, and thinking, after all, is difficult work. When I was fifteen my father told me that I would never be a writer because I wasn't hungry enough, by which I think he meant that there would always be some man to feed me. I accepted his pronouncement as I accepted, at that age, all pronouncements which had an air of finality, and began making other career plans.

My task, it seemed to me, was to find a man in whom there resided enough power to justify my acting the child, that is, to justify my acceptance of my own femininity. For I regarded myself as feminine only in my childlike aspect; when I presented myself as a thinking person I felt entirely sexless. The boys in my class regarded me as an intellectual and showed an almost unanimous disinterest in my company. When I was in the eighth grade I lived in trepidation lest I be cited as class bookworm, and defended myself against that threat by going steady with what surely must have been the dumbest boy in our set. He was no fonder of me than I was of him; we needed each other because you had to be part of a couple in order to get invited to parties.

I did not get the opportunity to demonstrate my skill as a child-woman until I became old enough to go out with college boys. My training had equipped me only to attract intelligent men, and a boy who was no brighter than I held no power for me. But for a man who could act as my teacher I could be submissive and seductive—I *felt* submissive and seductive; my awe of the male mind translated easily into an awe of the male person.

I was, I realize now, in tune with the demands of my time. This was in the late Fifties, Marilyn Monroe was the feminine archetype of the period, and Marilyn Monroe was sexy because of her childishness. It is not much of a step from seeing oneself as a child in relation to men to seeing oneself as their victim; obviously a child is powerless before adults. All children are potential victims, dependent upon the world's goodwill. My sense of powerlessness, of feminine powerlessness, was so great that for years I trusted no man who had not indicated toward me a special favor, who had not fallen in love with me. And even toward those who had, I acted the victim, preferring to believe myself the one who loved most, for how could a man retain his power in loving me unless I gave it back to him through my submission? Years later I heard a story about how Bob Dylan so tormented a groupy that she jumped out a window while ten people looked on, and recognized the spirit of adolescence. I never got myself into a situation even comparably extreme, my fundamental self-protectiveness having permitted me to allow only minor humiliations, but the will was there.

Masochism as clinically defined is more or less exclusively a sexual disorder: masochists are people who derive sexual pleasure from pain. Freudian psychiatrists claim that all women are to one degree or another masochistic in the sexual sense (the male penetrates the female, presumably he hurts her, and presumably she enjoys the pain as part of the pleasure), and many Freudian thinkers extend the use of the term out of the area of sex into the social area and argue that the womanly woman is correctly masochistic, must be masochistic in order to accept the male domination which is necessarily a part even of her extra-sexual life. It seems to me more useful to define masochism, insofar as the word is to be used to describe a non-clinical emotional condition, as the doing of something which one does not enjoy because someone else demands it or even because one's conscience demands it. In this sense clinical masochism can be said to be non-masochistic: if one enjoys being whipped, one is acting directly upon one's own needs, whereas if one allows oneself to be whipped for someone else's pleasure without deriving any pleasure from the act, one is behaving masochistically. A person who acts upon someone else's will, or in accordance with someone else's image of her, or who judges herself by someone else's standards, has allowed herself to be made into an object. A masochist, as I define the term, is a person who consents to be made an object. It is in that sense that I think most women are, or have been at some time in their lives, masochists. For insofar as a woman lives by the standards of the world, she lives according to the standards set by men. Men have laid down the rules and definitions by which the world is run, and one of the objects of their definitions is woman. Men define intelligence, men define usefulness, men tell us what is beautiful, men even tell us what is womanly. Constance Chatterley was a male invention; Lawrence invented her, I used to think, specifically to make me feel guilty because I didn't have the right kind of orgasms.

Lionel Trilling wrote in an essay on Jane Austen that it is the presumption of our society that women's moral life is not as men's, and that therefore we do not expect from women, in fact do not condone in them, the same degree of self-love which we expect and encourage in men. What he meant, I think, was that since women are in a sense given their lives, since women customarily choose a lifestyle by choosing a man rather than a path, they do not need the self-love which is necessary to carry a man to the places he has to go. Self-love is indeed a handicap to a being whose primary function is supportive, for how is a woman adequately to support another ego when her self-love demands the primacy of her own? Women learn in many ways to suppress their selfishness, and by doing so they suppress also their self-esteem. If most men hold women in contempt it is no greater than the contempt in which women hold themselves. Self-love depressed becomes self-loathing. Men are brought up to command, women to seduce; to admit the necessity of seduction is to admit that one has not the strength to command. It is in fact to accept one's own objecthood, to internalize one's oppression.

Still, I picked up some interesting lore from men, while I was studying to please them. I learned about Eliot from one boy, and about Donne from another, and about Coltrane from a third. A lover turned me on to drugs and also showed me how you were supposed to act when you were high—that is, as if you were not high. I was not surprised that he was better at this than me, cool was beginning to seem more and more a masculine talent, and I had even taken to physical retaliation in arguments, having given up the idea that I would ever win anything by verbal means. I went to Sarah Lawrence instead of Barnard because my boyfriend thought Sarah Lawrence was a more "feminine" school. My parents got divorced and I sided with my father, at least at first, because his appeared to me to be the winning side. Men, I believed, were automatically on the winning side, which was why my oldest brother could afford to withdraw in moral outrage from my father's advances; there was for *him* no danger of branding himself a loser by consorting with my mother. Yet I envied his integrity. How could I maintain integrity when I was willing to sell out my principle for the sake of masculine attention?

I went to Sarah Lawrence and got to love it without ever taking it very seriously, which I also supposed was the way the boys I loved in those days felt about me. In fact, Sarah Lawrence appeared to me and to most of my friends there as a sort of symbol of ourselves: like the college, we were pretty and slightly prestigious and terribly self-serious in private, but just as we laughed at the school and felt embarrassed to be identified with it publicly (I always felt that if I had been a real student I would have gone to Barnard), so we laughed publicly at our own aspirations. "I like Nancy," a Princeton boy said to me, "except she always starts talking about Kafka promptly at midnight." And I laughed, god how I laughed, at Nancy—how *Sarah Lawrency* to carry on about Kafka—and, by implication, at myself. For I too expressed by my intellectualism in effusions. Men expected the effusions, even found them charming, while treating them with friendly contempt. It was important to be charming. A passion for Marxism, stumblingly expressed, an interpretation of *Moby Dick,* these tokens we offered our lovers to prove we were not simply women, but people. Yet though we displayed strong feelings about art and politics, we behaved as if we had not really done the reading. To argue a point logically was to reveal yourself as unfeminine: a man might respect your mind, but he would not love you. Wit, we believed, is frightening in a woman.

In my senior year I met a girl who knew the editor of *The Village Voice,* and after graduation she got me a job there. I went to work as a reporter without having the slightest notion of how to conduct an interview and so, to cover myself I made up a couple of pieces out of whole cloth. They were about drugs and hippies and homosexuals, the sort of scene pieces *The Voice* later specialized in, but nobody much was writing about that stuff in 1964, and I got several book offers and invitations to cocktail parties, and my father's friends started writing me letters full of sports analogies, saying it was time I entered a main

event. In fact, I felt terribly guilty about writing those pieces because they seemed frivolous and sensationalistic, the sort of thing emptyheaded girl reporters did when they were too dumb to write about politics, but on the other hand they got me attention, which writing about politics would never have done. I agonized all summer, publicly and privately, over this dilemma, often spending hours telling big strong male reporters how unworthy I felt. They seemed to like it.

I had never thought of myself as ambitious; actually, I think I was too convinced of my basic incompetence to be constructively ambitious, but I quickly saw that a lady journalist has advantages denied to men. For one thing she never has to pick up a check. For another thing, if she is even remotely serious, people praise her work much more than they would praise the work of a comparably talented man; they are amazed that a woman can write coherently on any subject not confined in interest to the readers of a woman's magazine. And finally, people tell her things they would not tell a man. Many men think the secrets they tell a woman are automatically off the record. They forget that the young woman hanging on their every word is taking it all down—often they confuse her attention with sexual interest. (That is not such an advantage. Some men, rock stars for instance, simply assumed that sex was what I had come for. They would expend a little flattery to assure me that they regarded me as a cut above other groupies, and then they would suggest that we get down to balling. They were often nasty when I refused.)

At any rate, the work was nice, and it gave me a higher status as a sexual object than I had ever had before. But it was also scary. If I was to do well at it I had to take it seriously. In the Autumn of 1964 I fell in love with a boy who was not sure he was in love with me, and by the time he decided he was I had quit my job and moved with him to Boston. He styled himself a revolutionary and thought the content of my work hardly worth the effort it took to produce it: I accepted his opinion with relief, telling myself that in any case I had not the emotional energy to handle both a lover and a job. My feeling for him evaporated fairly soon after I discovered that it was reciprocated, though I lived with him for several months after that, partly out of guilt and partly because living with a man made me feel grown-up in a way holding a job never could have done. But finally I left him and took a job as a staff writer on a national magazine, a classy job but underpaid. Instead of complaining about the salary, I took to not showing up for work, justifying my laziness by telling myself that I was selling out anyway by taking an up-town job and that the sooner I rid myself of it, the sooner I would regain my integrity.

In the meantime I had met a grown-up man who was powerful and smart and knocked out by my child act. We spent a few months seducing each other—"You're too young for me," he would say, and I would climb upon his lap, figuratively speaking, and protest that I was not. It was no more disgusting than most courtships. In the end we got married.

Of course, I had to marry a grown-up, a father figure if you will, and my husband, as it turned out, had to marry a child. That is, he had to have an intelligent woman, but one whose intelligence had been, as it were, castrated by some outside circumstances. My youth served that purpose; my other handicaps had not as yet emerged.

Anyway, our romantic personae lasted about a year. For a year he was kind to me and listened to my problems and put up with the psychosomatic diseases which marriage had induced in me, and for a year I brought joy and spontaneity into his drab grown-up existence. Then he began to get tired of being

a father and I to resent being a child, and we began to act out what I think is a classic example of contemporary marriage.

It had turned out, I realized with horror, that I had done exactly what middle-class girls are supposed to do. I had worked for a year in the communications industry, and my glamorous job had enabled me to meet a respectable, hardworking man who made a lot of money at *his* glamorous job, and I had settled down (stopped screwing around) and straightened myself out (went into analysis), and all that was missing was babies. I defended myself by assuming that we would be divorced in a year, and sneered a lot at Design Research furniture and the other symbols of middle-class marriage, but still I could not escape the feeling that I had fallen not just into a trap but into a cliche. On the other hand, I loved my husband, and I was still a writer, that is to say, a privileged woman with a life of her own. I could afford, as I began to at that time, to read feminist literature without really applying it to my own situation.

My husband, although he is nice to women, is a male supremacist, very much in the style of Norman Mailer. That is, he invests women with more or less mystical powers of control over the inner workings of the world, but thinks that feminine power is strongest when exercised in child rearing and regards contraception as unnatural. When I had my first stirrings of feminist grievance, he pronounced the subject a bore; I used to follow him from room to room, torturing him with my recitals of the sexist atrocities I was beginning to find in my favorite novels, and when I complained that magazines were paying me less than they paid men, he accused me of trying to blame the world for my own crazy passivity. But we were engaged at that time in the usual internal power struggle, and my feminism seemed to both of us more an intellectual exercise than a genuine commitment. It was not until many months later that he began to accuse me of hating men.

We already knew that he hated women, even that he had good reasons for hating women, but I had up to that time put on such a good display of being cuddly, provocative, sexually uninhibited and altogether unlike those other women that the subject of my true feelings about men had never come up. He knew that I had a compulsion to seduce men, which argues a certain distrust of them, but as the seductions, since our marriage, were always intellectual rather than sexual, they could, if you didn't want to consider their implications, be put down simply as insecurity. I don't think even I realized how I felt. Once I told my husband about a rigmarole a friend and I had made up to dismiss men we didn't like—we would go through lists of names, pointing our fingers and saying, "Zap, you're sterile," and then collapse into giggles; my husband, who has a psychoanalytical turn of mind, thought that was Terribly Revealing and I agreed that it was, but so what? And also, I agreed that it was Terribly Revealing that I like to pinch and bite him, that I made small hostile jokes and took an almost malicious pleasure in becoming too involved in work to pay attention to him (but only briefly; I never for very long attempted to work when he had other plans), that I would go into weeklong depressions during which the bed never got made nor the dishes washed. But the degree of my hostility didn't reveal itself to me until a pattern began to emerge around our quarrels.

We had, since early in the marriage, periodically engaged in bitter fights. Because my husband was the stronger, and because he tends to be judgmental, they usually started when he attempted to punish me (by withdrawing, of course) for some offense. I would dispute the validity of his complaint, and the quarrel would escalate into shouts and blows and then into decisions to terminate the marriage. In the first year my husband always beat me hollow in those battles. I used to dissolve into tears and beg his forgiveness after twenty minutes; I could not bear his rejection and I had no talent at all for conducting a quarrel. I won only when I succeeded in making him feel guilty; if he behaved badly enough I automatically achieved the moral upper hand for at least a week following the quarrel. But after a while, the honeymoon being over, he began to refuse to feel guilty and I began to resent his superior force. Things rested there until, in the third year of our marriage, we went to live in Los Angeles because of my husband's work. During the year we spent away from home I found that I could not work, and that he was always working, and we suddenly found ourselves frozen into the textbook attitudes of male-female opposition. We fought continually, and always about the same things. He accused me of making it impossible for him to work, I accused him of keeping me dangling, dependent upon him for all emotional sustenance, he accused me of spending too much money and of keeping the house badly. I accused him of expecting me continually to subordinate my needs to his. The difficulty, I realized over and over again without being able to do much about it, was that I had gotten myself into the classic housewife's position: I was living in a place I didn't want to be, and seeing people I didn't like because that was where my man was, I was living my husband's life and I hated him for it. And the reason this was so was that I was economically dependent upon him, having ceased to earn my living I could no longer claim the breadwinner's right to attention for my special needs.

My husband told me that I was grown-up now, twenty-six years old, there were certain realities which I had to face. He was the head of the household: I had never questioned that. He had to fulfill himself: I had never questioned that. He housed me and fed me and paid for my clothes, he respected my opinions and refused all his opportunities to make love to other women, and my part of the bargain should have become clear to me by now. In exchange for those things, I was supposed to keep his house and save his money and understand that if he worked sixteen hours a day for a year it was no more than necessary for his self-fulfillment. Which was all quite true. Except that it was also necessary for his fulfillment that I should be there for those few hours when he did not, and that I should adapt myself to his situation or else end the marriage. It never occurred to him to consider adapting himself to mine, and it never occurred to me. I only knew that his situation was bad for me, was alien, was in fact totally paralyzing, that it kept me from working, that it made me more unhappy than I had been in my life.

I knew that I was being selfish. But he was being selfish also, the only difference being that his selfishness was somehow all right, while mine was inexcusable. Selfishness was a privilege I had earned for a while by being a writer, that is, a person who had by male standards a worthwhile place to spend her time. As soon as I stopped functioning as a writer I became to my husband and to everyone else a mere woman, somebody whose time was valueless, somebody who had no excuse for a selfish preoccupation with her own wants.

I used to lie in bed beside my husband after those fights and wish I had the courage to bash in his head with a frying pan. I would do it while he slept, since awake he would overpower me, disarm me. If only I dared, I would mutter to myself through clenched teeth, pushing back the realization that I didn't dare not because I was afraid of seriously hurting him— I would have loved to do that—but because

even in the extremity of my anger I was afraid that if I cracked his head with a frying pan he would leave me. God, how absurd it was (god, how funny, I would mutter to myself, how amusing, oh wow, what a joke) that my whole life's effort had been directed toward keeping men from leaving me, toward placating them, submitting to them, demanding love from them in return for living in their style, and it all ended with me lying awake in the dark hating my husband, hating my father, hating all the men I had ever known. Probably I had always hated them. What I couldn't figure out was whether I hated them because I was afraid they would leave me or whether I was afraid they would leave me because I hated them.

Because one cannot for very long support such a rage without beginning to go crazy, I tried to think of the problem in political terms. It seemed to me too easy to say that my hatred for men was a true class hatred, that women hate men because women are an oppressed class hungering for freedom. And yet wherever there exists the display of power there is politics, and in women's relations with men there is a continual transfer of power, there is, continually, politics. There are political analogies even to our deepest, most banal fantasies. Freud maintains that the female terror of the penis is a primary fear, and that the male fear of castration by the vagina is merely a retaliatory fantasy, a guilty fear of punishment. The serf fears the overlord's knout, the overlord, guilty, fears the serf's revenge. Women are natural guerrillas. Scheming, we nestle into the enemy's bed, avoiding open warfare, watching the options, playing the odds. High, and made paranoiac by his observance of my rage, my husband has the fantasy of woman with a knife. He sees her in sexual ecstasy with her eyes open to observe the ecstasy of her partner, with her consciousness awake, that even in moments of greatest abandon, I always kept some part of my mind awake: I always searched for clues. Is he mine now, this monster? Have I disarmed him, and for how long? Men are beasts, we say, joking, parodying the Victorian rag, and then realize to our surprise that we believe it. The male has force almost beyond our overpowering, the force of laws, of science, of literature, the force of mathematics and skyscrapers and the Queensboro Bridge; the penis is only its symbol. We cannot share men's pride in the world they have mastered. If you follow that symbolism to its conclusion, we are ourselves that conquered world.

It is because they know that this is true, know it in their bones if not in their heads, that men fear the hatred of women. For women are the true maintenance class. Society is built upon their acquiescence, and upon their small and necessary labors. Restricted to the supportive role, conditioned to excel only at love, women hold for men the key to social order. It is a Marxist truism that the original exploitation, the enslavement which set the pattern for everything which came later, was the enslavement of women by men. Even the lowest worker rests upon the labor of his wife. Where no other claim to distinction exists, a man defines himself by his difference from the supportive sex; he may be a less than admirable man, but at least he is a man, at least he is not a woman.

And if women have fought, they have fought as guerrillas, in small hand-to-hand skirmishes, in pillow wars upon the marriage bed. When they attack frontally, when they come together in groups to protest their oppression, they raise psychic questions so profound as to be almost inadmissable. In E. E. Cummings' play *Him,* there is a scene in which two women sit in a Paris cafe and order men served up to them like plats du jour; it is an inexpressibly sinister sequence, and it has its counterparts elsewhere in the avant-garde literature of the Twenties. I do not imagine that Cummings approved of men using women like meat, but I am quite sure that he could not have treated the situation with such horror had the sexual roles been reversed. Cummings, like Leonid Andreyev and the other modernists who dealt in surreal images of female dominance, was writing during the early period of feminist protest, and I think they were expressing a fear basic to every man confronted with the idea of women's liberation. When men imagine a female uprising they imagine a world in which women rule men as men have ruled women: their guilt, which is the guilt of every ruling class, will allow them to see no middle ground. And it is a measure of the unconscious strength of our belief in natural male dominance that all of us, men and women, revolt from the image of woman with a whip, that the female sadist is one of our most deep-rooted images of perversion.

And although I believe this male fantasy of feminine equality as a euphemism for feminine dominance to be evidence of the oppressor's neurosis rather than of any supporting fact, it was part of the character of my resentment that I once fancied wresting power from men as though nothing less than total annihiliation would satisfy my rage. The true dramatic conclusion of this narrative should be the dissolution of my marriage; there is a part of me which believes that you cannot fight a sexist system while acknowledging your need for the love of a man, and perhaps if I had had the courage finally to tear apart my life I could write you about my hard-working independence, about my solitary self-respect about the new society I hope to build. But in the end my husband and I did not divorce, although it seemed at one time as if we would. Instead I raged against him for many months and joined the Woman's Liberation Movement, and thought a great deal about myself, and about whether my problems were truly all women's problems, and decided that some of them were and that some of them were not. My sexual rage was the most powerful single emotion of my life, and the feminist analysis has become for me, as I think it will for most women of my generation, as significant an intellectual tool as Marxism was for generations of radicals. But it does not answer every question. To discover that something has been wrong is not necessarily to make it right: I would be lying if I said that my anger had taught me how to live. But my life has changed because of it. I think I am becoming in many small ways a woman who takes no shit. I am no longer submissive, no longer seductive; perhaps it is for that reason that my husband tells me sometimes that I have become hard, and that my hardness is unattractive. I would like it to be otherwise. I think that will take a long time.

My husband and I have to some degree worked out our differences; we are trying to be together as equals, to separate our human needs from the needs imposed upon us by our sex roles. But my hatred lies within me and between us, not wholly a personal hatred, but not entirely political either. And I wonder always whether it is possible to define myself as a feminist revolutionary and still remain in any sense a wife. There are moments when I still worry that he will leave me, that he will come to need a woman less preoccupied with her own rights, and when I worry about that I also fear that no man will ever love me again, that no man could ever love a woman who is angry. And the fear is a great source of trouble to me, for it means that in certain fundamental ways I have not changed at all.

I would like to be cold and clear and selfish, to demand satisfaction for my needs, to compel respect rather than affection. And yet there are moments, and perhaps there always will be, when I fall back upon the old cop-outs. Why should I trouble to win a chess game or a political argument when it is so much easier to lose charmingly? Why should I work when my husband can support me, why should I be a human being when I can get away with being a child?

Woman's Liberation is finally only personal. It is hard to fight an enemy who has outposts in your head.

Consciousness ♀

Vivian Gornick

Vivian Gornick, a staff writer for the *Village Voice* from 1969 to 1971, has written articles on a wide range of social issues. She is the coeditor of *Woman in Sexist Society,* a collection of feminist writings, and the author of *In Search of Ali Mahmud: An American Woman in Egypt.*

In a lower Manattan office a legal secretary returns from her lunch hour, sinks into her seat and says miserably to a secretary at the next desk: "I don't know what's happening to me. A perfectly nice construction worker whistled and said, 'My, isn't *that* nice,' as I passed him and suddenly I felt this terrific anger pushing up in me. . . . I swear I wanted to *hit* him!"

At the same time, a thoughtful 40-year-old

mother in a Maryland suburb is saying to a visiting relative over early afternoon coffee: "You know, I've been thinking lately, I'm every bit as smart as Harry, and yet he got the Ph.D. and I raised the girls. Mind you, I *wanted* to stay home. And yet, the thought of my two girls growing up and doing the same thing doesn't sit well with me at all. Not at all."

And in Toledo, Ohio, a factory worker turns to the next woman on the inspection belt and confides: "Last night I told Jim: 'I been working in the same factory as you 10 years now. We go in at the same time, come out the same time. But I do all the shopping, get the dinner, wash the dishes and on Sunday break my back down on the kitchen floor. I'm real tired of doin' all that. I want some help from you.' Well, he just laughed at me, see? Like he done every time I mentioned this before. But last night I wouldn't let up. I mean, I really meant it this time. And you know? I thought he was gonna let me have it. Looked mighty like he was gettin' ready to belt me one. But you know? I just didn't care! I wasn't gonna back down, come hell or high water. You'll just never believe it, he'd kill me if he knew I was tellin' you, he washed the dishes. First time in his entire life."

None of these women are feminists. None of them are members of the Women's Liberation Movement. None of them ever heard of consciousness-raising. And yet, each of them exhibits the symptomatic influence of this, the movement's most esoteric practice. Each of them, without specific awareness, is beginning to feel the effects of the consideration of woman's personal experience in a new light—a political light. Each of them is undergoing the mysterious behavioral twitches that indicate psychological alteration. Each of them is drawing on a linking network of feminist analysis and emotional upchucking that is beginning to suffuse the political-social air of American life today. Each of them, without

ever having attended a consciousness-raising session, has had her consciousness raised.

Consciousness-raising is the name given to the feminist practice of examining one's personal experience in the light of sexism; i.e., that theory which explains woman's subordinate position in society as a result of a cultural decision to confer direct power on men and only indirect power on women. The term of description and the practice to which it alludes are derived from a number of sources—psychoanalysis, Marxist theory and American revivalism, mainly—and was born out of the earliest stages of feminist formulation begun about three years ago in such predictable liberationist nesting places as Cambridge, New York, Chicago and Berkeley. (The organization most prominently associated with the growth of consciousness-raising is the New York Redstockings.)

Perceiving that woman's position in our society does indeed constitute that of a political class, and, secondly, that woman's "natural" domain is her feelings, and, thirdly, that testifying in a friendly and supportive atmosphere enables people to see that their experiences are often duplicated (thereby reducing their sense of isolation and increasing the desire to theorize as well as to confess), the radical feminists sensed quickly that a group of women sitting in a circle discussing their emotional experiences as though they were material for cultural analysis was political dynamite. Hence, through personal testimony and emotional analysis could the class consciousness of women be raised. And thus the idea of the small "woman's group"— or consciousness-raising group—was delivered into a cruel but exciting world.

Consciousness-raising is, at one and the same time, both the most celebrated and accessible introduction to the woman's movement as well as the most powerful technique for feminist conversion known to the liberationists. Women are *drawn,* out of a variety of discontents, by the idea of talking about themselves, but under the spell of a wholly new interpretation of their experience, they *remain.*

Coming together, as they do, week after week for many months, the women who are "in a group" begin to exchange an extraordinary sense of multiple identification that is encouraged by the technique's instruction to look for explanations for each part of one's history in terms of the social or cultural dynamic created by sexism—rather than in terms of the personal dynamic, as one would do in a psychotherapist's group session. (Although there are many differences between consciousness-raising and group therapy—e.g., the former involves no professional leader, no exchange of money—the fundamental difference lies in this fact: in consciousness-raising one looks not to one's personal emotional history for an explanation of behavioral problems but rather to the cultural fact of the patriarchy.)

Thus looking at one's history and experience in consciousness-raising sessions is rather like shaking a kaleidoscope and watching all the same pieces rearrange themselves into an altogether other picture, one that suddenly makes the color and shape of each piece appear startlingly new and alive, and full of unexpected meaning. (This is mainly why feminists often say that women are the most interesting people around these days, because they are experiencing a psychic invigoration of rediscovery.)

What *does* take place in a consciousness-raising group? How *do* the women see themselves? What *is* the thrust of the conversation at a typical session? Is it simply the manhating, spleen-venting that is caricatured by the unsympathetic press? Or the unfocused and wrong-headed abstracting insisted upon by the insulated intellectuals? Or yet again, the self-indulgent contemplation of the navel that many tight-lipped radical activists see it as?

"In this room," says Roberta H., a Long Island housewife speaking euphemistically of her group's meetings, "we do not generalize. We do not speak of any experience except that of the women here. We follow the rules for consciousness-raising as set out by the New York Radical Feminists and we do not apply them to 'woman's experience'—whatever on earth that is—we apply them to ourselves. But, oh God! The samenesses we have found, and the way in which these meetings have changed our lives!"

The rules that Roberta H. is referring to are to be found in a mimeographed pamphlet, an introduction to the New York Radical Feminists organization, which explains the purpose and procedures of consciousness-raising. The sessions consist mainly of women gathering once a week, sitting in a circle and speaking in turn, addressing themselves—almost entirely out of personal experience—to a topic that has been preselected. The pamphlet sets forth the natural limitations of a group (10 to 15 women), advises women to start a group from among their friends and on a word-of-mouth basis, and suggests a list of useful topics for discussion. These topics include Love, Marriage, Sex. Work, Femininity. How I Came to Women's Liberation, Motherhood, Aging and Competition With Other Women. Additional subjects are developed as a particular group's specific interests and circumstances begin to surface.

When a group's discussions start to revolve more and more about apparently very individual circumstances, they often lead to startling similarities. For instance, a Westchester County group composed solely of housewives, who felt that each marriage represented a unique meaning in each of their lives, used the question, "Why did you marry the man you married?" as the subject for discussion one night. "We went around the room," says Joan S., one of the women present, "and while some of us seemed unable to answer that question without going back practically to the cradle, do you know?, the word love was never mentioned *once.*"

On the Upper West Side of Manhattan, in the vicinity of Columbia University, a group of women between the ages of 35 and 45 have been meeting regularly for six months. Emily R., an attractive 40-year-old divorcee in this group, says: "When I walked into the first meeting, and saw the *types* there, I said to myself: 'None of these broads have been through what I've been through. They couldn't possibly feel the way I feel.' Well, I'll tell you. None of them *have* been through what I've been through if you look at our experience superficially. But when you look a little *deeper*—the way we've been doing at these meetings—you see they've *all* been through what I've been through, and they all feel pretty much the way I feel. God, when I saw *that!* When I saw that what I always felt was my own personal hang-up was as true for every other woman in that room as it was for me! Well, that's when *my* consciousness was raised."

What Emily R. speaks of is the phenomenon most often referred to in the movement, the flash of insight most directly responsible for the feminist leap in faith being made by hundreds of women everywhere—i.e., the intensely felt realization that what had always been taken for symptoms of personal unhappiness or dissatisfaction or frustration was so powerfully and so consistently duplicated among women that perhaps these symptoms could just as well be ascribed to *cultural* causes as to psychological ones.

In the feminist movement this kind of "breakthrough" can occur no place else than in a consciousness-raising group. It is only here,

during many months of meetings, that a woman is able finally—if ever—to bring to the surface those tangled feelings of anger, bafflement and frustrated justice that have drawn her to the movement in the first place. It is only here that the dynamic of sexism will finally strike home, finally make itself felt in the living detail of her own life.

Claire K., a feminist activist in Cambridge, says of women's groups: "I've been working with women's groups for over two years now. The average life of a group is a year to 18 months, and believe me, I've watched a lot of them fold before they ever got off the ground. But, when they work! There is a rhythm to some of them that's like life itself. You watch a group expand and contract, and each time it does one or the other it never comes back together quite the same as when the action started. Something happens to each woman, and to the group itself . . . But each time, if they survive, they have *grown.* You can see it, almost smell it and taste it."

I am one of those feminists who are always mourning after the coherent and highminded leadership of the 19th century. Often, when I observe the fragmented, intellectually uneven, politically separated components of the woman's movement I experience dismay, and I find myself enviously imagining Elizabeth Cady Stanton and Lucretia Mott and Susan B. Anthony sitting and holding hands for 40 years, sustaining and offering succor to one another in religious and literary accents that make of their feminism a heroic act, an act that gave interwoven shape to their lives and their cause. And I think in a panic: "Where would we all be without them? Where would we be? They thought it all out for us, and we've got not one inch beyond them." Lately, however, I have changed my mind about all that . . .

I was on my way to a meeting one night not too long ago, a meeting meant to fashion a coalition group out of the movement's many organizations. I knew exactly what was ahead of me. I knew that a woman from NOW would rise and speak about our "image"; that a Third Worlder would announce loudly she didn't give a good goddamn about anybody's orgasms, her women were starving, for chrissake; that a Radicalesbian would insist that the woman's movement must face the problem of sexism from within *right now;* and 10 women from the Socialist party would walk out in protest against middle-class "elitist" control in the movement. I knew there would be a great deal of emotional opinion delivered, a comparatively small amount of valuable observation made, and some action taken. Suddenly, as the bus I was on swung westward through Central Park, I realized that it didn't matter, that none of it mattered. I realized it was stupid and self-pitying to be wishing that the meeting was going to be chaired by Elizabeth Cady Stanton; what she had done and said had been profoundly in the idiom of her time, and in the idiom of *my* time no woman in the movement was her equal, but something else was: the consciousness-raising group.

I saw then that the small, anonymous consciousness-raising group was the heart and soul of the woman's movement, that it is not what happens at movement meetings in New York or Boston or Berkeley that counts, but the fact that hundreds of these groups are springing up daily—at universities in Kansas, in small towns in Oregon, in the suburbs of Detroit—out of a responsive need that has indeed been urged to the surface by modern radical feminism. It was here that the soul of a woman is genuinely searched and a new psychology of the self is forged. I saw then that the consciousness-raising group of today is the true Second Front of feminism; and as I thought all this I felt the ghost of Susan B. Anthony hovering over me, nodding vigorously, patting me on the shoulder and saying: "Well done, my dear, well done."

That ghost has accompanied me to every movement meeting I have attended since that night, but when I am at a consciousness-raising session that ghost disappears and I am on my own. Then, for better or worse, I am the full occupant of my feminist skin, engaged in the true business of modern feminism, reaching hard for self-possession.

And now let's go to a consciousness-raising session.

Early in the evening, on a crisp autumn night, a young woman in an apartment in the Gramercy Park section of Manhattan signed a letter, put it in an envelope, turned out the light over her desk, got her coat out of the hall closet, ran down two flights of stairs, hailed a taxi and headed west directly across the city. At the same time, on the Upper West Side, another woman, slightly older than the first, bent over a sleeping child, kissed his forehead, said goodnight to the babysitter, rode down 12 flights in an elevator, walked up to Broadway and disappeared into the downtwon subway. Across town, on the Upper East Side, another woman tossed back a head of stylishly fixed hair, pulled on a beautiful pair of suede boots and left her tiny apartment, also heading down and across town. On the Lower East Side, in a fourth-floor tenement apartment, a woman five or six years younger than all the others combed out a tangled mop of black hair, clomped down the stairs in her Swedish clogs and started trudging west on St. Marks Place. In a number of other places all over Manhattan other women were also leaving their houses. When the last one finally walked into the Greenwich Village living room they were all headed for, there were 10 women in the room.

These women ranged in age from the late 20's to the middle 30's; in appearance, from attractive to very beautiful; in education, from bachelor's degrees to master's degrees; in marital status, from single to married to divorced to imminently separated; two were mothers. Their names were Veronica, Lucie, Diana, Marie, Laura, Jen, Sheila, Dolores, Marilyn and Claire. Their occupations, respectively, were assistant television producer, graduate student, housewife, copywriter, journalist, unemployed actress, legal secretary, unemployed college dropout, schoolteacher and computer programer.

They were not movement women; neither were they committed feminists; nor were they marked by an especial sense of social development or by personal neurosis. They were simply a rather ordinary group of women who were drawn out of some unresolved, barely articulated need to form a "woman's group." They were in their third month of meetings; they were now at Marie's house (next week they would meet at Laura's and after that at Jen's, and so on down the line); the subject for discussion tonight was "Work."

The room was large, softly lit, comfortably furnished. After 10 or 15 minutes of laughing, chatting, note and book exchanging, the women arranged themselves in a circle, some on chairs, some on the couch, others on the floor. In the center of the circle was a low coffee table covered with a coffeepot, cups, sugar, milk, plates of cheese and bread, cookies and fruit. Marie suggested they begin, and turning to the woman on her right, who happened to be Dolores, asked if she would be the first.

Dolores (the unemployed college dropout): I guess that's okay. . . . I'd just as soon be the first . . . mainly because I hate to be the last. When I'm last, all I think about is, soon it will be my turn. *(She looked up nervously.)* You've no idea how I *hate* talking in public. *(There was a long pause; silence in the circle.)* . . . Work! God, what can I say? The whole question has always been absolute hell for me. . . . A lot of you have said your fathers ignored you when you were growing up and paid attention only to your brothers. Well, in my house it was just the opposite. I have

two sisters, and my father always told me I was the smartest of all, that I was smarter than he was, and that I could do anything I wanted to do . . . but somehow, I don't really know *why,* everything I turned to came to nothing. After six years in analysis I still don't know *why. (She looked off into space for a moment and her eyes seemed to lose the train of her thought. Then she shook herself and went on.)* I've always drifted . . . just drifted. My parents never forced me to work. I needn't work even now. I had every opportunity to find out what I really wanted to do. But . . . nothing I did satisfied me, and I would just stop. . . . Or go on a trip. I worked for a big company for a while. . . . Then my parents went to Paris and I just went with them. . . . I came back . . . went to school . . . was a researcher at Time-Life . . . drifted . . . got married . . . divorced . . . drifted. *(Her voice grew more halting.)* I feel my life is such *waste.* I'd like to write, I really would; I feel I'd be a good writer, but I don't know. I just can't get going. . . . My father is so disappointed in me. He keeps hoping I'll really do something. *Soon. (She shrugged her shoulders but her face was very quiet and pale, and her pain expressive. She happened to be one of the most beautiful women in the room.)*

Diana (the housewife): What do you think you *will* do?

Dolores (in a defiant burst): Try to get married!

Jen (the unemployed actress) and Marie (the copywriter): Oh, no!

Claire (the computer programer): After all that! Haven't you learned yet? What on earth is marriage going to do for you? Who on earth could you marry? *Feeling* about yourself as you do? Who could save you from yourself?
Because that's what you *want.*

Marilyn (the school teacher): That's right. It sounds like "It's just all too much to think out so I might as well get married."

Lucie (the graduate student): Getting married like that is *bound* to be a disaster.

Jen: And when you get married like that it's always to some creep you've convinced yourself is wonderful. So understanding. *(Dolores grew very red and very quiet through all this.)*

Sheila (the legal secretary): Stop jumping on her like that! I know *just* how she feels. . . . I was *really* raised to be a wife and a mother, and yet my father wanted me to do something with my education after he sent me to one of the best girls' schools in the East. Well, I didn't get married when I got out of school like half the girls I graduated with, and now seven years later I'm *still* not married. *(She stopped talking abruptly and looked off into the space in the center of the circle, her attention wandering as though she'd suddenly lost her way.)* I don't know how to describe it exactly, but I know just how Dolores feels about drifting. I've always worked, and yet something was always sort of confused inside me. I never really knew which way I wanted to go on a job: up, down, sideways. . . . I always thought it would be the most marvelous thing in the world to work for a really brilliant and important man. I never have. But I've worked for some good men and I've learned a lot from them. But *(her dark head came up two or three inches and she looked hesitantly around)* I don't know about the rest of you, but I've always wound up being propositioned by my bosses. It's a funny thing. As soon as I'd being doing really well, learning fast and taking on some genuine responsibility, like it would begin to excite them, and they'd make their move. When I refused, almost invariably they'd begin to *browbeat* me. I mean, they'd make my life miserable! And, of course, I'd retreat. . . . I'd get small and scared and take everything they were dishing out . . . and then I'd move on. I don't know, maybe something in my behavior was really asking for it, I honestly don't know anymore. . . .

Marie: There's a good chance you *were* asking for it. I work with a lot of men and I don't get propositioned every other day. I am so absolutely straight no one *dares.* . . . They all think I am a dike.

Sheila (plaintively): Why is it like that, though? Why are men like that? Is it something they have more of, this sexual need for ego gratification? Are they made differently from us?

Jen (placing her coffee cup on the floor beside her): No! You've just never learned to stand up for yourself!And goddammit, they *know* it, and they play on it. Look, you all know I've been an actress for years. Well, once, when I was pretty new in the business, I was playing opposite this guy. He used to feel me up on the stage. All the *time.* I was scared. I *didn't* know what to do. I'd say to the stage manager: That guy is feeling me up. The stage manager would look at me like I was crazy, and shrug his shoulders. Like: What can *I* do? Well, once I finally thought: I can't stand this. And I bit him. Yes, I bit the bastard, I bit his tongue while he was kissing me.

A Chorus of Voices: You *bit* him????

Jen (with great dignity): Yes, dammit, I bit him. And afterward he said to me, "Why the hell did you do that?" And I said, "You know goddam well why I did that." And do you know? He respected me after that. *(She laughed).* Didn't *like* me very much. But he respected me. *(She looked distracted for a moment.)* . . . I guess that *is* pretty funny. I mean, biting someone's tongue during a love scene.

Veronica (the assistant TV producer): Yeah. Very funny.

Laura (the journalist): Listen, I've been thinking about something Sheila said. That as soon as she began to get really good at her job her boss would make a pass—and that would pretty much signal the end, right? She'd refuse, he'd become an S.O.B., and she'd eventually leave. It's almost as if sex were being used to cut her down, or back, or in some way stop her from rising. An *instinct* he, the boss, has—to sleep with her when he feels her becoming really independent.

Lucie (excitedly): I'll buy that! Look, it's like Samson and Delilah in reverse. *She* knew that sex would give her the opportunity to destroy his strength. Women are famous for wanting to sleep with men in order to enslave them, right? That's the great myth, right? He's all spirit and mind, she's all emotion and biological instinct. She uses this instinct with *cunning* to even out the score, to get some power, to bring him down—through sex. But, look at it another way. What are these guys always saying to us? What are they always saying about women's liberation?—"All she needs is a good—." They say that *hopefully. Prayerfully.* They know. We *all* know what all that "All she needs is a good—" stuff is all about.

Claire: This is ridiculous. Use your heads. Isn't a guy kind of super if he wants to sleep with a woman who's becoming independent?

Marie: Yes, but not in business. There's something wrong every time, whenever sex is operating in business. It's always like a secret weapon, something you hit your opponent below the belt with.

Diana: God, you're all crazy! Sex is *fun.* Wherever it exists. It's warm and nice and it makes people feel good.

Dolores: That's a favorite pipe dream of yours, isn't it?

Sheila: It certainly doesn't seem like very much fun to me when I watch some secretary coming on to one of the lawyers when she wants a raise, then I see the expression on her face as she turns away.

Marie: God, that sounds like my mother when she wants something from my father!

Veronica (feebly): You people are beginning to make me feel *awful!* (Everyone's head snapped in her direction.)

Marie: Why?

Veronica: The way you're talking about using sex at work. As if it were so horrible. Well, I've *always* used a kind of sexy funniness to get what I want at work. What's wrong with that?

Lucie: What do you do?

Veronica: Well, if someone is being very stuffy and serious about business, I'll say something funny—I guess in a sexy way—to break up the atmosphere which sometimes gets so heavy. You know what I mean? Men can be so pretentious in business! And then, usually, I get what I want—while I'm being funny and cute, and they're laughing.

Diana (heatedly): Look, don't you see what you're doing?

Veronica (testily): No, I don't. What am I *doing?*

Diana (her hands moving agitatedly through the air before her): If there's some serious business going on you come in and say: Nothing to be afraid of, folks. Just frivolous, feminine little me. I'll tell a joke, wink my eye, do a little dance, and we'll all pretend nothing's really happening here.

Veronica: My God, I never thought of it like that.

Laura: It's like those apes. They did a study of apes in which they discovered that apes chatter and laugh and smile a lot to ward off aggression.

Marilyn: Just like women! Christ, aren't they always saying to us: *Smile!* Who tells a man to smile? And how often do you smile for no damned reason, right? It's so *natural* to start smiling as soon as you start talking to a man, isn't it?

Lucie: That's right! You're right! You know—God, it's amazing!—I began to think about this just the other day. I was walking down Fifth Avenue and a man in the doorway of a store said to me, "Whatsamatta, honey? Things can't be *that* bad." And I was startled because I wasn't feeling depressed or anything, and I couldn't figure out why he was saying that. So I looked, real fast, in the glass to see what my face looked like. And it didn't look like anything. It was just a face at rest. I had just an ordinary, sort of thoughtful expression on my face. And he thought I was depressed. And, I couldn't help it, I said to myself: "Would he have said that to you if you were a man?" And I answered myself immediately: "No!"

Diana: That's it. That's really what they want. To keep us barefoot, pregnant, and *smiling.* Always sort of *begging,* you know? Just a little supplicating—at all times. And they get anxious if you stop smiling. Not because you're depressed. Because you're *thinking!*

Dolores: Oh, come on now. Surely, there are lots of men who have very similar kinds of manners? What about all the life-of-the-party types? All those clowns and regular guys?

Claire: Yes, what about them? You never take those guys seriously. You never think of the men of real power, the guys with serious intentions and real strength, acting that way, do you? And those are the ones with real responsibility. The others are the ones women laugh about in private, the ones who become our confidantes, not our lovers, the ones who are *just like ourselves.*

Sheila (quietly): You're right.

Lucie: And it's true, it really does undercut your seriousness, all that smiling.

Sheila (looking suddenly sad and very intent): And underscore your weakness.

Dolores: Yes, exactly. We smile because we feel at a loss, because we feel vulnerable. We don't quite know how to accomplish what we want to accomplish or how to navigate through life, so we act *feminine.* That's really what this is all about, isn't it? To be masculine is to take action, to be feminine is to smile. Be coy and cute and sexy—and maybe you'll become the big man's assistant. God, it's all so sad. . . .

Veronica (looking a bit dazed): I never thought of any of it like this. But it's true, I guess, all of it. You know *(and now her words came in a rush and her voice grew stronger),* I've always been afraid of my job, I've always felt I was there by *accident,* and that any minute they were gonna find me out. Any minute, they'd know I was a fraud. I had the chance to become a producer recently, and I fudged it. I didn't realize for two weeks afterward that I'd done it deliberately, that I don't *want* to move up, that I'm afraid of the responsibility, that I'd rather stay where I am, making my little jokes and not drawing attention to myself . . . *(Veronica's voice faded away, but her face seemed full of struggle, and for a long moment no one spoke.)*

Marilyn (her legs pulled up under her on the couch, running her hand distractedly through her short blond hair): Lord, does *that* sound familiar. Do I know that feeling of being there by accident, any minute here comes the ax. I've never felt that anything I got—any honor, any prize, any decent job—was really legitimately mine. I always felt it was luck, that I happened to be in the right place at the right time and that I was able to put up a good front and people just didn't *know* . . . but if I stuck around long enough they would. . . . So, I guess I've drifted a lot, too. Being married, I took advantage of it. I remember when my husband was urging me to work, telling me I was a talented girl and that I shouldn't just be sitting around the house taking care of the baby. I wanted *so* to be persuaded by him, but I just couldn't do it. Every night I'd say: Tomorrow's the day and every morning I'd get up feeling like my head was full of molasses, so sluggish I couldn't *move.* By the time I'd finally get out of that damn bed it was too late to get a baby-sitter or too late to get to a job interview or too late to do anything, really. *(She turned toward Diana).* You're a housewife, Diana. You must know what I mean. *(Diana nodded ruefully.)* I began concentrating on my sex life with my husband, which had never been any too good, and was now getting really bad. It's hard to explain. We'd always been very affectionate with one another, and we still were. But I began to *crave . . .* passion. *(She smiled, almost apologetically.)* What else can I call it? There was no passion between us, practically no intercourse. I began to *demand* it. My husband reacted very badly, accused me of—oh God, the most awful things! Then I had an affair. The sex was great, the man was very tender with me for a long while. I felt *revived.* But then, a funny thing happened. I became almost hypnotized by the sex. I couldn't get enough, I couldn't stop thinking about it, it seemed to consume me; and yet, I became as sluggish now with sexual desire as I had been when I couldn't get up to go look for a job. Sometimes, I felt so sluggish I could hardly prepare myself to go meet my lover. And then . . . *(She stopped talking and looked down at the floor. Her forehead creased, her brows drew together, she seemed pierced suddenly by memory. Everyone remained quiet for a long mement.)*

Diana (very gently): And then?

Marilyn (almost shaking herself awake): And then the man told my husband of our affair.

Jen: Oh, Christ!

Marilyn: My husband went wild . . . *(her voice trailed off and again everyone remained silent, this time until she spoke again.)* He left me. We've been separated a year and a half now. So then I *had* to go to work. And I have, I have. But it remains a difficult, difficult thing. I do the most ordinary kind of work, afraid to strike out, afraid to try anything that involves real risk. It's almost as if there's some *training* necessary for taking risks, and I just don't have it . . . and my husband leaving me, and forcing me out to work, somehow didn't magically give me whatever it takes to get that training.

Laura (harshly): Maybe it's too late.

Diana: Well, that's a helluva thought. *(She crossed her legs and stared at the floor. Everyone looked toward her, but she said no more. Jen stretched. Claire bit into a cookie, Lucie poured coffee and everyone rearranged themselves in their seats.)*

Marie (after a long pause): It's your turn, Diana.

Diana (turning in her chair and running thin hands nervously through her curly red hair): It's been hard for me to concentrate on the subject. I went to see my mother in the hospital this afternoon, and I haven't been able to stop thinking about her all day long.

Jen: Is she very sick?

Diana: Well, yes, I think so. She underwent a serious operation yesterday—three hours on the operating table. For a while there it was touch and go. But today she seemed much better and I spoke to her. I stood by her bed and she took my hand and she said to me: "You need an enormous strength of will to live through this. Most people need only one reason to do it. I have three: you, your father and your grandmother. And suddenly I felt furious. I felt *furious* with her. God, she's always been so strong, the strongest person I know, and I've loved her for it. All of a sudden I felt tricked. I felt like saying to her: "Why don't you live for yourself?" I felt like saying: "I can't take this burden on me! What are you doing to me?" And now suddenly, I'm here, being asked to talk about work, and I have nothing to say. I haven't a goddamn thing to say! What do I do? After all, what do I *do?* Half my life is passed in a fantasy of desire that's focused on leaving my husband and finding some marvelous job. . . . At least, my mother worked *hard* all her life. She raised me when my real father walked out on her, she put me through school, she staked me to my first apartment, she never said no to me for anything. And when I got married she felt she'd accomplished

everything. That was the end of the rainbow. . . .

Dolores (timidly): What's so terrible, really,
your mother saying she lived for all of you?
God, that used to be considered a moral virtue. I'm sure lots of men feel the same way,
that they live for their families. Most men
hate their work. . . .

Marilyn: My husband used to say that all
the time, that he lived only for me and the
baby, that that was everything to him.

Lucie: How did you feel about that? What
did you think of him when he said it?

Marilyn (flushing): It used to make me feel
peculiar. As though something wasn't quite
right with him.

Lucie (to Diana): Did you think something
wasn't *quite right,* when your mother said what
she said?

Diane (thinking back): No. It wasn't that
something wasn't quite right. It seemed "right,"
if you know what I mean, for her to be saying
that, but terribly wrong suddenly.

Lucie: That's odd, isn't it? When a man says
he lives for his family it sounds positively unnatural to me. When a woman says it, it sounds
so "right." So expected.

Laura: Exactly. What's pathology in a man
seems normal in a woman.

Claire: It comes back, in a sense, to a woman
always looking for her identity in her family
and a man never, or rarely, really doing that.

Marie: God, this business of identity! Of
wanting it from my work, and not looking for
it in what my husband does. . . .

Jen: Tell me, do men ever look for their
identities in their wives' work?

Veronica: Yes, and then we call them Mr.
Streisand. *(Everybody breaks up, and suddenly cookies and fruit are being devoured. Everyone stretches and one or two women walk
around the room. After 15 minutes . . .)*

*Marie (peeling an orange, sitting yogi-fash-
ion on the floor):* I first went to work for a
small publicity firm. They taught me to be a
copywriter, and I loved it from the start. I
never had any trouble with the people in that
firm. It was like one big happy family there.
We all worked well with each other and everyone knew a bit about everybody else's work.
When the place folded and they let me go I
was so depressed, and so *lost.* For the longest
time I couldn't even go out looking for a job. I
had no sense of how to go about it. I had no
real sense of myself as having a transferable
skill, somehow. I didn't seem to know how to
deal with Madison Avenue. I realized then
that I'd somehow never taken that job as a
period of preparation for independence in the
world. It was like a continuation of my family.
As long as I was being taken care of I functioned, but when I was really on my own I
folded up. I just didn't know how to operate.
. . . And I still don't, really. It's never been the
same. I've never had a job in which I felt I was
really operating responsibly since that time.

Sheila: Do you think maybe you're just
waiting around to get married?

Marie: No, I don't. I know I really want to
work, no matter what. I know that I want some
sense of myself that's not related to a husband,
or to anyone but myself, for that matter. . . .
But I feel so lost, I just don't know where it's
all at, really. *(Five or six heads nodded
sympathetically.)*

Claire: I don't feel like *any* of you. Not a
single one.

Dolores: What do you mean?

Claire: Let me tell you something. I have
two sisters and a brother. My father was a
passionately competitive man. He loved sports
and he taught us all how to play, and he treated
us all exactly as though we were his equals at
it. I mean, he competed with us exactly as
though we were 25 when we were 8. Everything: sailing, checkers, baseball, there was
nothing he wouldn't compete in. When I was a
kid I saw him send a line drive ball right into

my sister's stomach, for God's sake. Sounds terrible, right? We loved it. All of us. And we thrived on it. For me, work is like everything else. *Competitive.* I get in there, do the best I can, compete ferociously against man, woman or machine. And I use whatever I have in the way of equipment: sex, brains, endurance. You name it, I use it. And if I lose I lose, and if I win I win. It's just doing it as well as I can that counts. And if I come up against discrimination as a woman, I just reinforce my attack. But the name of the game is competition.

(Everyone stared at her, openmouthed, and suddenly everyone was talking at once; over each other's voices; at each other; to themselves; laughing; interrupting; generally exploding.)

Laura (dryly): The American dream. Right before our eyes.

Diana (tearfully): Good God, Claire, that sounds awful!

Lucie (amazed): That's the kind of thing that's killing our men. In a sense, it's really why we're here.

Sheila (mad): Oh, that love of competition!

Marie (astonished): The whole idea of just *being* is completely lost in all this.

Jen (outraged): And to act *sexy* in order to compete! You degrade every woman alive!

Veronica (interested): In other words, Claire, you imply that if they give you what you want they get *you?*

Diana (wistfully): That notion of competition is everything we hate most in men, isn't it? It's responsible for the most brutalizing version of masculinity. We're in here trying to be men, right? Do we want to be men at their worst?

Lucie (angrily): For God's sake! We're in here trying to be *ourselves.* Whatever that turns out to be.

Marilyn (with sudden authority): I think you're wrong, all of you. You don't under-stand what Claire's really saying *(Everyone stopped talking and looked at Marilyn.)* What Claire is really telling you is that her father taught her not how to win but how to lose. He didn't teach her to ride roughshod over other people. He taught her how to get up and walk away intact when other people rode roughshod over *her.* And he so loved the idea of teaching *that* to his children that he ignored the fact that she and her sisters were girls, and he taught it to them, anyway. *(Everyone took a moment to digest this.)*

Laura: I think Marilyn had a very good point there. That's exactly what Claire has inside her. She's the strongest person in this room, and we've all known it for a long time. She has the most integrated and most *separate* sense of herself of anyone I know. And I can see now that that probably has developed from her competitiveness. It's almost as though it provided the *proper* relation to other people, rather than no relation.

Sheila: Well, if that's true then her father performed a minor miracle.

Jen: You're not kidding. Knowing where *you* stand in relation to other people, what you're supposed to be doing, not because of what other people want of you but because of what you want for yourself . . . *knowing* what you want for yourself . . . that's everything, isn't it?

Laura: I think so. When I think of work, that's really what I think of most. And when I think of *me* and work, I swear I feel like Ulysses after 10 years at sea. I, unlike the rest of you, do not feel I am where I am because of luck or accident or through the natural striving caused by a healthy competitiveness. I feel I am like a half-maddened bull who keeps turning and turning and turning, trying to get the hell out of this maze he finds himself in. . . . I spent 10 years not knowing what the hell I wanted to do with myself. So I kept getting married and having children. I've had three children and as many husbands. All nice men, all good to me, all meaningless to me. *(She stopped short, and seemed to be groping for words. . . .)* I wanted to *do* something. Something that was real, and serious, and would involve me in a struggle with myself. Every time I got married it was like applying Mercurochrome to a festering wound. I swear sometimes I think the thing I resent most is that women have always gotten married as a way out of the struggle. It's the thing we're encouraged to do, it's the thing we rush into with such *relief*, it's the thing we come absolutely to *hate*. Because marriage itself, for most women, is so full of self-hatred. A continual unconscious reminder of all our weakness, of the heavy price to be paid for taking the easy way out. Men talk about the power of a woman in the home. . . . That power has come to seem such a lopsided and malevolent thing to me. What kind of nonsense is that, anyway, to divide up the *influences* on children's lives in that bizarre way? The mother takes care of the *emotional* life of a child? The vital requirement for nourishment? Out of what special resources does *she* do that? What the hell principle of growth is operating in *her?* What gives a woman who never tests herself against structured work the wisdom or the self-discipline to oversee a child's emotional development? The whole thing is crazy. Just crazy. And it nearly drove me crazy. . . . What can I say? For 10 years I felt as though I were continually vomiting up my life. . . . And now I work. I work hard and I work with great relish. I want to have a family, *too*. Love. Home. Husband. Father for the children. Of course, I do. God, the loneliness! The longing for connection! But work first. And family second. *(Her face split wide open in a big grin.)* Just like a man.

Lucie: I guess I sort of feel like Laura. Only I'm not sure. I'm not sure of anything. I'm in school now. Or rather "again." Thirty years old

and I'm a graduate student again, starting out almost from scratch. . . . The thing is I could never take what I was doing seriously. That is, not as seriously as my brother, or any of the boys I went to school with, did. Everything seemed too long, or too hard, or too something. Underneath it all, I felt sort of *embarrassed* to study seriously. It was as if I was really feeling: "That's something the *grownups* do. It's not something for *me* to do." I asked my brother about this feeling once, and he said most men felt the same way about themselves, only they fake it better than women do. I thought about that one a long time, and I kept trying to say myself: What the hell, it's the same for them as it is for us. But . . . *(she looked swiftly around the circle)* it's not! Dammit, it's *not!* After all, style is content, right? And ours are worlds away. . . .

Veronica: Literally.

Lucie: I don't know. . . . I still don't know. It's a problem that nags and nags and nags at me. So often I wish some guy would just come along and I'd disappear into marriage. It's like this secret wish that I can just withdraw from it all, and then from my safe position look on and comment and laugh and say yes and no and encourage and generally play at being the judging mother, the "wise" lady of the household. . . . But then I know within six months I'd be miserable! I'd be climbing the walls and feeling guilty. . . .

Marilyn: Guilty! Guilty, guilty. Will we *ever* have a session in which the word guilty is not mentioned once? *(Outside, the bells in a nearby church tower struck midnight.)*

Diana: Let's wrap it up, okay?

Veronica (reaching for her bag): Where shall we meet next week?

Marie: Wait a minute! Aren't we going to sum up? *(Everyone stopped in mid-leaving, and sank wearily back into her seat.)*

Lucie: Well, one thing became very clear to

me. Every one of us in some way has struggled with the idea of getting married in order to be relieved of the battle of finding and staying with good work.

Diana: And every one of us who's actually done it has made a mess of it!

Jen: And everyone who *hasn't* has made a mess of it!

Veronica: But, look. The only one of us who's really worked well—with direction and purpose—is Claire. And we all jumped on her! *(Everyone was startled by this observation and no one spoke for a long moment.)*

Marilyn (bitterly): We can't do it, we can't

admire anyone who *does* do it, and we can't let it alone. . . .

Jen (softly): That's not quite true. After all, we *were* able to see finally that there was virtue in Claire's position. And we *are* here, aren't we?

Marie: That's right. Don't be so down. We're not 102 years old, are we? We're caught in a mess, damned if we do and damned if we don't. All right. That's exactly why we're here. To break the bind. *(On this note everyone took heart, brightened up and trooped out into the darkened Manhattan streets. Proof enough of being ready to do battle.)*

The March of the Real Women
Jill Johnston

Jill Johnston, writer and feminist activist, writes a weekly column for the *Village Voice.* She participated in the feminist forum at Town Hall in 1970 and is the author of *Marmalade Me,* a collection of her early essays. Her most recent book, *Lesbian Nation,* is her personal account of her emergence as a political and social lesbian.

It was common report or it was generally believed or I heard it said that something or other something. I went to a meeting which I almost never do and I had a good time and tried to claim the credit for doing everything wrong again. I went to this same meeting two weeks before and distinguished myself by sitting in a corner and pretending to be invisible. The irkstwhile expresident of now and then ordered me from the back of her head not to write about it so I won't. These meetings every tuesday over at the illogical seminary on 20th and ninth have concerned the august 25 strike and march of women and this last meeting could perhaps be characterized as a struggle to determine what we mean by women. Ostensibly it

was a parliamentary battle over the speakers. The truth of the matter was out near the end when a particularly disagreeable disgrumpled 50ish member of our own sex I think said passionately *we want real women speaking,* and other things like you people have your own gay liberation day etc. although this woman was not representative in her style of the other straights there or anyplace else necessarily she does I believe typify the entire right wing of feminism which doggedly resists the logical outcome of the struggle against the patriarchy. The great confrontation within the movement continues to be that between the straights and the lesbians. A reliable source tells me that at this date 60 per cent of the radical feminist organization has come out and the rest remain predictably defensive and deprecatory. Another organization of feminists is by point of order either lesbian or celibate. The evidence is overwhelmingly that it is not gay women who are becoming straight. The violence and ardour of this next to last meeting before the march was paradigmatic of the intensity of the issue within the movement. Many straight women translate their personal problem into a movement rhetoric that goes something like but we can't alarm all those women out there across amerika especially the women we want to know about feminism who don't know about it yet and they'll all be saying see I told you so they were right the woman's movement really is a bunch of lesbians. This attitude belongs to the well known standard conservative media approach to public taste and opinion geared to maintaining the status quo which no matter how you look at it is patriarchal. For example at the meeting the expresident I mentioned jackie ceballos stood and made an impassioned plea for a speaker or speakers who would look *(look)* conservative enough to appeal to all those women out there, whoever they are. Her remark set me thinking about another great split which to my knowledge hasn't been articulated in feminist analysis and that is the split in amerika that originated in the '50s and culminated in the '60s dividing the country into straights and freaks in the most general sense crossing color sex age and class lines. The best known agents of this revolution were the psychedelic drugs. As recently as 1970 I for one regarded people as open or closed by virtue of natural or induced freakouts and imagined that the key to survival was an unqualified expansion of consciousness. Now if you weld the counterculture onto feminism or vice versa I think it can be seen that right wing and reformist feminism is represented by women who like their old culture men never turned on tuned in and dropped out or did any of those

things thought to be subversive of the continuation of sanity and order. A number of feminists beginning at least with valerie solanis have noted the ironies of the sexual revolution what that meant for women in its updated counterculture form: more and better women to fuck by the new pleasure oriented freaks. The counterculture may be at heart a new mystique of masculine aggression, and a lot of those turned on tuned in dropt out women may still be hauling pots in the kitchens of the wonderful free communes but sexist consideration aside (if that's possible), there remains the phenomenon of mind expansion and concomitant revolutionary attitudes by which women as well as men can be distinguished from each other in what leary has called the struggle of the flower people against the metal men. Not that the flower people are supposed to be struggling. A subsplit within the counterculture occurred with the campus activists and now the whole movement seems confused by the generalized public co-option of the various styles which once indicated who was what. Anyway as to feminism I hazard my own statistics that old culture women or women you'd call straight in the straight freak dichotomy are overwhelmingly the women we also call straight in the straight lesbian confrontation and that the counterculture women within feminism are those who were lesbian to begin with and or those who were and remain the most amenable to the idea of discovering the superior pleasures of lesbian sex. That's a gross generalization. There are many freaky straights and many straight freaks and indeterminate combinations thereof. I guess off and on radical women like to think of themselves as swingers or something. I don't know what those women are doing if they're not yet turned on to feminism. I imagine that by now even if they're not aligned with feminist organizations they've absorbed the reformist feminist lines and they have their old men *help*ing them haul those pots in the kitchens. I think it's fair to say that freaky straights seriously in the feminist movement don't stay sexually straight for very long. I don't think these women would say any more as a couple of them did two years ago in some feminist essay we don't carry with us, as part of our movement baggage, an understanding of homosexual technique . . . (!) I mentioned something called a straight freak above and I'm not sure what'that is. There are some old dyke heads around, dykes who still think they're queer, i.e. different, dykes who still think you have to work with men, dykes who still think their lifestyle is a bedroom issue or that they're a special interest group whose interests are secondary to that of straight feminists, dykes who might deep down rather be straight themselves in other words who still think they're queer and have to explain and apologize and all that. It's the difficulty of dykes assuming their own vanguard position that divide the dykes and threaten to undermine certain major important confrontations with the straight feminists. The feminists always trot out that line about sexual orientation and how it isn't supposed to matter and of course it isn't but it very much does right now in this pre and post stage of human liberation (I mean when we are humanly liberated sexual orientation *won't* matter) especially since almost all the feminists complaints and demands revolve around their heterosexuality whether they say so or not. Thus their sexual orientation matters a lot. This is a difficult challenge for the dykes who naturally see themselves as much more than sexual women and who're sensitive already to the use of their own word as a discriminatory practice to describe a woman as nothing more than sexual. Thus the dykes have to say both things at once. That sexuality absolutely is at the core of the feminist revolution, and that the revolution also transcends our particular sexualities in the sense that our erotic life should

be a component in the life of a totally functioning satisfied woman. But when that happens we'll all be a woman since you are who you sleep with and to continue sleeping with the man is to remain only half a woman and a half a woman is not the ideal functioning satisfied woman. Anyway the present local politics of inter-dyke struggle is a reality in the ongoing conflict with the straight women.

The meeting I went to was as I see it a major victory for the feminist/lesbian approach to feminism, it was an uproarious and horrendous and hilarious evening at the end of which both dykes and straights were astonished that we had somehow managed to nominate and elect at least five upfront lesbians as speakers for the march and two others we think might be and one who isn't upfront and one who's pending, this was at least a dramatic reversal of one of the first marches when as martha shelley tells it she had to storm the mikes (by kate's permission who was speaking) to speak for lesbians that year they didn't even elect a *token*. The substruggle of the dykes surfaced at the end of the meeting last tuesday. Ostensibly a few personalities were involved and the issue seemed to be the disagreement between dyke separatists and dyke collaborators meaning dykes who work with men at GAA. I suspect the conflict is a lot deeper and that this particular disagreement is symptomatic of that difficulty I mentioned of moving into our own vanguard position. To any old dyke head the token situation is still the proper place. Whatever the conflict it was actually two dykes at the end who initiated the move to reverse everything and eliminate speakers altogether. For myself I don't think it's all that important whether you have speakers or not but clearly in this case to eliminate them would have meant a setback to a critical feminist/lesbian victory. Everybody was screaming and out of order. I yelled sour grapes. Someone yelled fuck the democratic process, let's have a queen. Some woman was yelling at me that it was all my fault, that this sort of thing happened whenever I came. And the dykes as I said were turning against themselves in some weird political myopia that only the inside inside might be able to understand as sue schneider said when she came out of the closet she heard the door slam behind her, meaning I think that a lot of dykes didn't hear the noise. So anyhow a vote was called and I thought that was it that all was lost but I was wrong and a clear majority voted to keep the speakers. Before that when this woman was carrying on and accusing us of coming in a bloc which we did although I said I came as myself which was also true and anyway what is the straight faction if it isn't a bloc even if they don't admit that most of their issues (abortion prostitution sterilization contraception child care marriage and divorce) are heterosexual issues it seems ironic to me they should be accusing us of wanting to know if the candidates were "gay" especially since so many "gay" women are themselves "experts" on heterosexual issues, like marriage and divorce, both as "gay" and "straight" women, and since so many "gay" women are centrally involved in these very heterosexual projects like abortion again as sue schneider said one half to more women working on the abortion project in new york are dykes who help with counseling and putting up women from all over and she thinks moreover that if we dyke-otted the women's movement it would fall apart in two days. As to the march this should be the first year of clarity for lesbians who constitute the revolutionary pivot of the feminist revolution until this time trapped as token between gay males and straight women that's sort of what I really wanted to say to that woman at the meeting that lesbians are fucking really tired of being tokens and of many feminists not declaring their own conversion and telling like it is how

the entire straight feminist movement is sexually confused sick celibate furious at men unable to be fucked by men any more unwilling and scared and discovering the (still criminal) pleasures of love and sex with their sisters. Like when're they gonna start telling their stories. As to maintaining a conservative stance and soft-playing to all the sisters "out there" in middle amerika I could quote phyllis chesler here saying women, including many feminists, respond more positively to those projects which ease the burdens of the female status quo rather than to those projects which attempt to redefine or abolish the stotus quo. Easing the burdens of motherhood and supporting abortion reform are essential tasks, yet both imply a continuation of a powerless female responsible for children and for birth control. Endquote. The feminists in amerika are still not recognizing their most powerful force for change in their most independent aggressive and sexually alive women. A strong feminist in london told me right off that the lesbians there are in the vanguard of the movement and this was a woman who lives with a husband and a child. The only feminist who has asserted herself in this manner in this country is ti-grace atkinson who has apparently been so well treated by the movement that she is now supporting the mafia. People like midge decter I dunno they're so far out in left (or right) field that at this stage of revolution in a city like new york at least you wonder if they ever saw the ball at all. She's one of those who never considered sexuality without a man ever not even with an asparagus or a rhubarb. So what do these women think when they know that most of the women marching in the women's march august 25 are the dangerous dykes of that great original broadeyed sunken race called women. A logistically very easy and tactically correct maneuver. We're not coming to take over as sue said we're coming to get your attention for awhile. She said in missouri they used to say we'd have to hit the mule over the head with a two by four to get their attention so you could talk to them. I don't care about marches or meetings or any of it. I don't care what the straight women think unless they agree with us we're oppressed and we want woman power and revolution should be fun or we should forget it. The Cistercians, or somebody, is Coming! A Torrential Rain often accompanies a Major Eruption. Then we go away to the country and say after the butterfly is formed it must rest and realize its being as a butterfly.

The Outs Become Ins: The 1972 Democratic Convention

Since I've been aware of the world, all the national elections have been times for focusing feelings: Kennedy in 1960 helped awaken students and young people to politics; Johnson in 1964 confirmed a growing sense of betrayal; Nixon and Humphrey in 1968 shaped a universe without alternatives.

And now after all this history comes a man, George McGovern, with the rhetoric in part of the Port Huron Convention of ten years ago. Is it a measure of the New Left's success, or are we being absorbed into the status quo?—Tom Hayden, *Rolling Stone* interview.

Even for Tom Hayden, principal author of the SDS founding document, the Port Huron Statement, there is no clear-cut answer to the alternatives he poses. "Both are true; neither are true. Whatever happens this November radicalism will find its way through a lot of dead ends," he replies. But more than any answer he might give, Hayden's question points up the importance of the 1972 Democratic Convention as a measuring rod for twelve years of social turmoil. For by 1972 those who had pinned their hopes on the 1960s becoming an era of political change had come of age. They had seen the programs of the Great Society fail in a variety of ways, faced up to the disaster of the war in Vietnam, and learned that the police of Chicago could be just as brutal as the police of Birmingham, Alabama in putting down demonstrations that took to the street.

When the McGovern forces came to Miami in 1972, it was this heritage—from the war in Vietnam to bossism within the party—that they sought to change. But they sought to change it from a position of strength. The McGovern guidelines were in force at the convention, which meant more blacks, more women, more young people than ever before. Even Mayor Daley could be sent home when the delegation he led did not conform to party rules. Yet, if the McGovern delegates represented a new populism, it was a special kind of populism with few places for old people or working people or white ethnics. In a country where only 4 percent of the population goes to graduate school, 39 percent of the McGovern delegates had gone; and on income the McGovernites were just as different. Of the McGovern delegates, 31 percent earned $25,000 or more per year, as compared with 6 percent of the entire population; 6 percent of the McGovern delegates earned less than $5,000 as compared with the national figure of 18 percent. Most interesting of all, perhaps, was the difference between the number of delegates McGovern could claim and the overall voting results of the Democratic primaries:

Candidate	*Votes*	*Percentage*
Hubert Humphrey	4,051,134	26.5%
George McGovern	3,950,394	25.8%
George Wallace	3,612,650	23.6%

The new journalism collected here follows closely the operation of the McGovern forces at the Democratic Convention, sometimes dealing with the political strategy they adopted, other times with the positions they took on busing or abortion or family income. The reportage in all cases was completed before the November election in which McGovern was so badly defeated, but the judgments it requires take us directly from an assessment of the election to an assessment of the mood of the country. Was it the radical nature of McGovern's program that brought about his defeat? Or the degree to which he embraced traditional political strategies in order to gain votes? If the latter—does it suggest the country had within it a capacity for a new politics of expectation that went untapped? If the former—does it indicate that the amount of change since 1960, and especially since 1965, was the reason people voted for the man John Kennedy defeated when he ran for President?

In his "Making Crowds," the playwright Arthur Miller provides a pro-McGovern interpretation of the Democratic Convention. For Miller, a Connecticut delegate in 1968 and 1972, the convention "signified a renovation of politics, a major party opened at last to the streets, the teacher, the student, the amateur." Only "the legitimizing weight of the working

class was not there to make it the real reflection of the America it wanted
to be," he contends. Miller sees the differences between the 1968 and 1972
Democratic Conventions reflected most transparently in the style and conduct of the delegates. "Nobody vomiting rye or smoking Admirations, no
rebel yells from blue-eyed Yahoos, and surely the highest I.Q. level in any
Convention history." But as he goes on to observe, "It was not merely that
there were so many blacks and actual girls in jeans rather than fat ladies
from hard precinct chairs. It was that—had McGovern not been nominated—they would have burst the form itself, abandoned the Convention
and burst through the streets and real life." The McGovern phenomenon
in Miller's eyes is the creation of a "New Crowd," and his reportage turns
on the potential of that crowd, "forming itself not only among the previously ignored and dispossessed, but also in some undetermined degree among
that eight or ten percent of the straight people as well."

In Wilfrid Sheed's "Donkey Serenade" the difference between Chicago
in 1968 and Miami in 1972 is also central. "As a tale of cold-blooded
vengeance," the 1972 Convention "was worthy at least of a Sam Peckinpah
movie," he writes. "The villains of '68 were cornered and gunned down one
by one. Some, like Mayor Daley, went down snarling. Others, the Larry
O'Briens, recanted and promised to reform, but they were gunned down
anyway." But Sheed, in contrast to Miller, traces the differences between
the two conventions to the time when the "McGovern committee had
calmly sat down and redesigned the Democratic Party, while the men
laughingly called pros had dozed their long off-year's nap." It is these new
rules that Sheed sees as responsible for the uniqueness of the 1972 Democratic Convention, and the question he continually asks in his analysis of
the McGovern forces is, "How clever is too clever?" The result is an
account in which Sheed continually shifts from his admiration for the
McGovern effort to his worry that it depends on trickery.

The remaining pieces in this section all offer a harsher view of the Democratic Convention. In Hunter S. Thompson's "Fear and Loathing in Miami:
Old Bulls Meet the Butcher" the real business of the Convention is seen
happening as usual "on secret-numbered telephones or behind closed
doors." For Thompson, the "only real question in Miami was whether or
not McGovern might be stripped of more than half of the 271 delegates he
won in the California primary." It is this problem that he sees as the overriding concern of the McGovern staff, and his story details the way in
which the McGovern forces deliberately lost a credentials fight over the
South Carolina delegation in order to make sure they were in a position to
win the California challenge. In the end, Thompson finds the political
need to win dominating the McGovernites like everyone else and even
carrying over to the way they celebrate their defeat of Humphrey. "The
atmosphere at the victory party was not much different from the atmosphere of the Convention itself: very cool and efficient, very much under

control at all times . . . get the job done, don't fuck around, avoid violence, shoot ten seconds after you see the whites of their eyes."

Germaine Greer's "McGovern, The Big Tease," begins with her grudgingly acknowledging her hopes for McGovern. "I struggled to retain a modicum of Marxian good sense, but the drag of desire pulled me away so many times that despite myself I began to hope madly that McGovern was a superman, that the convention was open, that the people were really the people, autonomous and honest, and not mere pawns for the men who were marketing McGovern." But in the end Greer finds herself just as trapped by contradictory feelings. "I wish and painfully hope that the women, the kids, the blacks, the Latins, and the 'intellectual pseudosnobs' bring off the impossible for him in November, in spite of himself, his baloney machine, and his Machiavellis, even though they will take credit for it." Greer sees McGovern as the only alternative for the country in 1972, but for her he is essentially the lesser of two evils. The more closely she scrutinizes the Convention, the more she finds it a reflection of marketing techniques in which "God, Conscience, Sincerity, the dead Kennedys, the suffering Vietnamese, and, above all, the People were all on the side of the Democrats." It is a conclusion that goes a long way toward explaining why the very hopes McGovern aroused also played a role in eroding his support.

Making Crowds
Arthur Miller

Arthur Miller, who was a delegate to both the 1968 and 1972 Democratic conventions, is best known as one of America's most important contemporary dramatists. His plays include *Death of a Salesman, The Crucible,* and *After the Fall.*

As in Chicago so in Miami—this had to be the Last Convention. So said half-a-dozen newsmen of my acquaintance and I felt the same myself a good part of the time. There is the shock and charm of the American crowd in all its variety and sheer animal power, but in any real sense the thing simply cannot work. How can the same man "represent" Richard Daley and Bella Abzug? For that matter how could Franklin Roosevelt stand for the principles of Georgia's Governor Talmadge and his red suspenders and simultaneously for the young trade-union movement whose organizers were being crucified in the South?

But this is too rational. Democracy is first of all a state of feeling. A nominee, and later a President, is not a sort of methodical lawyer hired to win a client's claim, but an ambiguously symbolic figure upon whom is projected the conflicting desires of an audience. Like the protagonist in a drama he rises to a level of the fictional. As he comes closer to being the nominee he becomes less an ordinary man than a performer who is merely like a man. One proof of this is that we demand a perfection of character of him which would be absurd and childish were he not a nominee but which is somehow reasonable as he approaches that status. For he is now a hero who must act out what we would believe is the best in our own faulted personalities.

So it is inevitable that the Issues dim in a Convention quite as they do in a good play whose moral conclusions and thematic point, while necessary to give it form, recede in importance for the mind which is swayed by personalities, color, the surprises and sudden switches of the action itself.

As a Connecticut delegate in '68 I was at first surprised by the relative impotence of the Issues for the Humphrey men who made up the bulk of our delegation. I had assumed that as machine politicians whose very livelihoods depended on winning the election, they would be ruled by this consideration, but I could not find one who believed Humphrey had a chance against Nixon. One would assume they would therefore be casting about for an alternative. This would be rational. Nor were they under the illusion that continuing the war would do anything but hurt their cause. Yet they would not hear of any idea to set themselves against Johnson's policy, which had no hope of bringing peace reasonably soon.

It was clear then that it came down to their *belonging* somewhere, the way people belong in a certain neighborhood and are strangers in another in no objective way different than their own. Win or no win, issues or no issues, they belonged with Humphrey and the binding tie was visceral. And when I thought about it later in the calm of total disaster for our side, I found my own case too similar. Had Humphrey by some miracle turned against the war and come out for immediate withdrawal I knew it would be hard for me to go with him. I did not belong with him. Objectively, his record on other issues was as good or better than McCarthy's, yet in his camp I'd have been a stranger and at odds with myself. It is a bit like asking an audience in the last act of *Hamlet* to side with the King. Assume we suddenly learn that the King might well be literally innocent of the murder of Hamlet's father, could it change our non-identification with him? Hamlet has already said too many things which moved us and carried us with him, and mere facts could never prevail over expended feelings.

It could have been a feeling of *déjà vu* which made the Miami thing seem so manifestly theatrical an occasion, but there were also striking signs that whatever principles they had come to fight for the delegates were *on;* they had come to symbolize, not merely to transact public business. It was another element in the transformation of the Party which had now become contemporary. Nobody vomiting rye or smoking Admirations, no rebel yells from blue-eyed Yahoos, and surely the highest I.Q. level in any Convention in history—they actually kept up with most of the parliamentary maneuvering which was lost on the crowd in Chicago. To be sure there was the same air of total disorientation in the first days, like a freshman class at a large university asking where the gym is, but these people bore a double perspective; like actors they related to the reality around them, but at the same time they played it for the home screen.

One could remember when people went shy and reticent before the TV lights and camera, and the old-time delegate caught by a TV interviewer would either puff himself up and try to look like a statesman, or wave to his mother through the lens. These young, suckled on TV, knew that you never look into the lens and that you have to condense the statement of your position or be cut off, and they did both with ease and naturalness. The old guard had been more cagey than this before the camera, suspicious of the interloper, for a Convention was an authentic rather than an artistic occa-

sion. The new understood that the camera is the main thing and that nothing could be said to *happen* until it had been filmed.

These shadings are politically instructive. The men of Chicago knew it was all as staged a performance as *The Follies* and that their part in it was to obey instructions while evincing the requisite enthusiasms on cue. They too were acting, but the difference was that they believed in the form itself while the new delegates were ironical toward the very idea of a Convention and even the Party. After all, McGovern had let slip that if he lost the nomination he would bolt. They were here to win their demands upon society, would use the form as long as it was usable and if the form failed them they were capable of walking off the stage and out of the theatre. For the old, the stakes used to be the Party and the Convention. For the young it was to dominate the age itself, and when the young were tapped by the TV men they played it fully, not strategically and strained as the old men used to. In theatre terms, the classic fourth wall of the stage was no more—they were trying to mingle with the audience, but they were playing nonetheless.

It has been said that this Convention had much more content than previous ones but it was not merely that there were so many blacks, and actual girls in jeans rather than the fat ladies led in from hard precinct chairs. It was that—had McGovern not been nominated—they would have burst the form itself, abandoned the Convention, and burst through into the streets and real life. No such implicit threat hung over Chicago against the possibility of a Humphrey defeat. So in Chicago and Miami were two levels of art, one more naïve than the other perhaps, but both were performances. And in the mind vague prospects rose of some more authentic means of choosing the most powerful officeholder on the planet.

This performance-orientation, I thought,

suppurated the city itself, the people's tone of voice became unreal and emblematic. Unable to park the car I had foolishly rented I reverted to cabs and I had no sooner sat down in one than the driver in his New York accent announced, "I'm a Republican, been one thirty-five years. Who likes Nixon? You can't like Nixon. But I'm a Republican. Because my father-in-law's a Democrat." He laughed. "I like to get the knife in. It's all shit." I hadn't mentioned I was a writer, but it wasn't necessary—we are a nation of the interviewed.

This outer-directedness took stranger forms than usual in Miami. Flamingo Park, normally a preserve for the arthritic aged, the pensioner and the baby-sitter, had by mutual agreement become a corral for the Outraged, the much-feared Hippies who now lay about in the shade of dusty palms like the cast of an abandoned show. Some, veterans of the Chicago battles, others new recruits, they sent up dutiful wisps of grass smoke, demonstrating, as it were, their fundamental intelligence rather than the advertised rage. In fact, by the middle of our Passion Week the TV people had already sucked the marrow of their news and had abandoned them to life's ironies, which can be crueler than the clubs of the police. Even the lawn looked tired. I heard through the terrible moist heat the voice of a girl and The Gospel According to Saint Matthew.

At an impromptu pulpit made of a crate over which a faded purple cloth was draped, she stood alone, reading the Bible to Miami, a pretty seventeen-year-old totally ignored by the few strollers from the straight world who had come to see the animals, and unheard by her contemporaries who blinked cruddy eyes at the morning sun or stared dead-brained at the old, half-crippled Jews sliding the shuffle-board disks along the baking concrete slabs. The dust, it seemed, had settled again, and America had once more transformed her revolutionaries into screwballs, as in my youth she had hung the Hobo's mask on the Depres-

sion unemployed who, in their hour, had made a bid to characterize the country and had failed. Then I heard actual Hebrew.

A small drooping pup tent, one of several propped up on these deserted fairgrounds, and before it stood a young Jew with a yarmulke on his head, doing something with a man of sixty-five or so who wore a brown felt hat, a blue vest without a shirt, and had a two-day grey stubble on his cheeks. Amazed and unbelieving, I approached—the young Jew was teaching the old man how to wind phylacteries around his arm! I saw now that under the old guy's hat brim was the single strand of leather attached to which was the leather box containing the Holy Word pressed to his forehead. He was having trouble learning how to wind the leather reins around his fingers, but the young teacher was patiently redoing the procedure. And all the while a few yards away stood another Orthodox, a confederate of nineteen who, as I came near, asked if I wanted to be next.

"Are you proselytizing?" I asked.

"No, we don't proselytize. We're only interested in Jews. Come on, try it."

"I gave that up when I was fourteen."

"Try it. You might like it again."

The confederate's sublime arrogance, irritating as it was, nevertheless contrasted with the surrounding air of cultivated purposelessness, and was strangely fitting in this highly political, outer-directed city. But the worst was yet to come—I heard the old pupil *counting*. I went closer to hear what to my atavistic heart seemed an abomination, for when you wind the phylacteries you are talking to God. But he was, he was counting even as he at last had managed to correctly wind the narrow leather rein around his fingers and up his arm.

"One thousand, two thousand, three thousand," he muttered, hardly moving his lips. Why was he counting? And why did not the young Orthodox soul-fisher seem to notice? Was this all a mockery, and the two young

Jews acting out some kind of travesty of holy instruction, hoping to kill their parents with heart attacks? But now the old pupil glanced past me and I followed his gaze to another man, a companion his own age, who was standing there photographing his friend's conversion with a home movie camera.

The old pupil, who to the naked eye, or rather to the silent film, was the very picture of the hatted old pious Jew performing one of the most ancient of rituals, now lowered his arm and having rehearsed sufficiently ordered his cameraman to begin shooting; "Count to ten, one thousand, two thousand, up to ten," he instructed him, and then turned back to perform the winding of the phylactery. Meanwhile, the shill never ceased inviting me to join the fun, but the thing that brought me back to my twentieth-century senses was the fact that the two Orthodox, who I have no reason to think were anything less than sincere fishers of men, were also cooperating and knew how to place themselves on each side of the new convert so that their ministrations would show to good effect on film. Meanwhile—and this is the final note on this edifying scene—the convert put on a look of such powerful piety as he performed his newly rediscovered Godly duty that I had to wonder whether this was as faked as it appeared to be. For all I know he would from that day return to the Synagogue and the Jewish life, the more so when it has all been filmed, registered, you might say, in God's very eye. Flamingo Park, this whole city in fact, had taken on the air of scenery, the MGM back lot in whose perfect imitations of streets the extras and featured players filled up waiting time with games, naps and horseplay while the stars and the producers worried out the continuity in closed rooms somewhere up high.

Which reminds me of my shock on first learning that Eisenhower had his makeup man. But what did I expect—a Presidential candidate sweating on television and his wrinkles showing? What is this nostalgia for the authentic? Must not Lincoln have had some crowd-related object in mind when he trimmed his beard just so? Still, the idea of Lincoln pausing for his pancake and going over in his mind. "Fourscore and seven years ago. . . ."

And were we not set up for this by the Renaissance painters who made the miserable Magdalen so beautiful, Jesus so unearthly? Was it at least part of his motivation in a Roman colony where every official action was surrounded with show business that Jesus knew he must really die to break through with the message? Did the wild men of the '68 Chicago streets understand that they'd be clowns until they bled real blood on a medium where blood was as catsup theretofore?

It seems that even George Meany was carried away by the pull of the symbolic. One assumed an ideological cleavage behind his and I. W. Abel's refusal to go with the Convention's choice, and the cynical would make the stakes even more material—McGovern was not in debt to labor and so would be independent of its claims on the Presidency. But surely Meany knew what later was revealed, that the pro-McGovern unions controlled more campaign money than the unions he and Abel held in their grip, so we are face-to-face again with symbolic gestures. To Meany and such standard types this Convention might as well have been a Mayan ritual whose application to himself or anyone he knew was simply not possible. The whole thing just wasn't real, a lot of kids acting out a drama of power politics when they had never even *worked,* owned businesses, met a payroll or paid homage to the industrial machine in any form. They watched it all like Legionnaires at a convention in Sandusky, Ohio, before a performance of *Waiting for Godot* or *The Bald Soprano.* What the hell is this?

You can call it a culture gap but you'd think that, faced with another four Nixon years, they would have been able to temper outrage if only for the sake of the lesser evil. Men acting rationally surely could have done so. But they had been reached where art reaches men—in the hollows of disgust and primordial rage, until they left their famous hardheaded objectivity behind and retreated to a gesture of revolt which had to be mostly empty since the forces to inflict damage were not theirs to command. And so George Meany for a moment joined the cast, long enough to curse a world he never made and departing a play too spurious for any belief. It was a revulsion of taste, but taste is always a matter of identification, as the history of art makes clear enough.

When I went to Miami Beach it was with the near certainty that the pros would rob George McGovern of the nomination; after a day in the lobbies looking in vain for the Old Boys I was afraid he would win everything but the power that goes with the nomination. It seemed to me then that, underneath the conflict of issues and life-styles and the rest, what we were witnessing, and still are as the election battles shape up, is the most complicated and ambiguous construction man makes—the Crowd.

To put it briefly, a Crowd is not merely a large collection of people but an organism in itself, having its own energies which are aimed at a discharge. The McGovern phenomenon can be seen as the creation of a new Crowd whose existence, in terms of its individual members, was previously known, but as a Crowd was unforeseen. The common assumption was that the two parties—that is, the two Crowds—had preempted the field and the most that could happen was perhaps a lowering of the age of the Democratic crowd which would demand a quicker peace in Vietnam and some changes in the tax and welfare sys-

tems. What McGovern demonstrated, surprisingly, was that a new Crowd has in fact secretly been forming itself not only among the previously ignored and dispossessed, but also in some undetermined degree among that eight or ten percent of the straight people as well, that mercurial group of the unaligned which may shift to or away from either party and decide an election. By pulling out, the Meanys are signaling their hope and belief that this new construction is merely that—a rather adventitious seizure of party power by a fragment which is not, in fact, a crowd at all but a self-announced facsimile.

A merely random collection of people becomes an operative Crowd at the point when each of its members begins to feel a strong sense of equality with all the others. This must not be mistaken for a virtue or an evil; a Nazi crowd and a Democratic one are subject to the same generic sensations regardless of their opposing ideologies. William L. Shirer once told me that when he attended Hitler's mass meetings as a hostile reporter he often felt the skin crawling on his neck as he realized that something within him was being sucked into the general sweep of the crowd's fused identity. Whatever the crowd's larger social purposes its first purpose is to exist as a crowd, and it achieves its existence when differences have been eradicated among its members. At this moment, like any organism, a crowd tends to expel what is alien to itself, and that is when its Crowd-life begins. The phenomenon is common in the theatre where a lot of unrelated people gather and only fuse if and when a common, equal response is ignited in them by what they are seeing. The play which fails, in effect, to make a crowd out of a disparate collection of people has simply left their differences intact. So it is that the politician, like the writer or actor, must make a crowd for himself by providing that locus around which a great many people may transcend their ordinary bounds of feeling and join in the crowd's equality.*

What has misled observers of the McGovern phenomenon is that its adherents' viewpoints and class memberships are so various and even conflicting. A great many well-to-do people, for example, have contributed a lot of money even in the face of McGovern's announced intention to raise their taxes; the professional women continue working for him despite a nearly total refusal on his part to adopt their positions; blacks who until very recently swore to support only candidates vowing fealty to their cause have gone for McGovern who has not. And so on. Contrariwise, the Jews, or a lot of them, have conceived McGovern as lukewarm at best about Israel despite his avowals of continuation of past U.S. policy.

Something more than the sheer consideration of issues is working here, and it is obviously so when Wallaceites can regard McGovern without falling to pieces.

To put it this way is not to make Issues disappear but to set them in their place below the question of symbolic identification. At the least, it is certain that McGovern's Crowd is a real one and not a facsimile, and that it has important possibilities for growth. But this is due as much to the openness—you might call it vagueness—of his positions as their sharpness. With some surprise I found, for whatever one man's experience may be worth, that to his own followers McGovern stands for more than his orientation toward Issues, and this may be the basic reason why the Republicans—at least around Convention time—had stopped laughing.

Driving to my lodgings in the small hours, I picked up hitchhikers, all of them the McGovern Young. At half-past four one morning my headlights flashed on a girl walking alone

*A neglected book, Crowds and Power by Elias Canetti, Viking Press, 1963, has some startling insights into this entire business.

along Collins Avenue. She was twenty-one, short-bobbed, wore white slacks with fake stiff lace around the bells, a black jersey, and came all the way from Alaska to this hot place. But she was not even a delegate, just a "worker" for George; she had scraped the fare together and was now stone broke, trying to walk the seven miles way out to her motel in the next town, Hollywood. In fact, she was eating once a day at the canteen in the Convention Hall where the Democratic Party provided fried chicken to just such faithful. I offered to give or loan her money but she refused, either on some arcane principle or for fear of a sexual approach. In any case, she was placidly resentful that McGovern workers were not being paid as evidently they had been promised. This did not amount to a betrayal in her mind, but simply a fact. Like the other Georgeans I came to meet, she was remarkably factual. For example, she had accompanied an Eskimo delegate (there exploded in my mind a furred man in this frightful heat) who also had to surmount barriers in order to get here. "He had to borrow his brother's plane to fly to Nome."

She said this with a certain hurt. I doubt that in all the history of revolutionary gatherings a delegate has been reduced to borrowing his brother's plane, but in surreal Miami I must admit that this piece of information seemed perfectly ordinary. And what, I asked, had moved her toward McGovern? The war? Ecology? The Alaskan pipeline?

"I wouldn't say it was those things," she said, and her tone made "those things" seem distant indeed. "I just wanted to participate."

It was a longer drive to Hollywood than I had booked in my mind when I picked her up and in the surrounding blackness between the towns our interview gave way to conversation. She was studying biology and lived alone in a cabin heated by a kerosene stove on the outskirts of whatever Alaskan town, eating out of cans. Her parents were divorced. I looked at her more carefully now—she was rather plain, a turned-up nose, round face, straight black hair, pudgy. A lonely girl. One understood the issue. It is not to denigrate it or its political force to make note of it this way. She had felt the pull of her Crowd and had answered it as she never could have by watching it all on the tube.

I had told her I also was for McGovern and before her motel door she smiled for the first time and offered her hand. In the morning she would awaken hungry and suffer through the day until the Democratic fried chicken in the evening. But, as she said, it was helping her to lose weight. The whole experience had innumerable benefits, and should Nixon solve the war before election time or even make the air pure, she would remain a McGovern worker. And this is strength, not weakness, in a political movement.

In full sunlight another partisan, a boy from Vermont, sat beside me on the way to the Doral Hotel, McGovern's headquarters, but he was not only a delegate; he had been on TV as the youngest delegate in history, eighteen. He seemed extremely tired with an inner exhaustion known especially to performers who must go on despite everything. Yet he was already a little sick of his notoriety, he said. "I'm not sure I'll go on in politics. I don't feel like it right now."

Had something disillusioned him?

"Not exactly. But I don't think he should have said that to Wall Street."

Said what?

"How they hadn't to worry none about his tax reforms. He had no call saying a thing like that to Wall Street. I mean is he serious?"

Then you've gone sour on him?

"No—no, I'm for him. But I wish he hadn't said those things."

And what had brought him in? The war? Ecology? Unemployment?

He glanced at me. I could, I thought, hear his mind saying, "What war?"—he gave me that kind of blank. But what had brought him out to do political work?

"It was interesting. I met a lot of people and I enjoy that. I don't know, I just felt I wanted to get into it. But I don't think I'd make it a life's work."

A third was Boston Irish and feverish with all his appointments and the caucuses; red-haired, twenty-three, he was having the time of his life. But he was serious. "I think we can take Massachusetts."

And why was he in it? The war? Ecology? What?

Again that surprised look.

Or maybe, I said, you're Irish and just like the game.

He laughed, "It's not the Irish, but I do, I like the game. I want to do it all my life."

Why? What's there about it?

"I just like it. I like doing it. I think we can take Massachusetts."

There would be an opportunity later to learn about those issues (or the lack of them) and the young, but a conversation over breakfast reminded me of the complications in the hearts of the other Crowd, the one that had stopped growing. Two or three times I had passed these two immense men in the Americana lobby—I would go there to sleep in my room or simply because, as Muskie's headquarters, it was the only place you could park. As in Shakespeare, it was separated from the chief contenders' camps, housing Meany's entourage as well as John Bailey's Connecticut troops. Thus it was the quietest lobby of all and you could find middle-aged and elderly John of Gaunts bemoaning the partition of this England, this blessed Isle and so forth. I had exchanged waves with these two giants who, I figured, must know my face, so polite and friendly were they every time our paths crossed. On this morning I found myself at the next table and since they looked kind of lonely and in need, for some reason, of my company I moved over and joined them over eggs. I discovered they had merely waved to be friendly. Also, to talk with someone who might, hopefully, help them understand what had happened to their kind in Miami.

This was Wednesday, when McGovern had already turned back the California challenge and had the nomination in the bag.

I asked, "You fellas for Humphrey?"

"I am. He's for Muskie," said the black-haired man, relieving his thick wrist by stretching his watch band which was extended near to bursting.

"You delegates?"

"No. Just here. You?"

"No, I'm trying to write about it."

"The papers."

"Magazine. But I'm for McGovern."

"I seen you somewhere."

I knew he wouldn't like what he dimly saw and I waited and he finally pointed a finger. "You were with the McCarthy side at the '68 Convention."

"That's it. I'm Miller."

"Oooh ya." Then he turned to his friend. "He's that writer."

"O-o-h ya," the brown-haired man said. Their curiosity overtook their distaste. The black-haired man's eyes flickered at notoriety so close. "Well, he'll never win Connecticut."

"Still, he certainly came up fast for the nomination."

"He got that for one statement. When he said he'd end the war on Inauguration Day."

"That's how Eisenhower beat Stevenson, wasn't it? When he said he'd go to Korea? Stevenson said we'd have to fight on forever."

"That's true." He opened a little, his uncertainty peeked out. "You think he's got a chance?"

"What've you got against him?"

"He's not honest." And the brown-haired friend nodded.

"By the way, where you from?"

"Hartford."

"What do you do?"

"I'm a Sheriff. We both are." The brown-haired man nodded again, and said, "Sheriffs." I could see them both emerging from the squad car, chests immense, holsters shining, Americans in charge.

"How do you mean, not honest?"

"Well, Humphrey . . . a man goes out and works for him, he takes care of you. McGovern, I'm afraid, is gonna tell you if you don't qualify, get out."

Unhorsed by his unblinking honesty, the whole Convention came alive for the first time. "But you could work with him, couldn't you? With his people?"

The brown-haired man spoke; "They've got no use for ethnics. I'm a Ukrainian. You don't see any Ukrainians up there" (on the Convention platform).

"Or Poles either. I'm a Pole. Fifteen percent of the delegates are black. Which is all right, but where's the others?"

They looked hurt. Beetle-browed, appealing for justice. "You're right about that. He's going to have to come to you people."

"I don't know what you are, but. . . ."

"I'm Jewish."

"Okay. If Ribicoff was made Vice-President. . . ."

"He won't take it. I just talked to him."

"Sure he won't take it," the Pole said; "he's not going to sink with a loser."

"I don't think that's it. He's been sponsoring McGovern for years. He just doesn't want any more than he's got. He's a Senator and that's what he likes."

"And he's got the scratch," the Pole said.

"Plenty," the Ukrainian added, rubbing two fingers.

"But say he was Vice-Presidential nominee," the Pole said; "that'd be a terrific feather in your cap, now wouldn't it."

"Sure."

"Well that's it."

The point driven home, they both leaned back heavily in their chairs. But they wanted another move; mine. It surprised me.

"Under Roosevelt they had all kinds of Democratic clubs where I come from. Ukrainian, Polish, Irish, Lith. . . ."

"Sure!" the Pole agreed. "Roosevelt *came* to the ethnic people."

"Supposing McGovern came to you people. Is it too late? Could he make a difference now?"

"He won't do it. He comes from that place out there. They got no ethnics out there."

"But if he did, would you accept him?"

"You can't live on 'ifs.' What he likes is these Hippies. If it wasn't for them in Chicago, where they made such a bad impression, Humphrey'd have been elected. Those riots destroyed the Democratic Party."

"The war did that."

"Well, naturally the war. Without the war it'd been heaven. Even now, people don't realize there's a lot of boys out there."

"McGovern's trying to bring them home."

"That's right." They both nodded agreement. They believed or disbelieved each separate thing separately. There was no ideology to wrack falsehoods into a straight line. I didn't think they were lost to McGovern at all. If he cared enough, and if he, as native as an Indian, could project himself into the immigrant heart which is torn between shame of the old-country beginnings and resentment of that shame. Their most heartfelt emotion is a piece of the dignity pie which Nixon even more than McGovern cannot ever give them. I have heard deeply anti-Communist, Catholic Poles evince pride that Poland is advancing, has stood up to Moscow and can boast of artists and writers, even if they are Reds. Similarly Italians. McGovern, strange as it sounds, is in the best position to fire these people up. Nobody is more American than he, none could more legitimately show them the recognition that would bring them home. Looking at these men I was mystified that they had been left so far out on a limb. Is it possible McGovern thinks they are lost to him? Or can he really lack the requisite sympathy as they suppose? Or is it that they represent the outer limits of the new Crowd? Surely a Kennedy would have long since visited Hamtramck and Hartford by this time. But the Kennedys are immigrants.

"A politician, like a playwright, has to work with his viscera as well as his head or he's no good. Humphrey, Daley, Meany, Muskie cannot feel the changes in the country."—Senator Abe Ribicoff at eight-thirty in the morning in the lobby of the Americana. His car was waiting outside the revolving door to take him over to McGovern at the Doral, but he sat down to talk; he has evidently learned how to relax into the moment and not be rushed by time. In Chicago on the worst night of the carnage in the streets, he had stood at the podium of the Convention over the heads of the Illinois delegation and, looking directly down at Richard Daley, had been the first official Democrat to flash the facts of life to the grand and doomed machine, declaring his horror that the Chicago Police Department was using "Gestapo tactics." At which the crevasse opened and the waters of Miami rushed through the dikes, for that was when Daley had drawn a finger over his throat as he glared up at Ribicoff and told him to drop dead. Connecticut had been placed on Illinois' flank so that I was close to Daley's troops whose size-eighteen necks swelled, there seeming, for a moment, that if Daley gave the signal they would have gladly rushed the platform and torn Abe's head from his shoulders. The parliamentary system is a paraphrase for murder and Abe could feel the killing waves. I thought I saw his hand shake, but he stood and nodded back to Daley's gesture and curse, affirming again what he had declared. If there was a single instant when the new Crowd split from the old and began to form a separate entity it was then, when Ribicoff's heel drew the borders of the old Crowd's growth.

Apart from his courage, and it took a great deal of it in that moment of ignition, I suppose he could be the one to tell the Party the time of day because there is something in him that has had enough of politics. I wanted to know if he would accept the Vice-Presidential nomination, about which there was much talk. "I'm going to tell them that after thirty-nine years in politics I'd prefer to run for local office with McGovern. It's the only enthusiasm I have left for politics. There are other things I want to do with my life." A recent widower, he seemed to see the turmoil through the quietus of mortality. For over two years he has been McGovern's sponsor in the Senate and, from all accounts, foresaw every step of his rise from what at first seemed an impossibly obscure beginning. In fact, he sensed early on the real extent of the new third Crowd—McGovern's—and now showed no surprise that it turned out to be there. But at least until very recently the general opinion of McGovern was that he was too colorless, even mildly professorial and no leader. "McGovern is a very ambitious man. I asked him two years ago, 'But are you ready to give up everything for this? Your family life, your own peace, every minute of your existence?' He said, 'I want to be President.' He's a very great organizer and he's tough. I believe he's going to make it."

I thought again of our mythmaking apparatus. For no solid reason I can name I also had

had the idea of a professorial McGovern, the first Ph.D. since Wilson to run for high office, but two years ago he had shown up at my neighbor's house at a party for Joe Duffey's campaign for the Senate and he looked to me then like a beautifully tailored, middle-aged cowboy with that long blue gaze and thick thumbs. Maybe it was his dovish anti-war stance that had characterized him so softly, or maybe just the journalistic shorthand which bedevils us all. I could not help thinking of our other great figures of myth, movie stars when there still were stars, and the hilarious misapprehensions of their characters which the public, especially intellectuals, devour. It is a rule never to be broken that the most lasting picture of a star is always created by his or her earliest interviews. The reason is simply that lazy journalists forever after unearth the file and basically rewrite what was written before. The same is true of politicians who are tagged early on. Someone somewhere must have portrayed McGovern as an overcivilized professor when in fact he is the most direct political descendant of the Kennedy operational technique.

That technique was most spontaneously demonstrated not so much on the podium in Miami but in the lobby of the Doral Hotel when about three hundred Hippies, S.D.S., Progressive Labor Party, and assorted Outraged suddenly filed in and sat down on the floor, demanding to see McGovern who had to explain himself then and there as to why, the previous evening, he had stated that he would retain the U.S. armed presence in Thailand. The entire hotel was promptly shut down tight, the management cutting off the elevators for fear the invasion would spread through the upper floors. A squad of police soon arrived and were quickly ordered out, for violence in that narrow lobby would have left a lot of red meat lying about. Besides, it is a part of our awareness in post-Chicago times that the young savages are daughters and sons of the middle class and bear a political legitimacy which, as always in every era, is the reward given the violent and the brave. In the bargain, you can see long-haired cops everywhere now, four years after Chicago.

But arriving quite by chance an hour or more after the sit-down had begun it was hard to gauge the beat. Beneath the uproar the kids were clearly disciplined and when a thin girl of nineteen or so ordered them through a bullhorn to sit, they formed in ranks and sat facing her as in class. Many were shirtless, and all were styled in the latest Army & Navy store bargains. I could not help my mind's resurrection of the continuity here—the last sit-down I had seen was in Flint, Michigan, in 1936 when the auto workers shut down Fisher Body Plant Number 2, and this was a reassurance, for the act of sitting together on signal is political, not temperamental, a call for parley rather than riot. Nevertheless even to the untutored eye the taunting factions stood out, primarily the Zippies who clustered—all fifteen of them—in one corner with their own portable p.a. system, holding up a six-by-ten-foot photo of Johnson which they had stolen out of the Convention Hall where it had hung in a line of the Great Democratic Leaders of the past. Over L.B.J.'s forehead they had stuck a McGovern bumper sticker. The echo of their yells and latter-day Dadaist ebullience, rapping against the marble lobby walls combined with the rhythmic chants of the sitters led by the young girl, left all options open. Three TV cameras with their crews were ranged on a platform to one side, but no photo lights were on yet, the opening curtain evidently being delayed, for what cause no one seemed to know. It needs be mentioned that in a more open area nearer the entrance doors a dozen or so straights in conventional clothes were standing around, people with Mid-western eyeglasses and flowered dresses, who looked

on with more curiosity than the apprehension which the occasion seemed to deserve; their estimate of the mood turned out to be quite correct, probably because the riots they had seen on TV numerous times had never harmed them.

The sitters, split though they were among their factions, were nevertheless united in one object, to force McGovern down from his suite; understanding the program, the TV men were not wasting light and tape on the preliminaries. "We want McGovern! We want McGovern!" For half an hour the demand repeated itself under the orchestrating arms of the young girl at their head, and now, having achieved the inner organization of a true Crowd, which was their mutual equality and unanimity, a victory or discharge beyond mere chanting had to be found. But nothing of that kind seemed about to happen, so hands were raised quite as in the classroom, their sole previous experience of purposeful action, and from the floor came proposals to climb the stairs to McGovern or to physically force the management to turn an elevator on. Now the TV men stirred but continued smoking and drinking their Cokes. Meanwhile the Zippies, mocking McGovern as well as the political purposefulness implied in the surrounding orderliness, had raised the volume of their p.a. to drown it all. Long since used to the blasts of rock music, the seated majority was immune to interruption. That pall of stalemate descended when anything can happen; they had committed themselves symbolically and there could be no retreat this side of confrontation or violence. And the sense of timing in headquarters upstairs caught the danger by some telepathic means, for an elevator door opened and Mankiewicz appeared. A roar of curses, applause and yells greeted him. He seemed an even smaller and more fragile man than he is, possibly because by this time the girl leader was sitting on the shoulders of a boy and was bent over looking down at him, while she carefully held her microphone close to her mouth so that her rage would carry throughout the lobby's chaotic acoustics.

Now one camera was trucking into the center of the lobby from the common roost at one side, and the Outraged carefully made way for it. From the ranked P.L. group came the rhythmic chant, "Fuck McGovern!" but the camera's lights were not yet on and this soon died away. Now the Zippies, who had been left behind by the moving camera, pressed ahead into the crowd with their immense Johnson photograph, screaming at lung-bursting levels through their p.a., but suddenly going silent to hear the camera crew's advice not to block the entire view. They moved accordingly and, once properly positioned, resumed their particular version of passion, grouped at the right-hand bank of elevators opposite the Progressive Laborites who were standing on the other flank of the sitting majority. So we had the full panoply—against the left wall the P.L.'s program summed up in Fuck McGovern, in the center the bulk of the sitters waiting for orders from the sharp-faced girl perched next to a very serious if not humiliated Mankiewicz, and on the right flank the Zippies carrying on where Tristan Zara had left off in Zurich, 1924.

I can't vouch for the accuracy of Mankiewicz' dialogue with the girl leader because his appearance caught me so by surprise. A moment before his arrival I had seen three boxes of a dozen eggs each handed up from the crowd on the floor to the leadership around the girl—food had been brought in for a long sit, if necessary—and even she had involuntarily to register a disclaimer, however humorously, of the purpose these potential missiles would serve. Laughing, she said they were hard-boiled, but there was room for doubt. The vision of McGovern being pelted by three dozen eggs from a crowd of young, usually identified as his most fervent supporters, would on TV

have changed even bad odds to none at all. In addition, as these boxes of eggs were moving from hand to hand up to the front, a haggard, bearded fellow in torn cut-off-at-the-knee dungarees came up to me and said he had played in *The Crucible* in college and thought now that he should straighten me out as to what was happening here. Indicating the Progressive Laborites and their Fuck McGovernism, he said, "They're trying to puddle him right here and now. They think the Vietcong are bourgeois and Mao is ready for his Cadillac. You're looking at the stormbirds of American fascism—the worse it gets the quicker the workers will turn against capitalism, you see?" I saw. He looked sickened, in which case what was he doing here at all? "I thought we had to call McGovern on that statement he gave out about keeping forces in Thailand. But this is therapy time and it's going through the roof. He's out of his head if he comes down now. They'll ruin him right in the living room. It's awful. We're in prime time now."

I caught the end of the Mankiewicz confrontation. The girl, beet red in the face, arching over from her perch on the boy's shoulders, was screaming, "Okay, in fifteen minutes we're either getting an answer or McGovern is coming down. Within fifteen minutes, is that right?"

Mankiewicz kept his eyes down. He had evidently agreed to this already but she wanted it loud and clear. I thought I could hear his teeth gritting. "That's right."

"Okay, get going!" she dismissed him. He disappeared to the triumphant screams of the mob, and she turned with electric eyes to the whooping audience, a thin-lipped grin gashing her face. A stout girl in a once-white blouse and a skirt stepped up beside her with a pad and pencil and called out, "Okay, cool it. Now let's get the issues!"

As slices of white bread and pieces of cheese were being handed around and the Dada's were going wild with satire of this participatory democracy, the white-bloused girl was having trouble dredging issues from the orderly majority. "Abortion!" finally sounded loud and clear, and she dutifully wrote it down and turning her eyes over the whole assembly for its agreement, said "Abortion, right?" "Right on!" Then after some more soul searching in which hiatus it was clearer than ever that the issues were being dragged behind them rather than leading them forward, they resurrected the litany of the vanguard. A P.L. boy cried out, "Socialism now!" but was cut off by his fellows who knew better. They were still seated on the floor but pressing on into history and scrambling for their declarations, their flags, as it were, and the only sure thing in them was their existence now that the perhaps future President of the United States was descending from his sequestered throne room to pay homage to their power. For myself, a mixture of resentment and a hard-to-win confession; they were right in insisting McGovern face the contradiction of his peace position which his previous night's statement clearly implied, perhaps even at the cost of his national humiliation on the tube, for betrayal by politicians has been the brand upon the forehead of this system. But I was flummoxed by their contempt for human dignity, let alone the dignity of their own demand for honesty. Mankiewicz, after all, was still a human being and the girl had all but urinated on his head to the crowd's apparent appreciation. No country could be led by such contempt, excepting to a very dark place.

Like heavy cannon the two remaining TV cameras lumbered into place amid the crowd which now got to its feet as the TV lights burst on, illuminating the bottom of a curving stairway to one side of the lobby. My mind was on three dozen eggs secreted somewhere, cradled in pairs of children's hands. McGovern arrived at the bottom of the stairs to find the girl leader swaying over his head with her microphone pressed to her mouth. I cannot recall her lines,

but the command in them was filled to bursting with the audience's fantasy of power which had been sucked up from so many sources—the snarling orders of the tough cops on TV, the Chinese students' interrogations of erring professors and landlords, Perry Mason, and their dreams dreamed not long ago in Larchmont bedrooms surrounded by the hated chintz. Surely, an authentic rather than a role-playing voice here could not have sought to demean the one Senator who had stood alone for so many years against their hated war. But despite myself I realized now that McGovern had correctly chosen to recognize his duty to answer for his press statement which had trimmed his peace position.

McGovern appeared in the white light at the foot of the stairway and if an observer had arrived at that very moment he could not have known whether the roar of the crowd was hostile or friendly. For the crowd had already won by this giving-birth and the sound was the sound of relief after labor, from enemy and friend alike. He spoke right through the din of the Zippies' mockery and the counter-incoherence of his supporters, in a voice amazingly the same as it had been in my neighbor's house, without a trace of apology or trepidation and yet not with that false charm designed to kid away the conflict. His references are from within. There was about him not the slightest air of being put-upon, no sign of anger, but an even estimation of the trouble he was in, neither more nor less. All three cameras were on now and he was speaking on prime time to America but the inevitable tension of performing fused with his being here before this particular group of young. It was the first authentic feeling any of them had heard since the demonstration began.

He came directly to the issue of his previous press statement and overrode it; he would say now precisely what he had been saying all along, that on Inauguration Day the war would end and all American forces would be out of Indochina within ninety days. The inevitable cheer went up and the inevitable digging in of heels—what about abortion, a guaranteed annual wage, legalization of pot, amnesty? He lobbed the ball back—surely they accepted that human beings could not agree on absolutely everything. This summoning up of their own creed derailed them, for it did not sound strategic or cynical but a genuine aspect of his character. He had still left unexplained his paradoxical statement, but it had fallen away, lost in the discharge of their feelings of common identity which had succeeded in materializing him before them as though they had created him. The sharp-faced girl yelled on in vain, and when he said that they would surely understand he had a lot of things he must do and waved farewell, the applause swept up to the ranks of the P.L.'s who were now mounted on each other's shoulders, middle fingers raised, hands jerking upward in the air, shouting, "Fuck McGovern!" But they had fallen into place, they too were enjoying now, and the fabled Issues had gone by, were merged in the climactic fact that he had come down because they had demanded him, had grown him. Moses smashed the Tablets in a fury with the Jews for their failure to rise to the sublime Commandments, but despite everything he had forged a Tribe of many disparate peoples, for what mattered was not the words but the mime, the fact that they had been present when he went up and when he came down from the Lord, and if few would remember exactly what was said or settled, none would forget the essential—that they had been there when for their sake he had climbed Sinai, they had seen it and had been the cause and were the sinews of a leader and thus transcended.

As they dispersed and the white lights of the cameras flowed out, I walked out into the heat of night and was stopped by another bearded one naked to a pair of murky shorts. "I played in *The Crucible* at Louisiana State. Terrific, wasn't it?" I wasn't so sure, although I was surer than I had been ten minutes earlier. He was an associate professor somewhere. I was curious whether he dressed like this for class. No, of course not—"This is theatre," he said with a pleased smile, "you don't go onstage in your ordinary clothes." We both laughed. "Come over to Flamingo Park in the morning. I'll show you our plans to trash the Republicans in August." It was precisely the same tone a director might use toward his next production, that suppressed brag about a coming masterpiece, that basic joyfulness in being an artist at all.

I find I have left the Convention itself for last, and it isn't by accident since it was so anticlimactic after the second day. Certainly it signified a renovation of politics, a major party opened at last to the streets, the teacher, the student, the amateur. It showed that a new machine has been born, but the question remains the depth of its reach into the country. The truth is that the legitimitizing weight of the working class was not there to make it the real reflection of America it wanted to be. If only for this absence it can be but a stage along the way. But it is equally true that there never has been a new movement, be it Abolition, the New Deal, or Wilson's New Democracy, which did not first arrive in the heads of intellectuals. Still, there was not yet Power, only an aversion for what is, and these are not the same. So there was a certain surreality, as though a new king had just been crowned, but the old one had neither died nor could he be located, he had simply wandered off.

Which probably symbolizes the pervading sense of an inner unrelatedness in the country itself. Ours is a President whose paternality has never settled on him. Patricides, we live now in the shadow of something homogenized, whose leadership consists at best of a benign distrust between the people and itself, and at worst of its implicit violence. This vagueness of a ruling personality had to enter the Convention where, quite strangely, the enemy Nixon's name was barely mentioned at all. The one moment when an authentic emotion was felt was Teddy Kennedy's evocation of the nostalgia of the past when indeed there had been kings even if you didn't altogether admire them. But otherwise there was nothing handed down, no grail, no flag, no helmet emptied of its immortal knight, and so nothing was quite won, not yet. But something may have created itself if history is kind.

It was literally as though we had no past at all. A man from Mars must surely have wondered if this race was new. Yet we live under the oldest continuous government on earth and, strangely, the Convention could not find one old man loved enough to bless the new leader and send him forth with something memorable and good. Within the bounds of conventioneering there was less a classic conflict with the dying than a sheer assertion of new birth, a dangerously immaculate conception.

But it could turn out yet to have been realer than it seemed. Within America a certain Crowd has certainly lost its old cohesion and the lines of force no longer hold. The vote is floating. As late as Jack Kennedy's campaign one could still speak of Left and Right, but this time only of a mood. What else than a mood could have found a leader for so city-bred a revolution in a man from the sparsest population in the country? If historical formulations had their classic impress, how could so ministerial a man be leader of an avant-garde whose advertised faith is in smoke, a movement of women clamoring for the right to abort, students for whom the conventional disciplines are laughable?

It may be that in some primordial way there is a reaching back to roots in the raising up of George McGovern. Even for his enemies his menace is not radicalism but righteousness, that quality which always hovers on the ridiculous but when it stands and holds can smash through all confusion. It could well be that righteousness is all we have left. If Kennedy was of the Left, if only symbolically, he was also as much the author of the Green Berets and the war as any man was, and if Nixon is the Right he has thrown the line to China. Yet few know how to call Kennedy bad and this country has enormous trouble trying to think of Nixon as good. But it is indeed a word McGovern suggests to the mind despite everything, not that one really knows his character but that he seems to be seriously obsessed with the creativity of the people rather than the manipulability of institutions. If he truly is so, and can make it palpable, anything can happen.

As for Conventions themselves, they will surely have to go. Perhaps a national primary is the answer, something at least more straightforward than this travesty which all of us know is but a time-honored means of manipulating symbols. The much-touted finesse of the new machine is a doubtful achievement, finally; it has only proved that amateurs can learn cynicism fast. The nominees will have to make the fight at the supermarket and on film, which brings us back to where we started—to the man on the stump attempting with directness to make his Crowd.

Donkey Serenade

Wilfrid Sheed

Wilfrid Sheed, novelist and critic, was a nominee for the National Book Award in 1966 for his novel *Office Politics.* Other novels include *Max Jamison* and *A Middle Class Education.* He has been a critic for the *New York Times Book Review,* a film critic for *Esquire,* and a book review editor for *Commonweal.* His latest novel is *People Will Always Be Kind.*

Miami Beach, Fla.—For days the writers circled like buzzards waiting for one small rabbit to die. There just wasn't going to be enough convention to go around. "How about doing a story about the *writers* at the convention?" said the first five writers I met. The search for angles was as grim as anything in nature. Norman Mailer announced he was doing his piece in three days, presumably underwater—so that was one angle gone. Jerry Rubin and Abbie Hoffman trapped Theodore White in the lobby of the Fontainebleau (I believe they thought he was I. F. Stone) and tried to wring his secrets from him. "Do what I do," snapped White. "Make it up."

By the second day the writers were telling each other that this was the dullest convention they'd ever attended. Nothing novel about that; it's quite correct to be bored at conventions. In this case it meant that the new young delegates weren't nearly as much fun as the old warlords: They were earnest and righteous, and there was no way you could get them drunk. In fact, all that was left of the dirty old days were the writers themselves. The buzzards eyed one another narrowly: "Why don't you go home and leave this to me?"

Actually, it was a fascinating convention, but not in the usual sense. Abbie Hoffman said it looked like an early SDS rally, and so it did in spots. But the young delegates were not going to be cheated out of a dull convention. The kids and women and blacks were fascinated with their new toy, parliamentary procedure, and so the world's freshest delegates produced the world's ploddingest politics. "It's just like a law court," my thirteen-year-old daughter said approvingly. At that particular moment the rules committee was taking a vote on whether to vote on whether to vote, and someone was objecting to the whole schlemozzle. A generation raised on *Perry Mason* had arrived and was wallowing in stuffiness.

Likewise on the floor itself, now that youth was present, the carnival flavor was all but gone. No funny hats or snake dances for this crowd, no "Kiss me, I'm a Democrat." America had come of age. "We shall overcome" was still okay, but "The monkey wrapped his tail around the flagpole" was definitely out.

Still, it *was* fascinating, in its dull way, especially for those of us who had felt the policemen's cattle prods in Chicago, 1968. As a tale of cold-blooded vengeance, it was worthy at least of a Sam Peckinpah movie. The villains of '68 were cornered and gunned down one by one. Some, like Mayor Daley, went down snarling. Others, the Larry O'Briens, recanted and promised to reform, but they were gunned down anyway. Old pros muttered about ruthlessness. The Toby Jugs with the cigars who had smirked at us in Chicago ("Grow up, kid") saw with frozen horror how well their advice had been taken. The question of the week was whether the party could stand such a blood-letting. An academic question, of course. You can't deny a revolutionary his purge.

The real story, it seemed, had taken place four years ago and had been covered by no writers at all. The McGovern committee had calmly sat down and redesigned the Democratic party, while the men laughingly called pros had dozed their long off-year's nap. The breathtaking incompetence of the pros followed them right into the convention hall. Hubert Humphrey looked at the delegations with wild surprise: the Californians, who resembled a United Nations Christmas card; New York, which might have been a class at the New School; and New Jersey, a crowd of Republican-type commuters waiting for a bus. Was this what had hit him? A cardiogram would probably have shown that the fight went out of him then and there. Only the grim, flinty labor faces from states like Indiana, Ohio, and Pennsylvania kept him company in that bright, steaming barn.

Confronted with this, the pols began feverishly to praise the wonderful diversity of the convention—what other party would let such riffraff in? Larry O'Brien welcomed the women and children as if he'd invited them himself, reminding one somehow of W. C. Fields patting Baby Le Roy on the head with a rolled newspaper containing a brick. With sour irony, the pros grabbed every chance they could find to throw McGovern's rules back at him, challenging his own apparent breach of them in California, but this merely confirmed the new rules, the new party, and it didn't even save them California.

From the first it was clear that the McGovern rules could lead only to a McGovern candidacy because he alone understood them. Even the press could not sustain the suspense for long. The rumor mill in the Fontainebleau insisted that Humphrey and Muskie were meeting upstairs to settle George's hash and even told us what they were saying. But then Humphrey and Muskie marched out of the same room and said they hadn't been meeting at all—it was like two kids caught smoking. So much for the stop-McGovern movement. Now George was in the awkward position of having no one to compromise with. If he compromised anyway, it would be from no visible pressure—unless you call Scoop Jackson visible pressure. The question, the only question for the last two or three days, was: How was George using his freedom? In a temporarily open sea, would he tack to the left or to the right?

The sea wasn't really open; it only seemed that way. A word here about how trivia can affect history. The salamilike shape of Miami Beach stretches the hotels that housed the delegates along the longest possible line, and it was quite possible not to meet an enemy the whole time you were there. It took a long hike in a boiling sun or at least a glum taxi creep to get from the New York delegation to, say, Scoop Jackson's sarcophagus. And it was tempting to stay close to one's own pool and one's own kind. Another city and another weather forecast might have produced a different convention.

As it was, McGovern's enemies seemed somewhat unreal to his friends. To the right, there were phantom labor leaders munching on dead cigars (with George Meany owning the cartoon rights) and, to the left, the scrawny crowd at Flamingo Park—zapped-out stand-ins for the peace movement, yip-hip-zippies who could have been hired by central casting. When they marched on Senator McGovern, they conveyed just enough empty menace to make him look like quite a fellow for confronting them and to show the TV audience what dragons he had to appease on his left. But there was no real indication of what waits for him outside the dingy wonderland of Miami Beach. The state of the nation has to be guessed.

My old friends from the class of '68, two generations back as the new politics go, seemed to feel that a slight collapse to the center would help, nationally speaking. Chicago had left them with a healthy, perhaps too healthy, respect for the power of the old bosses. They couln't really be dead so soon, could they? "Tricks, we won by tricks," said Joe Duffey of Connecticut. "Next time *they'll* know the tricks." Duffey once sneaked a nomination himself (for the Senate in '70) and lost an election, and he knows how different the two arts are. You can pay dearly for pulling a boss's nose when you show up in his district.

That was one school of thought, very big everywhere except in the McGovern delegations. People who had limped out of Chicago more dead than alive were suddenly recommending that we try to save Mayor Daley's face and all the lesser faces that run our rundown cities—all of whom would have made invaluable allies from a '68 point of view and reputedly are still able to get the dead to vote twice, even if they can't get the kids.

Flag a passing McGovernite and you heard a different tale. The bosses couldn't get out the vote in the primaries, so why go crawling to them now? "Suppose Daley withdraws his support, and we take Illinois anyway, where does that leave the bum?" One more question: Are you drunk with power, sir? Maybe, the answer went, but a new party is a new party. If we load it up with old bosses, what have we changed? And if "boss" was a dirty word in '68, what has happened since then to clean it? If they're nicer to us now, it's only because they need us. And we have our own people to reward. Meanwhile, picture King Lear in a Humphrey but-

ton, wandering the lobbies while his children are dividing the kingdom.

More prosaically, there was some question of whether the McGovern high command controlled the delegates through too many compromises on personalities. When the famous McGovern boiler room sent up word to support a compromise plan on the Illinois delegation (one-half vote to each of Daley's people and one-half vote to each of the challengers), the delegates would have none of it. In fact, their greatest outbursts of stubbornness were not on issues, on which they showed a most unyouthlike willingness to compromise, but precisely on personalities: the "get Daley" issue, the vice presidential nomination, the unseating of Chairman O'Brien.

The vice president mini-mutiny (Eagleton got more votes from Alabama Wallaceites than from some McGovern sectors) was a break for George, because it gave him a line for his acceptance speech about how he had not really controlled the convention at all. From all accounts, he and his boys controlled the hell out of it. A New Jersey delegate told me that they had telephone instructions on everything but how to brush their teeth. And although too many people were chasing too few phones, the system worked so smoothly that in the case of the South Carolina challenge they were able to manipulate the vote up and down until Ohio, the chief enemy, fell on its fanny.

How clever is too clever? The McGovernites have spent their lives, even as you and I, hearing about liberal losers and radical bumblers, and they could hardly be blamed for trying their hands at ruthless efficiency. As a radical bumbler of long standing myself, I was sorry to see them doing all the shabby things necessary to win—the sellout of the women in South Carolina, the apparent deal with the Wallaceites over the Alabama challenge—but I guessed they *were* necessary, and I didn't want to see the smirk on the Toby Jugs again. But occasionally the McGovern people seemed to overmanage just for the fun of it. On the abortion issue, I was told, the first signal was palms down, or "vote your conscience," but the second was thumbs down, or better forget your conscience for now. To have control of such a machine is intoxicating, and rumor has it that different boilermakers took a turn at it—Pierre Salinger over Vietnam, Rick Stearns or someone else over abortion. The very minor revolt over the vice presidency was a low growl from the beast at the receiving end.

By the last day one was so conscious of the machine that the candidate himself had all but disappeared. He was, for most writers, unavailable, but a staffer told me that he had botched the black caucus, as usual (by now he must be so selfconscious about that particular communication problem as to be completely tongue-tied), and was out of favor with Mexican-Americans, who had learned that he didn't need them any more. Several close supporters were quite lukewarm about him personally, but this is common among candidates' staffs: As you approach the presidency, no one seems worthy of it, since it wasn't designed for a human in the first place. The striking thing about this campaign is that the leader's personality doesn't seem to matter. When McGovern finally appeared on the platform, I felt that half the crowd was roaring for Gene and half for Bobby, and that the man who had finally dragged the flag to the top of the hill was incidental.

The hot gossip seemed to bypass McGovern and land squarely on his staff. Rumors of gorgeous power struggles gurgled through the turgid air. (The crowd seemed to have absorbed all the air conditioning, and I found myself attending any press conference that was held in a cool room. Hence I have invaluable scoops on John Gilligan and Mike Gravel.) A writer who'd been chasing Frank Mankiewicz onto elevators for four days said he thought he'd been chasing the wrong man— Gary Hart had grabbed the hot crown for the moment. Others said to watch Rick Stearns— McGovern's chief delegate counter—on the rail. These rumors are self-generating. It looks as if a flock of talented adventures, every bit the equal of Jack Kennedy's, is on the wing, and there are bound to be stories about them.

In fact, there is a whole new era of gossip, which is one of the blessings of the two-party system. Politics is basically gossip anyway, and a convention is its World Series. The women, blacks, and youth quickly opened their own gossip branches. The women, of course, had the big names, and this was some of the stuff you heard. On the first night Betty Friedan told me that Gloria Steinem and Bella Abzug were giving up too much woman power in order to help McGovern—a shrewd prophecy, since McGovern's brain trust had ordained not only the defeat of the women's challenge in South Carolina but also the precise score, in order to save George's bacon in California. But on the second night we saw Bella tearing like a red-crested mongoose into Shirley Mac-Laine because *Shirley* had given up too much for George by helping to dump the abortion plank. So the lines were not that clear.

Ms. Steinem lost her preternatural cool on the same issue, calling the McGovernites "bastards" for their pains, and she later caught an edge of Mankiewicz's tongue that can't have sent her home happy. Mank had just finished announcing George's choice for v.p., and Gloria asked if she could hold a women's caucus on the subject. Frank said, "You can use this hall any time you like, Gloria, and you can do whatever you like in it. But not on my time." That's the kind of thing that men have been saying to women for years, and that has caused all the trouble.

Did the women feel sold out? That depends on which women you're talking about. They got Jean Westwood as party chairman [sic], a significant wedge into the party structure, and this may be all some of them expected this time around. As usual, one felt that all the deals had been made offstage and we were watching a laborious charade. But anyone who thinks of political woman as a monolith has met only one of them, and the only thing they all agree on is that they learned a lot from their freshman (fresh-person?) hazing.

It seemed that every second time one passed an open door there was a woman inside saying, "What we've got to do next time. . . ." There was some furry tongue tangling over the right to be cochairpersons, a word that will never trip lightly off anyone's lips, and some fairly wild swipes, but the general tone was one of precision and parliamentary patience, learned in the PTA wars and elsewhere. (In fact, some women now get more political practice than men, and it shows.) Some hard-liners will probably never be satisfied. On the last day I heard a group complaining about Gloria Steinem's make-up. "How can she ask us not to be sex objects when she wears eye-shadow?" From a quick squint around, I would say this was like Fat Jack Leonard and Eddie the Dwarf discussing Clark Gable's uppity mustache.

Every *first* door you passed there was a Negro saying, "What we've got to do next time. . . ." In my hotel the Alabama challenge delegation held closed meetings that you could hear two floors away, and feeling ran even higher. The black caucus, which McGovern failed to dominate, degenerated into a rumble over who would be the fairest black in the new administration. (This meeting, too, was closed, but Kenneth Gibson may well have been one of the rumblers, and you have to bet that Jesse Jackson was in there somewhere. Old Jesse liked to stir things along, while re-

maining a cool operator inside.) The most moving speech from the platform was by Willie Brown on the California challenge, when he demanded, "Give me back my delegation," and the most moving one off the platform was by Shirley Chisholm, asking for black delegates to come on over. White observers felt that she could have led a gospel-singing march on the hall then and there, but this could be a failure to understand black rhetoric and the real purpose of Ms. Chisholm's speech. She is both bright and passionate, which is more than could be said for any of the other candidates, but these gifts were being put to the service of a clumsy stop-McGovern move, plus a bad-tasting piece of self-promotion.

Anyone who feared that the new "quota" system would flood the place with mediocrities could be assured at first glance. Prigs there were aplenty, especially in the New York delegation. But the blacks, youth, and women all looked smarter than the old pols ever did, and they sure as heck paid more attention. Television does not convey the heat and glare through which they sat for eight hours at a stretch, nor the diet of dehydrated ham sandwiches and Pepsi-Cola on which they fed themselves. The floor is a dislocating place, the kind where you suddenly wonder where you are and how the devil you got there. The din is incessant and meaningless, and there is none of the tidy organization you see on the screen. Like-minded delegations may be so far apart that coordinated action seems a miracle.

Yet for all that, the floor work of the freshman McGovernites was at least relatively smooth. Several times they broke with the old American tradition of not listening to the speeches, and they rejoiced in the crazy schedule by which numerous important issues were settled after their elders' bedtime. (When Larry O'Brien woozily suggested adjourning "until 7 p.m. tomorrow morning," they shouted for him to continue.)

The other fear, voiced or whined by a South

Carolinian, that white Protestant males are now a helpless minority, also seems exaggerated. The new delegates do not form a solid bloc. A black from Pennsylvania told me that Julian Bond was a pimp. And the women and children were bad-mouthing each other just as merrily. Beyond that, blacks, youth, and women are three totally different categories of human beings, and their popular front should spring the usual leaks shortly. A Negro spoke against the women of South Carolina, pointing out that blacks had done extremely well in that delegation—we've got ours, Jack. Then the women who *had* made the original S.C. delegation "proudly" cast all their votes against their challenging sisters— we've got ours, too.

Meanwhile other minorities were chaffering. The Chicano caucus, or rather jamboree, decided that the blacks were getting altogether too much attention and that maybe a little good Chicano action was called for. They failed to come up with anything special this time, but they've got four years to think of something truly spectacular. Meanwhile organized labor could split like a fire-work ("George Meany is just an embarrassment," said a machinist) instead of ticking like a soggy bomb. And where were the Italians? One wound up feeling that this convention was only a rehearsal for a real blowout, with party manners suspended, which might juut occur in time to catch the bicentennial festivities in 1976. My daughter, who'll be eighteen in time to vote that year, wants to be an alternate delegate, and I can't see her behaving that quietly.

"Bring back Chicago," said a saucy newsman. "That was a real convention, boy." This certainly was a tea party in comparison. The deskman at our hotel feared the worst. "Too many hands have been tied in this town," he said ominously. But they were tied just right. When the yippies tried a skinny dip in Flamingo Park, the cops just said, "We'll drain the pool, son." When they wanted to march on the hall, they were allowed to march until the hot smog shredded them. After all, Hoffman and Rubin were on the other side now, with a change of T-shirts every day, and there were more kids in the hall than out. This is McGovern's basic issue. He brought the dissenters in, and he got *them* to vote against the abortion plank and against the Gay Liberation plank and the $6,500 guaranteed income and all the stuff they'd been screaming for. If the old men had done it, the place would have been in flames.

Now that the convention has dispersed, McGovern is free to make whatever deals he feels necessary with the old guard, without fear of floor demonstrations and candle-lit marches. And my guess is he'll make plenty. But his issue remains intact. The old liberal principle, co-opt the enemy, is once again being tested. Given the opportunity, the new groups did not go berserk: On the contrary, they behaved with almost humorless responsibility and were the first to discipline their own crazies. Father Flanagan would have loved it.

It's probably only a breather in this tangled nation of ours. God knows what disillusionments, new factions, brand-new diseases lie ahead. But, in the meantime, what a relief to be bored at a convention again. And after Nixon has stolen all the other issues, ended the war on election eve, and injected the economy with meltable silicone, McGovern will still have this to take to the country: Isn't it nice to have your children back again? Or, if you're sick to death of youth, women, and blacks (as many of them are themselves), he can say, behind his hand: Well, I listened. Maybe they'll quiet down now. If they get Nixon again, they'll raise the sky with their screams.

It might just do it.

Fear and Loathing in Miami: Old Bulls Meet the Butcher

Hunter S. Thompson

Hunter S. Thompson describes his past occupations as those of journalist, dope addict, thief, bagman, and author. He was involved in the drug culture in the San Francisco Bay area and wrote *Hell's Angels: A Strange and Terrible Saga* on the basis of his personal experiences with the Hell's Angels. Mr. Thompson has written for several magazines and has been national affairs editor for *Rolling Stone.* He is the author of *Fear and Loathing in Las Vegas: A Savage Journey to the Heart of the American Dream* and *Fear and Loathing on the Campaign Trail '72.*

> Do not go gentle into that good night.
> Rage! Rage! Against the dying of the light.
> —Dylan Thomas

Sunday is not a good day for traveling in the South. Most public places are closed—especially the bars and taverns—in order that the denizens of this steamy, atavistic region will not be distracted from church. Sunday is the Lord's day, and in the South he still has clout—or enough, at least, so that most folks won't cross him in public. And those few who can't make it to church will likely stay home by the fan, with iced tea, and worship Him in their own way.

This explains why the cocktail lounge in the Atlanta airport is not open on Sunday night. The Lord wouldn't dig it.

Not even in Atlanta, which the local chamber of commerce describes as the Enlightened, Commercial Capital of the "New South." Atlanta is an alarmingly liberal city, by Southern standards—known for its "progressive" politicians, non-violent race relations and a tax structure agressively favorable to New Business. It is also known for moonshine whiskey, a bad biker/doper community, and a booming new porno-film industry.

Fallen pom-pom girls and ex-cheerleaders from Auburn, 'Bama and even Ole Miss come to Atlanta to "get into show business," and those who take the wrong fork wind up being fucked, chewed and beaten for $100 a day in front of hand-held movie cameras. Donkeys and wolves are $30 extra, and the going rate for gangbangs is $10 a head, plus "the rate." Connoisseurs of porno-films say you can tell at a glance which ones were made in Atlanta, because of the beautiful girls. There is nowhere else in America, they say, where a fuck-flick producer can hire last year's Sweetheart of Sigma Chi to take on 12 Georgia-style Hell's Angels for $220 & lunch.

So I was not especially surprised when I got off the plane from Miami around midnight and wandered into the airport to find the booze locked up. What the hell? I thought: This is only the *public* bar. At this time of night—in the heart of the bible belt and especially on Sunday—you want to look around for something *private.*

Every airport has a "VIP Lounge." The one in Atlanta is an elegant, neoprivate spa behind a huge wooden door near Gate 11. Eastern Airlines maintains it for the use of traveling celebrities, politicians and other conspicuous persons who would rather not be seen drinking in public with the Rabble.

I had been there before, back in February, sipping a midday beer with John Lindsay while we waited for the flight to L.A. He had addressed the Florida state legislature in Tallahassee that morning, the Florida primary was still two weeks away, Muskie was still the front-runner, McGovern was campaigning desperately up in New Hampshire and Lindsay's managers felt he was doing well enough in Florida that he could afford to take a few days off and zip out to California. They had already circled June 6th on the Mayor's campaign calendar. It was obvious, even then, that the California primary was going to be The Big One: Winner-take-all for 271 delegate votes, more than any other state, and the winner in California would almost certainly be the Democratic candidate for President of the United States in 1972.

Nobody argued that. The big problem in February was knowing which two of the 12 candidates would survive until then. If California was going to be the showdown, it was also three months and 23 primaries away— a long and grueling struggle before the field would narrow down to only two.

Ed Muskie, of course, would be one of them. In late February—and even in early March— he was such an overwhelming favorite that every press wizard in Washington had already conceded him the nomination. At that point in the campaign, the smart-money scenario had Big Ed winning comfortably in New Hampshire, finishing a strong second to Wallace a week later in Florida, then nailing it in Wisconsin on April 4th.

New Hampshire would finish McGovern, they said, and Hubert's ill-advised Comeback would die on the vine in Florida. Jackson and Chisholm were fools, McCarthy and Wilbur Mills were doomed tokens . . . and that left only Lindsay, a maverick Republican who had only recently switched parties. But he had already caused a mild shock wave on the Democratic side by beating McGovern badly— and holding Muskie to a stand-off—with an 11th hour, "Kennedy-style" campaign in non-primary Arizona, the first state to elect delegates.

Lindsay's lieutenants saw that success in Arizona as the first spark for what would soon be a firestorm. Their blueprint had Lindsay compounding his momentum by finishing a strong third or even second in Florida, then polarizing the party by almost beating Muskie in Wisconsin—which would set the stage for an early Right/Left showdown in Massachusetts, a crucial primary state with 102 delegates and a traditionally liberal electorate.

The key to that strategy was the idea that Muskie could not hold the Center, because he was basically a candidate of the Democratic Right, like Scoop Jackson, and that he would move instinctively in that direction at the first sign of challenge from his Left—which would force him into a position so close to Nixon's that eventually not even the Democratic "centrists" would tolerate him.

There was high ground to be seized on The Left, Lindsay felt, and whoever seized it would fall heir to that far-flung, leaderless army of Kennedy/McCarthy zealots from 1968 . . . along with 25 million new voters who would naturally go 3-1 against Nixon—unless the Democratic candidate turned out to be Hubert Humphrey or a Moray Eel—which meant that almost anybody who could strike sparks with the "new voters" would be working off a huge and potentially explosive new power base that was worth—on paper, at least—anywhere between five percent and 15 percent of the total vote. It was a built-in secret weapon for any charismatic Left-bent underdog who could make the November election even reasonably close.

Now, walking down a long empty white corridor in the Atlanta airport on a Sunday night in July, I had a very clear memory of my last visit to this place—but it seemed like something that had happened five years ago, instead of only five months. The Lindsay campaign was a loose, upbeat trip while it lasted, but there is a merciless kind of "out of sight, out of mind" quality about a losing presidential campaign . . . and when I saw Lindsay on the convention floor in Miami, sitting almost unnoticed in the front row of the New York delegation, it was vaguely unsettling to recall that less than six months ago he was attracting big crowds out on Collins Avenue—just one block east of his chair, that night, in the Miami Beach convention hall—and that every word he said, back then, was being sucked up by three or four network TV crews and echoed on the front pages of every major newspaper from coast to coast.

As it turned out, the Lindsay campaign was fatally flawed from the start. It was all tip and no iceberg—the exact opposit of the slow-building McGovern juggernaut—but back in February it was still considered very shrewd and avant-garde to assume that the most important factor in a presidential campaign was a good "media candidate." If he had Star Quality, the rest would take care of itself.

The Florida primary turned out to be a funeral procession for would-be "media candidates." Both Lindsay and Muskie went down in Florida—although not necessarily because they geared their pitch to TV; the real reason, I think, is that neither one of them understood how to *use* TV . . . or maybe they knew, but just couldn't pull it off. It is hard to be superconvincing on the tube, if everything you say reminds the TV audience of a Dick Cavett commercial for Alpo dogfood. George McGovern has been widely ridiculed in the press as "The ideal anti-media candidate." He looks wrong, talks wrong, and even acts wrong—by conventional TV standards. But McGovern has his own ideas about how to use the tube. In the early primaries he kept his TV exposure to a minimum—for a variety of reasons that included a lack of both money

and confidence—but by the time he got to California for the showdown with Hubert Humphrey, McGovern's TV campaign was operating on the level of a very specialized art form. His 30-minute biography—produced by Charley Guggenheim—was so good that even the most cynical veteran journalists said it was the best political film ever made for television . . . and Guggenheim's 60-second spots were better than the biofilm. Unlike the early front-runners, McGovern had taken his time and learned how to use the medium—instead of letting the medium use him.

Sincerity is the important thing on TV. A presidential candidate should at least *seem* to believe what he's saying—even if it's all stone crazy. McGovern learned this from George Wallace in Florida, and it proved to be a very valuable lesson. One of the crucial moments of the '72 primary campaign came on election night in Florida, March 14th, when McGovern—who had finished a dismal sixth, behind even Lindsay and Muskie—refused to follow their sour example and blame his poor showing on that Evil Racist Monster, George Wallace, who had just swept every county in the state. Moments after both Lindsay and Muskie had appeared on all three networks to denounce the Florida results as tragic proof that at least half the voters were ignorant dupes and nazis, McGovern came on and said that although he couldn't agree with some of the things Wallace said and stood for, he sympathized with the people who'd voted for "The Governor" because they were "angry and fed up" with some of the things that are happening in this country.

"I feel the same way," he added, "But unlike Governor Wallace, I've proposed *constructive solutions* to these problems."

Nobody applauded when he said that. The 200 or so McGovern campaign workers who were gathered that night in the ballroom of the old Waverly Hotel on Biscayne Boulevard were not in a proper mood to cheer any praise for George Wallace. Their candidate had just been trounced by what they considered a dangerous bigot—and now, at the tail end of the loser's traditional concession statement, McGovern was saying that he and Wallace weren't really that far apart.

It was not what the ballroom crowd wanted to hear, at that moment. Not after listening to both Lindsay and Muskie denounce Wallace as a cancer in the soul of America . . . but McGovern wasn't talking to the people in that ballroom; he was making a very artful pitch to potential Wallace voters in the other primary states. Wisconsin was three weeks away, then Pennsylvania, Ohio, Michigan—and Wallace would be raising angry hell in every one of them. McGovern's braintrust, though, had come up with the idea that the Wallace vote was "soft"—that the typical Wallace voter, especially in the North and Midwest, was far less committed to Wallace himself than to his thundering, gut-level appeal to rise up and smash all the "pointy-headed bureaucrats in Washington" who'd been fucking them over for so long.

The root of the Wallace magic was a cynical, showbiz instinct for knowing exactly which issues would whip a hall full of beer-drinking factory workers into a frenzy—and then doing exactly that, by howling down from the podium that he had an instant, overnight cure for all their worst afflictions: Taxes? Nigras? Army worms killing the turnip crop? Whatever it was, Wallace assured his supporters that the solution was actually real simple, and that the only reason they had any hassle with the government at all was because those greedy bloodsuckers in Washington didn't *want* the problems solved, so they wouldn't be put out of work.

The ugly truth is that Wallace had never even bothered to *understand* the problems—much less come up with any honest solutions—but "the Fighting Little Judge" has never lost much sleep from guilt feelings about his personal credibility gap. Southern politicians are not made that way. Successful con men are treated with considerable respect in the South. A good slice of the original settlers of that region were men who'd been given a choice between being shipped off to the New World in leg-irons, or spending the rest of their lives in English prisons. The Crown saw no point in feeding them year after year, and they were far too dangerous to turn loose on the streets of London—so, rather than overload the public hanging schedule, the King's Minister of Gaol decided to put this scum to work on the other side of the Atlantic, in The Colonies, where cheap labor was much in demand.

Most of these poor bastards wound up in what is now the Deep South, because of the wretched climate. No settler with good sense and a few dollars in his pocket would venture south of Richmond. There was plenty of opportunity around Boston, New York and Philadelphia—and by British standards the climate in places like South Carolina and Georgia was close to Hell on Earth: Swamps, alligators, mosquitos, tropical disease. . . . all this plus a boiling sun all day long and no way to make money unless you had a land grant from the King. . . .

So the South was sparsely settled, at first, and the shortage of skilled labor was a serious problem to the scattered aristocracy of would-be cotton barons who'd been granted huge tracts of good land that would make them all rich if they could only get people to work it.

The slave-trade was one answer, but Africa in 1699 was not a fertile breeding ground for middle-management types . . . and the planters said it was damn near impossible for one white man to establish any kind of control over a boatload of black primitives. The bastards couldn't even speak English. How could a man get the crop in, with brutes like that for help?

There would have to be managers, keepers, overseers: White men who spoke the language, and had a sense of purpose in life. But where would they come from? There was no middle class in the South: Only masters and slaves . . . and all that rich land lying fallow.

The King was quick to grasp the financial implications of the problem: The crops *must* be planted and harvested, in order to sell them for gold—and if all those lazy bastards needed was a few thousand half-bright English-speaking lackeys, in order to bring the crops in . . . hell, that was easy: Clean out the jails, cut back on the grocery bill, jolt the liberals off balance by announcing a new "Progressive Amnesty" program for hardened criminals. . . .

Wonderful. Dispatch royal messengers to spread a good word in every corner of the kingdom, and after that, send out professional pollsters to record an amazing 66 percent jump in the King's popularity . . . then wait a few weeks before announcing the new 10 percent sales tax on ale.

That's how the South got settled. Not the whole story, perhaps, but it goes a long way toward explaining why George Wallace is the Governor of Alabama. He has the same smile as his great-grandfather—a thrice-convicted pig thief from somewhere near Nottingham, who made a small reputation, they say, as a jailhouse lawyer, before he got shipped out.

Indeed. With a bit of imagination you can almost hear the cranky little bastard haranguing his fellow prisoners in London's infamous Hardcase jail, urging them on to revolt:

"Lissen here, you poor fools! There's not much time! Even now—up there in the tower—they're cookin up some kind of cruel new punishment for us! How much longer will we stand for it? And now they want to ship us

across the ocean to work like slaves in swamp with a bunch of goddamn Hottentots!

"We won't go! It's asinine! We'll tear this place apart before we'll let that thieving old faggot of a king send us off to work next to Africans!

"How much more of this misery can we stand, boys? I know you're fed right up to *here* with it. I can see it in your eyes—pure misery! And I'm tellin' you, we don't have to stand for it! We can send the king a message and tell him how we feel! I'll write it up myself, and all you boys can sign it . . . or better still, I'll go talk to the king personally! All you boys have to do is dig me a little hole over there behind the gallows, and I'll. . . .

Right. That bottom line never changes: "You folks be sure and come to see me in the White House, you hear? There'll be plenty of room for my friends, after I clean house . . . but first I need your vote, folks, and after that I'll . . ."

George Wallace is one of the worst charlatans in politics, but there is no denying his talent for converting frustration into energy. What McGovern sensed in Florida, however—while Wallace was stomping him, along with all others—was the possibility that Wallace appealed instinctively to a lot more people than would actually vote for him. He was stirring up more anger that he knew how to channel. The frustration was there, and it was easy enough to convert it—but what then? If Wallace had taken himself seriously as a presidential candidate—as a Democrat or anything else—he might have put together the kind of organization that would have made him a genuine threat in the primaries, instead of just a spoiler.

McGovern, on the other hand, had put together a fantastic organization—but until he went into Wisconsin he had never tried to tap the kind of energy that seemed to be flowing, perhaps by default, to Wallace. He had given it some thought while campaigning in New Hampshire, but it was only after he beat Muskie in two blue-collar, hardhat wards in the Middle of Manchester that he saw the possibility of a really mind-bending coalition: A weird mix of peace freaks and hardhats, farmers and film stars, along with urban blacks, rural chicanos, the "youth vote" . . . a coalition that could elect almost anybody.

Muskie had croaked in Florida, allowing himself to get crowded over on the Right with Wallace, Jackson and Humphrey—then finishing a slow fourth behind all three of them. At that point in the race, Lindsay's presumptuous blueprint was beginning to look like prophecy. The New Hampshire embarrassment had forced Muskie off-center in a mild panic, and now the party was polarized. The road to Wisconsin was suddenly clear in both lanes, fast traffic to the Left and the Right. The only mobile hazard was a slow-moving hulk called "The Muskie Bandwagon," creeping erratically down what his doom-stricken Media Manager called "that yellow stripe in the middle of the road."

The only other bad casualty, at that point, was Lindsay. His Wisconsin managers had discovered a fatal flaw in the blueprint: Nobody had bothered to specify the name of the candidate who would seize all that high ground on Left, once Muskie got knocked off center. Whoever drew it up had apparently been told that McGovern would not be a factor in the later stages of the race. After absorbing two back-to-back beatings in New Hampshire and Florida, he would run out of money and be dragged off to the nearest glue factory . . . or, failing that, to some cut-rate retirement farm for old liberals with no charisma.

But something went wrong, and when Lindsay arrived in Wisconsin to seize that fine high ground on the Left that he knew, from his blueprint, was waiting for him—he found it already occupied, sealed off and well-guarded on every perimeter, by a legion of hard-eyed fanatics in the pay of George McGovern.

Gene Pokorny, McGovern's 25-year-old field organizer for Wisconsin, had the whole state completely wired. He had been on the job, full time, since the spring of '71—working off a blueprint remarkably similar to Lindsay's. But they were not quite the same. The main difference was painfully obvious, yet it was clear at a glance that both drawings had been done from the same theory: Muskie would fold early on, because The Center was not only indefensible but probably nonexistent . . . and after that the Democratic race would boil down to a quick civil war, a running death-battle between the Old Guard on the Right and a gang of Young Strangers on the Left.

The name-slots on Lindsay's blueprint were still empty, but the working assumption was that the crunch in California would come down to Muskie on the Right and Lindsay on the Left.

Pokorny's drawing was a year or so older than Lindsay's, and all the names were filled in—all the way to California, where the last two slots said, "McGovern" and "Humphrey." The only other difference between the two was that Lindsay's was unsigned, while Pokorny's had a signature in the bottom right hand corner: "Hart, Mankiewicz & McGovern—architects."

Even Lindsay's financial backers saw the handwriting on the wall in Wisconsin. By the time he arrived, there was not even any low ground on the Left to be seized. The Lindsay campaign had been keyed from the start on the assumption that Muskie would at least have the strength to retire McGovern befored he abandoned the center. It made perfect sense, on paper—but 1972 had not been a vintage year for paper wisdom, and McGovern's breakthrough victory in Wisconsin was written off as "shocking" and "freakish" by a lot of people who should have known better.

Wisconsin was the place where he found a working model for the nervous coalition that made the rest of the primary campaign a downhill run. Wisconsin effectively eliminated every obstacle but the corpse of Hubert Humphrey—who fought like a rabid skunk all the way to the end; cranked up on the best speed George Meany's doctors could provide for him, taking his cash and his orders every midnight from Meany's axe-man Al Barkan; and attacking McGovern savagely, day after day, from every treacherous angle Big Labor's sharpest researchers could even crudely define for him. . . .

It was a nasty swansong, for Hubert. He'd been signing those IOUs to Big Labor for more than 20 years, and it must have been a terrible shock to him when Meany called them all due at the same time.

But how? George Meany, the 77-year-old quarterback of the "Stop McGovern Movement," is said to be suffering from brain bubbles at this stage of the game. Totally paralyzed. His henchmen have kept him in seclusion ever since he arrived in Florida five days ago, with a bad case of The Fear. He came down from AFL-CIO headquarters in Washington by train, but had to be taken off somewhere near Fort Lauderdale and rushed to a plush motel where his condition deteriorated rapidly over the weekend, and finally climaxed on Monday night when he suffered a terrible stroke while watching the Democratic Convention on TV.

The story is still shrouded in mystery, despite the best efforts of the 5000 ranking journalists who came here to catch Meany's last act, but according to a wealthy labor boss who said he was there when it happened—the old man went all to pieces when his creature, Hubert Humphrey, lost the crucial "California challenge."

He raged incoherently at the Tube for eight minutes without drawing a breath, then suddenly his face turned beet red and his head swelled up to twice its normal size. Seconds later—while his henchmen looked on in mute horror—Meany swallowed his tongue, rolled out of his chair like a log, and crawled through a plate glass window.

THE YOUNG BULLS TAKE CHARGE; CRONKITE & THE WIZARDS TAKE A FALL; HUMPHREY CROAKED AND THE SQUEEZE PLAY EXPLAINED ON THE BEACH

"The confrontations with the Old Guard seldom come in public. There are conversations on the telephone, plans are laid, people are put to work, and it's done quietly. California is a classic. There will never be a case in American politics of such a naked power grab—straight power, no principle, straight opportunism. I wasn't aware of it. I thought it was a purely defensive move to protect themselves against attack. We were naïve. It never occurred to me that anybody would challenge California—until the last 36 hours before the credentials committee meeting. Then we really got scared when we saw the ferocity of their attack."

—George McGovern, talking to *Life* reporter Richard Meryman in Miami

What happened in Miami was far too serious for the kind of random indulgence that Gonzo journalism needs. The Real Business happened, as usual, on secret-numbered telephones or behind closed doors at the other end of long hotel corridors blocked off by sullen guards. There were only two crucial moments in Miami—two potential emer-

gencies that might have changed the outcome—and both of them were dealt with in
strict privacy.

The only real question in Miami was whether
or not McGovern might be stripped of more
than half of the 271 delegates he won in the
California primary—and that question was
scheduled to come up for a vote by the whole
convention on Monday night. If the "ABM
Movement" could strip 151 of those delegates
away, McGovern might be stopped—because
without them he had anywhere from 10 to 50
votes less than the 1509 that would give him
the nomination on the first ballot. But if
McGovern could hold his 271 California delegates, it was all over.

The "ABM Movement" (Anybody but
McGovern) was a coalition of desperate losers,
thrown together at the last moment by Big
Labor chief George Meany and his axe-man,
Al Barkan. Hubert Humphrey was pressed
into service as the front man for ABM, and he
quickly signed up the others: Big Ed, Scoop
Jackson, Terry Sanford, Shirley Chisholm—
all the heavies.

The ABM movement came together,
officially, sometime in the middle of the week
just before the convention, when it finally became apparent that massive fraud, treachery
or violence was the only way to prevent
McGovern from getting the nomination . . .
and what followed, once this fact was accepted
by all parties involved, will hopefully go down
in history as one of the most shameful episodes
in the history of the Democratic process.

It was like a scene from the final hours of the
Roman Empire: Everywhere you looked, some
prominent politician was degrading himself in
public. By noon on Sunday both Humphrey
and Muskie were so desperate that they came
out of their holes and appeared—trailing a mob
of photographers and TV crews—in the lobby
of the Fountainebleu, the nexus hotel about

500 yards down the beach from the Doral,
racing back and forth from one caucus or press
conference to another, trying to make any
deal available—on any terms—that might possibly buy enough votes to deny McGovern a
first-ballot victory.

The ABM strategy—a very shrewd plan, on
paper—was to hold McGovern under the
1500 mark for two ballots, forcing him to peak
without winning, then confront the convention
with an alternative (ABM) candidate on the
third ballot—and if that failed, try *another*
ABM candidate on the fourth ballot, then yet
another on the fifth, etc. . . . on into infinity,
for as many ballots as it would take to nominate somebody acceptable to the Meany-Daley
axis.

The name didn't matter. It didn't even make
much difference if He, She or It couldn't possibly beat Nixon in November . . . the only
thing that mattered, to the Meany-Daley
crowd, was *keeping control of The Party;*
and this meant the nominee would have to be
some loyal whore with more debts to Big Labor
than he could ever hope to pay . . . somebody
like Hubert Humphrey, or a hungry oppor-
tunist like Terry Sanford.

Anybody but George McGovern—the only
candidate in Miami, that week, who would
be under no obligation to give either Meany
or Daley his private number if he ever moved
into the White House.

But all that noxious bullshit went by the
boards, in the end. The ABM got chewed up
like green hamburger on opening night. They
were beaten stupid at their own game by a
handful of weird-looking kids who never even
worked up a sweat. By midnight on Monday
it was all over. Once McGovern got a lock on
those 271 delegates, there was never any doubt
about who would get the nomination on
Wednesday.

The blow-by-blow story of how McGovern beat the ABM will become an instant fixture in political science textbooks, regardless of who wins in November—but it's not an easy thing to explain. If a transcript existed, it would read more like an extremely complicated murder trial than the simple, out-front political convention that most people think they watched on TV. Trying to understand the byzantine reality of that convention on TV—or even on the floor, for that matter—was like somebody who's never played chess trying to understand a live telecast of the Fisher-Spassky duel up in Iceland.

The bedrock truths of the McGovern convention were not aired on TV—except once, very briefly on Monday night; but it hardly mattered, because all three networks missed it completely. When the deal went down, Walter Cronkite saw green and called it red, John Chancellor opted for yellow, and ABC was already off the air.

What happened, in a nut, was a surprise parliamentary maneuver—cooked up by over-ambitious strategists in the Women's Caucus—forcing a premature showdown that effectively decided whether or not McGovern would get the nomination. The crisis came early, at a time when most of the TV/Press people were still getting their heads ready to deal with all the intricate possibilities of the vote on the ABM challenge to McGovern's California delegates . . . and when Larry O'Brien announced a pending roll-call vote on whether or not the South Carolina delegation included enough women, very few people on the Floor or anywhere else understood that the result of that roll-call might determine exactly how many delegates would later vote for McGovern on the California challenge, and then on the First Ballot.

On the evidence, less than a dozen of the 5000 "media" sleuths accredited to the convention knew exactly what was happening, at the time. When McGovern's young strategists deliberately lost that vote, almost everybody who'd watched it—including Walter Cronkite—concluded that McGovern didn't have a hope in hell of winning any roll-call vote from that point on: Which meant the ABM could beat him on the California challenge, reducing his strength even further, and then stop him cold on the first ballot.

Humphrey's campaign manager, Jack Chestnut, drew the same conclusion—a glaring mistake that almost immediately became the subject of many crude jokes in McGovern's press room at the Doral, where a handful of resident correspondents who'd been attached to the campaign on a live-in basis for many months were watching the action on TV with press secretary Dick Dougherty and a room full of tense staffers—who roared with laughter when Cronkite, far up in his soundproof booth two miles away in the Convention hall, announced that CBS was about to switch to McGovern headquarters in the Doral, where Dick Schumacher was standing by with a first-hand report and at least one painfully candid shot of McGovern workers reacting to the news of this stunning setback.

The next scene showed a room full of laughing, whooping people. Schumacher was grinning into his microphone, saying: "I don't want to argue with you, Walter—but why are these people cheering?"

Schumacher then explained that McGovern had actually won the nomination by losing the South Carolina vote. It had been a test of strength, no doubt—but what had never been explained to the press or even to most of McGovern's own delegates on the floor, was that he had the option of "winning" that roll-call by going either up or down . . . and the only way the ABM crowd could have won was by juggling their votes to make sure the South Carolina challenge *almost* won, but not quite. This would have opened the way for a series of potentially disastrous parliamentary moves by the Humphrey-led ABM forces.

"We had to either win decisively or lose decisively," Rick Stearns explained later. "We couldn't afford a close vote."

Stearns, a 28-year-old Rhodes Scholar from Stanford, was McGovern's point man when the crisis came. His job in Miami—working out of a small white trailer full of telephones behind the Convention Hall—was to tell Gary Hart, on the floor, exactly how many votes McGovern could muster at any given moment, on any question—and it was Stearns who decided, after only 10 out of 50 states had voted on the South Carolina challenge, that the final tally might be too close to risk. So he sent word to Hart on the floor, and Gary replied: "Okay, if we can't win big—let's lose it."

"The old bulls never quit until the young bulls run them out. The old bulls are dead, but don't forget that the young bulls eventually become old bulls too."

—James H. Rowe, "an old professional from FDR's days," in *Time* Magazine

The next time I saw Rick Stearns, after he croaked the Humphrey/Meany squeeze play on Monday night, was out on the beach in front of the Doral on Saturday afternoon. He was smoking a cigar and carrying a tall plastic glass of beer—wearing his black and red Stanford tank shirt. I sat with him for a while and talked as the Coast Guard cutters cruised offshore about a hundred yards from the beach and National Guard helicopters and jets thundered overhead. It was the first time in ten days I'd had a chance to feel any sun and by midnight I was burned, drunk and unable to get any sleep—getting up every 15 minutes to rub more grease on my head and shoulders.

(Airplane)
HST: I was reading Haynes Johnson's thing in the Washington Post about how you won South Carolina. He mainly had it from Humphrey's side; he cited the fact that it fooled almost everybody. He said only a few McGovern staffers knew.

Stearns: No, that's not true. The guys in the trailer operation knew. The floor leaders, the ones who paid attention, knew; but some of them were just following instructions.

HST: That was it, more or less?

Stearns: That was it, although if you have that many people who know, chances are . . .

HST: Well, I was standing with Tom Morgan, Lindsay's press secretary; I don't know if anybody told him, but he figured it out. Then I went out in the hall and saw Tom Braden, the columnist. He said, "Oh, Jesus! Terrible! A bad defeat." Then I was really confused.

Stearns: Johnny Apple of the New York Times rushed out and filed the story which went to [Times Managing Editor] Abe Rosenthal. Rosenthal was sitting watching Walter Cronkite sputter on about the great setback the McGovern forces had, you know, the terrible defeat. So he killed Apple's story.

HST: Oh, Jesus!

Stearns: Apple got on the phone to Rosenthal and they had a shouting match for 30 minutes that ended with Apple resigning from the NY Times.

HST: Cazart!

Stearns: But he was hired back at the end of the next day. They never ran his story, but he was hired back at what I assume was a substantial increase in his salary.

HST: There was a reference in Johnson's story to a private discussion on Sunday. He said you'd explained the strategy 24 hours earlier.

Stearns: Let's see. What could that have been? The floor leaders meeting?

HST: He didn't say. You saw it coming that early? Sunday? Or even before that? When did you see the thing coming?

Stearns: It became clear during the maneuvering that went on the week before the Convention when we were trying to define several key parliamentary points.

HST: You'd seen this coming up all the week before during this maneuvering with Larry O'Brien and James G. O'Hara, the convention parliamentarian?

Stearns: Well, I'd seen it as of Thursday when we began to get some idea of how O'Brien and O'Hara intended to rule on the two issues, but as early as then we were going over a whole war game of possible parliamentary contingencies. The Humphrey camp would have never turned to procedural chicanery if they'd really had a working majority on the floor. The essential point is that procedure is the last defense of a vanishing majority.

First, who could vote, under the rules, on their own challenge? Did the rule which says a delegate can vote on anything but his own challenge mean that the 120 McGovern delegates from California not being challenged would be able to vote? We contended that they could. Eventually the chairman agreed.

The second and most important question was the question of what constituted a majority—whether it was a constitutional majority, or, as we originally contended, a majority of those present-and-voting. The chair's decision on that was a compromise between the two rules—that the majority would be determined by those *eligible* to vote. And he ruled then that since everyone but 153 bogus delegates from California were eligible, the majority on the California question would be 1433. So, in other words, we won the first point on who could vote. On the second point we came up with a compromise which was really to our advantage . . .

HST: What did you lose on that?

Stearns: Well, the only thing we lost was that, if it had been present-and-voting, it would have meant that we could have picked up extra votes by urging people just not to vote: if they were caught between pressures from labor on one hand and us on the other and couldn't find any way out of the dilemma, they could leave, and their absence then would lower the majority.

On the third issue we . . .

(Helicopter)

HST: Damm! Fuck! I can't believe those fuckin' helicopters! Christ! I'll leave it on the tape just to remind me how bad it was.

Stearns: The LEAA [the Federal Law Enforcement Assistance Act] . . .

HST: Oh, it's one of those pork barrel . . .

Stearns: . . . One thing Jerry and Abbie did for the city of Miami was to beef up the technology of the police department with that grant Miami got to buy all this stuff.

Well, the third point—which we lost and which we were arguing obviously because it was in our interest—was that the challenges ought to be considered in the order of the roll-call. This would have put California first and would have avoided the problem entirely, of course. On that, the chair ruled against us, and I think fairly. He followed the precedent of the last Conventions, which was that challenges were to be considered in the order in which the Credentials Committee had discussed them. That meant that we had South Carolina, Alabama, Georgia and Kentucky—four possible test cases—coming before we got to the California vote.

Kentucky we got withdrawn, eliminating one of them. Cashin's Alabama challenge was the same challenge he brought in '68. It's not a very attractive challenge. A lot of people felt that they had been misled by Cashin in '68, including blacks, and were not disposed to work for him again. He was trying to get Wallace thrown out of the Convention. Wallace's slate had been openly elected. Alabama was one of the first states in the country to comply with the reform rules. Voters happened to choose Wallace delegates. [*Airplane*] So we knew the Alabama challenge would be defeated on a voice vote. On Georgia, Julian [Bond] and Governor Jimmy Carter worked out a compromise. South Carolina was the only possible test vote to come up before the California challenge.

There were two procedural issues that the Humphrey coalition wanted to settle on the South Carolina challenge. The first was that question of *who* could vote. The chair ruled that there were nine South Carolinian women who had not been challenged, who would be entitled to vote on the challenge. It is a 32-member delegation, which meant that there were then 23 South Carolinians who were disqualified.

The second area of challenge—and the most troublesome—is what constituted a majority. That was what the Humphrey people went after first. The maneuvering that was going on! There was only one way that that question of what constituted a majority could arise, and that was if either side prevailed in the range of 1497 to 1508 votes. If either side prevailed by more than a constitutional majority, 1509, the question is moot.

It sounds impossible to maneuver a vote into that area, but in fact it's very easy if you have a Humphrey delegation controlled as well as Ohio. Ohio passed and passed and passed. All Frank King, their chairman, had to do was sit there, add correctly, cast the vote accordingly and we would have been in that area. Not only that, we would have been sucked into that area with an *artificial* vote from the Ohio delegation, which means that on the procedural test . . .

(Helicopter)

HST: You son of a bitch!

Stearns: If we'd let ourselves be sucked into that trap, I think we would have lost both the procedural tests.

HST: I see. They could lend you votes on one roll call, then take them back to the next one.

Stearns: A bogus count. If you look at the tally on the South Carolina challenge, the Minnesota delegation on which Humphrey had 35 hard-core votes went 56-to-8 for the South Carolina challenge, so there were at least 35 votes that the Humphrey coalition could have manipulated. In Ohio, Humphrey had as many as 80 votes that could have been cast any way that Humphrey forces chose to cast them.

So our problem was to maneuver ourselves around the Ohio delegation in a way that the Ohio votes could not be cast to force us into a test vote on California before we got to the real issue. And remember, to win a procedural test on California, it would only require turning out 1433 votes, but South Carolina would have had to have 1497 votes to win the same procedural question as to who could vote and what constituted a majority.

HST: That's why you wanted to put it off till California?

Stearns: The numbers were much better for us on California than they were on South Carolina.

HST: I was asking [McGovern pollster] Pat Caddell why you didn't just get it over with, and he was running back and forth on the floor and just said, "Well, we want to wait for California." But he never explained why.

Stearns: It was the difference in what was the working majority on the floor. Plus, it's much harder to hold delegates on procedural questions since they don't understand the significance of a parliamentary point. Everyone had gotten clear enough instructions on how to handle California that I think they were aware of the procedural problem if it had arisen with the California vote, which it did.

My instructions to our floor leaders and to our delegation chairman was that on the first 12 tallies we would go all out to win the South

Carolina minority report challenges. Perhaps not *all* out. We would go out to win, but not to the extent of jeopardizing votes we had on the California challenge. If there was somebody whose support we knew we had on California, but weren't sure if he would be able to withstand pressure from labor, Humphrey or whoever else, they were not to bother the guy. We didn't want to sacrifice votes on California. But that aside, we went after that challenge. That didn't quite work, because I had a number of passes in the first 12 states that reported, which meant that I put off the decision another eight or nine tallies.

HST: The passes weren't for political reasons, but because they couldn't make up their minds?

Stearns: Well, one for political reasons— that was the Ohio delegation, which was passing so it could put itself in the position of voting last so it could maneuver the vote and throw us into the procedural test. The others, just because it took a long time to get the counting done in the delegation.

HST: What was the woman's angle? It was talked about like it was some kind of shameful trip or something.

Stearns: The Women's Caucus was disputing the fact that only nine members of the 32-member delegation were women. The women made the South carolina Minority Report their test vote to the Convention. I personally don't think they had a terribly good case.

Their case was based on a misunderstanding of the McGovern guidelines. The misunderstanding was thinking that quotas had somehow been established. What the McGovern commission argued was that quotas would be imposed if the state did not take effective steps to see that women were represented in reasonable proportions. That is, they had to take down all the barriers to women being elected, but there was no guarantee in the guidelines that because a woman was a woman,

she was necessarily going to be elected. The guidelines attempted to give women the same chance of election that men had, removing some of the obstacles that kept them off slates in the past.

It was not a terribly good challenge in the first place, but no credentials challenge has ever really been decided strictly on the justice and merits of the challenge. They all come down to essentially political questions and in that case the Women's Caucus made what was in effect a weak challenge into a political issue. So it had to be treated seriously. This is why we set out at the beginning to try to win it, to try to see if we had the votes to win it the first time around.

HST: It was sort of forced on you.

Stearns: Well, it was, but I don't think the Women's Caucus really understood the significance of an early test vote. I would have much preferred that they would have picked— well, they had a much better case in Hawaii, for example, because the challenge came up after both the California and Illinois decisions. If we had to have a test vote on a women's issue, I'd rather they had picked a stronger case, Hawaii, which also would have moved the test vote after California.

HST: Why did they insist on being first?

Stearns: I'm not sure of the process they went through to pick South Carolina, but they had chosen it, and that made the issue of South Carolina one that one had to respond to as a political question.

HST: But they weren't somehow hooked into the Chisholm/Humphrey/stop-McGovern thing in order to get some bargaining power?

Stearns: I think there may have been some thought of that—the fact that it was to come first would give them some leverage with us that they might otherwise not have had. My intentions were to win that California challenge.

(Also on the beach is Bill Dougherty,

Lieutenant Governor of South Dakota, long-time McGovern crony and a key floor leader who worked under Stearns. Forty-two years old, he is wearing trunks and a short-sleeve shirt and staring at the surf.)

Dougherty: You know, this is the first time I've ever seen the ocean. Oh, I *saw* it out in California, but not like this. Not close up.

HST: Were you over there for the Democratic National Committee meeting?

Dougherty: Shit, I never got out of bed all day yesterday. I'm on the national committee. I've got McGovern really pissed at me. I never showed up. I couldn't move. I absolutely couldn't move yesterday. I was sick. I was just sick, physically.

HST: Well, there's a lot of people that are sick.

Stearns: I've never been as exhausted as I was.

Dougherty: I was going home yesterday. I'm not going home till Sunday, 'cause I couldn't get to the airport. No shit. I got down Wednesday, I think it was or something, and I don't think I ever sat down until yesterday, 'cause I was working hotels.

Stearns: Two hours of sleep in three days.

HST: This had been the least fun to me of all the things since I've been on this trip. It seems like it would have been at least . . . this is the first time I've been on the beach.

You worked with Bill on the Monday night floor fight through your incredible trailer/ boiler room/delegation phone system.

Stearns: Gary Hart and I came down in May to talk to Southern Bell and outline the communications equipment we wanted for the Convention. See, we ran a two-tier operation. We had 250 whips on the floor, people we'd selected from each delegation to make sure that somebody was talking to the individual delegate. We had one person in every row of the Convention giving instructions somewhere.

Then we had our floor leaders, Bill, Pierre Salinger and so on and then our delegation chairman. We had two ways to get to them. We had a boiler room here at the hotel, which was plugged into the SCOPE system. You'd call in at whip level.

HST: Which color phone did that come into?

Dougherty: White.

HST: And you had a different color. A red phone?

Dougherty: Blue phone.

Stearns: We had a blue phone for the floor leaders and delegation chairman.

HST: Who was there in the boiler room at the hotel?

Stearns: There were ten people. The Western director was Barbara McKenzie. Doug Coulter did the Moutain states. Judy Harrington did the Plains states. Scott Lilly did the Central states, Illinois, Missouri, Kentucky. Gail Channing did Ohio and Michigan. Laura Mizelle did the Pennsylvania, New Jersey, Delaware area. Tony Babb did the NY delegation, Puerto Rico; and Alan Kriegle did the New England states. They were in charge of the whips who were on the floor. They had worked for over a year in Washington as the liaison with regional areas of the campaign, handling the detail work, running to the delegates and the group we had in the trailer were the best of our field organizers.

HST: Were the hotel boiler room phones wired right to the floor, or into the trailer?

Stearns: Right to the floor. . . . I had a point-to-point line between them and me. Then that red phone in the office, I'd pick that up and it rang automatically at the hotel.

Dougherty: We on the floor could get either place.

HST: Was it completely triangular?

Stearns: Oh no. We oversaw a full communication system. You could go anywhere with the communications we had.

HST: There wasn't one main nexus where everything had to go through?

Stearns: There was a switchboard here at the Doral. The way instructions went out is that I would stand up in the back of the trailer and shout "NO" and then pick up that red phone which would ring automatically here and someone would pick it up and I'd say "NO" and then everyone knew that they were to instruct everyone to vote no on that. That way you had two trys at making sure the instructions got through.

Dougherty: David Shumacher of CBS has a film of you in the trailer with a cigar in your mouth shouting "NO." They're gonna run it Sunday night.

Stearns: When will it be on?

Dougherty: I think *Sixty Minutes.* He said you got a cigar in your mouth. He said, "Boy, Dougherty, does this spoil the grass-roots flavor of your campaign." Of course, Shumacher just loves it.

HST: Let's get back. You came down in May to set up your communications.

Stearns: We had to protect the communications system in the trailer and the communications system in the hotel, so we traced the telephone lines and there were two points where it was vulnerable. In the Convention center it was behind five link fences and pretty well guarded; but you had open manhole covers. The telephone lines here are laid very close to the surface—it's an artificial peninsula and you hit water if you dig any deeper than 12 feet—so anyone who could open a manhole cover could get to any of the telephone lines. . . .

HST: If they knew where they were.

Stearns: If you knew where they were. But chances are any manhole cover you pick up in this city you're gonna find telephone lines laid under it. We pointed that out to Southern Bell, and they suggested that we weld the manhole covers down, which we agreed to.

The only other vulnerable point was in the hotel itself. There is a switching room at the backside of the hotel behind the room where all the press equipment was set up. That was the other vulnerable spot. So we had an armed guard placed on that. A guy with an axe could have demolished that communications system in 30 seconds.

Dougherty: You can do some of those things at a Convention, 'cause everybody forgets about it five days after it happens. Once the vote goes in, they don't recall any situation where even the crookedest of things may have changed it. There's no protest. There have been terrible things that happen at Conventions.

HST: Yeah, I'm surprised this thing went off as well as it did. You got a gang of real scum, the kind of people Barkan [AFL-CIO] and those people could have brought in. Between Daley and Barkan they could have brought. . . .

Stearns: Well, they did. They brought them in, but we beat them. . . .

HST: I mean people with axes—that kind of thing.

Dougherty: I'll tell you, one of the things we had going for us: You know how tough it is to keep communications going in one camp? The Stop McGovern movement had to keep communications going in *four* camps— try to coordinate all the communications of four camps.

We could have won the South Carolina Challenge if we were absolutely sure of every vote. We were getting votes out of places like Minnesota that we never expected. But we had Ohio waiting with a delegation that Humphrey . . . I mean they had 80 or 90 votes with which they could have done the same thing we did.

HST: Was that Humphrey's accordian delegation—Ohio?

Stearns: Yes. With the 80 or 90 Humphrey

delegates, Frank King could have sat up and read any set of figures he wanted. We had a few delegations like that, too, as you saw in the last moments of that challenge.

HST: Oh yeah, but I forget which ones. . . .

Stearns: Colorado, Wisconsin, Nebraska, Rhode Island. In the last seven or eight minutes of that challenge we didn't even bother to poll the delegations; I was just reading the numbers that we expected them to cast. That was the best moment of the Convention: when [ex-Governor of Nebraska] Frank Morrison's first instructions were to cut that vote down to 14 and then Bill came rushing up the aisle to take four more.

Dougherty: No, it was 17, and then I changed it to 14. I was whispering right in his ear. They got a shot of that on TV, I guess.

Stearns: I heard.

HST: Was the Humphrey guy next to you? When you came up to Morrison, was there somebody there who knew what you were saying to him?

Dougherty: Johnny Apple [New York Times reporter] caught me.

HST: Kirby [Jones, McGovern press assistant] said that King was aware that one of your people was on him.

Dougherty: Oh, they were aware of it on the floor.

Stearns: That was Dick Sklar standing next to King. He was our liaison for the Ohio delegation. He and Frank King did not get along.

Dougherty: That South Carolina deal with me, who loves politics, and this is my third Convention, it was so great. . . .

HST: It strikes me as being the key thing.

Stearns: Bill can describe it—I mean, I can describe what it was like sitting in the trailer—but Bill can describe it working on the floor.

Dougherty: Oh, this is perfect. When I got the word to shave, I had about ten minutes. I couldn't go to the other side after the first night, 'cause I damn near got in a fist fight

with the governor. See, he moved in—you know he moved in a couple of alternates on us, and I wouldn't let him do it. And, God, he got madder 'n hell and he never spoke to me the rest of the Convention. So I had to go way over to the other side because I couldn't use that girl, 'cause she was sittin' right next to the Governor, and I had to lean over him to talk to her. And he was ready to punch me every time I leaned over.

So I ran clear out the other side and got ahold of him and then I came back around and got ahold of Mondragon and Ortez, or whatever his name is. Then I told him I wanted to get as many votes as I could get and it wasn't very many.

HST: When did you suddenly decide to start shaving?

Dougherty: Oh, Kansas was the key.

Stearns: Yeah, we pared it down to Kansas and then made the decision at that point that we were not going to win with a working majority of our own.

HST: How far along was that?

Stearns: That was the 11th or 12th vote.

Dougherty: But see, you didn't know because Ohio would pass.

Stearns: Ohio would pass, is what screwed us up. So I had to wait for another four or five votes. We had New York pass.

HST: What number was Ohio?

Stearns: Ohio was, I think, 11.

Dougherty: Kansas was 11, wasn't it?

Stearns: That's right, Kansas.

Dougherty: Frank King, with his Ohio delegation, has passed on every roll call since. . . .

HST: It's sort of a political habit. You always want to have that leverage at the end, I suppose.

Dougherty: In the legislature you get the same thing, you get guys who pass all the time and wait to see how the vote is.

Stearns: But, the question was whether we would throw New York's votes behind the challenge or hold New York out, but when they held out Ohio, I gave instructions to our New York delegates to pass the first time.

HST: That gave you a helluva cushion, right?

Stearns: Yeah, there was a lot to work with there.

Dougherty: Then we started shaving.

Stearns: Then we heard a few more votes just to get a better sense of where things were going, and then the instructions went out to start cutting.

Doughtery: See, we were afraid the Humphrey forces were gonna start going the other way, which, if they were really coordinated, they could have done.

HST: Yeah. Well, wait a minute. What would have happened then?

Stearns: The game that was going on was to see who could push who over the 1509 mark first. If they'd pushed us up above 1509 with a lot of bogus votes, it would have been very hard to persuade our people to cut back then, 'cause if you think you've won, then the instinct is to go out and fight for every vote you can get your hands on. We tried to hold the obvious switches to the end. We started cutting votes at that point—hold the obvious ones to the end and suddenly throw a lot of votes on them, push them up over 1509, and then at that point the only way they can get out from under that is by abandoning one of their own. Governor West of South Carolina. They would have thrown him to the wolves at that point.

HST: What do you mean by them? You people have been around longer than I have. What do you mean—exactly what would they have done to Governor West?

Dougherty: Well, they'd have to abandon him to the South Carolina challenge by changing their vote.

Stearns: Once they'd gone over 1509, they had seated Governor West's delegation.

Dougherty: So to get back down under, they had to abandon him.

Stearns: When it really came down to it, they had less guts than we had. We were willing to sell out the women, but they weren't willing to sell out a Southern governor.

HST: When did King figure it out?

Stearns: Well, I think we were ahead of them almost from the beginning. It turned out our strategy confused them almost as much as it may have confused our own supporters.

HST: Johnson in the Post said it confused Jack Chestnut [Humphrey's floor manager]. Johnson said the Humphrey people bought it completely as they were sitting there with Humphrey watching it on TV.

Stearns: Oh, they did. His aides interpreted it as a great victory. What confused them was the fact that we went out to win it at the beginning. They've been reading the columnists for a month about undisciplined, unruly McGovern delegates, and I think once they saw us start to win the South Carolina challenge, I think they relaxed. That was just what they wanted us to do. We needed to set out to win for some political reasons because we couldn't sell out the women completely. If there was a chance to win it, then we had the obligation to try and win.

Dougherty: What did Chestnut say to Humphrey?

Stearns: He said, "We've given a great setback to McGovern." But Humphrey was smarter: Humphrey said, "No, they ran that deliberately. . . ."

HST: Yeah, Humphrey said, "They're pulling it back." There was a TV pool reporter with him at the hotel. I was watching Humphrey's face, and Jesus, it just turned to wax. He looked the worst I've ever seen him—which makes me very happy, that son of a bitch. He should be buried with his head down in the sand. I've never been so disgusted with a human being in politics.

Dougherty: One thing, Humphrey isn't dumb. He's got a bunch of dumb guys around him.

Stearns: He's smart—he's been around a long time. He was the only one of that group who knew what was going on.

HST: According to Johnson, they thought they had it locked up until about halfway through—then all of a sudden they realized. . . .

Stearns: Yeah, but we really did try to win at first, and I think they relaxed then. But with Ohio coming in, we had 30 bogus votes from Minnesota on that total. Maybe a few others—I have to go over the totals again—but Minnesota was what I caught, and then we had Ohio holding out to the end.

Stearns: King passed twice to make sure that his was the last vote that was cast. At that point I was trying to cut our total down to the point where no matter how he cast those votes, no matter how or what they did with those Ohio votes, there was no way they could push us into that area.

HST: So you just wanted to get as low as you could, once you decided to go down?

Stearns: Well, I didn't want to go as low I could. I wanted a good vote for women's challenge, but I wanted it just low enough that there was nothing King could do to re-write it.

HST: So it had to be almost 80 votes low.

Stearns: Yeah, I think we came in at about 1420 or 1430. And we were prepared to go lower. The number that I was aiming to get us down to was about 1410 and we had those lined up, but as we started taking the votes off, finally King gave up and went ahead and cast his vote. I think we cut it down to the figure where King couldn't win, and I think he realized that.

HST: When you say dropping it down, now, you mean changes?

Dougherty: When we had time, we shaved them and shaved again.

Stearns: Yeah, we cut them as they were cast and we were ready to change them after.

HST: Did you have to go back and do it? I've forgotten.

Stearns: A few of them we did. We went back to Wisconsin. Wisconsin originally came through at 54, then we cut it down to 37. Oregon came through at 33 and we cut it down to 17 or whatever the figure was. I had Rhode Island ready to, I mean, they would have moved all 22 votes. . . .

HST: You were hung between 1410 and a possible 1500?

Stearns: What I was aiming for was the figure at which Ohio could not have made a difference.

HST: Yeah, but the most you could have gotten—if you hadn't had that option of losing, when you saw you might not win—you think it was about 1500?

Stearns: Well, my feeling was that on the issue of the challenge itself, we were stuck at around 1500. That was clear from the beginning, and it would have been disastrous. To keep them from playing with the vote, we had to show them that we had the discipline on the floor, that there was nothing they could do at that point.

Dougherty: But it got tougher to hold that discipline as it went along.

HST: What Gary Hart was quoted as saying was that you couldn't afford to let them know you had control of the floor. Is that right?

Stearns: No, I think it's just the opposite. We wanted them to think that we had the control. Otherwise we would have been shifting votes all night.

HST: How long did that fencing with King go on? Did he fuck you up at any time?

Stearns: No, that was their one attempt at that.

HST: All he did was pass twice?

Stearns: No, Ohio passed three times, but I think they realized the fourth time they came around that it was hopeless. They knew we had control.

HST: He didn't really make any moves except passing.

Stearns: He kept passing. His strategy was to

have Ohio cast their votes last so they could manipulate the Ohio votes in a way that would have thrown us into the procedural test.

Dougherty: We had some hard votes in Ohio, too—ones they couldn't move.

Stearns: Right, they couldn't move our Ohio votes, and as we begun cutting that figure down, we finally got to the point where they realized we'd cut it down to zero if we had to.

HST: So his thing was mainly just waiting.

Stearns: To wait until the truth began to dawn on them, that we controlled the votes on the floor.

Dougherty: What we couldn't afford— hell, it became so obvious—we didn't want to get the women mad at us.

Stearns: Bill's point is very good: it got harder as you went along because the more that vote was pushed to 1509, the more our delegates wanted to go majority. That's just what the Humphrey coalition was trying to lure us into, trying to go all out to win the thing, win it with their votes which could have been pulled out from under us, and at that point psychologically to get our supporters to change would have almost been impossible.

Dougherty: I was getting nervous, myself.

Stearns: I know, I was getting the calls back, but. . . .

Dougherty: The delegates were all bitchin' at me. And I was pissed off.

HST: Why?

Dougherty: I was so worried about our delegates gettin' pissed off, 'cause they're all such a great bunch of nonpolitical professionals. I thought, "Ooh shit!" 'Cause, jeez, they got mad at me when I started shaving votes on some of those delegations. You know, "What are you trying to do?" and all that. . . . I didn't have time to explain it. I just had to be hard and say, "Goddamn it! That's the way it's gonna be!"

HST: You mean the delegates themselves didn't know what was going on?

Dougherty: No! Shit, they weren't aware.

Stearns: Well, our whips knew. I held a briefing session with them on Monday, and I spent an hour and a half going over the possible parliamentary contingencies.

Doughtery: But the average delegate didn't know.

Stearns: There were perhaps 250 people on the floor who had a good idea of what was going on. There were another 50 or 60 who had a pretty *complete* idea of what was going on. And then there were about 20 who *knew* what was going on.

HST: Did state-level leaders like Diane White or Dick Perchlick in the Colorado delegation know what was happening?

Stearns: No.

HST: That's amazing. Amazing you could do it. It must have been hell on the floor.

Stearns: It was. That one woman in Nebraska got so damn mad. Oh God, she was mad! But after they saw what it led to in the California vote, then we had a couple of days where we could say almost anything and people realized that we weren't trying to. . . .

Dougherty: That's when they learned discipline.

HST: Well, Jesus. It was really a helluva gamble then, wasn't it, given the kind of delegates that were there.

Stearns: Yeah, but you had to take it. We had a nomination at stake.

HST: What was the point then in sending Mankiewicz and Salinger and Hart out to call it a terrible defeat on the floor? After it was over—not before, but after.

Dougherty: Well, on account of the women.

Stearns: We sure didn't want to get the women angry for us on the California challenge.

Dougherty: The women didn't catch on, though. They still haven't. It's so complicated that they haven't figured it out.

Stearns: I felt sort of guilty about what we'd done to the Women's Caucus. Afterwards I went around the trailer saying how bad I felt that we'd done it, but. . . .

HST: What was the long-range effect of that, anyway? Was it just a symbolic thing that you'd done?

Dougherty: McGovern never did have that women's meeting yesterday. You know the Women's Caucus called me up and I was in bed. I just hung up. I said, "I can't help it," and I hung up.

Stearns: They called me at 7:30 in the morning after I'd just gone to bed, and my response was, "If you really have to meet with him, I'll arrange it, but the fact that you want to meet with him at 10:00 when the Democratic National Committee is going to convene and elect its first woman chairman in the history of the party shows us how wrong you've been all along, all you're interested in is the form, not the substance. The substance is going to happen over at the National Committee meeting and if you want to do something meaningful, you should go there at 10:00." So whoever it was hung up. Maybe they went to the committee meeting. Silly. I mean, they want to meet with McGovern while they're electing their first woman national chairman of the party.

Doughtery: The one that was raisin' all the hell was the delegate from South Dakota.

Stearns: She caught me about 7:00 in the coffee shop as I was finally getting breakfast.

Dougherty: You know what she's done for the Democrats? Nothin', ever. For George McGovern or anything. I really chewed her out on the floor, I said, "Instead of going around startin' all this trouble, you should be goin' around puttin' out the fires."

HST: What was the loss they had? What did the women suffer?

Dougherty: That wasn't what they complained about. They were complaining there wasn't enough input from women in the campaign.

HST: Was there any permanent damage done? Or tangible damage?

Dougherty: No, I don't think so.

HST: The networks must have caught on at some point. I remember I went somewhere and came back and saw Mike Wallace saying what a brillant move it had been.

Dougherty: I went back to that airlines lounge in the hall, and watched TV a little bit and had coffee after I finished all that sweatin'. And Cronkite is on there saying that McGovern forces have suffered a serious setback and all of a sudden they switched him to the Doral Hotel. There's David Shumacher who says, "Well, I'm sorry Walter, maybe they suffered a serious defeat, but when they lost, everybody in the boiler room cheered."

HST: That probably will go down in the annals of political history.

Stearns: It was the greatest moment in my political career. I'd say I've spent four years studying for the ten minutes on that vote, being able to make the right decision in that circumstance. Learning the names of all those delegates, how they'd been chosen, how the whole thing was put together, what the parliamentary situation might be.

HST: What are the most obvious things that could have gone wrong? In your place, on the floor, or at the Doral boiler room?

Stearns: Well, the most obvious thing that could have gone wrong was if we'd lost control of the Convention. The other issue at stake on that South Carolina vote was whether or not we could control our own delegates and whether we could impose the discipline that was going to lead to a working majority that could nominate George McGovern.

HST: Without them even knowing what you were doing.

Stearns: That was the whole question the press was raising right before the Convention.

The Humphrey campaign had all this fantastic strategy about how McGovern supporters, because they were ideologically inclined to proportional representation, would desert us on the California issue and then they'd cut us apart from the black caucus by releasing to Chisholm and the women would come running at us in another direction. So the question was whether we could keep control, and that was the most important thing that could have gone wrong, just a complete inability. . . .

HST: What would have been the first manifestation?

Stearns: Well, South Carolina. . . .

HST: No, I mean, even while it was going on. If somebody just stood up and told you to fuck off and "What's wrong with you. . . ."

Stearns: If Bill had gone to Pat Lucy and said, "We want you to cut back to 37 on this" and Pat had turned around to his delegation and said, "I need 20 people to step forward and change their votes." And people said "Go to hell."

HST: And you didn't think that that could have happened?

Stearns: Oh yeah, it could have happened. But we had a bunch of delegates down here that wanted to win. . . .

Dougherty: After Tuesday night though, they got . . .

Stearns: They got a little restless. I mean after Monday night, they were willing to follow us anywhere, because they realized what we'd done. . . .

HST: On the Daley challenge they didn't. That was Monday night, wasn't it? What caused that? Why did some of them desert you on the Daley thing?

Stearns: You mean on the compromise? Our hard core supporters didn't desert us. We pulled exactly . . .

Dougherty: We needed a two-thirds vote from the whole convention on that one.

Stearns: We pulled exactly the vote of ab-

solutely loyal supporters we had. The people who screwed us on that were the Humphrey and Muskie people who were still convinced that they were gonna win. We got Alderman Singer and Jesse Jackson to agree to publicly announce the compromise . . .

Dougherty: Let me tell you this story. I was on the floor with John Bailey [Chairman of the Connecticut delegation, and past Chairman of the Democratic National Committee] right when Frank Morrison had the deal in his hand to give it.

See, you could divide that motion in two, parliamentary-wise, and I asked Bailey to give it, to make the motion to suspend the rules. If Bailey made the motion for two-thirds to suspend the rules, I think it would have passed. Then I'd have Frank Morrison make the motion to seat both delegations and it only takes a majority to do that.

HST: So if you separated the two motions, you could have got it.

Dougherty: See, if John Bailey had made the motion to suspend the rules . . . I wanted to divide the question: have John Bailey make the motion to suspend the rules, then have Frank Morrison make the motion to have the compromise, and it only would have taken a majority on the compromise, see. And we could let some of our people vote the other way and we still could have won it.

HST: Why didn't Bailey make it?

Dougherty: I was talking to him right on the phone while we were gettin' ready to do it. I was right there on Frank Morrison's phone, and he says, "I won't do it, because the Mayor [Daley] hasn't agreed to it."

And I says, "This is the only chance, John, this is the only chance we've got, otherwise we're gonna kick him right out of the Convention." I pleaded with him, I said to him, "For the good of the Democratic party." And he wouldn't do it.

Stearns: The Humphrey coalition's last

hope at that point was that we would be willing to sell out Singer and Jackson, who came through for us and did everything we asked them to do on that California vote and on the compromise.

HST: Why did Singer and Jackson go for the compromise? Were they just thinking about carrying Illinois in November?

Stearns: They're politicians.

Dougherty: You remember me on the floor. I was mad, because I thought those guys, Jackson and Singer, wouldn't support it either, but they did! See, that just killed any chance Daley had of being seated.

Stearns: That's when I decided to go all out for Jackson. When they kept their word on that, then that's fine with me—we'd keep our word, too.

Dougherty: I'll tell you this. I wanted Daley in that Convention so bad I could taste it.

Stearns: He should have been there.

Dougherty: There's a legal question on it, too. I mean those guys, the Jackson delegation, weren't exactly legally seated, if you really want to be honest about it. I guess they were on the reform rules, but there was nobody running against them.

Stearns: I agree. The Daley side had a good argument. The Jackson side had a good argument, and the compromise would have settled the whole thing.

The problem at that point was to convince the Humphrey coalition that the compromise was the only way they were going to keep Daley in the Convention. But they wouldn't believe us. Their last hope was that we would not keep that agreement, that we would sell out Singer and Jackson, so that then they could have come back on the majority report, and at that point carry a disaffected Illinois delegation, because whether Daley had been seated or not, at that point the Singer-Jackson delegation would have gone on voting until a majority report had passed.

HST: I don't follow that.

Stearns: Temporary rule votes until you get all through the credential challenges. That is, those 151 unseated delegates from California went on voting right to the end of the evening until the majority report was passed. The same was true of Illinois: the Singer-Jackson delegation would have voted right to the end, regardless of whether Daley had been seated or not. The last hope the Humphrey people had was that we would desert Jackson, that is betray our word on that agreement, and then be able to use that Illinois delegation plus the 151 votes from California to defeat the passage of the majority report on credentials, which would have put us right back at the beginning again. But we kept our word.

HST: I didn't know that. Even the people who had been unseated could vote on the final passage.

Stearns: They would vote on the passage of the final report. And if we did not keep our word—if Jackson had been unseated—he might be angry enough to go out and by that point we would have also offended the women, and would have offended the blacks, and then they could have put together enough of a vote to defeat the passage of the majority report. But by the time we finished that night, they were so demoralized that they just let it go through on a voice vote. They lost their appetite to fight. On the next morning, Muskie and Humphrey were through.

HST: According to the Haynes Johnson story, they pretty well gave up at the end of the South Carolina roll call. They knew it.

Stearns: It was obvious. But even as late as the nomination roll call, I had an AFL-CIO guy come up to me and tell me that we only had 1451 votes for the nomination. What he was telling me was my *own* figure, from our absolutely hard count on the California thing, not realizing we just seated 151 delegates from California to take the total up to 1600.

HST: How important was O'Hara's ruling then? What accounts for the worry over O'Hara's ruling? And the tremendous spread that you got in the end? O'Hara's ruling wouldn't matter, it would appear.

Dougherty: Yeah, it would have. If he'd ruled different, we wouldn't . . . it kinda broke things, and we needed a break at that point.

Stearns: You not only deal with numbers at a Convention, you deal with psychology.

Dougherty: When a train starts leaving the station . . .

Stearns: If people think you're gonna lose, votes can just melt away.

Dougherty: See, just like on the Eagleton vote, there were all kinds of rumors around the floor that we didn't have the votes.

HST: Yeah, I was on the floor. People were trying to leave.

Stearns: We didn't turn it on at that point because we knew we had the votes, and if we turned it on, we would have destroyed the atmosphere for McGovern's presentation.

HST: For good or ill.

Dougherty: It's the first time for the history of this country that the presidential nominating speech was given at three o'clock in the morning.

Stearns: It was one of the best hours in the history of the Democratic party, that hour. I almost cried.

HST: That was the best speech I've ever heard him give. I've been following the campaign ever since way back in New Hampshire, and that's the best I've ever heard him speak.

Dougherty: He had 126 guys writing his speech for him, but I think he wrote it himself.

HST: Whose idea was it to put in the line about you won't have Nixon to kick around anymore? I thought that was the best part of the . . .

Stearns: That was his. "I want those doors open and that war closed" was also his idea.

HST: That was a good shot at Nixon. I saw it was almost over, so I decided to flee. I was in the cab listening to it on the way back, and the cab driver—a total stranger—just turned around and laughed, as if I understood somehow, too.

HST: Where are you going now?

Stearns: I'm getting my assignments these days from the New York Times. There are things that I read about in the Times before anybody talked to me. As I understand it from Jim McNaughton's latest story, I'm supposed to take the states west of the Mississippi.

HST: Is that in today?

Stearns: It was in the Times yesterday. First I ever heard of it. It really pissed me off. I mean, somebody ought to tell me before . . .

Dougherty: That's George McGovern for ya.

Stearns: Yeah, but if you got time to talk to Jim McNaughton, you got time . . .

Dougherty: What about Dick Stout's Newsweek story?

Stearns: I didn't see that.

Dougherty: Did you see that one Monday? About Dick Dougherty being press secretary and Mankiewicz traveling. Hart being in charge of the campaign.

Stearns: Oh yeah, they had you in there as a seasoned political pro.

Dougherty: Yeah. He got that in Maryland the day I was out there with McGovern. I found out it was gonna be in there. So I went to Dick Stout and I said, "Where in the hell did you get that?" Dick Stout said he ran into Fred Dutton comin' outta the bank in Washington and Fred told him the whole deal. Then Dutton came to me and he said, "I wonder if Cunningham [McGovern's administrative assistant] and those guys know about it." So I said, "I haven't heard anything about it."

When I got in town I got ahold of Dick Dougherty [McGovern's Press Secretary] and told him the whole deal and he said, "For chrissakes." So he got ahold of Dick Stout and found out exactly how much was gonna be in that story and then I went to Gary and I said, "Here's what's gonna be in Newsweek on Monday. I think some of these guys should be aware." Cunningham wasn't even aware, or any of them. But that's typical George Mc-Govern, you know.

(Garbled conversation. Whistling. Clicks. Airplane.)

HST: You taking off today?

Stearns: No, I think not. If I can get on a plane tomorrow. I feel like sitting out here on this bench and drinking for awhile.

THE LATE, LATE SHOW; TIME TO FLEE AGAIN

It was somewhere around eight-thirty or nine on Sunday evening when I dragged myself off the plane from Miami. The '72 Democratic Convention was over. McGovern had wrapped it up just before dawn on Friday, accepting the bloody nomination with an elegant, finely crafted speech that might have had quite an impact on the national TV audience . . . (Time correspondent Hugh Sidey called it "perhaps as pure an expression as George McGovern has ever given of his particular moralistic sense of the nation.") . . . but the main, middle-American bulk of the national TV audience tends to wither away around midnight, and anybody still glued to the tube at 3:30 A.M., Miami time, is probably too stoned or twisted to recognize McGovern anyway.

A few hundred ex-Muskie/Humphrey/Jackson delegates had lingered long enough to cheer Ted Kennedy's bland speech, but they started drifting away when George came on— hurrying out the exits of the air-conditioned hall, into the muggy darkness of the parking lot to fetch up a waiting cab and go back to whichever one of the 65 official convention hotels they were staying in . . . hoping to catch the tail end of a party or at least one free drink before catching a few hours' sleep and then heading back home on one of the afternoon planes: Back to St. Louis, Altoona, Butte . . .

By sundown on Friday the "political hotels"

were almost empty. In the Doral Beach— McGovern's ocean-front headquarters hotel— Southern Bell Telephone workers were dragging what looked like about 5000 miles of multicolored wires, junction boxes and cables out of the empty Press/Operations complex on the mezzanine. Down in the lobby, a Cuban wedding (Martinez-Hernandez: 8:30–10:30) had taken over the vast, ornately-sculptured Banquet Room that 24 hours earlier had been jammed with hundreds of young, scruffy-looking McGovern volunteers, celebrating the end of one of the longest and most unlikely trips in the history of American politics . . . it was a quiet party, by most Convention standards: Free beer for the troops, bring your own grass, guitar-minstrels working out here and there; but not much noise, no whooping & shouting, no madness. . . .

The atmosphere at the victory party was not much different from the atmosphere of the Convention itself: very cool and efficient, very much under control at all times . . . get the job done, don't fuck around, avoid violence, shoot ten seconds after you see the whites of their eyes.

It was a McGovern party from start to finish. Everything went according to plan—or *almost* everything; as always, there were a few stark exceptions. Minor snarls here and there, but not many big ones. McGovern brought his act into Miami with the same kind of fine-focus precision that carried him all the way from New Hampshire to California . . . and, as usual, it made all the other acts look surprisingly sloppy.

I was trapped in the Doral for 10 days, shuttling back & forth between the hotel and the Convention Hall by any means available: Taxi, my rented green convertible, and occasionally down the canal in the fast white "staff taxi" speedboat that McGovern's people used to get from the Doral to the Hall by water, whenever Collins Avenue was jammed up with sight-seer traffic . . . and in retrospect, I think that boat trip was the only thing I did all week that I actually enjoyed.

There was a lot of talk in the press about "the spontaneous outburst of fun and games" on Thursday night—when the delegates, who had been so deadly serious for the first three sessions, suddenly ran wild on the floor and delayed McGovern's long-awaited acceptance speech until 3:30 A.M. by tying the convention in knots with a long outburst of frivolous squabbling over the vice-presidential nomination. Newsweek described it as "a comic interlude, a burst of silliness on the part of the delegates whose taut bonds of decorum and discipline seemed suddenly to snap, now that it didn't make any difference."

There was not much laughter in Miami, on the floor or anywhere else, and from where I stood that famous "comic interlude" on Thursday night looked more like the first scattered signs of mass Fatigue Hysteria, if the goddamn thing didn't end soon. What the press mistook for relaxed levity was actually a mood of ugly restlessness that by 3:00 A.M. on Friday was bordering on rebellion. All over the floor I saw people caving in to the lure of booze, and in the crowded aisle between the California and Wisconsin delegations a smiling freak with a bottle of liquid THC was giving free hits to anybody who still had the strength to stick their tongue out.

After four hours of listening to a seemingly endless parade of shameless dingbats who saw no harm in cadging some free exposure on national TV by nominating each other for vice-president, about half the delegates in the hall were beginning to lose control. On the floor just in front of the New York delegation, leaning against the now-empty VIP box once occupied by Muriel Humphrey, a small blonde girl who once worked for the Lindsay campaign was sharing a nasal inhaler full of crushed amyls with a handful of new-found friends.

Each candidate was entitled to a 15-minute nominating speech and two five-minute seconding speeches. The nightmare dragged on for four hours, and after the first 40 minutes there was not one delegate in 50, on the floor, who either knew or cared who was speaking. No doubt there were flashes of eloquence, now and then: probably Mike Gravel and Cissy Farentholt said a few things that might have been worth hearing, under different circumstances . . . but on that long Thursday night in Miami, with Sen. Tom Eagleton of Missouri waiting nervously in the wings to come out and accept the vice-presidential nomination that McGovern had sealed for him 12 hours earlier, every delegate in the hall understood that whatever these other seven candidates where saying up there on the rostrum, they were saying for reasons that had nothing to do with who was going to be the Democratic candidate for vice-president in November . . . and it was *not* going to be ex-Mass. governor "Chub" Peabody, or a grinning dimwit named Stanley Arnold from New York City who said he was The Businessman's Candidate, or some black Step'n'Fetchit-style Wallace Delegate from Texas called Clay Smothers.

But these brainless bastards persisted, nonetheless, using up half the night and all the prime time on TV, debasing the whole convention with a blizzard of self-serving gibberish that drove whatever was left of the national TV audience to bed or the *Late Late Show*.

Thursday was not a good day for McGovern. By noon there was not much left of Wednesday night's Triumphant Warrior smile. He spent most of Thursday afternoon grappling with a long list of vice-presidential possibilities and by two, the Doral lobby was foaming with reporters and TV cameras. The name had to be formally submitted by 3:59 P.M., but it was 4:05 when Mankiewicz finally appeared to say McGovern had decided on Senator Thomas Eagleton of Missouri.

There is a very tangled story behind that choice, but I don't feel like writing it now. My immediate reaction was not enthusiastic, and the staff people I talked to seemed vaguely depressed—if only because it was a concession to "the Old Politics," a nice-looking Catholic boy from Missouri with friends in the Labor Movement. His acceptance speech that night was not memorable—perhaps because it was followed by the long-awaited appearance of Ted Kennedy, who had turned the job down.

Kennedy's speech was not memorable either: "Let us bury the hatchet, etc. . . . and Get Behind the Ticket." There was something hollow about it, and when McGovern came on he made Kennedy sound like an old-timer.

Later that night, at a party on the roof of the Doral, a McGovern staffer asked me who I would have chosen for VP. I finally said I would have chosen Ron Dellums, the black congressman from Berkeley.

"Jesus christ!" he said. "That would be suicide!"

I shrugged.

"Why Dellums?" he asked.

"Why not?" I said. "He offered it to Mayor Daley before he called Eagleton."

"No!" he shouted. "Not Daley! That's a lie!"

"I was in the room when he made the call," I said. "Ask anybody who was there—Gary, Frank, Dutton—they weren't happy about it, but they said he'd be good for the ticket."

He stared at me. "What did Daley say?" he asked finally.

I laughed. "Christ, you *believed* that, didn't you?"

He had, for just an instant. After all there was a lot of talk about "pragmatism" in Miami, and Illinois was a key state. . . . I decided to try the Daley rumor, on other staff people, to see their reactions.

But I never got around to it, I forgot all about it, in fact, until flipping through my notebook on the midnight jet from Atlanta. I came across a statement by Ron Dellums. It depressed me, for some reason, but it seems like a good way to end this goddamm thing. Dellums writes pretty good, for a politician. It's part of the statement he distributed when he switched his support from Shirley Chisholm to McGovern:

"The great bulk of that coalition committed to change, human freedom and justice in the country has moved actively and powerfully behind the candidacy of Senator McGovern. That coalition of hope, conscience, morality and humanity—of the powerless and the voiceless—that did not exist in 1964, that expressed itself in outrage and frustration in 1968, and in 1972 began to form and welded itself imperfectly but courageously and lifted a man to the brink of the Democratic nomination for the Presidency of the United States, and within a short but laborious step from the Presidency of the United States. The coalition that has formed behind Senator McGovern has battled the odds, baffled the pollsters, and beat the bosses. It is my conviction that when that total coalition of the victims in this country is ever formed, this potential for change would be unheralded, for it could pose a real alternative to expediency and status quo politics in America."

—Ron Dellums: July 9, 1972

McGovern, the Big Tease

Germaine Greer

Germaine Greer, a native Australian now living in England, came to prominence with the English and American promotional tours for her book *The Female Eunuch*. She was formerly a teacher of English literature and enjoyed a reputation as an underground journalist. Ms. Greer was the featured participant in the Town Hall panel on feminism in 1970.

The weather in Miami reminded me of Vietnam, the same rank heaviness in the air whacking sullenly against the rotor blades of the military helicopters and the same filthy skirts that the airliners trailed across the livid sky. The fumes that clouded the freeway came from the exhausts of vast carapaces of metal shielding their soft-bodied drivers instead of the million Hondas that infest South Vietnam, but the root cause of the ecological disaster is the same. The soldiers billeted in Miami Beach High School had the faces of American soldiers anywhere, and the nondelegates lived like refugees in their pup tents in Flamingo Park. The whores threading through the gloaming of the plush bars used the same lines and chewed the same gum.

Saturation bombing and defoliation and cloud-seeding are not the only disasters that the U.S.A. has inflicted upon Vietnam; they may not even be the worst. American money is the central reality in the war-made metropolis of Saigon; it reaches into every area of life, civil and military, so that it has almost destroyed the last vestiges of an individual civilization. The withdrawal of every last American soldier will not eradicate the traces of big business and gangsterism, even though the money will depart when the soldiers can no longer protect its interests and consume its heroin, and when the military supplies no longer stock the black market and there are no more lucrative currency deals to be made. America will leave behind a nation of whores,

pushers, beggars, spies, petty spivs, racketeers, cripples, and disaffected mercenaries who have learned how to use their guns for robbery and looting.

It is not only American policy that has laid waste Vietnam, but the nature of the American economy and the cast of its civilization. Buy or die is the message. Those who buy the free enterprise system escape massacre and economic ostracism, but their culture grows leperous with the absorption of cannibal values. Imperialism is not a vice practiced by certain depraved characters, but the mode of operation that characterizes economies that must keep expanding in order to survive. To blame Richard Nixon is weak-minded; to hope that a nice man from South Dakota will reverse the process is plumb crazy—but that is what I and thousands of other radic-libs did.

Who knows? Economic analyses of American hegemony might be false, might be emotional reactions caused by an overaesthetic response to Holiday Inns and Thick Shakes. Perhaps distrust of international corporate capitalism is but a feeling after all, seeing how few radicals really understand it, business know-how on that level being a prerogative of the practitioners.

It has become for many of us essential to believe that there is a way out. Humanists are not anxious to accept the idea that man is now ruled by the machine. Democrats believe that the people can take power again in the name of the Constitution, notwithstanding Nixon's accomplishments without a Republican majority in either house. If the President's personal power makes him virtually uncontrollable, the solution is not to abolish the office, it seems, but to choose a good man for President (as if Nixon were not himself, by his own lights, an extremely virtuous person, appalled by dirty words, if not by dirty money). The most cynical of us needs to sing "We Shall Overcome" occasionally. After years of guilt about our standard of living and education, the color of our skins, and our unconscious assumption of ethnic superiority, the middle-class radic-libs desperately need a chance to feel *good* again.

I struggled to retain a modicum of Marxian good sense, but the drag of desire pulled me away so many times that despite myself I began to hope madly that McGovern was a superman, that the convention was open, that the people were really the people, autonomous and honest, and not mere pawns for the men who were marketing McGovern. From the first time I had ever heard the man's name, he had been praised by people I loved and respected. Americans Abroad for McGovern. At best, so it was said, he was incapable of lying, at worst he was our Only Hope.

If I were going to hold hard to my economic analysis of American politics, then I could most easily be seduced into support for McGovern by a better economist. When Kenneth Galbraith beamed on me with all the tender optimism he had been amassing during the campaign, irrational hope gained another toehold. When Arthur Miller explained fervently how important it was that McGovern get a chance to realize the issues for which American liberals had been fighting against tremendous odds all their lives, I felt like a destructive child wrecking my own source of happiness. Amerika cannot be willed out of existence, so it must be changed. Violent revolution is more likely from the military-industrial complex than from the faction-torn,

informer-ridden, rhetoric-stoned Left, whose futile gestures toward it simply provide the sanction for more grinding forms of repression. Nonviolent revolution would require more time than anybody thinks we have. McGovern offered a chance, albeit slender, of a change for the slightly better: more Nixon threatened a change for the much worse. Arthur Miller announced the familiar warning: "If this man wins another term, the Supreme Court will be castrated, and the *New York Times* will be a single mimeographed page." Upon reflection, neither eventuality seemed as unlikely as it should have.

For many, McGovern appeared like a new prophet, a healer of society who could not function without faith. "You gotta *believe*," they would say. Flo Kennedy, the black attorney from New York who had arranged the Feminist party activities at the convention, explained it in her own vivid way. "Honey, this man McGovern is like a paper cup. You turn him up empty and put a chair leg on him and he'll collapse. You fill him up with sand and put a lid on him and turn him up, and he'll hold the chair and anyone who sits on him. The people are the sand; they've gotta make him what they want him to be." Lack of faith in McGovern was lack of faith in oneself, or loserism, as Flo calls it. "There's a whole lotta people out there who are afraid to win because they don't think of themselves as running the show. They've been niggerized, the only way they know is suckin'. They'll bitch their own people and chop down their own supports. It's all part of horizontal hostility, see." Maybe part of my dubiousness about McGovern stemmed from that sort of a feeling. Kurt Vonnegut said once that there was no worse experience than seeing the guys who were in high school with you in charge of the world. As a small-time academic, McGovern came from a class I was contemptuously familiar with; I did not want to think I mistrusted him on that ground.

The myths of the Republican regime are repulsive. Nixon has survived on the notions that the poor remain poor through their own fault; that America lacks the resources to assure every American the fundamental necessities of life; that national health services are too expensive to maintain; that unemployment is essential to the American economy—and that all these notions shelter beneath the banner of the New Prosperity.

The New Mythology of the Democratic party is more attractive, although softer-headed, than the nastiness of the GOP. "Power to the People" is a slogan that will warm the heart, especially when set to music by John Lennon and bawled in the streets by the young, the gifted, and the black. We would all so very much like to agree, to feel our energies flow for altruism, and to believe that the issues are not so complicated as to evade our grasp. "Intellectual pseudosnobs" are ill-equipped by their cultural traditions to accept dialectical materialism that denies the individual will, is anti-Protestant, substitutes determinism for heroism. Such a philosophy is dehumanizing, degrades the individual, phallus and all, to mere reagency. The middle-class radical can easily be persuaded to forgo it in his fantasy, and the best educated are the most vulnerable in this respect. The cultural revolution that Marxism entails is an unbearable impoverishment, a forfeiting of the intellectual's most cherished heritage; Yevtushenko and Solzhenitsyn remind him horribly of the price that the proletarian dictators must exact, in return for the least amelioration in the condition of the masses.

The softening up that the Democrats had planned was bound to draw us in: no bourgeois Marxist really sees himself as an anomaly or expects to be massacred by the proletariat; he has not the sense of grievance necessary to believe that he could cut the throats of the White House incumbents, although they could turn the M16 rifles of the National Guard upon him without turning a hair. His intellectual passion for truth and justice and equality and tolerance cannot join in battle with the irrational hostility of a race brutalized for generations by anality, competition, and sexual repression. The idealist Democrat cannot kill for his ideals. We all needed so intensely to believe that our case was not hopeless and that we were not totally hypocritical in our well-fed radicalism, we were so ready to love the man who would agree to represent us (yes, me too) that within hours of arriving in Miami Beach we were all maudlin and ripe for being screwed in every orifice of the mind and heart.

GOD BLESS AMERICA

At a meeting of the National Women's Political Caucus on the morning after I arrived, I caught sight of my fellow Yippie, Abbie Hoffman, covering the meeting for the book he is doing with Jerry Rubin and Ed Sanders. Abbie looked odd with the unsolicited nose job he had as a result of a police beating in Washington last May, but odder still was the something soft and questing, even mawkish in his expression. "Ah, come on, Geegee," he pleaded with me. "Don't be so down on everything! We gotta chance this time, Geegee!" "But Abbie," I replied faintly, "it can't work this way. What kind of bargaining power have these people got? Remember your Marx, man, and the nature of capitalism." "Aw Gee, I never read Marx, but Lenin woulda liked it." I realized with a guilty creak of the heart that Abbie was sick of trashing and being trashed, tired of the feds infesting the staircase of his apartment, tired of informers and spying, too intelligent not to see that most of his activities had had the net result of intensifying oppression while revolution remained as far off as ever. Besides, he loved America.

"It's terrific, Gee. We're inside the hall this time. All these women and blacks and young kids, it's terrific! Ya been down to the Park? Ya gotta come down, and there's a poetry reading—ya wanna read a poem?"

I had been to the Park—the night before, with a young reporter who had lurched at me with his lips puckered when we were on our way in the cab. I ducked; he asked me why. I thought the overriding question was why he had lurched in the first place, having received no encouragement. What I did not realize is that a political convention is still a convention, that all the males-away-from-home expect to let their hair down, make love to strange women, dance all night and all that.

I have seen a good many People's Corrals in my time, and Flamingo Park must rate as one of the nicest. It was warm; there were lavatories and even a swimming pool, and the retaining wire was hidden by blossomy hedges, and Green Power was handing out nourishing food. Best of all, there was hardly anybody there. A drug entirely appropriate to the strategies of containment had appeared, a muscle relaxant called Quaalude. The nondelegates sprawled about, enervated and content. The Democrats could expect little needle from that quarter.

By way of relating to the disenfranchised poor of South Beach, the slogan of the nondelegates might have been "Think Jewish," not the Jewish of Meyer Lansky or Moshe Dayan or even Trotsky, but the Jewish of chicken soup. Allen Ginsberg was into wearing a yarmulke and intoning Yiddish mantras. Abbie Hoffman produced a poem abusing Nixon in Yiddish. The Zippies were fed up with the schmaltzy complacency of the Yippies, and a few abortive trashings ensued,

but the truth about Flamingo Park was that nothing was happening there. As Jerry Rubin said when I met him on the convention floor, "The action is here, man. The Park is a drag," and he went off to secure himself a nomination for the Vice-Presidency from the New York delegation. It felt like the end of an era.

The nondelegates' finest hours were spent in the Doral Hotel lobby demanding an explanation from nominee McGovern of his words to the POW and MIA families: "While I am fully confident that there would be no such need, I would also retain the military capability in the region—in Thailand and on the seas—to signal and fulfill our firm determination on this issue [the release of all prisoners and a full accounting of all missing in action]."

The irritating thing about that statement was the impression it gave that McGovern had only recently grasped the practical difficulty of withdrawing from Vietnam, and that only in the vaguest way. He was saying what the families of POWs and MIAs wanted to hear, just as he constantly produced the stirring promises that the antiwar lobby wanted to hear, regardless of U.S. commitments in Southeast Asia and size and scope of the American operation there. Five hundred people marched on the Doral to hear his explanation. They arrived at noon; McGovern could not be coaxed from the seclusion of his suite until nearly seven o'clock. A little straight talking could have had them on their way in minutes, and yet the Democrats were amazed and impressed that McGovern agreed to talk to them at all, and overcome with admiration of his cunning in getting it together for prime time viewing, LIVE!! I stood and waited with them for a couple of hours off and on. Arthur Miller was standing near me, appalled by the self-consciousness of what he saw. A demagogue from the Park came up to me and asked for $60 to buy the people food. I dug my last $37 out of my pocket. "That's no good, man," he wailed. "I need sixty." "You're damn lucky to get more than half of it at your first touch. You get and raise the rest, you asshole," I snapped. "They're publicity hounds, provocateurs," Arthur was saying miserably.

The most vociferous of the invaders of the Doral were probably no more than self-seekers and stoned demagogues, but there were more perilous infiltrations into the ranks of the non-delegates. The Yippies smelled a grand jury and more conspiracy trials in the offing and clammed up, but the vets, the most persuasive antiwar group in the country, were not so fly. As a result of the infiltration of their open Southeast regional planning meeting held in Florida a month before, more than twenty vets were served with subpoenas to appear before a federal grand jury in Tallahassee on Monday morning, the first day of the Democratic Convention. The scale of the operation was unprecedented, the number of men expected to testify on one day apparently preposterous.

The Democrats' wholehearted support of the vets was a mark in their favor, even if one considered that it was more closely connected with anti-Nixon feeling than a genuine understanding of the issue. Anti-Nixonism is probably the main reason the convention was so ready to accept the contention of the People's coalition for Peace and Justice that U.S. Air Force jets have been repeatedly and deliberately bombing the dikes in North Vietnam, despite official disclaimers from the White House and the Pentagon. By the last night of the convention, the dikes had become an instant cause célèbre; the vets marched silently through the streets carrying torches and bags of sand to patch a symbolic dike. A huge banner appeared in the convention hall: STOP BOMBING THE DIKES. A journalist standing near me asked, "Is that a Gay Liberation sign?"

SHIRLEY MACLAINE IN TEARS

The Democratic Convention also represented the first emergence of women as a significant group in electoral politics. The National Women's Political Caucus was only a year old, and its first big opportunity had arrived. There was almost no hope that it could have developed voting strength and practical strategies in such a short time, but in the unkind way of history it was about to be tested and a precedent set. The intensity of my irrational hope that the course of American politics could be changed with respect to its foreign policies was compounded by the fervidity of my desire to see the women distinguish themselves and win some representation in the party platform and some power to implement their own will. After several days of following their activities I found myself in a morass of passionate wishing and utter disappointment.

When I got to the National Women's Political Caucus meeting in the Napoleon Room at the Deauville Hotel on Sunday morning, Gloria Steinem was speaking, and the controlled jubilation of her tone pushed my tormenting hopes up to fever pitch. She spoke of councilmen being ousted by housewives, of women forming 46 per cent of the attendance at precinct meetings in one state. "The political process has been changed," she sang, "and it will never be the same again." Women had challenged their way to being 40 per cent of the delegates, with 38 per cent of the vote; they had made the McGovern-Fraser guidelines work for them. Of course, some delegations had simply stacked themselves with token females, wives and daughters and whomever, in order to escape a challenge, and for them at least new activism among women had nothing to do with it, but the atmosphere was so electric, the women's enthusiasm so contagious, that I for one could not keep my heart from beating faster.

Bella Abzug took over, vowing staunchly that Yvonne Brathwaite Burke was not going to be Lawrence O'Brien's right-hand man, that women would not be McGovern's sacrificial lamb, coming down heavy on every last syllable as if to nail her meaning to the Democratic masthead.

A bevy of women paused in the doorway, their heads moving with odd self-consciousness, and minced extravagantly to a row of empty seats. One of them a delegate from New Mexico, festooned with Zuni jewelry, her hair elaborately teased into a modified braid, was smoking a small blue enameled pipe. Her eyes slid round the room, under their carefully slanted false eyelashes, Fifth Avenue Indian style. The blonde next to her suddenly said, in a skittish, unnecessarily piercing voice, "Ah think we'd do a lot better down in our room"— at which signal they rose, clattering and clinking and excuse-meing at the tops of their voices. Even Bella paused in her orations to demand the cause of the disturbance, but the ladies, swinging their rumps like ponies, were gone.

Bella brought up the question of the minority report on control of one's reproductive destiny. To bring abortion into the Democratic party platform might seem unwise, she argued, but the issue concerned a fundamental human right that could not be denied by those who chose to live by a different code. There was a brief debate on the subject; some delegates argued that it was a state matter, and inappropriate therefore in the party platform. Another woman said she was against abortion and she was sure that more than half the women there were on her side. A show of hands was called for; five went up. A tension had crept into the high-spirited meeting. Bella's attitude had been doggedly apologetic, and she did not expound any strategy for the defense of the abortion report. Her windup left us in even more doubt about how the women were to proceed: it was

our overriding priority to dump Nixon, she said, even if we had to waive the immediacy of certain demands. "Womanpower is a growing thing that must live."

Betty Friedan, introduced as "the mother of us all," took the floor and reminded us that in 1968 there was not one word about women in the Democratic party platform. Women had figured as miniskirted greeters or invisible wives who had lunches with each other. This year, she announced proudly, "women are gonna make policy, not coffee." The women's duty at the convention was to make "what may not be realistic today, realistic tomorrow." Her words suggested another possible strategy for the women, to make sure that abortion entered the Democratic party platform, because the Democratic candidate was unlikely to win in '72: by '76 they would have had to develop a way of handling it. I wondered if abortion would have a chance if Kennedy ran in '76. By this time it was obvious no clear guidelines for feminist action at the convention could be expected from the NWPC. Most of their talk was self-congratulation for what had already been achieved, but it was early days yet and the meeting was very small.

In the days that followed I went to many women's meetings. Women for McGovern debated the credentials' challenges, which I had great difficulty in following and for which, in any event, the strategies would be directed by telephone from the McGovern campaign trailer. The caucus met again on Sunday afternoon to discuss strategy, but while I was there I heard only Bella's oratorical chariot riding over the voices of dissent. Gloria and her cohorts withdrew to the Betsy Ross Hotel to prepare for the meeting with the caucus of women delegates and to throw a fund-raising party, while I went down to the Shore Club Motel for a sing-in with the Feminist party, whose various educational activities, such as public burning of antifeminist religious quotations, went largely unnoticed. (Apparently the fires in the Playboy Bunny wardrobe were caused by electrical faults: such a symbolic conflagration could have been claimed by a women's guerrilla organization notwithstanding, but it wasn't.)

The Feminist party had arrived at the Shore Club only to find that the motel had netted some bigger spenders than the poor women who had come by bus and train to sleep two or three in a room and eat fried chicken out of cardboard boxes; their block booking had been summarily shifted to another hotel. They had printed all their literature with the HQ address of the Shore Club, so Flo Kennedy announced her intention of squatting bag and bagging in the foyer until the Shore Club honored its obligation. The bastions fell at one blast of her trump, and the women moved in.

Jammed together in a steaming cardroom, the Feminists relieved their hearts by roaring, "I'm tired of bastards fuckin' over me," and, "Move on over or we'll move on over you." We allowed ourselves the luxury of believing that sisterhood is strong, although the events of the day had left me feeling that the mere fact of femaleness does not constitute sisterhood, and sisterhood itself does not automatically confer power.

The next morning I dashed down to the Carillon for the big womanpower meeting of the caucus of women delegates. This was going to be it: here I would see 40 per cent of the delegates emerging as a powerful voting bloc, disciplined and agreed on all essential points. When I arrived, Gloria Steinem was calling the roll. The delegates sat at tables set in semicircular tiers and sprang to their feet cheering themselves whenever the name of their delegation was called. Their jollity was infectious, but I was feeling slightly appalled that the business of the day seemed to be self-congratulation and laurel-counting rather than hard plotting for the long nights ahead. There were

even a few indications that some wheeling and dealing was being attempted offstage, contrary to the stated spirit of the proceedings. Even Gloria's relentless prominence in all affairs began to disturb me and most of all her occasional wistful mention of the "smoke-filled rooms where the decisions are made." Either this convention was going to drag the naked screaming decisions out of the smoke-filled rooms, or it was going to be defeated in its essential purpose. It was hard to be pessimistic with the women howling with glee as their states were named, leaping in the air and beaming all around, but I persisted in wondering how many floor leaders were absent because they were at McGovern's briefings on the night's strategies.

The miserable fact was that the women's caucus was not a caucus in any meaningful sense: the McGovern machine had already pulled the rug out from under them. Even if they had had microphones on the floor at their meetings and had thrashed out the issues, polled the women present, and based a feminist strategy on the results of the poll, they would not have had much more bargaining power than they had had before they ever attended a precinct meeting. They were in Miami as cards in McGovern's hand, to be led or discarded as he wished, not as players at the table. He could rely on the intensity factor to work them hard and stack the hall with his supporters, and he was not obliged to offer them a bent nickel in recompense; they would vote him to the nomination because they had no alternative. The right wing could threaten him with secession, but not his captive women, blacks, Latins, and kids. They were just not cynical enough to grasp the fact, or else they would have considered an alternative play, a vote for Humphrey or even for Nixon. As Flo said bitterly, "Honey, if you'll fuck for a dime, you can't complain because somebody else is getting a fur coat." Womanlike, they did not want to get tough with their man, and so, womanlike, they got screwed.

I began to fear that I could no longer maintain my journalistic pose of calm impartiality, and so I bolted from the room to the Latin caucus next door. It was every bit as muddled and bombastic as the women's. Later glimpses of the black caucus and the youth caucus indicated what I had feared all along. None of the caucuses really existed as policy-making bodies or influential entities on the convention floor. A spurious leaderism ripped them all off and masqueraded as the collective voice, without one firm position sanctioned by the collectivity out of which a hard deal could be made. Spokesman after spokesman claimed to have secured this or that, on a collateral of hot air, and the women's caucus was no exception.

When I got back to the Carillon, newspeople were scurrying everywhere, like bedbugs when you turn the light on. A clot of men in suits was moving like the Blob From the Swamp toward the room where the women's caucus was. I squirmed through the cameramen up behind the Blob. In its heart was McGovern: it was the first time I had seen him since I arrived, except for a glimpse of him, as coquettish as any sultana riding in her palanquin, as he was borne out of the Fontainebleau after a press conference. I had seen a smallish man, with an engagingly shy list to his head, his teeth as well capped and his jowls as well shaven and powdered and his shoes as shiny as you would expect of one who is desirous of being a Presidential candidate.

McGovern was eventually decanted from his escort's collective embrace and faced the women's caucus. They threw themselves at his head, cheering, climbing on chairs for a better look at him, yelling endearments. If ever he doubted that he had them in the palm of his hand, he could no longer doubt it. He

might be an expert in the techniques of coquetry, but his women were a pushover. I raged inside, to think what such spontaneity and generosity could cost them. Liz Carpenter introduced him with a gesture so fulsome that it almost overbalanced itself. A woman beside me muttered, "What a hypocrite. Everyone knows she was for Humphrey."

Liz said, "We are all here because of him." Cheers and tears. McGovern took the floor and uttered the boo-boo that revealed that he had utterly no understanding of the temper of feminism. To have passed off responsibility for the women's presence from himself to Eve would have been bad enough, with all its pious reference to the anti-feminine Judeo-Christian tradition, but to put it down to Adam! He must have been reassured, for the women forgave him at once. There were a few cries of "Shame!" and "Pig!" but you would have thought they were more endearments. He swung into an explanation of the California delegate dispute and on into his stock speech on Vietnam. Suddenly there was an interruption. Jacqui Ceballos, deadly pale, was on her feet just below the stage.

"What about the right to control our own bodies?" she cried. "We'll never be free until we have that!"

I could hear her from where I was standing, halfway down the hall, but Bella and Gloria stared glassily out into the room, as if they were deaf or entranced. Without a microphone, Jacqui could not hope to compete with McGovern's hugely amplified voice. He faltered, and in the brief silence Jacqui's voice wailed. "We must control our bodies, otherwise we'll never be free." McGovern resumed, sailing crescendo into the familiar finale: "I want us to resolve that once that tragedy is put behind us, never again will we send the precious young blood of this country to die trying to bail out a corrupt dictatorship."

I would have been happier if he had also

said that America would never again send her precious intelligence to set up corrupt dictatorships, but everybody else was deliriously happy with McGovern's oratory. He and his acolytes proceeded past me, women reaching out to touch him and take his hand. Shirley MacLaine trod softly behind him, her eyes awash with tears. The women's last chance to negotiate had been washed out in a tide of soupy emotion.

Why had Bella and Gloria not helped Jacqui to nail him on abortion? What reticence, what loserism had afflicted them then? I wondered if they had already made some sort of a deal. They may have thought they had: perhaps they had agreed not to embarrass him with the minority report on reproduction, but what on earth would they get in exchange? South Carolina? What could be worth it?

A TALE TOLD TO A PIOUS IDIOT

What happened on the first night of the convention is now a matter of record. McGovern's nomination was safe before the official proceedings had even started, when he and Abraham Ribicoff had persuaded Lawrence O'Brien to rule that the credentials issues should be settled by a majority of those delegates eligible to vote. South Carolina, *pace* the women, was thrown out to avoid a ticklish dispute over the definition of a majority before the California vote was settled. It was, after all, a numbers game. The delegates did as they were told; onlookers who marveled at their biddability ought to have spared a thought for their lack of any organization except McGovern's. I hardly understood what was happening, my eardrums perforated by Sammy Spear's hypodermic sound, penned in a dark gallery on the wrong side of a TV catwalk where you couldn't see the convention floor or the large TV screens. I had read that George Wallace's campaigns were a new kind

of carnival, which mixed revivalism, jingoism, and populism in a new and heady brew, and it seemed to my unseasoned eye that the Democratic National Convention had modeled itself on his scenario. An overamplified choir had screamed rousing songs in bursts for an hour or so; flags had paraded around the hall to shrieking brass, a cleric had prayed for the proceedings. God, whom I had thought of as a Nixon intimate, was continually invoked.

The presentation of the New Mythology was as remorseless and simplistic as any advertising campaign. I had become familiar with the principal gimmicks by watching the telethon the night before, and in Lawrence O'Brien's opening address we got most of it over again. Like all marketing techniques it worked by manipulating emotions, at the most accessible level, and even as you recognized the facileness of the technique, it got to you. God, Conscience, Sincerity, the dead Kennedys, the suffering Vietnamese, and, above all, the People were all on the side of the Democrats. Gloria Steinem said that the McGovern-Fraser guidelines had had the effect of making the convention floor "look like the country": the Democrats cited this single factor tirelessly in their own praise, but actually the change stopped right there. The convention floor only *looked like* the country. The presence of women, blacks, and youth was visible; what had changed was the party's *image,* so crucial in the age of media politics. The attributes one could not see, like class, income, and education, are more fundamental to politics in many ways than the obvious sexual and ethnic differentiations, and when it came to representing these less obvious categories the Democratic National Convention was markedly inadequate. More than two-thirds of the delegates came from the over-$15,000-a-year bracket, which accounts for only 23 per cent of the American population; 39 per cent of the delegates had done postgraduate work, when only 4 per cent of the population has enjoyed that privilege. The insolvency of the Democratic party had affected its ability to bring the lower-paid workers to Miami Beach, just as the lower-paid workers have not the expensive leisure to undertake political campaigning. One delegate told me that the first question the party had put to her, when she announced her desire to become a delegate, was her name; the second was, "Can you pay your own way to Miami Beach in July?" Some of the delegations had been subsidized not, it seems, by the party but by the McGovern machine.

The Democrats knew that the faces of the delegates were their most valuable stock-in-trade (closely followed by the pious memories of the Kennedys and the quotability of JFK). They used them over and over again, in their official publication, "Democrats in Convention," in the telethon, then in Lawrence O'Brien's opening address. The precedent was well established for depiction of the vital, glowing eager faces in all the news media. The long nights that followed were bearable only because the eye could be guided from the dreariness of the rostrum to the ferment beneath. Film of prettily lit, prettily shot faces of every racial cast, but all of them agreeable, fleshed out the platitudes of O'Brien's opening speech. The dialectic was that of sentient flesh and soul against the giant machine: the language was the same that Goldwater had used, of moral revival, righteous disquiet, and the ground swell of public feeling. The Democratic party was the party-of-the-smaller-man-than-ever-before.

In depicting the people, the image-makers for the Democratic party allowed no dissident voices, no one who said, "If we don't fight them in Vietnam, we'll be fighting them in our own backyards," as the people can be heard to do, not a queer-basher or a law-and-order addict among them. The people on the convention floor were only too happy to applaud this charming image of themselves as simple folks; direct, honest, and profound in their candid appraisal of the political malaise of America, tolerant of all human failings, but hell on institutions. A great foam of enthusiasm rolled off them, and O'Brien's speechwriter worked them further, using that special variety of meaningless language that can elicit a consensus response. "It comes from the people up," he intoned with a throb in his voice, "these simple direct words sum up what many people have been saying . . . In good men—good women—good ideas—and good works, the Party of the People is unmatched." What was the use of drawing a polyglot convention from the intellectual elite, when you had to talk to them as if they were sentimental, tasteless, pious idiots?

Suddenly I realized that the most significant aspect of the convention was being lost on me, precisely because I was present. O'Brien was not speaking primarily to the delegates; he was speaking to the nation-at-large on prime-time TV. The delegates were no more than the studio audience, kicking the show along by cheering and laughing whenever the signal was given. O'Brien was not after all wearing pancake makeup for our benefit. In the fact that almost no significant contender for office appeared in public without cosmetics I found an interesting insight into the methods of political parley. Just as the man's face, authentic and expressive as it was, could not be allowed to make its own appeal to the public and stand or fall by the response, so also a politician's arguments could not be allowed to be clearly and faithfully expressed, but must cloak themselves in jargon and the fake resonance of the pulpit. To get people to believe the truth, the admen believe, it is necessary to lie. Before the convention had ever nominated him, McGovern's personality and beliefs were being falsified by those who sought to make the people buy him. His meaning had to be puffed into vagueness, because consensus politics means that you cannot afford to give the many-headed beast, the public, anything to vote *against,* for voting against is what gargantuan pseudodemocracy has to come down to.

The delegates were not wearing stage make-up though, and they were not talking to each other in the fervent hope of saying as little as possible. They were extraordinary, so proud and alive and earnest and so damnably naive that it swelled your heart and broke it to watch them, puzzling over the issues, doubting what was best to do, seeking guidance and being raked by the big guns of baloney-power. If only they had had the confidence of their own imagination and judgment instead of meekly allowing themselves to fall in line at the merest touch of a McGovern whip, he might have had to be their servant instead of their master. That is what was so maddening: there was a chance of something really new, but it was stifled at its birth.

For me, the clearest case of funk was the rail-roading of the abortion issue. The minority report on a "person's right to control his re-productive destiny" was, of course, treated as an abortion plank, although it applies equally to a man's right to have a vasectomy and a woman's right to refuse compulsory steriliza-tion. The delegates who were for McGovern first and the interests of the group they re-presented second argued that abortion was a state matter and had no place on a federal platform, which was irrelevant. What was in question was a *right,* to be established con-stitutionally and upheld by the Supreme Court. If state laws were in violation of the right of privacy, they must be declared unconstitution-al; for the women who have already spent millions of dollars and years of their lives battling the state legislatures on the issue, federal intervention has become an urgent necessity. If the "abortion" plank had been

adopted as part of the party platform, thou-sands of people with energy and experience would have campaigned for McGovern in a positive and intense way, just as they had done in the primaries; they might lose, but they would lose honorably.

By foul means I acquired a delegate's pass to get onto the floor for the debate. Betty Friedan had told me that the Idaho delegates had had the bright idea of asking the male dele-gates who were not interested in the issue to give up their seats to the women delegates who felt more directly concerned. As I asked around the floor it was clear to me that many delegations were ready to do this, but many of the willing men were for the adoption of the plank in any case. Too many of the women said that they were for the plank, but that they had agreed to vote against it for McGovern's sake. At least two women defied their entire delegations, which polled their single votes *for,* with a bad grace; most gave in.

When Eugene Walsh came out with the argu-ments of the Right-to-Lifers, not a single opinion in the convention hall was changed. If anything, his contorted face repelled, but Gloria was furious that he had been allowed to speak at all. "You promised us you would not take the low road," she said to Gary Hart. I was at a loss to explain her distress: the friends of the fetus do not have so much right on their side that their arguments must be stifled. Even more, I was outraged to think that nonsensical promises had been made in secret sessions, when the business of strengthening the women's caucus had been neglected. Shirley MacLaine's speech to the issue made one single point, which if it had been taken to heart would have lumbered McGovern with the "sensitive" issue he was now so anxious to avoid. Instead of speaking directly against abortion, which she could not in conscience do, despite the slot she chose to speak in, she begged the delegates to vote according to their consciences—but even as she spoke, the McGovern whips were instructing his delegates to avoid the necessity of a roll call by shouting the minority report down. Why Bella Abzug should have been so angry with her, on the ground that a "sister never goes against a sister," when sisterhood had not been adequate to bring Jacqui Ceballos' question to McGovern's notice, I could not understand either.

As I traveled home in the bus that night something happened that brought home to me in the most vivid way the fact that McGovern had not managed to please the sexual bigots by betraying the sexual liberals. A man sitting across the aisle from me suddenly burst out:

"What am I doing, sitting here all night letting them debate abortion? Suppose some broad does get herself knocked up, I don't give a shit!"

His wife's hands were loosely clasped on the skirt of her little-girl gingham dress. She was not listening.

A man on the other side said, "The country's not ready for that. It's a matter of education."

He went on for a bit in a calming way, and then suddenly overbalanced and began to say in a voice that rose higher and higher, "That sexual orientation stuff, that's what I don't like. I don't care what they do in private," (his voice said that he cared passionately) "but I don't want one teaching my kid! I just don't. I mean, how would you like it if some homo is getting at your kid . . ." By now he was screaming with disgust.

The other man joined in, "Yeah, You know, most of the elected officials in my state are *queer!* Every damn one of them."

They yelled insanely at one another until the first man capped it all by roaring, "You ever see McGovern walk? He's one of them, I tell you! He's one of them."

I looked around the bus looking for signs of ridicule or dismay. A boy with a Wallace button on his hat gazed at me as unwinkingly as a lizard. The two men had fallen to commiserating on their long years of service for the Democrats, and how they would have to abandon politics. It did not matter to them one bit that the distasteful reports had been voted down; McGovern's image was tainted with them anyway. Instead of carrying his stinking dead dog proudly through politics, he had hidden it under his coat.

The official sexuality of the Democratic party has not, of course, changed. The politicians' concubines sat in their seraglio at the side of the rostrum each night, until the debates got too tedious and they began to lose their beauty sleep, when they melted away. They were all coiffed and plentiful of eyelash and fixedly smiling. If you asked for information about any of them from their aides, the answer came, "She is lovely, truly lovely," or words to that effect. On all symbolic occasions the wives appeared, standing beside, behind, below, and smiling. The heterosexuality of the politicians was in plentiful evidence, but their virility was almost as important. Ladies of the Wallace persuasion, worried perhaps that the Gov'nah might not appear to be holding his own, volunteered the informatiom to me on three separate occasions that "he has all of his sexual faculties *unimpaired.*"

According to Rocky Pomerance, Miami chief of police, the Democratic Convention had not attracted the usual number of whores; a mere 18,000 had bothered to make the trip, and, said Pomerance, "That'll be 18,000 votes for Nixon." The ladies implied that they had been undercut by amateur competition from the large number of women delegates, but the fact of the matter is that few delegates or press men had the time or the energy for whoring. I hung out with the ladies who work the Fontainebleau one night, trying to get their angle, but there were so many newsmen trying to engineer newsworthy confrontations between us that I had to give it up. The newsmen wrote their stories just the same: the *Miami News* said that I told one girl "she was a disgrace to our sex," when really I don't think she is any more disgraceful than any politician's wife. *The Village Voice* imagined that a whore had upbraided me for prostituting myself to *Harper's* (as if they ever use the *word,* let alone figuratively). The only person who did that, in fact, was Norman Mailer.

The image-makers went to some pains to present Eleanor McGovern as a new sort of candidate's wife, careless of how history suffered in the process. Her least pronouncement was greeted with wonder and acclaim, as if it were remarkable that she could speak at all. One afternoon in the Doral, a woman for McGovern grabbed my arm: "Quick, Mrs. McGovern is going to speak, down there," and she spun me off down the lobby. "No, no," I heard them say crossly when I arrived in the room. "Mrs. McGovern is not going to speak," and they shrugged as if the whole notion were preposterous. I had got pretty used to Mrs. McGovern as the traditional smiling mute and was preparing to leave when my arm was grabbed again. "Come and meet Mrs. McGovern." I was dragged into the scrum that hid her tiny form from view. The press of advisers and trainbearers parted and catapulted her into my midriff. I took her hand, as cool and dry and still as a dead bird. "It must be so nice to be covering the convention," she said faintly. I choked on the desire to say that it was unmitigated mental torture and bleated something about how I'd rather have been involved. "Oh, no," she said, "much less exhausting. So much tension." Bending over at the waist to bring her voice within earshot, I felt like an intolerable, sneaking bully. "The Senator says Eleanor has an energy problem," someone said. A gigantic bouncer appeared from nowhere, clearing the room for the next

nonevent. Incredibly he was wearing a clergyman's dog collar.

Of all the extracurricular events Mrs. McGovern might have attended, the one she chose was a fashion show put on by Governor Askew's wife. I had come across it by accident, after seeing the tiny demonstration that trudged round and round in the Americana Hotel forecourt shouting, "The poor need food, the poor need clothes. What do we get? Fashion Shows!"

I ran the gamut of the security men and was gingerly welcomed by the hostesses. Until I saw the complimentary orange drink among the samples of suntan lotion and scent on the tables, I could not fathom why the hostesses were balancing giant orange paper roses on their heads, or why in that heat they were draped in orange capes with bobble trim. Even Mrs. Askew was starring in an imaginary commercial for Florida in her orange, green, and white dress oversewn with orange blossom. She mounted the podium to present the distinguished guests; "I want you to meet the women behind the men behind the wheels of the Florida government," she said.

Then she introduced us to all of her female relatives, in blood and in law; "It is a very special pleasure that we have our mothers with us at this convention." Mrs. Wilbur Mills and Mrs. Terry Sanford and a bevy of assorted wives were present, but the star had still to come. Eleanor McGovern's arrival was signaled by a panic of photographers. Under cover of the confusion, a few poor women laid down their $3 and moved quietly into the ballroom.

A small voice arose in the din: "This is what the poor woman is wearing this year, cut-down dungarees and levi jacket—" The genuine poor is more likely to be found in a wash-cotton dress and trodden-down slippers, but the women had a point and they were making it with a little wit. Crash! The security men moved in, lifting the girls bodily off the floor. One of the women had a very small baby. The police in their space-age helmets came running down, batons akimbo, to help. "You rich women—" one of the girls began to scream, but her voice was choked off in the rush that carried her clean out of the room. Mrs. McGovern curled a small white-shod foot around the leg of her chair. The Florida matrons clicked their tongues. "Publicity-seekers," they opined sagely. The models came out and gangled down the catwalk in ready-made stocklines from Saks Fifth Avenue. The poor had been phony poor, and the rich were not rich. Nothing in Miami was what it seemed.

As if I had not fallen foul of enough bamboozlement and forlorn hope in Miami Beach, I also had the misfortune to entangle with the Star. I was introduced to him in an elevator, so there was nowhere I could take cover when he bent his full charm on me. That charm is a work of kinetic art, and I am not one to sneer at artistic achievement. The raw material is not contemptible either; there are few flaws in the marble out of which the Star has hewn himself. We achieved the fifteenth floor and I prepared to make a dash for reality, but the Star caught my arm. "Can I have a meeting with you?" he asked as he drew me aside into a chair. "Do up that button," I said crossly. "You don't have to come on with your tits hanging out." Bless my soul if he didn't put his perfect fingers to the second button on his shirt. "I wasn't serious," I amended feebly. The Star leaned close. "Do you know I have been trying to find you? I even called the Chelsea." My palms began to sweat.

I don't remember too much of what ensued. The Star was upbraiding me for voicing my misgivings about the American political system on the Cavett show. He was leaning so close to me that I began to worry about my toothpaste, mainly because it was still in London, and I hadn't cleaned my teeth in days. I snatched at a toothpick and stuck it in my mouth. The Star leaned further forward, nipped the end of my toothpick in his perfect teeth and bit it off. I was so rattled I forgot the cash value of a toothpick curtailed by the Star and promptly broke it into tiny pieces and left it in the ashtray. The Star took my gnarled paw into his smooth hand.

"Why do you want to go to that meeting?" he asked. (Shirley MacLaine's voice was echoing from the meeting I had been on my way to attend.)

"Because I'm on an assignment and I like to be serious about serious things." I wasn't really too sure that the Democratic Convention was serious, but I was still giving it a chance.

I bolted from the chair. The Star ran after me. "Call me," he said. "Any time." He gave me his room number, which I instantly forgot. I could just see myself, trucking round Miami, sniffing at the Star's warm trail like a bloodhound. I knew I was being challenged, but I squirmed away. "Look, I'm pretty busy. Can't we play the game according to the old rules? You call me." I cut and ran.

When I tottered home to my air-conditioned nightmare that night, two messages were waiting. One said simply, "Please pursue." The more I thought about it, the more I thought that the whole encounter was phony. I was being vamped for McGovern, or maybe just so that the Star could test his artistic creation and find it still good. The next morning I sent him a dozen red roses and a note, "Sorry I was out when you called." The Star was not to be so easily snubbed. At length he left a note, "Can we go on like this?" Heartsick and teased beyond endurance by what the convention had become, I still managed to resist the promise of an intimacy that still struck me as illusory as everything else at the Democratic National Convention. I could see it as part of the whole process, the wooing and winning of vulnerable and hopeful people, for somebody's good, but not their own. I withheld belief, but I could not avoid him forever. We met again. He pleaded with me not to play into Nixon's hands by helping to destroy McGovern's credibility with the people who were the hard core of his support. I wanted so much to believe, found my skepticism so desolating, that I almost threw myself sobbing into his arms and signed on for the Presidential campaign trail, but the Star tired of his conquest before it had quite taken place. I was right after all, although he laughed uproariously when I accused him of vamping for McGovern; I was right, but I wished with all my heart I hadn't been.

A VAPID ANTHEM

The last night of the convention seemed to me the culmination of outrage. All week the McGovern machine had been soliciting for prospective candidates for Vice-President with connections among the labor unions and the Catholic Church. At the eleventh hour, Tom Who? came across with so much alacrity that suspicions must have been aroused. There was no time by then to check these out because the delegates had to be organized out of saddling McGovern with some woman or black or pot smoker. McGovern was running out of arm's reach of his core supporters to angle after the center and the centers of organized tyranny, but the exhausted delegates, after a week without sleep and a diet that should have given them kwashiorkor, were still supporting him as trustingly as ever. When the charade of voting was over and Teddy Kennedy had summarized the glorious traditions of the Democratic party, I walked among the delegates while they greeted their hero, issuing forth after three days in the tabernacle. I remembered how Valerie Kushmer had seconded his nomination, putting her suffering as a POW's wife at his disposal in simple

words, her nakedness almost obscene among the blarney that surged about our ears for so many days. It had seemed to me then a blasphemy to make such wanton use of sincerity and fervor in a vulgar tourney for power. Coming after her awesome act of faith in McGovern, Walter Fauntroy's speech sounded as false and mannered as any fraudulent preacher's pitch. The Philistinism of the famous litany shocked me almost to tears. Even the hard-bitten newshounds around me had looked sick. Respect for the language, for communication, is essential if ideas are to be respected; truth could never prevail in the guise of hucksterism. People around me laughed at my expression of consternation. "You're just not used to American politics. You have to learn to accept the ballyhoo."

"I won't and I don't," I said unsteadily, "especially when your precious party makes such a big song and dance about its new candor."

McGovern came among his people, painted the color of pigskin and gleaming with sweat. High on the podium, facing the raunchy disorder of the convention hall, he looked like a disposable paper man compared to the people who sent up such a blast of enthusiasm to him. Walking among them as they drank in his words was like moving about during the National Anthem. Perhaps tiredness had a good deal to do with it, but many eyes brimmed with tears of joy and thankfulness. I wanted to warn them that they were being teased and played upon, to beg them to keep some reserve, but I was too close to hysterical tears to speak at all. McGovern's words, the regulation mix of jingoism, pietism, and populism, were aimed at their heartstrings, working them over and over so that emotion roared about the hall in waves.

Come home, to the affirmation that we have a dream.
Come home to the conviction that we can move our country forward,

Come home to the belief that we can seek a newer world.

I should not have been surprised that Fauntroy's bombast had supplied the McGovern movement with a slogan, vapid as it was, or that McGovern was reduced to quoting jingoistic songs or that America was still committed to warlike policies everywhere else but Asia, as far as he was concerned. I passed a young black delegate, his hands clasped to his breast, his eyes shining adoration at the man who would bring him home. My resentment at the whole horrible travesty became unbearable. As I turned to get out of there before the kissing could begin, I heard McGovern intoning:

May God grant us the wisdom to cherish this good land and to meet the great challenge that beckons us home.

When the shouting was all over, I realized that despite the secret dealings, the hypocrisy, the tantalization and the bamboozlement, the coarsening and cheapening of every issue, the abandonment of imagination and commitment for the gray areas of consensus, there was no alternative for American liberals but to let McGovern tease them a little while longer. In their alienation, their impotence, and their guilt they have no other alternative. Through the disappointment and the dismay that clouded my mind, another flicker of hope began to burn, against all reason and probability. I wish and painfully hope that the women, the kids, the blacks, the Latins, and the "intellectual pseudosnobs" bring off the impossible for him in November, in spite of himself, his baloney machine, and his Machiavellis, even though they will take the credit for it. The Big Tease has just begun.